Sexual Knowledge, Sexual
knowledge about sex fr
account cognate sciences
the volume analyses the
came by 1900 to be called

Various contributions
sexual teachings, and the
empirical sexual knowled
tions. A major concern of
– in terms of group, clas
incorporated into system
sexual liberals and radic
science, sexual liberation
hand. With the modern
background of AIDS, su
Sexual Science offers histori

This volume forms par
with *The Enlightenment i*
Revolution in History (198
Siècle and its Legacy (199
Scientific Revolution in Na
Europe in Historical Contex
collections is to bring to
approaches to the history
thought and action.

- 8 JUN 2017

2 8 SEP 2018

- 3 SEP 2020

- 1 NOV 2021

This item must be returned or renewed before the last date stamped above.

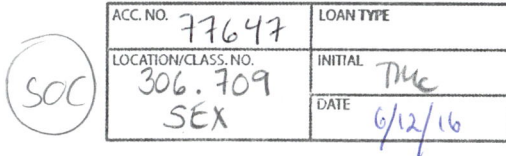

Volumes edited by Roy Porter and Mikuláš Teich

Already published

The Enlightenment in national context
Revolution in history
Romanticism in national context
Fin de siècle and its legacy
The Renaissance in national context
The scientific revolution in national context
The national question in Europe in historical context
The Reformation in national context (with R. W. Scribner)
Sexual knowledge, sexual science: the history of attitudes to sexuality

In preparation

The Industrial Revolution in national context: Europe and the USA
Drugs and narcotics in history
Nature and society in the development of
knowledge: a quest for missing links

SEXUAL KNOWLEDGE, SEXUAL SCIENCE

SEXUAL KNOWLEDGE, SEXUAL SCIENCE

THE HISTORY OF ATTITUDES TO SEXUALITY

EDITED BY

ROY PORTER

Professor of the History of Medicine, The Wellcome Institute for the History of Medicine, London

AND

MIKULÁŠ TEICH

Emeritus Fellow, Robinson College, Cambridge

Published by the Press Syndicate of the University of Cambridge
The Pitt Building, Trumpington Street, Cambridge CB2 1RP
40 West 20th Street, New York, NY 10011-4211, USA
10 Stamford Road, Oakleigh, Melbourne 3166, Australia

© Cambridge University Press 1994

First published 1994

Printed in Great Britain at the University Press, Cambridge

A catalogue record for this book is available from the British Library

Library of Congress cataloguing in publication data

Sexual knowledge, sexual science: the history of attitudes to
sexuality / edited by Roy Porter and Mikuláš Teich.
p.   cm.
"This book derives in part from a conference held at the Wellcome
Institute for the History of Medicine in the summer of 1991 and
organized by Michael Neve and Christine Stevenson" –
– Acknowledgements.
Includes index.
ISBN 0 521 44434 9 (hard). – ISBN 0 521 44891 3 (paper)
1. Sexology – History – Congresses. 2. Sex customs – History –
– Congresses. I. Porter, Roy, 1946– . II. Teich, Mikuláš.
HQ60.85 1994
306.7' 09 — dc20   93-28940   CIP

ISBN 0 521 44434 9 hardback
ISBN 0 521 44891 3 paperback

CONTENTS

Notes on contributors   page ix
Acknowledgements   xiii

Introduction   1

PART I: SEXUALITY BEFORE THE ERA OF FREUD

1 Sowing the field: Greek and Roman sexology   29
HELEN KING

2 Sadism, masochism and history, or When is behaviour sado-masochistic?   47
VERN L. BULLOUGH, DWIGHT DIXON AND JOAN DIXON

3 Some traditional Indian views on menstruation and female sexuality   63
JULIA LESLIE

4 Sexual knowledge in England, 1500–1750   82
PATRICIA CRAWFORD

5 The transformation of Eve: women's bodies, medicine and culture in early modern England   107
ROBERT MARTENSEN

6 The literature of sexual advice before 1800   134
ROY PORTER

7 The eclipse of sexual selection theory   158
SIMON J. FRANKEL

8 Mammals, primatology and sexology   184
LONDA SCHIEBINGER

| 9 | Krafft-Ebing's psychological understanding of sexual behaviour
RENATE HAUSER | 210 |

PART II: SEXOLOGY SINCE FREUD

10	The customs of the Magians: the problem of incest in historical societies MICHAEL MITTERAUER	231
11	Masculinity and the Decadence GEORGE L. MOSSE	251
12	'Not a stranger, a doctor': medical men and sexual matters in the late nineteenth century ANGUS MCLAREN	267
13	'May the doctor advise extramarital intercourse?': medical debates on sexual abstinence in Germany, *c.*1900 ANDREAS HILL	284
14	The development of sexology in the USA in the early twentieth century VERN L. BULLOUGH	303
15	Sigmund Freud and the sexologists: a second reading SANDER L. GILMAN	323
16	'The English have hot-water bottles': the morganatic marriage between medicine and sexology in Britain since William Acton LESLEY A. HALL	350
17	Tainted love RICHARD DAVENPORT-HINES AND CHRISTOPHER PHIPPS	367

Index   384

NOTES ON CONTRIBUTORS

VERN L. BULLOUGH is SUNY Distinguished Professor Emeritus in the SUNY College, in the School of Nursing, SUNY Buffalo. He was Garrison Lecturer at the American Association for the History of Medicine in 1988; was founder and editor of the *History of Nursing Bulletin* 1981–6; President of the Society for Scientific Study of Sex, 1981–3, and received its Distinguished Achievement Award in 1990. Continuing a prolific and scholarly output of articles and books, Professor Bullough's most recent publications include: with Bonnie Bullough, *Cross Dressing, Sex and Gender* (University of Pennsylvania Press, 1993); also with Bonnie Bullough, *Human Sexuality: An Encyclopedia* (Garland, late 1993) and *Science in the Bedroom: A History of Sex Research* (Basic Books, early 1994). He also edits a series on Human Sexuality for Prometheus Books.

PATRICIA CRAWFORD is an Associate Professor of History at the University of Western Australia. Books include *Denzil Holles 1598–1680* and *Women in Religion in England 1500–1720*. She has edited *Exploring Women's Past* and has published various articles, including a study of attitudes to menstruation in seventeenth-century England. Current research is a social history of women in early modern England with Sara Mendelson as co-author.

RICHARD DAVENPORT-HINES is an author whose books include *Sex, Death and Punishment* (1990) and *Vice: An Anthology* (1993). He is writing a biography of W. H. Auden.

DWIGHT and JOAN DIXON are a husband and wife team of sex therapists in San Diego, California, who also have an active research programme.

SIMON J. FRANKEL, a graduate of Yale Law School, studied history of science at Harvard, University College London, and Cambridge

University. His historical interests focus on the development of geological and evolutionary theory.

SANDER GILMAN is the Goldwin Smith Professor of Humane Studies at Cornell University and Professor of the History of Psychiatry at the Cornell Medical College. During 1990-1, he was Visiting Historical Scholar at the National Library of Medicine, Bethesda, Maryland. A member of the Cornell faculty since 1969, he is an intellectual and literary historian and the author or editor of over twenty-seven books, among the most recent being *Sexuality: an Illustrated History* (1989). He is author of the basic study of the visual stereotyping of the mentally ill – *Seeing the Insane* (1982).

LESLEY HALL is a professional archivist in the Contemporary Medical Archives Centre, Wellcome Institute for the History of Medicine, London, and has a Ph.D. (University of London) in history of medicine. Her book, *Hidden Anxieties: Male Sexuality 1900-1950*, was published by Polity Press, Cambridge, in 1991, and she has also written on masturbation, Marie Stopes, and venereal diseases. She is currently co-authoring *The Facts of Life* with Roy Porter.

RENATE HAUSER took her M.Phil. degree at Cambridge ('Emil Kraepelin and *dementia praecox*'). Her Ph.D. was 'Sexuality, Neurasthenia and the Law: Richard Von Krafft-Ebing (1840-1902)' (Ph.D. thesis, London University, 1992).

ANDREAS HILL is working as a doctor in psychiatry at the Medizinische Universität, Lübeck, in Germany. He studied medicine at Heidelberg and Lübeck Universities, at the Bremer Institut für Präventionsforschung und Sozialmedizin as well as at the Wellcome Institute for the History of Medicine, London, and various teaching hospitals in London and at the University of Illinois, Chicago. He received a scholarship from the Evangelisches Studienwerk Villigst. He is currently completing his medical-historical MD thesis on 'Medical Debates about Sexual Abstinence in Germany from 1900 to 1918' (Institut für Medizin- und Wissenschaftsgeschichte, Prof. v. Engelhardt, Medizinische Universität Lübeck).

HELEN KING is a Senior Lecturer in History at Liverpool Institute of Higher Education. Her first degree was in ancient history and social anthropology (University College London, 1980), and her doctoral thesis was on ancient Greek gynaecology in its cultural context (University of London, 1985). She has held research fellowships at Newnham College, Cambridge, and the University of Newcastle, and has published widely on ancient gynaecology and on the later history of gynaecology and midwifery.

JULIA LESLIE is Senior Lecturer in Hindu Studies at the School of Oriental and African Studies, University of London; and a Senior Member of the Centre for Cross-Cultural Research on Women at Queen Elizabeth House, University of Oxford. Her publications include: *The Perfect Wife: The Orthodox Hindu Woman according to the Strīdharmapaddhati of Tryambakayajvan* (Delhi: Oxford University Press, 1989); *Rules and Remedies in Classical Indian Law*, editor (Leiden: Brill, 1991); *Roles and Rituals for Hindu Women*, editor (London: Pinter, 1991; USA: Fairleigh Dickinson University Press, Associated University Presses, 1991; Delhi: Motilal Banarsidass, 1992). She is also the editor of the *Bulletin of the British Association for the Study of Religions*.

ROBERT MARTENSEN recently completed his doctoral dissertation, entitled 'The Politics of the Body in Early Modern England', at the University of California, San Francisco. He teaches the history of medicine at Harvard Medical School and practises medicine in Boston. In addition to early modern European medicine and culture, his research interests include the history of religion and medicine and the history of hospitals.

ANGUS MCLAREN is Professor of History at the University of Victoria. His many books include: *A History of Contraception* and *A Prescription for Murder: The Victorian Serial Killings of Dr Thomas Neill Cream*.

MICHAEL MITTERAUER is Professor of Social History at the University of Vienna where his initial work concerned medieval urban history and the history of the aristocracy, followed by projects on the social history of the family. Many of his publications deal with this topic, the most recent of these being: *Historisch-anthropologische Familienforschung*, 1990; *Familie und Arbeitsteilung*, 1992. The chapter in this volume has been developed from his study on 'Christianity and Endogamy' published in *Continuity and Change*, 1992. Professor Mitterauer is currently working on a volume entitled *Ahnen und Heilige: Namengebung in der europäischen Geschichte*.

GEORGE L. MOSSE is Professor Emeritus, University of Wisconsin-Madison and the Hebrew University, Jerusalem. Publications include *Towards the Final Solution: Nationalism and Sexuality*; *Fallen Soldiers: Reshaping the Memory of the World Wars*.

CHRISTOPHER PHIPPS was educated at the universities of Kent, Southern California, and London. He now works at the London Library.

ROY PORTER is Professor in the Social History of Medicine at the Wellcome Institute for the History of Medicine, London. He is currently working on the history of hysteria. Recent books include *Mind Forg'd Manacles: Madness in England from the Restoration to the Regency* (Athlone, 1987); *A Social History of Madness* (Weidenfeld and Nicolson, 1987); *In Sickness and in Health: The British Experience, 1650–1850* (Fourth Estate, 1988); *Patient's Progress* (Polity, 1989) – these last two coauthored with Dorothy Porter; and *Health for Sale: Quackery in England 1600–1850* (Manchester University Press).

LONDA SCHIEBINGER is Professor of History and Women's Studies at the Pennsylvania State University. She is author of *The Mind Has No Sex? Women in the Origins of Modern Science* (Cambridge, Mass.: Harvard University Press, 1989) and *Nature's Body: Gender in the Making of Modern Science* (Boston: Beacon Press, 1993).

ACKNOWLEDGEMENTS

THIS book derives in part from a conference held at the Wellcome Institute for the History of Medicine in the summer of 1991 and organized by Michael Neve and Christine Stevenson. We would like to express our gratitude to those authors who read papers at that conference and who have patiently waited to see this volume emerge; our thanks also to those other authors who have joined our enterprise at a later stage. We greatly value the advice of Michael Neve and Christine Stevenson in helping us to bring this volume to press.

We wish to acknowledge our gratitude to the Wellcome Trust for funding the original conference, and to Frieda Houser, without whose administrative expertise neither the conference nor the volume would have come about. Lastly, we would like to record our appreciation of the support given to us by William Davies of the Cambridge University Press, for encouraging the sequence of volumes on large themes that we have been editing with Cambridge since the late 1970s. It has been a pleasure to work with him.

INTRODUCTION

THIS book addresses not the history of sex[1] or sexuality but of sexual knowledge, from Antiquity to AIDS, from India to Indiana, home of the Kinsey Institute. This is not to claim that it is comprehensive – the 'state of the art' does not admit it. What it shows is the need to analyse changing attitudes towards and prejudices about sexual knowledge. In various societies and at different times, has it been thought desirable or dangerous to possess knowledge about the erotic? Who has a right to know? Who should know *what*? This leads to certain perennial questions. According to what value-systems has sexual knowledge been deemed essential to humanity or alternatively out of bounds? Through what procedures has it come about that certain sexual information has been denigrated and rendered taboo, rather as proficiency in the black arts became condemned in Europe as intrinsically improper knowledge, pursuit of which would betray depravity of soul or a Faustian pact with the devil?[2] How far has it been judged the case with sex, as with so many other matters, that a little learning is a dangerous thing? – the preferable alternatives therefore being blissful ignorance or profound erudition. One concern of this book is, in other words, to probe the imperatives of sexual secrecy and the agendas of sexual enlightenment.

The authors who have contributed to this collection also investigate the shaping of sexual knowledge, enquiring in what ways general awareness, experience and lore have been transformed into what has been touted as sexual 'science', indeed sexology – unsurprisingly, that term in its English form is of American origin, dating from the dawn of the twentieth century.[3] The history of the making of sexual science is obviously of great interest, not least because the very endeavour has had to overcome so many impediments. Sex was inseparably bound up with individual attitudes and actions that occurred within the private domain. How *could* it then become the subject of a precise, objective mode of enquiry, conducted through observation and experiment, answerable to the methodological rigour claimed by physics or pharmacology? Who could make the bedroom a laboratory? Could everyday, empirical knowledge of human sexual behaviour be transformed into a science?

To deal with these questions has been the aspiration of twentieth-century sex-researchers, not least that of the grandfather of American quantitative investigation, Robert Latou Dickinson, who thought, in classic positivistic mode, that all knowledge should be rendered scientific and that everything sexual should be amenable to measurement.[4] Alfred Kinsey was initially a professor of zoology at Indiana University, a specialist in wasps, a passionate collector and taxonomist; to Kinsey, study of human sex life was apparently of a piece with the pursuit of entomology. Kinsey seems to have had a touchingly naive faith in the validity of questionnaires, interviews and statistical tables (as well as a trusting, perhaps credulous, attitude to respondents' replies). It is now almost half a century since the publication of his *Human Behavior in the Human Male* (1948). The proliferation of Kinsey Reports since then, sponsored by the Kinsey Institute, and of Kinsey-type enquiries, shows that such scientific aspirations continue to command academic and scientific support and maybe even public respect. Does the fact that America has been sex-surveyed more thoroughly than Britain indicate an ardent New World faith in science (or sex) or a greater Old World prudery? (It may, of course, also show that the social sciences in general have enjoyed and still enjoy greater standing in America.)[5]

Many different kinds of investigative techniques into, and bodies of knowledge about, sex may lay claim to authenticity. Such knowledge might assert its truth status through Higher Authority, being graven upon tablets of stone or inscribed in Holy Scripture. It might be derived from ancient texts, comprising *ex cathedra* pronouncements from the golden age of heroic thinkers, Hippocrates, Plato, Aristotle: small wonder that England's first best-selling sex manual dubbed itself *Aristotle's Master-Piece*.[6] Alternatively, it might assert its foundations in basic biology or endocrinology: anatomy would thus spell sexual destiny.[7] It might be derived from the essential truths of natural history, primatology or ethology;[8] or it might square with psychological doctrines or philosophical views of human nature and fate.[9] Moreover, within such stately homes of sexual truth, there could be particular suites of expertise, an *ars erotica* for instance, the accumulated wisdom of amorous delight, or an erotic freaks' gallery.[10]

This book scrutinizes such diverse notions about the nature, order and validity of sexual science – and the controversies they have engendered – while, over the longer historical perspective, examining the successive erection, modernization and demolition of assorted sexual disciplines. From this, it will be possible to ask what such bodies of knowledge reveal about the ideological and practical ends sexual science has served, bearing in mind the rise of various sociologies of knowledge committed to viewing science, to a greater or lesser degree, as social relations refracted through the prism of fact and theory, and to seeing 'sciences' as entities that are culturally shaped or framed. It goes without saying that a central question posed in many of the contributions to this book regards the ontological and epistemological status of sexual science: is there an objective, neutral science of sex, or are such bodies of knowledge essentially objectified prejudice and prescription?[11]

Dialogues between sexuality and science have lengthy and contentious histories. Within certain creeds, admittedly, the truth about sex has, putatively, been rather straightforward. In the Garden of Eden, the Bible tells us, our first parents were created in a state of perfect innocence. Eve disobeyed the Lord's command; the bittersweet fruit of the tree of the knowledge of good and evil was tasted; Adam and Eve recognized they were naked, and a new consciousness came into the world: carnal knowledge.[12]

This carnal knowledge, according to emergent Christian dogmas that for two millennia commanded intellectual assent and institutional sanction, was a double-edged sword. After the Fall, the lapsarian world was plagued and tempted with the interdicted forms of knowledge that had flowed from the forbidden fruit or from Pandora's box. Certain forms of sexual knowledge, notably erotica, were obscene, unfit for modest ears and eyes, indelibly tainted with lust, lewdness and lechery. Yet, pastoral theologians maintained no less strongly, there was also a becoming sexual knowledge. This, directed principally to the generation of children ('Go forth and multiply', the original pair had been commanded) but also to conjugal consolation, had been inscribed in the Scriptures and decretals: it was, after all, better to marry than burn. Safe custody of this wisdom was entrusted to the theologian and canonist, the priest and the paterfamilias. It was essential to protect the innocent and susceptible from the depravity of false information and scandal. The Christian centuries undertook a delicate balancing act, cherishing and according *imprimatur* to true wisdom about generation, while silencing or at least rationing all that was treacherous, filthy and prohibited.[13]

There have long been self-proclaimed sexual liberators – never more so than in the last hundred years – seeking, as they would see it, to deliver mankind from the mind-forg'd manacles inflicted by bigoted zealots dedicated to keeping mankind in woeful captivity. Such liberators have come in many shapes and forms: from medieval heretics and the libertines of the Renaissance, Restoration and Enlightenment (in a tradition running from Rabelais to Casanova) through to nineteenth-century liberals, free-love crusaders and modern prophets of permissiveness.[14] Such libertarians (as they will collectively be styled in this Introduction) have long been influential in shaping the agenda and assumptions of our written histories of sex. Latterly hand-in-glove with the Freudo-Marxian Left,[15] such *soi-disant* liberators have characteristically chosen to see themselves as fighting the good fight in battles between darkness and light, morbid- and healthy-mindedness, puritanism and pleasure, ignorance and emancipation. On the one hand, there has been the silencing censorship of Inquisition and magistrates, and, on the other, the bold rebellion of humane freedom fighters, crusading against persecution and the gaolers of the mind.[16]

It will already be apparent from the thumbnail sketch earlier given of Christian tenets that this 'heroes and villains' history of sexual repression and sexual revolt, though popular, is grossly simplistic. Traditional Christian society was not 'against sex'; rather, as recent research has reiterated, it saw its task as prescribing certain sexual acts while proscribing others. And such a 'saints and sinners' history will seem all the more deficient when we enlarge our historical vision beyond Christianity's authorized versions of ethics and behaviours and examine pagan traditions of erotic *savoir-faire* and the bodies of carnal knowledge associated with Islam, Hinduism and other world-historical religions and cultures.[17]

This volume thus aims to avoid repeating this by-now hackneyed and discredited story (in the libertarian mould) of sexual repression and liberation. Nor does it mean to go to the opposite extreme, and to construct an out-and-out revisionist account, 'proving' (as has been attempted recently, in their different ways, by certain Foucaultians, radical feminists and polemicists from the radical right)[18] that self-styled sexual liberation has been nothing but a sham perpetrated on unsuspecting victims, seduced by specious erotic daydreams and the phoney rhetoric of free love. Rather than engaging in partisan polemics, the point of this volume is to analyse and reassess salient aspects of the history of *sexual knowledge*.

And here an intriguing feature requires consideration. For within the libertarian tradition, it was always taken for granted that the cause of sexual emancipation and the cause of sexual science were as one, comrades in arms. Sex is good; knowledge is good; sexual knowledge (so this liberal calculus would run) must therefore be a double desideratum. Increase of sexual knowledge, it has thus been assumed, will make for greater sexual freedom, heightened sexual pleasure, realization of human desires and drives, and truer psychosexual fulfilment.[19] Or, to look on the therapeutic side, dissemination of sexual knowledge (reformers have pronounced) would diminish frustration, enhance understanding of the roots of criminal psychopathology, aid fertility and conception where desired, improve contraceptive techniques, maximize fulfilment, and so forth. If erotic erudition was suspect within the Christian creed, for 'libertarians' the advancement of carnal knowledge was envisaged as pure gain, the union of truth and happiness.

Underpinning this implicit faith in the marriage of sexual liberation with sexual science, of sexual and intellectual freedom, have been shared assumptions, rarely made explicit but subtly reinforced in metaphor and emotionally charged symbols. The cause of sexual liberation has traditionally been represented as involving more successful, more frequent, more joyous penetration: erection, coition, orgasm, ejaculation have been central topics within sexology. Within what feminists typically term patriarchal societies, sexual liberation and scientific breakthroughs since the seventeenth century have been mutually, if mainly unconsciously, stimulated by penetrative images and viewed as equally desirable. Freud liked to portray himself as a *conquistador*, comparing the practice of psychoanalysis to making a conquest. Indeed, within certain radical traditions, from the Ranters after the English Civil War through to Freudo-Marxists like Wilhelm Reich, sexual emancipation has been presented as a politically revolutionary act, the paradigm case of human liberation.[20] Agenda of this kind, influential at least since Bacon's depiction of science as delving into and dominating a Nature understood to be female, have now been subjected to comprehensive critique by feminist historians and literary scholars.[21]

This convenient conflation of scientific enquiry and (essentially male) sexual activity has been influential since about 1980. It has reinforced all manner of earlier sexual campaigns of the twentieth century, notably lobbies for sex education and freedom of information about venereal diseases and contraception, battles for sexual rights (contraception), and for sexual free speech. And it has, not least, shaped the narratives and assumptions of received histories of sexual thinking.

But in recent years these commonplaces have been challenged, controversies have erupted, and revisions have been undertaken. A growing awareness of the mixed blessings brought by 1960s permissiveness to the 'pill generation', the formation of feminist and minority rights movements, the advent of AIDS and its accompanying homophobic and conservative backlash – all of these, as Richard Davenport-Hines and Christopher Phipps show below in their essay, 'Tainted Love' (chapter 17), have muddied the waters and washed away the once clear boundary-lines of the sexual debate. The old entrenched libertarian truths can no longer unquestioningly be accepted as factually, ethically or politically correct, and narratives about sex are undergoing rapid and radical transformation.[22] Liberationist renderings still command stalwart loyalties – few academics, fundamentally committed as they must be to intellectual freedom, could seriously countenance a reversion to censorship or seek the reimposition of conspiracies of sexual silence.[23] But recognition has grown that the liberal version at best tells one side of the story; and that those facts it does recount have been selective and ideologically loaded. They told the tale from the viewpoint of those who, traditionally the underdogs, were finally to become the winners – the sex doctors, anarchists, liberal crusaders and Freudian intellectuals. So if the narrative had a ring of radicalism, it was also banally Whiggish through and through; sexual truth was patent (to all with eyes to see) and time would secure its triumph. Not least, its register, accent and diction were male, middle-class and basically heterosexual. Liberal pieties about releasing the libido from customary shackles endorsed macho man (and his mates), entailing a view of sexuality, classically embodied in the Freudian theory of penis envy, that enshrined the 'healthy' heterosexual male libido as its yardstick. It was a view that, while often giving nods of sympathy to deviations from that norm, nevertheless saw them as *deviations* – albeit ones that might be treated or tolerated. At its blindest or most complacent, the liberal view offered a blanket denunciation of traditional teachings about sexuality as 'repression', while giving little serious consideration to sexualities other than the dominant paradigm: little recognition to female sexuality, to homosexualities, to non-genital, non-penetrative sexualities.[24]

All this encrusted 'truth', which set the mould for popular English-language texts like Gordon Rattray Taylor's *Sex in History*, published in 1954, Wayland Young's *Eros Denied* (1964), or Reay Tannahill's *Sex in History* (1980), has convincingly been challenged in recent years from many scholarly standpoints. For one thing, the biologism explicit or latent in received liberal versions has been detected and deplored: too often, we now see, advocacy of greater (male) sexual 'release' has been conflated with 'progress'. We now appreciate that a discriminating history of sex must go beyond questions of frequency statistics and bedroom gymnastics, for sex is rooted more in the head than in the bed. For another, the writings of Michel Foucault and his devotees have contended that the repression model, fundamental to the libertarian telling, is a myth. Libertarian claims to the contrary, Western sexual *mores* have been far from universally straitjacketed and silenced. Over the centuries, Europe enjoyed a crescendo of sexual discourse and erotic expression. Indeed, so runs the Foucaultian version, it may be the liberators' own 'knowledges' that have unwittingly promoted the greatest sexual compulsions and the most inhibiting doctrines, not least the modern orthodoxies that privilege sex as the quintessence of the self and the *primum mobile* of the good life. What is therefore historically puzzling, Foucault argued, is not 'repression' but rather the tenacity of the myth of repression, the upholding of which has depended on an unholy alliance of bad faith and false consciousness that itself requires further exploration.[25]

Foucault's convictions have been adopted in complex ways in many modes of textual analysis and literary criticism, notably post-structuralism and deconstructionism, that call into question any residual notions of sexual 'essentialism'. Such critics have maintained that sexuality makes no sense except as inscribed in language and discourse; hence study of sexuality, properly understood, must centre on discourses of desire, exploring words, language and symbols: sex is a semantic construct, contingent upon particular economies of representation.[26] Such views, in turn, have been adopted and developed by various historical subdisciplines – women's history, gay history, lesbian history, people's history – whose champions have insisted, following Foucault, that the liberal version imposes a repressiveness of its own, taking for granted a semblance of compulsory heterosexuality, ensconced in the fetish of the phallus (and for women, according to Freud, penis envy and the mature primacy of the *vaginal* orgasm).[27] In these rival, dissenting readings, sex and its history have become decentred, and the polymorphously perverse has come into its own. Not least, in reaction to the new politico-cultural conservatism rampant in Thatcher's Britain and Reagan's USA, and attending the profound rethinking and regroupings required by the AIDS epidemic,[28] the question has had to be posed: What does sex mean anyway? What is its essential identity, if it possesses such a thing? What is its value? Should sexuality command the limelight that it has enjoyed over the last thirty or forty years?

Notions of sexuality as a psychobiological entity possessed of a stable meaning may be dissolving. With the *fin de siècle* upon us, the sociologist Anthony Giddens has recently asserted, sex is being viewed less in terms of familiar, self-evident genitality (widely dismissed as a leftover from the world we have lost when sex was synonymous with reproduction), and is being transformed into a technique of self-fashioning within the wider politics of the self. Sex today appears to be having less to do with biological gender and genital manoeuvres; many regard it as concerned, rather, with self-definition and satisfaction, be it through models of restraint – even a new celibacy – or celebrations of narcissism and virtual-reality masturbatory fantasies proceeding from a self-stimulated erotics of the imagination.[29]

There is, in short, no longer – if ever there was – any consensus about how to tell the history of sexual knowledge and evaluate its ideological functioning in culture and society. Can it then be meaningful to speak of a rise of sexual science in the manner we surely can speak of the rise of astronomy? Can sexual chemistry be studied in the same way as chemistry itself? – precisely, of course, the question underlying Goethe's thought-experiment novel, *Elective Affinities*. Is it valid to speak about human sexuality as part of a continuum with the sexual biology of the animal kingdom? These are issues touched upon in many of the chapters in this book, and systematically discussed in Londa Schiebinger's 'Mammals, Primatology and Sexology', an exploration of Linnaeus's view of sex, gender and of *Homo sapiens*'s place in the economy of nature, and also Simon Frankel's 'The Eclipse of Sexual Selection Theory', which addresses Darwinian perceptions of human and animal relations in the first half of the twentieth century. Frankel makes the observation that we must resist taking evolutionary biology's accounts of animal sexual behaviour at face value, as if they were neutral and objective. In a manner offering parallels to Kinsey, Julian Huxley and fellow ornithologists systematically if unconsciously projected onto the animal kingdom certain moral norms of human sexual conduct, notably the commitment to monogamy they prized as the ideal in civilized society, and then offered inferences back for preferred human sexual behaviour – ones that explicitly rebutted the ideas of Freud and Havelock Ellis. It is surely also a mark of Huxley's own socially conservative and patriarchalist prejudices that his hostility towards Darwinian sexual selection involved a deep scepticism as to whether female birds and mammals truly 'chose' their males.[30]

The chapters in this volume explore the form and content of sexology roughly from Greek times to the present. The scene is set by Helen King's 'Sowing the Field: Greek and Roman Sexology', a wide-ranging introduction to the canons of sexual knowledge encoded and authorized in the writings of Antiquity, some biological, some erotic, and most the work of males (physicians, philosophers, poets) who, nevertheless, did not necessarily underwrite crassly phallocentric sexual dogmas. Finding Foucault's interpretation monolithic, King warns against adopting, with the dubious benefit of hindsight, too narrow and homogeneous a view of Graeco-Roman sexual teachings.[31]

Questions of hindsight are also raised in Vern Bullough's 'Sadism, Masochism and History, or When is Behaviour Sado-Masochistic?' (chapter 2), which juxtaposes the conduct and sensibilities of early Christians against the categories of late nineteenth-century sexology and against our own assumptions and asks: do we subscribe to the idea of a uniform underlying human sexual nature, or should we be thoroughgoing relativists? As Renate Hauser also demonstrates in chapter 9, Richard Krafft-Ebing and his late Victorian contemporaries developed a psychobiologistically essentialist notion of the presence of certain inherent propensities to sadism and masochism.[32] In Krafft-Ebing's opinion, sadism was the extreme form of the almost inevitable tendency to dominate that accompanied the male genitalia: masochism was likewise an inordinate expression of the natural female tendency to submission entailed by a biology of penetrability. Pioneer psychiatrists and sexologists commonly sought to discern various sexual pathologies latently present under other names in earlier epochs. Thus Krafft-Ebing, Freud and others took delight in revealing scandalous and unacknowledged sexual underpinnings of Christian asceticism. Mortification of the flesh was thus, in the eyes of science, a convoluted and self-deceiving technique for carnal gratification. How far can we still subscribe, it is one of Bullough's purposes to ask, to such 'objective' unveilings of sexual conduct? Bullough in effect reverses in his discussion the priorities of traditional sexologists. It is perhaps possible, with those pioneers, to read medieval behaviour in the light of modern sexology; but we must certainly, he suggests, turn the tables and comprehend modern sexology as shaped by medieval Christian culture. Why is it, Bullough asks, that preoccupations with sadism and masochism loom so large in the modern sexual imagination, professional and popular alike? To a greater or lesser degree, he answers, it is because of the profound cultural indoctrination wrought by Christianity, with its celebration of the agony of the Cross and its dream of redemption through Christ's suffering. Thus sexual dispositions and proclivities may be culturally deeply ingrained without being biological universals.[33]

A rather similar moral emerges from comparison of the discussions in three of the contributions below on pre-modern centuries: that by

King, already mentioned, Julia Leslie's 'Some Traditional Indian Views on Menstruation and Female Sexuality' (Chapter 3), and Patricia Crawford's 'Sexual Knowledge in England, 1500–1750' (Chapter 4). All three examine the framing of views of sex and gender difference, notably female subordination, on the basis of anatomical and physiological 'truths'. In the dominant discourses examined in these papers, menstruation was widely regarded as self-evident confirmation of a specific female inferiority – it proved that women were inherently 'wet', steadily accumulating and needing to discharge morbific wastes. But of the three cultures surveyed by these authors, it was only the medieval and early modern Christian milieu in which the female reproductive system served as the excuse for a shrill and systematic misogyny (characterized by the very epithet, 'the curse'). Various schools of scholarship, mainly informed by psychology or anthropology and some of them sympathetic to feminism, have sought to point to universal facets of the feminine, and amongst these menstruation has loomed large.[34] But the essays in this volume seek, by contrast, to stress the culture-specific aspects of the construal of female (and male) sexualities within particular bodies of sexual teachings. As Leslie points out, while traditional Hinduism doubtless attached certain stigmas to the female, it also esteemed the creative and pleasure-giving aspects of female sexuality; affording erotic delight formed an element in the equivocal vocation of the female.[35] Contrast of European and Indian teachings about the sexual role of women offered by these chapters demonstrates the diversity of inferences that culture may make from biology – or, more correctly, shows how biology itself largely lies in the eye of the beholder.

Thomas Laqueur has particularly argued that the very notion of what constitutes the differentiation of male and female – seemingly so elementary and natural – has been subject to radical transformation. Greek anatomy and medical theory bequeathed, he has argued, a 'one sex' model, that regarded the male as normative and the female as an inferior, even a 'monstrous' version of the male. It was not until the eighteenth century that, for complex physiological and socio-cultural reasons, the more familiar notion of 'opposite sexes' was constituted.[36] In 'The Transformation of Eve: Women's Bodies, Medicine and Culture in Early Modern England' (chapter 5), Robert Martensen broadly accepts Laqueur's programmatic assertion that a transformation in the conceptualization of gender came about in the early modern period, but argues that Laqueur is mistaken in concentrating upon anatomical evidence derived from the genitalia. For seventeenth-century medical anatomists, a key source of gender (and hence of sexuality) lay in the brain and the central nervous system. Modern concepts of sexual differentiation have hinged, Martensen argued, as much upon the concept of the greater nervous sensibility of the (putatively rational) female as upon crude distinctions between male and female genitals.

Crawford's chapter broaches a further key feature of the forging of sexual science: the role of printing and the printed book in the establishment and dissemination of new modes of knowledge. Elizabeth Eisenstein and other historians have argued that modern science is unthinkable without the printing revolution launched by Gutenberg: print gave a new solidity to knowledge while promoting possibilities of criticism.[37] At the same time, the printing revolution created limitless new possibilities for the dissemination and popularization of knowledge.[38] The consequence was, as Crawford demonstrates, the differential stratification of sexual knowledge in the early modern period – the learned and the popular, the academic and the lay, the 'scientific' and the 'superstitious', their identities largely hingeing on their rung on the written/oral ladder. A hierarchy of normative and prescriptive sexual knowledge became thereby established, with different sorts of truths (high and low, elite and popular), and with various links bridging them.

The impact of printed works upon sexual practices and sexual prohibitions has been a topic widely explored of late. Thomas Laqueur in particular has taken note of the vastly increased anxiety expressed in the eighteenth century concerning onanism. How do we explain the rise of the masturbation scare in the eighteenth century?[39] It was precisely because, suggests Laqueur, amongst other modes of sex liable to be regarded as dangerous and damaging, self-abuse was so closely implicated with approved knowledge, with the fashionable polite literature of the post-Addison Enlightenment. Masturbation was perceived to be a habit excited by reading and the stimulation of the imagination that reading provoked. Onanism was thus hardly likely to be regarded as a serious threat before the flowering of a society that read itself into identity. Self-abuse thus became entangled and confused with self-improvement, thereby adding another spiral to traditional fears about the dangers of learning, and not least of solitude and privacy.[40] Against this background, and by means of a general survey of sexual advice manuals, Roy Porter's 'The Literature of Sexual Advice before 1800' (chapter 6) explores the moral dilemmas, real or rhetorical, expressed by authors of such tomes and perhaps experienced by their readers: Was sexual knowledge a topic proper for mass and free dissemination through print? If so, what rules must govern its writing? How could one guarantee that edifying works would not fall into irresponsible hands? Might not the very existence of printed sexual advice prove a school of vice? Porter here points to a phenomenon also explored in other chapters of this book: the ease with which bodies of sexual information could double as science and as *erotica*.[41]

As emphasized by Foucault and explored in greater detail by such scholars as Cynthia Eagle Russett,[42] it was the second half of the nineteenth century that witnessed the great mushrooming of sexological writings – formulations that in a rather self-congratulatory way ordered and validated a body of sexual knowledge whose very objectivity would serve a double purpose, authorizing the claims of science and thereby dictating certain sexual norms. What is particularly noticeable about such medico-psychological writings is the immense anxiety often generated surrounding speaking about sex at all – it was often portrayed as a risky business, liable to injure one's professional reputation – and the equally strict insistence that only one group of people enjoyed the authorized credentials and hence were burdened with the onerous duty: scientific and medical men.[43] In '"The English Have Hot-Water Bottles": The Morganatic Marriage of Medicine and Sexology in Britain since William Acton' (chapter 16), Lesley Hall demonstrates the domination of British sexual discourse from the mid-nineteenth century, by the medical profession, a body extremely circumspect in regard to the crumbs of information it deigned to distribute to the lay public, believing the facts of life both inflammatory and 'somehow very distasteful'.[44] Examining a comparable era in central Europe, Andreas Hill's '"May the Doctor Advise Extramarital Intercourse?": Medical Debates on Sexual Abstinence in Germany Around 1900' (chapter 13) tells a partially similar but also a somewhat different story. In Germany, medical men were no less prominent in attempting to establish their credentials for monopolizing sexual discourse; but while British medical educators tended to be rather conservative, a significant group of energetic younger German physicians, especially those based in Berlin, took it upon themselves to spearhead campaigns for radical sexual and moral liberalization. Abandoning the blatant chauvinism of the double standard while declining to embrace the new puritanism, numerous physicians argued on personal and medical grounds for the healthiness of a freer sexual expression.[45]

Once again, ambiguities strike us about the new late nineteenth-century sexological discourses. For one thing, as Angus MacLaren's '"Not a Stranger, a Doctor": Medical Men and Sexual Matters in the

Late Nineteenth Century' (chapter 12) entertainingly discusses, medical men might themselves enjoy rather a rum public image. In certain eyes, notably their own, they were benefactors of humanity. In the view of others, they might be torturers of dumb animals, persecutors of prostitutes, enforcers of dangerous and coercive smallpox vaccination, and generally heartless monsters more interested in research than healing. It was widely rumoured that Jack the Ripper must have been a medical man.[46] Convictions of this nature had real justification, since MacLaren's tale is one in which, partly because of the ambivalent involvement of medical men in atrociously conducted illegal abortions, it readily became difficult, in some circumstances, to distinguish doctors from murderers and murderers from doctors.[47] The motives and roles of medical men who chose to busy themselves in the provision of sexual services were, to say the least, thus laid open to searching question.[48]

There was also something profoundly ambiguous about what the medical specialists were actually declaring about sexuality. It was a point of faith amongst those who, by the close of the nineteenth century, may without grave anachronism be called 'sexologists' that their investigations were humane and liberal: they were enlarging sympathetic understanding, instructing magistrates, senates and the courts, and therapeutically benefiting anguished individuals. But several of the chapters below convey the paradoxes of that enterprise, both in aspiration and effect: Renate Hauser's 'Krafft-Ebing's Psychological Understanding of Sexual Behaviour' (chapter 9),[49] George Mosse's 'Masculinity and the Decadence' (chapter 11), Sander Gilman's 'Sigmund Freud and the Sexologists: A Second Reading' (chapter 15), and Michael Mitterauer's 'The Customs of the Magians: The Problem of Incest in Historical Societies' (chapter 10). Dealing respectively with major sexological formulations in the period between the 1870s and the Great War, these authors show how sexologists addressed themselves to sources of historical, moral, religious and legal ambiguity and developed 'scientific' classes of sexual deviancy to encompass them: the categories of inverts and perverts, homosexuals, lesbians, degenerates, the understanding of incest and so forth. It was a science, but it was also often social rescue. For *fin de siècle* anatomists of sex, working within such youthful disciplines as forensic psychiatry and ethnography, were involved in attempts to shore up cultural order by reinforcing sex-roles and middle-class morality in the teeth of the unnerving perils and affronts of modern life: streetwalking, child prostitution, domestic violence, incest, and all the other festering moral scandals of the city of dreadful night – to say nothing of sexual anarchy amongst 'new women', Bohemian artists, intellectuals and other 'degenerates'.[50] Sexology was also proferring a practical toolkit, the classificatory and diagnostic expertise required to administer the asylums, hospitals, reformatories and gaols charged to cope with the chronic masturbators, simpletons, child molesters, rapists, pregnant teenagers, prostitutes, and other sex offenders who terrified nineteenth-century elders and legislators.

Facing disorder and delinquency, late Victorian sexual science tabulated the varieties of erotic disposition, devising criteria demarcating normal folk from psychopaths, defectives, recidivists and criminals; and in some cases detention or medico-psychological therapies were recommended. Responding to the needs of courts confronted with cases of rape, gross indecency, marital non-consummation, exhibitionism, incest, impotence and pederasty, the illustrious forensic psychiatrist, Richard von Krafft-Ebing, compiled his encyclopaedic *Psychopathia sexualis* (1886), which itemized, often for the first time, if occasionally in the decent obscurity of Latin, the bestiary of sexual transgressions, from adultery to zooerasty, by way of bestiality, coprolagnia, exhibitionism, fetishism, frottage, sado-masochism, satyriasis, urolagnia, voyeurism and a hundred other ready-named perversions. In a slightly uneasy way, Krafft-Ebing combined the humane tolerance of the scientist with a deep-seated conviction of the need to distinguish between 'healthy' and 'degenerate' sex, and a dread of sexual anarchy. Slightly later, Havelock Ellis's significantly titled *Studies in the Psychology of Sex* (1905–28) further carved out the taxonomy and terminology of psycho-sexual types since familiar: homosexuals, paedophiles, nymphomaniacs, fetishists, transvestites, zoophiles, and so forth – labels somewhat rare before the twentieth century. Thus homosexuality, as Mosse shows, was widely interpreted as psychologically based, though 'deviant' sorts were also believed to be scarred by some symptomatic physical trait: effeminacy in the male, dull eyes, thick lips, large labia, preternatural hairiness in the female (facets, Gilman shows, prominent in anthropological studies of Jewishness).[51] It is noteworthy that Ellis's very first volume, published in 1894, had been titled *Man and Woman*, presenting an inexhaustibly compendious account of secondary and tertiary sexual differences. Many other pioneers of *Sexualwissenschaft* around the turn of the century – Albert Moll, P. J. Moebius, Iwan Bloch, Magnus Hirschfield, and not least Freud himself in his *Three Essays on the Theory of Sexuality* (1905) – regarded this insistence upon the scientific reality of ingrained sexual pathologies as a blow for progress. 'Perverts', they claimed, were not 'wicked', they were simply born that way; their abnormality was a kind of sickness, hence they should not be punished. For many early sexologists, as Gilman shows in his contribution, sexual peculiarities were regarded as arising from a racial basis: Jewishness and sexual deviation (not least incest) were widely linked.[52]

Simultaneously examining the sexual history of races and the rise of their scholarly study, Michael Mitterauer in 'The Customs of the Magians: The Problem of Incest in Historical Societies' (Chapter 10), pursues a double enquiry. He examines the development of different rules and standards governing the prevention of incest in the Mediterranean world of Antiquity, while at the same time evaluating the attempts of the emergent sciences of anthropology, sociology, zoology and sexology to give scientific meaning (through notions of system and universality) to such conventions and codes.[53] Examination of the work of Eduard Sachau, Edward Westermarck, and, later, Lévi-Strauss reveals an ambivalent interest in ancient sexual and marriage customs. On the one hand, there was a scholarly and historical desire to recapture the habits and practices governing individual societies; on the other, there was the hope of finding universal and thereby putatively natural scientific laws, paralleling of course Freud's own formulations on the incest taboo and the Oedipus complex.

The founders of modern sexology thus staked their intellectual authority on the conviction that certain people were physically and psychologically predisposed to engage in abnormal, inadmissible and deleterious sexual activity. Of course, no one denied 'unnatural' acts had always been committed: time out of mind, everyone knew, men had engaged in buggery, flogging or bestiality, women had masturbated, pleasured themselves with lapdogs or dallied with tribadism. But until the Victorian era, these were largely regarded as vices that might be indulged by various immature, profligate, impressionable, foreign or oversexed individuals, succumbing to lust, intoxication, libertinism, opportunity or necessity (e.g., life in a nunnery or in the navy). Sodomy, self-abuse and so forth had not traditionally been interpreted by doctors or moralists as products of abnormal germ plasms or diseased personalities, or as diagnostic of a hereditary group or a psycho-physically bizarre subset. They had been seen rather as vices, committed on a casual, one-off basis by libertines and debauchees who, in the classic Wildean manner, could resist everything but temptation. It was the role of modern sexual science to shift attention from practices to psyches, and thereby systematically to pigeonhole such sorts as 'deviants', the invert or homosexual, the narcissist, masochist or exhibitionist; indeed, it first invented all the sexual '-ists' and '-isms'.[54]

An illuminating parallel and contrast is offered in Vern Bullough's 'The Development of Sexology in the USA in the Early Twentieth Century' (chapter 14). The new nation possessed an abundant faith in science. Its upbeat culture in the Progressive era fused the requirements of procreation with an optimistic individualism to create positive visions of sexuality, mirrored and magnified through the commercial and capitalist exploitation of eroticism. In such circumstances, it can hardly be surprising that sexology developed rapidly in North America. What, however, differentiates early American from European sexology, Bullough notes, is the overwhelming concentration in America upon the study of 'normal heterosexuality' as distinct from the attention given in the Old World to homosexuality, the perversions and sexual psychopathology.[55]

Alongside a new social history of medicine, we have become aware, during the last two decades or so, of the need for a re-examination of the social history of science and ideas. Thus during these years investigation of micro-reality has gained due prominence in history-writing – in exploration of the dynamics of gender, of parents and children, the tensions of family and household, masters and servants, workplace and shop-floor, probing the complexities of struggle and collusion, duplicity and complicity, hegemony and subversion, control and resistance, individuation and stereotyping, socialization and difference, that comprise interpersonal cultural politics. Beyond the limitations of quantification and the jargon of sociology, richer histories of private life, popular culture, life-style and representations are being constructed, histories 'from below' that assume significance by being alert to cultural conflict, the construction of the self, the production and reproduction of power relations between the individual and collectivities, and, not least, the capacity of language and symbols to define reality.[56] One dimension that this new social history has been recapturing is sexuality. This volume is mainly about texts and teachings. But such matters cannot be divorced from social reality. Our hope is that these explorations of different dogmas will provoke further issues for the social history of sex.[57]

NOTES

1 It is worth saying at the outset that the very notion of the sexual is itself hotly debated: is it possible to draw a clear line between the erotic and, more broadly, the realm of gender, identity and the sensual? This Introduction will not explore that issue, but for illuminating discussion see Stephen Heath, *The*

Sexual Fix (New York: Schocken; London: Macmillan, 1982). There are some helpful general surveys of the history of sex. See Sander Gilman, *Sexuality* (New York: Wiley, 1989); Vern L. Bullough, *Sex, Society and History* (New York: Science History Publications, 1976). At a popular level, see Reay Tannahill, *Sex in History* (New York: Stein and Day, 1980); Gordon Rattray Taylor, *Sex in History* (New York: Vanguard, 1954; New York: Harper and Row, 1973); Harriett Gilbert, *A Women's History of Sex* (London: Pandora, 1987).

2 On the history of ambiguous attitudes towards knowledge in general, see Jean Delumeau, *Sin and Fear. The Emergence of a Western Guilt Culture, 13th-18th Centuries* (New York: St Martin's Press, 1990).

3 1902 in fact. On the rise of North American sexology, see chapter 14, Vern Bullough's essay, 'American Sex Research 1910-1930'. The term *Sexualwissenschaft* is often attributed to Iwan Bloch.

4 For the rise of sexological research, notably in North America, see Chapter 14 by Vern Bullough in this volume, which discusses Dickinson in some detail; Paul A. Robinson, *The Modernization of Sex: Havelock Ellis, Alfred Kinsey, William Masters and Virginia Johnson* (London: Harper and Row, 1976; Ithaca, N.Y.: Cornell University Press, 1989); and Janice M. Irvine, *Disorders of Desire: Sex and Gender in Modern American Sexology* (Philadelphia: Temple University Press, 1990); see also Vincent Brome, *Havelock Ellis: Philosopher of Sex* (Boston: Routledge and Kegan Paul, 1979).

5 Alfred Kinsey et al., *Human Behavior in the Human Male* (Philadelphia: W. B. Saunders, 1948); idem, *Sexual Behavior in the Human Female* (Philadelphia: W. B. Saunders, 1953). On Kinsey, see W. B. Pomeroy, *Dr Kinsey and the Institute for Sex Research* (London: Nelson, 1972). The sorry history of the latest Kinsey report, commissioned in 1970, appearing in 1990, shows, *inter alia*, a breaking down of any consensus that may once have existed as to the true disciplinary basis of a sexual science. See the revealing Introduction by Hubert J. O'Gorman to Albert D. Klassen, Colin J. Williams and Eugene E. Levitt, *Sex and Morality in the U.S.: An Empirical Enquiry under the Auspices of the Kinsey Institute* (Middletown, Conn.: Wesleyan University Press, 1989). It will be remembered of course that Mrs Thatcher, while Prime Minister, vetoed a survey of sexual habits proposed by her own Department of Health and Social Security, on the grounds that it would be an intrusion into privacy. That is peculiar, since her administration intruded into people's privacy more than any previous one.

6 For instances of sexual knowledge grounded in early philosophy, see Johannes Morsink, *Aristotle on the Generation of Animals: a Philosophical Study* (Washington, D.C.: University Press of America, 1982). For *Aristotle's Master-Piece*, see Roy Porter, '"The Secrets of Generation Display'd": *Aristotle's Master-piece* in Eighteenth-Century England', in R. P. Maccubbin (ed.), *Unauthorized Sexual Behavior during the Enlightenment* (*Special Issue of Eighteenth Century Life*), 3 (May 1985), 1-21.

7 For the grounding of sexual knowledge in anatomy and biology, see Thomas W. Laqueur, *Making Sex. Gender and the Body from Aristotle to Freud* (Cambridge, Mass.: Harvard University Press, 1990); Thorkil Vangaard, *Phallos: A Symbol and its History in the Male World* (London: Jonathan Cape, 1972); T. P. Lowry (ed.), *The Classic Clitoris: Historic Contributions to Scientific Sexuality* (Chicago:

Nelson Hall, 1978); John S. Haller and Robin M. Haller, *The Physician and Sexuality in Victorian America* (Urbana: University of Illinois Press, 1974); Sandra Harding and Jean F. O'Barr (eds.), *Sex and Scientific Inquiry* (London and Chicago: University of Chicago Press, 1987). Complex versions of essentialism appear in Germaine Greer, *Sex and Destiny* (London: Secker and Warburg, 1984). For exposure of such 'essentialism', see Lynda Birke, *Women, Feminism and Biology: The Feminist Challenge* (Brighton: Wheatsheaf Books, 1986).

8 See chapters 8 and 7 below, Londa Schiebinger's 'Mammals, Primatology and Sexology', and Simon Frankel's 'The Eclipse of Sexual Selection Theory'. For instances of sexual knowledge grounded in ideas of evolution and primate behaviour, see Donna Haraway, *Primate Visions: Gender, Race and Nature in the World of Modern Science* (New York/London: Routledge, Chapman and Hall, 1989). For social Darwinist and sociobiological constructions of sex and gender difference, see E. O. Wilson, *Sociobiology: The New Synthesis* (Cambridge, Mass.: Harvard University Press, 1975) and Lionel Tiger, *Men in Groups* (London: Nelson, 1969). Opposing these are R. C. Lewontin, Steven Rose and Leon Kamin, *Not in Our Genes: Biology, Ideology and Human Nature* (New York: Pantheon Press, 1984), and Ruth Hubbard, Mary Sue Henifin and Barbara Fried (eds.), *Biological Woman – The Convenient Myth* (Cambridge, Mass.: Schenkman, 1982).

9 For sexual knowledge grounded in psychology, psychiatry and ideas of human nature see N. O. Brown, *Life Against Death* (London: Routledge and Kegan Paul, 1959); Juliet Mitchell, *Psychoanalysis and Feminism* (London: Allen Lane, 1974); F. Sulloway, *Freud: Biologist of the Mind* (New York: Basic Books; London: Burnett Books, 1979); and Jeffrey Moussaieff Masson, *A Dark Science. Women, Sexuality, and Psychiatry in the Nineteenth Century* (New York: Farrar, Straus and Giroux, 1986).

10 Interesting on the *ars erotica* is Michel Foucault, *Histoire de la sexualité*, vol. I: *La Volonté de savoir* (Paris: Gallimard, 1976); trans. Robert Hurley, *The History of Sexuality: Introduction* (London: Allen Lane, 1978).

11 This view presupposes certain general notions of a sociology of knowledge and of science. For illuminating discussions, see Barry Barnes and Steven Shapin (eds.), *Natural Order: Historical Studies of Scientific Culture* (Beverly Hills, Calif., and London: Sage Publications, 1979); Barry Barnes, *Interests and the Growth of Knowledge* (London: Routledge and Kegan Paul, 1977); D. Bloor, *Knowledge and Social Imagery* (London: Routledge and Kegan Paul, 1976); Harry Collins, *Changing Order: Replication and Induction in Scientific Practice*, (Beverly Hills and London: Sage, 1985); H. M. Collins and T. J. Pinch, *Frames of Meaning: The Social Construction of Extraordinary Science* (London: Routledge and Kegan Paul, 1982); R. M. Young, 'Science *is* Social Relations', *Radical Science Journal*, 5 (1977), 65–129. A good survey is offered in Barry Barnes, 'Sociological Theories of Scientific Knowledge', in R. C. Olby, G. N. Cantor, J. R. R. Christie and M. J. S. Hodge (eds.), *Companion to the History of Modern Science* (London: Routledge, 1990), 60–76. On the idea of 'framing,' see Charles E. Rosenberg and Janet Golden (eds.), *Framing Disease: Studies in Cultural History* (New Brunswick, N.J.: Rutgers University Press, 1992).

12 See E. Pagels, *Adam, Eve and the Serpent* (London: Weidenfeld and Nicolson,

1988); Mieke Bal, 'Sexuality, Sin, and Sorrow: The Emergence of Female Character (A Reading of Genesis 1–3)', in Susan Rubin Suleiman (ed.), *The Female Body in Western Culture: Contemporary Perspectives* (Cambridge, Mass.: Harvard University Press, 1986), 317–38; Frank Bottomley, *Attitudes to the Body in Western Christendom* (London: Lepus Books, 1979); Peter Brown; *The Body and Society: Men, Women and Sexual Renunciation in Early Christianity* (New York: Columbia University Press, 1988).

13 For balanced views of sexual propriety, permission and prohibition within pre-industrial Christendom, see Jean-Louis Flandrin, *Les Amours paysannes: amour et sexualité dans les compagnes de l'ancienne France (XVIe–XIXe) siècle* (Paris: Editions Gallimard Hulliard, 1975); idem, *Familles, parenté, maison: sexualité dans l'ancienne société* (Paris: Hachette, 1976); idem, 'Repression and Change in the Sexual Life of Young People in Medieval and Early Modern Times', *Journal of Family History*, 2 (1977), 196–210; idem, 'La Vie sexuelle des gens mariés dans l'ancienne societé', *Sexualités Occidentales. Communications*, 35 (Paris, 1982), 102–15; idem, 'Amour et mariage', *Dix-Huitième Siècle*, 12 (1980), 163–176; idem, *Le Sexe et l'occident: évolution des attitudes et des compartiments* (Paris: Seuil, 1981); idem, *Un temps pour embrasser: aux origines de la morale sexuelle occidentale (VIe–XIe siècle)* (Paris: Editions de Seuil, 1983); Vern Bullough and James Brundage, *Sexual Practices and the Medieval Church* (Buffalo, N.Y.: Prometheus, 1982); James A. Brundage, *Law, Sex and Christian Society in Medieval Europe* (Chicago: University of Chicago Press, 1988); Joan Cadden, *The Meanings of Sex Difference in the Middle Ages: Medicine, Natural Philosophy, and Culture* (Cambridge: Cambridge University Press, 1992); Danielle Jacquart and Claude Thomasset, *Sexualité et savoir médical au moyen âge* (Paris: Presses Universitaires de France, 1985), trans. by Matthew Adamson as *Sexuality and Medicine in the Middle Ages* (Cambridge: Polity Press, 1989); Beryl Rowlands, *Medieval Woman's Guide to Health: The First English Gynecological Handbook* (Kent, Ohio: Kent State University Press, 1981); Mary F. Wack, *Lovesickness in the Middle Ages: The 'Viaticum' and its Commentaries* (Philadelphia: University of Pennsylvania Press, 1990).

14 See, for instance, Paul A. Robinson, *The Sexual Radicals: Reich, Roheim, Marcuse* (London: Maurice Temple Smith, 1970); for an earlier tradition, see David Foxon, *Libertine Literature in England 1660–1745* (New York: University Books, 1965); Peter Wagner, *Eros Revived: Erotica in the Age of Enlightenment* (London: Secker and Warburg, 1986).

15 Herbert Marcuse, *Eros and Civilization* (Boston: Beacon, 1966).

16 For instances of this 'heroic' history see Fraser Harrison, *The Dark Angel: Aspects of Victorian Sexuality* (London: Sheldon Press, 1977); Richard Davenport-Hines, *Sex, Death and Punishment: Attitudes to Sex and Sexuality in Britain since the Renaissance* (London: Collins, 1990).

17 See Julia Leslie's essay in this volume (chapter 3) and also Basim Musallam, *Sex and Society in Islam: Birth Control before the Nineteenth Century* (New York: Cambridge University Press, 1983); Sudhir Kakar, *Intimate Relations: Exploring Indian Sexuality* (Chicago: University of Chicago Press, 1989).

18 See Andrea Dworkin, *Pornography: Men Possessing Women* (New York: Perigee Books, 1981); idem, *Intercourse* (London: Secker and Warburg, 1987); Sheila Jeffreys, *The Spinster and Her Enemies: Feminism and Sexuality, 1880–1930* (London:

Pandora Press, 1985); *idem, Anti-climax: A Feminist Perspective on the Sexual Revolution* (London: Women's Press, 1990); R. Scruton, *Sexual Desire* (Weidenfeld and Nicolson, 1985). These views are fiercely criticized in Camille Paglia, *Sexual Personae* (New Haven: Yale University Press, 1990).

19 This set of views is very clear in Wayland Young, *Eros Denied: Studies in Exclusion* (London: Weidenfeld and Nicolson, 1964).

20 Christopher Hill, *The World Turned Upside Down: Radical Ideas during the English Revolution* (Harmondsworth: Penguin, 1978); I. D. McCalman, 'Females, Feminism and Freelove in an Early Nineteenth Century Radical Movement', *Labour History*, 38 (1980), 1–25; *idem*, 'Unrespectable Radicalism: Infidels and Pornography in Early Nineteenth Century London', *Past and Present*, 104 (1984), 74–110. On Reich, see Paul A. Robinson, *The Sexual Radicals*. On Freud's macho imagery, see Lisa Appignanesi and John Forrester, *Freud's Women. Family, Patients, Followers* (New York: Basic Books, London: Weidenfeld and Nicolson, 1992).

21 Brian Easlea, *Science and Sexual Oppression: Patriarchy's Confrontation with Women and Nature* (London: Weidenfeld and Nicolson, 1981); *idem, Fathering the Unthinkable: Masculinity, Scientists and the Nuclear Arms Race* (London: Pluto, 1983); Ludmilla Jordanova, *Sexual Visions* (Hemel Hempstead: Harvester Books, 1989); Carolyn Merchant, *The Death of Nature: Women, Ecology and the Scientific Revolution* (New York: Harper and Row, 1980); Evelyn Fox Keller, *Reflections on Science and Gender* (New Haven, Conn.: Yale University Press, 1985); Mary Jacobus, Evelyn Fox Keller and Sally Shuttleworth (eds.), *Body/Politics: Women and the Discourses of Science* (New York: Routledge, 1990); John Christie, 'Feminism in the History of Science', in R. Olby, G. Cantor, J. R. R. Christie and M. J. Hodge (eds.), *Companion to the History of Modern Science* (London: Routledge, 1990), 100–9.

22 For new uncertainties, see Dennis Altman, *AIDS and the New Puritanism* (London: Pluto, 1986); Erica Carter and Simon Watney (eds.), *Taking Liberties: AIDS and Cultural Politics* (London: Serpent's Tail, published in association with the I.C.A., 1989); Simon Watney, *Policing Desire: Pornography, AIDS, and the Media* (Minneapolis: University of Minnesota Press, 1987); Cindy Patton, *Inventing AIDS* (New York and London: Routledge, 1990); Marilyn French, *The War Against Women* (London: Hamish Hamilton, 1992); Susan Faludi, *Backlash: The Undeclared War against Women* (London: Chatto and Windus, 1992).

23 Though there have been, for example, vocal feminist calls for the censorship of pornography. See Susan Griffin, *Pornography and Silence: Culture's Revenge against Nature* (New York: Harper and Row, 1981).

24 Points well made, for instance, by Jeffrey Weeks. See his *Coming Out: Homosexual Politics in Britain from the Nineteenth Century to the Present* (Totowa, N.J.: Barnes and Noble, 1977); *idem, Sex, Politics and Society: The Regulation of Sexuality since 1800* (London: Longman, 1981); *idem, Sexuality and Its Discontents: Meanings, Myths and Modern Sexualities* (London: Routledge and Kegan Paul, 1985). There is also now a vast feminist literature exposing the patriarchal prejudices of standard psychosexual teachings. See, for instance, Dale Spender, *Man Made Language* (London: Routledge and Kegan Paul, 1980); Mary Daly, *Gyn/ecology*

(Boston, Mass.: Beacon Press, 1978); Kate Millett, *Sexual Politics* (London: Virago, 1970). Juliet Mitchell's *Psychoanalysis and Feminism* (London: Allen Lane, 1974) attempts to demonstrate that feminism has much to learn from an understanding of Freud. For a historical dimension, see Ellen Herman, 'The Competition: Psychoanalysis, its Feminist Interpreters and the Idea of Sexual Freedom 1910–1930', *Free Associations*, 3 (1992), 391–438.

25 For Foucault's views see Michel Foucault, *Histoire de la sexualité*, vol. I: *La Volonté de savoir*, trans. Robert Hurley, *The History of Sexuality: Introduction*; vol. II: *L'Usage des plaisirs* (Paris: Gallimard, 1984); trans. Robert Hurley, *The Use of Pleasure* (New York: Random House, 1985); vol. III: *Le Souci de soi* (Paris: Gallimard, 1984); trans. Robert Hurley, *The Care of the Self* (New York: Random House, 1987); vol. IV: *Les Aveux de la chair*, announced by Gallimard, remained unfinished. There is now a vast and daily growing literature assessing these views. For the merest sample, see Arnold Davidson, 'Sex and the Emergence of Sexuality', *Critical Inquiry*, 14, 1 (1987), 16–48; Lois McNay, *Foucault and Feminism: Power, Gender and the Self* (Cambridge: Polity Press, 1992); Roy Porter, 'Is Foucault Useful for Understanding Eighteenth and Nineteenth Century Sexuality?' *Contention* 1 (1991), 61–82; and the fine chapter, 'Foucault on Sexuality', by Anthony Giddens in his *The Transformation of Intimacy. Sexuality, Love and Eroticism in Modern Societies* (Cambridge: Polity Press, 1992); John Forrester, *The Seductions of Psychoanalysis* (Cambridge: Cambridge University Press, 1990), 'Michel Foucault and the History of Psychoanalysis', 286–315. For the personal dimension, see Didier Eribon, *Michel Foucault: 1926–1984* (Paris: Flammarion, 1989).

26 See, amongst innumerable other texts, Lawrence Birken, *Consuming Desire: Sexual Science and the Emergence of a Culture of Abundance, 1871–1914* (London: G.M.P. Press, 1988; Ithaca/London: Cornell University Press, 1989); Jonathan Dollimore, *Sexual Dissidence: Augustine to Wilde, Freud to Foucault* (Oxford: Clarendon Press, 1991); Michael Worton and Judith Still (eds.), *Textuality and Sexuality: Reading Theories and Practices* (Manchester: Manchester University Press, 1993). Illuminating on the role of language are Dale Spender, *Man Made Language*, and Mary Daly, *Gyn/ecology*.

27 See the works of Sheila Jeffreys cited above in n. 18.

28 See, *inter alia*, V. Berridge, 'The Early Years of AIDS in the United Kingdom 1981–6: Historical Perspectives', in T. Ranger and P. Slack (eds.), *Epidemics and Ideas* (Cambridge: Cambridge University Press, 1992); Elizabeth Fee and Daniel M. Fox (eds.), *AIDS, The Burdens of History* (Berkeley, Los Angeles and London: University of California Press, 1988); *idem, Aids: The Making of a Chronic Disease* (Berkeley, Los Angeles and London: University of California Press, 1992); D. Fox, P. Day and R. Klein, 'The Power of Professionalism: AIDS in Britain, Sweden and the United States', *Daedalus* (winter 1989); Mirko Drazen Grmek, *History of AIDS: Emergence and Origin of a Modern Pandemic*, trans. Russell C. Maulitz and Jacalyn Duffin (Princeton, N.J.: Princeton University Press, 1990); Eric T. Juengst and Barbara A. Koenig (eds.), *The Meaning of AIDS: Implications for Medical Science, Clinical Practice and Public Health Policy* (New York: Praeger, 1989); Randy Shilts, *And the Band Played On: Politics, People, and the AIDS Epidemic* (London: Penguin, 1987); S.

Sontag, *AIDS as Metaphor* (Harmondsworth: Allen Lane, 1989); Simon Watney, 'Moral Panic Theory and Homophobia', in P. Aggleton and H. Homans (eds.), *Social Aspects of AIDS* (Lewes: Falmer Press, 1988).

29 See the valuable discussion in Anthony Giddens, *The Transformation of Intimacy*. For the sexual disruption characteristic of *fin de siècle*, see Roy Porter and Mikuláš Teich (eds.), *Fin de Siècle and its Legacy* (Cambridge: Cambridge University Press, 1990), and Elaine Showalter, *Sexual Anarchy* (New York: Viking, 1990).

30 On gender in nature and gender in society, see Haraway, *Primate Visions* and R. C. Lewontin, Steven Rose and Leon Kamin, *Not in Our Genes: Biology, Ideology and Human Nature* (New York: Pantheon Press, 1984).

31 For further studies of this era see Aline Rousselle, *Porneia: On Desire and the Body in Antiquity*, trans. Felicia Pheasant (New York: Basil Blackwell, 1988); John J. Winkler, *Constraints of Desire: The Anthropology of Sex and Gender in Ancient Greece* (New York: Routledge, Chapman and Hall, 1990); John Boardman, *Eros in Greece* (London: John Murray, 1978); Kenneth J. Dover, *Greek Homosexuality* (Cambridge, Mass.: Harvard University Press, 1978; updated with a new postscript, 1989); Eva Keuls, *The Reign of the Phallus: Sexual Politics in Ancient Athens* (New York: Harper and Row, 1985).

32 On the construal of the perversions in the latter part of the nineteenth century, see Renate Hauser, 'Sexuality, Neurasthenia and the Law: Richard von Krafft-Ebing (1840–1902)' (Ph.D. thesis, London University, 1992).

33 Illuminating are Joan Cadden, *Meanings of Sex Difference in the Middle Ages* (Cambridge: Cambridge University Press, 1993), and Joyce E. Salisbury (ed.), *Sex in the Middle Ages: A Book of Essays* (New York: Garland, 1991).

34 See, for instance, Janice Delaney, Mary J. Lupton and Emily Toth, *The Curse: A Cultural History of Menstruation* (New York: Dutton, 1976; rev. edn Urbana: University of Illinois Press, 1988) and (the significantly named) Penelope Shuttle and Peter Redgrove, *The Wise Wound: Menstruation and Everywoman* (London: Gollancz, 1978).

35 In questioning essentialism, we must beware any tendency to speak in a blanket manner of 'oriental sexuality'. For the East, and the sexual myths spun about it by Westerners and often perpetuated, unconsciously, by modern Western historians, see Ronald Hyam, *Empire and Sexuality in the British Experience* (Manchester: Manchester University Press, 1990); E. W. Said, *Orientalism* (Harmondsworth: Penguin, 1978); Kenneth Ballhatchet, *Race, Sex and Class under the Raj: Imperial Attitudes and Policies and their Critics 1793–1905* (London: Weidenfeld and Nicolson, 1980). For menstruation in Western thinking, see Charles T. Wood, 'The Doctor's Dilemma: Sin, Salvation and the Menstrual Cycle in Medieval Thought', *Speculum*, 56 (1981), 710–27; P. Crawford, 'Attitudes to Menstruation in Seventeenth-Century England', *Past and Present*, 91 (1981), 47–73; Martin Ingram, 'The Reform of Popular Culture? Sex and Marriage in Early Modern England', in B. Reay (ed.), *Popular Culture in Seventeenth-Century England* (London: Croom Helm, 1985), 129–65; John Addy, *Sin and Society in the Seventeenth Century* (London/New York: Routledge, Chapman and Hall, 1989).

36 A fine attempt to trace a cultural history of the human sexual body is Thomas

W. Laqueur's *Making Sex. Gender and the Body from Aristotle to Freud* (Cambridge, Mass.: Harvard University Press, 1990).
37 See Elizabeth Eisenstein, *The Printing Press as an Agent of Change: Communications and Cultural Transformations in Early-Modern Europe*, 2 vols. (Cambridge: Cambridge University Press, 1979).
38 See, for recent discussion, Roy Porter (ed.), *The Popularization of Medicine, 1650–1850* (London: Routledge, 1992).
39 On onanism, see Robert H. MacDonald, 'The Frightful Consequences of Onanism: Notes on the History of a Delusion', *Journal of the History of Ideas*, 28 (1967), 423–31; J. Stengers and A. Van Neck, *Histoire d'une grand peur: la masturbation* (Brussels: University of Brussels Press, 1984); Tristram Engelhardt, 'The Disease of Masturbation: Values and Concept of Disease', *Bulletin of the History of Medicine*, 48 (1974), 234–48; E. H. Hare, 'Masturbatory Insanity: The History of an Idea', *Journal of Mental Science*, 108 (1962), 1–25.
40 For further expositions of Laqueur's views see his 'The Social Evil, the Solitary Vice and Pouring Tea', in M. Feher (ed.), *Fragments for a History of the Human Body*, vol. III (New York: Zone, 1989), 334–65.
41 Valuable here are Angus McLaren, *Reproductive Rituals: The Perception of Fertility in England from the Sixteenth to the Nineteenth Century* (London and New York: Methuen, 1984); Janet Blackman, 'Popular Theories of Generation: The Evolution of *Aristotle's Works*: The Study of an Anachronism', in John Woodward and David Richards (eds.), *Health Care and Popular Medicine in Nineteenth-Century England: Essays in the Social History of Medicine* (London: Croom Helm, 1977), 56–88; P.-G. Boucé, 'Some Sexual Beliefs and Myths in Eighteenth-Century Britain', in P.-G. Boucé (ed.), *Sexuality in Eighteenth-Century Britain* (Manchester: Manchester University Press, 1982), 28–46. See also Alan Rusbridger, *A Concise History of the Sex Manual, 1886–1986* (London and Boston: Faber and Faber, 1986); Roy Porter, '"The Secrets of Generation Display'd": *Aristotle's Masterpiece* in Eighteenth-Century England', in R. P. Maccubbin (ed.), *Unauthorized Sexual Behaviour during the Enlightenment* (Special Issue of *Eighteenth-Century Life*), 3 (May 1985), 1–21; Otho T. Beall Jr, '*Aristotle's Masterpiece* in America: A Landmark in the Folklore of Medicine', *William and Mary Quarterly*, 20 (1963), 207–22; D'Arcy Power, 'Aristotle's Masterpiece', *The Foundation of Medical History*, Lecture vi (Baltimore, Md.: William and Wilkins Co., 1931); Thomas H. Johnson, 'Jonathan Edwards and the "Young Folks' Bible"', *The New England Quarterly*, 5 (1932), 37–54. For social background to early modern sexual practices, see G. R. Quaife, *Wanton Wenches and Wayward Wives: Peasants and Illicit Sex in Early Seventeenth Century England* (London: Croom Helm, 1979); Jean-Louis Flandrin, *Families in Former Times: Kinship, Household and Sexuality*, trans. Richard Southern (Cambridge: Cambridge University Press, 1976); Roger Thompson, *Unfit for Modest Ears: A Study of Pornographic, Obscene and Bawdy Works Written or Published in England in the Second Half of the Seventeenth Century* (London: Macmillan, 1979). These are issues well discussed in Peter Wagner, *Eros Revived: Erotica in the Age of Enlightenment* (London: Secker and Warburg, 1986).
42 For the rise of sexual science after 1850 see Cynthia Eagle Russett, *Sexual Science: The Victorian Construction of Womanhood* (London/Cambridge, Mass.:

Harvard University Press, 1989); Ornella Moscucci, *The Science of Woman: Gynaecology and Gender in England, 1800–1929* (Cambridge: Cambridge University Press, 1990).

43 Here men essentially means males, though in an age when women were breaking into science and medicine, females could assume such authority so long as they armoured themselves with appropriate professional qualifications. Marie Stopes routinely called herself 'Dr', though she was a Ph.D. not a doctor of medicine.

44 See also Lesley A. Hall, '"Somehow Very Distasteful": Doctors, Men and Sexual Problems between the Wars', *Journal of Contemporary History*, 20 (1985), 553–74; idem, 'From *Self-Preservation* to *Love Without Fear*: Medical and Lay Writers of Sex Advice from William Acton to Eustace Chesser', *Bulletin of the Society for the Social History of Medicine*, 39 (1986), 20–23; idem, 'An Unmanliness Despised by Men: Masturbation in Britain, 1850–1950' and 'Changing Perceptions of the Male Conjugal Role in Britain, 1850–1900', in Ad van Der Woude (ed.), *The Role of the State and Public Opinion in Sexual Attitudes and Demographic Behaviour* (Paris: International Commission of Historical Demography, 1990), 217–28 and 457–70; G. J. Barker-Benfield, 'The Spermatic Economy: A Nineteenth-Century View of Sexuality', *Feminist Studies*, 1 (1972), 45–74; idem, *The Horrors of the Half-known Life: Male Attitudes toward Women and Sexuality in Nineteenth-Century America* (New York: Harper and Row, 1976); M. Jeanne Peterson, 'Dr Acton's Enemy; Medicine, Sex, and Society in Victorian England', *Victorian Studies*, 29 (1986), 457–73, 569–90.

45 Regarding German developments, see Cornelie Usborne, *The Politics of the Body in Weimar Germany. Women's Reproductive Rights and Duties* (London: Macmillan, 1992). For background, see Iwan Bloch, *The Sexual Life of our Time, in its Relations to Modern Civilization* (New York: Allied, 1958; orig. publ., 1907); Vern L. Bullough, 'The Physician and Research into Human Sexual Behaviour in Nineteenth-Century Germany', *Bulletin of the History of Medicine*, 60 (1989), 247–67.

46 Judith Walkowitz, *The City of Dreadful Delight. Narratives of Sexual Danger in Late-Victorian London* (London: Virago, 1992); Nicolaas A. Rupke (ed.), *Vivisection in Historical Context* (London: Croom Helm, 1987), especially M. A. Elston, 'Women and Anti-Vivisection in Victorian England', 259–94.

47 On abortion see John Keown, *Abortion, Doctors and the Law: Some Aspects of the Legal Regulation of Abortion in England from 1803 to 1982* (Cambridge: Cambridge University Press, 1988).

48 Compare the eighteenth-century man-midwife: Roy Porter, 'A Touch of Danger: The Man-Midwife as Sexual Predator', in G. S. Rousseau and R. Porter (eds.), *Sexual Underworlds of the Enlightenment* (Manchester: Manchester University Press, 1988), 206-32.

49 Richard von Krafft-Ebing, *Psychopathia sexualis – With Especial Reference to the Antipathic Sexual Institute: A Medico-Forensic Study*, trans. Franklin Klaf from 12th German edn (New York: Stein and Day, 1978). For late nineteenth-century psychiatric renderings of sexuality, see Renate Hauser, 'Sexuality, Neurasthenia and the Law: Richard Von Krafft-Ebing (1840–1902)' (Ph.D. thesis, London University, 1992); Yannick Ripa, *Women and Madness: The*

Incarceration of Women in Nineteenth-Century France (Cambridge: Polity Press, 1990); Elaine Showalter, *The Female Malady: Women, Madness and English Culture 1830–1980* (New York: Pantheon Books, 1985; London: Virago, 1987).

50 For decadence and degenerationism see George L. Mosse, *Nationalism and Sexuality: Respectability and Abnormal Sexuality in Modern Europe* (New York: H. Fertig, 1985); Robert A. Nye, 'Degeneration and the Medical Model of Cultural Crisis in the French *Belle Epoque*', in Seymour Drescher, David Sabean and Allan Sharlin (eds.), *Political Symbolism in Modern Europe: Essays in Honor of George L. Mosse* (New Brunswick, N.J.: Transaction, 1982), 19–29; idem, *Crime, Madness, and Politics in Modern France: The Medical Concept of National Decline* (Princeton, N.J.: Princeton University Press, 1984); Daniel Pick, *Faces of Degeneration: Aspects of a European Disorder c. 1848–1918* (Cambridge and New York: Cambridge University Press, 1989). For the newly flourishing domain of studies of masculinity, see Peter Stearns, *Be a Man! Males in Modern Society* (New York: Holmes and Meier, 1979); Victor J. Seidler, *Rediscovering masculinity: Reason, Language and Sexuality* (London/New York: Routledge, Chapman and Hall, 1989); Lynne Segal, *Slow Motion. Changing Masculinities, Changing Men* (London: Virago, 1990); J. A. Mangan and James Walvin (eds.), *Manliness and Morality: Middle-Class Masculinity in Britain and America 1800–1940* (New York: St Martin's; Manchester: Manchester University Press, 1987); Heather Formaini, *Men. The Darker Continent* (London: Heinemann, 1990); Anthony Easthope, *What a Man's Gotta Do. The Masculine Myth in Popular Culture* (London: Paladin, Grafton Books, 1986); D. Bowskill and A. Linacre, *The Male Menopause* (London: Frederick Muller, 1976); Harry Brod (ed.), *The Making of Masculinities: The New Men's Studies* (Boston and London: Allen and Unwin, 1987); Arthur Brittan, *Masculinity and Power* (Oxford: Basil Blackwell, 1989); Victor J. Seidler (ed.), *The Achilles Heel Reader: Men, Sexual Politics and Socialism* (London: Routledge, 1991), and his *Recreating Sexual Politics: Men, Feminism and Politics* (London: Routledge, 1991). For male sexual problems see Lesley A. Hall, *Hidden Anxieties. Male Sexuality, 1900–1950* (Cambridge: Polity Press, 1991). For homosexuality see David F. Greenberg, *The Construction of Homosexuality* (Chicago, Ill.: University of Chicago Press, 1988).

51 Sander Gilman, *The Jew's Body* (New York and London: Routledge, 1991).

52 How far Freud's views on sexuality were influenced by current views about Jewish sexuality has been hotly discussed. See Sander Gilman, *The Jew's Body*, and, for a view playing down Jewishness in Freud's discourse, Peter Gay, *A Godless Jew: Freud, Atheism, and the Making of Psychoanalysis* (New Haven and London: Yale University Press, 1987).

53 Valuable here as a comparison is Carl Degler, 'Has Sociobiology Cracked the Riddle of the Incest Taboo?' *Contention*, 1 (1991), 109–30.

54 These points are well made in Jeffrey Weeks, *Against Nature* (London: Rivers Oram Press, 1991). See also Janice M. Irvine, *Disorders of Desire: Sex and Gender in Modern American Sexology* (Philadelphia: Temple University Press, 1990), 5f.

55 For background on the sexual revolution in the USA, see John D'Emilio and Estelle B. Freedman, *Intimate Matters: A History of Sexuality in America* (New York: Harper and Row, 1988). For the role of the doctor, see John S. Haller and Robin M. Haller, *The Physician and Sexuality in Victorian America* (Urbana:

University of Illinois Press, 1974).

56 For some introduction to this new social history, see the *History Workshop Journal*, the journal *Representations*, and Peter Burke, *New Perspectives on Historical Writing* (Cambridge: Polity Press, 1991).

57 For similar discussions of grassroots sex, see Françoise Barret-Ducrocq, *L'amour sous Victoria: sexualité et classes populaires à Londres au XIX siècle* (Paris: Plon, 1989); trans. John Howe, *Love in the Time of Victoria: Sexuality, Class, and Gender in Nineteenth-Century London* (London: Verso, 1991); Steve Humphries, *A Secret World of Sex: Forbidden Fruit, the British Experience 1900–1950* (London: Sidgwick and Jackson, 1988); John C. Fout (ed.), *Forbidden History: The State, Society, and the Regulation of Sexuality in Modern Europe* (Chicago: University of Chicago Press, 1992); G. S. Rousseau and Roy Porter (eds.), *Exoticism in the Enlightenment* (Manchester: Manchester University Press, 1989); R. P. Maccubbin (ed.), *Unauthorized Sexual Behaviour during the Enlightenment* (*Special Issue of Eighteenth-Century Life*), 3 (May 1985).

PART I

SEXUALITY BEFORE THE ERA OF FREUD

ONE

SOWING THE FIELD: GREEK AND
ROMAN SEXOLOGY

HELEN KING

WORK on all aspects of ancient sexuality has mushroomed in the last few years, following the publication in the 1980s of the two volumes of Foucault's *The History of Sexuality* that cover the classical world. These have provided a theoretical framework, based on the social construction of categories, which has rapidly become commonplace in classical studies. However, Foucault's use of the Greek and Roman past has not always been accepted uncritically: Amy Richlin has recently reminded us that Foucault's 'contemplative, self-disciplined, married pederasts', striving for mastery of self through control of their bodies, are also 'the men who made so many jokes objectifying women's bodies'.[1]

In this chapter I want to use the category of 'sexology' to examine not only what sort of information about sexual behaviours existed in the ancient world, but also the type of knowledge which was thought to be unnecessary or 'shameless'. Recent work on ancient sexuality has emphasized a number of interlocking features which may be taken as characteristic of sexual relations within both Greek and Roman culture, throughout the period of antiquity. Although there is certainly variation between, for example, Periclean Athens and late Republican Rome, or from late Republican Rome to the Roman Empire, and although further layers of complexity are added with the reception of Greek culture by the Romans, nevertheless four features remained largely constant.

First, the expression of sexuality was centred on a fundamental inequity, not only in male–female relationships, but also between male partners in a homosexual relationship. In literature, this inequity was represented by the imagery of predation, warfare, flight and pursuit.[2] Fear was believed to make a woman more attractive; this is particularly clearly expressed in the poets of the early Roman Empire. In Horace, Chloe shies away 'like a fawn seeking its frightened mother'.[3] Force is part of the game: Ovid gives the argument of the specific case ('she struggled like a girl who doesn't want to win'), of personal preference ('It only turns me on / when the girl says "I'm frightened"') and of general principle, since 'It's all right to use force – force of *that* sort goes down well with / The girls'.[4] But although women are presented as naturally passive and as terrified victims, they are simultaneously believed to be sexually voracious, insatiable creatures whose aim is to draw off men's seed.[5]

The second feature is more applicable to classical Greek culture. Male homosexual activity was, to some extent, seen as normal, but only if it was kept within certain clearly defined social parameters. Relationships between equals in age were frowned upon. In classical Athens, homosexual relationships ideally had some features of an initiation rite, being between a young, beardless boy and an older mentor.[6] However, even such relationships were hedged round with etiquette regarding the process of courtship and the giving and receiving of gifts and other signals, while a 'deep-rooted anxiety' about pederasty was expressed in classical Athenian law.[7] Aristotle argues that any enjoyment of what he saw as the subordinate, defeated role of the passive partner in a homoerotic relationship is unnatural;[8] on Athenian vase-paintings, the passive partner is never shown with an erection.[9] The Athenian figure of the *kinaidos*, the man who actually enjoys the passive role, is presented as a 'scare-figure', both socially and sexually deviant.[10] In Rome, male homosexual relationships were seen as 'Greek' and were acceptable for a citizen only if with a foreigner or a slave; relationships between partners of the same age were seen as particularly reprehensible, and only occur in anecdotes about the scandalous behaviour of certain emperors.[11] Again, inequity is seen to be central: sexual relations articulate a set of statements about social hierarchy.[12]

The third, closely related, feature is the importance of penetration; the main distinction in all sexual encounters, hetero- or homosexual, was presented as being between penetrator and penetrated. Jack Winkler's discussion of the second century AD *Dream Book* of Artemidoros shows how the meaning of dreams of sexual activity was centred on who penetrates whom, thus rendering a dream of sex with an animal 'unnatural' only in the sense that, in terms of social hierarchy, it is meaningless: 'If a man gains advantage over a sheep, so what?'[13] This focus on penetration may explain why lesbian relations are all but invisible, being seen as outside the realm of 'sexuality'.[14] About female homosexuality very little is known, and scenes of this kind are virtually absent from art;[15] for Greece, there are hints that the most common form was between a young girl and her chorus-leader, but it has been argued that reciprocity, the absence of the fixed roles of pursuer and pursued, was the main characteristic of such relationships.[16] The Roman attitude towards female homosexuality was even more negative than the Greek.[17]

A fourth constant is the objectification of women. In Greek myth the first woman, Pandora, is made by the gods for man; her attractive appearance conceals a ravenous belly and the mind of a bitch.[18] Women are often commodified as food, prepared for their consumption in such a deceitful way that the real is hard to glimpse beneath the facade, but then unwrapped and eaten.[19]

Within this context, what information on sexual behaviour was available in antiquity? It is not only the Greeks who 'had a word for it'; both Greek and Latin possess extensive sets of sexual vocabularies ranging from the technical to the everyday to the obscene.[20] They also seem to have had sex manuals; the names of writers of such works over the period from the fourth century BC to the first century AD survive, but mostly in the works of the Christian fathers such as Clement of Alexandria and Justin Martyr, who condemn these pagan works as licentious, immoderate and excessive.[21] The targets of such attacks, the manuals, are – with one important exception – lost. Thus this is 'a vanished literature, known only secondarily and from scraps'.[22]

What would be in such a sex manual? The Greek term for writers of these works was *anaiskhuntographoi*, literally 'writers of shameless things'.[23] The possession of sex manuals is linked by their critics to gluttony, drunkenness and buying sex, as evidence of the absence of a primary virtue of the ancient world, moderation.[24] It thus appears that pagans and Christians alike felt that there was something excessive about a book on the subject. It has also been argued by Holt Parker that men were supposed to know what to do without reading books, and were therefore rarely given much advice.[25] The content of such works was long assumed to have consisted simply of lists of positions for heterosexual intercourse. This assumption owes something to the desire to read back into antiquity an aspect of sexology which has received considerable attention from the marriage manuals of the 1920s and 1930s onwards.[26] However, support for the suggestion may be found in an ancient Greek prostitute called Cyrene, who was apparently known as '12 positions' because of the number of postures she offered. The tenth-century AD lexicon which mentions her also claims that the first to have written a sex manual was Astyanassa, Helen of Troy's body servant; it was she who was first both to discover positions for intercourse, and to write about them.[27] The theme of discovery, for all variations other than the face-to-face position, is taken up in the *Dream Book* of Artemidoros. Artemidoros notes that 'some say' the frontal position alone is 'natural'; he agrees with this assessment because, of the other animals, each species has its one proper sexual position. For man, all other positions were invented, as the result of insolence and dissipation.[28] Illustrations of the various positions in the manuals are also mentioned by the ancient sources, and may survive on Pergamene vases of the second century BC and in such buildings as the Regio VII brothel in Pompeii.[29] Such illustrations will be discussed in more detail below.

The most (in)famous proponent of the genre was a fourth-century BC woman, Philaenis, whose name then came to be used for sex manuals in general, and for prostitutes.[30] A few papyrus fragments of a work attributed to Philaenis, dating from the second century BC, were found in the early 1970s, thus giving us our first opportunity to find out what the Christian fathers found so outrageous. The editor of the fragments, Lobel, describes them as giving 'a systematic exposition of *ars amatoria* . . . summary and matter of fact'.[31] They suggest that there was more to such works than the lists of positions mentioned by her attackers, as sections 'On advances' and 'On kisses' were included; perhaps the material most talked about in antiquity was simply the lost final section 'On positions' of a manual which systematically progressed from attraction to consummation.[32]

The preamble to the text claims that it is written from personal experience, as an objective and scientific guide. Jeffrey Weeks, in a study of the history of sexology, is thus wrong to claim that 'new to the nineteenth century was the sustained effort to put all this on to a new, "scientific" footing';[33] on the contrary, the claim to scientific knowledge is central to the genre from the outset. The advice on flattery in the surviving fragments suggests telling an older woman she looks young, and an ugly woman that she is 'fascinating'. The genre thus teaches men how to deceive, although the very complaint they most commonly make about women is that the female sex is inherently deceptive, a feature derived from the first woman, Pandora, whose very nature was that of a beautifully wrapped package endowed by the gods with every charm, yet containing 'the mind of a bitch'.[34] This recalls Ovid's plea to his mistress, 'I wish you were less shapely or less slutty: / Such lovely shape doesn't mesh with wicked ways. / Your feats deserve hating, your face urges love.'[35]

Setting such works as the text of Philaenis within the context of the Hellenistic desire to classify in order to control, Holt Parker describes them as an 'ana-tomy' of sex, a cutting apart and naming of the components of attraction in an attempt to control them. They also comfort the male reader by assuring him that he will meet nothing unexpected in the sexual world.[36] I would add to this that they enable him to meet the deceitfulness of woman with deceit of his own.

The gender of the authors of such works, and in particular that of Philaenis, has long been debated. In antiquity there was a story that a man called Polycrates wrote a scandalous treatise on love, then attributed it to Philaenis, who strenuously denied her authorship.[37] Among modern commentators, Tsantsanoglou argues that the attribution to a woman is done simply to arouse the 'erotic curiosity' of the male reader; Parker suggests that since men are seen as capable of self-control, while women are represented as unrestrained, the cultural logic requires that books which are 'immoderate' must be ascribed to women; Myerowitz proposes that men write under female names because sex is 'women's business'.[38] In fact, all agree, this is literature produced by and for men, assuring them that what women really want is precisely what men want them to want.[39]

Another direction from which we can approach the largely lost contents of ancient sex manuals is by looking for parodies of the genre in the surviving literature.[40] The most famous passage to have been read in this way comes from the third book of Ovid's 'spoof-didactic'[41] poem *Art of Love* which, like the preamble to the papyrus Philaenis, makes claims to a scientific approach based on personal experience: 'This work is based / On experience: what I write, believe me, I have practised.'[42] In his advice to the women 'begging me for lessons'[43] the poet advises them to adopt a position which will show off their best features and disguise their physical imperfections; the woman with a good face should make sure she always lies on her back.[44] In this deliberately absurd parody of the sexual positions manual, women are objectified; there is no suggestion that they should choose a position based on their own pleasure. For a man, pleasure is gained by observing, and using, female beauty. If, as the papyrus fragments suggest, the Philaenis manuals covered considerably more than positions, then Ovid's advice on flattery should also be seen as a parody of this genre. The Philaenis papyrus suggests picking the woman's worst feature and then making it appear desirable. In his *Cures for Love*, Ovid advises the reader how to put himself off his former girlfriend by recalling, with comic over-exaggeration, her worst points.[45]

Another text which may owe something to the sex manual model is a fourth-century AD dialogue, Ps-Lucian's *Affairs of the Heart*. One of the speakers compares the pleasures of married love and the love of boys, recommending women over boys because they last longer; a woman is desirable from maidenhood to middle age, whereas boys pass their prime as soon as their beard starts to grow.[46] It is further suggested that heterosexual intercourse gives pleasure to both partners, while in homosexual love the passive partner derives none. Furthermore, a woman can be used like a boy, thus providing the male partner with two roads to pleasure.[47] The arguments in favour of love between men recall Aristotle's arguments for the *polis* as the highest form of human organization. Where Aristotle's *Politics* describes the village as adequate to supply subsistence needs, but the *polis* as necessary if man is to reach 'the good life', one speaker in Ps-Lucian argues that heterosexual relationships are about supplying basic needs, but love between men is superior precisely because, being unnecessary, it shows a higher level of civilization.[48] The speaker Theomnestos describes a ladder (Greek *klimax*) of pleasure for the lover of men: it is not sufficient to look at the loved one, but the progression runs from sight, to touch with the fingertips, to a light kiss, to opening the mouth, on to the use of the hands – squeezing a breast, grasping the belly throbbing with passion, touching the early down of puberty, and then on to 'warmer work', starting with the thighs and then hitting the target.[49] This 'ladder' model recalls the progression in the extant fragments of Philaenis, perhaps suggesting that this was the normal format of the lost sex manuals.

Sex manuals were not, however, the only books from which information on sexual behaviour could be gained. There is an ancient tradition of attributing sex manuals to midwives. The male authors of the medical canon show complete lack of faith in the medical aspects of such works; for example, Pliny claims that Lais and Elephantis disagreed in their recommendations for procuring abortion, and while one says that particular measures lead to fertility, the other says they will cause barrenness.[50] The main text on midwifery which survives from antiquity, Soranus's *Gynaecology*, is concerned more with the end product than with the beginning of the process. Other medical works too focus on fertility rather than on pleasure. The Hippocratic medical texts of the fifth/fourth century BC advise intercourse as a therapy for women's diseases, to moisten the womb. Here too there is a basic gender asymmetry, since, although men are also advised to balance their food, drink and exercise in order to maintain health, a woman's health is dominated by the sexual function.[51] These texts recommend spring as the best time for conception, and give practices to ensure that a child of the desired gender is conceived: tie off the right testicle if you want a girl, the left if you want a boy.[52]

Advice on positions for intercourse is not included, although marital intercourse is often recommended as a cure, or as part of the cure, for women's diseases. For example, in a chapter of the Hippocratic *Diseases of Women*, a woman whose phlegmatic menses and copious, sticky saliva show that she is 'too wet' is dried out by vapour baths, emetics and purges of the womb, while keeping to a dry diet and taking plenty of exercise. After the first menstrual period free of phlegm, she is told to sleep with her husband and continue aromatic, astringent fumigations to her womb. If her husband's seed does not fall out, she is given a further regimen which gradually reintroduces normal food to her diet. Intercourse can thus be used in conjunction with other elements of the medical repertoire.[53]

It is not only technical literature which could transmit some advice on sexual practice. Reading 'which lures the mind to sexual pleasures' appears in the therapeutic context of medical writing, sufferers from impotence being advised by Theodorus Priscianus to read 'tales of love'.[54] Longus's novel *Daphnis and Chloe*, a work in this genre from the early Roman empire, tells of the sexual awakening of the naive shepherdess, Chloe. Zeitlin argues that the novel works on the assumption that nature alone is insufficient as a form of sexual education; first Philetas instructs the pair, but tells them only about 'kisses, embraces, and lying down together naked',[55] then in the third book a neighbour's wife teaches the still-ignorant Daphnis the *techne* (craft) necessary in order to deflower Chloe, but puts him off by describing the painful and bloody process involved.[56] Only in the last words of the final fourth book of the novel does Daphnis do what he has been taught, and Chloe 'learn' that all until then had been merely play.

Generations of translators have had to cope with the significant amount of sexual information which appears incidentally in Greek and Latin poetry; until very recently, the usual strategy was simply to translate the offending passage into the *other* classical language. The seventh-century BC poet Archilochus describes a woman setting limits on how far the man can go; she suggests another woman of the household who would oblige if he is 'in a hurry'.[57] The man instead proposes a different 'pleasure of the goddess', to 'land in the grassy meadows'. Another fragment of Archilochus may describe fellatio: 'As on a straw a Thracian man or Phrygian / Sucks his brew, forward she stooped, working away.'[58]

A poem of Catullus describes how his girlfriend's sparrow is dead, the sparrow which 'never would wander from her lap' and which she could 'arouse to sharp bites'. This may be best understood as a description of impotence comparable to that of Ovid: 'And my girl didn't even disdain to incite you / softly with the motion of her hand. / But ... she saw no skill could make you rise.'[59] On more public occasions, Ovid boasts, he and his partner have been more successful: 'I've often petted to climax / with my darling at a party, hand hidden under her cloak.'[60]

Herodas, whose mimes were written 'for the amusement of the bookish intelligentsia of Alexandria'[61] in the third century BC, represents bored middle-class housewives who, once spied on while alone, are presented as sexually voracious. Koritto and Metro discuss the merits of the latest dildo, being passed round among their friends: 'No man has ever had a cock so very – / We are alone – so very stiff!'[62] But of course they are not alone; the reader is there too, sharing in this male image of what women are 'really' like.

No discussion of Greek and Roman sexology would be complete without mention of the visual arts, including such objects as vase-paintings, mirrors, lamps and engraved gems. Sutton estimates that only about 150 out of the 30,000 or 40,000 extant vase-paintings from classical Athens show copulation, although many others show symposia, drinking parties at which there is a strong sexual element. The heterosexual images, showing male use of women for the pleasure of the male, are mainly found on wine vessels dating from the period 575–450 BC, and Sutton suggests that their demise is linked to the rise of democracy leading to an emphasis on city values and less representation of individual gratification.[63] The tone of the homosexual paintings is very different; there is a more 'romantic' feel, while penetration is not shown, intercourse instead being intercrural.[64] Shapiro suggests that this representation of 'less than the reality' is because penetration is seen as demeaning to the recipient; to display a man being demeaned is thus seen as inappropriate.[65]

For the Roman Empire, in particular, evidence exists for sexually explicit pictures to hang on bedroom walls. These may have a direct relationship to the sex manuals of Philaenis and others. Ovid mentions 'small painted pictures' (*tabellae*), showing 'various sexual unions and positions', on the walls of the emperor Augustus's residences, while Suetonius's *Life of Tiberius* claims that this emperor had many highly lascivious pictures on his bedroom walls, together with the sex manual of Elephantis, so that nobody should lack an exemplar of the posture required.[66] Pictures which may fall into this category survive from the Roman world, some wall-paintings, others portable; descriptions of lost works are also preserved. The extant works are not always particularly well painted, Myerowitz noting that one of the difficulties for the artists seems to be 'what to do with all the arms and legs'. She has drawn attention to a first century AD Roman mirror-cover, showing a couple in bed making love, with an erotic *tabella* hanging on the wall over the bed.[67]

Such pictures can show generic couples, or mythical characters. The role of myth as a sexual exemplar is interesting, recalling Ovid saying of himself, 'My sex-life runs the entire / Mythological gamut.' In the *Art of Love* he jokingly suggests that the unhappy women of myth were ruined only through lack of sexual technique – the man who has done everything the characters of myth did is even able to give them advice on where they went wrong.[68]

The particularly explicit *tabellae* in the emperor Tiberius's bedroom were said to have included one by a famous painter of such pieces, Parrhasius of Ephesus.[69] This notorious picture showed one of the sexual positions of mythology, in which Atalanta orally satisfies Meleager (*in qua Meleagro Atalanta ore morigeratur*). Fellatio is shown more in Greek than in Roman representations, but Richlin points out that the central feature of Suetonius's Tiberius is that he is senile and impotent; he therefore needs to find ways of being fellated.[70]

The eighteenth-century *Monumens de la vie privée des douze Césars* of Pierre F. Hugues d'Hancarville, which falsely claims to be taken from a previously unknown Roman collection of cameos and medals, illustrates a number of the more scandalous scenes from Suetonius's *Lives*, such as Augustus prostituting himself to his great-uncle Julius Caesar.[71] One illustration in the fuller edition shows Tiberius admiring a painting in which Meleager sits while Atalanta kneels and fellates him.[72] Some of the plates were used to illustrate Karl Friedrich Forberg's *Apophoreta* or *Manual of Classical Erotology*, the German edition of 1824 listing 90 postures and illustrating 21 (taking XVIa and b as two), the English version of 1884 listing 90, but referring the reader to d'Hancarville for illustrations. Should we trust 'Baron' d'Hancarville's admittedly vivid imagination? There is some controversy as to whether Meleager or Milanion was Atalanta's successful suitor;[73] if Suetonius too was confused here, then the passage should perhaps be read in conjunction with Ovid's remark that 'Milanion bore Atalanta's legs on / His shoulders: nice legs should always be used this way'.[74] If this is combined with Suetonius, the infamous Atalanta position becomes something more complex than simple fellatio.[75] Hallett argues that the Latin may suggest *mutual* oral gratification in a standing '69' position: this position may be 'far more physically strenuous than the recumbent', but both Atalanta and her suitor were prototypes of physical fitness.[76] It is, however, necessary to set this incident in the wider context of the Atalanta myth. Sourvinou-Inwood has analysed it as a paradigm of 'wild marriage' in which the girl, rather than being 'tamed' by marriage, is made more wild; eventually she and Melanion have intercourse in a sanctuary, and are turned into lions.[77] Atalanta is thus a model of extreme sexual habits, and her sexual postures are not to be recommended.

Another notorious position in the ancient world, particularly in Greek culture, is for the woman to be 'on top', a position sometimes associated with another mythical couple, Hector and Andromache. Martial describes Andromache riding Hector as a horse, a position so exciting that it aroused the spectators to masturbation.[78] Andromache was, of course, Hector's wife; prostitutes would apparently refuse the position, or charge extra.[79] Catullus's presentation of himself to Ipsitilla supine, but 'prepared', may be interpreted as an invitation to his partner to ride him.[80] In Artemidoros, if a sick man dreams of sex with his mother, in which she is 'on top and "riding cavalry"', this means death, because the mother represents the earth, and to have earth on top of you means to be buried as a corpse. However, for a healthy man to have such a dream is not so bad, because this is the one sexual position in which 'the man takes pleasure without laboring'.[81] The worst possible dream for a man is to be fellated by his mother.

Myth may thus provide a language in which to speak of sexual variations, but the characters of myth are far from being models for mortals. Artemidoros here raises two further themes relevant to ancient sexology: the image of woman as earth, and the relationship between pleasure and labour. The dominant image of woman in classical culture is that of the field to be ploughed and sown. This combines the features of inequity, penetration and the objectification of women, and is explicit in many of the texts already discussed in this chapter. In the Hippocratic medical works, 'the young girl's flesh had to become porous and spongy, like earth that had been plowed for planting'; subsequent sexual ploughing promoted good drainage of the menstrual fluids.[82] The imagery of 'breaking up the earth' is used on Daphnis and Chloe's wedding night,[83] and Ovid's 'the wheat / Grows tallest in well-dug fields' suggests that frequent ploughing leads to healthy offspring.[84] The Roman agricultural manuals show a similar concern for ensuring that the soil is suitable for planting, while Cato advises that, having chosen a good farm, 'In his youth the owner should devote his attention to planting. He should think a long time about building, but planting is a thing not to be thought about, but done.'[85] Is one objection to the sex manuals that, in women as well as in fields, planting is a thing not to be thought about, but done?

The image of plough and field can also be turned upside-down for comic effect. Thus Catullus's mistress, 'Lesbia', is seen as a plough, running through the field of available men and injuring the little flower at the edge of the field which is Catullus.[86] Ovid argues that the earth is more powerful than the plough: 'the furrowed soil / Rubs away the curved ploughshare'.[87]

Carson has argued that work (Greek *ponos*), in sowing and ploughing, is used for the sexual act with the intention of producing legitimate children; play (Greek *paidia*) for everything else, producing pleasure.[88] A similar opposition has been detected by Zeitlin in *Daphnis and Chloe* where, before Chloe's marital defloration, all was 'pastoral play'.[89] This may suggest that sex manuals were about play rather than work, pleasure rather than labour. In the papyrus fragments of Philaenis, however, the author turns aside any such objections to her enterprise; it is *work*, rather than unnecessary play, she claims, basing her authority to speak on 'having worked hard (*ponesasa*) myself'.[90]

There was thus a range of information about sexual behaviour available in antiquity. Sex manuals seem to have given a ladder of pleasure, possibly culminating in lists of sexual positions. They sought to create control by cutting up the elements of sexual attraction, but they also taught deception, thus putting men, who should be able to master their bodies, on a level with unrestrained, shameless and deceptive women. There was considerable ambivalence towards 'unnecessary' sexual positions in antiquity, as part of a wider discussion on the relationship between pleasure and conception.[91] Sexual theory and practice were part of a debate on civilization, in which on the one hand it was believed that the 'unnecessary' was the more civilized, but on the other that 'natural' was best; however, the definition of 'natural' was itself the focus of disagreement, face-to-face being best in Artemidoros but, as far as conception is concerned, Lucretius favouring 'doing it in the manner of the beasts' with rear entry, the woman on all fours.[92] The question of the invention, or discovery, of sexual positions is in turn part of a wider discussion of whether sexual intercourse would happen at all unless men and women were first taught what to do.[93]

NOTES

1 M. Foucault, *The History of Sexuality*, vol. II: *The Use of Pleasure*, trans. R. Hurley (New York, 1985) and vol. III: *The Care of the Self*, trans. R. Hurley (New York, 1986). For a critique of Foucault's model of the ancient world, with particular reference to his treatment of the female, see L. A. Dean-Jones, 'The Politics of Pleasure: Female Sexual Appetite in the Hippocratic Corpus', *Helios*, 19 (1992), 72–91. B. Thornton, 'Constructionism and Ancient Greek Sex', *Helios*, 18 (1991), 181–93, criticizes what he sees as a reductionist use of Foucault in the work of classical scholars, while A. Richlin, 'Zeus and Metis: Foucault, Feminism, Classics', *Helios*, 18 (1991), 160–80, demonstrates how the

work of Foucault and his followers has written out not only the sexuality of ancient women, but also the pioneering feminist work on ancient sexuality published in the late 1970s and early 1980s.

2 For example, Ovid, *Amores* 1.9, line 3: 'Every lover is a soldier'; P. Bing and R. Cohen, *Games of Venus: An Anthology of Greek and Roman Erotic Verse from Sappho to Ovid* (New York and London, 1991), 6; on pursuit see J. Henderson, 'Greek Attitudes toward Sex', in M. Grant and R. Kitzinger (eds.), *Civilization of the Ancient Mediterranean. Greece and Rome*, vol. II (New York, 1988), 1249–63, pp. 1256–7; on military imagery see J. P. Hallett, 'Perusinae Glandes and the Changing Image of Augustus', *American Journal of Ancient History*, 2 (1977), 151–71. For the continuity of the idea that male pleasure lies in pursuit rather than in possession, see the sexologists of the 1920s and 1930s cited in M. Jackson, '"Facts of Life" or the Eroticization of Women's Oppression? Sexology and the Social Construction of Heterosexuality', in P. Caplan (ed.), *The Cultural Construction of Sexuality* (London, 1987), 52–81, p. 61. As P. Green, 'Sex and Classical Literature' (1983; reprinted in *Classical Bearings* (London, 1989), 130–50) has pointed out, all that remains in the ancient literature is what he calls 'sex in the head'; the relationship between this literature and actual sexual habits must remain uncertain.

3 Horace, *Odes* 1.23; Bing and Cohen, *Games of Venus*, 226; A. Richlin, 'Reading Ovid's Rapes', in A. Richlin (ed.), *Pornography and Representation in Greece and Rome* (New York and Oxford, 1992), 158–79; H. Montague, 'Sweet and Pleasant Passion: Female and Male Fantasy in Ancient Roman Novels', in Richlin (ed.), *Pornography and Representation*, 245.

4 Ovid, *Amores* 1.5: Bing and Cohen, *Games of Venus*, 263–4; *Amores* 3.4, trans. P. Green, *Ovid: The Erotic Poems* (London, 1982), 143–4; *Art of Love* 1.673–4, trans. Green, 187.

5 Passive: D. M. Halperin, 'Why is Diotima a Woman? Platonic *Eros* and the Figuration of Gender', in his *One Hundred Years of Homosexuality* (New York and London, 1990), 133; an abbreviated version appears in D. M. Halperin, J. J. Winkler and F. I. Zeitlin (eds.), *Before Sexuality: The Construction of Erotic Experience in the Ancient Greek World* (Princeton, N.J., 1990), 257–308. Insatiable: A. Carson, 'Putting her in her Place: Women, Dirt, and Desire', in Halperin et al., *Before Sexuality*, 135–69, p. 142; Halperin, 'Why is Diotima a Woman?', 129. On the related fear of adultery, D. Cohen, *Law, Sexuality, and Society: The Enforcement of Morals in Classical Athens* (Cambridge, 1991), 141–6.

6 K. J. Dover, *Greek Homosexuality* (Cambridge, Mass., 1978); F. Buffière, *Eros adolescens: la pédérastie dans la Grèce antique* (Paris, 1980); B. Sergent, *L'Homosexualité initiatique dans l'Europe ancienne* (Paris, 1986) and *L'Homosexualité dans la mythologie grecque* (Paris, 1984); trans. A. Goldhammer, = *Homosexuality in Greek Myth* (London, 1987); E. C. Keuls, *The Reign of the Phallus: Sexual Politics in Ancient Athens* (New York, 1985), 276–7.

7 The quotation is from D. Cohen, *Law, Sexuality, and Society*, 201. See also Keuls, *Reign of the Phallus*, 287–91; on the process of courtship, see Dover, *Greek Homosexuality*, 81–109; Sergent, *L'Homosexualité initiatique*; and E. Cantarella, *Bisexuality in the Ancient World*, trans. C. O'Cuilleanáin (New Haven and London, 1992), 17–21.

8 Aristotle, *Nicomachean Ethics* 1148b, discussed by Cohen, *Law, Sexuality, and Society*, 184 and 201; Halperin, 'Why is Diotima a Woman?', 131. On active/passive, see Dean-Jones, 'The Politics of Pleasure', 75.
9 Halperin, 'Why is Diotima a Woman?', 134.
10 Halperin, 'Why is Diotima a Woman?', 133; J. J. Winkler, 'Laying down the Law: The Oversight of Men's Sexual Behavior in Classical Athens', in Halperin et al., *Before Sexuality*, 171–209.
11 A. Richlin, *The Garden of Priapus* (New Haven and London, 1983), 220–6; J. P. Hallett, 'Roman Attitudes toward Sex', in M. Grant and R. Kitzinger (eds.), *Civilization of the Ancient Mediterranean. Greece and Rome*, vol. II (New York, 1988), 1265–78, p. 1272; Bing and Cohen, *Games of Venus*, 18; Hallett, 'Perusinae Glandes', 156; on Foucault's attempts to make the Romans more favourable to homosexuality than they appear to have been, see Richlin, 'Zeus and Metis', 170.
12 Halperin, 'Why is Diotima a Woman?', 130.
13 J. J. Winkler, 'Unnatural Acts: Erotic Protocols in Artemidoros' *Dream Analysis*', in *The Constraints of Desire* (New York and London, 1990), 17–44, p. 39. On Artemidoros see also S. R. F. Price, 'The Future of Dreams: From Freud to Artemidoros, in Halperin et al., *Before Sexuality*, 365–87, and S. MacAlister, 'Gender as Sign and Symbolism in Artemidoros' *Oneirokritika*: Social Aspirations and Anxieties', *Helios*, 19 (1992), 140–60. For an earlier recognition of the centrality of the opposition penetrated/penetrator, see M. B. Skinner, 'Parasites and Strange Bedfellows: A Study in Catullus' Political Imagery', *Ramus*, 8 (1979), 137–52, p. 142.
14 K. J. Dover, 'Classical Greek Attitudes to Sexual Behavior', *Arethusa*, 6 (1973), 59–73, pp. 72–3.
15 C. Johns, *Sex or Symbol: Erotic Images of Greece and Rome* (London, 1982), 103.
16 Halperin, 'Why is Diotima a Woman?', 136–7; on Sappho, Bing and Cohen, *Games of Venus*, 72, and M. Williamson, paper delivered at the conference 'Language and Gender', Loughborough, 2 May 1992 (forthcoming in the conference proceedings, ed. S. Mills, Longman, 1993); on Sappho's representation of woman as both subject and object, Winkler, *Constraints of Desire*, 162–87; for a general discussion of female homosexuality in antiquity, see Cantarella, *Bisexuality in the Ancient World*, 78–93. In a discussion of the Greek medical texts of the Hippocratic corpus, Dean-Jones argues that sexual relations between women were seen as medically inadequate; because a woman must be moistened by her husband's seed, neither lesbian sex nor masturbation can satisfy her 'real' needs: 'The Politics of Pleasure', 80.
17 J. P. Hallett, 'Roman Attitudes toward Sex,' 1266; in 'Female Homoeroticism and the Denial of Roman Reality in Latin Literature', *Yale Journal of Criticism*, 3 (1989), 209–27, Hallett argues that 'tribadism did go on in Rome and among the Romans of the classical period'.
18 On Pandora, see N. Loraux, 'Sur la race des femmes et quelques-unes de ses tribus', *Arethusa*, 11 (1978), 43–87 and J.-P. Vernant, 'Le mythe prométhéen chez Hésiode', in *Mythe et société en Grèce ancienne* (Paris, 1974), 177–94.
19 M. H. Henry, 'The Edible Woman: Athenaeus's Concept of the Pornographic', in Richlin (ed.), *Pornography and Representation*, 250–68.

20 J. N. Adams, *The Latin Sexual Vocabulary* (London, 1982); J. Henderson, *The Maculate Muse* (Yale, 1975) and 'Greek Attitudes toward Sex', 1254.
21 Clement of Alexandria, *Protrepticus* 4.53P; Justin Martyr, *Second Apology* 15.3.
22 H. N. Parker, 'Love's Body Anatomised: The Ancient Erotic Handbooks and the Rhetoric of Sexuality', in Richlin (ed.), *Pornography and Representation*, 90–111, p. 93.
23 For *anaiskhuntographoi*, see for example Polybius 12.13.1 on 'Botrys, Philaenis and other writers of shameless things'; discussion in Parker, 'Love's Body Anatomised', 91.
24 Dover, 'Classical Greek Attitudes to Sexual Behavior', 63; Parker, 'Love's Body Anatomised', 98; M. Nussbaum, 'Therapeutic Arguments and Structures of Desire', *differences* 2 (1990), 46–66, p. 49; on the combination of sexual and culinary indulgence, Winkler, *Constraints of Desire*, 114.
25 Parker, 'Love's Body Anatomised', 97. In his discussion of *Daphnis and Chloe* in *Constraints of Desire*, 101–26, Winkler shows that the novel plays on the opposition between instinct and learning, raising the question whether people need to be taught how to copulate.
26 Jackson, '"Facts of Life"?', 63–4.
27 On Cyrene and her postures (Greek *schemata*) see Aristophanes, *Frogs* 1327–8 and Suda, s.v. Dodekamechanon. Astyanassa (s.v.) 'discovered and wrote', *heure kai egrapse*, her postures.
28 'Natural' is *kata physin* (Artemidoros 1.79, translated in Winkler, *Constraints of Desire*, 214, and 91.12). See also Winkler's discussion in *Constraints of Desire*, 42. As with Cyrene, the verb used for the discovery of sexual positions is *heurisko*, which has the sense both of 'discovery' and of 'invention.'
29 M. Myerowitz, 'The Domestication of Desire: Ovid's *parva tabella* and the Theater of Love', in Richlin (ed.), *Pornography and Representation*, 150; Richlin, *The Garden of Priapus*, 228 n. 2. J. Boardman and E. La Rocca, *Eros in Greece* (London, 1978), 153–4, suggest that the six erotic schemes used on Pergamene vases of the second century BC could be based on the manual of Philaenis. For Pompeii, see J. E. G. Whitehorne, 'Filthy Philaenis (P. Oxy. xxxix 2891); A Real Lady?' in M. Capasso, G. Savorelli and R. Pintaudi (eds.), *Miscellanea Papyrologica in Occasione del Bicentenario dell'Edizione della Charta Borgiana* vol. I (Papyrologica Florentina XIX) (Florence, 1990), 531 n. 2.
30 Parker, 'Love's Body Anatomised', 93. Hallett, 'Female Homoeroticism', 215–16, discusses Martial's 'Philaenis', a lesbian with male genitalia who anally penetrates boys.
31 The papyrus fragments form P. Oxy. xxxix 2891. See E. Lobel, P. Oxy. xxxix (1972), 51 and the discussions of Q. Cataudella, 'Recupero di un'antica scrittice greca', *Giornale Italiano di Filologia*, 25 (1973), 253–63; K. Tsantsanoglou, 'The Memoirs of a Lady from Samos', *Zeitschrift für Papyrologie und Epigraphik*, 12 (1973), 183–95; M. Marcovich, 'How to Flatter Women: P. Oxy. 2891', *Classical Philology*, 52 (1975), 123–4; H. N. Parker, 'Another Go at the Text of Philaenis', *Zeitschrift für Papyrologie und Epigraphik*, 79 (1989), 49–50; Whitehorne, 'Filthy Philaenis'.
32 Whitehorne, 'Filthy Philaenis', 532.
33 Tsantsanoglou, 'The Memoirs of a Lady from Samos', 186, translates the

relevant words of Philaenis as 'those who want to live their life with scientific knowledge'. See J. Weeks, *Sexuality and its Discontents. Meanings, Myths and Modern Sexualities* (London, 1985), 65. *Contra* Parker, the existence of 'Philaenis' would suggest that men do *not* automatically know what to do – or at least that they need advice in how to obtain a woman with whom to do it.

34 See n. 18 above.
35 Ovid, *Amores* 3.11b: Bing and Cohen, *Games of Venus*, 273–4.
36 Parker, 'Love's Body Anatomised', 97–104.
37 Athenaeus, *Sophists at Dinner*, 335c.
38 Tsantsanoglou, 'The Memoirs of a Lady from Samos', 192; Parker, 'Love's Body Anatomised', 99; Myerowitz, 'The Domestication of Desire', 151.
39 Parker, 'Love's Body Anatomised', 106.
40 Ibid., 94.
41 Green, *Ovid: The Erotic Poems*, 339.
42 *Art of Love*, 1.28–9: Green, *Ovid: The Erotic Poems*, 167.
43 *Art of Love*, 2.745–6: Green, *Ovid: The Erotic Poems*, 213.
44 Parker, 'Love's Body Anatomised', 95–6.
45 *Cures for Love*, 323–40: Green, *Ovid: The Erotic Poems*, 248–9.
46 Ps-Lucian, *Affairs of the Heart*, 25–6; passage discussed by Halperin, 'Why is Diotima a Woman?' 135; on such comparisons between homosexual and heterosexual love, see Cantarella, *Bisexuality in the Ancient World*, 54–77.
47 Ps-Lucian, *Affairs of the Heart*, 27.
48 Ibid., 35.
49 Ibid., 53.
50 Pliny, *Natural History* 28.23 (81); on contraceptives and early stage abortifacients, see J. M. Riddle, *Contraception and Abortion from the Ancient World to the Renaissance* (Cambridge, Mass., and London, 1992); 82–4 discusses Pliny.
51 A. E. Hanson, 'Conception, Gestation, and the Origin of Female Nature in the *Corpus hippocraticum*', *Helios*, 19 (1992), 31–71, p. 57.
52 *Superfetation* 31 (ed. Littré, vol. 8, p. 500) cited by Hanson, 'Conception, Gestation, and the Origin of Female Nature', 45.
53 Dean-Jones, 'The Politics of Pleasure', 74; *Diseases of Women* 1.11 (ed. Littré, vol. 8, pp. 44–8).
54 Theodorus Priscianus, 2.11 (ed. Rose, p. 133), cited by H. Elsom, 'Callirhoe: Displaying the Phallic Woman', in Richlin (ed.), *Pornography and Representation*, 212–30, p. 215.
55 2.7.7; F. I. Zeitlin, 'The Poetics of *Eros*: Nature, Art, and Imitation in Longus' *Daphnis and Chloe*', in Halperin et al., *Before Sexuality*, 417–64, pp. 435 and 449. On the genre, see D. Konstan, 'Love in the Greek Novel', *differences* 2 (1990), 186–205.
56 3.15–20; Winkler, 'Unnatural Acts', 121; Zeitlin, 'The Poetics of *Eros*', 423; Montague, 'Sweet and Pleasant Passion', 242.
57 Bing and Cohen, *Games of Venus*, 54–6.
58 Iambic Fragment 42 (West) = Bing and Cohen, *Games of Venus*, 57.
59 Catullus 2, Bing and Cohen, *Games of Venus*, 197–8; see also Catullus 3. Ovid, *Amores* 3.7, trans. Bing and Cohen, *Games of Venus*, 43–4 and 269–72.
60 *Amores* 1.4, 47–8, trans. Green. Martial 9.22.4 suggests that the left hand, the

manus fututrix, is best for sexual manipulation (Bing and Cohen, *Games of Venus*, 266 n. 6).

61 M. B. Skinner, 'Nossis *thelyglossos*: The Private Text and the Public Book', in S. B. Pomeroy (ed.), *Women's History and Ancient History* (Chapel Hill, 1991), 20–47, p. 35.

62 Herodas, *Mime* 6.69–70: Bing and Cohen, *Games of Venus*, 174–7. For further discussion and paintings of dildos in use, Keuls, *Reign of the Phallus*, 82–6, who points out that these images are 'male notions of women's desires', and Dean-Jones, 'The Politics of Pleasure', 90 n. 45.

63 R. F. Sutton, 'Pornography and Representation on Attic Pottery', in Richlin (ed.), *Pornography and Representation*, 3–35, pp. 7–8. On pottery, see now M. F. Kilmer's systematic and well-illustrated book, *Greek Erotica on Attic Red-figure Vases* (London, 1993).

64 Dover, 'Classical Greek Attitudes to Sexual Behavior', 65–7; Sutton, 'Pornography and Representation', 14.

65 H. A. Shapiro, 'Eros in Love: Pederasty and Pornography in Greece', in Richlin (ed.), *Pornography and Representation*, 53–72, p. 57.

66 Ovid, *Tristia* 2; Myerowitz, 'The Domestication of Desire', 132; Suetonius, *Life of Tiberius*, 43.

67 Myerowitz, 'The Domestication of Desire', 133–4 and 146; also illustrated in Johns, *Sex or Symbol*, plate 35, and Boardman and La Rocca, *Eros in Greece*, 162–3.

68 Ovid, *Amores* 2.44; *Art of Love* 3.42, trans. Green, 215.

69 E.g. Pliny, *Natural History* 35.72, 'some smaller pictures of an immodest character'.

70 Johns, *Sex or Symbol*, 139; on the posture, see J. P. Hallett, '*Morigerari*: Suetonius, *Tiberius*, 44', *L'Antiquité Classique*, 47 (1978), 196–200; Richlin, *The Garden of Priapus*, 53 on Martial 9.67, in which fellatio is the 'something wickeder' demanded by the poet after anal intercourse with his girlfriend; Myerowitz, 'The Domestication of Desire', 137; Richlin, *The Garden of Priapus*, 91, and Hallett, 'Roman Attitudes toward Sex', 1275–6, discuss the wider problem of fiction versus fact in descriptions of the sexual proclivities of Roman emperors.

71 On d'Hancarville see Johns, *Sex or Symbol*, 22; F. Haskell, 'd'Hancarville: An Adventurer and Art Historian in Eighteenth-century Europe', in E. Chaney and N. Ritchie (eds.), *Oxford, China and Italy: Writings in Honour of Sir Harold Acton on his Eightieth Birthday* (London, 1984), 177–91; G. S. Rousseau, 'The Sorrows of Priapus: Anticlericalism, Homosocial Desire, and Richard Payne Knight', in R. Porter and G. S. Rousseau (eds.), *Sexual Underworlds of the Eighteenth Century* (Manchester, 1987), 101–53, p. 113; on eighteenth-century uses of Latin passages in sex guides, see P. Wagner, 'The Discourse on Sex – or Sex as Discourse: Eighteenth-century Medical and Paramedical Erotica', in R. Porter and G. S. Rousseau (eds.), *Sexual Underworlds of the Eighteenth Century* (Manchester, 1987), 46–68, p. 48. On the sexual image of Augustus, Hallett, 'Perusinae Glandes'.

72 P. F. Hugues d'Hancarville, *Monumens de la vie privée des douze Césars, d'après une suite de pierres et medailles, gravées sous leur regne* ([Rome], 1786), plate XIX and

85–8 (British Library PC 15.df.8); not included in the 1785 edition, which has only 24 engravings compared with the 50 engravings and fuller text of the later version. Another edition bearing the date 1786 (PC 13.ff.8) has different engravings.
73 Hallett, *'Morigerari'*, 199 n. 7.
74 Ovid, *Art of Love* 3.775–6 discussed by Richlin, *The Garden of Priapus*, 158–9; see illustrations 55 and 57 in A. Dierichs, 'Erotik in der Kunst Griechenlands', *Antike Welt*, 19 (1988), with 37 and 40 for vaginal intercourse in which the woman rests her legs on the man's shoulders. F.-K. Forberg, *Hermaphroditus*, translated into English by Viscount J. Smithson (1884), 61–3 cites this passage.
75 F.-K. Forberg's *Apophoreta*, the appendix to his *Hermaphroditus* (1824), notes the Ovid passage (p. 227) and in position VII gives the man standing while the girl is carried by him with her legs around his hips.
76 Hallett *'Morigerari'*, 199 and n. 9; for a rare representation of 69 in classical art, see the first-century AD Roman lamp illustrated by Johns, *Sex or Symbol*, 138. Cunnilingus is rarely mentioned in Greek literature, being seen as more distasteful than fellatio: Henderson, 'Greek Attitudes toward Sex', 1255; H. von Staden, 'Women and Dirt', *Helios*, 19 (1992), 7–30, p. 13 and p. 23 nn. 44–5. The Romans generally expressed considerable distaste towards the female genital secretions; see Richlin, *The Garden of Priapus*, 249 n. 18.
77 C. Sourvinou-Inwood, *'Reading' Greek Culture: Texts and Images, Rituals and Myths* (Oxford, 1991), 85–7.
78 Martial 11.104.11–14; Richlin, *The Garden of Priapus*, 159. Representations of this posture are more common in Roman than in Greek art: Johns, *Sex or Symbol*, 136–7.
79 Aristophanes, *Wasps* 500–2, *Women at the Thesmophoria*, 153; Machon, cited in Athenaeus 13.577d and 13.581c–f; Henderson, *The Maculate Muse*, 164; Henry, 'The Edible Woman', 264; Bing and Cohen, *Games of Venus*, 132.
80 Catullus 32; J. R. Heath, 'The Supine Hero in Catullus 32', *Classical Journal*, 82 (1986), 28–36; Bing and Cohen, *Games of Venus*, 202–3.
81 Artemidoros, *Dream Book*, trans. Winkler, 'Unnatural Acts', 214.
82 P. DuBois, *Sowing the Body: Psychoanalysis and Ancient Representations of Women* (Chicago, 1988), 67–81; ancient references to earth/woman listed by Halperin, 'Why is Diotima a Woman?', 283 n. 100. On medical texts, Hanson, 'Conception, Gestation, and the Origin of Female Nature', 41; J. R. Pinault, 'The Medical Case for Virginity in the Early Second Century C. E.: Soranus of Ephesus, *Gynecology* 1.32', *Helios*, 19 (1992), 123–39, pp. 129–30.
83 Winkler, *Constraints of Desire*, 124–5.
84 Ovid, *Art of Love* 3.101–103; Green, *Ovid: The Erotic Poems*, 217; on women as soil in relation to foetal growth, H. King, 'Making a Man: Becoming Human in Early Greek Medicine', in G. R. Dunstan (ed.), *The Human Embryo: Aristotle and the Arabic and European Traditions* (Exeter, 1990), 10–19.
85 Manuals listed by Varro 1.1.8–11, Cato, *On Agriculture*, 34–5 and 3.
86 Catullus 11: Bing and Cohen, *Games of Venus*, 37 and 201–2.
87 Ovid, *Art of Love* 2.474–5; Green, *Ovid: The Erotic Poems*, 180.
88 Carson, 'Putting her in her Place', 149–53.
89 Zeitlin, 'The Poetics of *Eros*', 425 and 458.

90 Tsantsanoglou, 'The Memoirs of a Lady from Samos', 187.
91 A. E. Hanson, 'The Medical Writers' Woman', in Halperin et al., *Before Sexuality*, 309-38, p. 316, argues that Hippocratic gynaecology is 'product-oriented', desire being encouraged because it is believed to lead to more perfect offspring.
92 Lucretius, *De rerum natura* 4.1259-62, recommends 'doing it in the manner of the beasts', to help women conceive more easily (see also Pliny, *Natural History* 10.63). This passage should be read within the wider context of Books 4 and 5, where Lucretius discusses the effect of social learning on erotic experience (Nussbaum, 'Therapeutic Arguments', 55-60).
93 The theme of this chapter has stimulated considerable interest among my colleagues; I thank them all for their enthusiasm, although I have considered it inadvisable to take up all their offers of assistance. The library staff of the Institute of Classical Studies helped with tracing bibliography, and I owe my initial interest in Philaenis to Dominic Montserrat.

TWO

SADISM, MASOCHISM AND HISTORY,
OR WHEN IS BEHAVIOUR
SADO-MASOCHISTIC?[1]

VERN L. BULLOUGH, DWIGHT DIXON AND JOAN DIXON

SADISM and masochism became pathological largely through the writings of Richard von Krafft-Ebing. In his *Psychopathia sexualis* (1886) sadism and masochism made up half of the four broad categories of sexual variation (the other two were fetishism and homosexuality) which he discussed at length.[2] Each successive edition of the book amplified and added cases but the basic structure remained the same.

Sadism was defined as the act of sexual arousal (including orgasm) produced by inflicting pain. Krafft-Ebing borrowed the term 'sadism' from the attitudes expressed in the novels of the Marquis de Sade (Louis-Donatien-François-Alphonse de Sade 1740–1814). De Sade had achieved notoriety from both his lifestyle and his fiction, particularly *Justine, ou les malheurs de la vertu* (published in 1791) and *Juliette ou les prospérités du vice* (1797).[3]

Masochism he defined as the opposite of sadism, since, instead of the desire to inflict pain and use force, the masochist has the desire to suffer pain and be subjected to force. He again turned to a literary figure for his term, this time the writings of Leopold von Sacher-Masoch (1836–1895), a historian, dramatist and novelist. Sacher-Masoch's fictional writings became stereotypes, almost always featuring a woman in furs (he had a fetish for furs) who, with a whip, symbolic of lust, scourged her male lover for his animal lusts. In his classic, *Venus in Pelz*, Wanda and Gregor are the active and passive participants in flagellation.[4]

Though Krafft-Ebing added more and more cases in each successive edition, he kept in a few incidents of historical sadism, mentioning the Caesars, Nero and Tiberius, who allegedly delighted in having maidens slaughtered before their eyes, and Gilles de Rayes, who was executed in 1440 on account of the mutilation and murder of more than 800 children.[5] His only reference to a historical case of masochism was that of Jean Jacques Rousseau, who described in his *Confessions* his desire to be subjected and whipped by a woman.[6]

Krafft-Ebing argued that sadism was a pathological intensification of the masculine character and masochism a pathological degeneration of the distinctive psychical peculiarities of women, although he included examples of female sadists and male masochists. His concepts of sadism and masochism as examples of individual psychopathology have become part of modern sexology as well as popular culture.

Many of those who followed his diagnosis and classification disagreed with him on details but did not challenge his assumptions about its pathological nature. Albert von Schrenk-Notzing (1894) preferred to use the term 'algolagnia' (a lust or craving for pain) for masochism and argued that the two phenomena of sadism and masochism were linked together.[7] Although the term 'algolagnia' has not generally been accepted, other investigators also emphasized the complementary emotional states. Havelock Ellis went further and argued that sado-masochism was not necessarily based upon cruelty, but instead might be motivated by love: 'The masochist desires to experience pain, but he generally desires that it should be inflicted in love; the sadist desires to inflict pain, but in some cases, if not most, he desires it should be felt as love'.[8]

Further broadening the concept was Sigmund Freud, who introduced the popularly accepted term 'sado-masochism' as two forms of the same entity, often found in the same person. 'He who experiences pleasure by causing pain to others in sexual relations is also capable of experiencing pain in sexual relations as pleasure. A sadist is simultaneously a masochist, though either the active or the passive side of the perversion may be more strongly developed in him and thus, represent his preponderant sexual activity.'[9]

Freud's modification of Krafft-Ebing became institutionalized in psychoanalytic thought and for much of the twentieth century it was the Freudian version that dominated in both the popular and scholarly literature.[10] In general, sado-masochism has been visualized as intrinsically pathological and its participants as a particular kind of people for whom the behaviour is a symptom of some underlying personality problem. Both sadism and masochism are still listed as diagnostic categories in the American Psychiatric Association's *Diagnostic and Statistical Manual of Mental Disorders*.[11] Most psychiatrically oriented writers on the subject have emphasized the psychopathology of the individual, although they have usually confined their work to either the collection or presentation of individual case histories.[12]

In the past few decades there has been a tendency to extend the definitions even further to cover rapists as well as their victims, abused and abusing spouses, initiators of child abuse, and even certain kinds of suicides.[13] Such an inclusive definition was exemplified in the human sexuality text of Masters, Johnson and Kolodny published at the beginning of the 1980s. 'Forms of sadism run the entire gamut from "gentle," carefully controlled play acting with a willing partner to assaultive behavior that may include torture, rape, or even lust murder.'[14]

Increasingly, in fact, sado-masochism has been visualized as not only a pathology but a social behaviour since it entails an interaction of individuals. Thus the interrelationships among, and the social meanings underlying, such aspects of behaviour as dominance and submission, aggression and passivity, masculinity and femininity, all have implications for what is now commonly defined as sado-masochistic behaviour.

Weinberg, Williams and Moser protested against such 'over generalization' by professionals and instead attempted to develop a construct based on the views of the participants on what constitutes sado-masochism.[15] They challenged the essentialistic or traditional model of sado-masochism and urged that it be replaced by a more atomistic one. Defining the essentialist model as one which transformed 'doing' into 'being',[16] they held that it was a model imposed from the outside. They also argued that the traditional model was inaccurate because no such personality type had so far been found. Instead they used the term 'sado-masochism' to describe an activity and to focus more on roles than on persons. By emphasizing how people interpreted their own behaviour they argued they had eliminated the essentialist question of whether people or behaviours are, in and of themselves, 'really' sado-masochistic and instead looked at the participant's own application of the label 'sado-masochism'.

Thus sado-masochism for them became a social process involving a set of social practices that sustained a particular class of erotic fantasies and behaviour which in turn generated sexual arousal. Members of their study sample viewed sado-masochism as a sexual experience grounded in fantasy in which the voluntary partners played dominant/submissive roles that they defined as sado-masochistic. The social processes in their view involved dominance and submission, role-playing, consensuality, erotic meaning and mutual definition. Weinberg, Williams and Moser's ideas were not so much a new concept but a summary of much of the research that had immediately preceded their writing. Anticipating their emerging definition were several studies focusing on the interaction between individuals in the sado-masochistic groups and organizations.[17]

To adopt such a social definition either puts severe limits upon the kinds of behaviour which can be called sado-masochistic or forces a distinction between different kinds of sado-masochistic behaviour, the voluntary and permissive which Weinberg, Williams and Moser describe, and other types of behaviour which do not fit into their definition but which others would include as sado-masochistic. The question, however, becomes a more basic one, so far ignored by investigators, and that is whether sado-masochism itself can be defined as pathological. To answer this question, two other dimensions of the issues involved in sado-masochism need to be investigated, the physiological and the cultural.

PHYSIOLOGICAL IMPLICATIONS OF PAIN

Current research seems to emphasize that under certain conditions, such as when pain perception could disrupt effective coping, pain inhibition becomes more adaptive and is influenced by medial brain stimulation which can bring about both opioid and non-opioid analgesia. Morphine receptors in the brain have been known since 1973; these are designed to receive endorphins, morphine-like substances produced by the body that are both powerful pain-killers and antidepressants. Since the influence of endorphins can be inhibited by stress, it is possible in certain activities for an individual to get a high. Moreover, the individual can even develop a tolerance and dependence upon these self-induced opioid analgesics.[18] Extreme physical activity such as running pushes a person beyond the pain threshold into a kind of high and the abrupt termination of regular running exercises can lead to withdrawal symptoms. Even anticipation of pain can activate a general physiological arousal[19] which can be channelled into sexual feelings[20] or be regarded as such by its participants.[21]

Weinberg, William and Moser argued that whether pain was real or apparent, light or heavy, was not important to their definition but only to the interpretation that the participants put upon it. They reported on a 'female submissive' who liked to handle as much pain as was possible in her sado-masochistic encounters but was afraid of going to the dentist. Her boyfriend tried to help her by suggesting that she think of dental pain as an erotic experience but, though she tried, it did not work, and she remained afraid of dentists.[22]

Their definition gives as much emphasis to the psychological as to the physical and they held that feelings such as uncertainty, apprehension, embarrassment, powerlessness, anxiety and fear are produced through a variety of sado-masochistic practices which place a person in a position of 'power' over another. Humiliation, for example, can be verbal, while bondage is more physical. Alex Comfort added that struggling and being tied up were strong physical stimuli regardless of anything symbolic.[23] Bondage implies submission on the one hand and dominance on the other.

Each investigator seemed to add another dimension. Eric Fromm held that the victims in the sado-masochistic relationship responded paradoxically to isolation and powerlessness by bonding with their tormentors, accepting the abuse, and ultimately ended up by taking control over their powerlessness by 'voluntarily' inflicting ruin upon themselves. Masochists were said to increase their suffering in order to cope with it, and to achieve blissful union (confluence by destruction of self).[24]

CULTURAL DIMENSIONS

These new theories and explanations raise new kinds of problems about what can and cannot be defined as sado-masochistic behaviour. As early as 1969, Paul Gebhard had argued that sado-masochism was not so much a pathology as something that was deeply 'embedded in our culture since our culture operates on the basis of dominance–submission relationships, and aggression is socially valued'.[25] Historically, in fact, ecstasy has often been associated with pain. Cultural conditioning to pain and suffering have sequelae which have implications not only for the social toleration of pain as suffering and therefore as being good for one's soul but for the acceptance, and even at times encouragement, of sado-masochistic behaviour.

Moreover, pain itself has often been regarded as normative in sexual relations. Certainly biting, scratching, hitting and other such activity were subject-matter for the ancient sex manuals from India, China and elsewhere.[26] Such practices continue into modern times. Kinsey and his colleagues noted that scratching and biting were often part of precoital play in conventional sex and the physiological response to pain was similar to that of orgasm.[27] Studies of behaviour in such animals as minks, ferrets, sables and skunks indicated that they need to engage in combat to perform coitus.[28] Paul Gebhard, influenced by such data, speculated there was a phylogenetic basis for these activities among humans, although why some individuals were more likely to equate pain with pleasure than others was not clear to him. He suggested that it was a combination of factors: physiological, psychological and cultural ones were probably all involved.[29]

What has not been emphasized in this discussion of sado-masochism is just how deeply embedded the concepts of pain and suffering are in Western culture. Pope John Paul II, in his first public broadcast after he had been wounded by an assassin's bullet in May 1981, stated that he regarded his own sufferings as an offering to his church and to the world and seemed to imply that others would benefit from it.[30] In this respect the pope was part of a long Judaeo-Christian tradition of accepting pain and suffering as necessary, with the Jewish prophet Job and the Christian concept of Jesus serving as examples. Christianity, more than Judaism, however, is the focal point for the sources of Western sado-masochism, since in Western Christian teachings suffering marked the transference of Jesus as teacher to Jesus the Christ as saviour. Because Jesus had suffered martyrdom on the cross to 'save mankind', many Christians tried to undergo the same suffering as Jesus, believing either that they would achieve salvation sooner or that salvation itself was only possible to those who had suffered.

This ideology became effectively incorporated into Christian belief through the ascetic saints of the fourth and fifth centuries. We would hold that it was this ideology which has long made the Western world prone to accept and tolerate a wide variety of behaviours which have come to be called sado-masochistic but which before the term was coined were more or less normative in our culture. The best illustration of such a thesis comes from the examples in the lives of Christian saints, and it is the example of such saints, perhaps more in so-called Catholic countries than in Protestant ones, which established a mystical, and some might called it orgasmic, response to pain and suffering.

HISTORICAL CONCEPTS ABOUT PAIN AND SUFFERING

It was in the fourth and fifth centuries that the Christian Church changed from being a barely tolerated and sometimes persecuted minority group to an officially established religion favoured by the state. This new kind of status not only resulted in an influx of new members but brought a change in attitudes to many of the more traditional-minded members of the Church, who felt discouraged and even betrayed by the resulting compromises. One result was the attempt by some to escape the anxieties, pains and turmoils of the world in order to remain pure in heart.[31] There was also a widely prevalent belief that those who had not suffered in this world were condemned to suffer in the next world; similarly, any suffering endured on this earth would result in a corresponding purification of the soul in the next.[32]

The consequence was a deeply embedded inclination for masochism, since by suffering one could rapturously anticipate ultimate salvation and the wonderful pleasures awaiting those who suffered. As a corollary those who inflicted punishment or held others in submission, sadists if you will, could believe that they were also doing this not only for the salvation of the person being punished but for their own salvation as well. Once such a mindset became established in Western thought, it continued to influence Western culture; there is, in effect, a continuing progression from the early martyrs to the Marquis de Sade and Leopold von Sacher-Masoch.

Though few historians of the past have ever described these early Christian ascetics as masochists, the term sometimes used, 'competitive asceticism', indicates that they went beyond mere self-denial. Each tried to outdo the other in pushing the human body to new and greater abuse, and in the process their endorphins allowed them to experience the ecstatic pleasure of knowing they would be saved. This was important because, while there was uncertainty and ambiguity in early Christianity in describing heaven, perhaps in part because one person's utopia is not necessarily that of someone else, hell posed no such problems, because it has always been identified with the more horrifying aspects of life on earth. Thus for the fourth-century ascetics hell was real, and by struggling against the things of this world they could combat hell itself. Life in the next world was important, important enough to sacrifice everything in this world to attain. The response was the emergence of what Helen Waddell and others have called the Desert Fathers,[33] ascetics who believed it was necessary to suffer before one could enter heaven.

These ascetics could endure almost any kind of earthly suffering by contemplating salvation, thinking of heavenly bliss, anticipating the rapturous joys awaiting them in the next world. The result was that many not only took to inflicting pain and suffering upon themselves but went into ecstatic trances by so doing. A good illustration of such a case is Macarius the Younger (AD 394), who spent forty days every year keeping Lent and practising self-mortification in a dark cell in the ground. Palladius, the source of much of our information about these ascetic Fathers of the Church, described these cells as having no 'opening but a hole through which one could creep, for they were made in the inner desert to which no visitors were admitted'. Space was so restricted, he continued, 'that it was impossible even to straighten out one's legs in them'. Even this extreme of ascetic mortification, however, was not enough. Palladius reported that one day when Macarius was sitting in his cell, a gnat stung him on the foot. Feeling the pain he killed it with his hands, and it was gorged with his blood. He accused himself of acting out of revenge [thus killing one of God's creatures] and condemned himself to sit naked in the marsh of Skete out in the great desert for six months. Here the mosquitoes lacerate even the hides of wild swine just as wasps do. Soon he was bitten all over his body, and he became so swollen that some thought he had elephantiasis. When he returned to his cell after six months he was recognized as Macarius only by his voice.[34]

Accompanying this suffering were ecstatic visions which involved a 'high' similar to what some participants in sado-masochistic activities of today recount. For example, a sado-masochist in 1979, responding to a question as to why anyone would want to be dominated and punished by others given the risks inherent in such procedures, answered: 'Because it is a healing process ... the old wounds and unappeased hunger I nourish, I cleanse and close the wound. I devise and mete out appropriate punishments for old, irrational sins ... A good scene doesn't end with orgasm – it ends with catharsis.'[35]

Similarly, the idea of the Christian ascetics was to rid themselves of their old-style body, transforming their flesh through fasting and maceration until they arrived at a new psychological consciousness which they associated with a deified body and a near-miraculous state. The 'new' body was capable of overcoming the problems of space, of treating suffering with contempt, of passing through the centuries of time, and ultimately of having the substance and power of the angels.[36] Macarius himself in one of his *Spiritual Homilies* put the process simply: 'A Man cannot be considered a saint until he has purified the clay of his being.'[37]

St Jerome (AD 420) described the experience more personally:

There I sat, solitary, full of bitterness; my disfigured limbs shuddered away from the sackcloth, my dirty skin taking on the hue of the Ethiopian's flesh; every day tears, every night sighing; and if in spite of my struggles sleep would tower over and sink upon me, my battered body ached on the naked earth ... Yet that same I, who for fear of hell condemned myself to such a prison, I the comrade of scorpions and wild beasts, was there, watching the maidens in their dance; my face haggard with fasting my mind burnt with desire in my frigid body, and the fires of lust alone leaped before a man prematurely dead. So destitute of all aid, I used to lie at the feet of Christ, watering them with my tears, wiping them with my hair, struggling to subdue my rebellious flesh with seven days' fasting ... and, the Lord himself is witness, after many tears, and eyes that clung to heaven, I would sometimes seem to myself to be one with the angelic hosts.[38]

Masochistic reaction in the Christian ascetics often aroused erotic feeling. Ammonius, for example, who had cut off his left ear rather than leave his desert retreat, was reported never to have pampered his flesh. Yet when desires of the flesh 'rose up in revolt', the good saint 'heated an iron in the fire and applied it to his limbs, so that he became ulcerated all over'.[39] Palladius, the recorder of the lives of these early ascetics, wrote that he himself was often bothered by concupiscence. He finally consulted with a devoted monk by the name of Pachon who told him that the fight with one's passions was an almost never-ending one and that it was important not to relax or the earthly passions would win out. Ultimately, however, God would help those who persevered and suffered enough over their passions.[40] The faithful came, in fact, to believe that these tinglings of the flesh were put there by God to remind the sufferers that they were not yet quite exalted and to encourage them to continue to strive through suffering to achieve exaltation.[41]

The whole masochistic process might be described as a five-step model. First a desire to escape the sinfulness of oneself and the world around led (2) to self-punishment and suffering, (3) which brought on erotic feelings, (4) further punishment and (5) ecstatic climax. The climax, however, was only temporary and needed to be repeated again and again. The assimilation or union by destruction of self is essentially the same sensation that today's masochists report.

Once the model of masochistic mortification was set in the early Church, it continued through the Middle Ages. Periodically saints appeared who seemed to obtain satisfaction through their suffering. St Frances of Rome (1440), for example, was sorely tried all her life by visions which made her feel that her whole body was being assaulted. To rid herself of these visions she scourged herself with horsehair girdles and chains with sharp points. The more she punished herself, the more her visions and ecstasies appeared, until she was spending the whole night in prayer and ecstatic self-punishment.[42] St Felix of Cantalice (1587) wore a shirt of iron links and plates studded with iron spikes. To punish himself further he fasted on bread and water, picking out only the worst of foods for his own meal. The result was an ecstatic response: 'He tried to conceal from notice the remarkable spiritual favors he received but often when he was serving mass he was so transported in ecstasy that he could not make the necessary response.'[43]

Christian of Aquila (1543) practised such severe penance and devoted such long hours to prayer that she was transported into a rapt ecstasy.[44] St Lydwina of Schiedam (1433) believed that God had called her to be a victim for the sins of others. Once she had become convinced of this, suffering became her greatest joy. So severe were the pains that she inflicted upon herself that the pain spasms convulsed and contorted her body, causing her to vomit, and brought on a syncope of the heart which left her prostrated. Still she joyfully continued.[45] Rudolph M. Bell's collections of saints who deprived themselves of food and endured other deprivation in their mystical ecstasy add a large number of women to the group described above.[46]

The sexual connotations of these experiences are not just in the minds of researchers like ourselves who are diligently seeking out such correlations, but even in the minds of other scholars less inclined to make such an association. For example, the authors of *Butler's Lives of the Saints* describe St Arnulf of Villers (1228) thus:

> Every day he scourged himself, now with rods, now with thorny branches, now with a stick covered with a hedgehog's skin. Brothers whose duties took them near the cell adjoining the fruit barn, which was Arnulf's favorite retreat, asserted that as each lash descended upon his body he would *ejaculate* the name of a member of the community or some outside person on behalf of whom he was beseeching God's mercy.[47]

St Rita of Cascia (1451) was said from childhood on to have had a special devotion to the sufferings of Jesus, the

> contemplation of which would sometimes send her into an ecstasy, and when in 1411 she heard an eloquent sermon on the crown of thorns from St James della Marcca, a strange physical reaction seems to have followed. While she knelt absorbed in prayer she became acutely conscious of pain – as of a thorn which had detached itself from the crucifix and embedded itself in her forehead.[48]

One does not need to be a Freudian to see the sexual symbolism here.

But even if the saints were masochistic, does that mean that they were also sadistic? The interdependence of the two can best be illustrated by the story of Shenute, one of the early Desert Fathers. Shenute demonstrated his dedication to asceticism while still a child when he was herding a flock of animals. First he would deliberately stand out in the blazing sun to watch the flock, and then after he had bedded the animals down for the night he would set out for some irrigation ditch where he would stand neck-deep in water, praying for hours. Impressed by his devotion and suffering, his parents finally agreed to send him to a monastery when he was 14 years old. Here he fasted so much that his skin hung on his bones. Often he ate only once a week, and then sparingly. He hung himself on a cross and remained there for a week at a time. Eventually he went off alone to the desert, where he stayed for five years. When he returned from the desert, now a fully grown man, he established a monastery which included in its discipline systematic punishment as a necessary corollary to achieving a kind of collective ecstasy. Laughing or smiling led to a beating, as did any kind of minor infraction. Sometimes Shenute struck the monks so hard that they died. This was because both he and they believed that beating opened the doors to heaven.[49]

There seems to have been a 'necessity' for suffering either self-inflicted or inflicted by a beloved senior. St Benedict, for example, justified punishment as essential because an abbot was supposed to hate wrongful acts. The punishment, moreover, was best if the one who did the punishing did so on a person he loved. The monk, hating the powers of his will, embraced powerlessness, thereby annihilating his will for the love of God. By repressing his sexuality, St Benedict became a spiritual father of his flock, and in the process the sensual needfulness of the lover was sublimated into the moral needfulness of the saint.[50]

Rarely during the medieval period did writers object that the cultivation of fear and physical pain debased human souls into animality, an argument sometimes made now. Instead it was accepted as a kinaesthetic part of education, a sign of love between the dominant and subordinate partners. Both physical and mental pain were important because the sufferers were able to affirm that the virtuous should participate in the sufferings of Jesus and they were absolutely certain that Jesus 'wished' to suffer.[51] Convinced that they had the spirit of Jesus in them and their spirit was in him, they applied the tools of mortification and contrition to all that was lovable: to their companions on the way, to themselves, and eventually to all.

A good illustration of this mindset on a mass scale is the rise of the flagellants, groups of whom began to appear in the thirteenth century, and spread rapidly during the Black Death. Philip Ziegler described some of their practices as follows:

> A large circle was formed and the worshippers stripped to the waist, retaining only a loin cloth or skirt which stretched as far as their ankles. Their outer garments were piled up inside the circle and the sick of the village would congregate there in hope of acquiring a little vicarious merit ... The Flagellants marched around the circle; then at a signal from the Master threw themselves on the ground. The usual posture

was that of one crucified but those with special sins on their conscience adopted appropriate attitudes ... The master moved among the recumbent bodies, thrashing those who had committed such crimes or who had offended in some way against the discipline of the Brotherhood.[52]

During their collective flagellation exercises, each person carried a heavy scourge with three or four leather thongs, the thongs being tipped with metal studs. With these they began rhythmically to beat their backs and breasts. As the pace grew, many threw themselves on the ground, each trying to outdo the others in self-scourging, whipping themselves into a frenzy in which pain had no reality. From scourging themselves they turned to scourging others. Certain of the brethren alleged they could drive out the devils, heal the sick, and even raise the dead by flagellation.

Inevitably a tradition so deeply imbedded in Western Christian thinking was effectively communicated to Christian congregations everywhere. Cathedrals such as that of Beauvais had panels depicting punishment and subsequent salvation.[53] Scourging of evils even became a necessity for sinful kings. Henry II of England submitted to just such a scourging in 1174 when, in order to atone for his part in the murder of St Thomas à Becket, he walked barefoot into Canterbury Cathedral, throwing himself before Becket's tomb, and being whipped and scourged by a succession of bishops, abbots and monks.[54] When the seventh crusade led by Louis IX (Saint Louis) of France failed, he accepted scourging as part of his penance.[55]

The foundation of the medieval and early modern education was based upon scourging and pain, not only to achieve ecstasy, but to acquire knowledge. Teachers were told how to switch a pupil, with the result that Krafft-Ebing was able to include Rousseau among his masochists. In his *Confessions*, Rousseau tells how as a boy he was sent to a boarding-school where the director, a woman, spanked him, and this association of punishment with eroticism caused him so much enjoyment as a youth that he deliberately provoked such spanking. He added that later in his adult life he sought out women who would be willing to spank him.[56]

With Rousseau this account has come full circle, back to Krafft-Ebing who, without quite knowing it, made much of Western history a study of pathological behaviour. He constructed a new pathology of a behaviour which had been endemic in Western culture. Are we to label many of the Christian saints as examples of sado-masochistic pathology? Or are the definitions and social constructions of a Krafft-Ebing in need of a critical rethinking? In a sense such a rethinking is being done by some of the current generation of classifiers, who have extended sado-masochism to include perpetrators, and sometimes victims of spouse and child abuse, rape and similar activities.

It is not enough, however, to argue as Weinberg, Williams and Moser did, of the necessity to speak of different kinds of sadomasochistic behaviour. Rather, it seems to be critical that we begin to admit to ourselves that Western culture is permeated with sadomasochistic behaviour and each of us, as culture-bearers of past assumptions, probably have some elements of this in our own psyche. The problem then is not the existence of sado-masochistic behaviours, but the control of them. Making such behaviour pathological, as Krafft-Ebing did, is far too easy. Controlling it in ourselves in much more difficult.

NOTES

1 An earlier draft of this chapter was given over a decade ago at the Midwest Medieval Conference, Purdue University, 9 October 1982. The criticism and suggestions made at the conference have been incorporated into the text. A revised draft was later sent out to colleagues for criticism and final revision was put aside as other more pressing projects had to be completed. The Dixons then introduced their own thinking and this chapter now represents our thinking as of 1993.
2 His book went through numerous editions in German, and at least two different editions were translated into English, the seventh by Charles Gilbert Chaddock (Philadelphia: F. A. Davis, 1894); the twelfth and final edition by F. J. Rebman in 1906 (reprinted, Brooklyn, N.Y.: Physicians and Surgeons Book Company, 1922, 1933, and several times thereafter).
3 Marquis de Sade, *Juliette*, trans. Austry Wainhouse (New York: Grove Press, 1968) and *Justine*, trans. Richard Seaver and Austry Wainhouse (New York: Grove Press, 1965). During his confinement to an insane asylum during the last part of his life he wrote *Les 120 Journées de Sodome*, which remained unpublished until the twentieth century, when Iwan Bloch published it in both French and German.
4 Leopold von Sacher-Masoch, *Venus in Pelz* (reprinted Munich: Lichtenberg Verlag, 1967).
5 Krafft-Ebing *Psychopathia Sexualis*, 58 (7th edn) and 83 (12th edn).
6 Ibid. 119–20 (7th edn), 166–7 (12th edn). See p. 58 in this chapter.
7 Albert von Schrenck-Notzing, a reprint and translation, *The Use of Hypnosis in 'Psychopathia Sexualis'* (New York: Julian Press, 1946).
8 Havelock Ellis, *Analysis of the Sexual Impulse*, vol. III; *Studies in the Psychology of Sex*, 2nd edn, rev. and enlarged (Philadelphia: F. A. Davis, 1928), 160.
9 Sigmund Freud, 'The Sexual Aberrations', in *Basic Writings of Sigmund Freud*, ed. and trans. A. A. Brill (New York: Modern Library, 1938), 570.
10 Eugene E. Levitt, 'Sadomasochism', *Sexual Behavior* (6), 69–80.
11 American Psychiatric Association, *Diagnostic and Statistical Manual of Mental Disorders* 3rd edn (Washington, D.C.: American Psychiatric Association, 1980).

12 See, for example, Frank S. Caprio, *Variations in Sexual Behavior* (New York: Grove Press, 1955), and Wilhelm Stekel, *Sadism and Masochism* (reprinted New York: Grove Press, 1965).
13 Charles A. Moser, 'An Exploratory and Descriptive Study of a Self-Defined S/M (Sadomasochistic) Sample' (Ph.D. dissertation, San Francisco, Institute for Advanced Study of Human Sexuality, 1979).
14 William H. Masters, Virginia E. Johnson and Robert C. Kolodny, *Human Sexuality* (Boston: Little, Brown and Co., 1982), 349.
15 Martin S. Weinberg, Colin J. Williams and Charles Moser, 'The Social Constituents of Sadomasochism', *Social Problems*, 31 (1985), 379–89.
16 Kenneth Plummer, *The Making of the Modern Homosexual* (Totowa, N.J.: Barnes and Noble, 1981).
17 Judith Coburn, 'S & M', *New York Times*, 4 February, 1977, 43–50; G. W. Levi Kamel, 'Leathersex: Meaningful Aspects of Gay Sadomasochism', *Deviant Behavior*, 1 (1980), 171–91; John Allen Lee, 'The Social Organization of Sexual Risk', *Alternative Lifestyles*, 2 (February 1979), 69–100; Thomas S. Weinberg, 'Sadism and Masochism: Sociological Perspectives', *Bulletin of the American Academy of Psychiatry and the Law*, 6 (1978), 284–95; Thomas S. Weinberg and Gerhard Falk, 'The Social Organization of Sadism and Masochism', *Deviant Behavior*, 1 (1980), 379–93; Thomas S. Weinberg and G. W. Levi Kamel (eds.), *S and M: Studies in Sadomasochism* (Buffalo: Prometheus Books, 1983); Andreas Spengler, 'Manifest Sadomasochism of Males: Results of an Empirical Study', *Archives of Sexual Behavior*, 6 (1977), 441–56.
18 Gregory W. Terman, Y. Shavit, J. W. Lewis, J. Timothy Cannon and John C. Liebeskind, 'Intrinsic Mechanisms of Pain Inhibition: Activation by Stress', *Science*, 226 (1984), 1270–7.
19 Levitt, 'Sadomasochism', 69–80.
20 Sylvan S. Tomkins, *Affect, Imagery, Consciousness*, 2 vols. (New York: Springer, 1962).
21 Stanley Schacter, 'The Interaction of Cognitive and Physiological Determinants of Emotional Sate', in L. Berkowitz (ed.), *Advances in Experimental Social Psychology*, vol. II (New York: Academic Press, 1963), 49–80; and Elaine Walster and G. William Walster, *A New Look At Love* (Reading, Mass.: Addison Wesley, 1978).
22 Weinberg, Williams and Moser, 'Social Constituents of Sadomasochism', 379–89.
23 Alex Comfort, 'Pain/Pleasure', *Forum*, 3 (8) (1974), 46–9.
24 Eric Fromm, *Escape from Freedom* (reprinted New York: Avon, 1965), 161–5, 173–4.
25 Paul H. Gebhard, 'Fetishism and Sadomasochism', in Jules H. Masserman (ed.), *Dynamics of Deviant Sexuality* (New York: Grune and Stratton, 1969).
26 For discussion of various manuals, see Vern L. Bullough, *Sexual Variance in Society and History* (Chicago: University of Chicago Press, 1976), *passim*.
27 Alfred Kinsey, W. B. Pomeroy, C. E. Martin and Paul H. Gebhard, *Sexual Behavior in the Human Female* (Philadelphia: W. B. Saunders, 1953).
28 For various examples see the index in Clelland S. Ford and Frank A. Beach, *Patterns of Sexual Behavior* (New York: Harper and Brothers, 1951).
29 Paul H. Gebhard, 'Fetishism and Sadomasochism'.

30 As reported in the *New York Times*, 18 May 1981.
31 This is not so much my thesis as that of Ferdinand Lot, *The End of the Ancient World* (reprinted New York: Harper and Row, 1961).
32 Jacques LaCarrière, *The God Possessed*, trans. Roy Monkcom (London: George Allen and Unwin, 1963), 173-4.
33 Helen Waddell, *The Desert Fathers* (reprinted Ann Arbor, Mich.: University of Michigan Press, 1957).
34 Palladius, *The Lausiac History*, trans. and annotated by Robert T. Meyer (Westminster, Md.: Newman Press, 1965), 18.4, p. 59. See also A. Butler, *Butler's Lives of Saints*, ed., revised and supplemented by Herbert Thurston and Donald Attwater, 4 vols. (reprinted New York: R. J. Kennedy and Sons, 1962), vol. I, 19-21. See also *Acta Sanctorum* (Antwerp, 1632, in progress), 2 January.
35 Weinberg and Kamel, *Studies in Sadomasochism*, 134.
36 LaCarrière, *The God Possessed*, 205
37 Quoted by LaCarrière, *The God Possessed*, from the (Pseudo-) Macarius, *Spiritual Homilies*.
38 Jerome, *Ad Eustochium*, *EP* xxii, in J. P. Migne, *Patrologiae Latina*, henceforth *PL* (Paris: Garnier Fratres, 1887, vol. xxii). The English version is based upon that of Waddell, *Desert Fathers*, 27.
39 Palladius, *The Lausiac History*, 11. 4, p. 47.
40 Ibid., 23.1-6, pp. 81-3.
41 Ibid., 47.15-16, pp. 128-9.
42 *Acta Sanctorum*, 9 March (III) and *Butler's Lives of the Saints*, vol. I, 529-33.
43 *Acta Sanctorum*, 19 May (IV), and *Butler's Lives*, vol. II, 344-5. See also A. Kerr, *A Son of St Francis* (London: Sands and Company, 1900).
44 *Butler's Lives*, vol. II, 95-8; see also Philbert P. Seebock, *Die Herrlichkeit der Katholischen Kirche in ihren Heiligen und Seligen des 19 Jahrhunderts* (Innsbruck: F. Rauch, 1900), 297.
45 *Acta Sanctorum*, 15 April (II), and *Butler's Lives*, vol. II, 95-8.
46 Rudolph M. Bell, *Holy Anorexia* (Chicago: University of Chicago Press, 1985). We do not want to get into the controversy over whether the term 'anorexia' can be used to describe these women, but certainly their behaviour emphasized self-punishment which in our terms could be called masochistic. It also gave them a power base, a factor that cannot be overlooked in any discussion of masochism.
47 *Butler's Lives*, vol. II, 679, italics mine. I believe this is an accurate translation of the *Acta Sanctorum*, 30 June (VIII).
48 *Butler's Lives*, vol. II, 369-70; *Acta Sanctorum*, 22 May (V); Matthew J. Corcoran, *Our Own Saint Rita* (New York: Benziger Brothers, 1919).
49 LaCarrière, *The God Possessed*, 131-3; *Butler's Lives*, vol. II, 1-2; DeLacy O'Leary, *The Saints of Egypt* (New York: Macmillan, 1937), 25-55.
50 We base this argument on a discussion with Karl Morrison, who first expounded it in 'Holiness as an Expression of Acquired Maladaptive Behavior', an unpublished paper given at the Medieval Academy of America, 1982, meeting in Kalamazoo, Michigan.
51 St Ambrose, *PL*, vol. XVI, 1051-3.

52 Philip Ziegler, *The Black Death* (London: Collins, 1969), 87. See also William M. Bowsky (ed.), *The Black Death* (New York: Holt, Rinehart and Winston, 1971), 69.
53 Michael Cothren, 'The Iconography of Theophilus Windows in the First Half of the Thirteenth Century', *Speculum*, 59 (1984), 308–29.
54 P. Schaff, *History of the Christian Church* (New York: 1907), 5(1), 146–7.
55 Cothren, 'The Iconography of Theophilus Windows', 328.
56 Jean Jacques Rousseau, *The Confessions*, trans. W. Conygham Mallor (reprinted New York: Tudor, 1935), 19.

THREE

SOME TRADITIONAL INDIAN VIEWS ON MENSTRUATION AND FEMALE SEXUALITY

JULIA LESLIE

INTRODUCTION

Sudhir Kakar, the Indian psychoanalyst, argues that for the majority of Indian women female sexuality is 'a utilitarian affair', its primary value lying in 'its capacity to redress a lopsided distribution of power between the sexes'.[1] Since ancient times, however, that unequal distribution of power has been explained by the dominant (and predominantly male) ideology in terms of the inherent nature of women. This traditional view of women may be found encapsulated in myths and stories, or it may be confronted directly in treatises on the proper behaviour of men and women according to sacred norms (*dharma*). At its simplest, this view maintains that women are inherently wicked, that they are possessed of an uncontrollable and threatening inborn sexuality, and that they are innately impure.

In this chapter, I shall explore the link between notions of female sexuality and the idea of an inherent nature of women, within the narrower context of traditional Indian discourses on menstruation. First, I shall set the scene with a brief sketch of the debate on the inherent nature of women. I shall then relate two epic stories about female sexuality (one positive, one negative), and the dominant myth about the origins of menstruation. Finally, I shall look at the discourse on menstruation, and its implications for female sexuality, within three different indigenous frameworks. A reasonably objective, if not entirely accurate, account of menstruation may be found in the medical treatises of *āyurveda*, the 'science of life'. Revulsion for the female body is the keynote of the ascetic discourse, exemplified here by the debate on women in the texts of Jainism. The third framework is that provided by the religious ideology of orthodox Hinduism (that is, according to *dharmaśāstra*, 'the science or discipline of what is right'). While this last is the dominant voice of the culture, it is important that one does not generalize from it. Since Indian culture contains many subcultures, male and female, dominant and 'muted',[2] the frame of reference is vital.

THE INHERENT WICKEDNESS OF WOMEN

There is plenty of evidence in Sanskrit literature for the perceived inherent wickedness of women. Much of it is reproduced in the *Strīdharmapaddhati*, an eighteenth-century Sanskrit treatise on the proper behaviour of women.[3] The author, Tryambaka, concedes that women are indeed inherently wicked. However, he goes on to argue that they are not beyond religious instruction: they can learn how to behave. His scriptural proof is the famous saying, 'Good conduct destroys inauspicious marks.'[4] These 'marks' include the inauspicious potential of female nature. Tryambaka's meaning is clear. Women who listen to pandits like himself can learn to behave according to the codes of conduct (*dharma*) laid down for women. They should transform themselves into devoted wives in order that the inherent evil of their female natures may be annulled.[5] The rest of Tryambaka's treatise explains how this may be done.

THE INHERENT SEXUALITY OF WOMEN

The sexuality of women is closely related to the notion of inherent female nature. However, the familiar Indian equation between the inherent weakness and wickedness of women on the one hand and their inborn sexuality on the other is by no means obvious, for the sexuality of women is not invariably negative. In that same treatise on the perfect wife, Tryambaka recommends a 'bold confidence in sexual matters' (*prāgalbhyaṃ kāmakāryeṣu*).[6] His subsection on going to bed in the evening stresses her sexual initiative: 'After paying homage to her husband's feet, she should go to bed. Treating her beloved in a way that gives him pleasure (*āhlādasaṃyuktaṃ kṛtvā*), she should engage in sexual intercourse (*saṃyogam ācaret*; i.e. she should make love to him).'[7] In another section, he instructs the good wife to 'make sexual advances' (*upasarpati*) to her husband at the appropriate time.[8]

Further evidence both for and against female sexuality may be found in India's great epic, the *Mahābhārata*.[9] This vast poem, which probably evolved between 400 BCE and 200 CE, is primarily an exposition on *dharma*.[10] The well-known story of Bhaṅgāśvana is told in support of female sexuality; the equally well-known tale of Aṣṭāvakra and the female ascetic takes a negative stance.

Bhaṅgāśvana is a childless king who, in order to obtain children, performs a fire sacrifice disliked by the god Indra. Bhaṅgāśvana obtains a hundred sons but, in doing so, he enrages Indra, who transforms him into a woman. Abandoning both family and kingdom, the female Bhaṅgāśvana retires to the forest. There she meets a male ascetic with whom she has another hundred sons. Her ability to thrive infuriates Indra. This time, he causes the two sets of children to fight and kill each other. The carnage complete, Indra appears to Bhaṅgāśvana and (to cut a long story short) grants her a wish. Without hesitation, Bhaṅgāśvana asks the god to bring back to life the children she produced as a woman – on the grounds that the love of a woman is greater than that of a man.[11] Indra revives both sets of children, and grants Bhaṅgāśvana the further wish of choosing which sex he/she would like to remain for the rest of his/her life. Bhaṅgāśvana chooses to remain a woman – on the grounds that women experience greater pleasure in sexual intercourse than men.[12] This story makes a virtue of the much-maligned sexuality of women.

The fact remains, however, that most statements relating to female sexuality take the opposite view. The classic story in support of this view is that of the youth Aṣṭāvakra and the elderly female ascetic to whom he is sent in preparation for his marriage.[13] Despite her age, the ascetic repeatedly attempts to seduce the young man, assuring him that for women there is no greater delight and no more destructive urge than sex;[14] that even very old women are consumed by sexual passion;[15] and that a woman's sexual desire can never be overcome in all the three worlds.[16] In the *Mahābhārata*, this story is told by the revered elder statesman, Bhīṣma, to demonstrate the true nature of women. His point is that, even after the taking of ascetic vows, even in extreme old age, a woman cannot overcome her lustful nature, and therefore one should always beware of the sexuality of women.

Similar evidence can be found elsewhere. In one of the oldest and most important collections of myths and legends, the *Mārkaṇḍeyapurāṇa* (compiled about 300 to 600 CE), we learn that sex, described as the cause of death in the world, is also the direct result of the passionate nature of women.[17] The *Mahābhārata* links the origin of evil directly to the sexual passion of women.[18] The best-known work of *dharmaśāstra*, the *Manusmṛti* (compiled between 200 BCE and 200 CE), tells us that women are innately promiscuous, fickle-minded, lacking in love, and unfaithful to their husbands even when closely guarded; indeed, they have been possessed of an indiscriminate sexual desire since time began.[19] This is certainly the more common prejudice.[20]

THE INNATE IMPURITY OF WOMEN

The third point in the theory of inherent female nature is provided by the allegation of innate impurity. There are two main arguments in support of this view. First, women's lack of access to initiation and religious education means that they are unable to use sacred mantras to purify themselves.[21] Second, menstruation pollutes. Indeed, menstruation is perceived as the visible sign both of a woman's sexual appetite and of her innate impurity – and thus, arising from the combination of these two, of her propensity for evil.

At one level, of course, menstruation is simply one of the impurities of the body. The traditional list includes semen, blood, urine, faeces, ear-wax, nail-parings, phlegm, tears, dandruff, and sweat.[22] One might therefore assume that menstrual blood is no more polluting for women than, for example, semen is for men. But this is not the case. According to the powerful mythic context, menstrual blood is far more than a physical impurity; it is the inescapable reminder of women's collective guilt.

The story of Indra's brahminicide is told in a range of texts, one of the earliest and most authoritative accounts being that in the *Taittirīyasaṃhitā* (a liturgical text compiled between 800 and 500 BCE).[23] When the universe is threatened by Viśvarūpa, Indra destroys him. But Viśvarūpa is a brahmin and Indra is condemned as a brahmin-killer. To escape the consequences of this particularly dreadful crime, Indra persuades the earth, the trees and women to assume one-third of his guilt each. In return, he grants each a wish: the earth, when dug, will heal within one year; trees, when cut, will grow again; and women, unlike all other creatures, will enjoy sexual intercourse at any time, even in advanced pregnancy. In several variations on this theme in other texts, Indra distributes his brahminicide in four parts: among rivers, mountains, earth and women in one text;[24] among fire, trees, cows and women in another;[25] among trees, earth, water and women in a third.[26] In all versions, however, one recipient is constant: women. In some texts, Indra's sin causes the recipients to become impure; in others, the recipients are already impure. According to one source, Indra's guilt is offloaded onto 'foetus-killers'.[27] According to another, it is given to sinful brahmins whose crimes include such things as serving low-caste *śūdras*.[28] In yet another, it falls to those who kill brahmins.[29] In this somewhat confused context, the issue of which came first – the impurity of women or the assumption of Indra's guilt – is blurred.

Either way, the mark of Indra's guilt has two crucial implications: a cyclical fertility and a recurrent power to pollute. In the case of the earth, Indra's guilt takes the form of fissures in the ground during the dry season, the sign of an infertile (and hence inauspicious) land prior to the release of the monsoon rain. During this time, the earth should not be 'ploughed', an obvious metaphor for sexual intercourse. In the case of trees, Indra's guilt takes the form of sap, the vital juice that signals the fecundity of plant life and without which there can be no growth, no fruit; yet the not uncommon ruling that one should avoid the 'red secretions' and resin from cut trees demonstrates a power to pollute.[30] In the case of rivers, the swirling mud-red waters of the rainy season are described in terms of a symbolic menstruation: they are *rajasvalāḥ*, 'full of dirt' or 'full of passion', a word also applied (in both senses) to menstruating women. Such waters should not be entered for fear of pollution: a ruling that applies equally to muddy monsoon rivers and menstruating women.[31]

In women, Indra's guilt takes the form of menstrual blood. Menstruation is thus the sign of a woman's participation in brahmin-murder. It marks her innate impurity, her cyclical fecundity, her uncontrollable sexuality, and, by extension, the inescapable wickedness of her female nature. This is the mythic dimension of what we might call the socio-religious politics of menstruation. Before I elaborate on this further, I shall outline my three frameworks for the discourse on menstruation.

MENSTRUATION IN THE CONTEXT OF MEDICAL DISCOURSE

The earliest fully developed āyurvedic work, the *Carakasaṃhitā* (probably composed in the first or second centuries BCE, and further redacted over subsequent centuries), explains that there are four criteria of truth: scriptural testimony, direct observation, inference, and reasoning. Anything contrary to reason, we are told, should be rejected as untruth.[32] To these four may be added two more: tradition and analogy.[33] According to *āyurveda*, the human body is a microcosm of the universe. The aim of *āyurveda* is to provide information about the parts and functions of that microcosm.

According to Caraka, conception occurs inside the womb as a result of the union of three things: the male seed (*bīja*; or semen, *śukra*), the female seed (*strībīja*, *śoṇita*), and the descending spirit (*jīva*, *cetanādhātu*) impelled by the *karma* of former lives.[34] If the spirit does not descend, no life can be created and so conception does not occur. In medical texts, the 'female seed' is usually equated with the uterine blood of the mother (*śoṇita* means 'red'), and hence with menstrual blood.[35] The most common terms used to denote menstrual blood are:

ārtava, described by Bose et al. as 'a special and fiery variety of blood';[36] and *rajas*, defined as 'the blood of a woman that appears at the time of puberty'.[37] Sexual intercourse enables the man's semen to enter the woman's uterus, where it is united with her menstrual blood. The sex of the child depends on the preponderance of either semen or menstrual blood: the former produces a son, the latter a daughter; if the two exist in equal quantity, the resulting offspring is sterile, impotent, or a hermaphrodite (*napuṃsaka, klība*). We are also told that conception occurring on odd days of the menstrual cycle produces females because menstrual blood increases in quantity on those days.[38]

In order to create a normal foetus, both the man's semen and the woman's menstrual blood must be pure. Pure semen is described as transparent, fluid, glossy, sweet-smelling like honey, and like oil or honey in appearance. Pure menstrual blood resembles hare's blood or the colour of lac, and it leaves no stains in washed clothes.[39]

All the medical texts agree that the first three days and nights of the menstrual flow are unsuitable for conception: for then the semen is like an object cast into fast-flowing water and swept away by the stream.[40] During these three days, the menstruating woman should follow a strict regimen designed to encourage a successful pregnancy, a regimen deriving both from notions of health and from magical correlations relating to the future foetus. For example, she should not indulge in sexual intercourse.[41] She should eat only easily digested milk-based foods. She should not sleep too much, laugh too much, hear loud noises, and so on. Breaking these guidelines may injure the unborn child.[42]

At the end of the three days and nights, she should take a cleansing bath, put on fresh clothes and ornaments, and go to her husband. The following twelve days (or, according to some authorities, sixteen) are suitable for conception. This is the period when the woman is deemed to be in 'season' (*ṛtu*). After this period, her womb will not allow the man's semen to enter, just as the lotus closes itself at the end of the day.[43]

The resulting embryo inherits from its mother the soft parts of the body (skin, blood, flesh, fat, heart, liver, lungs, spleen, kidneys, stomach, intestines, and so on), and from its father the hard parts (bones, teeth, veins, tendons, ligaments, arteries, semen, hair and nails).[44] In particular, the child's heart is directly linked to its mother's through the umbilical cord and the placenta. Indeed, medical texts derive *dohada*, the term denoting the cravings of the pregnant woman, by folk etymology from *dvaihṛdaya*, meaning 'two-hearted', on the grounds that the hearts of mother and child are linked in this way.

Hence the ruling that one should never deny the cravings of the pregnant woman,[45] for in indulging the mother-to-be one is in fact indulging the child who still craves for the experiences of its former life.

After conception, the channels carrying the menstrual blood are obstructed by the foetus, which explains why pregnant women no longer menstruate. When a woman's blood is 'obstructed below' in this way, apart from flooding the placenta to nourish the foetus, it also moves up to her breasts where it forms the future mother's milk.[46] This point deserves emphasis. What in religious and mythic contexts is seen as the most polluting of all substances (i.e. menstrual blood) is transformed into what in those same contexts is one of the purest (i.e. breast-milk).[47] In the context of *āyurveda*, both blood and milk are perceived simply as sources of maternal nourishment, and the process of transformation from one to the other is a physical one.[48] For *āyurveda* is concerned primarily with what are perceived to be the physical facts. While āyurvedic texts inevitably reflect to some extent the assumptions and prejudices of the culture, there is little evidence of an ulterior motive of socio-religious control. Hence the view of menstrual blood and breast-milk as nourishment for the foetus, and the stress on the mechanics of conception. Sermons on the inherent wickedness of women, on the consequences of her innate sexuality, and the polluting powers of menstrual blood, are conspicuously absent.[49]

MENSTRUATION IN THE CONTEXT OF ASCETIC DISCOURSE

A totally different view of both menstruation and female sexuality is provided by the ascetic mode. In the case of Indian Buddhism, Prince Siddhārtha's transformation into Śākyamuni Buddha is marked by the sensitive young man's revulsion for the sweaty sexuality of dancing girls: 'And the Future Buddha awoke, and ... perceived these women lying asleep, ... some with their bodies wet with trickling phlegm and spittle; some grinding their teeth ...; some with their mouths open; and some with their dress fallen apart so as plainly to disclose their loathsome nakedness.'[50] A second-century retelling of the same episode describes how, when the prince saw these women lying dishevelled and twitching in their sleep, he was moved to scorn. This, he concluded, is the nature of women (*svabhāva*): 'impure and monstrous (*aśucir vikrtās ca*) in the world of living beings'.[51] Here is the standard (or male) ascetic identification of the phenomenal world with sensual pleasures, typified by women as essentially worldly and sexual beings. The future Buddha's aversion for the female body constitutes a step forward on his path to enlightenment.

The aversion displayed by Jain ascetic discourse is even more striking. The issue is this. The last great teacher of the Jains was Mahāvīra who may have lived around 599 to 527 BCE. He was a naked ascetic (*acelaka śramaṇa*). There is no disagreement on this point; disagreement arises only in the interpretation to be put upon this fact. Is nakedness an essential prerequisite of renunciation? Or is it merely an optional, if commendable, practice? Broadly speaking, by about 300 BCE, Jainism had split into two camps: on the one hand, the naked or 'sky-clad' Digambaras for whom nakedness was an essential part of the renouncer's path; and on the other, the 'white-clad' Śvetāmbaras for whom it was not. However, both sides agreed that women should never be naked in public – on grounds ranging from the fact of menstruation to the inherent sexuality of women, and even to their vulnerability to sexual harassment. Thus this major split came to focus on the question of whether or not women can attain salvation. For the Śvetāmbaras, initiation into the monastic life is sufficient proof of renunciation, both for men and for women (although it is conceded that the life of the renouncer is especially hard for women). For the Digambaras, the wearing of clothes (whether by men or by women) signals an incomplete renunciation, while the female body is itself proof of inadequate spiritual advancement. According to the Digambaras, then, it is impossible for a woman to attain liberation; to be more precise, the (non-gendered) individual self cannot attain salvation immediately after a lifetime as a woman. However pious she may be, the most that a woman can hope for is to be reborn in a male body; only then will she have access to the true path of renunciation (that is, the path of the naked male ascetic). This is the path which culminates in *mokṣa*, release from the cycle of rebirth.

The arguments for and against the likelihood of women attaining salvation are catalogued in the Jain texts.[52] Some of these arguments are familiar, even predictable: the male ascetic's rejection of the social and physical world; his contempt for women as the symbols of sexuality, procreation, and society in general; and so on. What is startling, however, is the unbridled disgust for women's bodies and, in particular, for that most physical (and, according to tradition, essentially sexual) process, menstruation. The latest contribution to the debate is found in the *Yuktiprabodha* ('Teaching Through Arguments') by the seventeenth-century Śvetāmbara author, Meghavijaya. In this work, Meghavijaya sets out to demolish eighty-six points of Digambara doctrine, including their much-disputed views regarding the salvation of women (*strīmokṣa*). The *Yuktiprabodha* includes the following statements of the Digambara point of view:

INDIAN VIEWS ON MENSTRUATION AND FEMALE SEXUALITY 71

> Women, namely, those beings who have the physical sign of the human female, do not attain moksa in that very life for their souls do not manifest that pure transformation which is called 'a Perfected Being' (Siddha).⁵³
> ... the biologically female is distinguished ... by the fact that she has an impure body, as is evident by the flow of [menstrual] blood each month.⁵⁴
> Moreover, it is said in the scriptures that on account of the constant flow of the menstrual blood, various types of minute beings are generated in the genitals of women; this also occurs on other parts of her body, such as the breasts.⁵⁵

This picture of women's genitals and breasts as prime sources of impurity, swarming with microscopic creatures, may be contrasted with the matter-of-fact āyurvedic statement that menstrual blood and breast-milk are sources of maternal nourishment. For the Jain theologians, however, menstruation is a form of violence (*hiṃsā*): the flow of blood destroys countless minute living beings (*aparyāpta*). Moreover, as a result of these bodily secretions and their inhabitants, women suffer from a constant itching which gives rise to continuous and uncontrollable sexual desire. This leads to the further violence of sexual intercourse. The *Yuktiprabodha* provides quotations to this effect:

> The Omniscients have said that when a man is overcome by sexual passion and engages in sexual activity, he kills 900,000 minute beings [i.e., the sperm cells in the ejaculate] ...
> In the vagina of a woman also, beings ... are born, numbering ... up to ... 300,000.
> When a man and a woman unite sexually, these beings in the vagina are destroyed, just as if a red-hot iron were inserted into a hollow piece of bamboo [filled with sesame seeds].⁵⁶

The logic is clear. How can women become renouncers when they are never free of sexual desire and when their very bodies form the site and source of violence against living beings?

Nor is menstruation condoned as an involuntary process. On the contrary, it is perceived as the consequence of 'a sexual volition ... comparable to a man's emission of semen in a dream'.⁵⁷ As a result, menstruation – together with its underlying cause, female sexuality – creates in women two powerful emotional forces: a deep sense of shame (which compels them to wear clothes in order to hide their bodies from men); and a constant fear of sexual assault (perceived as the male response to the sexually active woman). The constant presence of these powerful emotions of shame and fear (from which men by the very nature of their bodies are deemed to be free) renders women unfit to take the higher vows of the religious mendicant.

Now this is far more than the usual negative view of menstruation, the taboo that can be observed in so many traditional cultures all over the world. It constitutes an elaborate phobia about the reproductive process and a radical contempt for women's bodies. But perhaps we need to be reminded of the context of this alarming centuries-long debate. The issue of nakedness is part of an interminable battle of wits between two opposed sects. Given the attitudes towards women in Indian literature in general, and in ascetic discourse in particular, it is unlikely that any of the male debaters cared very deeply about the salvation of women. It is far more likely, as Goldman suggests, that the debate was 'a kind of protracted metaphor for a struggle over the spiritual validity of the two paths of Jaina mendicancy'.[58] This is the hidden agenda. For the Digambaras, this obsessive picture of menstruation and female sexuality is a vital part of their argument that their white-clad rivals are at the same secondary level of spiritual advancement as their own pious but white-clad Digambara women. By describing the female body, and menstruation in particular, in terms calculated to disgust, and by simultaneously equating these physical processes with the need to wear white garments, the Digambaras intended to tar the Śvetāmbaras with the same polluting brush.

MENSTRUATION IN THE CONTEXT OF NORMATIVE DISCOURSE

I shall now turn to *dharmaśāstra* and, in particular, to Tryambaka's views on menstruation in the *Strīdharmapaddhati*.[59] Under the general heading of 'duties common to all women' (*strīṇāṃ sādhāraṇā dharmāḥ*), Tryambaka groups together a variety of rulings to form nine sections, one of which details 'the duties of the menstruating woman' (*rajasvalādharmāḥ*).[60] This is a loosely structured section that touches on most of the points normally made on the subject in dharmaśāstric texts.

The woman herself is described in a number of different ways that together demonstrate the ambivalent attitudes towards her. For example, *puṣpiṇī* and *puṣpavatī* (meaning 'bearing flowers' or 'in bloom') are positive terms of almost horticultural heartiness.[61] In contrast, there is the blunt *malavadvāsas* ('she whose clothes are stained'), or the graphic *ārtavābhiplutā* ('overflowing with menstrual blood'). More euphemistic terms include *rajasvalā* ('full of impurity, or dirt, or passion'; recalling the mud-red monsoon rivers) and *strīdharmiṇī* ('she who has the duty or condition of women'). These last

INDIAN VIEWS ON MENSTRUATION AND FEMALE SEXUALITY 73

two terms manage to encapsulate within the definition of the menstruating woman our three themes of the inherent nature of women, sexual passion, and innate impurity.

The first point that Tryambaka makes is that 'the menstruating woman is impure for three (days and) nights'.[62] According to a famous quotation, 'On the first day, she is declared to be [as polluting as] an untouchable; on the second, [as polluting as] a brahmin-killer; on the third, [as polluting as] a washerwoman; on the fourth, she is purified.'[63] I have already discussed the significance of this impurity, and the traditional tracing of its origins to the story of Indra's brahminicide.

Equally predictable are the innumerable prohibitions relating to the menstruating woman. Some of these demonstrate her impure state: for example, the ruling that she should not touch (i.e. pollute) fire; that is, she should not cook.[64] Some strive to avoid deepening that state of impurity still further: for example, she should not cut her nails. Others demand that she should not make herself attractive: for example, she should not use collyrium for her eyes, comb her hair, take a bath, or massage her body with oil.[65] Nor should she in any way suggest that she is sexually available: for example, she should not eat from her husband's plate; she should not even look at her husband. In effect, she is in no fit state to do anything.

These prohibitions are reinforced by the threat of defects accruing to the unborn child. As in the āyurvedic context, the link often reflects a magical correlation. For example, if she uses collyrium, her child will be blind in one or both eyes. If she combs her hair, he will be bald. If she massages her body with oil, he will have a skin disease. If she takes a bath, he will die by drowning. If she cleans her teeth, his teeth will be discoloured. If she cuts her nails, his nails will be diseased. If she plaits rope, her child will hang himself. If she laughs, his palate, lips and tongue will be discoloured. If she talks a lot, he will be a chatterbox. If she hears a loud noise, he will be deaf. If she runs, he will be unstable. If she roams about, he will be insane. And so on.

The most important prohibition of all is the ban on sex. If a menstruating woman makes love during the crucial three days, her child will be an untouchable, or cursed. Hence the detailed prohibitions to ensure that she is neither available nor attractive to her husband at this time.

Next come the rulings regarding the ritual bath of purification. Towards the end of the morning on the fourth day, she should cleanse herself with sixty lumps of earth (the high number indicating the depths of her impurity).[66] Then she should clean her teeth, and take a ritual bath. Pure once more, she should gaze at the sun, pray for a male child, and attend to her 'women's duties'. According to one quotation, 'When she has bathed properly, she should look at her husband's face ... or (if he is away) she should look at the sun while meditating on her husband in her mind.'[67] That evening, she should make sexual advances to her husband. A second quotation is more explicit:

> Anointed with unguents of ground turmeric and saffron, wearing bright garments, thinking of her husband's lotus foot, gazing at her own toes [i.e. keeping her eyes cast down], not looking at other men, thinking only of her husband, thinking of him as light itself ..., beautifully dressed and ornamented and anointed with perfume, and in good spirits, she should go to bed.[68]

This is an entirely positive (if male-oriented) image of female sexuality. Within the framework of marriage, and in the wider context of the dharmaśāstric norm of the householder, sex in pursuit of progeny is appropriate. Within that context, female sexuality as an expression of fertility is highly auspicious.

But what if the menstrual flow does not cease on the morning of the fourth day? Tryambaka is quite clear. If bleeding continues after the fourth day, she is considered 'fit to be touched' by her husband and therefore pure with regard to sexual intercourse with her husband; that is, she should still make love to him. Until her menstrual flow has ceased altogether, however, she is not held to be 'of pure conduct' and therefore she is not 'fit to perform the ritual worship of the gods'.[69]

We may speculate on the hidden agenda here. I suggest that a number of issues are at stake. First, there is the overriding importance of establishing a pregnancy in the hope of producing sons. A blanket prohibition on sexual intercourse during the menstrual flow might prevent a couple from taking advantage of the woman's 'season'. Second, there is probably the desire to take the initiative out of the hands of women. A woman who does not wish to have sex, or who is anxious not to conceive, might use persistent bleeding as an excuse. Finally, vaginal bleeding remains a bodily impurity that requires some form of purification before any religious ritual. A ruling attributed to the *Smṛticandrikā*, a thirteenth-century collection of rulings on *dharma*, makes this clear: 'For women (who continue to bleed from the fourth) until the twelfth day, the purification (appropriate) for urine is required; a ritual bath is (prescribed for those who bleed from the twelfth) until the eighteenth day; after that, she is (again) impure for three days (i.e. it is assumed that another cycle has begun).' The distinction between vaginal bleeding and menstrual blood proper is a nice one: it gives a man maximum access to his wife's body; it makes the greatest possible allowance for pregnancy; and yet it continues to protect religious ritual from pollution.

This point is taken further. Still using the *Smṛticandrikā* as his source, Tryambaka explains that the menstruating woman loses two kinds of blood: 'That which occurs to women at the wrong time (i.e. outside the crucial three days) men call "blood" (*raktam*); that which occurs at the right time (i.e. within those three days) is called "menstrual blood" (*rajas*); as a result of the latter alone, she becomes impure.'[70] The distinction being made here is evidently not the āyurvedic one between pure and impure substances, between healthy and sickly menstrual blood: the consistency and colour of the blood is not discussed. Nor does it reflect the phobic response of the Jain ascetic to all female fluids. Rather it represents a clash of dichotomies. According to the pure/impure dichotomy, all impurities of the body (blood, semen, sweat and so on) render a person impure. According to the auspicious/inauspicious dichotomy, menstruation bears the added weight of two quite different elements: the mythological burden of Indra's sin of brahmin-murder, and the extreme inauspiciousness of infertility. On those first three days of her menstrual cycle, a woman is temporarily barren and, as in the case of the cracked dry earth before the monsoon rains, infertility makes her inauspicious. But on the fourth day of the menstrual cycle, whether or not the flow of blood ceases, women are deemed to be in 'season' once more, both fertile and auspicious. Here auspiciousness overrides impurity, not entirely, but with crucial effect: 'menstrual blood' (*rajas*) is redesignated '(ordinary) blood' (*raktam*). Fertility wins the day.

Another quotation provides a more detailed definition:

> The best of wise men know that the menstruation of women is of four kinds: that which is due to illness; that which is due to (a disturbance of) the emotions; that which is due to (an imbalance of) the humours; and that which occurs at the right time (of the monthly cycle; i.e. during the crucial three days).[71] Tryambaka concludes that only the fourth type of bleeding makes a woman ritually impure.

Finally, there are the rulings concerning the importance of making love at the proper time. These take the form of penalties or atonements enjoined for those husbands and wives who fail to take proper advantage of the opportunity to conceive. For example, 'A man who fails in his duty to his wife should put on the skin of a donkey with the hair turned outwards and go to seven houses calling (out to each in turn): "(Give) alms to a man who has failed in his duty to his wife!" And this should be his livelihood for six months.'[72] In fact, this ruling is normally cited in the context of adultery. A variety of penalties may be imposed on the wife who refuses to make love; and again, these are penalties usually associated with adultery. For example, according to one authority, she should perform a severe twelve-day penance every month for six months. According to another, she should be abandoned. According to a third, she should be devoured by dogs in a public place. An anonymous source maintains that she will be reborn as a bitch, a she-wolf, a female jackal or a female hog. Yet another authority enjoins that her husband should proclaim her publicly to be a foetus-killer and drive her out of his house. Tryambaka concludes by demonstrating that the woman who leaves her husband's house, even to return to her natal home, is assumed to be unfaithful.[73]

These rulings bring us full circle. The woman who refuses to make love with her husband at the auspicious time of her fertile season is demonstrating (albeit by implication) the promiscuity or negative sexuality commonly cited in discussions of the inherent wickedness of women. Sudhir Kakar describes this type of discourse as 'the cornerstone of the culture's official view of women', thereby acknowledging its power. These rules and images, which Kakar refreshingly dismisses as 'a collective fantasy of the wife',[74] focus on the possible sexual abandon of adult women, and the implications of that abandon for a culture that depends upon its ability to control the sexuality of women.

In contrast, the woman who makes sexual advances to her husband at the proper time makes both herself and her sexuality auspicious. For the auspiciousness of a wife lies in the gift of her fertility (and thus of progeny) to her husband and her husband's family. Puberty marks the onset of that fertility; hence the celebrations of the first menstruation in many parts of India. For the wife, the blood that signals the start of another menstrual period means several things: temporary impurity, certainly; but also proof of pregnancy lost, and thus of a temporary but exceedingly inauspicious barrenness. On the fourth day of the cycle, however, after her bath of purification, both fertility and auspiciousness return, and the scales tip the other way. Indeed the start of a woman's fertile 'season' is so powerfully auspicious that Tryambaka can write in his section on the inherent nature of women that menstruation is the mark of an all-encompassing purity unique to women: 'Women are incomparably pure; at no time are they defiled; for menstruation sweeps away their sins month after month.'[75]

CONCLUSIONS

So what conclusions can we draw? For *āyurveda*, the issue is the pragmatic one of healthy versus unhealthy substances. For the male ascetic, the motive force is renunciation of the physical and sexual world, and hence contempt for women's bodies as the epitome of both. For *dharmaśāstra*, dominated by the householder code with the reproductive power of women at its core, bodily fluids are impure but fertility is auspicious. This is the dominant voice of a culture that both controls and depends upon the sexuality of women. Within my three different frameworks, fascination, disgust and fear, all relate directly to the power of women to create and nourish life from the substance of their own bodies. The particular substance that serves to focus this confused attention is the essentially sexual fluid of menstrual blood.

NOTES

1 S. Kakar, *Intimate Relations: Exploring Indian Sexuality* (Delhi, 1989), 13.
2 For the classic statement on dominant and 'muted' groups see E. Ardener, 'Belief and the Problem of Women', in S. Ardener (ed.), *Perceiving Women* (London, 1975).
3 An analysis and partial translation of this work is presented in I. J. Leslie, *The Perfect Wife: The Orthodox Hindu Woman according to the Strīdharmapaddhati of Tryambakayajvan* (Delhi, 1989). All references to the *Strīdharmapaddhati* are to the reconstruction of the text in *The Perfect Wife*.
4 *Acāro hanty alakṣaṇam.* Cf. *Manusmṛti* 4.156 (V. N. Mandlik edn, Bombay 1886); *Vasiṣṭhadharmasūtra* 6.8 (A. A. Führer edn, Pune 1905); *Viṣṇusmṛti* 71.91 (V. Krishnamacharya edn, Adyar 1964, Mysore MS). For English translations of these works see W. Doniger and B. K. Smith, *The Laws of Manu* (London, 1991); G. Bühler, *The Sacred Laws of the Aryas* part II: *Vāsishtha and Baudhāyana* (Oxford, 1882); and J. Jolly, *The Institutes of Vishnu* (Oxford, 1880).
5 For an analysis of Tryambaka's discussion on this topic see I. J. Leslie, '*Strīsvabhāva*: The Inherent Nature of Women', in N. J. Allen, R. F. Gombrich, T. Rauchaudhuri and G. Rizvi (eds.), *Oxford University Papers on India*, vol. I, Part 1 (Delhi, 1986); and in Leslie, *The Perfect Wife*, 246–72.
6 *Strīdharmapaddhati* 22v.3–5; Leslie, *The Perfect Wife*, 274.
7 *Strīdharmapaddhati* 20r.6–7; Leslie, *The Perfect Wife*, 237.
8 *Strīdharmapaddhati* 40r.1; Leslie, *The Perfect Wife*, 286.
9 *Mahābhārata* 13.12 (see n. 10).
10 For the Sanskrit text in 19 volumes see V. S. Sukthankar et al. (eds.), *The Mahābhārata: Text as Constituted in the Critical Edition* (Poona, 1933–9). For a complete English translation by K. M. Ganguli in 12 volumes see P. C. Roy (ed.), *The Mahābhārata* (Calcutta, 1883–96). For a more accurate but as yet incomplete English translation see J. A. B. van Buitenen, *The Mahābhārata* (Chicago, 1973–).

11 *Mahābhārata* 13. 12. 42.
12 *Mahābhārata* 13. 12. 47.
13 *Mahābhārata* 13. 19 ff.
14 *Mahābhārata* 13. 20. 59–60, 64–7.
15 *Mahābhārata* 13. 22. 4–5.
16 *Mahābhārata* 13. 22. 9.
17 *Mārkaṇḍeyapurāṇa* 49. 28–9. For the Sanskrit text see the K. M. Banerjea edn (Calcutta, 1862); for an English translation see F. E. Pargiter, *The Mārkaṇḍeya Purāṇa* (Calcutta, 1904).
18 *Mahābhārata* 13. 40. 5–12.
19 *Manusmṛti* 9. 15.
20 In this context, it is no surprise that the independent or 'fierce' (*ugrā*) goddesses are perceived as 'wild destructive females associated with rampant appetite and sexuality, and the blood of battlefield, sacrifice and menstruation' (Leslie, *The Perfect Wife*, 320).
21 Some of the causes of this historical development are discussed in Leslie, *The Perfect Wife*, 36–8.
22 Cf. *Manusmṛti* 5.135.
23 *Taittirīyasaṃhitā* 2.5.1 ff. (Ānandāśrama edn, Pune 1900–8). For an English translation see A. B. Keith, *The Veda of the Black Yajus School, Entitled Taittirīya Saṃhitā* (Cambridge, Mass., 1914). For a discussion of the myth in the context of Vedic *śrauta* ritual see F. M. Smith, 'Indra's Curse, Varuṇa's Noose, and the Suppression of the Woman in the Vedic Śrauta Ritual', in J. Leslie (ed.), *Roles and Rituals for Hindu Women* (London, 1991), 17–45.
24 *Mahābhārata* 5.10.13.
25 *Mahābhārata* 12.329.28–41.
26 *Bhāgavatapurāṇa* 6.9.6–10 (E. Burnouf edn with French translation, 1840–98). For an English translation see G. V. Tagare, *The Bhāgavata Purāṇa* (Delhi, 1976–8).
27 *Atharvaveda*, S. D. Satvalekar edn, Bombay 1957; 522. For an English translation see W. D. Whitney and C. R. Lanman, *Hymns of the Atharva-Veda* (Cambridge, Mass., 1905).
28 *Skandapurāṇa* 5.3.118.141 (Veṅkateśvara Press edn, Bombay 1909–11). No English translation is available.
29 *Rāmāyaṇa* 8.86.10–16 (S. K. Śāstrigal edn, Madras 1958). For a complete English translation in three volumes see H. P. Shastri, *The Ramayana of Valmiki* (London, 1953–9). For a more accurate but as yet incomplete English translation see R. P. Goldman (ed.), *The Rāmāyaṇa of Vālmīki: An Epic of Ancient India* (Princeton, 1984–).
30 See, for example, *Manusmṛti* 5.6; *Taittirīyasaṃhitā* 2.5.4.
31 For a discussion of this point see R. Salomon, 'Legal and Symbolic Significance of the "Menstrual Pollution" of Rivers', in R. W. Lariviere (ed.), *Studies in Dharmaśāstra* (Calcutta, 1984), 152–78.
32 *Carakasaṃhitā, sūtrasthāna* 11.17–26. For the Sanskrit text with an English translation see P. V. Sharma, *Caraka-Saṃhitā* (Varanasi, 1981–5).
33 *Carakasaṃhitā, vimānasthāna* 8.33.
34 *Carakasaṃhitā, śarīrasthāna* 4.5.

35 Mention is also made of the 'semen' of women but, according to the *Aṣṭāṅgasaṃgraha* 2.1 (Āṭhavale edn, Pune 1980), this plays no part in the formation of the foetus. No English translation of the *Aṣṭāṅgasaṃgraha* is available. Cf. J. Jolly, *Medicin* (Strasburg, 1977), 61.
36 D. M. Bose, S. N. Sen and B. V. Subbarayappa (eds.), *A Concise History of Science in India* (Delhi, 1971), 242.
37 *Suśrutasaṃhitā* 1.14.2 (Jādavaji Trikamji edn, Bombay 1915). For an English translation see K. K. L. Bhishagratna, *An English Translation of the Sushruta Samhita* (Calcutta, 1907).
38 J. Jolly, *Medicin*, 63.
39 *Suśrutasaṃhitā* 3.2.17–18; *Aṣṭāṅgasaṃgraha* 2.1.196 ff; *Aṣṭāṅgahṛdaya* 2.1.10–19 (Kunte and Navre edn, Bombay 1939). For a German translation of the *Aṣṭāṅgahṛdaya* see L. Hilgenberg and W. Kirfel, *Vāgbhaṭa's Aṣṭāṅgahṛdaya saṃhitā: Ein Altindisches Lehrbuch der Heilkunde* (Leiden, 1941).
40 *Suśrutasaṃhitā* 3.2.31.
41 Somewhat at odds with this idea is the wish Indra granted to women. There are evidently two ways of approaching the question. As a general rule, *āyurveda* stresses the medical aspects and thus the prohibition on sex during pregnancy. *Dharmaśāstra* seems undecided. Some texts follow the myth, insisting that if a woman wants to make love, her husband should not refuse, right up to the delivery of her child; e.g. the *Mitākṣara* commentary on *Yājñavalkyasmṛti* 1.81 (Nārāyan Rām edn, Bombay 1949; no English translation); *Taittirīyasaṃhitā* 2.5.1.4–5. Others rule that she should avoid sex, e.g. *Strīdharmapaddhati* 41r.3–4 in the section on the duties of the pregnant woman (Leslie, *The Perfect Wife*, 289).
42 *Suśrutasaṃhitā* 3.2.25 ff.
43 *Suśrutasaṃhitā* 3.3.9; *Aṣṭāṅgasaṃgraha* 2.1.198.
44 *Carakasaṃhitā*, *śarīrasthāna* 3.6–7. According to this view, a child may be born of the combined seed of two women, but it will be a deformed child without bones, etc., for these are provided by the seed of the male (*Suśrutasaṃhitā* 3.2.47).
45 *Aṣṭāṅgahṛdaya*, *śarīrasthāna* 1.52–3; cf. *Strīdharmapaddhati* 41r.9–41v.2 (Leslie, *The Perfect Wife*, 289–90).
46 *Suśrutasaṃhitā* 3.4.24.
47 For the symbolism of blood and milk in purāṇic mythology see W. D. O'Flaherty, *Women, Androgynes, and Other Mythical Beasts* (Chicago, 1980), 40–3. For related ethnographic material see Patricia Jeffery, Roger Jeffery and Andrew Lyon, *Labour Pains and Labour Power: Women and Childbearing in India* (London, 1989):

> The mother's contribution to the baby's development, then, is towards its growth rather than its essential make-up – and that, too, using defiling blood (*ganda khūn*) ... Early in pregnancy, preparations begin for nurturing the baby after birth: some blood is believed to congeal into breast milk, which remains in the breast and becomes heavy or solidified and yellow in colour ('like pus'). (p. 76)

48 'The developing foetus takes its strength from the mother's retained menstrual blood' (Jeffery, Jeffery and Lyon, *Labour Pains*, 76).
49 This is not the only instance in which *āyurveda* stands out against the normative

tradition. Remedies are often prescribed without regard for the expectations of Hindu orthodoxy, and without either apology or explanation for breaking normative rules. For example, the wholesome properties of meat and alcohol are discussed without reference to the religious context (e.g. *Carakasaṃhitā, sūtrasthāna* 27.311; *cikitsāsthāna* 24.61). These are not the texts of unbelievers (atheists, *cārvākas*); the authors are pious enough, but their first allegiance is to the 'science of life' (*āyurveda*).

50 From the introduction to the *Jātaka* or 'Birth stories' of the Buddha, in H. C. Warren, *Buddhism in Translations: Passages from the Buddhist Sacred Books and Translated from the Original Pali*, (Cambridge, Mass., 1896), 60–1.

51 *Buddhacarita* 5.63–4. For both the Sanskrit text and an English translation see E. B. Cowell, *The Buddha-Karita or Life of Buddha by Asvaghosha* (Oxford, 1894).

52 See P. S. Jaini, *Gender and Salvation: Jaina Debates on the Spiritual Liberation of Women* (Berkeley, 1991).

53 *Yuktiprabodha* 1 (Jaini, *Gender and Salvation*, 162). The commentary explains: 'The specific use of the word "*dravyataḥ*" [i.e., biologically] indicates that males who possess the female libido (*bhāvataḥ*) [and thus can be considered psychologically female] are not inherently opposed to the attainment of mokṣa.' As the ensuing discussion makes clear, the Digambaras do not deny the possibility of salvation to men who are 'psychologically female' (i.e. homosexual), nor do they allow it to women who are 'psychologically male' (i.e. lesbian). The issue is not sexual or psychological orientation, or even spiritual advancement, but simply a matter of physical fact: the female body demonstrates the impurity of the soul within. The Digambara position on this point concludes: 'We therefore maintain that there is no mokṣa possible for those persons who are biologically female, because crookedness (kauṭilya) is their very nature ... As it is often said in the world: "Falsehood, rashness, deceitfulness, foolishness, excessive greed, lack of affection and pitilessness are the innate faults of women"' (*Yuktiprabodha* 2–8).

54 *Yuktiprabodha* 10 (Jaini, *Gender and Salvation*, 166).

55 *Yuktiprabodha* 12 (Jaini, *Gender and Salvation*, 166).

56 *Yuktiprabodha* 69 (Jaini, *Gender and Salvation*, 179). These statements are presented by the Śvetāmbara spokesman who, while evidently accepting their validity, argues that they do not apply to nuns who refrain from all sexual activity and who 'maintain extreme skillfulness and presence of mind'.

57 Jaini, *Gender and Salvation*, 13–14. Cf. *Yuktiprabodha* 89 and Jaini, *op. cit.*, 192–3 n. 49.

58 Foreword by R. P. Goldman, in Jaini, *Gender and Salvation*, xx.

59 See n. 3.

60 Leslie, *The Perfect Wife*, 283–8.

61 The implications of these terms may not be wholly positive. In *Bhagavadgītā* 2.42, for example, the adjective *puṣpita* ('flowered'; in this context, 'flowery' speech) suggests something without substance, bearing flowers but not the all-important fruit. I am grateful to Tuvia Gelblum for this suggestion. For the Sanskrit text with an English translation see R. C. Zaehner, *The Bhagavad-Gītā* (Oxford, 1969).

62 *Strīdharmapaddhati* 33v. 8–9 (Leslie, *The Perfect Wife*, 283).

63 *Strīdharmapaddhati* 36r. 2–3 (Leslie, *The Perfect Wife*, 283).
64 Leslie, *The Perfect Wife*, 284.
65 For some of the implications of rulings relating to a woman's appearance, see J. Leslie, 'The Significance of Dress for the Orthodox Hindu Woman', in R. Barnes and J. B. Eicher (eds.), *Dress and Gender: Making and Meaning in Cultural Contexts* (Oxford, 1992), 198–213.
66 This high number is exceeded by that stipulated for the polluting and inauspicious menstruating widow (Leslie, *The Perfect Wife*, 286).
67 *Strīdharmapaddhati* 37v.3–4 (Leslie, *The Perfect Wife*, 286).
68 *Strīdharmapaddhati* 37v.5–7 (Leslie, *The Perfect Wife*, 287).
69 *Strīdharmapaddhati* 36r.6–8 (Leslie, *The Perfect Wife*, 287).
70 *Strīdharmapaddhati* 35v.6–9 (Leslie, *The Perfect Wife*, 283–4).
71 *Strīdharmapaddhati* 35v.3–4 (Leslie, *The Perfect Wife*, 284).
72 *Strīdharmapaddhati* 37v.7–9 (Leslie, *The Perfect Wife*, 287).
73 Leslie, *The Perfect Wife*, 287–8.
74 S. Kakar, *Intimate Relations: Exploring Indian Sexuality* (Delhi, 1989), 18–19.
75 *Strīdharmapaddhati* 21v.9–10 (Leslie, *The Perfect Wife*, 254). In fact, this is the standard argument not for the purity of women *per se* but for the proper treatment of the wife who has been raped or abducted, or who has temporarily left her husband. When the next menstrual period demonstrates that she is not carrying another man's child, she may once more be accepted into the marital home. For some writers on *dharmaśāstra*, menstruation purifies a woman of 'mental adultery' such as impure thoughts but not of 'physical adultery'; for others, the issue is whether or not she conceives (see Leslie, *The Perfect Wife*, 254–5).

FOUR

SEXUAL KNOWLEDGE IN ENGLAND, 1500–1750

PATRICIA CRAWFORD

THIS chapter discusses how sexual knowledge was constituted in early modern England. Medical discourse about sex informs many aspects of early modern social life including theology and the law. Those ideas which physicians called knowledge can be analysed as an ideology which functioned as a means of reinforcing social distinctions and the differences between men and women. Together with theological discourse, that of medicine defined licit and illicit sexuality. Medical and theological writers claimed the power to define knowledge, but they were forced to recognize a competing female discourse. Women possessed sexual knowledge of a different and sometimes complementary kind. The first part of the chapter gives a brief account of the medical and theological discourses of early modern England about sexuality. Sex was construed unreflectingly 'as an inborn drive with a single natural goal'[1]. Medical writers claimed that their discourse constituted 'knowledge', and as an increasingly professional group they sought to distance themselves from other medical practitioners, particularly from women healers. Medical knowledge about sexuality and health changed over the early modern period, but it continued to inform contemporary discussion about marriage and reproduction. The second part of the chapter discusses popular understandings of sexuality. Men and women accepted many of these medical ideas as 'knowledge', but since their own sources of understanding were not exclusively medical and theological, the two sexes subverted the medical discourse. Many men ignored the moral framework in which sexuality was understood, and treated their sexual desires as imperatives. Women's own experiences and observations induced a degree of scepticism about medical theories. Men might be learned, observed the midwife Jane Sharp, but in childbirth 'It is not hard words that perform the work, as if none understood the Art that cannot understand Greek'.[2] Further, female gossip about sexuality could subvert the dominant discourse about male superiority by mocking men and their sexual prowess.

Apart from studies of erotica, the history of sexuality has been ignored until comparatively recently. Sexuality seemed natural, eternally the same over time, and therefore required no history. The studies of the *Annalistes* in France and the pioneering study of Lawrence Stone in English demonstrated that sexuality was socially constructed and had a history.[3] In much of the earlier work, the historians' attitudes and assumptions were relentlessly male. Thus Stone, for example, asserts that 'despite appearances, human sex takes place mostly in the head', ignoring the fact that for women sex usually occurs in the social context of possible pregnancy.[4] In recent social histories of the family in England, such as those of Houlbrooke and Macfarlane, comparatively little attention has been devoted to the subject of sexuality *per se*.[5] Those working on the church court records could not ignore the subject, but their prejudices have been limiting. Some work, such as that of Quaife and Addy, and even that of Ingram, accepts the perspective of the courts without questioning.[6]

The ideas of Michel Foucault have reshaped the history of sexuality, although his influence has perhaps been less in the early modern period than in later periods. Foucault's idea of power inhering in a dominant discourse is a particularly useful one.[7] This helps us to see how there was a range of ideas about sexuality in early modern England; some were classified as knowledge, others as foolish beliefs. While the ideas of the university-trained physicians were the main source of knowledge about sexuality, the observations and experiences of the populace at large provided an alternative knowledge. Debates about sexuality were arguments about rival sources of knowledge, and gender relations in early modern society.

MEDICAL AND THEOLOGICAL KNOWLEDGE IN EARLY MODERN ENGLAND

There were two main discourses about sexuality in early modern England, one religious, the other medical. The church viewed sexuality as a moral issue. Theologians, priests and ministers taught the populace the rights and wrongs of sexual matters through sermons, informal teachings and printed works. Basically, the church assumed that all sexuality should be heterosexual, genital, and confined to marriage. Before the Reformation, the clergy endeavoured to discipline and enforce their sexual teachings through the confessional and the church courts. From 1559 until 1641, the Anglican clergy endeavoured to control the sexuality of the laity through the church courts. These courts were abolished in 1641, but although they were re-established at the Restoration with much the same powers, in practice they were weaker.[8]

The Protestant clergy taught that sex was natural and God-given. The Bible showed that God had instructed Adam and Eve to multiply. Divines debated whether Adam and Eve had had sexual relations before the Fall. For example, William Gouge, a leading seventeenth-century divine, argued that sexuality was a consequence of sin, so that Adam did not 'know' Eve until after the Fall.[9] Nevertheless, most clergy agreed that one consequence of the Fall was that the sexual act was to be understood as involving shame. Nakedness was to be hidden. Pain was to attend woman's bringing forth of children as a punishment for her transgression.

According to the Protestant clergy, sexual relations played an important part in a happy, chaste marriage. Ideally, 'due benevolence', as sexual relations were termed, was a 'debt' which the couple owed to each other.[10] Those who could marry, according to William Perkins, were those capable of reproducing: 'The male is of a superior sexe, fit for procreation. The female is woman of an inferiore sexe, fit to conceive and bear children.'[11] Sexuality within marriage was good. Thus, although Stone argues that all non-procreative marital sex was attacked in the early modern period, the evidence does not support his contention.[12] Marital sex was not just allowable, it was good in itself. This 'duty', as Gouge called marital sexual intercourse, was one that husbands owed to wives who were barren, and to those who had passed the menopause. The husband and wife who 'mutually delight each in other', 'yielding that due benevolence one to another which is warranted and sanctified by God's word', would be protected from adultery.[13] Yet beyond the language of duties or debts which the couple owed to each other, Gouge depicted marital sexuality as a pleasure; husbands who did not delight in their wives were 'stock-like'. Gouge urged his readers to 'Read the Song of Songs', where they would find in the affection of Christ for his spouse their own model for marital love.[14] Other divines cited the example of Isaac sporting with his wife Rebekah in private as showing God's approval of marital sexual pleasure.[15] As the physician Lemnius pointed out, good sex made for domestic harmony.[16] Good sexual relations were thus a central part of married life.

Theological discourse about sexuality was influenced by the medical discourse. Physicians' knowledge was found in an international medical literature written in Latin. Initially circulated in manuscripts, medical knowledge was increasingly published in books from the sixteenth century onwards. Although the physicians jealously guarded their knowledge and attempted to control access to it, print offered an opportunity to popularize and to reach a wider audience. Some medical works were translated into English so that the literate could understand how to preserve their health.

Sexuality and health were linked. Medical theorists believed that men and women needed sexual activity. Seed in both men and women was part of a distillation of food and blood, a most precious bodily fluid. Seed accumulated in bodies from the time of adolescence, and the healthy body required either a discharge or a reduction in the amount produced. Thus marriage, the only site of lawful sexual activity, was necessary for the health of both sexes. If marriage were not possible, or one of the partners was absent, ill, or otherwise unavailable, the physicians recommended a sober diet and vigorous exercise. Those who overate were thought to be full of the spirit of fornication.[17] William Stout, a Lancaster shopkeeper, noted in his autobiography that illicit sexuality was 'mostly the effect or consequence of excessive eating and drinking of both men and woman [sic], and want of lawfull exercise'.[18] Sex was thus constructed as something to be released or controlled, a model that Martha Vicinus has characterized as an 'energy-control (or hydraulic) model'.[19]

Medical writers regarded the male body as the norm, superior to the female. Men were thought to be hotter, therefore they concocted more seed. As one physician, Nathaniel Highmore explained in 1651, males have 'more spirtualiz'd & subtile seeds' than females.[20] Since men produced more seed, their sexual urges were more powerful. From this, one lawyer extrapolated the conclusion that men were by nature less able to be chaste.[21] Nevertheless, medical writers recognized that women were sexual beings, and they recommended sexual activity as a remedy for certain female diseases, which they defined variously as 'mother fits', 'utero strangulato' and greensickness.[22] Lust, said one writer, was inevitable in the young, therefore marry them off.[23]

Early modern physicians needed knowledge about reproduction – 'generation' as they termed it – in order to assist men and women to a healthy reproductive life. During much of the sixteenth century, medical writers treated the ancient medical texts as authoritative and concentrated on expounding the ideas of Hippocrates, Aristotle and Galen as the basis of knowledge about conception. By 1500, the commonly accepted view of the theories of Aristotle and Galen was that the child was formed from the active principle in the male sperm shaping the female matter of menstrual blood. However, Hippocrates' view, that the child was formed from a mixture of the male and female seed was more popular.[24] In the early seventeenth century, the physician Helkiah Crooke explained the process as the male seed, leaping with greater violence, mingling with the female's. The woman snatched the man's seed into her womb, which then shut.[25] In 1634 the translation of Paré advised a husband how to time the release of his seed 'at the very instant or moment' that his wife perceived 'the efflux of her seed to approach', so that a conception could be made from 'the concourse or meeting of the seeds'.[26] Crooke did not insist that a simultaneous orgasm was necessary, but he concluded that it would hasten conception: 'there may be conception though it bee slower, if one come a little before or after another.'[27]

In the later seventeenth century, physicians developed new theories of generation, which shifted the paradigm of sexual knowledge. Most physicians were influenced by theories of the pre-formation of the child in the seed of either the man or the woman.[28] Some writers continued to follow the old theories. In 1696 McMath still insisted that a conception occurred from the mixture of the seeds of the man and the woman, though he admitted that others regarded the woman as 'the Field only, into which the Mans Seed is committed'.[29] Some of the divines were responding to the shift in medical ideas. Dean Comber praised procreative sex for women, citing the classical view 'that the Woman should not marry for any other end than that she may be a Mother'.[30] It was much easier to argue in the eighteenth century that good women did not enjoy sex.

Knowledge about sexuality was power in early modern times, and medical writers sought to control information. In the sixteenth century, much of the discourse about reproduction was in Latin, and anatomical, with questions of generation and reproduction central. Even diagrams of female anatomy in medical books were limited to male eyes only. That is, widespread anatomical knowledge was restricted. Plans to instruct midwives in anatomy by Peter Chamberlen in the 1630s and by Elizabeth Cellier in the 1680s were thwarted, the first by the midwives themselves, the second by the Royal College of Physicians.[31] Furthermore, in practice, physicians were reluctant to give their patients too much knowledge. They were unwilling to advise women about ways to precipitate menstruation, lest they provided women with a means of aborting themselves.[32]

Nevertheless, from the early to the mid-seventeenth century, especially during the Civil Wars and Interregnum, there was a movement to popularize medical knowledge.[33] Many Latin works were translated and simplified for a popular audience. Medical writers were troubled at the translation into English of Latin terms for sexual organs and for describing the process of reproduction. Translators feared that the English words were so associated with a variety of contexts, many of which were bawdy, that they would be accused of pandering to obscenity. Authors and publishers tried to assure readers, especially female readers, that their modesty was not threatened: 'There is nothing here that may be found harsh in the most Chastest Ear.'[34]

Physicians and theologians offered sexual advice about how to conceive healthy children.[35] Until the end of the seventeenth century, most writers insisted that sexual pleasure was necessary for conception. Culpeper advised that a woman could fail to conceive because there was 'very little or no pleasure in the act of copulation'.[36] If a wife hated her husband, her womb would not open.[37] But women's reports raised some doubts about the theory. Crooke admitted that while undoubtedly the man had to enjoy the encounter, women apparently did not: 'you shall heare many say that they haue no sense or inkling of pleasure at all'. However, on balance, he concluded that pleasure was a necessary part of the work of generation, otherwise men would be deterred by the 'scorn and detestation of so brutish and base a work' and women would be deterred by their fears of childbirth.[38]

Early modern advice for those who could not conceive was probably what would now be termed the 'rhythm method' of birth control. Physicians believed that a woman was most likely to conceive a son immediately after menstruation, and consequently they advised couples to concentrate their sexual activity on those days. If a wealthy wife were barren, her doctors might order her to take the waters at the baths, and have sex afterwards. Mary of Modena, for example, thought that she had conceived when the King came to her on Tuesday 6 September 1687 when she was at the baths.[39]

For women and men the implications of these theories differed. There were both positive and negative consequences for women in the theory that simultaneous orgasm was necessary for conception. They could veto a marriage partner whom they found sexually unattractive. As Queen Mary told a delegation beseeching her to marry, 'if she were married against her will she would not live three months, and would have no children'. One of Cecil's correspondents used similar arguments of Queen Elizabeth's marriage: she should marry according to her affections, 'whych shalbe the nerest wayes with the helpe of God to bryng us a blessed prynce'.[40] The negative implications were seen in legal attitudes to rape. If a rape were followed by pregnancy, the law deemed it no rape because the woman had, by definition, enjoyed the encounter.[41] By the eighteenth century, however, the change in medical theories of conception was reflected in the justices' handbooks; a charge of rape was allowed even if a woman were pregnant.[42]

Another consequence of the theory that sex was necessary for health was that celibacy was virtually impossible, thus making sin inevitable. Although there was always a strong school of thought which argued that sexual impulses could be reduced, abated and controlled, others thought that the power of sexuality was irresistible. Seminal secretion could not be stopped: 'Sleeping or Waking, the Spermaticks will do their Office.'[43] Much of the anti-Catholic propaganda of the sixteenth and seventeenth centuries focused on the inevitability of lust and illicit sexuality among monastic communities.[44] Protestants argued that the single state was unnatural. Although ideally men should not visit brothels, in practice the use of prostitutes by unmarried men was condoned. Reforming efforts were fruitless.[45] There was always an argument which had circulated since ancient times, that only the existence of prostitution allowed other women to walk the streets in safety.[46]

Physicians deemed excessive sex an evil, a danger to health.[47] Men throughout the early modern period expressed their anxiety about the deleterious effects of excessive sexual activity. Shakespeare castigated 'The expense of spirit in a waste of shame'.[48] Culpeper said that excessive sexual activity exhausted the spirits and dulled the mind, and Brooke said that it could lead to dulling and decay of sight.[49] Wilfully shedding sperm would harm a man 'more then if he should bleed fortie times so much'.[50] Popular superstition suggested that each act of sex shortened a man's life by a day. A woman who indulged excessively would become unable to conceive because her womb would be too moist and slippery, which, it was widely believed, was the reason why prostitutes bore few children.[51] Physicians and theologians also encouraged sexual restraint for eugenic purposes. Too much sex was believed to weaken the seed and stunt the child's growth. In 1633 Hart discussed the dangers of excess, citing with approval the doctrines of the Elizabethan theologian, Thomas Cartwright.[52] The dangerous effects of men's overindulgence in sexual activity both for the individual and the offspring were summed up by Gerrard Winstanley in the 1650s. Winstanley was radical in his economic ideas, but conventional in sexual matters. He censured the Ranters for their 'excess of Feminine society' which 'hinders the pure and naturall Generation of man, and spills the seed in vaine, and instead of a healthfull growth of mankind it produces weaknesse and much infirmnesse, through immoderate heat'. The Ranters' sexual indulgence meant that the mother either suffered excessively during pregnancy, or afterwards from the child's diseases. No child could live long, because it was 'a foole, or else a sickly weakly thing'.[53] The belief that immoderate sexual activity jeopardized people's progeny was constant during the early modern period. In the early eighteenth century, Defoe censured parents who weakened and diseased their progeny by excessive sexual activity.[54] Writers continued to argue that too much sex made people languid, and some claimed that it could engender gout or even lead to venereal disease itself.[55]

Theologians also attempted to regulate marital sexuality. Perkins regarded excessive sex even within marriage as no better than adultery.[56] Gouge taught that just as a man might surfeit at table, 'so may he play the adulterer with his own wife'.[57] Of course the perceptions of men and women about the amount of sex they deemed 'excessive' might differ. Divines and medical practitioners therefore endeavoured to suggest limits. The most usual advice was weekly sex, with one week's abstinence during the woman's menstruation. Daniel Rogers discussed what the ancients had allowed, and concluded that those with Christian liberty ought not to exceed the pagan prescription.[58] Nollius agreed that three times a month was best, as Solon had said.[59]

Sexual activity was to be restricted at certain times. The Bible prohibited sex during menstruation, as divines explained to their congregations.[60] Gouge advised husbands not to 'require this duty in that time' because 'such polluted copulation' would produce 'a leprous and loathsome generation'. Besides, it was expressly forbidden in Leviticus, under threat of capital punishment.[61] There was less agreement about sexual activity during pregnancy. Harris argued that beasts did not copulate with the pregnant females, and therefore men ought not to copulate with their pregnant wives.[62] Defoe too censured sex during pregnancy as 'a pollution in Nature', and rejected the popular idea that further sexual activity was necessary to finish the work of conception.[63] Divines and physicians also thought that husbands should abstain from sex with their breast-feeding wives, since sex spoilt a woman's milk and led to further conceptions.[64] Undoubtedly this medical theory had the effect of promoting the use of wet-nurses in families where their hire could be afforded. The widespread belief that the effects of sex on both pregnancy and lactation were harmful created a competition between a husband and his child for access to a woman's body. Finally, in cases where one of the parties was ill, the clergy did believe that the body's desires should be resisted: 'the body must bee beaten downe,' declared Gouge, 'and earnest prayer made for the gift of continency'.[65]

Clerical and medical discourse informed the laws which defined several kinds of sexual activity as illicit in early modern England. Premarital fornication was punished by the church courts. Mothers who bore children outside marriage were punished by the secular courts. The common law punished adultery by a married woman by depriving her of her dower or jointure. The 1650 Act which brought in the death penalty for adultery defined the crime as one which married women only could commit. Married men committed the crime of fornication.[66]

A range of sexual offences was punishable in early modern England. Prostitution was generally understood as an evil, and the women convicted were punished at Bridewell. Despite the sporadic onslaughts by the London civic authorities, pimps, brothel-keepers and clients were less harshly dealt with.[67] Some sexual offences, including bestiality and sodomy, were felonies which stipulated the death penalty on conviction. Attitudes to sodomy in early modern society are unclear. Although some historians have interpreted the case of the earl of Castlehaven as indicating an abhorrence of sodomy, Cynthia Herrup has argued that no such uniform attitude prevailed.[68] Lesbian sexual activity was not legally an offence. Lyndal Roper suggests that men found it difficult to think seriously of any sexual act which did not involve penetration, and thus they found it difficult to imagine what sexual activity between women could be, unless the women had recourse to manual objects.[69]

Other sexual activities were deemed undesirable but not criminal. Masturbation was less discussed as a sin in the early modern period than in the eighteenth and nineteenth centuries. In certain circumstances, physicians even recommended masturbation. Medical treatises indicated that the accumulation of seed could cause illness, and advised methods for relief. Physicians or midwives could masturbate their female patients to release the troublesome seed.[70]

Medical knowledge conformed to religious teaching, which defined deformed births as a punishment for sins. A 'monster' was born when parents engaged in excessive or illicit sexual practices.[71] Various defects were blamed on the mother's imagination, or frights she had had.[72] Abortive foetuses, known as 'moles', were said to be caused by a fault in the woman's seed.[73] The 1634 translation of Paré reported that some thought 'moles' were from a mixture of the woman's seed and menstrual blood without male seed, but Paré pointed out that Galen and Avicenna denied this.[74] At the end of the century, McMath explained that moles were fleshy tumours which could be caused by the congress of wanton lustful girls with old men. If an older man married a young wife, the greater quantity of seed produced by the lustier younger woman would overwhelm his seed in the womb and, instead of a healthy child, the woman would produce a 'mole'.[75]

All this theological and medical discourse established a sexual knowledge which was part of the means by which women were defined, and relations between the sexes regulated. Axiomatic to medical theory was that women were weaker. Man was the measure of all things, so woman's body was explained by the male model. In the sixteenth century, her ovaries were termed the 'female testes' or testicles, and her reproductive organs were described as 'no other than those of a man reversed, or turned inward'.[76] Belief in the primacy of the male over the female informed explanations of reproduction. The male foetus was perfect earlier than the female, received a soul sooner, and was born sooner.[77] As preachers explained, the Scriptures showed that the godly desired sons; medical discourse offered instructions on how a couple might produce a boy.[78] Medical discussion of various distinctive female bodily processes – menstruation, parturition and lactation – made the woman's body seem unstable and endlessly changing. Her menstrual cycle was linked with phases of the moon. Such ideas of physiological instability thus reinforced in turn the idea of the female person as unstable and changeable, at the mercy of the moon. Blood, seed and milk could all cause problems for a woman's health. Thus medical discourse defined marriage as the ideal stage of female life. In theory, a woman who had sexual conjunction with her husband enjoyed better health than at any other stage of her life.[79] The physiological state of the virgin and the widow were both problematical, in slightly different ways. Both suffered from disorders associated with the accumulation of seeds, which were variously interpreted as causing mother fits, suffocation of the womb, and greensickness. The widow was in greater danger because she had been exposed to sexual activity. Her imagination could stimulate unhealthy desire: 'A widow must restrain her memory and her fancy,' ordered Jeremy Taylor in his rules for widows.[80] Thus medical accounts of female physiology as unruly helped to justify female subordination.

POPULAR KNOWLEDGE ABOUT SEXUALITY

While medical and theological writers attempted to define medical knowledge, women and men had their own understandings, derived from observation and experience as well as from their reading or hearing of professionals' views. Popular knowledge about sexuality was based on a variety of sources, depending on sex, age, and level of literacy. Here I will argue that there were indeed separate male and female varieties of sexual knowledge, with some overlap between them. The sources for a study of popular beliefs are limited and difficult. Although some speech about sexual matters was reported in the courts, several censoring processes were at work. Women were usually careful about their speech in mixed company. Fewer women were literate, so fewer of their own words survive. Furthermore, what people said and what they did may have differed. Historians are well aware that the relationship of advice to practice is problematic; so, too, is that of words to deeds.

Although the educated male elite, a professional group, had established a discourse about sexuality, they did not have a monopoly on sexual knowledge. Even educated men relied at times upon female knowledge about sexual matters. The lawyers and judges in the civil and church courts made use of medical theories about sexuality for determining points relating to paternity, birth, and inheritance rights, and, as an educated male elite, they had access to the medical texts. But sometimes the information they sought was not provided by books. In cases of annulment of marriage on the grounds of non-consummation, for example, the courts needed to determine whether or not the woman concerned was still a virgin. In such a case, the court turned to an alternative source of authority, namely women, whose knowledge was based on observation and experience. Similarly, if a female offender sought to escape the death penalty on the grounds of pregnancy, then a jury of matrons was called to adjudicate.[81]

People needed and sought sexual knowledge for the conduct of their daily lives, but men's and women's purposes in seeking sexual knowledge may have differed. For women, knowledge about sexuality was generally associated with reproduction. According to the medical theories current, women had reason to believe that any pleasurable heterosexual genital contact could lead to pregnancy. Their attitudes varied as they feared or desired a child. Outside marriage, a pregnant woman faced social penalties. Consequently, for the unmarried woman, or for the wife whose husband was absent, or the mother who had too many children, knowledge about sexuality was necessary to prevent pregnancy. Married men sought healthy children. When men come to reason, claimed one popular medical treatise of 1736, 'they consider that there is no way of becoming immortal in this World, or at least of perpetuating themselves to the End of Time, but by being renewed in their Children'.[82] Depending upon their economic circumstances, however, the number of children may have been a burden. Some fathers may have sought to limit their family size while continuing their sexual activities. While both married women and men may have sought to use their knowledge of sexuality to restrict their family size, the interest of the unmarried man was often different. Ideally unmarried men were supposed to sublimate their sexuality by hard work and a spare diet. In practice, they may have been interested in sexual practices which would gratify their desires without causing them trouble. They feared venereal diseases. Nor did they wish to impregnate their lovers. They might be forced to marry them or face prosecution for maintenance payments in a bastardy case.

The populace at large derived its knowledge from a wide and varied range of sources. Although female literacy rates were lower than those of males, Slack suggests that by the year 1600 books were probably accessible to those who wanted them.[83] The increasing numbers of titles a century later shows that there was a lay audience for works providing information about sexuality and reproduction. Moreover, authors increasingly wrote specialized treatises. Authors of vernacular books may have had both a male and a female readership. Some medical practitioners and popularizers wrote specifically for a female audience. In the 1630s, one physician quoted Hippocrates' view that women should be instructed in knowledge about conception: 'Ignorance makes women become murderers to the fruit of their owne bodies.'[84] The preface to the translation of *The Expert Midwife* stated that midwives needed knowledge in order to help other women.[85] In the early eighteenth century, *The Rational Account* went through many editions. The preface to the 1736 edition promised that, by reading, women might remedy their own disorders,[86] but the 1739 edition declared that women had slender knowledge of their own infirmities.[87] In the late eighteenth century, John Leake published instructions for those women who were too far away from medical assistance or who could not afford it. He undertook not to confuse women with theories.[88] Some women writers directed their work to a female audience. Jane Sharp, in addressing her book to her 'Sisters', the midwives of England, tried to restrict her work to her own sex. She explained the process of generation so that women could understand how healthy babies could be conceived, nurtured in the womb, and reared through infancy and childhood.[89] Male writers, when addressing women, were conscious of the need to protect female modesty. McMath stated in his preface that he had omitted any account of the parts for generation, 'lest it might seem execrable to the more chast and shamefast, through Bawdiness and Impurity of Words'.[90] Both male and female authors, who expected women to be among their readers, deliberately chose sober titles for their books. They provided information about sexuality incidentally in the context of better health or of safer and healthier reproduction.

Other books about sexuality were directed to a male audience. Authors of Latin works addressed an educated, male audience, who thus had access to specialized information and a technical vocabulary. Some works which offered to reveal 'secrets' were directed to a wider audience. These books sold well in the sixteenth century, continued to sell in the seventeenth century, and flooded off the press in the eighteenth century.[91] Works purporting to be by Aristotle, such as *Aristotle's Masterpiece*, which contained 'secrets of generation', continued to find an audience into the twentieth century.[92] Literature for male eyes was signalled by titles such as *Rare Verities. The Cabinet of Venus Unlocked*.[93] Some authors aimed their work at the young and inexperienced, and under the guise of offering instruction, provided titillation.[94] Some of these publications could have reached a female audience.

Social level as well as gender affected access to information. Educated men gained knowledge not just from Latin medical works but also from the erotic writings of classical literature.[95] Poorer men might be literate, but they were restricted to works in English. All men and women had access to ballads and an oral culture, but the cultures of men and women were somewhat different. Women shared knowledge across social levels more than men did. A queen and a non-aristocratic midwife might discuss information.[96] While everyone could hear whatever knowledge the clergy had to offer about sexual matters, only the wealthy could consult physicians. Women relied more than men did on an oral culture about sexual knowledge. Attending each other's lyings-in, midwives and women of different social status exchanged information about sexuality and reproduction. Needless to say, women rarely talked about sexual matters before a mixed audience, and consequently their views are underrepresented in the written sources. The role of oral culture in transmitting knowledge is uncertain, but it is likely that as historians work further in the church court records, this subject will be illuminated.

There was a change in the mode of transmission of sexual knowledge over the period 1500 to 1750. In 1500, sexual knowledge, like all knowledge, was more likely to be transmitted orally; by 1650, there was a range of books. By 1700, women authors were contributing to the growing body of literature about women's bodies. In addition to Jane Sharp, women almanack writers such as Sarah Jinner and Mary Holden included useful information about sexual matters.[97] Print also gave a wider circulation to other sources of information. Stories, collections of jests, ballads and advertisements provided informal sources of sexual information and reached a wider audience than advice books. For example, the ballad 'A Remedy for the Greensickness' joked about sex as a cure for this common female ailment:

> A Handsom buxom Lass
> lay panting in her bed
> She lookt as green as grass
> and mournfully she said
> Except I have some lusty lad
> to ease me of my pain
> I cannot live
> I sigh and grieve
> My life I now disdain.[98]

Popular sayings reflected the same idea: 'Marry your daughters betimes lest they marry themselves' was a popular saw. Thus, although print was increasingly significant in the transmission of sexual knowledge to the populace at large, oral culture remained an important source of knowledge. Despite all the agonising of medical writers about the effects of translating discussion of reproduction from Latin into English, much sexual information was exchanged by word of mouth.

Talk was important in communicating sexual knowledge, especially among women, but here the sources are most difficult and elusive. Personal experience and observation clearly provided many people with their sexual knowledge. Observation of animal behaviour may have been another, if slightly misleading, source of information. (The distinctive relationship in the human female between ovulation and menstruation was not understood until the twentieth century.) Talk about sexual matters also took place between men and women outside marriage. From the correspondence between Dr William Denton and his nephew Sir Ralph Verney it is clear that Denton had talked with one of his female servants about sending Sir Ralph a female servant who 'will match your cock'.[99] Yet I would argue that a woman was liable to risk her modesty by engaging in such talk.

An important element of female socialization was the inculcation of a concept of modesty in women. The higher the social level, the more emphasis was placed upon proper bodily comportment and speech as the marks of a modest woman. In part, modesty meant not speaking about certain subjects before men, or, if speech were necessary, then she might employ circumlocutions. Modesty also involved women in guarding most areas of their bodies from male eyes. Female authors of midwifery treatises justified publication in terms of assisting women in preserving their modesty. For example, in 1737 Sarah Stone claimed that the modesty of 'our sex' would be lost unless women midwives mastered the difficulties of their work.[100]

In early modern England, there was a women's culture of shared knowledge about the distinctively female bodily functions. The main focus was the childbirth scene, a site at which a range of information about bodily matters was exchanged. While this female oral culture played an important part in providing sexual knowledge to women, it was not accessible to young unmarried women, who did not attend childbirths. Nor was it impervious to male influence.

Midwives had an important role in educating other women. Their knowledge was derived from a variety of sources. Some were educated enough to make use of books. Clearly in writing for midwives, authors such as Nicholas Culpeper and Jane Sharp thought that they had an audience. Experience was another teacher. The testimonials for midwives' licences usually refer to many years' experience and good success in practice.[101] In addition, midwives learned from men. Edward Poeton prepared a manuscript entitled *The Midwiues Deputy* for the use of his wife, a sworn midwife. He claimed that his material was collected from the works of Raynald, Guillemeau and Rueff, and explained in simple terms: 'I have striven . . . to use the most ordinary words and the playnest phrases.'[102] Furthermore, in the later seventeenth and early eighteenth centuries, several of the London women who served as medical practitioners for female disorders claimed that they had acquired their knowledge from their fathers or husbands. In some cases these men were physicians.[103]

Thus, although there was a separate female culture concerned with sexuality, it was not totally isolated from the male culture. We know that women did talk with men about conception. A group of women at a christening merrily advised Samuel Pepys about how to beget a child: they gave him ten points of advice, stressing that the foot of the bed should be higher than the head.[104] The boundaries for talk about sexual matters were drawn so that no modest unmarried woman discussed sexual matters in mixed company, and even married women were guarded about what they said before men in public. Thus the evidence from the court records was subject to a double censoring process: officials wrote down what they elicited in response to their questions, and women were careful what they said before the male court officials. Some women pleaded modesty for their refusal to talk: Ann Barnes complained that she was thrown to the ground by Nicholas Ames, 'and modesty does inforce me to forbeare the relacon of his unrulye behaviour'.[105] Yet despite modesty and self-censorship, the court records do show that, among themselves, some women did talk about sexual matters. However, so far the evidence from the church courts is insufficient to substantiate the fears of men, that women gossiped about male sexual prowess.

Female gossip about male sexuality could affect a man's reputation in early modern England. The Norwich Consistory Court heard how Ethelreda Baxter told her friends that William Noble, a married man, a maltster and a churchwarden, had solicited her as she was coming to her house. Furthermore, he 'did pull out his yard and put it into her hand', promising her that should she comply, she should want neither money nor malt nor anything. He boasted that 'his pintle was better than her husbands'.[106] These and other stories of sexual harassment were common knowledge among the witnesses against Noble. Ultimately the gossip spread; a few men heard about Noble putting his penis on a plank of a stile, and spilling his seed on the ground. Noble and his supporters counter-attacked with general allegations about the sexual reputation of the women.[107] Female gossip was equally explicit in 1707–9 among the women of a London Baptist congregation. There women alleged that their pastor, David Crosby, frequented brothels, tongue-kissed servant maids, and exposed himself. Such sexual talk was dangerous to women when it moved outside the all-female group. The congregation, when the minister was threatened, counter-attacked.[108] Whereas women needed to be explicit in their allegations about male sexual misconduct, men could damage women's social reputations by the generalized epithet of 'whore'.[109] Yet women's gossip had subversive power: their talk undermined male ideas of superiority.

Women's silences should be considered, as well as their talk. What is most puzzling is women's silence about sexuality in their diaries and letters. Although some female diarists did note that they thought they were pregnant, there are very few direct references to sexuality in women's diaries. Sarah Cowper, who recorded her distaste for sexual activity, seems a rare exception.[110] This contrasts with male diarists, who did mention sexual activity, albeit in shorthand and or in foreign languages.[111] Did marital loyalty or female modesty constrain most women? The silence of women diarists is in marked contrast with a range of popular literature about the merry meetings of gossips, where fictional female characters were quite explicit about all kinds of sexual matters.[112]

Books may have given men access to wider sources of information about sexuality than women had, but manuals about health and theologians' observations about illicit sexuality may have made men anxious about their sexuality. Evidence from popular literature reveals a wide range of male fears of women. Men worried lest women's powerful desires should prove irresistible, for they knew that the female seed had a 'greedy desire' for the male seed.[113] They feared that women would milk them of their seed.[114] Men knew of recipes for love philtres which would bewitch them, and were anxious about the food which women served them.[115] They suspected that women jested about male sexual prowess.[116]

Some men, as well as most women, were modest and embarrassed in discussing certain sexual matters both in public and in private. The almanack writer Sarah Jinner claimed that men and women suffered needlessly 'by their Modesty', because they were too shy to acquaint physicians with their symptoms.[117] William Whatley, a clergyman, realized that women were displeased by his public condemnation of sexual activity during the wife's menstruation. He protested that it could not be immodest for him to mention the matter, since the Holy Ghost had done so.[118] James II invited his Privy Council to be present at his wife's lying-in in 1688. He was able to explain to one councillor what was happening, saying 'you are a married man, and so may know these Matters'.[119] Samuel Jeake disguised his diary notations about sexual relations with his wife by writing in shorthand.[120] Samuel Pepys wrote his entire diary in shorthand, but when he described his sexual activities, he adopted the further disguise of a mixture of European languages.[121] To write of a homosexual act discomforted one gentleman, who referred to 'a most horrid and prodigious misdemeanour committed in our Towne this last weeke: there was (it seemeth) such obscenity and filthinesse acted publikely in the face of the Sun, that I am ashamed to mention it.' What he declared so abominable was 'the Sodomiticall kind of conjunction in the two men'.[122]

Sometimes the language used for sexual activity suggests that men saw sex less as a pleasure than a need. Common to the law courts was the expression, he had 'the use' of her body.[123] The language for the sexual act was of evacuation, expenditure, and the satisfaction of an itch. Some of the witnesses and recording clerks were explicit in discussing sexual matters, speaking of a man 'handling his prick', or of another coming to bed with 'nothing standing but his ears'.[124] 'Being naughty' was a common term for sexual intercourse in Chester diocese, and other church court records use the term 'to be naught' with someone.[125] In discussion of sexual matters, a man might use an animal analogy, suggesting that animal-breeding was another source of sexual knowledge. Alice Slaughter reported that her lover's alleged response to her claim that she was with child was: 'if I met with her I will give her a kick or two & make her Cast her Calfe'.[126]

A discussion of the means of family limitation illustrates the range of popular knowledge about an important aspect of sexual activity. Some historians have claimed that there was no family planning before the eighteenth century because people lacked both the desire and the means.[127] Certainly, there were arguments against family planning. There was a framework of God's providence: the Lord, not the individual, decided how many children would be born. Those who desired no children, wrote Hilder in 1653, 'have a diabolical spirit, they would counter God ... if possible'. God, he said, 'never makes mouths but he provides meat'.[128] In 1663 John Oliver professed that he was incapable of understanding how mothers of large families could ignore the mercy of God, and be grieved if they found themselves with child.[129] But undoubtedly, people were attempting contraception.[130]

Evidence suggests that men and women in early modern England sought to control their fertility for a variety of reasons by a variety of means. They knew that sexual abstinence prevented conception. (Cynics said that fear of the pox or of childbirth kept many chaste.)[131] Apart from abstinence, the most widely known method of contraception was probably *coitus interruptus*. Stone suggests that, while *coitus interruptus*, assisted by oral, manual and anal sex, could have been a technique thought up by each generation, such practices were more likely to have been culturally transmitted.[132] *Coitus interruptus*, known as onanism in the early modern period, may have been publicized by the clergy who preached against it: you who are married, warned Thomas Hilder, should mind the sin and punishment 'of a bird of your own feather, (viz) Onan, Gen. 38.9, 10.'[133] Both abstinence and withdrawal offered the possibility of success, although contemporaries believed that they were morally dubious. Likewise, as a method of preventing birth, abortion was successful. It was not a crime before the quickening of the child, and was under female control. McLaren suggests that women were undeterred by theological censures. There may have been a separate female sexual culture which exchanged such knowledge.[134] Infanticide, however, was illegal and was punishable by death. By the law of 1624, any unmarried woman who could not prove that her baby was born dead was presumed guilty of its murder.[135] Popular seventeenth-century medical works publicized a wide variety of contraceptives and abortifacients, and medicines were offered for sale in late seventeenth- and eighteenth-century London. Stone discounts the efficacy of such remedies, but the advertisements indicate that there was a thriving business in contraceptives and abortifacients in London.[136] In practice, women's knowledge must have been less effective than people believed, otherwise there would not have been so many unwanted pregnancies outside marriage.[137] But women may have rejected the option of abortion, fearing the danger to their bodies, or exercising moral scruples.

During the early modern period, there was a debate about the respective merits of medical 'knowledge' and popular, particularly female, 'knowledge'. Medical writers increasingly criticized and dismissed women's knowledge during this period. Cotta warned his readers against heeding women's advice seeing 'their authority in learned knowledge cannot be authenticall'.[138] Nevertheless, some men and women were sceptical about physicians' knowledge. When Deborah Brackley, a servant in Exeter, told her lover that she was pregnant, 'hee told her she could not be with Childe & though the docters tould her soe yet they were fooles'.[139] At the popular level, women continued to seek and heed the advice of midwives and other women. Although female talk may not have been knowledge according to the physicians, who were increasingly scornful of custom and oral traditions, the information which women exchanged may have helped to meet their needs. That is, I would argue against a medical monopoly of knowledge. For the populace at large, medical theories were too complicated to be readily useful. People selected elements which appealed. They were not restricted to the ideas of the university-trained, but could seek advice from a range of practitioners. Who was to say which of many remedies had helped?[140] Besides, there was a disjunction between medical theories and observations which encouraged scepticism. Women did conceive who reported no sexual pleasure at all.

Knowledge about sexuality gave its possessors some limited power in early modern England. Some Latin educated physicians withheld training about anatomy from women. Others physicians sought to inform the general public. Ideas about sexuality, conception and reproduction generally created a value system which enhanced male superiority. Men feared women's sexuality, and constructed a world in which their own sexual needs were prioritized. Women, however, continued to share a female culture in which knowledge about sexuality and reproduction was based on experience and observation.

ACKNOWLEDGEMENTS

Thanks to Jane Long, Roy Porter, and the participants in various seminars who have discussed these ideas with me; and especially to Sara Mendelson, for her careful and critical reading of the chapter.

NOTES

1 M. A. Warren, 'The Social Construction of Sexuality', in Norma Grieve and Ailsa Burns (eds.), *Australian Women. New Feminist Perspectives* (Melbourne, 1986), 143.
2 J. Sharp, *The Midwives Book* (London, 1671), 3–4.
3 J.-L. Flandrin, *Families in Former Times. Kinship, Household and Sexuality* (1976; trans., Cambridge, 1979); L. Stone, *The Family, Sex and Marriage in England, 1500–1800* (London, 1977).
4 Stone, *Family*, 483.
5 A. Macfarlane, *Marriage and Love in England. Modes of Reproduction 1300–1840* (Oxford, 1986); R. Houlbrooke, *The English Family 1450–1700* (London, 1984).
6 G. R. Quaife, *Wanton Wenches and Wayward Wives* (New Brunswick, 1979); J. Addy, *Sin and Society in the Seventeenth Century* (London, 1989); M. Ingram, *The Church Courts, Sex and Marriage in England, 1570–1640* (Cambridge, 1987); P. Hair, *Before the Bawdy Court* (New York, 1972). A valuable and informative study of reproduction is A. McLaren, *Reproductive Rituals. The Perception of Fertility in England from the Sixteenth Century to the Nineteenth Century* (London, 1984).
7 M. Foucault, *The History of Sexuality*, vol. 1: *An Introduction* (New York, 1978).
8 Ingram, *Church Courts*, 372; R. Houlbrooke, *Church Courts and the People during the English Reformation, 1520–1570* (Oxford, 1979); R. A. Marchant, *The Church under the Law: Justice, Administration and Discipline in the Diocese of York, 1560–1641* (Cambridge, 1969).
9 W. Gouge, *The Workes of William Gouge ... Domesticall Duties* (London, 1627), 116.
10 W. Whatley, *Bride Bush: or, A Direction for Married Persons* (London, 1619), 14.
11 W. Perkins, *Christian Oeconomie* (London, 1609), 24.
12 Stone, *Family*, 415–17.
13 Gouge, *Domesticall Duties*, 106, 130–1.
14 Ibid., 203–9. Gouge censured both those who were unwilling to engage in marital sex as well as those who engaged in too much; ibid., 130–1.
15 J. Dodd, *An Exposition of the Last Chapter of Proverbs* (London, 1614), 23.
16 L. Lemnius, *The Secret Miracles of Nature* (London, 1658), 18.
17 A. Dent, *The Plaine Mans Path-way to Heaven* (London, 1601), 72.
18 J. D. Marshall (ed.), *The Autobiography of William Stout of Lancaster, 1665–1752* (Manchester, 1967), 104.
19 M. Vicinus, 'Sexuality and Power', *Feminist Studies*, 8 (1982), 136.
20 N. Highmore, *The History of Generation* (London, 1651).
21 G. Mackenzie, *The Laws and Customes of Scotland* (Edinburgh, 1678), 185.
22 R. Bayfield, *Enchiridion Medicum* (London, [25 Aug.] 1651), 184.
23 R. Capel, *Tentations: Their Nature, Danger, Cure* (London, 1633), 374.
24 I. Maclean, *The Renaissance Notion of Woman* (Cambridge, 1980), 36–7; McLaren, *Reproductive Rituals*, 16–17.
25 H. Crooke, *Microcosmographia* (London, [1631]), 262.
26 A. Paré, *Works* (London, 1634), 889.
27 Crooke, *Microcosmographia*, 295.

28 McLaren, *Reproductive Rituals*, 22–5.
29 J. McMath, *Expert Mid-wife* (Edinburgh, 1694), 5.
30 T. Comber, *A Companion to the Temple*, vol. IV (London, 1684), 14.
31 J. Donnison, *Midwives and Medical Men. A History of Inter-Professional Rivalries and Women's Rights* (New York, 1977), 13–14, 18–19.
32 J. Astruc, *A Treatise on all the Diseases Incident to Women* (London, 1743), 74.
33 C. Webster, *The Great Instauration. Science, Medicine and Reform 1626–1660* (London, 1975), 264–73.
34 L. Lemnius, *A Discourse Touching Generation* (London, 1667), sig. A3v.-4.
35 P. Charron, *Of Wisdome* (London, 1606), 459.
36 N. Culpeper, *The Compleat Midwives Practice* (London, 1656), 67.
37 L. Riverius, *The Practice of Physick* (London, 1655), 503.
38 Crooke, *Microcosmographia*, 287.
39 *The Declaration ... concerning the Birth of the Prince of Wales* (London, [1688]), 34. The evidence is unclear about the relationship between these events and her menstruation. Mary was subsequently uncertain about which of two encounters had led to her conception.
40 Royall Tyler (ed.), *Calendar of State Papers, Spanish*, vol. XI, (13 vols., London, 1862–1945), 364, Renard to Emperor, 17 November 1553; PRO, SP 63/2, ff. 82–3, Earl of Sussex to Cecil, 1560. I owe this latter reference to the kindness of Susan Doran.
41 M. Dalton, *Country Justice* (London, 1655), 351 (cap. 107); (1666), 328–9.
42 W. Hawkins, *A Treatise of the Pleas of the Crown*, vol. I (2 vols., London, 1716), 108, questions Dalton; M. Hale, *Historia Placitorum Coronae* vol. II (2 vols., London, 1736), 630; R. Burn, *The Justice of the Peace*, vol. I (London, 1755), 314–15.
43 [B. Mandeville], *A Modest Defence of the Publick Stews* (London, 1725), 17.
44 T. Robinson, *The Anatomy of the English Nunnery at Lisborn* (London, 1622).
45 L. Roper, 'Discipline and Respectability: Prostitution and the Reformation in Augsburg', *History Workshop Journal*, 19 (1985), 3–28.
46 K. Thomas, 'The Double Standard', *Journal of the History of Ideas*, 20 (1959), 197–8.
47 P. Primaudaye, *The French Academie* (London, 1589), 225.
48 Shakespeare, Sonnet 129.
49 N. Culpeper, *Medicaments for the Poor* (London, 1656), 41; H. Brooke, *A Conservatory of Health* (London, 1650), 184–7.
50 W. Vaughan, *Natural and Artificial Directions for Health* (London, 1600), 47.
51 Lemnius, *Secret Miracles*, 31; L. Lemnius, *A Discourse touching Generation* (London, 1667), 128; R. B[unworth], *The Doctresse* (London, 1656), 50.
52 J. Hart, *Klinikh; Or, the Diet of the Diseased* (London, 1633), 328; J. Harris, *The Divine Physician* (London, 1676), 37.
53 Gerrard Winstanley, *A Vindication*, in G. Sabine (ed.), *The Works of Gerrard Winstanley* (Ithaca, N. Y., 1941), 400–1.
54 [D. Defoe], *Conjugal Lewdness: or, Matrimonial Whoredom* (London, 1727), 48, 62.
55 L. Lemnius, *The Touchstone of Complexions* (London, 1576), f. 105; [John Armstrong], *The Oeconomy of Love* (London, 1744), 72; [Defoe], *Conjugal*

Lewdness, 91.
56 Perkins, *Christian Oeconomie*, 113.
57 Gouge, *Domesticall Duties*, 303.
58 D. R[ogers], *Matrimoniall Honour* (London, 1642), 177–8.
59 H. Nollius, *Hermetical Physick* (London, 1655), 27–8
60 P. Crawford, 'Attitudes to Menstruation in Seventeenth-century England', *Past & Present*, 91 (1981), 57–8.
61 Gouge, *Domesticall Duties*, 131.
62 W. Harris, *An Exact Enquiry into, and Cure of the Acute Diseases of Infants* (London, 1693), 13–14.
63 [Defoe], *Conjugal Lewdness*, 302–3.
64 T. Raynalde, *The Birth of Mankynde* (London, 1565), ff. 102–102v; Harris, *Diseases of Infants*, 17.
65 Gouge, *Domesticall Duties*, 131.
66 K. Thomas, 'The Act of 1650 Reconsidered', in D. Pennington and K. Thomas (eds.), *Puritans and Revolutionaries. Essays in Seventeenth-Century History Presented to Christopher Hill* (Oxford, 1978), 261–3.
67 I. W. Archer, *The Pursuit of Stability. Social Relations in Elizabethan London* (Cambridge, 1991), 249–54.
68 C. Herrup, 'The Patriarch at Home: The Trial of the Earl of Castlehaven for Rape and Sodomy', unpublished paper. I am grateful to Dr Herrup for allowing me to cite this paper which is part of a larger study of law, sex and patriarchy. Cf. C. Bingham, 'Seventeenth-Century Attitudes towards Deviant Sex', *Journal of Interdisciplinary History*, 1 (1971), 447–68; A. Bray, *Homosexuality in Renaissance England* (London, 1982).
69 L. Roper, 'What is the History of Sexuality?', unpublished paper, ANU July 1986. I am grateful to Dr Roper for allowing me to cite this paper.
70 Paré, *Works*, 942. Most such advice was in Latin; W. Schleiner, 'The Moral Dilemma about Removing Seed', unpublished paper, Folger Library, 1991. I am grateful to Professor Schleiner for discussions about medical knowledge.
71 J. Sadler, *The Sicke Womans Private Looking Glasse* (London, 1636), 135–7; [J. Rueff], *The Expert Midwife* (London, 1637), 151–7.
72 Sadler, *Sicke Womans Private Looking Glasse*, 139–40.
73 W. Drage, *A Physicial Nosonomy* (London, 1663), 336.
74 Paré, *Works*, 925.
75 McMath, *The Expert Mid-wife*, 44–5.
76 T. Vicary, *A Profitable Treatise of the Anatomie of Mans Bodie* (London, 1577); J. Ferrand, *Erotomania. Or, a Treatise ... of Love* (Oxford, 1640), 11. Cf. T. Laqueur, *Making Sex. Body and Gender from the Greeks to Freud* (Cambridge, Mass., 1990), 24–113, who argues that in the early modern period the differences in the male and female were of degree, not kind.
77 Lemnius, *Secret Miracles*, 33, 302.
78 C. Hooke, *The Child-birth or Womans Lecture* (London, 1590); T. Chamberlaine, *The Complete Midwifes Practice Enlarg'd* (London, 1659), 288–90.
79 See, for example, N. Fontanus, *The Womans Doctour* (London, 1652), 4–6.
80 J. Taylor, 'Rules', in *The Whole Works*, vol. III (12 vols., 1848), 62. I owe this reference to the kindness of Catherine Coleborne.

81 J. C. Oldham, 'On Pleading the Belly: A History of The Jury of Matrons', *Criminal Justice History*, 6 (1985), 1-64.
82 *The Ladies Physical Directory*, 1736, preface. [Probably another edn of *Rational Account*, but the preface differs.]
83 P. Slack, 'Mirrors of Health and Treasures of Poor Men: The Uses of Vernacular Medical Literature', in C. Webster (ed.), *Health, Medicine and Mortality in the Sixteenth Century* (Cambridge, 1979), 240.
84 Sadler, *Sicke Womans Private Looking Glasse*, 142.
85 [Rueff], *Expert Midwife*, preface.
86 *The Ladies Physical Directory*, 1736, preface.
87 *The Ladies Physical Directory*, 7th edn, 1739, preface.
88 J. Leake, *Medical Instructions*, 5th edn, vol. 1 (2 vols., London, 1781), introduction, 39, 45.
89 J. Sharp, *The Midwives Book* (London, 1671).
90 McMath, *Expert Mid-wife*, preface.
91 Slack, 'Vernacular Medical Literature', 242, 246-7
92 *Aristotle's Master-piece* first published London, 1684. For the subsequent publishing history, see Janet Blackman, 'Popular Theories of Generation: The Evolution of Aristotle's Works. The Study of an Anachronism', in J. Woodward and D. Richards (eds.), *Health Care and Popular Medicine in Nineteenth-Century England* (London, 1977); R. Porter, ' "The Secrets of Generation Display'd": *Aristotle's Master-piece* in Eighteenth-Century England', in R. P. Maccubbin (ed.), *'Tis Nature's Fault. Unauthorized Sexuality during the Enlightenment* (Cambridge, 1985), 1-21.
93 *Rare Verities. The Cabinet of Venus Unlocked* (London, [8 Oct.] 1658).
94 R. Thompson, *Unfit for Modest Ears* (London, 1979), 173.
95 Ibid., 3.
96 For example, in 1688 Mary of Modena discussed plans and procedures for her delivery with her midwife; *The Declaration . . . concerning the Birth of the Prince of Wales*, 20-1.
97 Sharp, *The Midwives Book*; S. Jinner, *An Almanack or Prognostication* (London, 1658, 1659, 1660, 1664); M. Holden, *The Woman's Almanack* (London, 1688, 1689).
98 BL, C. 40. m. 10 (161).
99 M. Slater, *Family Life in the Seventeenth Century. The Verneys of Claydon House* (London, 1984), 72.
100 S. Stone, *A Complete Practice of Midwifery* (London, 1737), preface.
101 See, for example, London Guildhall MS 10,116/4, Licensing papers, 1665-6.
102 BL, MS Sloane 1954, E. P. of Petworth, *The Midwiues Deputy*, dedication.
103 P. Crawford, 'Printed Advertisements for Women Medical Practitioners in London, 1670-1710', *Society for the Social History of Medicine, Bulletin*, 35 (1984), 66-70.
104 R. Latham and W. Matthews (eds.), *The Diary of Samuel Pepys*, vol. v (10 vols., London, 1970-83), 222.
105 Norfolk RO, Ayl 347, 2 June 1661.
106 Norfolk RO, Consistory court depositions, Dep/43, 1637-9, f. 222v.-223.
107 Ibid., f. 248; DEP/44, ff.14-14v.

108 Regent's Park College, Angus Library, MS F PCEI, Cripplegate church book, ff. 32–49.
109 Amussen found that in half the cases men brought against women to the Consistory church in Norwich after 1660, there were specific allegations of sexual misconduct. She argues that a woman could dent a man's sexual reputation only with details; S. D. Amussen, *An Ordered Society. Gender and Class in Early Modern England* (Oxford, 1988), 104.
110 P. Crawford, 'Attitudes to Pregnancy, from a Woman's Spiritual Diary, 1687–8', *Local Population Studies*, 21 (1978), 43–5; Hertfordshire Record Office, Dame Sarah Cowper, Daily diary 1700–16, Panshanger MSS, D/EP/F29-35, p. 61. Special thanks to Sara Mendelson for this reference.
111 J. O. Halliwell (ed.), *The Private Diary of Dr John Dee*, Camden Society, 19 (1842); Pepys, *Diary*; H. W. Robinson and W. Adams (eds.), *The Diary of Robert Hooke, 1672–1680* (London, 1935), *passim*.
112 *A Whole Crew of Kind Gossips* (London, 1609); [H. Neville], *The Parliament of Ladies* (London, 1647).
113 Fontanus, *Womans Doctour*, 134, 193.
114 Lemnius, *Secret Miracles*, 185.
115 Hart, *Klinikh*, 352–3.
116 Bodl., Douce Ballads, *The Scolding Wives Vindication*; E. Gosynhill, *The Scholehouse of Women* (London, 1541).
117 Jinner, *An Almanack* (1659), preface to the reader.
118 Whatley, *A Bride Bush*, 23–4.
119 *The Declaration . . . concerning the Birth of the Prince of Wales*, 28–9.
120 M. Hunter and A. Gregory (eds.), *An Astrological Diary of the Seventeenth Century: Samuel Jeake of Rye 1652–1699* (Oxford, 1988), 25, 154, 187.
121 See, for example, Pepys, *Diary*, vol. IX, 144, 145, 337.
122 Norfolk RO, AYL/1/347, 4 Mar 1660[1].
123 For example, Oxfordshire CRO, MS Oxfordshire Dioc papers c. 96, no. 13.
124 Addy, *Sin and Society*, 133.
125 Ibid., 130; Hereford & Worcester R. O., Consistory court depositions, vol. 18, f. 374v.
126 Norfolk RO, AYL 347, 24 October 1664.
127 Stone, *Family*, 415–24.
128 T. H[ilder], *Conjugall Counsell* (London, 1653), 18, 20.
129 J. Oliver, *A Present for Teeming Women* (London, 1663), 17.
130 A. McLaren, *A History of Contraception From Antiquity to the Present Day* (Oxford, 1990), 141–77.
131 *The Comforts of Whoring* (London, [1694]), 42.
132 Stone, *Family*, 422.
133 H[ilder], *Conjugall Counsell*, 18; *Onania; or, the Heinous sin of Self-Pollution* (London, [1725?]).
134 McLaren, *Reproductive Rituals*, 5–6.
135 An Act to prevent the murthering of Bastard Children, 21 Jac. I c. 27.
136 Stone, *Family*, 423.
137 P. Laslett, *Family Life and Illicit Love in Earlier Generations* (Cambridge, 1977), 125.

138 J. Cotta, *A Short Discoverie of the ... Dangers of Several Sorts of Ignorant ... Practitioners of Physicke in England* (London, 1612), 25.
139 Devon RO, QSB Box 58, no. 21.
140 Cf. K. Hopkins, 'Contraception in the Roman Empire', *Comparative Studies in Society and History*, 8 (1965), 124ff.

FIVE

THE TRANSFORMATION OF EVE
WOMEN'S BODIES, MEDICINE AND CULTURE IN EARLY MODERN ENGLAND

ROBERT MARTENSEN

INTRODUCTION

In February 1650 a woman 'of very good family' complained of 'several months of pain' to her Oxford-trained physician, Thomas Willis (1621–75). The pain began in her stomach and radiated to her back. It was worse when she lay down, so much so that she spent 'whole nights sleepless'. 'Liable to headaches for several years', she suffered pain in her loins and upon urination. The doctor noted her condition 'is doubtless hysterical, having its origin from a foul vapour ascending from the uterus into the praecordia'.[1] Seventeen years later the doctor, by then Europe's most influential neuroanatomist and England's leading physician, had changed his mind. Concerned that 'any time a sickness happens in a Woman's Body ... we accuse the evil influence of the Womb (which for the most part is innocent)',[2] his anatomical studies and medical experiences had convinced him that hysteria was 'chiefly and primarily Convulsive, and chiefly depends on the brain and the nervous stock being affected'.[3]

The claim that women's bodies were governed by their brains and not their wombs and 'foul vapours' emanating from them represented a novel departure in English thought regarding women's physiology.[4] My concern in this chapter, however, is not with hysteria as such. Indeed, I will argue that seventeenth-century debates about hysteria, which at one level were about the differing nature of fluids and solids in both male and female bodies, were *really* about making both women's and men's bodies 'reasonable' and 'nervous' in a particular way. Hysteria, though it loomed large in medical practice and clinical texts, represented merely the 'last frontier' of traditional physiologies of fluids to Willis et al. who promoted a bodily paradigm in which the solid parts of the brain were paramount and the body and fluids (mainly blood) secondary. Traditional concepts of hysteria, and hence of women's physiology, had to be challenged if the 'neurocentric' body were to become canonical.

The overall medical result was a human body of sexless intelligence. Or was it? Debates about the nature and role of human fluids and solids in turn rested on the place of anatomy, medical chemistry and physiological experimentation in determining the body's truth. Embedded within these newly important methods of medical epistemology, however, were assumptions about gender that helped shape not only the 'neurocentric' model, but also the epistemological status of traditionally feminine ways of knowing. Both the processes and the conclusions were in turn taken up (or resisted) by a variety of women and men who sought to frame not only the medical but also the social and religious parameters of women's (and men's) behaviour and experience.

The 'nexus among ideologies of woman, nature, and science', to borrow Evelyn Fox Keller's characterization, has received considerable attention from historians in the past decade.[5] In addition to Fox Keller, Carolyn Merchant, Thomas Laqueur and Londa Schiebinger, to mention only a few, have all made recent contributions on one or another of the above topics in the early modern period.[6] To my knowledge, however, no one has yet attempted to articulate the historical context of this nexus regarding the new ontologies of mind, brain and body as they took form in early modern England.

TRADITIONAL ECONOMIES OF FEMALE MOISTURE

If a central issue in traditional theories of human reproduction was heat,[7] the central issue in traditional physiologies of women when they were of childbearing years, but not pregnant or infertile, was thought to be moisture.[8] The uterus was not only a cold organ, it was also the transit area and vessel for vast quantities of fluid. Unlike men, women regularly produced so much, both menstrual blood as well as ejaculate during orgasm. My premise is that these differences in kind and quality of fluid were perceived to constitute the (non-childbearing or nursing) female body as fundamentally different from the male.

Whereas men had less fluid, traditional theories accorded them more means of fluid elimination. Men could get rid of excess moisture by sweating, ejaculation, or extrude it to the skin's surface through their larger pores.[9] There it would turn into hair on contact with the air: women, after all, did not have beards. Women's coolness, however, made such coctions, or transformations, unlikely. Men's situation was akin to that of other animals, who extruded their excess fluids through their pores, where the residue became fur, horns or claws, or burned them up through intense physical activity.[10] Human females, however, were thought to be the only female animals who menstruated.[11] In addition, in both classical and medieval times it was felt that the normally flowing menstrual blood, being 'waste', was foul or worse. As recorded in the French medieval *Secrets des dames*: 'And whosoever were to take a hair from the pubis of a woman and mix it with menses and then put it in a dung-heap, would at the end of the year find wicked venomous beasts.'[12] Stories of the Venomous Virgin, widespread at the end of the thirteenth century, represented a synthesis of misogynistic thought on female fluids.[13]

Much of this kind of thinking, if not its overt misogyny, carried over into seventeenth-century thought regarding the etiology of hysteria. The anonymous author of *The Compleat Doctoress* (1656) divided female disease into four classes: (1) those common to all; (2) those affecting widows and virgins; (3) those affecting the barren and fruitful; and (4) women with child. Hysteria, the author argued, was the chief medical problem for women in categories 1 and 2. 'Stoppage of courses is the cause: ill vapours travel from matrix to brain.'[14] Nicholas Fontanus argued much the same in his *The Woman's Doctour* of 1652: 'by reason of the moisture wherewith those parts abound, the matrix is loosened, and exceedingly stretched: and this is the truth of the whole matter'.[15]

If the cause of woman's distress was considered to be almost exclusively a disorder of genital fluids and/or flesh, so too was the focus of traditional therapy. Achievement of female orgasm was considered the best therapy. For treatment of 'fits of the mother' in 1655, the prolific medical popularizer and herbalist Nicholas Culpeper advised prompt marriage 'to a lusty young man'. If that was not feasible, he suggested in his *Practice of Physick* 'that the genital Parts should be by a cunning Midwife so handled and rubbed as to cause an evacuation of the over-abounding sperm. But that being a thing not so allowable, it may suffice whilst patient is in bath to rub her belly in the Region of the Womb.'[16] According to its publisher, that advice went through eight printings totalling 15,000 copies.

Such mid-century characterizations of women's physiology were cited as a natural basis for a division of labour between men and women. According to *The Compleat Doctoress*: 'Women were made to stay at home and look after household employments . . . accompanied without any vehement stirring of the body . . . therefore hath provident Nature assigned them their monthly courses, that by the benefit of these evacuations, the feculent and corrupt blood might be purified, which otherwise, being the purest part of blood, would turn to rank poyson.'[17] Wives were more healthful than virgins and (chaste) widows because they were 'refreshed with man's seed, and therefore ejaculate their own, which being excluded, the cause of evil is taken away'.[18]

Women were also thought to be profoundly similar to men. Belief in the similarity and difference of female and male physiology and anatomy had coexisted at least since the time of Hippocrates. Specifically, that strain of Platonic thought that emphasized continuities fostered the tendency to conflate the sexes.[19] In this schema, women were physiologically like men, but less 'perfect' because possessed of less heat. Structurally, women and men were thought to be homologous: the female genitalia were but the male inverted.[20] Aristotelian thought, particularly the neo-Aristotelian thought of the later Middle Ages, was more comfortable with differences: women and men did not have the same seed, for instance. Man's seed was active; woman's passive.[21]

Recently the idea has been put forward that simultaneous acceptance of profound similarity and difference between the sexes was not the historical norm. Both Laqueur and Schiebinger have made much of pre-Enlightenment anatomical drawings which illustrated an isomorphism between female and male genitalia. Challenge, to paraphrase Laqueur, waited until the eighteenth and nineteenth centuries.[22] It was then, when there was the 'consolidation of a science-based profession' in the medical establishment, that the search for sex-based differences became intense.[23]

Even taken on its own terms, which is to say the structural isomorphism of male and female genitalia represented in medical and anatomical texts from classical times through the Renaissance, I have problems accepting the hegemony of the one-sex model in pre-Enlightenment Western thought. When one compares illustrations of male and female genitalia in Vesalius's *De humani corporis fabrica* (1543), for example, one cannot help noticing that the female genitalia depicted on the right-hand side of the page (fig. 5.1) resemble in shape the male genitalia depicted in two images on the lower half of the page (fig. 5.2). Does this mean they are the same? Yes, if one limits the observation to the shape of the depicted *organs*.

In terms of the *Gestalt* of the respective *pages*,[24] however, I would argue that a quite different comparison is also plausible. Whereas the page depicting the male devoted its top half to a truncal image of the opened male body, the page depicting the female used only its top left one-quarter to show the opened female. Furthermore, when one compares the respective portions devoted to depictions of the genitalia themselves, the page carrying the male showed two images of the

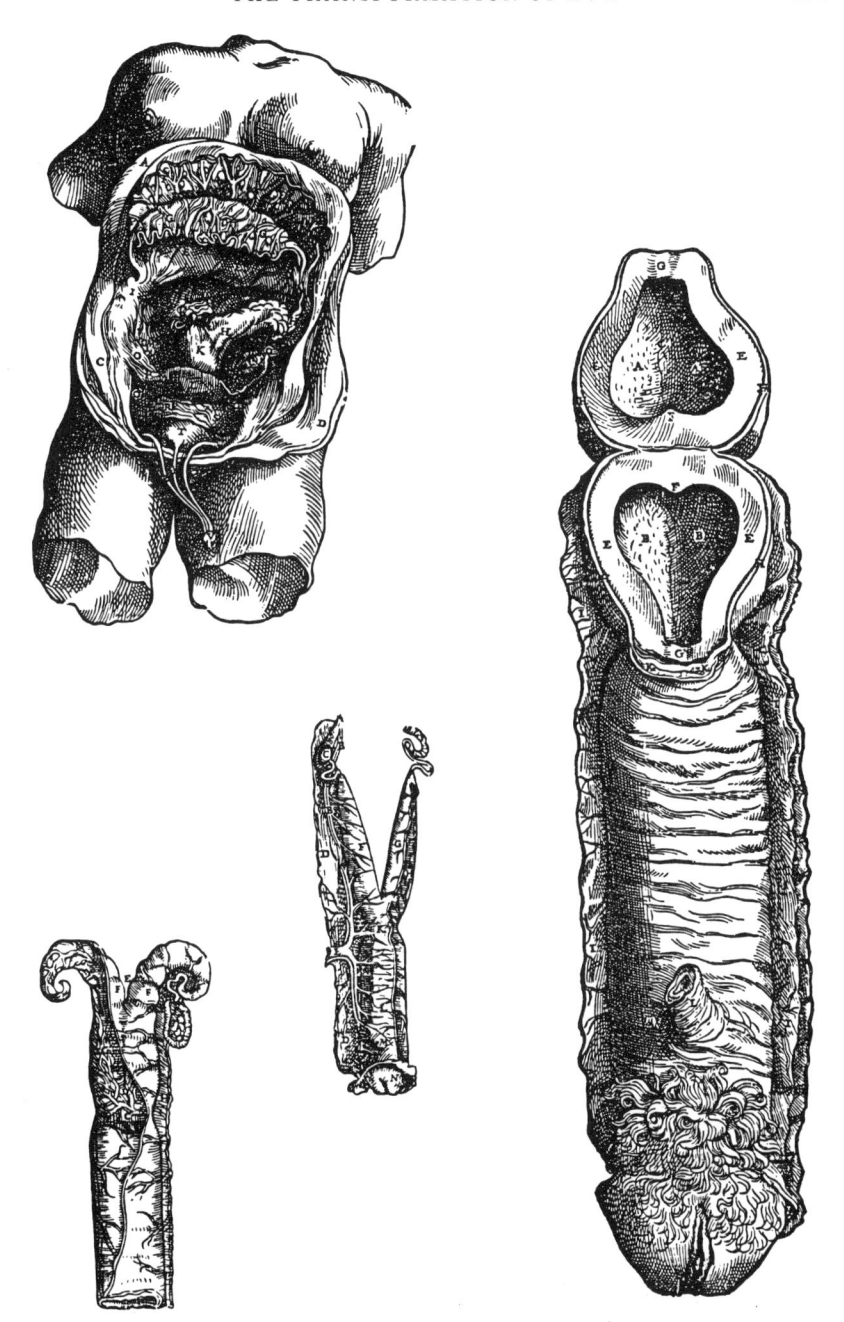

Fig. 5.1. Illustration of female genitalia from Vesalius's *De humani corporis fabrica* (1543).

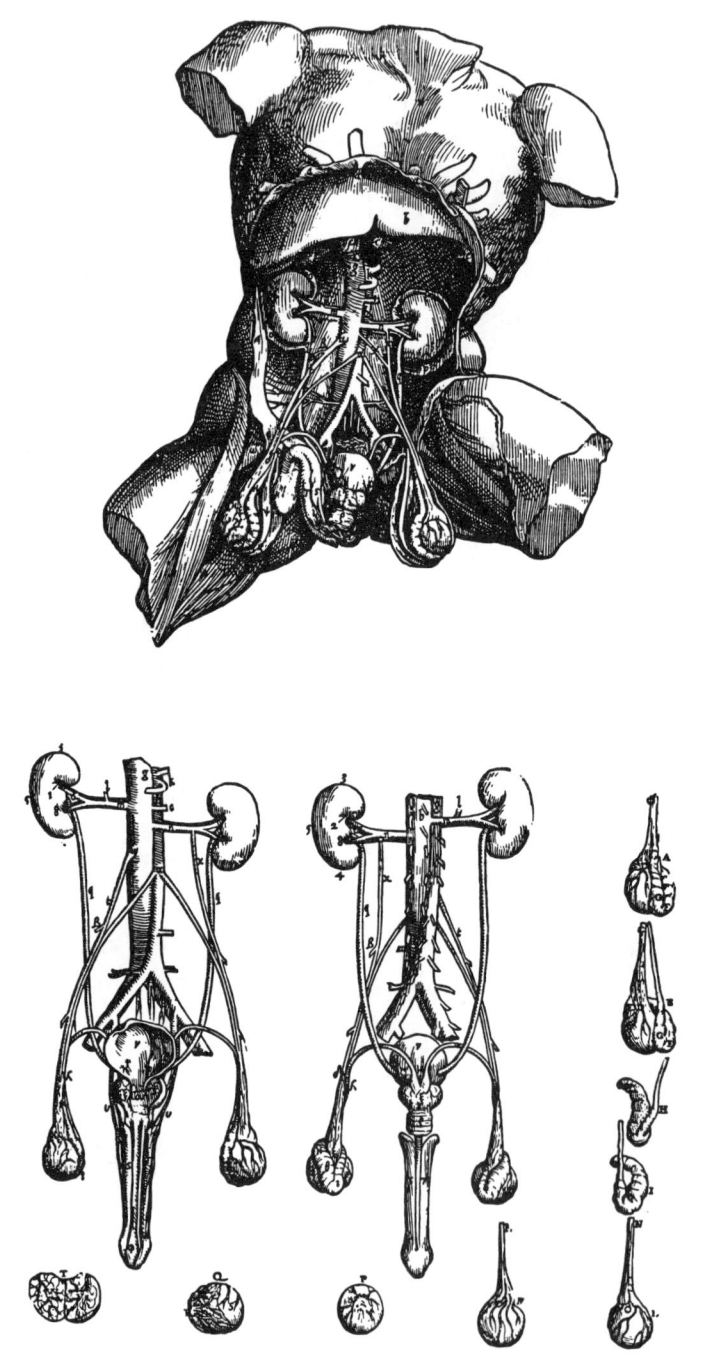

Fig. 5.2. Illustration of male genitalia from Vesalius's *De humani corporis fabrica* (1543).

genito-urinary system on its lower left and centre and nine smaller images of the testes and epididymides on its right-hand and bottom margins. In contrast, the page presentation of the female was quite different. Most notably for this discussion, the right-hand image of the female genitalia is the largest image on the page, approximately 1.75 times the length of the image of the female trunk which purportedly contains it. In contrast, the penises depicted on the preceding plate are only one-third the length of the corresponding truncal image of the male.

What I want to suggest through this exercise of image comparison is that it is quite plausible to read the respective images of male and female in Vesalius, and by extension in many other pre-Enlightenment texts, as representing male and female as both similar and different, as both one-sex and two-sex. The main theoretical cleavage point, as I have attempted to establish earlier, was the difference between male and female economies of fluid. Vesalius, I would argue, made the female genitalia so much larger than the corresponding male both in respect to each other and in respect to the bodies that putatively contained them because he and his audience assumed the womb and its fluids were much more important in women than the penis and its fluids in men.

The consensus between high and low cultures on the nature of women's physiology was reflected in the lack of substantial difference between learned and popular medical texts on women's health issues. When he asked rhetorically, 'How many incurable diseases are brought about by unhealthy menstrual discharges?', an elderly William Harvey did not sound very different from the popular authors cited above.[25] Common sense, empiric and folk treatments, and attention to astrological conditions characterized the content of texts on women's health. By and large women were taken care of by women, or by women or men who read women's health guides authored by men who pretended to be women.[26] The knowledge of midwives was on the same plane as the knowledge of university-educated (and hence male) physicians. Both the model and the consensus, however, were about to change.

WILLIS AND THE DOCTRINE OF THE BRAIN AND NERVES

When he took up the question of hysteria in earnest in 1667, Willis had already published his canonical text on the normal (un-sexed) brain and nervous system, *Cerebri anatome*, three years previously. Expensively produced with numerous engravings by Christopher Wren (1632-1723), it was a major assault on both the Galenic and

Aristotelian bodily paradigms that had emphasized the bodily primacy of either the triumvirate of liver, heart and brain (Galen) or heart (Aristotle.) Instead, for Willis the brain was the 'chief mover in the animal machine'.[27] Through complex interactions mediated by the nerves and various fluids, it was the prime minister of a body composed of important but inferior organs.[28]

Moreover, it was the solid aspects of the brain, not its spaces (the ventricles), that most engaged Willis and his colleagues. Like Harvey, whose early work on the heart as a pump exerted enormous influence at Oxford in the 1640s, they sought to treat the tissues of the brain and nerves themselves as objects and mechanisms.[29] This represented a considerable departure from previous thought on the importance of the brain and nerves. Even those writer(s) of ancient texts who most emphasized the role of the brain, such as the Hippocratic text (430–350 BC) on epilepsy, *The Sacred Disease*, described it primarily in terms of its status as a container and transit point for air from outside the body to the muscles and viscera.[30] Plato (429–347 BC), emphasizing the similarity between the 'round shape of the universe' and the head, found the brain 'the divinest part of us and lord over all the rest' because it served as a 'vessel' for 'Seed'.[31] In both cases, it was the brain's ventricles, the head as a vessel, that was given imaginative importance, not its grey and white matter and cranial nerves. Indeed, Plato seems to have believed that the fleshy parts of the body, including those of the head, were inferior.[32]

In contrast, in *Cerebri anatome*, Willis and his collaborators emphasized particular local and solid portions of the brain as control and stimulus-processing centres that communicated with the body through the cranial nerves. Whereas Galen described seven pairs of cranial nerves, Willis described ten pairs. Importantly for our discussion, Willis believed that the sixth, or 'intercostal', nerve (what nowadays is described as the sympathetic chain of ganglion) provided an *intracranial* connection to the face, viscera and heart, an anatomical finding which Willis believed demonstrated the primacy of the brain and nerves in governing emotion:

> Forasmuch as this nerve reaching forth into the praecordia and viscera of the whole abdomen is continued ... also into the eyes, as also into the parts of the mouth and face: certainly from hence a true and genuine reason may be given wherefore in every passion the eyes, face, and mouth do so correspond our mind, that oftentimes we are compelled to betray the most intimate sense of the heart by the countenance and aspect.[33]

Moreover, when he published *Cerebri anatome*, Willis considered the 'intercostal' innervation of the heart to be unique to humans.[34]

Also germane to our discussion was the cerebral location Willis assigned to the nervous fluid responsible for passionate behaviour. Traditional Galenic physiology emphasized the importance of the bodily humours. These had the power directly to affect emotion as well as any organ. By describing the brain in terms of its reservoirs (the ventricles) and not its parenchyma, Galen and his successors were reiterating their belief in the relative parity of brain and the lower body. In contrast, Willis assigned storage of nervous fluid to the (solid) annular protuberances of the cerebellum. These in turn communicated with the cerebrum directly, and via the 'intercostal' to the heart and viscera. Thus, messages from the blood and lower body were always to be mediated by the cerebrum and nerves.[35]

The physiological distance between mind, now firmly located in the brain, and body had increased. Unlike previous theories of interaction between the brain, nerves and visceral organs, Willisian neuroanatomy of the emotions minimized unmediated access by the lower body to the brain. Even fluid containing diseased material from the lower organs was presented to the brain by mediation of the nerves. Its message was then processed by the brain, which then sent its signals back to the body via the nerves. Transmission had characteristics of both particle flow and wave propagation. By these and other theories, Willis created a matrix of explanations that permitted him to argue a neurological origin for a large number of normal and abnormal mental and bodily situations from the autonomic to the volitional.

Much earlier, Plato had located reason in the head. The distinction, which I believe constituted a major difference between previous neurophysiologies and that of Willis et al., had to do with the role of the solid tissues of the brain. Whereas Plato (and Galen) ascribed them minimal importance, Willis made them, together with the nerves, paramount in the body. I will argue in the next section that it was a difference suffused with an implicit ideology of dominance (solid/male/cortex/'reason') and subordination (fluid/female/ body/ 'passion').

As an intellectual construct, woman's new 'nervous body' was expanded well beyond its uterine core. Directed by the brain and nerves, it was presented, like man's brain, as a complicated 'machine' subject to interplay between its end organs, chemical processes, and the ebb and flow of its many fluids. The physiological ground had been laid, in other words, for women to be viewed no longer primarily as expressions of their wombs.

At least in its pathological state, then, one could say that the 'neurocentric' body of the seventeenth century was relatively unsexed.[36] Differential capacity existed, but it was of insufficient magnitude to constitute a difference in kind. Mary Astell, a seventeenth-century feminist, agreed. Writing 'An Essay in Defence of the Female Sex' in 1696, she noted: 'If there be any defect in women it cannot be in the Body, (if I may credit the Report of learned Physicians) for there is no difference in the Organ of those Parts, which have any relation to, or influence over the Minds.'[37] In this regard, it was not so much that Willis did away with the potential for the visceral organs, including the womb, to turn 'evil'.[38] Instead, he proposed anatomical and clinical findings to suggest that the action was elsewhere.

It was an important paradigm that shaped learned English thought well into the eighteenth century. Working in an Enlightenment era dominated by a Newtonian world-view, physicians such as George Cheyne and Nicholas Robinson – fashionable 'nerve doctors' of early Georgian England – adopted enthusiastically the 'neurocentric' body first proposed by Willis et al. For Cheyne, for instance, hysteria, a nosological category which included everything from 'yawning and stretching up to a mortal Fit of an Apoplexy', was a nervous disease due to a 'relaxation and the Want of a sufficient Force and Elasticity in the Solids in general and the *Nerves* in particular'.[39]

MEDICAL EPISTEMOLOGY AND GENDER

Whereas for Vesalius and other sixteenth-century physicians, 'anatomy' was usually thought of in terms of the structure and function of the solid and visceral organs of 'normal' animal bodies, including humans, seventeenth-century English natural philosophers of the body had extended the concept of anatomy to include the blood and humours in healthy and sick individuals. In a passage reflective of this shift and extension of range, Francis Bacon encouraged anatomists to study bodily fluids: 'for the humours are commonly passed over in anatomy as loathsome and excrementous things; whereas it is highly useful and necessary to note their nature . . . the marks and impressions of diseases, and the changes and devastations they bring upon the internal parts, are to be diligently observed in different dissections.'[40]

Emblematic of this conception of anatomy as an aggressive way of knowing the natural world was Bacon's declaration that nature was an 'Other' that needed to be 'interrogated' and 'conquered' to yield its truth and riches. So, too, for Willis, who was perceived by his contemporaries as a 'Baconian'[41], the body was an entity whose 'secrets lay hidden'.⁴² Resolving in the 1660s to believe only 'Nature and ocular demonstrations', Willis began an extensive series of anatomies of invertebrates, mammals and humans in preparation of his *magnum opus* on the brain: 'I addicted my Self to the opening of Heads especially.'⁴³ The goal was to accumulate 'ocular demonstrations' that would provide a 'firm and stable basis' for a 'more certain Physiologie'.⁴⁴ So equipped, the anatomically informed philosopher would be able 'to unlock the secret places of Mans Mind'.⁴⁵

In this formulation reason was female and Willis the man-midwife who delivered her from Zeus's brain: 'Minerva was born from the Brain, Vulcan with his Instruments playing the Midwife: For either by this way, by Wounds and Death, by Anatomy, and a Caesarean Birth, Truth will be brought to Light, or for ever lye hid.'⁴⁶ In retelling the myth of Minerva's birth this way, I would argue that Willis's prose reflects a crucial shift regarding the relations of male and female in reference to each other at many levels in the early modern period. In the classical versions of the story, Minerva sprang fully formed and armoured from Zeus's head. Now she is passive and must be helped out by a man. Now it is the man who carries the metal. Moreover, it is only by this process, the violent but dispassionate methods of anatomy, that certain knowledge can be obtained.⁴⁷

The body had also become a battleground. Mid-century acceptance of Harveian ideas of the circulation stimulated English interest in the blood as a separate organ.⁴⁸ Amplifying this preoccupation was mid-century English learned medical interest in Paracelsian and Helmontian characterizations of disease as a 'poison' or 'outside force' that affected the body through the agency of blood.⁴⁹ Numerous theories of fevers and the chemical composition and physical characteristics of the blood were put forward in the 1650s, Willis's prominent among them.

Both the blood and disease had achieved an ontological status. As a consequence, the later Harvey, Willis, and many others promoted pathological and experimental 'anatomical' and 'physiological' investigations and experiments on healthy and sick animals and humans. As Willis wrote in 1675, the goal of 'rational' medicine was to find the 'weapons' whereby the medical 'system rightly framed' could conquer the 'martial field' of the human body.⁵⁰

Graphically, much the same set of dominance relations is told in the Vesalian imagery of the uterus discussed earlier. In both the right-hand and central images the margins of the female genitalia are serrated as though they had been ripped or torn. Apparently the organs *had* indeed *been* ripped, or at least rapidly cut. The corpse had been stolen from its tomb by Vesalius and his assistants. The woman's lover (a monk) and her parents complained to the city, and so Vesalius and his assistants deconstructed the corpse as rapidly as possible.[51] Stolen bodies were a mainstay of anatomical practice, however, especially in sixteenth-century Italy. What is striking about the depiction of the ripped edges in this image is that they are unique. The *De humani corporis fabrica* is filled with illustrations of flayed muscles and isolated body structures. In none of the others, however, was the raggedness of the dissection procedure made apparent.

In formulating his programme of human endeavour, Francis Bacon made explicit a credo of male dominance/female submission. Originally entitled *The Greatest Birth of Time* (*Temporis partus maximus*), but later retitled by Bacon as *The Masculine Birth of Time* (*Temporis partus masculus*), the fragment, consisting of a prayer and two chapters written when Bacon was in his forties, contains Bacon's 'straight answer from his (my) most inmost heart'[52] regarding ideal relations between man and nature:

> My intention is to impart to you, not the figments of my own brain, nor the shadows thrown by words, nor a decoction of religion ... No: I am come in very truth leading to you Nature with all her children to bind her to your service and make her your slave ... so may I succeed in my only earthly wish, namely to stretch the deplorably narrow limits of man's dominion over the universe to their promised bounds ...[53]

CONSENT

Willis anatomized in an era and country in which the hospital did not figure importantly as a setting of medical investigation. English physicians did not have the power to coerce patients (or their families) regarding the performance of a procedure. If anything, the reverse was true. In the absence of strong medical institutions and professional monopolies, wealthy patients were patrons; physicians attempted to satisfy their wishes.[54] Nevertheless, women from the Royalist upper classes formed an important component both of Willis's practice and of his research enterprise. In 1667, for instance, he reported autopsy findings on a 'noblewoman', a 'very noblewoman', and a child of the nobility. Indeed, the only post-mortem in which reference to the whole body was noted in his *Pathology of the Brain and Nervous Stock* of 1667 involved a female aristocrat.

A question arises: Why did elite women (or their families) permit themselves to be autopsied? After the death of one of his well-born female patients, Willis noted that 'it pleased her Friends, that her dead

Carcass, kept long opened for the Funeral, should be diligently inspected, so the genuine causes of the Disease and her Death, might be investigated'.[55] Of course, one might respond, he would hardly say otherwise. A lack of extant records from Willis's patients in this matter prevents a specific answer. That some permitted autopsies on themselves and watched autopsies on their friends and relatives, however, is not in doubt.[56] Margaret Cavendish (née Lucas) (1623–1673), Duchess of Newcastle, wrote extensively on natural philosophy in the 1660s.[57] For her, patient dissection was a matter-of-fact necessity in learned medicine. She did not want to see learned physicians criticized because they could not 'restore every Patient to this former health ... (when) they have only outward signs of inward distempers'. The problem was that 'all (people) are not dissected after they are dead, to inform Physicians of the true cause of their death'.[58]

Cavendish's approbation of pathological anatomy was one aspect of her more general embrace of elite learning and the social hierarchy of which it was a manifestation. Her reflections on this point foretell sentiment, more frequently expressed in genteel culture in the eighteenth century, that affluence was its own disease. For Cavendish, the elite were 'most commonly lazie and luxurious', conditions and habits which bred 'superfluities of humors, and these again breed many distempers'. As a consequence the nobility needed a learned medicine. Its 'lenitive' medicines and greater understanding would 'mediate' the disease burden of their 'luxurious' lives. By contrast, 'Country-people and Labourers take little or no Physick (medicine)', yet lived longer than 'Great and rich Persons'. Their longevity was attributable to their 'laborious exercises and spare diet'. Thus, learned 'Physicians with good and proper medicines, have, and do as yet rescue more people from death, than the Laws do from ruine'.[59]

Secondly, the Duchess, like many women and men of her social class, supported the concept of a privileged medical knowledge because she believed in the value of a rigid class system which placed her at the top. Luxury might bring with it the risk of increased disease, but the trade-off seemed worth it. After all, in the aftermath of the Civil War, which in the Newcastles' case had meant exile to France, their world had been turned upside-down. Thus, even though she was sceptical of aspects of the new investigational technologies supported by Willis and others, such as the microscope ('deluding glasses' to the Duchess), Cavendish supported elite versus popular medicine. To do otherwise, she believed, would be to support 'Hereticks'.[60]

THE NEW EVE

Learned physicians such as Willis published in Latin. Eventually, many of the more influential texts were translated into English as well as other European vernacular languages. Willis's major texts, for instance, were not 'Englished' until several years after his death. Although a reading knowledge of Latin would have been possessed by grammar-school graduates, knowledge of learned medical texts was primarily among a population that was overwhelmingly male and made up of university graduates, a group in which physicians and clerics formed the majority.

In both groups the Willisian 'neurocentric' body was an immediate hit. Not only were Willisian concepts the most influential in the College of Physicians in the late 1660s and 1670s, Willis himself became England's most prosperous medical practitioner.[61] In addition, the 'neurocentric' body, as well as Willis and some of his colleagues, were actively patronized by High Church leaders.[62] What I wish to emphasize here are those aspects of the Willisian paradigm that were utilized by politically conservative male Anglican leaders to shape an agenda for social relations between men and women.

Determined to maintain their newly won hegemony in English religious life, High Church clergy in the Restoration characterized their opponents of whatever stripe as sinful. To counter what they viewed as a national malaise, as well as to repress the potential for schism, they promoted a piety which emphasized obedience, repentance, and social and personal virtues.[63] If this led to what Richard Westfall has termed a 'spiritual mediocrity',[64] it nevertheless satisfied Anglican desires for an episcopally controlled piety that excluded religious and political dissent.[65]

The author of a number of conduct books first published for a genteel audience in the 1660s, Richard Allestree (1619–81) was a conservative Anglican divine who was a close friend of Willis's from his Oxford days as well as a cousin of Willis's occasional publisher, James Allestree.[66] The texts, with titles such as *The Ladies Calling, The Gentlemans Calling* and *The Whole Duty of Man*, went through many editions into the mid-eighteenth century.[67] At least the early ones were printed at the Sheldonian Theatre in Oxford, a structure that was the personal gift to the University from Gilbert Sheldon (1598–1677), Archbishop of Canterbury from 1663 to 1675 and Willis's principal patron.[68]

Regarding women's capacity for reason, Allestree noted, 'though I [he] do [did] not believe it', that he was not surprised that women's intelligence was felt to be 'Naturally' inferior to men's. How could it be otherwise when one took into account men's privileged access to learning? Improved by their education, men were like an 'inclosed piece of a Common, which by industry and husbandry become a different thing from the rest'. This made men 'artificial'. Women, in contrast, were 'natural'.[69] Such sentiments recall ancient attachments of women to 'nature' and men to 'art'.[70] In the same preface Allestree continued that women were not to accept the 'fictitious image' of themselves as 'silly and vicious creatures' put forward by 'unworthy men'. Instead, they should derive their 'descent from above the Stars' and 'claim cognation with Divinity'.

In the context of seventeenth-century male thought as expressed by Bacon, Willis and apologists for the Royal Society such as Thomas Sprat, its biographer, and Henry Oldenburg, its secretary, 'artifice' was a 'male' domain of high value. As the earlier citation from Bacon suggests, artifice, or the 'accompt ... of the ingenious', as the title pages of the *Philosophical Transactions* put it, was going to make nature ('her') perform. In Allestree's pastoral rhetoric above, the suggestion was that male activity ('husbandry') involved taking over part of the feminine 'Common' (nature) in order to make it more efficient. In sum, Allestree's language, as well as that of other mid-century putative spiritual directors, such as the prolific Jeremy Taylor (1613–67), suggested that women as well as the feminine generally, although existing in rough physiological parity with men, should be dominated by male enterprise in order to increase the production of wealth.

The body of *The Ladies Calling* laid out the social relations by which this would be achieved. Divided into two sections, the text of section one, entitled 'Virtues', listed five that were the special province of women. In order of presentation these were: modesty; meekness; compassion; affability; piety.[71] Women's lives were described as a continuum between maiden status, marriage and widowhood. Within the marriage relation there was a dramatic difference between the duties of the wife and those of the husband. Whereas the first duty of the wife (as well as that of the servant, which Allestree described subsequently) was 'Obedience ... in all lawful commands' to the husband, the husband's first task was to love his wife.

Wifely love, on the other hand, was number three on her duty list. This, in turn, was followed by the prohibition on wives to avoid 'forwardness', regardless of the husband's behaviour. Both husbands and wives had fidelity as their second duty.[72] As his third duty, the husband, 'to account his Wife as a part of his own body', had maintenance and provision. Both men and women in turn were to submit to God and Jesus as mediated by the 'lawful' priests of the newly restored Church of England. Like the 'Spartans ... not withstanding their ready address to military virtue', England would not be able 'address to Empire' if there were 'failing on the part of their Wives'.[73]

THE NEW ADAM

Within the male ethos itself, apologists for the 'new' philosophy argued that aspects of character such as deep feeling, sensitivity and the capacity for poetry should give way to the new 'solid' pursuits of invention and scientific investigation. Willis turned to anatomy, for instance, to overcome previous reliance on the 'suspicions and guesses of my [his] own mind'.[74] These in turn had been like 'a poetical philosophy and physick', no more real than a 'painter's fancy'.[75] Poets might talk of moral wisdom and the virtues of poverty, scoffed Thomas Sprat. Substantial men and men of property, however, followed natural philosophy, which had become the activity of prosperity.[76]

Furthermore, according to A. Cowley, whose poem to the Royal Society appeared in the dedicatory sections of Sprat's *History*, philosophy had became an exclusively male pursuit:

> Philosophy, I say, and call it He
> For Whatever the Painters Fancey be,
> It a Male Virtue seems to me.

Whereas Willis had identified Minerva with a reason that needed male intervention to become present, Sprat had banished her completely. In this regard it is worth recalling that Sprat's exemplary natural philosopher was Christopher Wren, chief illustrator of *Cerebri anatome*, architect of the Sheldonian Theatre, and an Anglican of impeccable background.

Poised as she was between the Court and her writing desk, the Duchess of Newcastle was alert to the shift in the ideology of male character described by Sprat above. Contrasting her husband to natural philosophers who spent 'most of their time in Dioptrical inspections', she praised him for not busying himself 'much with this brittle Art'.[77] She noted his collection and use of 'optick glasses', but she was pleased that he employed 'most of your [his] time in the more Noble and Heroick Art of *Horsemanship* and *Weapons*, as also in the sweet and delightful Art of *Poetry*, and in the useful Art of *Architecture*, etc.'[78] Newcastle's rhetoric recalls an idealized form of the knightly male character as described by Norbert Elias.[79] However, just as her husband did not get the post he coveted as Charles II's military chief, so, too, had a new male ethos of cool and disciplined aggression replaced an older form of male being.

Thus I want to suggest that in this new physiology of reason, the transformation of Eve went hand in hand with a transformation of Adam. Eve became 'reasonable' in a way women were not in the traditional formulations of a womb-dominated body, but she also became something of a physiological void. Curiosity, that delightful, fluid and troublesome character trait that had been ascribed to Western women since Genesis, had been universalized only to be appropriated and celebrated as a male character trait by male apologists for both the 'new' philosophy and the restored church. I would argue that the convergence of a bodily paradigm that emphasized the primacy of the solid parts of the brain with epistemological and theological strategies that emphasized the male nature of the 'solid' enquiry that produced it constituted an explicit male homoerotics that severely constrained women (and the 'feminine') at every level of their being.

WOMEN'S RESPONSES

An important consequence of this convergence was the tension it set up about the status of curious women. The shut-out was not lost on intellectually active women. Aware that the deck had been stacked, some, such as the Duchess of Newcastle, chose to participate in the game of natural philosophy. Speaking for her sex in 1668, she wrote: 'many of our Sex may have as much wit, and be capable of learning as well as Men, but since they want instruction, it is not possible they should attain to it'.[80] Known for her erudition, extravagant dress, and devotion to her husband, at the Court of Charles II, Margaret Cavendish was also known as 'mad Madge'. More telling, perhaps, of this new polarization of gender was Horace Walpole's eighteenth-century dismissal of her as a 'fertile pedant' with an 'unbounded passion for scribbling'.[81]

At the everyday level of health care as an artisanal undertaking, the epistemological methods that underwrote the 'neurocentric' body devalued the intellectual contributions of healers who were not university-trained. Learning of the kind Willis promoted was essential, for the 'unlearned' prescribed like 'people shooting at random'. That was a practice of 'quacking Jugglers and old Women'.[82] It didn't seem to matter that Willis's formative years had been spent learning medical recipes from the wife of his college canon.[83] Anatomically uninformed practice left medicine 'as if it were a Mystery', and it was no wonder that 'cynicks' as well as the 'vilest scum of the people fling dirt upon Physick'.[84]

Apologists for the new body of reason in effect declared that custom and intuitive knowledge, the traditional stock-in-trade of female healers of all kinds, including midwives, were no longer sufficient in the care of women. Her physiology no longer defined in terms of her sex, woman was presented as needing the advice of skilful male physician 'mechanicks'. Medical understanding depended on whole-body investigation of healthy and sick bodies and the 'rational therapies' derived from its lessons. In other words, in order to manage their minds and bodies, women required the authority of 'masculine' science and the control of its elite medical practitioners. However, to these spheres even elite women had no access, for the university and the profession were closed to them.

Jane Sharp, a midwife and author of the *Midwives Book* of 1671, protested this shift. In a phrase that ironically recalled the Royal Society's motto – 'nullius in verba' – she wrote: 'words are but the shell . . . It is commendable for men to empty their spare time in some things of deeper speculation than is required of the female sex, but the art of midwifery chiefly concerns us.'[85] Sharp was responding to another development in seventeenth-century treatment of women. If learned medicine as a system of thought – an *episteme* – was elevating the brain as it devalued the importance of the womb, male-authored empiric medicine, or medicine as *practica*, simultaneously asserted claims for control of the birthing process. Folding obstetrical forceps, the 'instruments of Vulcan' alluded to by Willis earlier, began being deployed by the Chamberlen dynasty in the middle decades of the seventeenth century. Existing on the margins of both elite medicine and midwifery, the Chamberlens and their followers nonetheless represented increasing competition to midwives who served the genteel classes.

It wasn't that midwives didn't try to organize on their own. In England two petitions for incorporation of midwives as a self-regulating body were presented to the king in the first half of the century. The first, organized by Chamberlen père in 1616 failed through a combination of opposition from the College of Physicians and several midwives. Organizing on their own in 1634, the midwives' petition for self-regulation was successfully opposed by the College of Physicians.[86] With the revival of episcopal licensing of crafts and professions in the Restoration, midwifery came under control of the Church.[87] The plan of Elizabeth Cellier in the 1680s to establish a self-regulating college for midwives also failed to gain crown support.[88] It was only in the eighteenth century that formal instruction in anatomy and obstetrics for midwives emerged in English lying-in hospitals. Then the initiators were male physicians who sought trained female assistants.

ALTERNATIVE VISIONS: THE CASE OF ANNE CONWAY

One of Willis's longest extant case notes[89] concerned Viscountess Anne Conway (née Finch) (1631-79), the noted vitalist natural philosopher[90] and correspondent whose household became a meeting-place for 'establishment' notables as well as religious dissidents in the 1670s.[91] Conway also spent virtually all her adult life in or near her bed. The sufferer of intense headaches from the age of 12 to her death, she was the recipient of medical attention from diverse healers and physicians including her kinsman, William Harvey, as well as Willis, Robert Boyle, Valentine Greatrakes, F. M. Van Helmont, and two presidents of the College of Physicians. Near the end of her life she became a religious 'enthusiast', joining the Society of Friends in 1677.

Placed in the context of her published philosophical thought, her own experience of her illness, when contrasted with Willis's interpretations, offers potential insight into the meaning of Fox Keller's 'nexus' as it was lived by an educated woman in the Restoration. To the extent that Anne Conway's natural philosophy, which she composed in notebooks near the end of her life, was a working out of the historical meaning of the new 'masculine' science as it had been applied to her body, aspects of her life as well as her published thought seem relevant to the general concerns of this essay.

For Willis, Anne Conway's headaches were ontological entities that manifested themselves as acquired structural abnormalities in the meninges (covering layers) of her brain. Employing military rhetoric to describe them, his language established the headache as an 'other', separate from Anne Conway the person. The headaches were 'Convulsive Distempers' that, 'having pitched the[ir] tents near the confines of the Brain, had so long besieged its regal tower, yet had not yet taken it; . . . for the sick lady . . . found the chief faculties of her soul sound enough'.[92] Valuing her as a 'most noble Lady . . . of a most beautiful form, and great wit, so that she was skilled in the Liberal Arts, and in all sorts of Literature, beyond the condition of her sex', he found her so favoured 'as if it were thought too much by Nature, for her to enjoy so great endowments, without some detriments, she was extremely punished with this Disease'.[93]

Tracing the origins of her headaches to a meningeal fever she had at the age of 12, Willis thought her meninges had 'contracted an habitual and indelible vice'. Assuming the problem to be a consequence of meningeal scarring in dura mater, 'the Pia mater being in the mean time safe', Willis described the meningeal disruption as the 'invincible and permanent ... yet not deadly causes'.[94] This conception was consistent with Willis's description of another woman whom he had treated for recurrent severe headaches. Unlike Conway, however, the other woman died six months after onset of symptoms. Opening her skull on post-mortem, Willis found a tumor 'three fingers broad' in her 'third sinus' which 'grew to the membranes' including the pia mater. Willis concluded 'from these observations the invincible and at length mortal cause of that Disease may plainly appear'.[95]

Most of Conway's extant letters contain at least one reference either to her pain or her current therapeutic regime. In both her life and natural philosophy, illness was part of the mystery of God's plan. Conway's affirmation of the value of patience and humility was in accord with her monistic theory of matter. Whereas her mentor, the Cambridge Neoplatonist Henry More (1614–87), maintained a distinction between matter and spirit, which was ubiquitous but immaterial, Conway joined the two: 'every Body is a Spirit, and nothing else, neither differs any thing from Spirit, but that it is more dark; therefore by how much the thicker and grosser it is become, so much the more remote is it from the degree of a Spirit, so that this distinction is only modal and gradual, not essential or substantial'.[96] Additionally, matter was not only interconvertible with spirit, it was also interconnected. Indeed, the 'Reasons and Causes of Things' depended on the fact that 'all Creatures from the highest to the lowest are inseparably united one with another'.[97] If that was understood, one might 'easily see into the most secret and hidden Causes of Things, which ignorant Men call occult Qualities'.[98] For Conway, matter also tended to become good. Even when it went into 'Eternal Torments' for an 'infiniteness of Ages'. 'Reason teacheth us' that 'it must at length return unto Good'.[99] 'Punishment', by which Conway meant suffering, was 'Medicinal', as it tended to restore goodness.[100]

Regarding the explicit gender of matter, a theme that underlay the alchemical theories with which she was familiar, Conway believed that matter, or a 'Body and Spirit' consisted of a 'more Active and a more Passive Principle, which may fitley be termed Male and Female'.[101] In contrast to Bacon's gender relations, however, relations between Conway's active and passive principles were not about domination and submission, but about 'Conjunction' and 'Cooperation'.[102]

The Quaker leader George Fox (1624–91), who visited Conway

twice in March 1678, put the matter of 'seed', by which he meant Christ's presence in the body, in female terms. Commenting in his *Journal* regarding 'hurtful' behaviour of the Quaker foe Rice Jones to some Quakers, he recounted that he told him, 'if he did wait in the fear of God for the Seed of the woman, Christ Jesus ... coming into him', that he 'might gather them [the Quakers] again'. A few lines later he reiterated the female nature of the divine: 'The Seed, Christ Jesus, the Seed of the woman'.[103]

Whereas Willis promoted a 'neurocentric' body, Conway, as did many others of diverse philosophical and political outlooks, believed that the essence of the body was in the blood.[104] Her belief in the fundamental unity of spirit and matter did not lead her to devalue reason, but she (like the Quakers) believed that access to the highest consciousness was through attention to an 'inner light'. Reason and goodness were inseparable. Indeed, to carry her thought on the ubiquity of life and potential goodness in all matter to its logical endpoint, Conway's vitalism made universal what the Quakers discussed primarily in reference to humans.

Perhaps the most striking difference between Conway's characterization of the material soul and Willis's was her confidence that its fundamental tendency was to goodness. The mature Willis, whose chemical ideas increasingly departed from the Helmontian and Paracelsian concepts which had been popular in the Oxford of his youth, had no such confidence in the ability of a person's innate nature to seek the good. Like the Anglican divines he prayed with, Willis believed that humans' ultimate principle was a 'striving after a divine state'.[105] However, this could not be achieved in one's lifetime. The sentient soul instead drove one towards a number of 'infinite wishes' based on emotional custom. When at full liberty, these 'wishes' in turn would have man 'role in the mud of sensual pleasure'.[106] Complete health required therefore not only a favourable constitution, appropriate medical care when ill, but a hierarchically ordered church to maintain an 'Empire of reason ... over the inferior faculties'.[107] When Conway and the Quakers sought to 'close with nature' regarding the body, to borrow Bacon's phrase, they did not separate, as Bacon and Willis did, the highest consciousness from a 'Form affirmative, solid and true and well defined'.[108] In contrast, for them the capacity for affirming the highest meaning was present in the body.

Moreover, both within the individual human body and within the community, Conway and the Quakers found a conjunction of the sexes that minimized the opposition between figure (male/active/ artificer) and ground (female/passive/nature) that had been central in

Bacon's thought, Willisian neuroanatomy, and Anglican gender apologetics. As Carolyn Merchant has noted, the Quakers, 'far more than the other Protestant sects, gave both men and women full equality'.[109] As opposed to Baconian 'interrogations' of (female) nature, Willis's anatomical 'conquering' of the 'martial field of the body', and Anglican calls for wifely submission, Quaker rhetoric emphasized cooperation: 'we shall be preserved near unto the ocean of all love'.[110]

Conway's burial directions give a sense of what she finally made of her long experience as an object of attention from orthodox religious (Henry More) and medical (Willis and others) advisers. She stipulated that 'rites and ceremonies of the so called Church of England may be wholly forborne at my buryall'.[111] Conway's final directive was that she 'would have no Cerecloth to avoid the coming of any men about hir, but desired that only Her Woman with the two maids should lay her in the Coffin, and to be kept here in the house till (Viscount Conway's) farther order'.[112]

CONCLUSION

Taken nominally – medical science is what it says it is – the theory that women were brain-directed and not womb-directed sought to overturn long-standing physiological ideas that characterized the non-reproducing woman as dangerous, unstable and demented. This new 'neurocentric' model of women was part of a larger scientific programme that sought to characterize female *and* male bodies as being under the leadership of the (unsexed) solid parts of the brain.

At a deeper level, however, I have suggested that the 'neurocentric' model developed by Willis and others naturalized social norms that were valued by a male subculture of scientific and religious leaders preoccupied with hierarchy, control and efficiency. Furthermore, the epistemological methods employed in development of this new model were based on assumptions about gender that promoted dominance and subordination as ideal relations between the (solid) brain and (fluid) body, men and women, and humans and the non-human natural world. Additionally, the Willisian ontologies of disease and mind represented a reification of human experience that increased the imaginative 'space' between what patients experienced (illness) and what physicians diagnosed and treated (disease).[113]

For English women in the later seventeenth century, I have argued that these new engenderings of the mind and epistemology led to alienation, in the form of new constraints on women's intellectual life and devaluation of the intuitive and customary knowledge base that had been a mainstay of female midwives and healers. Educated women, the primary female audience for these formulations, responded in a variety of ways. The duchess of Newcastle, identifying primarily with her social class, supported new epistemological concepts even as she bemoaned their implication for women (and perhaps went 'mad'). Women healers protested, sought professional autonomy, and coped as well as they could when their bid for incorporation was successfully repressed. Some, like Anne Conway, developed alternative philosophies that guided them to 'escape' into religious sects which attempted to practise a communal life based on co-operation between the sexes and a spiritual practice unmediated by male hierarchies.

NOTES

1. Thomas Willis, *Oxford Casebook*, ed. Kenneth Dewhurst (Oxford: Sandford, 1981), 92–4.
2. Thomas Willis, *An Essay of the Pathology of the Brain and Nervous Stock in which Convulsive Diseases Are Treat Of* (London, 1667). Originally published in Latin as *Pathologie cerebri et nervosi generis specimen*, in *Dr. Willis's Practice of Physick*, trans. S. Pordage (London, 1684), 69.
3. Ibid., 70.
4. According to Ilza Veith, Carolinus Piso (1563–1633) was the first European physician to argue unequivocally for a brain etiology of hysteria: *Hysteria: The History of a Disease* (Chicago: University of Chicago Press, 1965), 128–9. Unlike Willis, Piso did not publish a comprehensive theory of the body.
5. Evelyn Fox Keller, *Reflections on Gender and Science* (New Haven: Yale University Press, 1985), 61.
6. Carolyn Merchant, *The Death of Nature: Women, Ecology, and the Scientific Revolution* (New York: Harpers, 1980); Londa Schiebinger, 'Skeletons in the Closet: The First Illustrations of the Female Skeleton in Eighteenth-Century Anatomy', in Catherine Gallagher and Thomas Laqueur (eds.), *The Making of the Modern Body: Sexuality and Society in the Nineteenth Century* (Berkeley: University of California Press, 1987); Schiebinger, *The Mind Has No Sex?* (Cambridge, Mass.: Harvard University Press, 1989); Thomas Laqueur, *Making Sex* (Cambridge, Mass.: Harvard University Press, 1990); and 'Orgasm, Generation, and the Politics of Reproductive Biology', in Gallagher and Laqueur, *The Making of the Modern Body*.
7. See Everett Mendelsohn, *Heat and Life* (Cambridge, Mass.: Harvard University Press, 1964). For concepts of heat in reproduction, see Laqueur, *Making Sex* 27–9, 34–6, 44–50, 101–2.
8. Danielle Jacquart and Claude Thomasset, *Sexuality and Medicine in the Middle Ages*, trans. Matthew Adamson, (Princeton: Princeton University Press, 1988), 48–78.
9. Ibid., 73.
10. Ibid., 73 nn. 76, 77.
11. Ibid., 72.

12 *Les Secrets des dames*, ed. E. Rauneyre (Paris, 1880), 65–6. Cited in ibid., 76, n. 89.
13 Jacquart and Thomasset, *Sexuality and Medicine in the Middle Ages*, 75 n. 85.
14 Anonymous, *The Compleat Doctoress or, a Choice Treatise of all Disease Incident to Women* (London, 1656), Huntington Library 478273, p. 4.
15 Nicholas Fontanus, *The Woman's Doctour, or an Exact and Distinct Explanation of all such Diseases as are Peculiar to that Sex with Choice & Experimental Remedies against the Same* (London, 1652), 51, Wellcome Library 22842/A.
16 Nicholas Culpeper, *Practice of Physick* (London, 1655), 419, Wellcome Library 44145/C.
17 *Compleat Doctoress*, 1.
18 Ibid., 4.
19 Plato, *Republic*, in *The Collected Dialogues*, ed. E. Hamilton and H. Cairns (Princeton: Princeton University Press, 1963), 454c, 693.
20 Laqueur, *Making Sex*, 63–96; *idem*, 'Orgasm, Generation', 5–14; Schiebinger, 'Skeletons in the Closet', 47–8.
21 Aristotle, 'Generation of Animals', in *Complete Works of Aristotle* (2 vols., Princeton: Princeton University Press, 1984), 2.7161 5–7.
22 Laqueur, *Making Sex*, 69.
23 Ibid., 68.
24 Rudolph Arnheim, *Art and Visual Perception* (Berkeley: University of California Press, 1966), 213–92, 185–8.
25 William Harvey, *Exercitationes de generatione animalium* (1651) (London: Sydenham Society), cited in Porter, 'Hysteria: The Body and the Mind' (Unpublished MS, 1991), 37 n. 77.
26 John F. Benton, op. cit., 'Conclusion'.
27 Thomas Willis, 'Preface', to *Two Discourses on the Animal Soul* (1672), in *Dr Willis's Practice of Physick*.
28 Robert G. Frank, Jr, 'Thomas Willis and His Circle: Brain and Mind in Seventeenth-Century Medicine', in George S. Rousseau (ed.), *The Languages of Psyche* (Berkeley: University of California Press, 1990), 107–46; Diane Puklin, 'Medical Psychology in the Seventeenth Century: The Idea of a Neurological Emotion in the Thought of Thomas Willis' (Ph.D. dissertation, University of Chicago, 1980).
29 Robert G. Frank, Jr, *Harvey and the Oxford Physiologists* (Berkeley: University of California Press, 1980); Audrey B. Davis, *Circulation Physiology and Medical Chemistry in England 1650–1680* (Lawrence, Kans.: Coronado, 1973).
30 Hippocrates, *Œuvres complètes d'Hippocrate*, vol. VI, trans. E. Littré (Paris: Balliere, 1839–1861), 140, 387–9, 391–3, cited by Edwin Clarke and C. D. O'Malley, *The Human Brain and Spinal Cord*, vol. 1 (Berkeley: University of California Press, 1968), 4–5.
31 Plato, *The Timaeus*, trans. Benjamin Jowett, in *Plato: The Collected Dialogues*, 1195–6, 73b–d.
32 Ibid., 1198, 75e–76a; 1194–8, 70d–77.
33 Thomas Willis, *Cerebri anatome* (London, 1664), 117; see also Puklin, 'Medical Psychology', 112–40.
34 Puklin, 'Medical Psychology', 131.

35 Willis, *Cerebri anatome*, 120–2; Puklin, 'Medical Psychology', 133–5.
36 Thomas Willis, *Oxford Lectures*, trans. and ed. Kenneth Dewhurst (Oxford: Sandford, 1980), 87.
37 Mary Astell, 'An Essay in Defence of the Female Sex' (London, 1996), 12–13, cited in Schiebinger, 'Skeletons in the Closet', 47.
38 Willis, *Pathology of the Brain*, 69.
39 George Cheyne, *The English Malady* (London: Strahan and Leake, 1733), quoted in Richard Hunter and Ida Macalpine, *Three Hundred Years of Psychiatry, 1535–1860* (London: Oxford University Press, 1963), 184.
40 Francis Bacon, *Works*, ed. James Spedding, R. Ellis and D. Heath, vol. III (Boston: Friedrich Formann, 1860–64), 374–5, cited by Davis, *Circulation Physiology*, 153.
41 Willis, *Dr Willis's Practice of Physick*, 53. For Bacon and nature, see Carolyn Merchant, *The Death of Nature*, 179–86.
42 Willis, 'Preface to the Reader', *Cerebri anatome*.
43 Ibid.
44 Ibid.
45 Ibid.
46 Ibid.
47 Calvin used an image of God as midwife. See J. Jempsey Douglas, 'Calvin's Use of Metaphorical Language for God: God as Enemy and God as Mother', *Archiv für Reformationsgeschichte*, 87 (1986), 131, 133.
48 Davis, *Circulation Physiology*, 65–90; Frank, *Harvey and The Oxford Physiologists*, 169–88.
49 Davis, *Circulation Physiology*, 133–73; Peter H. Niebyl, 'Sennert, Van Helmont, and Medical Ontology', *Bulletin of the History of Medicine*, 45 (2) (1971), 115–37; Walter Pagel, 'Van Helmont's Concept of Disease – To Be or Not to Be? The Influence of Paracelsus', *Bulletin of the History of Medicine*, 46 (5) (1972), 419–54.
50 Willis, 'Preface to the Reader', in *Rational Therapeutics, the First and Second Part* (1675), in *Dr Willis's Practice of Physick*.
51 J. B. de C. M. Saunders and Charles O'Malley, *Vesalius: The Illustrations from his Works*, (Cleveland: World Press, 1950), 170.
52 Benjamin Farrington, '*Temporis partus masculus*: An Untranslated Writing of Francis Bacon', *Centaurus*, 1 (1951), 193–205, p. 204.
53 Ibid., 197; Fox Keller, *Reflections on Gender and Science*, 48.
54 Nicholas D. Jewson, 'Medical Knowledge and the Patronage System in Eighteenth-Century England', *Sociology*, 15 (1974), 370–85.
55 Willis, *Pathology of the Brain*, 75–8.
56 Edmund King, *Philosophical Transactions of the Royal Society*, 15 (1685), 228–31.
57 See Schiebinger, *The Mind Has No Sex?* 47–59.
58 Duchess of Newcastle, *Philosophical Letters or Modest Reflections upon Some Opinions in Natural Philosophy* (London, 1664), 352.
59 Ibid., 352–77.
60 Ibid., 377.
61 Harold Cook, *Decline of the Old Medical Regime in Stuart London* (Ithaca, N.Y.: Cornell University Press, 1986), 184–5.

62 Robert Martensen, '"Habit of Reason": Anatomy and Anglicanism in Restoration England', *Bulletin of the History of Medicine*, 66 (1992): 511–35, pp. 524–33.
63 John Spurr, 'Anglican Apologetic and the Restoration Church,' (Ph.D. dissertation, University of Oxford, 1985).
64 Richard S. Westfall, *Science and Religion in Seventeenth-Century England* (New Haven: Yale University Press, 1958), chapter 5.
65 Spurr, 'Anglican Apologetic'; Michael Heyd, 'The Reaction to Enthusiasm in the Seventeenth Century: Towards an Integrative Approach', *Journal of Modern History* 53 (June 1981), 258–80; Martensen, '"Habit of Reason"', 524–35.
66 J. Trevor Hughes, *Thomas Willis 1621–1675* (London: Royal Society of Medicine, 1991), 32–3.
67 Allestree's authorship of *The Whole Duty of Man* has been disputed.
68 Trevor Hughes, *Thomas Willis*, 34–5.
69 Richard Allestree, *The Ladies Calling* (Oxford: Sheldonian Theatre, 1673), 'Preface'.
70 See Merchant, *The Death of Nature*, 1–42.
71 Allestree, *The Ladies Calling*, 'Table of Contents'.
72 Ibid., 119–25.
73 Ibid., 'Preface'.
74 Willis, *Cerebri anatome*, 'Epistle Dedicatory'.
75 Ibid., 'Preface to the Reader'.
76 Thomas Sprat, *History of the Royal Society of London* (1667), ed. Jackson Cope and Harold Jones (London: Routledge, 1959), 403.
77 Duchess of Newcastle, *Observations Upon Experimental Philosophy to which is added the Description of a Blazing New World* (London, 1668), 'Dedication'.
78 Ibid.
79 Norbert Elias, *The History of Manners* (New York: Urizen, 1978), 191–217.
80 Duchess of Newcastle, *Observations*, 'To the Reader'; see also Schiebinger, *The Mind Has No Sex?* 47–59.
81 *Encyclopaedia Britannica*, vol. XVII (New York: Scribner, 1884), 381.
82 Willis, 'Preface to the Reader', in *Rational Therapeutics*.
83 Trevor Hughes, *Thomas Willis*, 9–10.
84 Willis, 'Preface to the Reader', *Rational Therapeutics*.
85 Jane Sharp, *The Midwives Book* (London, 1671), in Hilda Smith, 'Gynecology and Ideology in Seventeenth Century England', in Bernice Caroll, *Liberating Women's History* (Westport, Conn.: Greenwood, 1978), 112.
86 Thomas Forbes, 'The Regulation of English Midwives in the Sixteenth and Seventeenth Centuries', *Medical History*, 8 (1964), 235–44.
87 John R. Guy, 'The Episcopal Licensing of Physicians, Surgeons and Midwives', *Bulletin of the History of Medicine*, 56 (1982), 528–42.
88 Schiebinger, *The Mind Has No Sex?* 108–9.
89 Willis, *Two Discourses*, in *The Remaining Medical Works of ... Dr Thomas Willis* (London, 1681), quoted in Gilbert Owen, 'The Famous Case of Lady Anne Conway', *Annals of Medical History*, 4 (1937), 567–71.

90 *The Principles of the Most Ancient and Modern Philosophy* (1692), ed. Peter Loptson (The Hague: Martinus Nijhoff, 1982).
91 *The Conway Letters*, ed. Marjorie Hope Nicolson, revised Sarah Hutton (Oxford: Clarendon Press, 1992), 309–22, 378–84.
92 Willis, *Two Discourses*, cited in Owen, 'The Famous Case', 570.
93 Ibid., 569.
94 Ibid., 570.
95 Willis, *London Practice of Physick* (London, 1685), 283.
96 Conway, *Principles*, 164.
97 Ibid., 193.
98 Ibid., 164.
99 Ibid., 193.
100 Ibid., 188.
101 Ibid.
102 Ibid.
103 George Fox, *Journal*, rev. edn, ed. John L. Nickalls (Cambridge: Cambridge University Press, 1952), 336–9.
104 Conway, *Principles*, 218.
105 Willis, *Two Discourses on the Soul of Brutes*, in *Dr Willis's Practice of Physick*, 52.
106 Ibid.
107 Edward Stillingfleet, sermon preached before the King in 1667 (London, 1667).
108 Francis Bacon, 'New Organon', 4. 146, in *The Works of Francis Bacon*, ed. James Spedding, Robert Leslie Ellis and Douglas Denon Heath (14 vols., London, 1857–74); reprint edn, Stuttgart, 1962–3, cited by Ronald Levao, 'Francis Bacon and the Mobility of Science', *Representations* 40 (fall 1992), 1–32, p. 18.
109 Merchant, *The Death of Nature*, 256.
110 Robert Barrow, letter of 16 November 1690 regarding the 4,000 persons at George Fox's funeral (Huntington manuscript 27045).
111 Anne Conway's 'Will', in *Principles*, 481.
112 Ibid.
113 Leon Eisenberg, 'Disease and Illness: Distinctions between Professional and Popular Ideas of Sickness', in *idem, Culture, Medicine and Psychiatry*, vol. 1 (1977), 1–23.

SIX

THE LITERATURE OF SEXUAL ADVICE BEFORE 1800

ROY PORTER

RECENT decades have wrought a transformation in our understanding of past sexualities, stimulated largely by modern sexual liberationist campaigns, particularly those mounted by feminists and gays.[1] If once it seemed 'progressive' to argue that sex was a positive power long subjected to ignorance and oppression, and hence that the history of sexuality ought to be told as a story of official restraint, valiant opposition and eventual emancipation,[2] interpretations are now far more complicated. For one thing, the traditional tale now sounds excessively biologistic; most scholars would today stress the cultural conditioning and determination of sexual orientation, attitudes and activities. For another, it is also embarrassingly monolithic: we now talk not of sexuality but of varieties of sexualities. And, finally, it sounds crude and Whiggish, a self-satisfied saga of heroes and villains in which the desired outcome never was in doubt, the happy ending being only a matter of time.

Evaluation of the sexual orientations and experiences of earlier centuries is now much more ambiguous. Not least, we now have a far more realistic grasp of the limits of our knowledge. Once it was widely thought that the Victorians were sexually buttoned-up. Peter Gay and others have argued that they were more open: but the evidence adduced so far is sparse, and judgment on the swinging Victorians must be suspended.[3] Trends in family and community history over the last generation have led us to highlight the social pressures in the early modern era making for 'respectable' sexual restraint both before and within marriage. Revising this, Lawrence Stone's *Uncertain Unions* (1992) has offered extensive evidence, from church and secular courts, of apparently more free-and-easy sexual ways, or at least different conventions, which might involve suitors in genteel London middle-class homes around 1700 being invited by their sweetheart's mother to stay the night. Were these just the exceptions? Is that why these were the cases that ended up in the courts? It is very hard to decide and perhaps we will never know. Patricia Crawford has drawn attention (see chapter 4 above) to the paucity of direct, first-person recorded evidence as to what women made of their sexual lives.[4]

The early modern period also presents, as Crawford observes, a kind of theoretical void. There have been remarkable attempts to conceptualize Ancient and early Christian sexualities,[5] and a welter of readings of Victorian and post-Freudian times. The early modern era, by contrast, has seen fewer bold interpretations. And this is a gap accentuated by a glaring lacuna in the most ambitious attempt to trace sexualities, Michel Foucault's *Histoire de la sexualité*. Foucault sympathetically interpreted Ancient structures of feeling, showing the dialogue between eroticism and shifting concepts of the self; and he dazzlingly challenged conventional understandings of modern sexology. But, left tragically unfinished, Foucault's published volumes display a gigantic gulf between the teachings of St Augustine and the making of modern sexology in the nineteenth century, with its hysterization of women's bodies, pedagogization of children's sex, socialization of procreative behaviour and psychiatrization of perverse pleasure. The assumptions and methods used by Foucault in recovering former sexualities may be disputed: in my view he neglected, indeed often cavalierly dismissed, questions of class and gender, coercive power and conflict. But his goal – that of demonstrating the sequence of rational discourses within which sexuality has successively been inscribed – is surely fundamental to the enterprise of this volume.[6]

Foucault maintained that sexuality was discursive, that *savoir* and *pouvoir* were inseparable, and that power was not primarily negative. A key point of intersection of all these themes lies in writing.[7] Writing about sex has taken many forms, from bawdy jests to judicial records, from libertine verse to anatomical treatises.[8] A genre that assumed special significance in the early modern period, notably towards 1700, was printed sexual advice literature, a subset of the enormous dissemination of know-how on matters from medicine to manners, horsemanship to housekeeping, gushing from the presses in the post-Gutenberg era.[9] Popularization of expertise – itself a profoundly problematic concept[10] – was a major outcome of print culture, and sexual knowledge formed no exception. Underlying it, there was, of course, a learned tradition. Writing on *The 'Viaticum' and Its Commentaries*, Mary Wack has recently explored medieval concern with lovesickness; early in the seventeenth century, Jacques Ferrand produced *De la maladie d'amour*; his contemporary, Robert Burton, discussed erotic madness in the elephantine and erudite *Anatomy of Melancholy* (1621); twenty years later, Joannes Sinibaldus published his scholarly *Geneanthropeiae, sive de Hominis Generatione Decateuchon*, a ponderous tractatus on human sexuality.[11] Such works were learned, even Latinate; alongside these, from the late seventeenth century, popular vernacular manuals of sexual advice became widely available. First and foremost was the *Tableau de l'amour conjugal*, the pseudonymous work of the La Rochelle physician, Dr Nicolas Venette, published in 1696.[12] Venette's book constitutes a landmark in the annals of medically grounded sexual advice tomes. It was translated into English, German, Dutch and even Spanish – the first English version appeared in 1703 under the title of *The Mysteries of Conjugal Love Revealed*, priced at six shillings – and it became for over two centuries Europe's most popular sex guide, going through at least thirty-one French editions by 1800, and scores more in the nineteenth century and beyond (Flaubert never forgave Venette for his vast sales). Venette's text is precisely the tantalizing hotchpotch that might be expected in a work essaying a new form of writing. It is learned, but also popular; it is scientific, yet also ribald; it is earnest, it is playful. Quotations from the recently rediscovered Petronius jostle with autopsy reports; pieties from St John Chrysostom mingle with prurient accounts of African erotic practices, with purple passages about the power of Venus, and with pharmacological tips for restoring second-hand maidenheads.

Paralleling Venette's guide, the best-seller in the English-speaking world was *Aristotle's Master-Piece*, first published in 1684, and often issued together with other works also spuriously attributed to the Stagyrite: *Aristotle's Complete Midwife, Aristotle's Last Legacy* and *Aristotle's Book of Problems*.[13] Aimed at the common reader, *Aristotle's Master-Piece* had gone through at least forty-three editions by 1800, and quite probably scores more now unrecorded or lost. Blatantly trading on the magic of a great name, the work had no pretensions to be the last word in medical research. It was rather a codification of sexual folklore, with sections on palmistry, physiognomy and astrology, written for the class of reader who bought ballads and almanacs. And alongside such evergreens, dozen of other texts purveyed sexual knowledge with various emphases, some explaining the bedroom arts, others thundering prohibitions, some claiming to cure venereal disease, others centring on gynaecological mysteries. Our first really solid evidence of what literate Europe encountered by way of 'all you need to know about sex but never dared to ask' works, these texts are of profound historical interest. All the more surprising, then, that they have remained neglected. There is only one work in the English language devoted explicitly and exclusively to their study, Alan

Rusbridger's *Concise History of the Sex Manual*, and that is a jokey, prurient potboiler, with virtually no references before the 1880s – confirming how readily it is assumed that the history of sexuality is overwhelmingly a modern one.[14]

Foucault believed there had been a growing sexual garrulity: 'this is the essential thing,' he wrote, 'that Western man has been drawn for three centuries to the task of telling everything concerning his sex; that since the classical age [that is, the seventeenth century] there has been a constant optimization and an increasing valorization of the discourse on sex'.[15] Hence the 'repressive hypothesis' – the idea that sex was rendered taboo, unspeakable – was false. In many ways Foucault was right. The very existence of such works as the *Tableau de l'amour conjugal* and *Aristotle's Master-Piece* refutes without further ado the repressive hypothesis in its crassest form: evidently authors did not find such texts too abominable to write, magistrates did not outlaw them, or at least not always, and customers bought them. Yet naturally things were not so simple; censorship and repression work in subtle ways. Purchasers may not have handled their erotica in the same way as they handled other books. 'Away to the Strand to my bookseller's', Samuel Pepys notoriously wrote in his diary: 'and bought that idle, roguish book, *L'escholle des Filles*; which I have bought in plain binding (avoiding the buying of it better bound) because I resolve, as soon as I have read it, to burn it, that it may not stand in the list of books, nor among them, to disgrace them if it should be found.'[16] If magistrates did not burn erotica, it appears that buyers' superegos may have done their work for them, or at least felt the need to mouth such upright sentiments before the tribunal of their journal. Carnal knowledge was evidently a complex thing, desired, dangerous, denied all at once. And readers surely enjoyed playing with fire.

In the post-Gutenberg centuries, writers ceaselessly agonized over the act of creation: authorship.[17] And their anxieties applied with particular force to questions of sexual discourse, its legitimacy and especially its diffusion. Since the Fall, carnal knowledge had been original sin; could its propagation then be proper, or should it be kept under wraps? The shame of sexual knowledge according to the Christian creed meant, at the very least, that such dissemination could not be as unproblematic as the publishing of agricultural advice.[18] Yet, as Foucault implies, the game of testing the taboo, speaking the unspeakable, evidently spurred sly and devious pleasures. Defining, denying and defiling the conventions of writing sex perhaps gave frissons equivalent to delineating and desecrating the conventions of sex itself. And money must have talked. As popular culture grew commercialized in the Grub Street era, sex books became money-spinners, breeding profits through establishing a consumerism in erotica. Sex was prostituted in printed pornography; as with phone sex today, sex talk developed delights of its own.[19]

Hence an essential ingredient, even pleasure, of early sex manuals is the controversy they fomented about the legitimacy of sex literature itself. There were plenty of demurring voices – real and fantasized – claiming that writing sex was indecent and pernicious. These protests had to be rebutted. In the counter-arguments developed in these texts, professions of the public interest loomed large. Authors appealed to social need and popular demand. The nation was manifestly suffering sexual miseries and afflictions: impotence, infertility, venereal diseases. Such troubles were the outcome of ignorance, or, worse still, misinformation from false friends, overconfident *confidantes* or rapacious quacks. 'How many married Men and Women have complain'd to me of Seminal and other Weaknesses, Gleets, &c. to their depriving them of having Children?' thundered John Marten in his *Gonosologium novum: or, a New System of all the Secret Infirmities and Diseases, Natural, Accidental and Venereal in Men and Women* (1709), 'How many totally defective or incapable of performing the Conjugal Duty, being wholly abridg'd of that pleasing Sensation, and that from Venereal as well as Natural and Accidental occasions, is almost incredible to consider?'[20] Such victims solicited advice, *deserved* advice, retorted the obliging authors: people should not die, or suffer, from ignorance. Hence so long as vulgar errors were current and quacks were puffing erroneous opinions, responsible authors were duty-bound to counter lies with truth. He had been compelled to write on delicate matters, apologized Marten in his *Treatise of all the Symptoms of the Venereal Disease, in both Sexes*, 'that no Persons therefore for the future may be drove to the Necessity of Ship-wrecking their Bodies, Purses and Reputations upon those Rocks of Destruction, (I mean those wretched Ignoramus's QUACKS, MOUNTEBANKS and ASTROLOGERS that swarm in every Corner, imposing on the too credulous World their peddling insignificant *Remedies*)'.[21] Many judged this a case of the pot calling the kettle black, since Marten himself was widely branded as an empiric.

False views were apparently ubiquitous. Thus, a couple of generations later, the medical popularizer William Buchan denounced the widespread belief that a man could be cured of venereal disease by deflowering a virgin. The only way to scotch such 'absurd opinions', he argued, was through popular education. It was for this reason that he had penned his *Observations Concerning the Prevention and Cure of the Venereal Disease* (1796), maintaining that 'these hints' would 'conduce to put the young and unwary on their guard against the direful consequences of this insidious malady'. Public-spirited doctors had to be bold, because the venereally infected typically 'concealed' their conditions.[22]

There was thus the argument from necessity. There was also an assertion of right. Some authors intrepidly, in best Enlightenment *sapere aude* fashion, proclaimed the sovereignty of knowledge. Holding people in a state of ignorance was the ploy of princes and priests; knowledge was democratic and liberating. 'While men are kept in the dark,' proclaimed Buchan, 'and told that they are not to use their own understanding in matters that concern their health, they will be the dupes of designing knaves.' The thirst for knowledge could thus be portrayed not as idle curiosity, some questionable *libido sciendi*, but as integral to the humane and humanist quests for self-knowledge.[23] 'There is nothing human nature is more desirous of knowing', inserted Venette's English translator,

> than the origin of their being; which is explained in this little treatise; the admirable order of nature in the production of man, is exactly set forth for the satisfaction of every Reader. A young man may know, by this book, what constitution he is of, and whether he is disposed for continency or matrimony. He may learn at what age he ought to marry, that he may not be enervated in his younger years, and pass a considerable time of his life without pleasure.[24]

The mysteries of generation thus formed the key to the secrets of one's very being.

Necessity? Yes. Entitlement? Maybe. But surely hazards too. For might not trumpeting the ins and outs of sexual techniques put the innocent at risk? Would not publicizing cures for venereal diseases spare the guilty? Indeed, might not corruption of virtue be the diabolical motive of authors inflamed by prurience? Innocents, it was argued, no more needed to read sex handbooks to comport themselves properly than, in papal eyes, it was necessary to pore over the Bible to be suffused with grace.

Authors had their rejoinders at the ready. True innocence, they protested, would never be corrupted;[25] and it was a wicked world anyway, that would itself profane and deprave. 'It is impossible to prevent every thing that is capable of sullying the imagination,' argued the author of *Onania*, '*Dogs* in the Streets, and *Bulls* in the Fields may do mischief to Debauch's Fancy's, and it is possible that either Sex may be put in mind of Lascivious Thoughts, by their own *Poultry*.' Under such circumstances, it was surely preferable to reinforce modesty with knowledge, than wait until other 'Causes of Uncleanness in general, such as *Ill-Books, Bad-Companions, Love-Stories,* Lascivious Discourses, *and other Provocatives* to *Lust* and *Wantonness*' undermined unwary vulnerability.[26]

In works like Venette's that claimed to instruct in the arts of married love, the risk of corrupting innocence was not perceived as paramount, for heterosexual coitus was an act which, it was assumed, everyone would wish to perform, indeed, by nature's promptings and civic responsibility, *ought* to perform. The job of instruction manuals was thus principally to underscore nature and specify the optimal parties, times, circumstances and postures; for

> Constitution, age, climate, season, and our way of living, influence all our caresses. A man at twenty-five, of a hot complexion, full of blood and spirits, who lives in the fertile plains of Barbary, and in easy circumstances, is better able to kiss a woman five times a night in the month of April, than another aged forty of a cold constitution, who lives on the barren mountains of Sweden, and gets his bread with pain and difficulty, can once or twice a night in the month of January.[27]

Once a work like the *Tableau de l'amour conjugal* had stipulated that it was to be read exclusively by the married, there was little that it could be indecent to mention. Indeed, scanning them nowadays, we may find them notably anatomically explicit, graphic in their descriptions of male and female sexual equipment, the mechanics of foreplay and the optimal postures.

Considerations of innocence, however, weighed infinitely more heavily in the case of works handling masturbation. Rising from the anonymous *Onania* (1710) through Tissot's *Onanism* (1760)[28] and beyond, the masturbation panic has been explored by many historians, most thoroughly by J. Stengers and A. Van Neck in *Histoire d'une grande peur: la masturbation* (1984), and, most challengingly, by Thomas Laqueur.[29] There is no room here to explore the meaning of this *grande peur*,[30] though I shall briefly allude to it at the end. The special feature of masturbation is that it was portrayed as entirely pernicious – a vice doubly dangerous because it could be savoured in secret with the aid of nothing but a hand and a lurid imagination. Since it was assumed to be a sin of unmarried men and women, books opposing onanism were outwardly targeted at the juvenile and single. Such individuals had no business having a sex life at all: was it not, therefore, needlessly provocative to impart to them cognizance of forbidden practices? Was not the danger, critics thundered, that writings against self-abuse like *Onania, Or the Heinous Sin of Self-Pollution, And all its frightful Consequences, in both Sexes, Consider'd with Spiritual and Physical Advice to those, who have already injur'd themselves by this abominable practice. And seasonable Admonition to the Youth of the Nation, [of both Sexes] and those whose Tuition they are under, whether Parents, Guardians, Masters, or Mistresses* would instruct youngsters in a crime they had never even envisioned, would serve, in other words, as a school of vice?

It was an objection all authors condemning the solitary vice felt obliged to rebut. To speak or hold one's tongue? The author of *Onania* had his riposte. Precisely because masturbation was such a 'heinous sin', it was crucial that the warning be broadcast not just to *habitués* but also to adolescents who had 'who never contracted this guilt'.[31] For innocence would not prove a citadel against temptation. Hence the best philosophy was 'forewarned is forearmed'. *Onania* thus enunciated a robust policy to refute 'Those who are of Opinion, that notwithstanding the Frequency of this Sin, it never ought to be spoke of, or hinted at, because the bare mentioning of it may be dangerous to some, who without it, would never have thought of it'.[32] Reading about sex would not prove a dangerous thing, the Preface argued, so long as what was read was proper – that is, not fiction or any titillating matter but *Onania* itself and other pious, improving works. Of course, the line between the uplifting and the titillating was a fine one, but it was one that *Onania*'s author felt confident could be drawn. He was, he declared, 'fully persuaded, that there are very few Sentences throughout the Book, which do not more or less tend to the Mortification of Lust, and not one that can give Offence to the chastest Ear', even a female one.[33]

Not all were so readily convinced, the author allowed. In the Preface to the 7th edition he disclosed that, although, in earlier versions he had 'taken all imaginable Precaution against every Danger of raising impure Thoughts, even in the most Lascivious', he had, nevertheless, found to his 'sorrow, that some People, not only are Deaf to all wholesome Advice, but likewise will misconstrue and pervert the most candid Meaning' – indeed, 'some have accused me of writing obscenely and forwarding the Corruption of Manners'.[34] Hence, he had been led to ponder whether it might not be best to omit 'several Words and Passages, against which I know that Exceptions have been made'.[35] In other words, *Onania*'s advocacy of candour was shaky from the start: might not plain-speaking be obscene, if not in intention at least in effect? And the matter would not rest there. At the opening of the first chapter, the author returned to the problem that was fretting him: 'It is almost impossible to treat of this Subject so as to be understood by the meanest Capacities, without trespassing at the same time against the Rules of Decency, and making Use of Words and Expressions which Modesty forbids us to utter.'[36] At this point, the author seems to be changing tack, emphasizing that his goal was less truth than morality: 'As my great Aim is to promote Virtue and Christian Purity, and to discourage Vice and Uncleanness, without giving Offence to any, I shall chuse rather to be less intelligible to some, and leave several things to the Consideration of my Readers.'[37] For the risk was that 'by being too plain', he would 'run the Hazard of raising in some corrupt Minds, what I would most endeavour to stifle and destroy'. He would therefore, he confided, say rather little on the subject of how women masturbated with dildos because 'it would be impossible to rake in so much Filthiness, as I should be oblig'd to do, without offending Chastity'.[38] Indeed, even this much had to be said under cover of Latin: *'cum Digitis & aliis Instrumentis'*.[39] But, as will by now have become clear, the author, by a curious strategy, had been informing readers precisely what it was too inflammatory for them to be told. This is not, *ipso facto*, to adjudge him guilty of hypocrisy or bad faith; it is merely to point out the inescapable predicaments of talking the taboo.

The ultimate tactic lay in disavowal and offloading responsibility. 'It was reasonable to think', the author excused himself, 'that in the beginning of the Second Chapter, I had taken all imaginable Precaution against every Danger of raising impure Thought's, even in the most Lascivious.' Not so:

> But as I found to my sorrow, that some People, not only are Deaf to all wholesome Advice, but likewise will misconstrue and pervert the most candid Meaning, I would in the 4th 5th and 6th Editions, and likewise in this *Seventh*, to shew the integrity of my Intention, have omitted several Words and Passages, against which I know that Exceptions have been made.[40]

He would, he is here saying, happily have gone in for self-censorship. But he didn't – 'this, I say I would have done, had not some Gentlemen of great Piety as well as Penetration, diswaded me from it by this Argument', that an author 'ought never to be blamed for relating Facts as they are stated'.[41]

Having hence been persuaded by these upright gentlemen, the author was not answerable for his opinions. Indeed, in such professions of high-mindedness, whole batteries of higher authorities, especially the dead, were standardly invoked. Venette justified frank talk about matters sexual by contending that the Bible and the Church Fathers had set a wholesome precedent. And, in his turn, playing the martyred innocent, John Marten cited the Frenchman on this very matter. '*Venette* tells us,' he noted, deploying a double denial of responsibility,

> if modestly speaking of affairs of the *Secret Parts* be blamable, either St Austin, St *Gregory* of *Nice*, nor *Tertullian* should be perus'd, who all speak of Conjugal Affairs in such terms, as he durst not Translate. And by the same rule, one would suppress the Book of *Secrets of Women*, wherein he sets forth a great many things to provoke to Love. And in fine, the Books of Physicians and Anatomists ought not to be seen, if the Complaints above recited were just and reasonable.[42]

A couple of generations later, the excellent Tissot adopted an identical defence in *Onanism or a Treatise upon the Disorders Produced by Masturbation*. What was the proper idiom for sexual discourse?

> I have not neglected any precaution that was necessary to give this work all the decency, in point of terms, that it was susceptible of ... Should such important subjects be passed over in silence? No, certainly. The sacred writers, the fathers of the church, who almost all wrote in living languages, the ecclesiastical writers, did not think it proper to be silent upon crimes of obscenity, because they could not be described without words.[43]

Tissot thereby grounded his claim to speak on 'indecent' matters upon the Fathers – in the process, as Ludmilla Jordanova has remarked, enhancing his own prerogative to pontificate in quasi-religious tones.[44]

Friends and other authors, preferably deceased, were thus ultimately accountable for any alleged lewdnesses. As also were the readers. For the bottom line, claimed *Onania*'s author, was that purity or prurience lay in the reader's head. 'Therefore, as I shall be forc'd to make use of some expressions,' he explained in his second chapter,

> which tho' spoke with a Design the most remote from Obscenity, may, working by the reverse, perhaps furnish the Fancies of silly People with Matter for Impurity; therefore I say, I beg of the Reader to stop here, and not to proceed any further, unless he has a Desire to be chast, or at least be apt to consider whether he ought to have it or no.[45]

Caveat lector: but, one might respond, what surer come-on could there be than to beseech the reader to 'stop here'? A parallel might be seen in the disclaimer-cum-prompt offered in Venette's Preface, which insisted that his work was intended only for the 'small number of learned and judicious persons' who could be expected to share the pure love of 'naked truth' that he was imparting: which reader, at that point, would exclude himself?[46]

Thus the heart of the matter: if the heinous sin of self-abuse arose from mischievous knowledge, was not any or all information liable to be abused? *Onania* erected a pious warning notice: 'every Body, who would write profitably against any sort of Uncleanness whatever, and not do more Harm than Good by his Endeavours, ought to be very careful and circumspect as to this particular'.[47] But the writer's final ploy was to insist that his stance was at least franker and more effective than that adopted by others. In particular, he castigated 'the Learned *Ostervald*', author of the *Traité contre l'impureté*, published in Amsterdam in 1707 and translated into English in the next year as *The Nature of Uncleanness Consider'd . . . to which is added A Discourse Concerning the Nature of Chastity and the Means of Obtaining it*.[48] Ostervald, accused *Onania*, had, 'through an Excess of Modesty', completely omitted all discussion of masturbation whatsoever. By passing 'over this abominable Sort of Impurity in Silence', or by muttering about 'it in such general Terms, blending it with lesser Trespasses of the Uncleanness', Osterwald had 'failed of Representing the Heinousness that is in it'.[49] Interestingly, Ostervald had admitted as much. In his Preface, he had granted that, 'being too scrupulously modest', he had remained silent upon 'many particulars', whereon he had been 'forc'd to be defective'. Certain points, Osterwald conceded, 'should have been more enlarg'd upon; and some Objections more particularly consider'd; but this would have necessitated me to touch upon some Things, which Decency forbids. There are also divers Things, which I am oblig'd to express only in general Terms; others which I dare but just hint; and others again that I am forc'd totally to suppress.'[50]

Ostervald here put his finger on the problem. It was all very well for handbook authors to protest their writings could do no harm. Venette, for example, disavowed any danger by insisting that he was merely enunciating what comes naturally. 'We need no instructions ... to learn love,' he somewhat disingenuously upheld. His teachings were innocuous, because they were nature's promptings. 'Nature has taught', he claimed, 'both Sexes such Postures as are allowable; and that contribute to Generation; and Experience has shown those that are forbidden and contrary to health.' Hence, his treatise 'was not made to bring the work of generation or action of the genital parts, into a method ... That has been done before by the strength of Nature alone.' Yet such blather obviously begged all the questions. For if it were natural, why the need to teach it in the first place? If carnal knowledge had no power to corrupt, how could it have power to purify or fortify? Venette and others seemed to have trapped themselves in a self-contradictory denial of the medium through which they had chosen to express themselves. If not precisely duplicitous, the apologiae could hardly be convincing.[51]

It is not my purpose to catalogue the contents of early advice literature. Venette's *Tableau de l'amour conjugal* might be mentioned as not uncharacteristic. It was divided into four sections. Part I tackled the anatomy and physiology of the sexual organs, their mechanics and malfunctions, and remedies for defects. Part II then broached larger considerations of the nature of libido and love, discussing such issues as compatibility and the optimal frequency of coitus, and making recommendations for the best diet, times and seasons for copulation. Part III then examined the physiology of reproduction, adjudicating between rival embryological theories. And the last part broached some of the wider social, legal and religious issues arising out of love, sex and the family – including divorce on grounds of impotency, the supposed effects of witchcraft upon sexual capacity, heredity, monsters, hermaphrodites, and so forth. Like other writers, indeed influencing them, Venette developed an approach notable for its medicalizing tendency. Not surprisingly but surely very significantly, the routinization of sexual discourse at this time proceeded within the categories of the organic, or what would later be called the normal and the pathological. Perhaps because of this naturalistic, biological orientation, the trend-setting guidebooks endorsed and projected a rather upbeat, hedonistic philosophy.[52] Both Venette's *Tableau de l'amour conjugal* and *Aristotle's Master-Piece* assumed that, properly conducted, coitus ought to be a source of pleasure and well-being. Venette regarded libido as a barometer of bodily and spiritual health, and sexual performance as in itself therapeutic: 'There is nothing in the world more refreshing to those that are bilious than the caresses of women'.[53] Copulation was also a remedy for melancholy, hysteria and the green sickness (chlorosis). In short, 'there is no surer or safer means to preserve Health and avoid a sudden death than now and then to take a frisk with a woman'.[54] Such views were commonly expressed in the language of Enlightenment. 'The Venereal Act ... when it is performed in obedience to nature,' argued Robert Wallace, is 'highly delightful', while Erasmus Darwin insisted that 'animal attraction' was 'the purest source of human felicity; the cordial drop in the otherwise vapid cup of life'.[55] And to implement their meliorism, the sex manuals offered practical advice for overcoming obstacles. 'I knew a very lusty Man that married a very small Woman,' noted Marten in his *Gonosologium*, and by means of his *Yards* being of almost the longest Size, his Wife could not suffer him to have to do with her without a great deal of Pain; it was large as well as long, which largeness was judged, by a Physician or two they both apply'd to, to be the cause of that uneasiness, and order'd him Stiptick and Astringent Fomentations to reduce it, but in vain; he apply'd himself to me, and told me his Case, I presently apprehended 'twas the length of it that did the mischief, and to remedy it only advis'd him, from the Ingenious *Venette*, to make a hole through a piece of Cork, lin'd with Cotton on both sides of about an Inch and a half in thickness, and put his *Yard* through the hole, fastning the Cork with strings round his Waste, whenever he carress'd his Wife, which he did, and she never complain'd afterwards, but conceiv'd and had several Children, tho' before had been marry'd four Years, and never conceiv'd in all that time . . . As for the bigness of a Man's *Yard*, it very rarely happens that any Woman complains of it, or is any ways incommoded by it.[56]

We hear, superficially at least, a certain modern ring, even down to the macho braggadocio. But, as close attention to this passage reveals — for instance, its pronatalism — it would be wrong for us to presume too close an affinity between these early eighteenth-century sentiments and our erotic universe. The sexual mores of three centuries ago must not be elided with our own. After all, as earlier discussion of Foucault indicated, even the seemingly elemental components of the sexual economy are not timeless. As is made abundantly clear in works like Rudolf Dekker and Lotte Van de Pol's *The Tradition of Female Transvestism in Early Modern Europe* (1988), or Thomas Laqueur's *Making Sex* (1990),[57] early modern conceptions even of maleness and femaleness and their affiliations are poles apart from our own. So, it seems right to ask: what was sex in the eyes of the manuals?

Sex was to obey a value-system and a scheme of activity that — as the quotation from Marten indicates — prioritized a social economy of procreation. Without exception, the sex that was correct and approved according to the early modern manuals was coitus between conjugally bonded men and women, sex likely to culminate in the making of babies. Such erotic activity was perfectly epitomized in the short title of the English translation of Venette's work: *Conjugal Love; or, The Pleasures of the Marriage Bed*. Sex was pleasurable, but Nature had made it pleasurable because her design lay in the perpetuation of the species. According to *Aristotle's Master-Piece*, marriage had been instituted in Paradise as the hallowed vehicle for peopling the world. *Aristotle's Master-Piece* carried a pronatalist message unambiguously in favour of early nuptials and hostile to impediments to matrimony.[58]

Sexual activities were thus approved or rejected precisely in so far as they were liable to produce legitimate offspring. It goes without saying, therefore, that same-sex coitus was unequivocally disapproved. In the *Oeconomy of Love: A Poetical Essay* (1736), John Armstrong denounced what he regarded as the pernicious drift towards homosexuality:

> But in these vicious Days great Nature's Laws
> Are spurned; eternal Virtue, which nor Time,
> Nor Place can change, nor Custom changing all,
> Is mocked to scorn; and lewd Abuse instead,
> Daughter of the Night, her shameless Revels holds
> O'er half the Globe, which the chaste face of Day
> Eclipses at her Rites. For Man with Man,
> And Man with Woman (monstrous to relate!)
> Leaving the natural Road, themselves debase
> With Deeds unseemly, and Dishonour foul.
> Britons, for shame! Be Male and Female still.
> Banish this foreign Vice; it grows not here,
> It dies neglected; and in Clime so chaste
> Cannot but by forc'd Cultivation thrive.[59]

It is entirely characteristic of British sexual moralists to assume that gay sex is a perversion introduced by foreigners.[60]

Equally powerful, as we have seen, was the interdiction against masturbation, a practice judged to reduce capacity for fruitful coitus. One of the points most trenchantly made throughout *Onania* was that self-pollution must be evil because the sole lawful goal of sex was procreation: 'the Inclinations ... were given us for the continuance of our Species, and no other End'.[61]

And so, even within heterosexual coitus, positions and practices were to be ranked according to the probability of pregnancy. Herein lay the justification or rationalization for the rejection of sex with the woman on top. Any possible children of such unions, Venette warned, were likely to be 'Dwarfs, Cripples, Hunch-back'd, Squint ey'd, and stupid Blockheads, and by their Imperfections would fully evidence the irregular Life of their Parents, without putting us to the trouble to search the Cause of such Defects any further'.[62] And utterly inadmissible was oral or anal sex. In his *A Treatise of all the Symptoms of the Venereal Disease*, Marten explained that sex performed 'by a Man's putting his erected *Penis*, into another Persons ... Mouth, using Friction, &c. between the Lips' was 'so very Beastly and so much to be abhorr'd, as to cause at the mentioning or but thinking of it, the utmost detestation, and loathing'.[63]

Not least, practices with abortive or contraceptive tendencies or intentions were roundly condemned, notably *coitus interruptus*. *Aristotle's Master-Piece* made censorious reference to couples 'that desire not to have children and yet are very fond of nocturnal embraces'.⁶⁴ And certain editions of *Onania* included a letter from a man with a large brood, who, because of destitution, was limiting family size through the withdrawal method. This was wholly condemned by the author, who reproved 'Married Persons, who commit a heinous Sin to God, by frustrating what he has appointed for the Multiplication of our Species'.

> They indulge themselves in all the Pleasures of Sense, and yet would avoid the Charges they might occasion; in order to which they do what they can to hinder Conception. What I mean is, when the Man, by a criminal untimely Retreat, disappoints his Wife's as well as his own Fertility. This is what truly may be call'd a Frustraneous Abuse of their Bodies, and must be an abominable Sin. Yet it is certain, that Thousands there are in the Married State, who provoke and gratify their Lust, as far as is consistent with this their destructive Purpose, and no farther.⁶⁵

There were, of course, emphatic religious, moralistic and medical reasons for these erotic prejudices. But wider social imperatives were also, it must be stressed, in operation. Depopulation was the dread of mercantilist policy-makers in early modern Europe. Manpower had to be maintained for military, strategic and economic ends. We may assume – we have just seen the evidence – that certain poor or prudent couples were less than enthusiastic about producing unlimited families, or maybe about starting families at all; especially thanks to Angus McLaren's distinguished recent studies, we have become better aware of the wide range of prophylactic measures then practised.⁶⁶ In such circumstances, it is not surprising that propaganda stipulated the correct wedding of sexual pleasure with social responsibility. A deluge of pamphlets appeared in Britain around 1700, designed to counter the antipathy to matrimony developing, it was said, not least amongst women. Numerous books like *Marriage Promoted in a Discourse Of Its Ancient and Modern Practice, Both under Heathen and Christian Common-Wealths. Together with their Laws and Encouragements for its Observance* (1690)⁶⁷ carried messages echoing those of the manuals: marriage was the institution that united love, sex and conjugality; sex outside marriage was unsatisfactory, leading to sterility and disease. And if hesitations were entertained about matrimony, these could be smoothed away by the promise of a blissful bed life. Venette similarly argued that humans were moved by a double drive: sexual appetites and the passion of love. The rite that united them was marriage. Father of twelve children, Venette was frank and worldly-wise about the throb of the flesh: 'Conjugal caresses are the ties of love in matrimony ... they make up the essence thereof.'[68] Nearly a century later, the Scottish sex-advice author, James Graham, deplored the alleged national descent into luxury and depopulation. To counter this, it was everyone's duty, as a human, as a Briton, to marry and reproduce, for 'the most important business of everything in the animal creation', he judged, 'is to propagate the number of its species'. Such views obviously grew more problematic after Malthus.[69]

This whistle-stop tour of the sex-advice literature of three centuries ago – it has omitted major topics, like the construal of gender[70] – has raised, I wish to suggest in conclusion, issues of general relevance for the history of sexual knowledge. First, the problem of text and context in time. The sex manuals I have been surveying crystallized around the turn of the eighteenth century. One can see reasons for that. Print culture had been growing; in the early Enlightenment the dictates of the churches were ripe for challenge; medicine was gaining authority, while some of the characteristic anxieties of bourgeois society were beginning to surface. The books discussed – notably the *Tableau de l'amour conjugal* and *Aristotle's Master-Piece* – remained in print for well over two centuries. During that period, sundry alterations were made to their texts, long, of course, after the death of the author – though, medico-scientifically speaking, they were certainly not kept up to date. Hence something paradoxical seems to have been afoot. For some reason, the sexual knowledge people were acquiring through print, in the eighteenth and nineteenth centuries, was old-fashioned. Why? Was that the way people wanted it? Did the name of Aristotle give legitimacy or respectability? Did the antiquated air of such books help validate them with censors? These questions have hardly begun to be addressed. To progress further, we need to bring to bear all the best insights of the '*livre et société*' school of history, the techniques of the history of reading pioneered by Roger Chartier and Robert Darnton, and to learn from existing studies of chapbooks and fairy tales: how far were the uses of sex literature mythic?[71]

Second, and an obviously related question, that of reading itself. A great merit of the critical literary theory of the last twenty years has been to teach us the need for subtler techniques with texts. This is patent in the case of the handbooks here under consideration. They were often anonymous or pseudonymous, and they were revised, obviously by some publisher's hack, through successive scissors-and-paste editions. We generally know nothing of the author's intentions. Equally, because of the somewhat shameful nature of their subject-matter, we are ignorant about how they were actually read or used, beyond the crude fact that some of those I have mentioned sold and sold and sold, and so must have answered *some* want in the public.[72]

In particular, we need to be sensitive to profound ambiguities, to conspiratorial and collusive double-meanings and double-readings, to ways the texts may not be saying what they mean, or meaning what they say. These works uniformly protested their high-mindedness. But were they written as smut? Were they sold as smut? Were they read as smut? Did they primarily trade on the taboo? Such is the interpretation that has forcefully been advanced by Peter Wagner. In 'The Veil of Science and Morality: Some Pornographic Aspects of the ONANIA', he has contended that this genre of work had a hidden agenda and should be construed as concealed pornography: 'the hidden aim in every case', he argues, 'was the sexual stimulation of the reader'. In other words, anti-masturbation literature, like *L'Escholle des filles* for Pepys, was literature with which to masturbate.[73]

In a parallel manner, it may be argued that the advice literature was meant to be read, or at least *was* read, via exercises in reversal. Such texts formed instruction manuals in the forbidden. Angus McLaren has particularly observed the helpful interdictions that fill the manuals. *Aristotle's Master-Piece* cautioned husbands not to withdraw too rapidly; women were advised to lie still after coition and in particular to avoid sneezing. Why? Because all such acts would hinder pregnancy. Venette listed the coital postures to be avoided because they were unlikely to lead to conception. Was not all this a veiled form of contraceptive guidance? Were these works then the devil's manuals? The questions are crucial, but the answers elude us. For we are confronted with a profound problem.[74]

Alongside the immemorial history of sex, print culture brought sex books into prominence. Thereafter people had sex, and people had sex books. Some had one, some had the other, some had both. The relations between writing sex books, reading sex books, and having sex are profoundly enigmatic, and subject to Shandeian regressions.[75]

For the fact of the matter is that Foucault was only half right in his demolition of the 'repressive hypothesis'. The crude hypothesis is false; there was, as he stressed, ever more writing about sex, writings that were rarely wholly banned. Nevertheless, Foucault was misleading on another issue. For, in a certain regard, sex was indeed comprehensively silenced. Despite all the coitus going on, despite all the copies of erotica in circulation, our hard evidence about the sexual lives, thoughts and feelings of Europeans in 1650, 1750 or 1850 remains pathetically meagre, because it was a domain of life that was furtive and shameful, as was the body itself, whose fragmented past is only now being pieced together. Hundreds of British working-class autobiographies survive from this period, but hardly any mention sex.[76] On the positive side, we do have the texts I have been discussing. We must never mistake texts for people; but texts, properly read, can illuminate. And on the positive side, over the last generation, social historians have been rediscovering the history of the silenced, the micro-realities of the dynamics of gender, of parents and children, family and household, masters and servants, probing the interpersonal complexities of struggle and collusion, duplicity and complicity, control and resistance, individuation and stereotyping, socialization and difference. Richer histories of private life, of popular culture, of life-style, of representations, are being constructed, histories from below that avoid the trivialities of traditional social history – history with the politics left out – and assume significance by being alert to culture and gender conflict, the construction of the self, the production and reproduction of power relations, and, not least, the capacity of language and symbols to define reality.[77] One dimension this new social history can reclaim is sexuality.

NOTES

1 Good evidence is offered by the new *Journal of the History of Sexuality*, and, to name just a few books, Frank Mort, *Dangerous Sexualities: Medical–Moral Politics in England* (London: Routledge and Kegan Paul, 1987); Alan Bray, *Homosexuality in Renaissance England* (London: Gay Men's Press, 1982); Jeffrey Weeks, *Sex, Politics and Society: The Regulation of Sexuality since 1800* (London: Longman, 1981); idem, *Sexuality and its Discontents: Meanings, Myths and Modern Sexualities* (London: Routledge and Kegan Paul, 1985); Lawrence Birken, *Consuming Desire: Sexual Science and the Emergence of a Culture of Abundance, 1871–1914* (Ithaca and London: Cornell University Press, 1989). Excellent recent feminist studies include Ludmilla Jordanova, *Sexual Visions. Images of Gender in Science and Medicine between the Eighteenth and Twentieth Centuries* (London: Harvester Wheatsheaf, 1989); Lynne Nead, *Myths of Sexuality: Representations of Women in Victorian Britain* (Oxford: Basil Blackwell, 1988); Cynthia Eagle Russett, *Sexual Science. The Victorian Construction of Womanhood* (Cambridge, Mass.: Harvard University Press, 1989); Londa Schiebinger, *The Mind Has No Sex? Women in the Origins of Modern Science* (Cambridge, Mass.: Harvard University Press, 1989); Elaine Showalter, *The Female Malady: Women, Madness and English Culture 1830–1980* (London: Virago, 1987).

2 In this category we might place popular works such as Gordon Rattray Taylor, *Sex in History* (New York: Vanguard, 1954); Reay Tannahill, *Sex in*

History (New York: Stein and Day, 1980); and Wayland Young, *Eros Denied. Sex in Western Society* (New York: Grove, 1964). Such works depend heavily upon the researches of early twentieth-century sexologists such as Iwan Bloch, for whom see, for instance, *The Sexual Life of Our Time*, trans. M. Eden Paul (London: Rebman, 1909); idem, *Sex Life in England Illustrated: As Revealed in its Obscene Literature and Art*, trans. Richard Deniston (New York: Falstaff, 1934); idem, *Sexual Life in England Past and Present*, trans. William H. Forstern (London: Arco, 1958); idem, *A History of English Sexual Morals*, trans. W. H. Fostern (London: Francis Aldon, 1938).

3 Peter Gay, *The Bourgeois Experience – Victoria to Freud*, vol. I: *Education of the Senses* (New York: Oxford University Press, 1984); idem, *The Bourgeois Experience – Victoria to Freud*, vol. II: *The Tender Passion* (New York: Oxford University Press, 1986); idem, 'Victorian Sexuality: Old Texts and New Insights', *American Scholar*, 49 (1980), 372–7; Steven Marcus, *The Other Victorians: A Study of Sexuality and Pornography in Mid-Nineteenth Century England* (New York: Basic, 1964); Carl N. Degler, 'What Ought to Be and What Was: Women's Sexuality in the Nineteenth Century', *American Historical Review*, 79 (1974), 1467–90; Wendell Stacy Johnson, *Living in Sin: The Victorian Sexual Revolution* (Chicago: Nelson-Hall, 1979); F. Barry Smith, 'Sexuality in Britain, 1800–1900: Some Suggested Revisions', in Martha Vicinus (ed.), *A Widening Sphere: Changing Roles of Victorian Women* (Bloomington: Indiana University Press, 1977), 182–98.

4 Lawrence Stone, *Uncertain Unions. Marriage in England 1660–1753* (Oxford: Clarendon Press, 1992).

5 See, for instance, Aline Rousselle, *Porneia: On Desire and the Body in Antiquity*, trans. Felicia Pheasant (New York: Basil Blackwell, 1988); Peter Brown, *The Body and Society. Men, Women and Sexual Renunciation in Early Christianity* (London: Faber, 1989).

6 Michel Foucault, *Histoire de la sexualité*, vol. I: *La Volonté de savoir* (Paris: Gallimard, 1976); trans. Robert Hurley, *The History of Sexuality: Introduction* (London: Allen Lane, 1978); idem, vol. II: *L'Usage des plaisirs* (Paris: Gallimard, 1984); trans. Robert Hurley, *The Use of Pleasure* (New York: Random House, 1985); idem, vol. III: *Le Souci de soi* (Paris: Gallimard, 1984); trans. Robert Hurley, *The Care of the Self* (New York: Random House, 1987); vol. IV: *Les Aveux de la chair*, announced by Gallimard, remained unfinished. For some discussion, see Roy Porter, 'Is Foucault Useful for Understanding Eighteenth and Nineteenth Century Sexuality?', *Contention*, 1 (1991), 61–82.

7 For studies of a reflective, critical and philosophical nature that deal with the interface of writing and sexuality, see F. Barker, *The Tremulous Private Body* (London: Methuen, 1984); Michael Worton and Judith Still (eds.), *Textuality and Sexuality. Reading Theories and Practices* (Manchester: Manchester University Press, 1993).

8 For a popular introduction, see David Loth, *The Erotic in Literature: A Historical Survey of Pornography as Delightful as it is Indiscreet* (London: Secker and Warburg, [1961]/1962); Alan Bold (ed.), *The Sexual Dimension in Literature* (Totowa, N. J.: Barnes and Noble, 1983).

9 For some discussion of the ambiguities of the genre of popularized knowledge,

see the Introduction to Roy Porter (ed.), *The Popularization of Medicine, 1650–1850* (London: Routledge, 1992); Elizabeth Eisenstein, *The Printing Press as an Agent of Change: Communications and Cultural Transformations in Early-Modern Europe*, 2 vols. (Cambridge: Cambridge University Press, 1979).

10 For such complexities see Jay Mechling, 'Advice to Historians on Advice to Mothers', *Journal of Social History*, 10 (1975–76), 44–63.

11 Mary F. Wack, *Lovesickness in the Middle Ages: The 'Viaticum' and its Commentaries* (Philadelphia: University of Pennsylvania Press, 1990); Robert Burton, *Anatomy of Melancholy*, ed. Floyd Dell and Paul Jordan-Smith (New York: Tudor Publishing Co., 1948; Oxford: John Lichfield, 1621); Jacques Ferrand, *A Treatise on Lovesickness*, trans. and ed. Donald A. Beecher and Massimo Ciavolella, 1st edn (Syracuse, New York: Syracuse University Press, 1990); Joannes Sinibaldus, *Geneanthropeiae, sive de hominis generatione decateuchon* (Rome: Caballus, 1642).

12 See discussion in Roy Porter, 'Love, Sex and Medicine: Nicolas Venette and his *Tableau de l'amour conjugal*', in Peter Wagner (ed.), *Erotica and the Enlightenment* (Frankfurt: Lang, 1990), 90–122; idem, 'Spreading Carnal Knowledge or Selling Dirt Cheap? Nicolas Venette's *Tableau de l'amour conjugal* in Eighteenth-Century England', *Journal of European Studies*, 14 (1984), 233–55.

13 See Roy Porter, '"The Secrets of Generation Display'd": *Aristotle's Master-piece* in Eighteenth-Century England', in R. P. Maccubbin (ed.), *Unauthorized Sexual Behaviour during the Enlightenment (Special Issue of Eighteenth Century Life)*, NS 3 (May 1985), 1–21; Otho T. Beall Jr, '*Aristotle's Masterpiece* in America: A Landmark in the Folklore of Medicine', *William and Mary Quarterly*, 20 (1963), 207–22; Janet Blackman, 'Popular Theories of Generation: The Evolution of *Aristotle's Works*: The Study of an Anachronism', in John Woodward and David Richards (eds), *Health Care and Popular Medicine in Nineteenth-Century England: Essays in the Social History of Medicine* (London: Croom Helm, 1977), 56–88; D'Arcy Power, 'Aristotle's Masterpiece', *The Foundation of Medical History*, Lecture vi (Baltimore, Md.: William and Wilkins Co., 1931); Thomas H. Johnson, 'Jonathan Edwards and the "Young Folks' Bible"', *The New England Quarterly*, 5 (1932), 37–54.

14 Alan Rusbridger, *A Concise History of the Sex Manual, 1886–1986* (London and Boston: Faber and Faber, 1986).

15 Foucault, *The History of Sexuality*, vol. 1, *Introduction*, 23.

16 Samuel Pepys, *Diary*, 9 February 1668.

17 For agonizings over authorship, see John W. Saunders, *The Profession of English Letters* (London: Routledge and Kegan Paul/ Toronto: Toronto University Press, 1964).

18 For discussion of the history of the idea of forbidden knowledge, see Jean Delumeau, *Sin and Fear. The Emergence of a Western Guilt Culture, 13th–18th Centuries* (New York: St Martin's Press, 1990).

19 For Grub Street, see Pat Rogers, *Grub Street: Studies in a Subculture* (London: Methuen, 1972); Philip Pinkus, *Grub Street Stripped Bare* (London: Constable, 1980); and above all Peter Wagner, *Eros Revived: Erotica in the Age of Enlightenment* (London: Secker and Warburg, 1986).

20 John Marten, *Gonosologium novum: or, a New System of all the Secret Infirmities and*

Diseases, Natural, Accidental, and Venereal in Men and Women, 6th edn (London: Crouch, 1709), A3.
21 John Marten, *A Treatise of all the Symptoms of the Venereal Disease, in both Sexes . . .* (London: S. Crouch, 1709), xxxiii.
22 W. Buchan, *Observations Concerning the Prevention and Cure of the Venereal Disease* (London: Printed for T. Chapman, Fleet Street, and Mudie and Sons, Edinburgh, 1796), i–ii, xvi.
23 Ibid., 3.
24 Nicholas Venette, *Conjugal Love; Or, The Pleasures of The Marriage Bed Considered. In Several Lectures On Human Generation.* From the French of Venette, 20 edn (London: Printed for the Booksellers, 1750), iii.
25 This was a line still convenient in Freud's day. Justifying his sexually explicit interrogation of 'Dora', Freud riposted, 'There is never any danger of corrupting an inexperienced girl. For where there is no knowledge of sexual processes even in the unconscious, no hysterical symptom will arise; and where hysteria is found, there can be no longer any question of "innocence of mind" in the sense in which parents and educators use the phrase': Sigmund Freud, 'Fragment of the Analysis of a Case of Hysteria', in *The Standard Edition of the Complete Psychological Works of Sigmund Freud*, vol. VII trans. and ed. James Strachey et al. (London: Hogarth Press and the Institute of Psycho-Analysis, 1953–74), 1–122, p. 49.
26 *Onania, Or the Heinous Sin of Self-Pollution, And all its frightful Consequences, in both Sexes, Consider'd with Spiritual and Physical Advice to those, who have already injur'd themselves by this abominable practice. And seasonable Admonition to the Youth of the Nation, [of both Sexes] and those whose Tuition they are under, whether Parents, Guardians, Masters, or Mistresses.* The Eighth Edition, Corrected, and Enlarg'd to almost as much again, as particulariz'd at the End of the Preface; and are all the Additions, that will be made to this Book, how often ever it may come to be Reprinted, 130–2.
27 Venette, *Conjugal Love; Or, The Pleasures of The Marriage Bed Considered*, 111.
28 S.-A.-A.-D. Tissot, *Onanism: or, a Treatise upon the Disorders produced by Masturbation: or, the Dangerous Effects of Secret and Excessive Venery*. By M. Tissot, MD Fellow of the Royal Society of London. Member of the Medico-Physical Society of Basle, and of the Oeconomical Society of Berne. Translated from the last Paris edition By A. Hume. (London: printed for the translator, sold by J. Pridden, 1761); See on Tissot Ludmilla Jordanova, 'The Popularisation of Medicine: Tissot on Onanism', *Textual Practice*, 1 (1987), 68–80.
29 See Robert H. MacDonald, 'The Frightful Consequences of Onanism: Notes on the History of a Delusion', *Journal of the History of Ideas*, 28 (1967), 423–31; J. Stengers and A. Van Neck, *Histoire d'une grande peur: la masturbation* (Brussels: University of Brussels Press, 1984); Tristram Engelhardt, 'The Disease of Masturbation: Values and Concept of Disease', *Bulletin of the History of Medicine* 48 (1974), 234–48; E. H. Hare, 'Masturbatory Insanity: The History of an Idea', *Journal of Mental Science*, 108 (1962), 1–25.
30 Consult Thomas Laqueur, 'The Social Evil, the Solitary Vice and Pouring Tea', in M. Feher (ed.), *Fragments for a History of the Human Body*, vol. III (New York: Zone, 1989), 334–65.

31 *Onania, Or the Heinous Sin of Self-Pollution*, 8th edn, 3.
32 Ibid., A/A.
33 Ibid., A/A.
34 Ibid., A/A.
35 Ibid., A/A.
36 Ibid., 3.
37 Ibid., 3.
38 Ibid., 4.
39 Ibid., A/A.
40 Ibid., A/A.
41 Ibid., A/A.
42 Marten, *Gonosologium novum*, A4v.
43 Tissot, *Onanism*, 4.
44 Ludmilla Jordanova, 'The Popularisation of Medicine: Tissot on Onanism', *Textual Practice*, 1 (1987), 68-80.
45 *Onania, Or the Heinous Sin of Self-Pollution*, 8th edn, chapter 2, opening.
46 Venette, *Conjugal Love; Or, The Pleasures of The Marriage Bed Considered*, 26.
47 *Onania, Or the Heinous Sin of Self-Pollution*, 8th edn, 3.
48 Jean Frédéric Osterwald, *Traité contre l'impureté* (Amsterdam: T. Lombrail, 1707; translated into English 1708 as *The Nature of Uncleanness Consider'd . . . to which is added A Discourse Concerning the Nature of Chastity and the Means of Obtaining it*, London: R. Bonwicke, 1708).
49 *Onania, Or the Heinous Sin of Self-Pollution*, 8th edn, 4.
50 Quoted in ibid., 5.
51 Venette, *Conjugal Love; Or, The Pleasures of The Marriage Bed Considered*, 114.
52 For wider contextualization, see Roy Porter, 'Sex and the Enlightenment in Britain', in P.-G. Boucé (ed.), *Sexuality in Eighteenth-Century Britain* (Manchester: Manchester University Press, 1982), 1-27; especially Angus McLaren, *Reproductive Rituals: The Perception of Fertility in England from the Sixteenth to the Nineteenth Century* (London and New York: Methuen, 1984).
53 Venette, *Conjugal Love; Or, The Pleasures of The Marriage Bed Considered*, 141.
54 Ibid., 147.
55 Porter, 'Sex and the Enlightenment in Britain', 8f.
56 Marten, *Gonosologium novum*, 16.
57 Rudolf M. Dekker and Lotte C. Van de Pol, *The Tradition of Female Transvestism in Early Modern Europe* (New York/London: Macmillan, 1988); Thomas W. Laqueur, *Making Sex. Gender and the Body from Aristotle to Freud* (Cambridge, Mass.: Harvard University Press, 1990).
58 The pronatalist implications are stressed in Roy Porter, '"The Secrets of Generation Display'd": *Aristotle's Master-piece* in Eighteenth-Century England', in R. P. Maccubbin (ed.), *Unauthorized Sexual Behaviour during the Enlightenment* [*Special Issue of Eighteenth Century Life*], NS 3 (May 1985), 1-21.
59 John Armstrong, *The Economy of Love*, 3rd edn (London: T. Cooper, 1739), quoted in McLaren, *Reproductive Rituals*, 80.
60 For contemporary views of homosexuality see Alan Bray, *Homosexuality in Renaissance England* (London: Gay Men's Press, 1982); Richard Davenport Hines, *Sex, Death and Punishment. Attitudes to Sex and Sexuality in Britain since the*

Renaissance (London: Collins, 1989); Paul-Gabriel Boucé, 'Aspects of Sexual Tolerance and Intolerance in Eighteenth-Century England', *British Journal for Eighteenth-Century Studies*, 3 (1980), 173–89; D. A. Coward, 'Attitudes to Homosexuality in Eighteenth-Century France', *Journal of European Studies*, 10 (1980), 231–55; Randolph Trumbach, 'London's Sodomites: Homosexual Behavior and Western Culture in the Eighteenth Century', *Journal of Social History*, 11 (1977), 1–33; Robert P. Maccubbin (ed.), *Unauthorized Sexual Behavior during the Enlightenment* (Williamsburg, Va.: College of William and Mary, 1985).

61 *Onania, Or the Heinous Sin of Self-Pollution*, 8th edn, 87.

62 Roy Porter, 'Love, Sex and Medicine: Nicolas Venette and his *Tableau de l'amour conjugal*', in Peter Wagner (ed.), *Erotica and the Enlightenment* (Frankfurt: Lang, 1990), 90–122, p. 119.

63 Marten, *A Treatise of all the Symptoms of the Venereal Disease, in both Sexes*, 68.

64 *Aristotle's Master-piece* (12th edn: undated, but early eighteenth century), 39; see the discussion in Angus McLaren, *Reproductive Rituals*, 80.

65 *Onania, Or the Heinous Sin of Self-Pollution*, 8th edn, 100.

66 McLaren, *Reproductive Rituals*; idem, *History of Contraception* (Oxford: Basil Blackwell, 1990); see also John D'Emilio and Estelle B. Freedman, *Intimate Matters: A History of Sexuality in America* (New York: Harper and Row, 1988); Rosalind Mitchison and Leah Leneman, *Sexuality and Social Control: Scotland 1660–1780* (Oxford: Basil Blackwell, 1989); J.-L. Flandrin, *Families in Former Times: Kinship, Household and Sexuality*, trans. Richard Southern (Cambridge: Cambridge University Press, 1976).

67 [?R. Baldwin], *Marriage Promoted in a Discourse Of Its Ancient and Modern Practice, Both under Heathen and Christian Common-Wealths. Together with their Laws and Encouragements for its Observance. By a Person of Quality* (London: Printed for Richard Baldwin, near the *Black-Bull* in the *Old-Bayly*. 1690).

68 Nicholas Venette, *The Mysteries of Conjugal Love Reveal'd*, done into English by a Gentleman (London, no publisher, 1712), 80.

69 James Graham, *Lecture on the Generation, Increase and Improvement of the Human Species* (London: M. Smith, 1780), 3.

70 See, for instance, R. W. Connell, *Gender and Power: Society, the Person and Sexual Politics* (Cambridge: Polity Press, 1987).

71 R. Darnton, 'The High Enlightenment and the Low-Life of Literature in Pre-revolutionary France', *Past and Present*, 51 (1971), 81–115; repr. in his *The Literary Underground of the Old Regime* (Cambridge, Mass.: Harvard University Press, 1982), 1–40; idem, *The Great Cat Massacre and other Episodes in French Cultural History* (New York: Basic Books, 1984; repr. Harmondsworth: Penguin, 1985); R. Darnton and Daniel Roche (eds.), *Revolution in Print: The Press in France 1775–1800* (Berkeley: University of California Press, 1989); Roger Chartier, *Cultural History. Between Practices and Representations* (Ithaca: Cornell University Press, 1988; Cambridge: Polity Press, 1989); Isabel Rivers (ed.), *Books and their Readers in Eighteenth-Century England* (Leicester: Leicester University Press, 1982).

72 See Mary Fissell, 'Readers, Texts and Contexts: Vernacular Medical Works in Early Modern England', in Roy Porter (ed.), *The Popularization of Medicine,*

1650–1850 (London: Routledge, 1992), 72–96 and the items referred to in the footnotes.

73 See the excellent writings of Peter Wagner: 'The Pornographer in the Courtroom; Trial Reports about Cases of Sexual Crimes and Delinquencies as a Genre of Eighteenth-Century Erotica', in P. G. Boucé (ed.), *Sexuality in Eighteenth-Century Britain* (Manchester: Manchester University Press, 1982), 120–40; *idem*, 'Researching the Taboo: Sexuality and Eighteenth-Century Erotica', *Eighteenth-Century Life*, 3 (1983), 108–15; *idem*, 'The Veil of Science and Mortality: Some Pornographic Aspects of the ONANIA', *British Journal for Eighteenth-Century Studies*, 4 (1983), 179–84; *idem*, *Eros Revived: Erotica in the Age of Enlightenment* (London: Secker and Warburg, 1986); *idem*, 'The Discourse on Sex – or Sex as Discourse: Eighteenth-Century Medical and Paramedical Erotica', in George S. Rousseau and Roy Porter (eds.), *Sexual Underworlds of the Enlightenment* (Manchester: University of Manchester Press, 1987), 46–68; *idem*, *Eros Revived: Erotica of the Enlightenment in England and America* (London: Secker and Warburg, 1988).

74 McLaren, *Reproductive Rituals*.

75 Roy Porter, '"The Whole Secret of Health": Mind, Body and Medicine in *Tristram Shandy*', in John Christie and Sally Shuttleworth (eds.), *Nature Transfigured* (Manchester: Manchester University Press, 1989), 61–84.

76 David Vincent, 'Love and Death and the Nineteenth-Century Working Class', *Social History*, 5 (1980), 223–47.

77 Peter Burke (ed.), *New Perspectives on Historical Writing* (Cambridge: Polity Press, 1991).

SEVEN

THE ECLIPSE OF SEXUAL SELECTION
THEORY

SIMON J. FRANKEL[1]

IN OCTOBER 1922, Julian S. Huxley, grandson of Thomas Henry Huxley and himself one of the most well-known and influential biologists of this century, delivered a paper entitled 'Sex Biology and Sex Psychology' to the British Society for Sex Psychology.[2] At the time, Huxley was probably the pre-eminent authority on – and most vocal critic of – Charles Darwin's theory of sexual selection, the concept that, in many species of animals, competition among males for reproductive access to females has resulted in significant evolutionary developments, especially among males. This theory, set out at length in Darwin's 1871 work, *The Descent of Man, and Selection in Relation to Sex*,[3] provided a powerful stimulus for the development of the emerging discipline of sexology in the decades around 1900.[4] Indeed, pioneering works such as Havelock Ellis's *Man and Woman: A Study of Secondary and Tertiary Sexual Characters* (1894) and *Studies in the Psychology of Sex*, the fourth volume of which was entitled *Sexual Selection in Man* (1905), can be seen as drawing on Darwin's work as a basis for the study of human sexuality.[5]

Sexual selection is now an active area of theoretical and empirical research in evolutionary biology. Yet ironically, while the outlines of Darwin's theory were contributing to emerging approaches to human sexuality, the early decades of this century witnessed the general rejection of sexual selection theory by naturalists. By the end of the 1930s, it was regarded by biologists as an insignificant evolutionary mechanism, and much of what Darwin had considered evidence of sexual selection was reinterpreted and explained as evidence supporting his theory of natural selection. This approach to sexual selection continued during both the 'eclipse of Darwinism'[6] early in this century and the formation of the evolutionary synthesis in the 1930s and 1940s.

Julian Huxley, one of the architects of the evolutionary synthesis, played a central role in the decline of the Darwinian concept of sexual selection. Although Huxley's approach to sexual selection can to some degree be attributed to his unflagging belief in the power and sufficiency of natural selection as a mechanism of evolution,[7] his extensive writings in this area strongly suggest that his attitudes concerning human sexuality deeply influenced his observations and conclusions regarding animal mating and evolution. Specifically, Huxley's clear preference for studying monogamous species, where sexual selection is generally less significant, and his doubts about the operation of female choice, which lies at the heart of sexual selection, contributed to his conclusion that sexual selection was a minor phenomenon in the natural world and that, to the degree that sexual selection was operative, it simply acted as a form of natural selection.

This chapter is not a survey of Julian Huxley's influence on evolutionary thinking, an account of the impact of Darwinian thinking on studies of human sexuality, or a full chronicle of the history of sexual selection theory since Darwin. Rather, it seeks to trace the treatment of sexual selection theory early in this century, particularly in the investigations and writings of Julian Huxley.

DARWIN'S THEORY OF SEXUAL SELECTION AND THE RESPONSE OF WALLACE

Darwin formulated his theory of sexual selection to account for two major phenomena not explained by his theory of natural selection: differences in form between males and females within a species, or sexual dimorphism, and, associated with this, the persistence of characters, particularly in males, which appear to be disadvantageous, hindering survival. He had touched on the question of explaining these phenomena in the *Origin of Species*, where he noted that

> what I call Sexual Selection ... depends, not on a struggle for existence, but on a struggle between the males for possession of the females; the result is not death to the unsuccessful competitor, but few or no offspring ... The war is, perhaps, severest between the males of polygamous animals ... sexual selection will often have largely modified the external characters of animals having a will, to give one male an advantage in fighting with another or in charming the females.[8]

Using his analogy with artificial selection, Darwin remarked, 'if a man can in a short time give elegant carriage and beauty to his bantams, according to his standard of beauty, I can see no good reason to doubt that female birds, by selecting, during thousands of generations, the most melodious or beautiful males, according to their standard of beauty, might produce a marked effect.'[9] Darwin used the term 'secondary sexual' for those characters which resulted from this selective process.

Twelve years later, in his *Descent of Man, and Selection in Relation to Sex*, Darwin elaborated at length on this evolutionary mechanism, which, as he explained, 'depends on the advantage which certain individuals have over other individuals of the same sex and species, in exclusive relation to reproduction'.[10] Sexual selection was, he noted, 'an extremely complex affair, depending, as it does, on ardour in love, courage, and the rivalry of the males, and on the powers of perception, taste, and will of the female'.[11] Darwin divided 'the sexual struggle' into two categories: 'in the one it is between the individuals of the same sex, generally the male sex, in order to drive away or kill their rivals, the females remaining passive; whilst in the other, the struggle is likewise between the individuals of the same sex, in order to excite or charm those of the opposite sex, generally the females, which no longer remain passive, but select the more agreeable partners'.[12] Hence weapons such as antlers and horns evolved for combat between males in order to 'win' females, while ornaments and other features evolved for attracting females in order to mate; the classic example of the latter category is the stunning tail of the male peacock.

On the question of female choice, Darwin did not explain exactly why females of a given species prefer certain males, but he suggested that species have differing standards of beauty, not necessarily (though often) corresponding to human ones.[13] He suggested that there was a deliberate process of decision-making on the part of the female, noting that 'Sexual selection . . . implies the possession of considerable perceptive powers and of strong passions'.[14] Darwin asked, 'Does the male parade his charms with so much pomp and rivalry for no purpose? Are we not justified in believing that the female exerts a choice, and that she receives the addresses of the male who pleases her most? . . . [S]he is most excited or attracted by the most beautiful, or melodious, or gallant males'.[15] As one evolutionary biologist has recently noted, 'The bulk of Darwin's reasoning was directed at establishing that females actually demonstrated choice, and that mating was not left to chance or to the first suitor that approached the female'.[16]

In distinguishing sexual from natural selection, Darwin explained that 'Sexual selection depends on the success of certain individuals over others of the same sex in relation to the propagation of the species; whilst natural selection depends on the success of both sexes, at all ages, in relation to the general conditions of life'.[17] Significantly, features which help an organism in this struggle to inseminate may be unrelated to or indeed hinder it in its struggle to survive, and so be harmful to the species.[18] Darwin noted that 'the most refined beauty may serve as a charm for the female and for no other purpose'.[19] Hence the two selective processes may well work in opposing ways, as in the male bird's ornament which helps it to attract females but inhibits its ability to escape predators by flight or makes it more visible to predators. Or they may work together, as in the case of the prehensile organs of certain crustaceans which, Darwin suggested, originated to help the male hold onto the female during copulation in open waters.[20] While Darwin admitted that in many cases 'it is scarcely possible to distinguish between the effects of natural and sexual selection',[21] he clearly saw them as two distinct processes, with sexual selection centring on the male's ability to gain mating access to females.

The naturalist Alfred Russel Wallace at first cautiously accepted Darwin's concept of sexual selection, but he soon came to reject it as unworkable and unnecessary. Wallace was a vociferous advocate of the power and efficacy of natural selection, and so he had little room or need for sexual selection as another significant evolutionary mechanism. For twenty years, though most intensely in 1867 and 1868, Darwin and Wallace carried on a debate in their writings and correspondence over the origins of sexual dimorphism and the significance of sexual selection,[22] and some of Wallace's views are worth noting, for they were echoed by later naturalists.

Wallace opposed the theory on several grounds. He reasoned that the exaggerated colours and characters of males were the natural state, augmented by what he assumed to be the more active physiology of males in general; it was the absence of extravagant features in most females which must be explained. 'It seems a fair conclusion', Wallace argued, 'that colour *per se* may be considered to be normal, and to need no special accounting for; while the absence of colour or the prevalence of certain colours to the constant exclusion of others, must be traced, like other modifications in the economy of living things, to the needs of the species'.[23] Wallace suggested that drabness in females was favoured by natural selection because the females would otherwise be vulnerable to predators as they nested.[24] In addition, Wallace maintained that it was not possible for an animal without developed intelligence to make aesthetic choices, and so he virtually eliminated female choice. Female animals were not swayed by slight differences in plumage or colour (which they probably could not detect at all); if they were swayed at all between different suitors, it would be by those males which were more active and vigorous. But since these animals were already favoured in the struggle for existence, the effects of such female 'choice' would simply parallel those of natural selection, presumably without intensifying them. Similarly, Wallace believed that male competition for females would essentially parallel competition for food and other resources and so could be subsumed within natural selection.[25]

JULIAN HUXLEY AND THE ECLIPSE OF SEXUAL SELECTION

As John Durant has remarked, the theory of sexual selection had a 'rough ride' in the late nineteenth century and was generally not well received,[26] suffering from both neglect and attack in the decades around 1900.[27] In part, this was due to the emergence of a naturalist tradition, deriving from Wallace's approach and fully articulated by Edward Poulton, explaining all colour and its apparent use in terms of natural selection.[28] While Poulton, like Wallace, had some initial enthusiasm for the theory of sexual selection, he soon relegated it to being 'relatively unimportant' in evolution, and his influential writings emphasized the adaptive role of animal coloration in providing protection and species recognition.[29] More generally, perhaps, sexual selection, like bad stock in a bear market, suffered especially as natural selection went through a period of relative neglect.[30] The mutation theory of evolution, which enjoyed a vogue around the turn of the century, had little room for either natural or sexual selection. T. H. Morgan devoted a chapter of his influential *Evolution and Adaptation*, published in 1903, to suggesting that secondary sexual characters were actually the result of mutation.[31] Douglas Dewar and Frank Finn argued similarly, noting that 'it is absurd to credit birds with aesthetic tastes', especially since females simply yielded to more vigorous males.[32] Neo-Lamarckians such as Joseph T. Cunningham also rejected Darwin's explanation for secondary sexual characters,[33] as did some who favoured natural selection.[34] When the avid bird-watcher Edmund Selous presented his findings on avian courtship early in the century, he saw his support of the role of female choice as something of a 'rearguard action' against prevailing biological views. His observations showed that many, though not all, bird courtship antics played an important role in mate selection.[35] Though Selous's findings had some influence, notably on the early work of Julian Huxley, Selous's own obscurity among naturalists, the difficulty of his prose, and his habit of burying his conclusions amidst pages and pages of detailed field observations no doubt helped to minimize the impact of his writings.[36]

Indeed, it is a striking facet of the history of evolutionary theory that, while Selous and a few other naturalists continued to take sexual selection theory seriously as a framework for their field observations, the theory lost ground among the theoretical and experimental biologists who were coming to dominate the science. By the second decade of the century, extensive genetic experiments with *Drosophila* fruit flies were well under way, and some investigators applied their methods to Darwin's second theory. In 1915, A. H. Sturtevant, then working under T. H. Morgan in the famous 'fly room' at Columbia, published a paper on 'Experiments on Sex Recognition and the Problem of Sexual Selection in *Drosophila*', later regarded as one of the classics of early *Drosophila* work. Sturtevant's central experiment assessed the role of male wing-waving in the courting of females. In separate experiments, he found that males whose wings had been clipped had a lower chance of copulating with females than did normal males. However, if a female was placed in a vial with a normal male and a male whose wings had been clipped, she was equally likely to mate with either. Sturtevant concluded that the normal male's wing-waving actions 'made the female ready to copulate, but that she would then mate with either male'. He therefore denied that Darwinian female choice was exercised by fruit flies. '[T]he wings are of value in courtship,' he admitted, 'but the effect probably is to produce sexual excitement in the female, rather than to cause her to select a male that uses his wings. No "choice" is involved.' While noting that 'the effect, in nature, would be strongly in favor of the normal male', he concluded that 'sexual selection is not involved in any of these cases'.[37] Sturtevant did not reassess what was meant by 'choice' in an evolutionary context, nor did he recognize that female fruit flies were in practice preferring to mate with males possessing characters which stimulated them in a particular way. This was left to biologists decades later.[38] Instead, Sturtevant concluded that the females essentially had no flexibility in their mating. Sturtevant's conclusion that courtship was a primarily and unspecifically stimulative process in which 'neither sex exercises any "choice" in the selection of a mate'[39] was echoed by many biologists in the years that followed (particularly in the work of Julian Huxley, discussed below).

In a 1920 paper on hybridization between two species of *Drosophila*, Sturtevant suggested that a possible role for secondary sexual characteristics might be mate recognition as a 'means whereby the two species are kept from crossing' – that is, as an *inter*specific selective mechanism, rather than the explicitly *intra*specific process Darwin had described.[40] Sturtevant's mentor T. H. Morgan devoted a monograph of 1919 to *The Genetic and Operative Evidence Relating to Secondary Sexual Characters*. Far from the mutation theory he had espoused in 1903,[41] Morgan still opposed Darwin's explanation for secondary sexual characters, now attributing such characters to natural selection rather than to mutation. Even while noting that Darwinian 'choice' theoretically need not involve an 'aesthetic sense', Morgan agreed with Sturtevant that precopulatory displays by the male serve more to excite the female to copulate, rather than to mate with a particular male, and therefore had no relation to Darwinian sexual selection theory.[42] 'I can not but think', he declared, 'that at present we have a good deal to lose in the way of scientific procedure and nothing to gain of scientific value in accepting Darwin's interpretation of sexual selection based on the display of the male as furnishing an opportunity to the female to make the "best" selection amongst her suitors on the basis of his adornment.'[43]

Julian Huxley built on this *Drosophila* work in his widely influential studies on the courtship habits of birds. While it was not until the late 1930s that Huxley wrote on broad theoretical questions connected with Darwinian sexual selection, his own early fieldwork was very much connected with the theory. In general, his early work on bird courtship and sexual selection was marked by an emphasis on the progressive character of evolution, a tendency to reject Darwin's 'female choice' as a phenomenon rarely observed in the wild, and an emphasis on the efficacy and sufficiency of natural selection.

Before 1914, Huxley seems to have maintained some role for sexual selection along the lines suggested by Darwin. In a 1912 article on the courtship of the redshank, Huxley, building on earlier observational work by Edmund Selous,[44] noted that

> Selous' and my observations ... are ... enough to establish one important point, namely, that the actions of the birds which lead up to each single act of pairing are explicable only on the Darwinian theory of Sexual Selection, or on some modification of that theory.
>
> On the one hand, there is a very marked *display* by the male ...
>
> On the other hand, there is an equally marked *power of choice* shown by the female ...
>
> Thus, though the male in this particular species has the *initiative*, the *final decision* must rest with the female.[45]

Yet even as he appeared to corroborate Darwin's theory, Huxley expressed some dissatisfaction with the fact that sexual selection theory could not explain why, in the case of some characters, both sexes possessed them but only the male used them in display.[46] More significant, he remarked of male display in the redshank, that the fanning of the tail in the first two stages, the lifting and fluttering of the wings, and the high-stepping with the legs in the second stage, are all obviously calculated to show off to the best advantage certain conspicuous markings which are usually concealed, while the rattling note of the second stage *is to my mind equally to be considered as an excitant.*[47]

Echoing the work of Sturtevant and Morgan, Huxley interpreted his conclusion that the male's noises served to excite, rather than simply attract, the female as suggesting that female 'choice' was far less important – or even existent – in mating practices than Darwin had suggested; and this was a position Huxley propounded more strongly within a few years. In another 1912 piece, Huxley proposed the term 'epigamic', borrowed from Poulton, to describe structures used by both sexes in courtship and suggested that such 'secondary sexual' characters should generally not be considered products of sexual selection in the strict sense, since they did not really serve to determine mating patterns.[48]

Huxley's views on female choice in courtship developed and took shape in the years just after 1912, and his emerging ideas were strongly influenced by contemporary research on physiological regulation, especially hormonal activity, which suggested to Huxley that individuals' actions during courtship might be determined more by physiological factors than by anything one might consider 'choice.'[49] In particular, Huxley seems to have been influenced by W. P. Pycraft's 1913 book, *The Courtship of Animals*.[50] Building on the work of Lloyd Morgan and E. H. Starling on the emotions and hormones, Pycraft suggested that courtship activities served to influence the glandular activity of the participants, leading in turn to heightened physiological states and a higher chance of successful reproduction. 'Where these stimulants [secretions of the "sexual glands"] are lacking,' Pycraft wrote, 'there will be no desire, no display, and no pairing.'[51] Hence Pycraft saw the actions of sexual selection as reducible to physiological changes stemming from 'glandular secretions' and leading to successful reproduction. Notably, he did not consider that such physiological dynamics had an evolutionary history shaped by selective processes. While Pycraft dwelled little on the implications of his conclusions for evolutionary theory, he did note that 'Much hitherto attributed to the action of "Sexual Selection" alone, it is now evident is largely due to their activity [i.e. glandular secretions]'.[52]

In his well-known 1914 paper on 'The Courtship-habits of the Great Crested Grebe',[53] Huxley adopted Pycraft's position and went a step beyond his own earlier work, emphasizing primarily the ability of the male to excite the female physiologically so that she would be sexually synchronized with him and would reproduce efficiently; that is, she must be receptive not so much to him – that is not much at issue – but to his sperm. His article described in detail the courtship patterns of the grebe, and he suggested that in bird mating practices (and, he hinted, mating practices in general) there is very little 'sexual selection in the ordinary sense of the word'.[54]

After dividing bird courtship habits into 'solitary actions' (performed by the male) and 'combined actions' (performed by both male and female), Huxley undermined the distinction by positing that both kinds of actions, and the structures upon which they are based, were generally the products of the same evolutionary process – and not Darwinian sexual selection. Manifesting his Adamic urge to name things, Huxley suggested that the process at work was

> Mutual Selection ... in a way a blend between Sexual and Natural Selection. The structures and actions arising under it have their immediate origin in the preferences of individual birds, not in anything outside the species ... [but] the activities of both birds taken together, may be of use to the species as a whole, in keeping the sexes together when necessary.[55]

Here Huxley was stressing the strengthening of the pair bond, a benefit to the species. This supports John Durant's suggestion that Huxley's belief in the generally progressive nature of evolution led him to downplay Darwinian sexual selection, which could produce extravagant and otherwise deleterious features such as the peacock's tail.[56]

Huxley's analysis makes clear that what he was really concerned with were not characters in the male which lead the female to choose to mate with him in particular, but characters or practices in the male which excite the female to mate and, more precisely, to mate well – that is, with reproductive success. 'Display and ornament', Huxley explains, 'do not act on the aesthetic sense of the female, but on her emotional state; they are – using the words in no narrow or unpleasant sense – excitants, aphrodisiacs, serving to raise the female into that state of exaltation when alone she will be ready to pair.'[57] Analogously, mutual displays are simply to ensure synchronization so that the male and female reach the correct sexual pitch simultaneously, again ensuring efficient reproduction. In essence, Huxley subsumed the phenomenon of sexual selection within natural selection, for, within Darwin's framework, reproductive efficiency would be regarded as part of the province of natural selection, since it would be generally advantageous even if mating were random, and would tend to benefit the species as a whole. Huxley explained that,

> If display is normally an excitant, then there is no 'need' for ... actual rivalry between several males ... The female does not choose the 'best' out of a bunch of suitors; but those males in which the ornaments and display-habits do not reach a certain standard, will not be able to raise the female's emotional state to the requisite pitch.[58]

Males, then, must simply have characters of 'a certain standard' in order to excite the female physiologically; a 'sub-standard' male may get to copulate, but it will be in vain if the female is not biologically receptive. It is not mate choice but reproductive efficiency which is at stake.

In this 1914 paper and in other articles published in the following years, Huxley focused most of his attention on the 'love-habits'[59] of the birds he was studying – that is, on the immediate events leading up to successful coition. As a result, he generally tended to be far more concerned with the evolutionary significance of pair-bonding activities than with the events which lead to the formation of particular pairs. Even his discussion of 'active display by one or both sexes' is focused on displays *after* 'the birds have already paired-up into couples, but [when] coition has not yet taken place'.[60] Hence, Huxley ignored the actions which a male takes to attract a female to 'pick' him in particular; taking it all but for granted that the female has already paired with a male, Huxley's focus is on the actions of the male which help to prepare the female physiologically for intercourse.[61]

This approach related to another aspect of Huxley's work. As he joined many late nineteenth-century thinkers, such as Wallace, in intuitively regarding female choice as logically unlikely, so Huxley appears to have simply accepted monogamy as the proper and higher norm in the animal, as in the human, world. While Darwin himself had suggested that female choice and sexual selection in general play a more significant and obvious role in polygamous species, Huxley focused his studies almost exclusively on monogamous animals. In a 1916 paper, he wrote, 'Do not think me fantastic if I say that, even in birds, I believe that the finest emotions and most comfortable happiness are, as in man, associated with that form of monogamy in which male and female bear approximately equal parts.'[62] Of course Huxley acknowledged the existence of many species of polygamous birds,[63] but his studies consistently focused on monogamous territorial birds, and he clearly saw them as more evolutionarily developed forms – and he tended to generalize broadly about evolutionary mechanisms on the basis of such limited studies. Indeed, Huxley frequently employed human norms and practices in his discussions of animal interactions, as when he used the term 'love-habits' for the phenomena he observed (primarily in monogamous species)[64] or when he remarked of courtship in the grebe, 'Again we exclaim, how human! ... [when] we see to what a pitch of complexity the bird's emotional life is tuned.'[65] And, it is worth noting, Huxley was hardly a radical social reformer. His writings yield a consistent picture of a careful, conservative, and, one is tempted to say, late Victorian social outlook with respect to personal and sexual relations.[66]

Huxley's distinctive approach to courtship in birds marked his studies in the years that followed, leading him to suggest that Darwinian sexual selection was largely unimportant in the evolutionary history of display practices.[67] In a long article on the 'Courtship Activities in the Red-Throated Diver', published in 1923, Huxley again argued from observations of a monogamous species that strict sexual selection had only very limited applicability, restating his tenet that 'it is impossible ... to maintain that Darwin's original theory of sexual selection is adequate to explain the origin of most of the sexual ceremonies and adornments to be found in monogamous birds'.[68] Referring to Sturtevant and Morgan's work with *Drosophila*, Huxley generalized that female choice need not be explained, for females rarely actually appeared to choose; rather, they were primarily 'stimulated to action'.[69] Like Sturtevant, Huxley did not recognize the possibility that the differential stimulation of females could be a component of a modified but intact version of Darwinian sexual selection.

To some degree, of course, Huxley realized that his conclusions effectively grouped most sexual behaviour under the operation of natural selection. In a letter to *Nature* in December 1921 in which he suggested that sexual selection in the strict sense had been relatively unimportant, Huxley explained that in many cases 'sexual selection cannot be operative. The effect of the ceremonies ... is not the selection of one rather than another out of several possible mates, but simply a facilitation of the union of the gametes', a facet of natural selection. He went on to note that many structures once explained as products of sexual selection were really precisely the same, in an adaptive sense, as sex organs: '[W]herever mating displays and ceremonies, and the colours and structures associated with them, have this purely stimulative function they cannot be supposed to stand in any relation to sexual selection, but resemble copulatory organs in being solely subservient to efficiency in securing union of the gametes.'[70] As such, they would be 'genuinely beneficial characteristics', advantageous to both the individual and the species. To Huxley, this reflected the explanatory adequacy of natural selection which, as

Durant has observed, Huxley tended to identify with general evolutionary progress, despite Darwin's rejection of this view.[71] Huxley's broad conclusions, coupled with his growing influence among biologists, helped to undermine further the role of female choice in evolutionary thinking.

At the same time, Huxley's early writings on bird behaviour suggest that he never viewed male combat, the other main component of Darwinian sexual selection, as a particularly important evolutionary mechanism. This again was probably partly due to his preoccupation with monogamous species, for, like female choice, male conflict plays a more significant role among polygamous animals. In his 1914 paper on the great crested grebe, Huxley mentioned male combat only in passing: in the course of his discussion of the importance of certain actions in exciting one or both partners to a suitable and synchronized sexual pitch, he remarked that sexual excitement 'includes mere sexual desire, and also includes the fighting of males among each other as a result of sexual desire'.[72] By giving a mechanical (that is, physiological) explanation for male combat, while ignoring the possibility and significance of an evolutionary explanation for it as well, Huxley reduced male competition to an epiphenomenon of the sexual excitement which he found so central. In his 1923 piece on the red-throated diver, he again referred briefly to 'the direct competition among males, which was one of the main points of Darwin's theory of sexual selection', but he dismissed it as a rare occurrence; and, like Wallace, he assumed that if male combat did have any effect, it would simply parallel that of natural selection.[73] With his faith in evolutionary progress, Huxley once more ignored the possibility that the two selective processes might sometimes operate in conflict.

Following his research in bird behaviour, Huxley's investigations in an entirely different area also worked to undermine the concept of male combat. Again, his emphasis on natural selection led him to downplay the role of sexual selection. During the 1920s and early 1930s, Huxley studied the phenomenon of relative growth – the way in which different body parts of an animal maintain certain size ratios throughout development. Other researchers had already done some quantitative work in this area,[74] but Huxley's rigorous and extensive work has long been regarded as the foundation of what soon came to be known as allometry.[75]

In the 1920s, Darwinian evolution was still largely out of favour among biologists. While Huxley no doubt found his allometric studies interesting and worthwhile for the mathematical growth relationships they yielded, his investigations were in large part motivated by a desire to refute certain tenets of the anti-Darwinian theory of orthogenesis, then one of the more serious alternatives to Darwinism. Scientists such as Henry Fairfield Osborn maintained that most evolutionary change was due to involuntary trends developing along preset paths, without reference to the actual needs of organisms.[76] In his 1918 book, *The Origin and Evolution of Life*, Osborn explained that '[O]ur general principle [is] that every character has its own rate of velocity [of change] . . . [C]*hanges of Proportion* make up the larger part of mammalian evolution and adaptation . . . No form of sudden change of character . . . or of the chance theory of evolution [i.e. Darwinian natural selection] accounts for such precise steps in mechanical adjustment.'[77] What did account for these steps, Osborn argued, was an inherent and determined set of progressive developments, an evolutionary trend, which caused change over time in particular characters and their proportions. In this way, orthogenesis accounted for such occurrences as the enormous antlers of deer, huge horns of rhinoceroses, and even extended forceps of insects. Many of these phenomena, of course, were characters which Darwin had explained with reference to their utility in male combat.[78]

Huxley's work on relative growth refuted the orthogenetic position by arguing that many growth relationships follow certain simple equations. Such a set relationship would be due to a physiological mechanism, as yet unknown. Hence if there were a certain allometric link between body size and antler size in deer, then selection for larger body size over time (a well-known occurrence) would result in an *apparent* orthogenetic drive towards larger antlers, though this would really only be an epiphenomenon of a trend towards larger body size, which itself was explained by natural selection.[79]

In the first piece he wrote on allometry, a letter to *Nature* in December 1924, Huxley made clear the significance of these growth relationships. He explained that allometric findings have 'an important bearing on evolutionary and genetic theory. If (1) a mechanism for the [allometric] development of any character occurs throughout a group, and (2) the evolution of the group has been on the whole from small to large size, we shall get apparent orthogenesis of the character.' In fact, size increase has occurred in almost all groups of mammals, due to the 'biological advantage conferred . . . by increased size', and so, 'the apparent orthogenesis of horns, etc., in mammals, especially urged . . . by Osborn . . . is no true orthogenesis at all . . . On the contrary, it would be automatically brought about by the increase of absolute size of the whole animal . . . together with the existence of the same type of developmental mechanism for horn-growth throughout the group.'[80]

Huxley's argument was not entirely new – indeed, it had been suggested briefly by A. H. Sturtevant in 1924[81] – but his was by far the most forceful and thorough articulation of it. From 1924 until the mid-1930s, Huxley wrote a dozen articles in this area: in these pieces, most of which did not address theoretical questions, Huxley reported on allometric growth patterns in sheep, herring, crabs,[82] deer,[83] and a variety of insects,[84] among others. When he discussed the significance of his findings, Huxley noted their support for his theme noted above: relative antler size, he wrote, 'is primarily a function of absolute body-size, and not a diagnostic genetic character', while the mandibles of stag-beetles 'are purely growth-forms and have no systematic significance'.[85]

While dissolving much evidence for anti-Darwinian orthogenesis into the mechanism of Darwinian natural selection, Huxley's allometric work also disposed of significant evidence for Darwinian sexual selection; as noted above, most of the characters which he explained in terms of growth relationships had been interpreted by Darwin as evolutionary products of male combat. Huxley made this clear in his landmark 1932 work, *Problems of Relative Growth*, a compilation of much of his previous theoretical and empirical work on allometry. He argued that the prevalence of allometric growth patterns meant that unusually and even deleteriously large characters of many species need not be explained, whether as adaptive or otherwise. Once these growth relationships are clear, 'we are justified in concluding that the *relative* size of horn, mandible, or other ... organ is automatically determined as a secondary result of a single common growth-mechanism, and *therefore is not of adaptive significance*'.[86] Such a view, Huxley realized, 'makes it extremely difficult to assign any adaptive value' to the features,[87] but this also 'relieve[s] us of the necessity for seeking utilitarian explanations for the correlated changes'. Evolutionary criteria 'need not be invoked to account for the details of such characters'[88] – evidence which might well support sexual selection theory was not evidence at all.[89]

Julian Huxley's work in both bird courtship and allometry was extremely influential. Building as it did on the sense among biologists that sexual selection was not of particular significance, it gave many naturalists reason to devote little attention to Darwin's second theory. The prominent neo-Lamarckian E. W. MacBride saw Huxley's concept of 'epigamic' characters leading to mutual arousal as 'the best solution of the riddle' of secondary sexual characters, and A. F. Schull cited Huxley and Morgan in support of the same conclusion.[90] In a 1927 article, influential in its own right, on 'Sexual Selection and

Allied Problems in the Insects', O. W. Richards, who had worked with Huxley at Oxford, took his colleague's work as a starting-point.[91] Generally, Richards attributed nearly all secondary sexual characters to different forms of natural selection. He did not bother to suggest a functional role for the very large horns in the larger members of a family of beetles; citing Huxley's early work on allometry, Richards explained that it was 'unlikely that the horns can be of much direct use. The development of such structures is probably controlled by the existence of a logarithmic relation between the size of the outgrowth and that of the whole body.'[92] And he suggested that many male characters served to overcome the 'coyness' of females, so reducing the time taken by mating and ensuring the female was ready to copulate.[93]

Huxley himself summarized his views on sexual selection in two 1938 articles that are probably the most frequently cited pieces on the subject published in the first half of the century.[94] Huxley presented a general view which varied little from that set out in his studies of bird behaviour two decades earlier. As in his previous formulations, he elided sexual selection into natural selection, primarily by emphasizing the role of secondary sexual characters and display activities in gender and species recognition and as sexual excitants. As John Durant has remarked, 'Huxley gave Darwin fulsome credit for developing a principle whose significance he then proceeded to minimalize and marginalize at almost every turn.'[95] 'It has now become clear', Huxley declared, 'that the hypothesis of female choice and of selection between rival males irrespective of general biological advantage is inapplicable to the great majority of display characters.'[96] Returning to his earlier division between 'threat displays [which] promote both general and sexual vigour, and epigamic displays [which] stimulate the female's reproductive physiology',[97] Huxley summarized that display 'may induce a psycho-physiological state of readiness to mate, irrespective of any possibility of choice. In birds, display may synchronize male and female rhythms of sexual behaviour ... and initiate physiological changes leading to ... ovulation ... These effects directly promote effective reproduction and need no special category of "sexual selection" to explain their origin.'[98] As display will 'often be of advantage to the species in promoting more effective reproduction' and in species recognition, 'Any resultant selection will therefore come under the head of Natural Selection, not Sexual Selection in Darwin's sense.'[99] Huxley suggested that 'The term *sexual selection* as used by Darwin should be replaced by two terms – *epigamic selection* and *intra-sexual selection*. The latter will apply to all selection involving competition between individuals of one sex in the struggle for reproduction, while the former will include selection involving display-characters common to both sexes.'[100]

'Epigamic selection', then, would essentially be a form of natural selection for more efficient mating, while 'intra-sexual selection' would, as Wallace had suggested, simply mirror the effects of natural selection, as the more vigorous males succeeded in sex, as in life in general. Huxley, determined to emphasize the importance of natural selection, continued to ignore Darwin's point that the two selective processes could work in opposite directions, as sexual selection develops otherwise maladaptive characteristics. In addition, Huxley's indifference, if not hostility, to polygamy led him to argue that there is really little to be explained by sexual selection anyway, since 'competition between males for mates, accompanied by any form of female choice, is not the common phenomenon postulated by Darwin, but apparently confined to the relatively few species practising polygamy or with a high excess of males'.[101]

Confusing as these articles may have been, they clearly suggested that sexual selection was a relatively insignificant evolutionary mechanism, and for two decades they provided a convenient reference point for biologists who paid little attention to the theory.[102] The influence of these articles is suggested by Ernst Mayr's remark, when asked why he and others involved in working out the evolutionary synthesis in the 1940s paid so little attention to sexual selection, that they thought Huxley had said all there was to say on the topic and shown it to be worth little further attention.[103] Indeed, the theory received very little attention in the major books of the synthesis published around 1940, including, unsurprisingly, Huxley's pioneering *Evolution, the Modern Synthesis* (1942), in which he repackaged secondary sexual characters into mating efficiency and mate recognition – all in under three pages.[104] Choice, then, was essentially dropped out of sex. Males rarely battled each other over particular females. Females did not actually choose males with which to mate; they merely reproduced efficiently by responding to physiological fate, hormonal drives brought on by certain characteristics of males.[105]

EPILOGUE

Julian Huxley himself certainly saw his work in animal mating as having implications for understanding human sexuality, and his appearance before the British Society for Sex Psychology in 1922 suggests that those studying human sexuality saw connections as well. In the paper he presented on that occasion, he surveyed work, including his own, on animal reproductive practices and their links to hormonal regulation and then discussed human sexuality in general terms. He told his audience his general view that 'a large number of animals appear not to mate unless their emotional state has been raised to a certain level', and he made clear that 'emotional state' was a product of hormonal activity.[106] Huxley's discussion and citations make clear he was familiar with works of Freud, Jung, Ellis, and others, but found their focus on psychological processes misplaced. In general, he concluded, 'biological investigation ... shows us how certain abnormalities of sexual psychology may be more easily interpreted as caused by comparatively simple physical abnormalities than by the more complex distortions of psychological origin dealt with by psycho-analysis'.[107] Again looking to research on the role of endocrines in animals, Huxley suggested that variations in hormonal processes may account for much of 'abnormal sexual behaviour', and he remarked that, 'gonad secretion and the balance of all the endocrines has to be taken into account far more than is done by the average psycho-analyst'.[108] Interestingly, Huxley asked whether, if psychoanalysis is correct that sex plays an enormous role 'in the genesis of our mental organization, is it desirable that the average adult or adolescent should, by analysis, be given full self-knowledge on the subject?'[109] Huxley's answer was clear: as he noted, 'Knowledge of the processes of digestion is not necessary to digest well.'[110]

While Huxley was thus aware of the parallels between his own investigations in natural history and the contemporary work on human sexuality by researchers such as Freud and Ellis, he saw the two fields as fundamentally distinct approaches to a general set of phenomena. In retrospect, one similarity stands out. For as many researchers in the emerging field of sexology appear to have approached 'normal' sexual behaviour, and distinguished it from the 'abnormal', largely in terms of their own values, assumptions, and expectations,[111] so Julian Huxley's attitudes about human sexuality appear to have influenced deeply his approach to studying mating practices among animals. In both disciplines, researchers tended to privilege monogamy and reproduction, still powerful ideas in much thinking concerning human and animal sexuality.

NOTES

1 Work on this chapter was supported by a National Science Foundation Graduate Fellowship (Grants RCD-8651742 and RCD-8758005). Any opinions, findings, conclusion, or recommendations expressed herein are those

2 Julian S. Huxley, 'Sex Biology and Sex Psychology', in *Essays of a Biologist* (New York: Alfred A. Knopf, 1923), 133–73.
3 Charles Darwin, *The Descent of Man, and Selection in Relation to Sex* (2 vols., London: John Murray, 1871).
4 See Jeffrey Weeks, *Sexuality and its Discontents: Meanings, Myths and Modern Sexualities* (London: Routledge and Kegan Paul, 1985), 64–7, 83; Frank J. Sulloway, *Freud, Biologist of the Mind* (New York: Basic Books, 1979), 252–4, 301–2; Gert Hekma, 'A History of Sexology: Social and Historical Aspects of Sexuality', in Jan Bremmer (ed.), *From Sappho to de Sade: Moments in the History of Sexuality* (London: Routledge, 1989), 173–187. Sulloway notes that 'Freud's medical generation witnessed, under the general influence of Darwin and evolutionary theory, a major revival of interest in sexual etiology' (*Freud, Biologist of the Mind*, 256–7).
5 See, for example, Havelock Ellis's references to Darwin's *Descent of Man* in his *Studies in the Psychology of Sex: Sexual Selection in Man*, vol. IV (Philadelphia: F. A. Davis, 1905), v–vi.
6 A phrase coined by Julian Huxley in *Evolution, The Modern Synthesis* (London: George Allen and Unwin, 1942), 22–8; see also Peter J. Bowler, *The Eclipse of Darwinism: Anti-Darwinism Evolution Theories in the Decades around 1900* (Baltimore: Johns Hopkins University Press, 1983). Peter O'Donald appears to have first used the phrase 'eclipse of sexual selection'. See Peter O'Donald, *Genetic Models of Sexual Selection* (Cambridge: Cambridge University Press, 1980), 10.
7 See, for example, John R. Durant, 'Julian Huxley and the Development of Evolutionary Studies', in Milo Keynes and G. Ainsworth Harrison (eds.), *Evolutionary Studies: A Centenary Celebration of the Life of Julian Huxley* (London: Macmillan, 1989), 26, 32.
8 Charles Darwin, *On the Origin of Species* (London: John Murray, 1859), 120, 128. Darwin also mentioned the concept of sexual selection briefly in his sketch of 1842, his essay of 1844, and his 1858 Linnean Society paper; see Carl Jay Bajema, *Evolution by Sexual Selection Theory Prior to 1900* (New York: Van Nostrand Reinhold, 1984), 98–109.
9 Ibid., 89.
10 Darwin, *The Descent of Man*, vol. I, 256.
11 Ibid., vol. I, 296.
12 Ibid., vol. II, 398.
13 See the discussion in Andrew Pomiankowski, 'Sexual Selection: "Good Genes" or "Aesthetic" Preference' (Ph.D. dissertation, University of Sussex, 1987), 178–9.
14 Darwin, *The Descent of Man*, vol. I, 377.
15 Ibid., vol. II, 123.
16 Pomiankowski, 'Sexual Selection: "Good Genes" or "Aesthetic" Preference', 178.
17 Darwin, *The Descent of Man*, vol. II, 398.
18 Ibid., vol. I, 279.

19 Ibid., vol. II, 92.
20 Ibid., vol. I, 257.
21 Ibid., vol. I, 257; and see Stevan J. Arnold, 'Sexual Selection: The Interface of Theory and Empiricism', in Patrick Bateson (ed.), *Mate Choice* (Cambridge: Cambridge University Press, 1983), 70–1.
22 This debate has been chronicled in full elsewhere. See Malcolm J. Kottler, 'Darwin, Wallace, and the Origin of Sexual Dimorphism', *Proceedings of the American Philosophical Society*, 124 (1980), 203–26; idem, 'Charles Darwin and Alfred Russel Wallace: Two Decades of Debate Over Natural Selection', in David Kohn (ed.), *The Darwinian Heritage* (Princeton: Princeton University Press, 1985), 367–432.
23 Alfred Russel Wallace, *Natural Selection and Tropical Nature* (London: Macmillan, 1891), 360.
24 During the 1860s, Wallace studied the relationship between birds' nesting habits and their plumage and found that the females which incubated on open nests tended to be duller than those of species which did not; see ibid., 34–90, 118–40, and 338–94; and Pomiankowski, 'Sexual Selection: "Good Genes" or "Aesthetic" Preference', 185–6.
25 See, e.g., Wallace, *Natural Selection and Tropical Nature*, 374, 409; idem, *Darwinism* (London: Macmillan, 1889), 286. See also R. A. Fisher, *The Genetical Theory of Natural Selection* (Oxford: Oxford University Press, 1930), 134; Helena Cronin, *The Ant and the Peacock: Altruism and Sexual Selection from Darwin to Today* (Cambridge: Cambridge University Press, 1991), 102–3, 114, 131–3; and Pomiankowski, 'Sexual Selection: "Good Genes" or "Aesthetic" Preference', 183–4.
26 John R. Durant, 'The Conflict between Science and Ideology in the Evolutionary Thought of Julian Huxley', paper delivered at Cambridge University seminar, 19 May 1988, esp. 11.
27 But see G. W. Peckham and E. G. Peckham, 'Observations on Sexual Selection in Spiders of the Family *Attidae*' (Milwaukee: Natural History Society of Wisconsin, 1889), which investigated the theory carefully.
28 See, e.g., E. B. Poulton, *The Colours of Animals: Their Meaning and Use, Especially Considered in the Case of Insects* (London: Kegan Paul, 1890); and Pomiankowski, 'Sexual Selection: "Good Genes" or "Aesthetic" Preference', 190.
29 E. B. Poulton, *Charles Darwin and the Theory of Natural Selection* (London: Cassell, 1896), 79; idem, *The Colours of Animals*; Cronin, *The Ant and the Peacock*, 163; and Pomiankowski, 'Sexual Selection: "Good Genes" or "Aesthetic" Preference', 184, 190. For an example of the influence of Poulton's interpretive tradition, see R. W. G. Hingston, *The Meaning of Animal Colouration and Adornment* (London: Edward Arnold, 1933).
30 See generally Bowler, *The Eclipse of Darwinism*. Interestingly, sexual selection theory does not appear at all in Bowler's book.
31 T. H. Morgan, *Evolution and Adaptation* (New York: Macmillan, 1903), chapter 5; Bowler, *The Eclipse of Darwinism*, 204.
32 Douglas Dewar and Frank Finn, *The Making of Species* (London: John Lane/The Bodley Head, 1909), 298; and O'Donald, *Genetic Models of Sexual Selection*, 10–11.

33 Joseph T. Cunningham, *Sexual Dimorphism in the Animal Kingdom* (London: A. and C. Black, 1900); and Bowler, *The Eclipse of Darwinism*, 90.
34 See, e.g., T. H. Montgomery, Jr, 'The Significance of the Courtship and Secondary Sexual Characters of Araneids', *American Naturalist*, 44 (1910), 151–77.
35 Edmund Selous, 'Observations Tending to Throw Light on the Question of Sexual Selection in Birds, Including a Day-to-Day Diary on the Breeding Habits of the Ruff', *The Zoologist*, 10 (1906), 201–19, 285–94, 419–28; 11 (1907), 60–5, 161–82, 367–81, esp. 11, p. 163, where Selous displayed some bitterness that so many naturalists discarded sexual selection without first pursuing evidence for it; and Durant, 'The Conflict between Science and Ideology in the Evolutionary Thought of Julian Huxley', 11. In 'The Nuptial Habits of the Blackcock', *The Naturalist*, 673 (1913), 98, Selous commented that he had 'produced immensely strong evidence in favour of the Darwinian theory of sexual selection. It would seem, however, that, since the theory itself is (officially) out of favour, such evidence is not wanted.' See also John R. Durant, 'Innate Characters in Animal and Man: A Perspective on the Origins of Ethology', in Charles Webster (ed.), *Biology, Medicine and Society, 1840–1940* (Cambridge: Cambridge University Press, 1981), 178–80; and Richard W. Buckhardt, Jr, 'Julian Huxley and the Rise of Ethology', paper delivered at Julian Huxley Centenary, Rice University, October 1987, 8–10.
36 See, e.g., W. H. Thorpe, *The Origins and Rise of Ethology* (London: Heinemann, 1979), 30.
37 A. H. Sturtevant, 'Experiments on Sex Recognition and the Problem of Sexual Selection in *Drosophila*', *Journal of Animal Behavior*, 5 (1915), 351–66, reprinted in E. B. Levis (ed.), *Genetics and Evolution: Selected Papers of A. H. Sturtevant* (San Francisco: W. H. Freeman, 1961), 24–37, esp. 31–5. It is worth noting that Sturtevant cited, though he did not discuss, J. B. Watson's 1914 book, *Behavior* (New York: Henry Holt and Co., 1914).
38 See, e.g., J. Maynard Smith, 'Sexual Selection', in S. A. Barnett (ed.), *A Century of Darwin* (London: Heinemann, 1958), 231–44; *idem*, 'Fertility, Mating Behaviour and Sexual Selection in *Drosophila subobscura*', *Journal of Genetics*, 54 (1956), 261–79.
39 Sturtevant, 'Experiments on Sex Recognition and the Problem of Sexual Selection in *Drosophila*', 36. Sturtevant restated these conclusions in his widely cited monograph, *The North American Species of Drosophila* (Carnegie Institution of Washington, Publication no. 301, 1921), 9–11. Cf. Frank E. Lutz, 'The Effect of Sexual Selection', in *Experiments with Drosophila ampelophila Concerning Evolution* (Carnegie Institution of Washington, Publication no. 143, 1911), 36–7.
40 Sturtevant, 'Genetic Studies on *Drosophila simulans*, I: Introduction, Hybrids with *Drosophila melanogaster*', *Genetics*, 5 (1920), 499.
41 See T. H. Morgan, *A Critique of the Theory of Evolution* (Princeton: Princeton University Press, 1916).
42 T. H. Morgan, *The Genetic and Operative Evidence Relating to Secondary Sexual Characters* (Carnegie Institution of Washington, Publication no. 285, 1919), 47, 60–1.

43 Ibid., 51; also 98-9.
44 Selous, 'Observations Tending to Throw Light on the Question of Sexual Selection in Birds'.
45 Julian S. Huxley, 'A First Account of the Courtship of the Redshank', *Proceedings of the Zoological Society of London* (1912), 654 (emphasis in original).
46 Darwin himself spent some time grappling with this question, turning to an inconsistent invocation of the laws of inheritance; see the discussion in Pomiankowski, 'Sexual Selection: "Good Genes" or "Aesthetic" Preference' 179-82.
47 Huxley, 'A First Account of the Courtship of the Redshank', 654 (emphasis added). As Helena Cronin has noted, 'This approach was anticipated by the notoriously anti-Darwinian critic St George Mivart: "the female does not select; yet the display of the male may be useful in supplying the necessary degree of stimulation to her nervous system".' *The Ant and the Peacock*, 157, quoting [St George Mivart], Review of Darwin's *Descent of Man*, in *Quarterly Review*, 131 (1871), 62. Only with Huxley's writings, however, did this approach gain wide acceptance.
48 Julian S. Huxley, 'The Great Crested Grebe and the Idea of Secondary Sexual Characters', *Science*, NS 36 (1912), 602.
49 Huxley's familiarity with, and interest in, the growing literature on hormonal regulation is manifest in his piece 'Sex Biology and Sex Psychology', in *Essays of a Biologist* (New York: Alfred A. Knopf, 1923), 133-73.
50 Huxley noted in a postscript to his 1914 paper on the Great Crested Grebe that 'it was unfortunately only after the completion of the MS of this paper that I was able to read [Pycraft's book]'. Yet Huxley actually cited the book in the body of his paper. See Julian S. Huxley, 'The Courtship-habits of the Great Crested Grebe: With an Addition to the Theory of Sexual Selection', *Proceedings of the Zoological Society of London* (1914), 523, 559. Anyway, it is clear that Huxley and Pycraft were in friendly contact with each other during 1911-13, sharing manuscripts and ideas. See W. P. Pycraft, *The Courtship of Animals* (London: Hutchinson, 1913), 153.
51 Pycraft, *The Courtship of Animals*, 154-5.
52 Ibid., 16.
53 Huxley, 'The Courtship-habits of the Great Crested Grebe'. This article was later regarded as something of a founding document for the study of ethology, especially ritualization; see, e.g., Thorpe, *The Origins and Rise of Ethology*, 33; and Buckhardt, 'Julian Huxley and the Rise of Ethology'.
54 Huxley, 'The Courtship-habits of the Great Crested Grebe', 522.
55 Ibid., 524 (emphasis omitted). What is really meant by 'mutual selection' is not at all clear. Huxley himself may not have been entirely clear (in the same article, he noted, without further explanation, that 'Mutual Selection has a certain similarity with assortative mating, but it is by no means the same thing'), and he almost never used the concept in his subsequent writings. The concept appeared very briefly in one of his 1916 articles discussed below and not at all in his *Evolution, The Modern Synthesis* (London: George Allen and Unwin, 1942).

56 Durant, 'The Conflict between Science and Ideology in the Evolutionary Thought of Julian Huxley', 12.
57 Huxley, 'The Courtship-habits of the Great Crested Grebe', 559.
58 Ibid., 560.
59 Ibid., 491.
60 Julian S. Huxley, 'Bird Watching and Biological Science: Some Observations on the Study of Courtship in Birds', *Auk*, 33 (1916), 147, 149.
61 See ibid., 157. Some of Huxley's later writings suggest he was not unaware of his assumptions here, but he continued to generalize broadly about the shortcomings of sexual selection theory. See, e.g., his *Bird-watching and Bird Behaviour* (London: Chatto and Windus, 1930), 77.
62 Ibid., 147.
63 See, e.g., Huxley, 'Bird Watching and Biological Science: Some Observations on the Study of Courtship in Birds'.
64 See Huxley, 'The Courtship-habits of the Great Crested Grebe', 491.
65 Julian S. Huxley, 'Ils n'ont que de l'âme: An Essay on Bird-Mind', in *Essays of a Biologist* (New York: Alfred A. Knopf, 1923), 121.
66 See Julian S. Huxley, *Memories* (London: George Allen and Unwin, 1970), e.g. 85; see also, *idem* 'The Dominant Sex', in *Essays in Popular Science* (New York: Alfred A. Knopf, 1927), 65-9 (originally published in *The Spectator*, 131 [15 Sept. 1923], 355).
67 See Julian S. Huxley, 'Note on the Drumming of Woodpeckers', *British Birds*, 13 (1919), 41; *idem*, 'Some Points in the Sexual Habits of the Little Grebe, with a Note on the Occurrence of Vocal Duets in Birds', *British Birds* 13 (1919), 156; see also, *idem*, 'Bird Watching and Biological Science', 158.
68 Julian S. Huxley, 'Courtship Activities in the Red-throated Diver; Together with a Discussion of the Evolution of Courtship in Birds', *Journal of the Linnean Society (Zoology)*, 35 (1923), 269.
69 Ibid., 270.
70 Julian S. Huxley, 'The Accessory Nature of Many Structures and Habits Associated with Courtship', *Nature*, 108 (1921), 565-6.
71 Durant, 'The Conflict between Science and Ideology in the Evolutionary Thought of Julian Huxley', 12, 14.
72 Huxley, 'The Courtship-habits of the Great Crested Grebe', 527.
73 Huxley, 'Courtship Activities in the Red-throated Diver', 286.
74 See, e.g., W. Bateson and H. H. Brindley, 'On Some Cases of Variation in Secondary Sexual Characters, Statistically Examined', *Proceedings of the Zoological Society of London* (1892), 585-94.
75 Unsurprisingly, it was Huxley himself who named it such; see Julian S. Huxley and G. Tessier, 'Terminology of Relative Growth', *Nature*, 137 (1936), 780. While it might be regarded as anachronistic to use the term 'allometry' when discussing relative growth work prior to this christening, I do so for the sake of clarity and consistency.
76 See Bowler, *Eclipse of Darwinism*, 7, 141-81.
77 Henry Fairfield Osborn, *The Origin and Evolution of Life* (London: G. Bell and Sons, 1918), 265, 268.
78 See, e.g., Darwin, *The Descent of Man, and Selection in Relation to Sex*, vol. II, 252.

79 See Cronin, *The Ant and the Peacock*, 95–6.
80 Julian S. Huxley, 'Constant Differential Growth-ratios and their Significance', *Nature*, 114 (1924), 895–6. Cf. J. B. S. Haldane, *The Causes of Evolution* (London: Longmans, Green and Co., 1932), 23–8.
81 A. H. Sturtevant, 'An Interpretation of Orthogenesis', *Science* 59 (1924), 579.
82 Julian S. Huxley, 'The Variation in the Width of the Abdomen in Immature Fiddler Crabs Considered in Relation to Relative Growth-rate', *American Naturalist*, 58 (1924), 468–75; *idem*, 'Notes on Differential Growth', *American Naturalist*, 65 (1931), 289–315.
83 Julian S. Huxley, 'The Annual Increment of the Antlers of the Red Deer', *Proceedings of the Zoological Society of London*, 67 (1926), 1021–36; *idem*, 'The Relative Size of Antlers in Deer', *Proceedings of the Zoological Society of London* (1931), 819–64.
84 Julian S. Huxley, 'Discontinuous Variation and Heterogony in *Forficula*', *Journal of Genetics*, 17 (1926), 309–27; *idem* 'The Bimodal Cephalic Horn of *Xylotrupes gideon*', *Journal of Genetics*, 18 (1927), 45–53; *idem*, 'Further Work on Heterogonic Growth', *Biologisches Zentralblatt*, 47 (1927), 151–63; *idem*, 'Relative Growth of Mandibles in Stag-Beetles', *Journal of the Linnean Society (Zoology)*, 37 (1927), 675–703.
85 Huxley, 'The Relative Size of Antlers in Deer', 862; *idem*, 'Relative Growth of Mandibles in Stag-Beetles', 702.
86 Julian S. Huxley, *Problems of Relative Growth* (London: Methuen, 1932), 214 (emphasis in original).
87 Ibid., 219.
88 Ibid., 221.
89 More recent work has suggested that competition for females among males may to a significant degree account for the adaptive force behind the allometry of antlers. See the discussion of studies in Cronin, *The Ant and the Peacock*, 96–7.
90 E. W. MacBride, 'Zoology', in *Evolution in Light of Modern Knowledge: A Collective Work* (London: Blackie, 1925), 218–19; and A. F. Schull, *Evolution* (New York: McGraw Hill, 1936), 194–8. Cf. Haldane, *The Causes of Evolution*, 128.
91 O. W. Richards, 'Sexual Selection and Allied Problems in the Insects', *Biological Reviews*, 2 (1927), 298–360. The text of Richards's article makes clear that he had worked closely with Huxley on the topic. See, e.g., pp. 298, 345.
92 Ibid., 304.
93 Ibid., 324–5, 344–5. For the influence of Richards on the genetical ecologist E. B. Ford, see R. A. Fisher and E. B. Ford, 'The Variability of Species in the Lepidoptera, with Reference to Abundance and Sex', *Transactions of the Royal Entomological Society of London*, 76 (1928), 377–8. See also the important book, G. C. Robson and O. W. Richards, *The Variation of Animals in Nature* (London: Longmans, Greed and Co., 1936), 291–300; and Cronin, *The Ant and the Peacock*, 157–9.
94 Julian S. Huxley, 'Darwin's Theory of Sexual Selection and the Data Subsumed by it in Light of Recent Research', *American Naturalist*, 72 (1938),

416; and 'The Present Standing of the Theory of Sexual Selection', in G. R. de Beer (ed.), *Evolution: Essays on Aspects of Evolutionary Biology* (Oxford: Clarendon Press, 1938), 11. A third article by Huxley, 'Threat and Warning Coloration in Birds, with a General Discussion of the Biological Functions of Colour', *Proceedings of the Eighth International Ornithological Congress* (1934), 430, presented most of the same ideas, but much more briefly.
95 Durant, 'The Conflict between Science and Ideology in the Evolutionary Thought of Julian Huxley', 12. Ironically, Huxley commented that 'None of Darwin's theories have been so heavily attacked as that of sexual selection', (Huxley, 'The Present Standing of the Theory of Sexual Selection', 11).
96 Huxley, 'The Present Standing of the Theory of Sexual Selection', 20–1.
97 Ibid., 18.
98 Huxley, 'Darwin's Theory of Sexual Selection and the Data Subsumed by it in Light of Recent Research', 422–3.
99 Huxley, 'The Present Standing of the Theory of Sexual Selection', 20.
100 Huxley, 'Darwin's Theory of Sexual Selection and the Data Subsumed by it in Light of Recent Research', 431.
101 Ibid., 417.
102 The influence of Huxley's 1938 articles is the reason most frequently given by recent biologists to explain the lack of attention paid to sexual selection at mid-century. See, e.g., Robert L. Trivers, 'Parental Investment and Sexual Selection', in Bernard Campbell (ed.), *Sexual Selection and the Descent of Man, 1871–1971* (London: Heinemann, 1972), 165; G. A. Parker, 'Sexual Selection and Sexual Conflict', in Murray S. Blum and Nancy A. Blum (eds.), *Sexual Selection and Reproductive Competition in Insects* (New York: Academic Press, 1979), 123; Randy Thornhill, 'Male and Female Sexual Selection and the Evolution of Mating Strategies in Insects', in Blum and Blum (eds.), *Sexual Selection and Reproductive Competition in Insects*, 81; and O'Donald, *Genetic Models of Sexual Selection*, 10, 14–15. See also John R. Durant, 'Julian Huxley and the Development of Evolutionary Studies'.
103 Durant, 'The Conflict between Science and Ideology in the Evolutionary Thought of Julian Huxley'.
104 Huxley, *Evolution, The Modern Synthesis*, 35–7. Mayr treated secondary sexual characters similarly in his important book *Systematics and the Origin of Species*, concluding that 'many phenomena that have been recorded in the past as furthering intraspecific sexual selection are actually specific recognition marks'. Ernst Mayr, *Systematics and the Origin of Species* (New York: Columbia University Press, 1942), 254. Mayr here cited Huxley's 1938 articles and O. W. Richards's 1927 piece, 'Sexual Selection and Allied Problems in the Insects'. See also Mayr, *Animal Species and Evolution* (Cambridge, Mass.: Belknap/Harvard University Press, 1963), 96, 126–7.
105 The beginnings, or at least the roots, of a revival of Darwinian sexual selection theory can be seen in R. A. Fisher's 1930 book, *The Genetical Theory of Natural Selection*. Fisher was the first to integrate natural selection and Mendelian genetics to explain a great deal of evolutionary change, showing that characters conferring a very small selective advantage would still be subject to strong selection over time. In one chapter of his book, he provided

a sympathetic and sophisticated theoretical treatment of sexual selection theory and gave an explanation for the adaptive basis of female choice, which Darwin had largely assumed. Fisher, *The Genetical Theory of Natural Selection*, chapter 6. See also O'Donald, *Genetic Models of Sexual Selection*, 6–9.

Portraying sexual selection as a significant evolutionary process, Fisher noted that 'If . . . we consider that the tastes of organisms, like their organs and faculties, must be regarded as the products of evolutionary change . . . it appears . . . that occasions may be not infrequent when a sexual preference of a particular kind may confer a selective advantage, and therefore become established in the species' (Fisher, *The Genetical Theory of Natural Selection*, 135–6). Fisher went on to explain that if, say, a particular plumage gave 'an initial advantage not due to sexual preference, which advantage may be quite inconsiderable in magnitude', and if there were 'an additional advantage conferred by female preference' for that character, then

> The intensity of [female] preference will itself be increased by selection so long as the sons of hens exercising the preference most decidedly have any advantage over the sons of other hens, whether this be due to the first or to the second cause. The importance of this situation lies in the fact that the further development of the plumage character will still proceed . . . so long as the disadvantage [in natural selection] is more than counterbalanced by the advantage in sexual selection.
>
> Ibid., 136–7

Despite Fisher's 1930 contribution, sexual selection was essentially left out of the evolutionary synthesis and received little serious scientific attention until the 1960s. The definition of evolutionary fitness developed by geneticists in the synthesis, as the contribution to the gene pool of the next generation rather than in Darwin's more everyday sense of being well adapted and improving chances of survival, emphasized the similarities, rather than the differences, between natural and sexual selection, so undermining any distinction between the two mechanisms. Burney J. Le Beouf, 'Sex and Evolution', in Thomas E. McGill, Donald A. Dewsbury and Benjamin D. Sachs (eds.), *Sex and Behaviour: Status and Prospective* (New York: Plenum Press, 1978), 5; Mary Jane West-Eberhard, 'Sexual Selection, Social Competition, and Speciation', *Quarterly Review of Biology*, 58 (1983), 156; Ernst Mayr, *The Growth of Biological Thought: Diversity, Evolution, and Inheritance* (Cambridge, Mass.: Belknap/Harvard University Press, 1982), 596. As Ernst Mayr has remarked, 'something rather important was lost in the process' (Ernst Mayr, 'Sexual Selection and Natural Selection', in Bernard Campbell (ed.), *Sexual Selection and the Descent of Man, 1871–1971* (London: Heinemann, 1972), 88). In addition, the mathematical models formulated in the 1930s and 1940s tended to assume random mating, while a defining component of sexual selection is some deviation from panmixia. Finally, geneticists' enthusiasm for natural selection, once mathematical models had proved it could account for far more evolutionary change than previously thought possible, probably minimized their interest in other evolutionary mechanisms; see William B. Provine, 'The Role of Mathematical Population Geneticists in the Evolutionary Synthesis of the 1930s and 1940s', *Studies in History of Biology*, 2 (1978), 175.

Sexual selection, however, was not lost forever. Perhaps, as two writers

have recently suggested, more liberal social attitudes in the second half of this century rendered the study of female choice less problematic. See M. B. Andersson and J. W. Bradbury, 'Introduction', in J. W. Bradbury and M. B. Andersson (eds.), *Sexual Selection: Testing the Alternatives* (Chichester: John Wiley and Sons, 1987), 2. Building on Fisher's insights, naturalists in the 1950s, 1960s and 1970s revived and reformulated Darwin's second theory, producing an evolutionary model of female choice that has fostered extensive theoretical and empirical work. For a discussion of the beginnings of this revival, see Simon J. Frankel, 'The Eclipse of Sexual Selection' (M. Phil. dissertation, Cambridge University, 1988), 27–51.
106 Huxley, 'Sex Biology and Sex Psychology', 135.
107 Ibid., 171.
108 Ibid., 150. Huxley commented that 'the Freudian is robbed of some of his most cherished examples' by the results of investigations on the role of hormones. Ibid., 150.
109 Ibid., 157.
110 Ibid., 168–9.
111 See, for example, Sulloway, *Freud, Biologist of the Mind*, 297–315; Weeks, *Sexuality and its Discontents*, 85–9, 102; and Michel Foucault, *The History of Sexuality*, vol. 1: *An Introduction*, trans. Robert Hurley (New York: Random House, 1978).

EIGHT

MAMMALS, PRIMATOLOGY AND SEXOLOGY

LONDA SCHIEBINGER

IN 1758, in the 10th edition of his *Systema naturae*, Carolus Linnaeus introduced the term 'Mammalia' into zoological taxonomy. In his revolutionary classification of the animal kingdom – hailed in the twentieth century as the starting-point of modern zoological nomenclature – Linnaeus devised this term, meaning literally 'of the breast', to distinguish the class of animals embracing humans, apes, ungulates, sloths, sea-cows, elephants, bats, and all other organisms with hair, three ear bones, and a four-chambered heart. In so doing, he idolized the female mammae as the icon of that class.

In examining the evolution of Linnaean nomenclature, historians of science have tended to confine their study to developments within the scientific community. They trace the history of classification from Aristotle through Conrad Gesner and John Ray, culminating ultimately with the triumph of Linnaean systematics.[1] Linnaeus's nomenclature is taken more or less for granted as part of his foundational work in zoology. No one has grappled with the social origins or consequences of his term Mammalia. Certainly no one has questioned the gender politics informing Linnaeus's choice of this term.

It is also possible, however, to see the Linnaean coinage as a political act. The presence of milk-producing mammae is, after all, but one characteristic of mammals, as was commonly known to eighteenth-century European naturalists. Furthermore, the mammae are 'functional' in only half of this group of animals (the females) and, among those, for a relatively short period of time (during lactation) or not at all. As we shall see, Linnaeus could indeed have chosen a more gender-neutral name, such as Pilosa (the hairy ones – though the significance given to hair, and especially beards, was also saturated with gender),[2] for example, or Aurecaviga (the hollow-eared ones).

In what follows we consider first the emergence of the Linnaean term from natural history, retracing traditional history of science in order to understand naturalists' concerns as they attempted to devise categories for classification. What alternatives were available to Linnaeus as he thought about how to join humans to the animal kingdom, and how did other naturalists react? Crucial to my argument is the fact that Linnaeus could have derived a term from a number of equally unique, and perhaps more universal, characters of the class he designated mammals.

Traditional historians of science might stop short after describing struggles within scientific communities. But there is more to the story than that. To understand more fully the meaning of Linnaeus's term requires a foray into the cultural history of the breast. Though Linnaeus's term may have been new to zoology, the female breast carried within it deep, wide-ranging and often contradictory currents of meaning. As we shall see, there were also more immediate and pressing political trends that prompted Linnaeus to focus scientific attention on the mammae. Linnaeus venerated the maternal breast at a time when doctors and politicians had begun to extol the virtues of mother's milk (Linnaeus was a practising physician and father of seven children). Eighteenth-century middle-and upper-class women were being encouraged to give up their wet nurses; a Prussian law of 1794 would go so far as to require that healthy women nurse their own babies. Linnaeus was involved in the struggle against wet nursing, a struggle which emerged alongside and in step with political realignments undermining women's public power and attaching a new value to women's domestic roles.

MAMMALIA – THE GENEALOGY OF A TERM

It has been said that God created nature and Linnaeus gave it order.[3] Carolus Linnaeus, also known as Carl von Linné, 'Knight of the Order of the Polar Star', was, indeed, the central figure in developing European taxonomy and nomenclature. His *Systema naturae* treated the three classical kingdoms of nature – vegetable, animal and mineral – growing from a folio of only twelve pages in 1735 to a three-volume work of 2,400 pages in the 12th and last edition revised by Linnaeus himself in 1766. In the epoch-making 10th edition, Linnaeus gave binomial names (generic and specific) to all the animals known to him, nearly 4,400 species.[4]

Linnaeus divided animals into six classes: Mammalia, Aves, Amphibia, Pisces, Insecta and Vermes.[5] Though he had based important aspects of plant taxonomy on sexual dimorphism, the term

Mammalia was the only one of his major zoological divisions to focus on reproductive organs and the only term highlighting a character associated primarily with the female.[6] The names of his other classes come, in many cases, from Aristotle: Aves simply means birds; Vermes derives from the colour (red-brown) of the common earthworm; Amphibia emphasizes habitat; Insecta refers to the segmentation of the body. Scientific nomenclature has been a conservative enterprise; suitable terms tend to be conserved and new terms derived by modifying traditional ones. Linnaeus, however, devised the term Mammalia wholly new.

In coining the term 'mammals', Linnaeus abandoned Aristotle's canonical term, Quadrupedia. For more than 2,000 years most of the animals we now designate as mammals (along with most reptiles and several amphibians) had been called quadrupeds. While Aristotle had never intended to develop a definitive taxonomy, his analytical distinctions set out in his *Historia animalium* laid the groundwork for European taxonomy. Using a number of diagnostics – mode of subsistence, locomotion and reproduction – he arranged animals hierarchically along what later would be called the *scala naturae*. Aristotle began by dividing animals into two main groups according to the quality of their blood. 'Blooded animals' had warm, red blood and superior qualities of 'soul' (*psyche*) – sharp senses, great courage and intelligence; 'bloodless animals' had a colourless liquid analogous to blood but with no essential heat. Quadrupeds, then, formed a major category within blooded animals and included all animals going on four feet. Aristotle further separated quadrupeds into two groups: (1) viviparous (bearing live young and including many of the animals we now call mammals) and (2) oviparous (egg layers, what we now call reptiles and also some amphibians). Birds formed another group within the blooded animals; they were bipedal but not erect. Fish, the final group, were considered imperfect, lacking legs, arms and wings, and living in water.[7]

John Ray (1627–1705), the great English naturalist, presented the first serious challenge to Aristotelian classification. Aristotle's primary division of animals into blooded and bloodless, Ray noted, was not strictly accurate, since all organisms have a vital fluid. The division of animals into viviparous and oviparous was similarly flawed because all animals come from eggs (either internal or external to the mother's body). More specific to our theme, Ray was the first to question the appropriateness of the term 'quadruped'. Whales, porpoises and manatees, he pointed out, share key features with quadrupeds (red blood, a heart with two ventricles, and lungs), but do not have four feet. In his 'Table of Classification', Ray correctly removed these animals from the fishes and grouped them with other viviparous quadrupeds. He also suggested that the term 'quadruped' be dropped.[8]

Naturalists did not immediately act on Ray's suggestions. Linnaeus, in the first edition of his *Systema naturae* (1735), continued to use Aristotle's traditional term, Quadrupedia. He did, however, raise eyebrows and ire by including humans (rather uncomfortably) among quadrupeds. Indeed it was the question of how to place humans in nature more than anything else that led Linnaeus to abandon the term Quadrupedia and search for something more appropriate. In setting humans among quadrupeds, Linnaeus called attention to their hairy bodies, four feet (two for locomotion and two for gripping, as he later explained)[9], and the viviparous and lactiferous nature of the females. On the basis of similarities in their teeth (namely, four incisors) he further included humans in his order Anthropomorpha (a term he borrowed from Ray) along with apes, monkeys and sloths. Anthropomorpha was changed to primates only in the 1758 edition.

Linnaeus's ranking humans among quadrupeds outraged naturalists. They found repugnant his characterization of rational man as a hairy animal with four feet and four incisors. The French naturalist Georges-Louis Leclerc, Comte de Buffon, born the same year as Linnaeus and his principal rival, made the obvious point that many of the creatures included among Linnaeus's Quadrupedia were not quadrupeds at all: humans have two hands and two feet; bats have two feet and no hands; apes have four hands and no feet; and the manatee have only two hands.[10] Louis Daubenton, Buffon's assistant at the Jardin des Plantes, denounced Linnaeus's entire system as 'false' and 'inaccurate'.[11] Finally, many naturalists rejected as heretical the notion that humans are essentially animals. Holy Scripture, after all, clearly taught that man was created in God's image. It should be recalled that while Aristotle had included humans among viviparous quadrupeds, in the course of the Middle Ages scholastics removed humans from nature, emphasizing instead their proximity to angels.[12]

In defence of his new term, Linnaeus remarked that even if his critics did not believe that man originally walked on all fours, surely every man born of woman must admit that he was nourished by his mother's milk.[13] Linnaeus thus called attention to the fact, commonly known since Aristotle, that hairy, viviparous females lactate. Linnaeus was also convinced of the diagnostic value of the teat. As early as 1732, in his *Tour of Lapland*, he had already announced: 'If I knew how many teeth and of what peculiar form each animal has, as well as how many udders and where situated, I should perhaps be able to contrive a most natural methodical arrangement of quadrupeds.'[14] In the first edition of his *Systema naturae* (1735) he used the number and position of teats or udders to align orders within his class of Anthropomorpha (complicating factors being that females and males often have different numbers, and that females of the same species may also vary in the number of their teats). In 1758, Linnaeus finally announced the term Mammalia with the words: 'Mammalia, these and no other animals have mammae [mammata].' He seemed quite unconcerned that mammae are not a universal character of the class he intended to distinguish. 'All females', he wrote on the following page, 'have lactiferous mammae of determinate number, as do males (except for the horse).'

Mammalia resonated with the older term Animalia, derived from *anima* meaning the breath of life or vital spirit.[15] The new term also conformed to Linnaeus's own rules for zoological terms: it was pleasing to the ear, easy to say and to remember, and not more than twelve letters long.[16] For the rest of his life Linnaeus fiddled with his system, moving animals from order to order, creating new categories and combinations the better to capture nature's order. Yet he never felt the need to rechristen mammals.

The term Mammalia won immediate acceptance, though there were also detractors of note. Buffon took particular offence at the prominence Linnaeus gave the mammae: 'A general character, such as the teat, taken to identify quadrupeds should at least belong to all quadrupeds' (Buffon, like Linnaeus, noted that stallions have no teats).[17] Buffon also complained that Linnaeus's order Anthropomorpha lumped together things as different as man, the ape and the sloth. This 'violence' was wreaked on the natural order, he lamented, all because there was 'some small relationship between the number of nipples or teeth of these animals, or some slight resemblance in the form of their horns'.[18]

Other taxonomists – including Felix Vicq-d'Azyr and Thomas Pennant – continued to use the traditional term Quadrupedia. Still others developed their own alternatives. The Frenchman Henri de Blainville in 1816 tried to rationalize zoological nomenclature, calling mammals Pilifera (having hair), birds Pennifera (having feathers), and reptiles Squammifera (having scales).[19] In England, John Hunter proposed the term Tetracoilia, drawing attention to the four-chambered heart.[20]

These critics met with little success. Mammalia was adopted by the English as 'mammals', though 'mammifers' was also occasionally used, and as one commentator has suggested the science treating mammals was rather awkwardly rendered as 'mammalogy', meaning literally 'a study of breasts' (and not of breast-bearing animals, which would be more properly 'mammology' or 'mammalology').[21] The French devised *Mammifères*, or the breast-bearers (not *Mammaux*, nicely analogous to *animaux*). The Germans refocused matters sightly, creating *Säugetiere*, or 'suckling animals', which appropriately drew attention away from the breast and highlighted the act of suckling (though no distinction was made between a mother giving suck and a newborn taking milk). Linnaeus's term Mammalia was retained even after the Darwinian revolution and is today recognized by the International Code of Zoological Nomenclature.

HOW SIGNIFICANT ARE THE MAMMAE?

Were there good reasons for Linnaeus to name mammals 'mammals'? This question implies a logic uncharacteristic of the naming process. Names of taxa collect over time, and unless there is a technical problem – as was the case with the term Quadrupedia – they pass unchanged from generation to generation. Naturalists also name plants and animals for other than empirical reasons. Pleasing plants or animals are often named after a wife or colleague, while a particularly odious species might be given the name of a professional rival (e.g, *Siegesbeckia*, a small and unpleasant flowering weed that Linnaeus named after Johann Siegesbeck, a critic of his sexual system).[22]

Zoological nomenclature – like all language – is to some degree arbitrary; naturalists devise convenient terms to identify groups of animals. But nomenclature is also historical, growing out of specific contexts, conflicts and circumstances, and it is the job of the historian to ask why a certain term was coined. In creating the term Mammalia, Linnaeus intended to highlight an essential trait of that class of animals. Etienne Geoffroy Saint-Hilaire and Georges Cuvier, in their article 'Mammalogie' for the *Magazin encyclopédique* of 1795, summed up the practice of eighteenth-century taxonomists, stating that primary organs determine classes, while secondary organs determine orders. In 1827, Cuvier continued to argue that the mammae distinguish the class bearing their name better than any other external character.[23]

Is Cuvier's statement, in fact, true? Does the longevity of Linnaeus's term reflect the fact that he was simply right, that the mammae, indeed, represent a primary, universal and unique character of mammals (as would have been the parlance of the eighteenth century)? Yes and no. Palaeontologists today identify the mammary gland as one of at least six uniquely mammalian characters.[24] Linnaeus himself, though, was perhaps overly exuberant in singling out the breast or teat itself – a sexually charged part of the female body – rather than its function. Indeed one could argue that the term Lactantia (the lactating ones, derived from Linnaeus's own description of female mammae) would have better captured the significance of the mammae; certainly Linnaeus was wrong to think that the number and position of the teats themselves were significant. But Lactantia still refers exclusively to females. Lactentia or Sugentia ('the sucking ones') would have better universalized the term, since male as well as female young suckle at their mothers' breasts.

The fact remains that the mammae was only one among several traits that could have been highlighted. Even by eighteenth-century criteria, there was not one single character that could determine class assignment. As Buffon recognized, species – defined as members of a group of individuals that can mate and produce fertile offspring – is the only taxon that exists in nature. Even today, this does not mean that higher units (genera, families, orders, classes, and on up) are arbitrary; these must be consistent with evolutionary genealogy.[25] Yet, as we have seen, Linnaeus could have chosen from a number of equally valid terms, such as Pilosa, Aurecaviga, Lactantia, or Sugentia. Because Linnaeus had choices, I will argue that his focus upon the breast responded to broader cultural and political trends.

BREASTS AND MOTHER'S MILK: PROBLEMATIC ICONS

Long before Linnaeus, the female breast had been a powerful icon within Western cultures, representing the sublime and bestial in human nature.[26] The grotesque withered breasts on witches and devils represented temptations of wanton lust, sins of the flesh, and humankind fallen from paradise. The firm spherical breasts of Aphrodite, the Greek ideal, represented an otherworldly beauty and virginity. In the French Revolution, the bared female breast – embodied by the strident Marianne – became a resilient symbol of freedom.[27] From the multi-breasted Diana of Ephesus to the fecund-bosomed Nature, the breast symbolized generation, regeneration and renewal.

As we have seen, Linnaeus created his term Mammalia in response to the question of humans' place in nature. In his quest to find an appropriate term for what we would call a taxon uniting humans and beasts, Linnaeus made the breast – and specifically the fully developed female breast – the icon of the highest class of animals. By privileging a uniquely female characteristic in this way, it might be argued that Linnaeus broke with long-standing traditions that saw the male as the measure of all things. It is important to note, however, that in the same volume in which Linnaeus introduced the term mammalia, he also introduced the term *Homo sapiens*. This term – 'man of wisdom' – was used to *distinguish* humans from other primates (apes, lemurs and bats, for example). In the language of taxonomy, *sapiens* is what is known as a 'trivial' name (Linnaeus at one point pondered the choice of the name *Homo diurnus*, designed to contrast with *Homo nocturnus*).[28] From a historical point of view, however, the choice of the term *sapiens* is highly significant. Man had traditionally been distinguished from animals by his reason; the medieval apposition, *animal rationale*, proclaimed his uniqueness.[29] Thus, within Linnaean terminology, a female character (the lactating mammae) ties humans to brutes, while a traditionally male character (reason) marks our separateness from brutes.

The notion that woman – lacking male perfection of mind and body – resides nearer the beast than does man is an ancient one. Among all the organs of a woman's body, it was her reproductive organs that were considered most animal-like. For Plato, the uterus was an animal with its own sense of smell, wandering within the female body and leaving disease and destruction in its path.[30] The Greek physician Galen and even the great anatomist Andreas Vesalius (for a time) reported that the uterus had horns. Milk-production in the female breast had already been seen as linking humans and animals. Aristotle, in his *Historia animalium*, had recognized that all internally viviparous animals – women, sheep, horses, cows and whales, for example – nurse their young. Beyond noting how breast size relates to milk production, and noting the number and position of teats in the various animals, however, Aristotle was not much interested in the breast itself. His interest lay more in the utility and variety of milk from different animals – which among these makes the tastiest cheese and which grasses promote milk production.[31]

In Judaic traditions, too, the discomfort women feel during menstruation and childbirth were considered curses, rendering them unclean, undesirable and beastlike. The disgust associated with menstruation also sullied lactation; Aristotle's theory that lactation was related to menstruation remained current in the West well into the eighteenth century. For Aristotle, milk was concocted blood that, in the male, was secreted as semen. In the female, it was secreted as menstrual fluid (in non-pregnant women), as a vital fluid nourishing the embryo (in pregnant women), and as milk for the newborn (in postpartum women).[32]

Myths and legends also portrayed suckling as a point of intimate connection between humans and beasts, suggesting the interchangeability of the maternal breast in this respect. A nanny-goat, Amaltheia, was said to have nursed the young Zeus.[33] A she-wolf served as the legendary nurse to Romulus and Remus, the founders of Rome. From the Middle Ages to the seventeenth and eighteenth centuries, bears and wolves were reported to have suckled abandoned children. Children were thought to imbibe certain characters of the animals that nursed them – the 'wild Peter' found in northern Germany in 1724 was thought to have grown thick hair all over his body as a result of his nurturance at the breast of a bear. Linnaeus believed that ancient heroes, put to the breast of lionesses, absorbed their very great courage along with their milk.[34] In rarer instances, humans were reported even to have suckled animals. Veronica Giuliani, beatified by Pius II (1405–64), took a real lamb to bed with her and suckled it at her breast in memory of the lamb of God.[35] European voyagers reported that natives of South America kept their breasts active by letting animals of all kinds feed from them.[36] In Siam, women were said to suckle apes.

Linnaeus thus followed well-established Western conceptions when he suggested that women belong to nature in ways that men do not. As Carolyn Merchant has shown, nature itself has long been conceived as female in most Western intellectual traditions.[37] The influential eighteenth-century artists and engravers, Gravelot and Cochin, personified Nature as a virgin, her breasts dripping with milk (fig. 8.1).

It is significant that Linnaeus used the mammiferous Diana of the Ephesians, an ancient symbol of fertility, as the frontispiece to his *Fauna Suecica*, where he first defended including humans among the quadrupeds (fig. 8.2).[38] Linnaeus's Diana, half-captive in the fecund earth, emerges to display her womb – the centre of life – and her nourishing breasts.[39] In the classic image, her curiously immobilized trunk is covered with symbols of both fertility (bees, acorns, bulls, crabs) and chastity (stags, lions and roses), with those of fertility outnumbering those of chastity. Her pendulous breasts, heavy with milk, represent the life force of nature – mother and nurse of all living things.

For Linnaeus to suggest, then, that humans shared with animals the capacity to suckle their young was nothing new. This uniquely female feature had long been considered less than human. But it had also been considered more than human. In the Christian world, milk had been seen as providing sustenance – for both body and spirit. Throughout the Middle Ages, the faithful cherished vials of the Virgin's milk as a healing balm, a symbol of mercy, an eternal

Fig. 8.1. Nature portrayed as a young virgin. Though a virgin, her breasts are shown dripping with mother's milk (the virgin mother is a persistent theme in Christianity, where the ideal female is both chaste and fecund). Nature's nudity expresses the simplicity of her essence. The lion and stag are symbols of chastity. The multi-breasted Diana of the Ephesians in the background represents the Ancients' image of nature, 'the Mother of all Being'. From Charles Cochin and Hubert François Gravelot, *Iconologie par figures, ou traité complet des allégories, emblêmes &c* (1791; Geneva: Minkoff Reprint, 1972), s.v. 'Nature'.
Courtesy of The Pennsylvania State University Libraries.

Fig. 8.2. Frontispiece to Linnaeus's *Fauna Suecica* (1746), featuring a many-breasted Diana. Linnaeus's Diana is relatively modest with only four breasts; earlier depictions often featured twenty-eight or more breasts, sometimes encircling her entire upper body. Diana's breasts, spouting water, also became a favourite motif for fountains (those at Villa d'Este, Trivoli, for example). By permission of the Staatsbibliothek zu Berlin, Preußischer Kulturbesitz (Sign.: Lv 11 575).

mystery. As Marina Warner has pointed out, the Virgin Mary endured none of the bodily pleasures and pains associated with childbearing – menstruation, sexual intercourse, pregnancy and labour – except for suckling. The tender Madonna suckled the infant Jesus both as his historical mother and as the metaphysical image of nourishing Mother Church.[40] During the twelfth century, maternal imagery – particularly suckling and nurturing – extended also to Church Fathers. Abbots and prelates were encouraged to 'mother' the souls in their charge, to expose their breasts and let their bosoms expand with the milk of consolation.[41] Even the full breasts of God the Father were said to be milked by the Holy Spirit into the cup of the Son of God.[42]

In subcurrents of religious traditions, mother's milk was thought to impart knowledge. Philosophia-Sapientia – the traditional personification of wisdom – suckled philosophers at her breasts moist with the milk of knowledge and moral virtue (fig. 8.3). Augustine of Hippo, too, imagined himself drinking from the breasts of Sapientia.[43] Centuries later, men of science still sought the secrets of (female) Nature within her bosom, though now with a rather different end. Goethe, probing her innermost recesses, waxed poetic on the point: 'Infinite Nature, where are thy breasts, those well-springs of all life on which hang heaven and earth, toward which my withered breast strains?'[44] For Goethe, at least, the scientists' new desire was not to suckle at the breast of Nature, but to imitate the nourishing power of Nature.

Mother's milk was valued for its medicinal as well as its spiritual virtues. Sicilians drank the milk of a woman who had borne a first son as a cure for deafness. It was used as an abortifacient in sixteenth-century Germany. In Alsace, it served as a remedy for consumption. It was also used for healing earaches, fevers and sores.[45] Linnaeus recommended it to adults as a laxative.

In a certain sense, Linnaeus's focus on the milk-bearing breast was at odds with trends that found beauty (though not necessarily salvation) above all in the virginal breast. In both the Greek and Christian traditions the ideal breast was an unused one – small, firm and spherical; the process of milk swelling the breast was thought to deform it. Mythical female figures – the goddesses Artemis and Aphrodite, the martial Amazons (who burned away one breast so that their bows would lie flat against their chests), and the nursing mother of Christ – were all virgins.[46] Of all the female Virtues, only Charity possessed a non-virginal body – infants drank maternal bounty, love and humility from her breasts.[47]

The classic ideal of the firm, unused breast was indeed realized in

Fig. 8.3. Sapientia (the personification of wisdom) suckling two philosophers from a fifteenth-century German manuscript, reproduced in Lieselotte Möller, 'Nährmutter Weisheit', *Deutsche Vierteljahrsschrift*, 24 (1950), fig. 2, facing p. 351.

the bodies of many upper- and middle-class European women who relieved themselves of the burden of suckling their own children. Wealthy women bore children, but most often did not nurse them. For this task, they employed women who were considered closer to nature – peasants and, in overseas colonies, native and Negro women ('often but one remove above a brute', in the words of one observer) – to suckle their children.[48]

Colonial relations also shaped perceptions of the breast. Late nineteenth-century anthropologists classified breasts by beauty in the same way that they measured skulls for intelligence (fig. 8.4). The ideal breast – for all races – was once again young and virginal. Europeans preferred the compact 'hemispherical' type, found, it was said, only among whites and orientals. The much maligned breasts of African (especially Hottentot) women were dismissed as flabby and pendulous, similar to the udders of goats. When women of African descent were portrayed sympathetically, they were typically shown having firm spherical breasts, as in John Stedman's illustration of his 15-year-old mulatta mistress and later his wife, Joanna.[49] For Charles White, the Manchester physician and notorious racist, the hallmark of European superiority was found on the bosom of European women: 'In what quarter of the globe shall we find the blush that overspreads the soft features of the beautiful women of Europe, that emblem of modesty, of delicate feelings, and of sense? ... Where, except on the bosom of the European woman, two such plump and snowy white hemispheres, tipt with vermilion?'[50]

Linnaeus's fixation upon the female mammae, then, though new to the zoological tradition, emerged from deep cultural roots, which may help explain, at least in part, its easy acceptance within both science and the broader culture.[51]

GENDER POLITICS IN TAXONOMY

Europeans' fascination with the female breast provided fertile ground for Linnaeus's innovation. But more immediate political concerns compelled him to focus scientific attention on the mammae. His scientific vision arose alongside and in step with important political trends in the eighteenth century – the restructuring of child care and of women's lives as mothers, wives and citizens.

Most directly, Linnaeus joined the ongoing campaign to abolish the ancient custom of wet-nursing.[52] The eighteenth century was the heyday of wet-nursing. More Europeans – including not just aristocrats and wealthy merchants but farmers, clergy and artisans – than ever

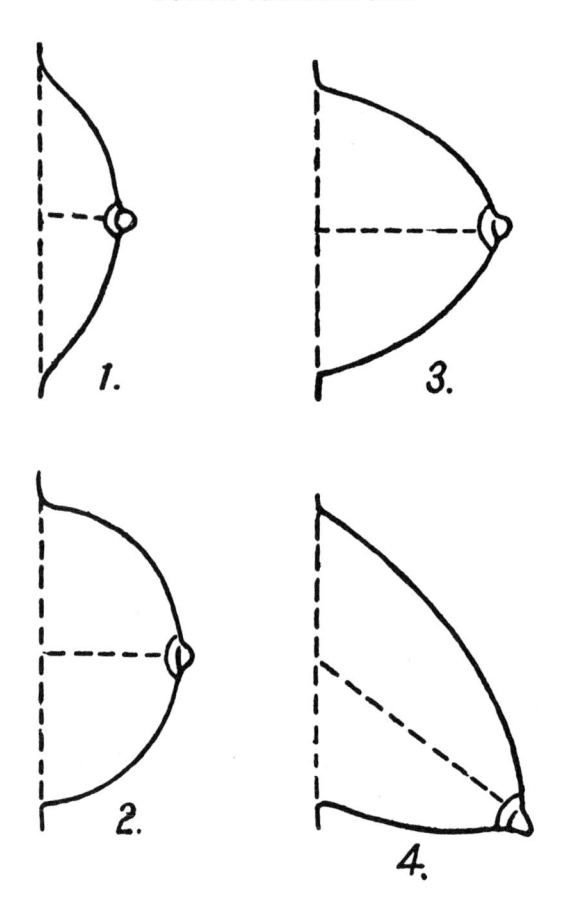

Fig. 8.4. Breast shapes among humans from Ploss, Bartels and Bartels's *Woman*, vol. 1, 399. The first is described as *bowl-shaped*, the second is *hemispherical* (characteristic of whites and orientals and identified by the authors as beautiful), the third *conical*, and the fourth (found primarily in blacks) *elongated*, as in 'the udder of the goat', with nipples pointed downward.

before sent their children to the countryside to be nursed.[53] Though wet-nursing had provided a solution to the problem of child-rearing for middle- and upper-class mothers and fathers, it also resulted in high infant mortality (these rates were also often exaggerated by state ministers).[54] Women's desire and, more often, need to engage like men in productive lives increasingly came into conflict with government policies to reverse population trends. Fears began to grow that Europe was losing population at a time when governments were looking for increased manpower to fuel both military and economic expansion. Concern to increase population was so great in Denmark, for example, that a law was passed in 1707 authorizing young women to bear as many children as possible even if they were bastards.[55] Joseph Raulin, physician to Louis XV of France, judged children 'the wealth of nations, the glory of kingdoms, and the nerve and good fortune of empires'.[56]

The preservation of family and maternal duties became important matters of state.[57] For state ministers, the simplest way to increase birth-rates was to reduce infant mortality through improved training for obstetricians, midwives and – most importantly – for mothers. A central element in this campaign was the health and conduct manuals written for women by medical doctors. In this context Linnaeus – himself a practising physician – prepared a dissertation against the evils of wet-nursing in 1752, just a few years before coining the term Mammalia and while watching his own children suckle (his wife bore seven children between 1741 and 1757). In his 'Step Nurse' (translated into French as 'La Nourrice marâtre, ou Dissertation sur les suites funestes du nourrissage mercenaire') Linnaeus sounded the themes of the Enlightenment attack on wet-nursing.[58] First and foremost, wet-nursing violated the laws of nature. Nature – herself 'a tender and provident mother' – had set the course for female reproduction; digression from her laws endangered both mother and child. Linnaeus recognized (as did other physicians and midwives) that a newborn nursed by another woman is deprived of the mother's first milk, colostrum, crucial for purging the child of meconium. He also warned that, because most nurses came from the poorest classes, they ate fatty foods, drank too much alcohol, were ridden with pox and venereal disease – all of which produced unhealthy, if not lethal, milk. He also emphasized that forcing the milk back might prove harmful to the mother. Uterine contractions after birth forced the voluminous humours associated with pregnancy to flow towards the breasts; if these humours did not emerge as milk, the woman might fall ill. For Linnaeus, the laws of nature thus dictated the road to health for both mother and child.

Here, in this 1752 pamphlet, Linnaeus alluded to his subsequent nomenclature by contrasting the barbarity of women who deprive their children of mother's milk with the gentle care of great beasts – the whale, the fearsome lioness and fierce tigress – who willingly offer their young the breast.[59] The idea that women should follow the example of beasts was a common feature of the anti-wet-nursing literature flooding Europe.[60] Appealing to natural law and order, the

French midwife Marie Anel le Robours pleaded with women to follow the 'animal instinct' that prompts a mother to care for her young immediately after birth. Women were admonished to disregard the wishes of husbands who sought to rid the house of troublesome infants and to cultivate instead the 'superior attachment that animals have for their young'. Women were also advised to disregard the advice of midwives who failed to recognize the value of colostrum (it was customary for women to wait twenty-eight hours after parturition before nursing). Infants, just like other small animals, she explained, will search for the breast immediately after birth.[61]

These and other critiques of baby farming went a long way towards countering the ignorance and abuses surrounding wet-nursing. Babies in this period did, in fact, have a better chance of surviving when nursed by their mothers than by women hired to do the task. The anonymous author of *The Ladies Dispensatory* may have exaggerated, though, when charging that sending a child out to a wet-nurse was little better than exposing it to die in the street.[62] More plausible were the reports of abuses, especially in France, where nurses often took in too many nurslings in their attempt to make ends meet.[63] Yet many of the attacks on wet-nursing also reiterated age-old myths and superstitions. Linnaeus, for example, cautioned that the character of the upper-class child could easily be corrupted by the milk of lower-class nurses. Using examples drawn from Erasmus, he blamed the bitter, wicked milk of nurses for Nero's addiction to alcohol and for Caligula's tyranny.[64] While authors of pamphlets showed genuine concern for the well-being of mothers and of children of their own classes, they seldom considered the evils of the wet-nursing business for the 'lower classes of mankind' (as one influential voice in the anti-wet-nursing movement, called them).[65] Children of wet nurses were often neglected or even 'disposed of' (for a small fee, no questions asked).[66]

The attempt to abolish wet-nursing was tied to another aspect of the restructuring of reproduction in the eighteenth century – the displacement of midwives by male physicians. The story of the demise of the midwife and rise of the male expert is well known.[67] University-trained physicians' move to professionalize women's health care (and in so doing to drive traditional female practitioners from the field) extended also to the management of newborns. The English physician William Cadogan, perhaps the most emphatic on this point, encouraged fathers – who often considered breast-feeding something low and degrading – to have their children nursed under their 'own eye'. Nursing, in his view, should not be one of 'the mysteries of the *Bona Dea*, from which men are excluded'. Supervision of the care of children had been 'too long fatally left to the management of women, who cannot suppose to have proper knowledge to fit them for such a task, notwithstanding they look upon it to be their own province'. The 'grandmothers' should be moved aside, along with their herbs, roots and other traditional practices.[68]

Medical authority and the legal system worked together to create new interest in maternal breast-feeding. As prescribed in Jean Jacques Rousseau's influential *Emile*, breast-feeding became fashionable among French upper-class women for a short period in the late eighteenth century.[69] In Germany, leading medical doctors advocated laws that would force healthy women to nurse their own infants.[70] Such laws were put into effect in Prussia in 1794, just a few years after Frederick the Great installed a modern version of Diana of the Ephesians in his Potsdam garden.[71]

Authors of anti-wet-nursing literature – including Linnaeus, Cadogan, Rousseau and Anel le Robours – were highly moralistic about returning women to their rightful place as loving and caring mothers. This, despite the fact that Rousseau placed his own five children in foundling homes, not even bothering to record their sex or dates of birth.[72] Women's attempts to contravene the laws of nature were seen as a matter of vanity. Cadogan prevailed upon every woman to give up 'a little of the beauty of her breast' to feed her young. Linnaeus charged that women only pretended to be unable to breast-feed and ridiculed their many excuses: that they did not have enough milk, or could not be deprived of fluids precious to their own health, or were overloaded with domestic affairs. But the real reason for such a reluctance, Linnaeus imagined, was a disinclination to deprive husbands of the pleasures of marriage – a characteristic, he noted, of all quadrupeds (it was thought that nursing mothers should refrain from sexual intercourse). Rousseau, not so sanguine on this point, charged that wet-nurses freed the upper-class mother to return to the gay entertainments of the city, not necessarily her husband's bed.[73]

Returning to nature and its laws was seen as the surest way to end corruption and regenerate the state, morally as well as economically. Rousseau, the era's self-appointed spokesman for nature, saw the refusal of mothers to nurse as the source of national depravity. 'Everything follows successively from this first depravity. The whole moral order degenerates; naturalness is extinguished in all hearts.' The bond between mother and child created through maternal nursing was idealized as the cement of civil society, fostering love of sons for mothers, returning husbands to wives. The infant was imagined to imbibe with the mother's milk her noble character, her love and virtue. 'Let mothers deign to nurse their children,' Rousseau preached, 'morals will reform themselves, nature's sentiments will be awakened in every heart, the state will be repeopled.'[74] For the enlightened of Europe, the breast symbolized the synthesis of nature and society, the bond between the private and public worlds.[75]

It is remarkable that in the heady days of the French Revolution, when revolutionaries marched behind the martial and bare-breasted Liberty,[76] the maternal breast became nature's sign that women belonged in the home. Delegates to the French National Convention used the breast as a natural sign that women should be barred from citizenship and the wielding of public power. In this case, 'the breasted ones' were to be confined to the home. In denying women political power, Pierre-Gaspard Chaumette, *procureur* of the Paris Commune, asked indignantly:

> Since when is it permitted to abandon one's sex? Since when is it decent for women to forsake the pious cares of their households and the cribs of their children, coming instead to public places, to hear speeches in the galleries and senate? Is it to men that nature confided domestic cares? *Has she given us breasts to feed our children?*[77]

This message was embodied in the 'Festival of Unity and Indivisibility' of 1793, celebrating the first anniversary of the Republic. David's carefully orchestrated festival featured a Fountain of Regeneration built on the ruins of the Bastille, the symbol of absolutism (fig. 8.5). As described in the popular press, eighty-six (male) deputies to the National Convention drank joyfully from the spouting breasts of 'Nature', personified as Isis, the Egyptian goddess of fertility.[78] While the male deputies publicly drank the maternal 'milk' of national renewal from the breasts of the colossal Isis, exemplary republic mothers quietly re-enact the scene giving their virtuous milk to future citizens of the state.

The year 1793 marked the fateful repression of women's demands for citizenship and also, as Lynn Hunt has shown, a turning-point in republican images of women. When publicly represented, women were no longer cast as the strident Marianne, the symbol of Liberty, but were increasingly relegated to motherly roles. Festivals featured parades of pregnant women; women featured in ceremonies, such as the Festival of the Supreme Being of 1794, were all wives and mothers, many pressing nurslings to their breasts.[79]

I would suggest, then, that Linnaeus's term Mammalia helped legitimize the restructuring of European society by emphasizing how

Fig. 8.5. The 'Fountain of Regeneration' by Jacques-Louis David, the famous eighteenth-century French painter. From Charles Monnet, *Les Principales Journées de la Révolution* (Paris, 1838). Spencer Collection, the New York Public Library, Astor, Lenox and Tilden Foundations.

natural it was for females – both human and non-human – to suckle and rear their own children. Linnaean systematics had sought to render nature universally comprehensible, yet the categories he devised infused nature with European notions of gender. Linnaeus saw females of all species as tender mothers, a vision he (wittingly or unwittingly) imprinted on Europeans' understandings of nature.

The story of the origins of the term Mammalia provides yet another example of how science is not value-neutral but emerges from complex cultural matrices. The term Linnaeus coined in 1758 solved the problem of how to class the whale with its terrestrial congeners and did away with Aristotle's outmoded term 'quadruped'. But more than that it provided a solution to the place of humankind within nature and ultimately of womankind within European culture.

ACKNOWLEDGEMENTS

A special thanks to the Guggenheim Foundation and the National Science Foundation for support for this project. I would also like to thank the Office of Research and Graduate Studies and the Institute for the Arts and Humanistic Studies at the Pennsylvania State University for their kind support. Portions of this essay first appeared in *The American Historical Review*, 98 (1993) and in *Nature's Body: Gender in the Making of Modern Science* (Boston: Beacon Press, 1993).

NOTES

1 Literature on Linnaeus is voluminous. Gunnar Broberg is one of the few to consider broader contexts. See his *Linnaeus: Progress and Prospects in Linnaean Research* (Stockholm: Almqvist and Wiksell International, 1980) and *Homo sapiens L.: Studier i Carl von Linnés naturuppfattning och människolära* (The Swedish History of Science Society, 1975).
2 Londa Schiebinger, *Nature's Body: Gender in the Making of Modern Science* (Boston: Beacon Press, 1993), chapter 4.
3 Broberg, *Linnaeus*, 34.
4 W. T. Stearn, 'The Background of Linnaeus's Contributions to the Nomenclature and Methods of Systematic Biology', *Systematic Zoology*, 8 (1959), 4–22.
5 Carl Linnaeus, *Systema naturae per regna tria naturae*, 10th edn (Stockholm, 1758).
6 Londa Schiebinger, 'The Private Life of Plants: Sexual Politics in Carl Linnaeus and Erasmus Darwin', in Marina Benjamin (ed.), *Science and Sensibility: Gender and Scientific Inquiry 1780–1945* (Oxford: Basil Blackwell, 1991), 121–41.
7 Aristotle, *Historia animalium*; G. E. R. Lloyd, *Science, Folklore and Ideology* (Cambridge: Cambridge University Press, 1983), 16.

8 Despite these objections, the term figured prominently in the title of his book. John Ray, *Synopsis methodica: animalium quadrupedum et serpentini generis* (London, 1693), 55. See also Charles Raven, *John Ray, Naturalist: His Life and Works* (Cambridge: Cambridge University Press, 1950).
9 Carl Linnaeus, *Fauna Suecica* (Stockholm, 1746), Preface.
10 Georges-Louis Leclerc, Comte de Buffon, *Histoire naturelle, générale et particulière*, vol. XIV (Paris, 1749–67), 18.
11 Cited by Jean Baptiste-Bory de Saint-Vincent, *Dictionnaire classique d'histoire naturelle*, vol. VIII (Paris, 1825), 270.
12 On this point, see Gunnar Broberg's excellent, '*Homo sapiens*: Linnaeus's Classification of Man', in Tore Frängsmyr (ed.), *Linnaeus: The Man and His Work* (Berkeley and Los Angeles: University of California Press, 1983), 156–94.
13 Broberg, *Homo sapiens L.*, 176.
14 Carl Linnaeus, *Lachesis Lapponica, or a Tour in Lapland*, vol. I, trans. John E. Smith (London, 1811), 191, sightly modified.
15 Theodor Gill, 'The Story of a Word – Mammal', *Popular Science Monthly*, 61 (1902), 434–8, p. 435.
16 Stearn, 'The Background of Linnaeus's Contributions to the Nomenclature', 8.
17 Buffon, *Histoire naturelle*, vol. I, 38–40.
18 Ibid. See also Phillip Sloan, 'The Buffon–Linnaeus Controversy', *Isis*, 67 (1976), 356–75; and James Larson, 'Linné's French Critics', in Broberg, *Linnaeus*, 67–79.
19 Henri de Blainville, 'Prodrome: d'une nouvelle distribution systématique du règne animal', *Journal de Physique*, 83 (1816), 246.
20 John Hunter, *Essays and Observations on Natural History, Anatomy, Physiology, Psychology, and Geology*, vol. I, ed. Richard Owen (London, 1861), 25.
21 Gill, 'The Story of a Word – Mammal', 436–7. See also *Dictionnaire pittoresque d'histoire naturelle*, vol. IV (1836), s.v. 'Mammifères'.
22 Ronald King in Robert Thornton, *The Temple of Flora* (1799; Boston: New York Graphic Society, 1981), 9.
23 Georges Cuvier, *Le Règne animal* (Paris, 1817), vol. I, 76.
24 See D. M. Kermack and K. A. Kermack, *The Evolution of Mammalian Characters* (London: Croom Helm, 1984), vii; also T. S. Kemp, *Mammal-like Reptiles and the Origin of Mammals* (London: Academic Press, 1982).
25 Stephen Jay Gould, 'A Quahog is a Quahog', in *The Panda's Thumb: More Reflections in Natural History* (New York: Norton, 1980), 204–7.
26 See Marina Warner's *Alone of All Her Sex: The Myth and the Cult of the Virgin Mary* (New York: Alfred A. Knopf, 1976) and her *Monuments and Maidens: The Allegory of the Female Form* (New York: Atheneum, 1985) along with Caroline Bynum's *Jesus as Mother: Studies in the Spirituality of the High Middle Ages* (Berkeley and Los Angeles: University of California Press, 1982); Heinz Kirchhoff's 'Die künstlerische Darstellung der weiblichen Brust als Attribut der Weiblichkeit und Fruchtbarkeit als auch der Spende der Lebenskraft und der Weisheit', *Geburtshilfe und Frauenheilkunde*, 50 (1990), 234–43; Erich Neumann's *Die Grosse Mutter* (Zurich: Rhein Verlag, 1956); Anne Hollander, *Seeing through Clothes* (New York: Penguin Books, 1975); Françoise Borin, 'Arrêt sur image', in Natalie Davis and Arlette Farge (eds.), *Historie des femmes en occident*, vol. III

(Paris: Plon, 1991), 213–19; and the anecdotes collected by Gustave-Jules Witkowski, including *Les Seins dans l'histoire* (Paris: A. Maloine, 1903). A good cultural history of the breast and mother's milk is much needed.

27 See Lynn Hunt, *Politics, Culture, and Class in the French Revolution* (Berkeley and Los Angeles: University of California Press, 1984), esp. part 1; also Warner, *Monuments and Maidens*, chapters 12 and 13.

28 Broberg '*Homo sapiens*', 176.

29 Linnaeus saw reason as the principal character distinguishing humans from other animals. In the preface to his *Fauna Suecica* (1746) he called reason 'the most noble thing of all' that places man above all others.

30 Plato, *Timaeus*, 91c. Also Ian Maclean, *The Renaissance Notion of Woman: A Study in the Fortunes of Scholasticism and Medical Science in European Intellectual Life* (Cambridge: Cambridge University Press, 1980), 31.

31 Aristotle, *Historia animalium*, 500a, 521b and 582a. Throughout the Middle Ages, there was little interest in mammae as a marker of sexual difference. See Joan Cadden, *Meanings of Sexual Differences in the Middle Ages: Medicine, Natural Philosophy, and Culture* (Cambridge: Cambridge University Press, 1992).

32 Aristotle, *Generation of Animals*, 776a–777a.

33 Warner, *Alone of All Her Sex*, 194.

34 Carl Linnaeus, 'Nutrix noverca', respondent F. Lindberg (1752), *Amoenitates academicae*, vol. III (Erlangen, 1787), 262–3. Goats and other animals were used to suckle syphilitic children in foundling hospitals in the eighteenth century or when there was a shortage of human nurses. Valerie Fildes, *Wet Nursing: A History from Antiquity to the Present* (Oxford: Basil Blackwell, 1988), 147.

35 Mervyn Levy, *The Moons of Paradise: Some Reflections on the Appearance of the Female Breast in Art* (London: Arthur Barker Limited, 1962), 55.

36 Hermann Ploss, Max Bartels and Paul Bartels, *Woman: An Historical Gynecological and Anthropological Compendium*, vol. III, ed. Eric Dingwall (St Louis: C. V. Mosby Co., 1936), 211.

37 Carolyn Merchant, *The Death of Nature: Women, Ecology, and the Scientific Revolution* (San Francisco: Harper and Row, 1980).

38 Linnaeus, *Fauna Suecica*, frontispiece.

39 Neumann, *Die Grosse Mutter*, 128.

40 Warner, *Alone of All Her Sex*, 192, 200; idem, *Monuments and Maidens*, 283.

41 Bynum, *Jesus as Mother*, 115. See also Erwin Panofsky, *Abbot Suger* (Princeton: Princeton University Press, 1946), 30–1, and Sander Gilman, *Sexuality: An Illustrated History* (New York: John Wiley and Sons, 1989), 144.

42 Warner, *Alone of All Her Sex*, 194.

43 The pictorial representation of *sapientia lactans* dates to the early fifteenth century. *Sapientia lactans* was incorporated into the seal of Cambridge University which shows the naked *Alma Mater Cantabrigia* with milk streaming from her breasts (W. S. Heckscher, 'Spiritualia sub metaphoris corporalium', *University of Toronto Quarterly*, 16 (1946–7), 212 n. 9). See Klaus Lange, 'Geistliche Speise', *Zeitschrift für deutsches Altertum*, 95 (1966), 81–122, and Lieselotte Möller, 'Nährmutter Weisheit', *Deutsche Vierteljahrsschrift*, 24 (1950), 347–59.

44 Johann Wolfgang Goethe, *Faust: Eine Tragödie* (1808–32; Munich: Deutscher Taschenbuch Verlag, 1962), 19.

45 Ploss et al., *Woman*, vol. III, 233–4.
46 On Amazons, see J. A. Fabricius, 'Dissertatio critica', cited in T. Bendyshe, 'The History of Anthropology', *Memoirs Read Before the Anthropological Society of London*, vol. I (London, 1865), 415–16. Saints Agnes and Barbara were depicted having their breasts cut off as a form of torture in grotesque art of the late Middle Ages (Margaret Miles, *Carnal Knowing: Female Nakedness and Religious Meaning in the Christian West* (Boston: Beacon Press, 1989), 156).
47 Warner, *Monuments and Maidens*, 281. Ideals of the breast also changed over time. Barbara Gelphi has traced the stunning way in which, after roughly the 1750s, the maternal breast vied with the virginal for cultural hegemony (*Shelley's Goddess; Maternity, Language, Subjectivity* (New York: Oxford University Press, 1992), 43–60).
48 John Pinkerton, *A General Collection of the Best and Most Interesting Voyages and Travels in all Parts of the World*, vol. XI (London, 1808), 194.
49 John Stedman, *Narrative of a Five Years Expedition against the Revolted Negroes of Surinam* (1796; Baltimore: Johns Hopkins University Press, 1988), 89.
50 Charles White, *An Account of the Regular Gradation in Man and in Different Animals and Vegetables* (London, 1796), 134.
51 It is unclear how aware the Protestant Linnaeus was of this multifarious heritage, though as a university-educated man, he was well versed in both the classics and Scripture.
52 Dissatisfaction with wet nursing began in the 1680s; the height of the campaign, however, came in the eighteenth century. Valerie Fildes, *Breasts, Bottles and Babies: A History of Infant Feeding* (Edinburgh: Edinburgh University Press, 1986); and Randolph Trumbach, *The Rise of the Egalitarian Family: Aristocratic Kinship and Domestic Relations in Eighteenth-Century England* (New York: Academic Press, 1978). Dry-nursing under the mother's direct supervision was also advocated but led to even higher infant mortality.
53 George Sussman, *Selling Mothers' Milk: The Wet-Nursing Business in France, 1715–1914* (Urbana: University of Illinois Press, 1982), 20; see also Nancy Senior, 'Aspects of Infant Feeding in Eighteenth-Century France', *Eighteenth-Century Studies*, 16 (1983) 367; Mary Sheriff, 'Fragonard's Erotic Mothers and the Politics of Reproduction', in Lynn Hunt (ed.), *Eroticism and the Body Politic* (Baltimore: Johns Hopkins University Press, 1991), 14–40.
54 Senior, 'Aspects of Infant Feeding', 367–8. See also George Sussman, 'Parisian Infants and Norman Wet-Nurses in the Early Nineteenth Century', *Journal of Interdisciplinary History*, 7 (1977), 637.
55 Reported in Henry Home, Lord Kames, *Sketches of the History of Man*, vol. I (Dublin, 1775), 169.
56 Joseph Raulin, *De la conservation des enfants*, vol. I (Paris, 1768), 'épitre au roi'.
57 See, e.g., ibid.; J. E. Gilibert, 'Dissertation sur la dépopulation, causée par les vices, les préjugés et les erreurs des nourrices mercénaires', preface, *Les Chef-d'oeuvres de Monsieur de Sauvages*, vol. II (Lyon, 1770).
58 Linnaeus, 'Nutrix noverca', trans. Gilibert as 'La nourrice marâtre, ou dissertation sur les suites funestes du nourrissage mercénaire', *Les Chef-d'oeuvres de Monsieur de Sauvages*, vol. II, 215–44.
59 Linnaeus, 'Nutrix noverca', 258.

60 This argument dates at least to the seventeenth century (Guérin, 1675); see Senior, 'Aspects of Infant Feeding', 378–9. On the theme of women following the example of beasts in suckling their young, see also William Cadogan, *An Essay upon Nursing and the Management of Children* (London, 1748), 7; Raulin, *De la conservation des enfans*, vol. I, xxv–xxviii; Jacques Ballexserd, *Dissertation sur cette question: quelles sont les principes de la mort d'un aussi grand nombre d'enfans* (Geneva, 1775), 64; Charles Whitlaw, *New Medical Discoveries, with a Defence of the Linnaean Doctrine*, vol. I (London, 1829), 233.; and *Der Patriot*, 27 January 1724, cited in Mary Lindemann, 'Love For Hire: The Regulation of the Wet-Nursing Business in Eighteenth-Century Hamburg', *Journal of Family History*, 6 (1981), 381. The anonymous 'Sophia' used a similar argument to try to convince men to let their wives breast-feed (*Woman not Inferior to Man* (London, 1739), cited in Vivien Jones (ed.), *Women in the Eighteenth Century: Constructions of Femininity* (New York: Routledge, 1990), 225).

61 Marie-Angelique Anel le Robours, *Avis aux mères qui veulent nourrir leurs enfans*, 3d edn (Paris, 1775), esp. ix, 53, 92–3.

62 Cited in Jones, *Women in the Eighteenth Century*, 85.

63 Abuses related to financial concerns were greater in France than in England. Fiona Newall, 'Wet-Nursing and Child Care in Aldenham, Hertfordshire, 1595–1726', in Valerie Fildes (ed.), *Women as Mothers in Pre-Industrial England* (London: Routledge, 1990), 129.

64 Linnaeus, 'Nutrix noverca', 265. Though this argument was heard less frequently, it was still prominent in the eighteenth century.

65 Cadogan, *An Essay upon Nursing*, 7.

66 Fildes, *Wet Nursing*, 193. A few medical men noted the high mortality rates among wet-nurses' own children (e.g., Linnaeus, 'Nutrix noverca', 264; see also James Lehning, 'Family Life and Wetnursing in a French Village', *Journal of Interdisciplinary History*, 12 (1982), 651).

67 See Jean Donnison, *Midwives and Medical Men: A History of Inter-Professional Rivals and Women's Rights* (London: Heinemann, 1977); Ornella Moscucci, *The Science of Woman: Gynaecology and Gender in England, 1800–1929* (Cambridge: Cambridge University Press, 1990), 42–57.

68 Cadogan, *An Essay upon Nursing*, 3, 24.

69 Jean Jacques Rousseau, *Emile, ou de l'éducation* (1762) in *Œuvres complètes*, ed. Bernard Gagnegin and Marcel Raymond, vol. IV (Paris: Gallimard, 1959–69), 254–64.

70 Lindemann, 'Love for Hire', 391.

71 *Allgemeines Landrecht* (1794), part II, title II, art. 67, in Susan Bell and Karen Offen (eds.), *Women, the Family and Freedom: The Debate in Documents 1750–1880*, vol. I (Stanford: Stanford University Press, 1983), 39. See also Doris Alder, 'Im "Wahren Paradies der Weiber": Naturrecht und rechtliche Wirklichkeit der Frauen im Preussischen Landrecht', in Viktoria Schmidt-Linsenhoff (ed.), *Sklavin oder Bürgerin: Französische Revolution und neue Weiblichkeit, 1760–1830* (Frankfurt: Jonas Verlag, 1989), 206–22.

72 William Kessen, 'Rousseau's Children', *Daedalus*, 107 (1978), 155; ironically, Emile was brought up by a wet nurse in the country (Senior, 'Aspects of Infant Feeding', 385).

73 Rousseau, *Emile*, 255.
74 Ibid., 258.
75 Ludmilla Jordanova (ed.), *Languages of Nature* (New Brunswick: Rutgers University Press, 1986), 97; Warner, *Monuments and Maidens*, 282.
76 See Hunt, *Politics, Culture, and Class in the French Revolution*, chapters 2, 3.
77 Darline Levy, Harriet Applewhite and Mary Johnson (eds.), *Women in Revolutionary Paris, 1789-1795* (Urbana: University of Illinois Press, 1979), 219. See also Dorinda Outram, *The Body and the French Revolution: Sex, Class and Political Culture* (New Haven: Yale University Press, 1989).
78 Claudette Hould, *Images of the French Revolution* (Quebec: Les Publications du Québec, 1989), 378-9. See also Mona Ozouf, *Festivals and the French Revolution*, trans. Alan Sheridan (Cambridge, Mass.: Harvard University Press, 1988), 84; and Viktoria Schmidt-Linsenhoff, 'Frauenbilder der Französische Revolution', in Schmidt-Linsenhoff (ed.), *Sklavin oder Bürgerin*, 451-2; and Mary Jacobus, 'Incorruptible Milk: Breast-feeding and the French Revolution', in Sara Melzer and Leslie Rabine (eds.), *Rebel Daughters: Women and the French Revolution* (New York: Oxford University Press, 1992), 66-8.
79 Lynn Hunt, *The Family Romance of the French Revolution* (Berkeley: University of California Press, 1992), 151-91, esp. 153-5.

NINE

KRAFFT-EBING'S PSYCHOLOGICAL UNDERSTANDING OF SEXUAL BEHAVIOUR[1]

RENATE HAUSER

RICHARD VON KRAFFT-EBING (1840–1902) was an Austrian mainstream psychiatrist, who practised in the latter half of the nineteenth century. He was a university lecturer and asylum director in Graz and in Vienna (from 1889), and was probably the most prolific writer on his subject amongst his contemporaries. His interests ranged from the study of organic neurological conditions, such as peripheral paralyses and paralysis of the insane, to psychological issues such as obsessional thoughts and the therapeutic value of hypnosis. At the root of much of his work was his interest in forensic psychiatry, in which he was the leading German-speaking expert of his time. He wrote what was to become the most important German textbook of forensic psychiatry in 1879 and reviewed virtually all the forensic literature for the main psychiatric journals throughout his career. His work on sexuality (one aspect of which will be discussed below) stemmed from his legal interests, but was to develop in a more psychological direction later.

Despite Krafft-Ebing's broad range of interests, it was his contribution to the study of sexuality which made his name. He is above all remembered as the author of the first medical classification of sexual disorders, the *Psychopathia sexualis* (1886). Within this context Freud scholars have seen him as a representative of mainstream Viennese psychiatry and as one of the many who disagreed with Freud's ideas. More recently (and convincingly), however, they have begun to see him as a significant influence on Freud's own revolutionary work on sexuality.

For more than twenty-five years Krafft-Ebing published his ideas on human sexual behaviour. From his first important paper of 1877, through his famous *Psychopathia sexualis* of 1886, to his last two theoretical contributions in 1901, his views changed significantly.[2] His original motive for studying the subject was forensic, but this changed over time to a more psychological and clinical approach. Thus he was in the early 1870s and late 1880s amongst the first to describe sexual behaviour within a framework of disease categories – a methodology essential for giving psychiatric opinions in legal cases. One reason for his change of direction away from forensic objectives was probably his direct contact with a new therapeutic technique – hypnotism. Krafft-Ebing first had the opportunity to practise hypnosis himself in Graz, in the autumn of 1887.[3] By chance, Ilma, the young woman on whom he first practised his hypnotic skills, was sexually attracted to women, a feeling and behaviour Krafft-Ebing successfully influenced by hypnosis. For several years thereafter he used hypnotic therapy to treat homosexuality. This treatment of specific modes of sexual behaviour led to a development of his views on sexuality.

Most characteristic of Krafft-Ebing's new psychological understanding of sexuality, was the model of sadism and masochism (and the broadening of the definition of fetishism) which he introduced into the medical literature in 1890 and understood as exaggerated male (sadistic) or exaggerated female (masochistic) behaviour.[4] Masochism was clinically more important than sadism and accordingly was given more attention. Not only were these new terms seen as extremes on a graded scale of health and illness (rather than as categories, as in the earlier model) but they were also diagnosed on the grounds of the inner feelings instead of the behaviour of the patient. Since they focused on the internal, subjective experience of the individual, as opposed to emphasizing observable, external behaviour, they shifted the whole scientific discussion away from an exercise in pathology to a psychological project. It is within Krafft-Ebing's work that we can see most clearly a move towards modern psychology with its preoccupation with subjective experiences. The new terms were also significant because they were not disease labels but rather described extremist expressions of normal attitudes.

This novel psychological understanding was not thought of as addressing the cause of the problem. Whilst the latter remained hereditary, the psychological explanation helped to evoke sympathy with the afflicted individual. Characteristically, Krafft-Ebing's psychological programme went together with a change in style, best observed in the different editions of the *Psychopathia sexualis*: whereas the cases in the first edition of 1886 were on the whole short and factual, later editions of the book contain more extensive analyses. Many of these, but especially the explicit autobiographical accounts, which were sent to him as letters, read like novels. Both these letters and Krafft-Ebing's connecting texts also increasingly added literary references, quoting works from Antiquity to novels by Zola and Sacher-Masoch. In addition there were almost journalistic descriptions of events such as the regular ball, the 'Woman-haters' ball, held by homosexuals in Berlin.[5] This certainly made for 'spicy' reading for some, and in reaction to this Krafft-Ebing increasingly used Latin passages to obscure the most explicit details of the text (a strategy which, incidentally, did not work).

So what made Krafft-Ebing broaden his enterprise? There are several possible answers to this question, but perhaps it was above all the sheer experience of having collected many cases and keeping an open mind. His encouragement of homosexuals to share their stories with him had by that time led to a veritable flood of letters. Reading these accounts, Krafft-Ebing was not only struck by the degree of subjective suffering (a point he spelt out repeatedly), but also, and not unrelatedly, he noted the closeness of the experiences to those of 'normal people'. Confronted with these complex inner worlds he could not help seeing the parallels with general human issues.

MASOCHISM

Krafft-Ebing's starting-point was the 'fact' – described by him as 'either an original fact or an inbred condition' – that the man normally plays the active, even aggressive, and the woman the passive, defensive role in the relationship of the sexes. The conquest of the woman by the man was a 'psychologically vital factor' which had undergone changes in history from 'primitive times and peoples, who used brute force, rape and even the rendering unconscious of the woman by knocking her out with a club'. Such practices, we learn, have today been replaced by civilized forms of courtship, seduction and ruse. This, Krafft-Ebing implied, was the norm, whilst it was 'undoubtedly pathological when the man seeks his sexual pleasure in a maltreatment by the woman and enjoys himself in the position of the conquered instead of the victor'.[6]

Women and men were not measured by the same yardstick; rather, behaviour which would undoubtedly be labelled masochistic in a man was seen as normal when displayed by a woman: 'The voluntary subordination of woman under the other sex is a physiological phenomenon. Due to her passive role in procreation and to traditional social conditions, a woman necessarily associates sexual relationships as such with the image of subordination. This image constitutes, as it were, the overtone, which characterises the timbre of female emotions'.[7]

Depending on the man involved, this nature-given female inclination may vary, but the woman always enjoys her role: 'The barbarian lets the woman overwork; the philistine gets her to fill his pipe. This she does not do under compulsion, but with joy'.[8]

Krafft-Ebing added that women, in fact, needed their very status in society for their happiness, especially in some regions:

> Incidentally many young women like nothing better than to go down on their knees in front of their husbands or lovers. It is said that lower class women in all Slav peoples are unhappy when they do not get beaten up by their husbands.
>
> A Hungarian informant tells me that the peasant women of the county of Somogy do not believe themselves to be loved by their husbands, until they have received the first slap in the face as a token of love.[9]

The wish of a man to be conquered by the woman or, in the case of a woman, to exaggerate the natural imbalance of power, was called masochism. This term, coined after the contemporary Austrian novelist Sacher-Masoch,[10] was introduced into the medical literature by Krafft-Ebing, but it was not his personal invention. The label 'masochism' had been suggested to him by an anonymous man in Berlin, who wrote him a long autobiographical letter and subsequently became his main informant on this condition.[11] This man had found consolation in reading Rousseau and Sacher-Masoch.[12] Whilst Krafft-Ebing almost certainly knew of Rousseau's sexual inclinations – Julius Möbius had published a psychological analysis of Rousseau in 1889[13] – he may not have been familiar with Sacher-Masoch's novels prior to receiving this letter. The most famous of these was *Venus in Furs*, a transparently autobiographical story of a male hero who demands of his lover that she dresses up in fur and flogs him.

The Berlin letter was full of references to what its author (who had so strongly resonated with Sacher-Masoch's literary descriptions) experienced as an unhealthy fantasy life: as a youngster he would spend hours fantasizing prison scenes in which he was tortured by mighty women. He would imagine scenes of kneeling down in front of an ideal mistress, chained in heavy chains, exposed to humiliations and tortures designed to amuse her. During the same years he developed a liking for velvet and fur and found it sexually exciting to touch these materials.[14] He claimed that the reason for his not achieving anything was his extensive fantasy life: which blocked his actions, and indeed spoke of 'orgies of fantasy'.[15] After many years of solitary fantasies he took a first step towards a more real sex life: 'after I had partially conquered my fear of people and my inclination to dreaming about, a change occurred in my sexual thinking in as much as my interest now turned towards real people'.[16]

This was followed a few years later by a brave but unsuccessful attempt to act out his masochistic fantasies in practice by instructing a prostitute.

> I finally conquered my last inhibitions and one day, in order to realise my dreams, I let myself be flagellated by a prostitute. The effect was a great disappointment. What happened with me here was to my taste coarse, repulsive and ridiculous at the same time. The flogging caused me nothing but pain, the rest of the situation disgusted and humiliated me. In spite of this I mechanically forced an ejaculation by using my fantasy to alter the real situation into the one I desired. This, the truly desired situation, was essentially different from the actual one in that I imagined a woman who would afflict the maltreatment upon me with the same lust as I wanted to receive it.[17]

This differentiation between behaviour and imagination, or between the physical and the psychological aspect of sexual life, became vital for Krafft-Ebing.[18] Other diagnostic labels within his sexual psychopathology were traditionally defined by objective behaviour: either the object or the act performed was abnormal. Now for the first time Krafft-Ebing used a model which emphasized the psychological attitude behind the objective behaviour. Krafft-Ebing's informant experienced the (subjectively) wrong kind of ejaculation in the arms of that prostitute, because she did not inflict the flogging on him with the right mental motivation. Her actual sexual behaviour, we may assume, was exactly according to his instructions, but he saw her as failing him on a psychological level.

This essential distinction, first defined by the Berlin informant and merely quoted as such by Krafft-Ebing, was subsequently expressed in different places all through his work. It served, amongst other purposes, to defend the terminology chosen in 1890. In 1892 Krafft-Ebing heard of a lawyer from Mitau, Kurland, who had invented the broader term passivism, a term which included what Krafft-Ebing described as sexual dependence and which he still saw as a physiological phenomenon.[19] Another term in contemporary use was Algolagnia, which Albert von Schrenck-Notzing and Albrecht von Eulenburg tried to promote and on which Krafft-Ebing commented critically in 1895.[20] Algolagnia, derived from the Greek word for pain, missed the point according to Krafft-Ebing, because it was not straightforward physical pain that the masochist was seeking. The important factor was the individual's mental image of being conquered by another person.

Apart from these attempts to clarify and defend his terms, Krafft-Ebing increasingly used the same type of psychological argument in various contexts. For example, expressions like psychologically dissatisfied or psychological orgy (by which was meant indulgence in sexual fantasies and which was distinguished from masturbation) recurred.[21]

One case in an article on the lack of sexual feelings – 'On inborn sexual anaesthesia'[22] – represents another excellent example of the broad psychological definition of sexual feelings that he used in his later works. A 29-year-old merchant consulted Krafft-Ebing about his abnormal sexual life before getting married for social reasons. He reported that after masturbating from the age of 17 to 19, he had become neurasthenic, and therefore had started to replace the health-damaging masturbation by regular visits to brothels. His potency was always fine and he experienced an agreeable feeling. However, he was very worried because he 'never had any emotion during the act, in particular any directed towards the woman, whom he experienced as lifeless and as "a piece of wood"'.[23]

The patient was further concerned about his lack of interest in nude women and his general dullness with them, especially given that he had 'full interests in the arts'. Neither did he hate women – he simply saw them as 'instruments for his coarser sensual needs' and did not understand the infatuation or jealousy of other men.[24] By diagnosing this man as suffering from sexual anaesthesia Krafft-Ebing once more defined healthy sexual functioning as something more than a physical ability to have intercourse.

This shift towards psychology was only part of a wider development within the field of the sexual sciences. Sex had moved from the physical body into the 'soul' and was no longer located in the genitals, but rather in the brain. Krafft-Ebing was familiar with the anatomical and physiological work of his day.[25] The clearest explanation of these ideas can be found in an article on the sexual functioning of women published in 1894. Here he subscribed fully to the thesis that the sexual centre in the brain was as important as the sexual organs of the body.[26] This led to conclusions about both pathological and normal female sexual functioning. For example, hysteria, according to Krafft-Ebing, was never due to mere physical disorder or simple abstinence; rather it always took a 'psychological factor' such as a 'physically and psychologically unsatisfactory coitus'.[27] As for the ideal sexual harmony between a couple, Krafft-Ebing, speaking from a male point of view, argued that the sexual satisfaction of the wife was very important for the pleasure of the husband. Again he made a clear distinction between the physiological and the psychological aspects of (male) sexuality:

[intercourse] is for the husband not only a spinal reflex, but a complicated psychocerebral act. If this was not the case, coitus for a man would be merely a masturbatory act in the body of a woman ... The ancient cynical remark *sublata lucerna nullum discrimen inter foeminas* [remove the light and there is no discriminating between women][28] is only justified in as far as an animalistic man can experience lust with any woman in whose vagina he manages to ejaculate. That this constitutes only one part of a man's sexual pleasure is proven by so many husbands' confidential complaints to the doctor of the frigidity of their wives.[29]

In 1892 Krafft-Ebing published a psychological essay which went further in its attempts at explaining human nature and sexual attraction than any other of his work: 'Comments on "sexual dependence" and masochism'.[30] The article was inspired by the lawyer from Mitau, Kurland, and heavily indebted to an anonymous correspondent of Krafft-Ebing's from Berlin, who was most probably the one who had directly influenced him in coining the term 'masochism'.[31] Its goal was to distinguish the clearly pathological masochism, as defined two years earlier, from 'sexual dependence'. The latter was seen as a phenomenon located in a grey area between the normal and the pathological, but ultimately still within the boundaries of physiology since 'the balance ... between the intense sexual drive ... and the minimal will-power ... is different in degree and not in quality as is the case in masochism'.[32]

Sexual dependence was therefore not seen as perverted, but at the extreme of normality. The motive behind acts committed by the enslaved partner, Krafft-Ebing said, was exclusively the possession of the beloved person – there was no independent, pathological reason. Sexual dependence only occurred after the love for a particular individual had been awoken. By contrast, the decisively pathological masochist longed for submission before having met any particular object of love. As he put it: 'the motive behind the actions and sufferings of the enslaved partner is here the charm of the tyranny as such. ... [these acts] are not a means to an end, but the end itself.'[33]

Masochism is, however, connected with sexual dependence in that it can develop from the latter. Thus acts of tyranny can become the goal of an enslaved person, as he continuously associates the tyranny with the beloved. Literary examples of sexual dependence (and not masochism!) are, according to Krafft-Ebing: *Manon Lescaut* by Prévost, *The Gambler* by Dostoevsky, *Leone Leoni* by Georges Sand and 'Käthchen von Heilbronn' by Heinrich von Kleist. All these examples had been labelled differently by other authors and Krafft-Ebing himself, in an earlier work, had interestingly called Kleist's heroine 'the most notable example of female masochism in the novel-literature'.³⁴

A certain amount of dependence, on the other hand, was necessary in sexual relationships in order to strengthen the bond. The typical shape of this dependence, created by law and morality and changing over time, is vital in addressing the question of levels of dependence in individual relationships. As Krafft-Ebing put it: 'Morals and customs prescribe gifts to the beloved woman, but the man who has fallen into unusual dependence, lavishes his whole fortune to the last penny upon her. Law prescribes that woman should help her husband by working in the household, but the dependent wife overworks to keep a do-nothing of a husband'.³⁵

Although there are many examples of sexual dependence in men, he continued, many more women than men become dependent. The reason for this is simply that 'Love is for a man almost always only an episode next to which he has many and important interests, whilst for a woman it is the main object of her life'.³⁶

If such sentences implied a natural difference between man and woman, Krafft-Ebing also showed a clear awareness of the legal and social double standard:³⁷ 'the man who is ruled by his sexuality can find satisfaction everywhere' (an obvious allusion to prostitution) whilst the woman is 'tied to one man, if she has one at all' – especially if she belongs to the higher levels of society.³⁸ In addition, law and customs between man and woman are far from being equal and in themselves contain a predominant dependence of woman. Therefore 'there are the ever increasing insatiable demands of men, who are determined to profit from their advantage and who turn the exploitation of the limitless female ability to make sacrifices into an industry'.³⁹

Krafft-Ebing states that sexual dependence was highly important in criminal justice because many crimes had been committed in order to possess a partner sexually. He then carried on to make further gender-conscious remarks: Men in their short-sightedness, he said, have summed up this truth in the sentence 'cherchez la femme', as they have also created the myth of Eve who gave Adam the apple, but 'If the history of mankind is, in fact, the history of one sex only, it is indeed woman who is the temptress. But if woman's actions and sufferings are weighed, the myth is reversed and it is Adam who gives Eve the apple. "Cherchez l'homme" is more frequently justified than "cherchez la femme".'⁴⁰

In one sense Krafft-Ebing was offering a feminist argument here. This is in keeping with other similar remarks found elsewhere in his work: for example, in the first chapter of his *Psychopathia sexualis* he accused Islamic religion of giving women a distinctly unequal status. His views were, however, of the kind that confirmed women's inferior status in society by arguing that the biological difference should lead to a different legal treatment of women. Such reasoning can be found in various passages in his work where he claimed at the same time that female infidelity deserved tougher punishment than its male counterpart, a claim based on such fundamental assumptions as that woman was by nature monogamous, whereas man was polygamous, and that a 'mentally normal and well educated woman had a minimal sensual desire'.[41] A similar argument was put forth at its strongest in Krafft-Ebing's very last monograph: 'Psychosis menstrualis. A Clinico-forensic Study' (*Psychosis menstrualis. Eine Klinisch-forensische Studie*, 1902), in which once more special laws should apply to women – in this case menstruating women – who were seen as not fully responsible for their deeds, since they suffered from a kind of periodic madness.[42]

In this text Krafft-Ebing first stated that legal punishment should be reduced if a sexually enslaved person had been motivated by the partner to commit a crime. Given that sexual dependence was more frequent in women, and given, further, that it was difficult to assess in court, Krafft-Ebing went as far as arguing for separate measures for the two sexes:

> One could well consider that the criminal codes dealing with incited crimes, should include as a mitigating factor the female sex. This would be similar to the mitigation on the grounds of youth, which is regulated by § 57 in the German code for the age up to 18, and in the Austrian code by § 46a up to the age of 20. It is an injustice to treat one sex as inferior in civil law (marital law) and to treat it as equally responsible in criminal law.[43]

Masochism was an important cultural phenomenon and, according to Krafft-Ebing, on the increase. As proof for this claim he quoted advertisements in newspapers, such as the following: 'Educated ladies who love the works of Sacher-Masoch are asked to answer this advertisement. Answers labelled J. F. will be conveyed by Rudolf Mosse, Berlin S. W.'[44]

His choice of name for the condition was clearly becoming fashionable and was a source of pride – he also said in an aside, that some of Sacher-Masoch's followers had objected to the use of his name in this context.[45] Through his patients he also learned of the widespread knowledge about masochistic techniques amongst prostitutes and of the equipment, such as whips, that was available in brothels.[46]

Another, equally significant sign, was 'the traces of masochism in the modern novel-literature, which might well be worth following up'.[47] Novels quoted by Krafft-Ebing (some of which he took directly from letters from his patients) included the several novels by Sacher-Masoch and his wife and Balduin Groller's *Gräfin Aranka*, Zola's *Um eine Liebesnacht*, Richepin's *La Glu*,[48] J. P. Jacobsen's *Niels Lyhhe*, and the two volumes of collected lyrical work of Johannes Wedde (edited posthumously in 1894).[49] The editor of Wedde's texts said in his introduction that he wanted to give back the power to the eternally feminine element, which had been eliminated by the reigning Christian doctrine. Krafft-Ebing obviously went along with this idea, which, at its strongest, implied that masochism was a reaction to the traditional humiliation of women: 'There is an important characteristic of masochism in this opinion [of Wedde's editor] which is trying to create a domina out of the submissive servant to which Christian doctrine has humiliated woman.'[50]

Apart from collecting contemporary literary examples, Krafft-Ebing also quoted some more exotic ones, which he obtained from learned informants: one Professor E. Deák from Pest (Budapest) told him, for example, that ancient Indian literature had already used the picture of a masochistic man being ridden as a horse by a woman (in a story entitled 'Female Moods' in the *Tantschatantra*). Benfey, editor of this Indian book, also referred to a Buddhist story of a wise man called Rishi who carried a woman on his shoulders and thus lost his wisdom.[51] Such literary examples presumably convinced Krafft-Ebing that his category of masochism referred to something real that was described by others. The masochists who read Krafft-Ebing's book found the examples exciting.[52]

On a more speculative level Krafft-Ebing volunteered several different explanations of masochism. His earliest such attempt argued that although Antiquity – he quoted Horace and pointed out that 'domina' was a frequent term in classical literature – gave examples of how a lover could feel dependent on his mistress, the real change came with the knights of the Middle Ages. Courtly love, he said, was a paradox in the history of morality and as yet unexplained. He suggested that during this period, which was 'full of unusual psychoses', the worship of women caught on and 'following the law of mass-psychoses, spread through the world by infection until it reached us'.[53] This explanation was not, however, repeated in later texts.

Krafft-Ebing also reported on the treatment of masochists. This consisted of a combination of good advice and hypnotic therapy, as was the case for the treatment of homosexuals. There are fewer cases of masochism than of homosexuality, and correspondingly fewer therapies described. One such illustrative case was a 30-year-old Hungarian man, who wrote to Krafft-Ebing in January 1891 asking for hypnotic treatment.[54] The autobiographical report gave many of the usual details: several years of masturbation in his teens, recognition of the health hazards involved, abstinence, lack of interest in women, and sexual attraction to young men which revolved around fantasies of getting punished (beaten on the bottom), finally two brothel visits where he found himself to be impotent with women. After reading Krafft-Ebing's texts he had diagnosed himself as homosexual and now hoped to get cured through hypnotism because he wanted to get married. Krafft-Ebing invited the man for a consultation (February 1891) – 'for reasons of humanity and scientific interest' – and rediagnosed him as masochistic. He subsequently ran a short course of hypnotic sessions, suggesting that the patient should:

(a) resist masturbation;
(b) become disinterested in his own sex and in ideas of flogging – both in a wakeful state and in his dreams;
(c) direct his libido only towards women, get erections when seeing beautiful female shapes, be fully potent with women and dream exclusively of women.[55]

After a very few days the patient reported that he no longer had any interest in men, but an increasing interest in women – he had started to dream of women. Three days later he felt free of his masochistic fantasies, no longer took an interest in whips, but still had dreams of flagellations centred around men. Some days later he made an attempt at intercourse in a brothel where he achieved only a partial erection, abandoned the attempt, decided that his sexual drive towards women was after all on the weak side, but nevertheless remained optimistic, since he experienced a decrease in his pathological ideas. Unfortunately, therapy was prematurely terminated when the patient was called home to Hungary because of urgent family duties.

Other patients initially tried to cure themselves without Krafft-Ebing's help. A 47-year-old man of independent means, for example, reported that he had never taken any interest in women, his sexual fantasies revolved around men from the lower classes, preferably dirty and with big, rough hands such as sailors, day-labourers, servants and coachmen.[56] With such men, whom he met by visiting disreputable pubs in disguise, he enjoyed himself in a passive, female role. Since there were too few opportunities to enact his sexuality, he temporarily settled for masturbation, became neurasthenic and – sent to Italy for recovery – discovered that social laws were different and more open there and that it was easy to find what he wanted. Returning home after six months, he fell back into his old misery of sexual frustration. He then tried to improve his situation by carefully instructing paid subjects; he indeed managed to find at least one man who was able to play the pre-planned comedy to his satisfaction.

These last two cases raise the question of the relationship between homosexuality and masochism. There were contemporary discussions about this, arguing that effeminate, homosexual men often showed masochistic traits (following the equation: masochistic = effeminate). Albert von Schrenck-Notzing, among others, promoted this idea, which Krafft-Ebing accepted.[57] In addition to the category of masochistic homosexuality Krafft-Ebing also described a few cases of sadistic homosexuality.[58]

FETISHISM

In 1889, in the 4th edition of the *Psychopathia sexualis*, Krafft-Ebing first introduced the term 'fetishism' into his work, acknowledging Cesare Lombroso as his immediate source.[59] Lombroso had used the phenomenon of fetishism as an explanatory model in his introduction to the Italian translation of the *Psychopathia sexualis* (1889).[60] In later editions of the *Psychopathia sexualis* Krafft-Ebing also quoted the Frenchman Binet in this context.[61]

Before fetishism acquired its new medical meaning, the word had referred to the religious worship of relics and holy objects. Krafft-Ebing modified this meaning as the worship of objects belonging to a beloved person (such as shoes), or sometimes parts of the body (hair), and a sexual desire directed exclusively towards these objects.

Fetishism was not a newly observed phenomenon, but a mere relabelling of data already collected: thus several of Krafft-Ebing's cases illustrating it had been described in earlier versions of his book, but had so far been listed under the general heading 'other paradoxical actions'.[62] The cases were, moreover, mostly taken from the literature and not observed by Krafft-Ebing himself; of thirteen cases of fetishism described in 1889 only one was Krafft-Ebing's; the majority were French or Italian, and there is a brief reference to a case dating back to 1838 (by Diez, published in his book *Suicide*).[63] The patients were obsessed by shoes, handkerchiefs, toiletries, ladies underwear or nightcaps. Each desired object was used differently: one man robbed two ladies of their shoes in an open street in New York; others masturbated with them: Blanche's patient, for example, was arrested causing public annoyance by masturbating in front of a shoemaker's shop; and a 50-year-old priest was in the habit of regularly hiring a prostitute's shoes without wanting the girl herself. Another needed elegant, black and high-heeled boots (and, in this case, the woman who wore them).[64] In a later work, Krafft-Ebing described more eccentric cases, such as the 19-year-old student who could not resist finger-rings, especially those made of gold (and therefore unaffordable), or the homosexual fetishist who was aroused by the sight of a young man wearing the sign of grief on his arm (*Trauerflor*: a black band on the upper arm worn after the death of a relative). This man, a lawyer who was completely unable to explain his strange taste, also felt attracted to warts, freckles, ulcers and other skin-diseases in men.[65] Krafft-Ebing's psychological explanation of fetishism followed Binet and used the model of association. He argued that the patient had experienced a sexual feeling in the past at a time when he was exposed to the later fetish. The brain then connected the two events.

Originally Krafft-Ebing saw fetishism as pathological,[66] but later introduced a distinction between physiological and pathological fetishism, thus broadening the term. This fundamental step was a good example of the way Krafft-Ebing was beginning to psychologize the subject of psychopathology. He went as far as to single out physiological fetishism as the principle which guarantees specific love:

> These physiological facts of fetishism often account for the affections that suddenly arise between man and woman, the preference of a certain person to all others of the same sex.[67]
> ... the phenomena of physiological fetishism [are] conditions for an individualisation of love, [and] important institutions of nature for the education of individuals, as well as [resulting in] monogamous connections between man and woman, which are useful for the next generation and hence also for society.[68]

The specific attraction between two individuals, the result of which is the desired monogamy, can, in other words, be explained by fetishism. Far from fetishism remaining a clear-cut medical category describing sexual pathology, it seems that it had been elevated to the status of the real glue between people: fetishism was what held together the institution of marriage. Once more Krafft-Ebing was not particularly original here. Above all he quoted Binet,[69] but also psychological or literary authors like Magnan, Max Dessoir (a psychologist from Munich), Jäger (a German contemporary psychologist, author of *Discovery of the Soul*), Molière and Belot (author of *Les Baigneuses de Trouville*).

Simultaneously, and also in line with the above authors, Krafft-Ebing's list of possible fetishes became longer, including quite abstract characteristics of a beloved partner. Heading the list of fetishes a woman might possess are – next to pieces of clothing like shoes – the hair, the hand, the foot and the expression of the eye. By way of proof, attention is drawn to the care taken by women with their hair: the 'often unreasonable amount of time and money spent upon its cultivation' and the frequency with which '*coiffures*' appear as female conversation topics. As for 'masculine virtues' that 'impose on woman', the list included, in addition to physical features, several character traits and talents: physical strength, courage, nobility of mind, chivalry, self-confidence, even self-assertion, insolence, bravado, a conscious show of mastery over the weaker sex, military uniforms (a cavalryman), the beard (the emblem of virility and the secondary symbol of generative power), the singing voice (tenor) and, lastly, mental superiority.[70]

Krafft-Ebing made his comments on fetishism an integral part of the later editions of his *Psychopathia sexualis* by repeating them in the first chapter ('Fragments of a Psychology of Sexual Life'). He thus signalled his increasing belief in the importance of this psychological concept. More generally Krafft-Ebing, who had drawn up a medical categorization of pathological sexual behaviour in 1886, had shifted focus to a significant degree over the following years. Whilst keeping a safe foot within mainstream psychiatry with its predominantly biological explanations, he was also influenced by the psychological explanations of his time, particularly those of Binet (with his association theory) and several of the leading figures of therapeutic hypnosis such as Moll and Forel of the Bernheim school.

His model of sexual behaviour, originally emphasizing clear-cut categories within a biological–medical framework (to render it suitable for his expert legal activity), became a much broader enterprise with its inherent claim to explain aspects of healthy human sexuality.

NOTES

1 This chapter is based on chapter 6 of my Ph.D. thesis: Renate Hauser, 'Sexuality, neurasthenia and the Law: Richard von Krafft-Ebing (1840–1902)', Ph.D. thesis, University College London, 1992.
2 Richard von Krafft-Ebing, 'Ueber gewisse Anomalien des Geschlechtstriebs und die klinisch-forensische Verwerthung derselben als eines wahrscheinlich functionnellen Degenerationszeichens', *Archiv für Psychiatrie und Nervenkrankheiten*, 7 (1877), 291–312; idem, 'Ueber sexuelle Perversionen', in Ernst von Leyden and Felix Klemperer (eds.), *Die deutsche Klinik am Eingang des 20 Jahrhunderts in akademischen Vorlesungen*, vol. VI, part 2 (1906) (14 vols., Berlin

and Vienna: Urban and Schwarzenberg, 1903–13), 113–54; *idem*, 'Neue Studien auf dem Gebiete der Homosexualität', *Jahrbuch für sexuelle Zwischenstufen*, 3 (1901), 1–36.

3 Hauser, 'Sexuality, Neurasthenia and the Law', 264–306.

4 Krafft-Ebing, *Neue Forschungen auf dem Gebiet der Psychopathia sexualis. Eine medizinisch-psychologische Studie* (Stuttgart: Enke, 1890). (Re-edited in 1891 as: *Neue Forschungen auf dem Gebiet der Psychopathia sexualis. Eine medizinisch-psychologische Studie*, 2nd edn, revised and enlarged (Stuttgart: Enke, 1891)). The ideas of the text were subsequently used in the 6th edition (1891) and the text was fully integrated into the 7th edition of Krafft-Ebing's most famous book, the *Psychopathia sexualis*.

5 See the lengthy quote from 'a Berlin newspaper of February 1884' in Krafft-Ebing, *Psychopathia sexualis mit besonderer Berücksichtingung der conträren Sexualempfindung; eine medicinischgerichtliche Studie für Aerzte und Juristen*, 14th (enlarged) edn, ed. Alfred Fuchs (Stuttgart: Enke, 1912), 441–3. (This passage was not quoted in the earlier editions of the book, but from the 10th edn of 1898.)

6 All quotations in this paragraph are from Krafft-Ebing, *Neue Forschungen*, 1st edn, 1.

7 Ibid., 28.

8 Ibid., 28.

9 Ibid., 28–9.

10 Sacher-Masoch was not only a novelist, but also a historian and a black sheep on the faculty board of Graz University. See Walter Höflechner, 'Leopold Sacher-Masoch Ritter von Kronenthal und die Universität Graz', in Hermann Wiesflecker (ed.), *Publikationen aus dem Archiv der Universität Graz*, vol. IV (Graz: Akademische Druck u. Verlagsanstalt), 125–38.

11 This letter was published by Krafft-Ebing, *Neue Forschungen*, 1st edn, 15–22.

12 Ibid., 17.

13 Ibid., 5.

14 Ibid., 16.

15 Ibid., 22.

16 Ibid., 18–19.

17 Ibid., 19–20.

18 Thomas Laqueur has presented some very inspiring work (so far unpublished) at a recent Wellcome Symposium as a seminar: Medicine, Masturbation, and Sociability, 1700–1990; read at The History of Medical Attitudes to Sexuality Symposium, 20 June 1991.

19 Krafft-Ebing, 'Bemerkungen über geschlechtliche Hörigkeit und Masochismus', *Jahrbücher für Psychiatrie*, 10 (1892), 199–211.

20 Krafft-Ebing, 'Beiträge zur Kenntniss des Masochismus' (1895). Reprinted in *Arbeiten aus dem Gesammtgebiet der Psychiatrie und Neuropathologie*, vol. IV (1899), 127–8 (the same article was originally published in 1895 in the *Internationales Centralblatt für die Physiologie und Pathologie der Harn und Sexualorgane*, 6 (1895), 353–60).

21 See Krafft-Ebing, 'Beiträge zur Kenntniss des Masochismus', *Arbeiten*, vol. IV, 129, and also p. 137 of his second article on masochism: Krafft-Ebing 'Beiträge

zur Kenntniss des Masochismus', 2nd article, *Arbeiten*, vol. IV, (1899), 131–60.
22 Krafft-Ebing, 'Ueber Anästhesia sexualis congenita', *Arbeiten*, vol. IV, 175–80.
23 Ibid., 179.
24 Ibid., 180.
25 For example, in Krafft-Ebing, 'Neuropathia sexualis feminarum', in W. Zülzer, *Klinisches Handbuch der Harn- und Sexualorgane* (Leipzig: F. C. W. Vogel, 1894), section 4, 80–103, he quoted whole lists of German, as well as foreign authors (85–8): Féré, Chambard, Guttzeit, Hammond, Glaevecke, Hegar, Schmalfuss, Bruntzel, Köberle, Tissier, Spencer-Wells, Kisch and Börner.
26 Krafft-Ebing, 'Neuropathia sexualis feminarum', 88.
27 Ibid., 91.
28 Or: all cats are grey in the dark.
29 See Krafft-Ebing, 'Ueber das Zustandekommen der Wollustempfindung und deren Mangel (Anaphrodisie) beim sexuellen Akt', *Internationales Centralblatt für die Physiologie und Pathologie der Harn und Sexualorgane*, 2 (1891), 94–106, p. 105 (reprinted in *Arbeiten*, vol. IV (1899) and Krafft-Ebing, 'Neuropathia sexualis feminarum'. 93. (The text is here identical with the exception that the earlier version speaks of a 'normal' man where the later one uses the term 'animalistic'; possibly another indication of the shift towards psychological understanding and away from a mechanical concept.)
30 Krafft-Ebing, 'Bemerkungen über geschlechtliche Hörigkeit'.
31 Ibid., 12, mentions one Mr N. from Berlin, who had generally inspired Krafft-Ebing to writing the article and with whom he had corresponded about a lawyer, von Stefanowsky (see also p. 11), inventor of a broader term, 'passivism'. A very similar note of acknowledgement to a (probably the same) correspondent in Berlin can be found in Krafft-Ebing's earlier text, *Neue Forschungen*, 1st edn, 13; the same text reprinted this man's autobiographical account (pp. 15–22), including the statement that he had found his favourite ideas described in Sacher-Masoch's novels.
32 Krafft-Ebing, 'Bemerkungen über geschlechtliche Hörigkeit', 199–200.
33 Ibid., 208.
34 Krafft-Ebing, *Neue Forschungen*, 1st edn, 29. See also Krafft-Ebing, 'Bemerkungen über geschlechtliche Hörigkeit', 210–11. Von Stefanowsky, the lawyer from Mitau, had used the other examples to illustrate his category passivism.
35 Krafft-Ebing, 'Bemerkungen über geschlechtliche Hörigkeit', 202.
36 Ibid., 204.
37 For a general article on the double standard, see Keith Thomas, 'The Double Standard', *Journal of the History of Ideas*, 20 (1959), 195–216.
38 Krafft-Ebing, 'Bemerkungen über geschlechtliche Hörigkeit', 204.
39 Ibid., 204.
40 Ibid., 206.
41 Krafft-Ebing, *Psychopathia sexualis*, 10.
42 Krafft-Ebing, *Psychosis menstrualis. Eine klinisch-forensische Studie* (Stuttgart: Enke, 1902).
43 Krafft-Ebing, 'Bemerkungen über geschlechtliche Hörigkeit', 207.
44 This example, which had appeared in an Austrian newspaper (*Vossische Zeitung*)

on 29 June 1895, was quoted as typical by Kraff-Ebing (second essay on masochism (1899) *Arbeiten*, vol. IV, 132n).
45 Second essay on masochism (1899) *Arbeiten*, vol. IV, 131–2.
46 Ibid., 132.
47 Ibid., 142.
48 Ibid., 140.
49 Ibid., 142.
50 Ibid., 143.
51 Ibid., 143–4.
52 Krafft-Ebing knew that reading cases in the medical literature excited some patients. For example he quoted in the same essay (pp. 153–4) a patient who 'went into ecstasy when reading a case by Moll' (Albrecht Moll, who followed in Krafft-Ebing's footsteps in many respects in his books on sexual pathology).
53 Krafft-Ebing, *Neue Forschungen*, 1st edn, 27.
54 Krafft-Ebing, second essay on masochism, *Arbeiten*, vol. IV, 134–6.
55 Ibid., 136.
56 Ibid., 151–4.
57 Ibid., 142, 145.
58 See pp. 166–7 of Krafft-Ebing, 'Zum Sadismus', *Arbeiten*, vol. IV, 160–9.
59 See p. 62 of the 4th (1889) German edition of the *Psychopathia sexualis*.
60 Lombroso's introduction to Krafft-Ebing's book (the 1st Italian edition was based on the 2nd German version of 1887) not only praised Krafft-Ebing's enterprise but put it firmly within the context of his own (Lombroso's) degenerationist views by adding substantially new ideas. Lombroso, for example, reprinted elaborate tables from his own works (with which Krafft-Ebing did not agree – see his early review of Lombroso: Krafft-Ebing, 'C. Lombroso di Pavia: *La medicina legale delle alienazioni mentali, studiatta col metodo esperimentale*, 1865, 47 pp.', *Allegemeine Zeitschrift für Psychiatrie*, 25 (1868), 269. Fetishism (*Feticismo*) was, next to atavism and epilepsy, used as an explanatory model for various sexual behaviours by the Italian. See Lombroso's comments on pp. xixff, of Krafft-Ebing, *Le psicopatie sessuali, con speciale considerazione alla inversione sessuale: studio clinico-legale* (*1889*), trans. Enrico Sterz and Luigi Waldhart. Introduction by Prof. Cesare Lombroso (Turini Bocca).
61 See, for example, Krafft-Ebing, *Psychopathia sexualis*, English edn, 208. The only authorized English trans. of the 10th German edn is by F. J. Rebman (Chicago: W. T. Keener and Co.). In fact, Binet was probably the first to use the term in this sexual-pathological context (in his paper of 1887: 'Du fétischisme dans l'amour', *Revue Philosophique*) and is quoted by both Krafft-Ebing and Lombroso. See also Annemarie and Werner Leibbrand-Wettley, *Formen des Eros: Kultur- und Geistesgeschichte der Liebe*, vol. II (2 Vols., Freiburg: K. Alber, 1972), 575, who add that the term itself was first used by Charles de Brosses in 1760 in a work on fetish gods.
62 Some examples of cases which were labelled 'paradoxical actions' in the 1st edition of the *Psychopathia sexualis* and 'fetishism' in the 4th edition are: case 12 of the 1st edn (46–7) became case 28 in the 4th edn (63); case 14 of the 1st edn (48) became case 34 of the 4th edn (66–7); case 15 of the 1st edn (48–9) became case 35 of the 4th edn (67–8) (indeed this case had already been

known to Krafft-Ebing in 1879 when he mentioned it in a review on the literature (see Krafft-Ebing, 'Jahresbericht über', 441–2); case 16 of the 1st edn (49–50) became case 36 of the 4th edn (68) (also already mentioned in a review in 1879; ibid., 440–1); case 17 of the 1st edn (50) became case 37 of the 4th edn (69). None of these cases underwent any change in content; the identical stories were merely labelled differently.

63 Krafft-Ebing, *Psychopathia sexualis*, 4th edn, 63–9.
64 All of these examples, ibid., 63–9.
65 Krafft-Ebing, 'Zum Fetischismus', *Arbeiten*, vol. IV, 172–4.
66 *Psychopathia sexualis*, 4th edn, 63.
67 10th edition (1898) of the *Psychopathia sexualis*, quoted after the English Rebman edition of 1901, 19.
68 Krafft-Ebing, 'Ueber sexuelle Perversionen', 146.
69 Quoted from the English Rebman edition of 1901 (which is the 10th edition (1898) of the *Psychopathia sexualis*), 20–3.
70 Ibid., 23–4.

PART II

SEXOLOGY SINCE FREUD

TEN

THE CUSTOMS OF THE MAGIANS: THE PROBLEM OF INCEST IN HISTORICAL SOCIETIES[1]

MICHAEL MITTERAUER

> Beast-like men have confused marriage, which God established in his wonderful care for the continuation of our nature and the propagation of our race: not as in animals, which have no understanding, but in an order suited to rational beings, the bond of love between a man and his wife in a pure, lawful union ... There are people who dare to approach the wives of their fathers, their fathers' brothers, their aunts, sisters, daughters-in-law, daughters, step-granddaughters or stepdaughters (as the Magians do), or their sisters-in-law, as Jews do, or unbelievers like the heathen. On this point we command ... and confirm according to the holy Scriptures: Let no believer dare to live in such an unlawful union, or to corrupt and confuse the rules of lawful marriage, which were established by God in his ineffable wisdom to strengthen our rationality.

With these words Mar Aba, the Patriarch of Seleucia-Ctesiphon around the middle of the sixth century, impressed upon the Nestorian Christians in the Sasanian Empire the need to distance themselves from the marriage customs of their non-Christian neighbours.[2] Transgressors were forbidden to attend church or receive the sacraments, and, he added,

> no Christian layman may accompany them on the day of their death, follow their bier during the funeral rites, or bury them, either openly or secretly, on the day of their death. For by their doings they have cut themselves off from the Christian life and, like mindless beasts, have polluted themselves in unlawful marriage; and so, even in death, they must be cut off from all communion with believers. They should be buried like asses, the beasts they resembled in life.[3]

Mar Aba's words of condemnation in his canon on marriage present various points of interest for students of incest. Firstly, they allude to the culture which, so far as we know, subjected the incest taboo to more radical questioning than any other in the history of mankind: the followers of Zoroaster (Zarathustra), whose beliefs were the state religion of the Persian Empire during the Sasanian period, and who were known as the Magians (or Magi), after a tribe which originally performed priestly functions. Mar Aba mentions them elsewhere: 'The peculiar idea of justice among the followers of Ormuzd is fulfilled when a man has had sexual relations with his mother, his daughter and his sister.'[4] Thus, such relationships were not merely permitted among the Zoroastrians, they were a religious duty – a cultural phenomenon which appears to be unique.[5]

However, the list of forbidden partners in Mar Aba's canon on marriage is by no means confined to close kindred. The 'father's brother's wife' appears on it, together with the step-granddaughter. Mar Timotheos, Patriarch of the Nestorians some time after Mar Aba, in *circa* 800, considerably lengthened the list, even to nephew's widow and sister-in-law's sister, and adds with mechanical regularity, 'for such are the customs of the Magians'.[6] Many of the marriages forbidden to those Nestorian Christians do not seem at all incestuous by modern standards. This also applies to marriage with a brother's widow, which induced Mar Aba to include both Jews and Magians among the 'beast-like men'. According to Mosaic law it was obligatory for a Jew to marry his childless brother's widow and engender an heir to the brother's name.[7] What seemed to Jews a religious duty seemed to others an attack on the created order. Such contradictions make it difficult for the historian to see the incest taboo as an unchanging anthropological constant.

Mar Aba's condemnation of marriage between near relations in the Persian Empire is also of interest for its comparison of human and animal behaviour: the avoidance of sexual relations with close relatives is the mark of rational man, whereby he distinguishes himself from irrational beasts. It is not only because it symbolizes shame that Mar Aba uses the ass as example. Matings between domestic animals of the same strain must have been commonplace in his world. His assumption that abhorrence of incest is unique to humans is equally applicable today. It leads directly from the foundations of canon law in Sasanian Mesopotamia to modern scientific controversies over the conflicting influences of nature and culture on human sexuality.

In the scientific literature, the term 'incest taboo' has become standard for the avoidance of near relations as sexual partners. The ethnologist George P. Murdock concluded from the study of 250 different societies that 'In no known society is it conventional or even permissible for father and daughter, mother and son, or brother and sister to have sexual intercourse or to marry.'[8]

By 'incest taboo', most authors mean a prohibition on so-called 'nuclear family incest'. Within these limits, it is claimed, the incest taboo is universally valid. The question of universality is linked to the fundamental problem of interpretation: is the incest taboo rooted in human nature, or is it a socially established sexual norm, like many others, but exceptionally widespread? The French cultural anthropologist Claude Lévi-Strauss, whose ideas on the incest taboo have strongly influenced contemporary scientific opinion, says:

> Let us suppose then that everything universal in man relates to the natural order and is characterized by spontaneity, and that everything subject to a norm is cultural and is both relative and particular ... The prohibition of incest ... presents, without the slightest ambiguity, and inseparably combines, the two characteristics in which we recognize the conflicting features of two mutually exclusive orders. It constitutes a rule, but a rule which, alone among all the social rules, possesses at the same time a universal character ... The prohibition of incest has the universality of bent and instinct, and the coercive character of law and institution.[10]

Whatever we may think of the author's attempt to reconcile the irreconcilable, the tension between nature and culture (or society), which governs human sexuality in relation to incest, is particularly obvious in this passage. What the incest taboo actually *is* is an open question; the same could be said of the many and varied attempts to find an explanation for it. They also relate to the tension between nature and culture, and so lead into the interesting interspace between different scientific disciplines. A summary of these opinions is given below.[11]

The first, primarily biological, approach could be called the theory of inbreeding avoidance: the taboo on incest stems from the danger of inbreeding. Investigation of both humans and animals seems to show that inbreeding has genetically negative consequences for the offspring. In humans, the children of close relatives show a distinctly greater incidence of disease and deformity. This is often referred to as 'inbreeding degeneration'. It seems incontestable that the phenomenon exists. What is questionable is whether it was formerly obvious enough to motivate a ban on incest.

A second approach, which has recently won strong support from behavioural scientists, is the 'theory of indifference'. It assumes an innate aversion from sexual intercourse between persons who have lived together from early youth. Ethological studies of various animal species have shown that animals, if offered a choice of sexual partners, will prefer non-siblings to siblings with which the animal has grown up. Sociological research points in the same direction. For example, boys and girls who have grown up in the same child-group of a kibbutz *never* enter upon love relationships or marriage in later life.[12] The same conclusions were reached by social anthropologists studying 'Sim-pua' marriages in northern Taiwan.[13] This is a traditional type of marriage in which the bride is taken into the bridegroom's house as an adopted daughter at a very early age – usually three or less – and so grows up with him. In comparison with marriages from the same area in which the partners come together only at the marriage itself, Sim-pua couples evince a striking lack of sexual interest in each other. What is notable about the theory of indifference is that the deciding factor in the aversion to incest is not biological relationship but social proximity – though the latter may follow behavioural patterns rooted in human nature.

The explanatory model preferred by cultural anthropologists is Lévi-Strauss's 'theory of exchange'. He holds that the incest taboo is not so much a ban on marrying one's mother, sister or daughter as a command to give them to a man from another group. Societies consist of a series of exchanges among sub-societies, and the most valuable items of exchange are women. Thus, the incest taboo is in fact a rule of reciprocity; but it is by no means a purely social rule. Rather it is 'the fundamental step because of which, by which, but above all in which, the transition from nature to culture is accomplished'.[14] Lévi-Strauss's ideas are complex and hard to follow; nonetheless they have become widely known, and have been accepted by many authors.

A fourth theory, popular with sociologists, is based on a desire for stability in family roles and relationships. It is assumed that the main function of the incest taboo is to avoid tensions which might be created by uncertainty over roles within the family. The male child of a father–daughter relationship, for example, is both son and brother to his mother, son and grandson to his father. Still weightier must be the argument that the incest taboo prevents potentially intolerable sexual rivalries within the family. Brothers would fight over sisters, daughters rival mothers. If we explain the incest taboo by this tension-avoiding function, however, we must bear in mind that many family structures, past and present, are wider than the parent–child group which is fundamental to the concept of the incest taboo as a ban on 'nuclear family incest'.

The theories of individual historians play no part in the controversy over the incest taboo, although the material on which it is based derives to no small extent from historical research. It seems to be a question of approach. Social historians view the incest taboo primarily as a social rule. They ask whether, among all the forbidden sexual relations between relatives, 'nuclear family incest' is really so exceptional that it can justifiably be set apart from other forms. From a historical viewpoint there is also the question whether the three types of relationship included in the incest taboo – mother–son, father–daughter and brother–sister – were actually lumped together by past cultures, as the unified notion of incest would suggest. Finally, any examination of the universality of social rules concerning incest must also consider the respective roles of nature and culture in their production.

Surviving sources and historiographical priorities have meant that historians are best informed about the marriage customs of royal and noble houses. If we were to conclude from this evidence that similar practices extended to the societies ruled by such groups, we should soon abandon the notion that the incest taboo was universal. However, such an approach is deeply problematic. So-called 'dynastic incest' is a special case.[15]

There are reports of marriages between (above all) brothers and sisters, but also fathers and daughters, and even mothers and sons, in ruling families from all parts of the world and all historical periods.[16] The kings of Hawaii regularly married their sisters. Among the Polynesian Tonga the chief's son had to marry his sister, especially if she preceded him as first-born. In the Hima kingdoms around the great African lakes, incestuous dynastic marriages were known up to the 1960s. In the Inca kingdom of the Andes, the marriage of siblings was an express privilege of the royal house. In addition to his sister-wife or 'Coya', the ruler had a number of concubines, but the succession was confined to the sons of the Coya. The most frequent, and also the oldest, evidence for dynastic incest comes from the Near East. The Persian dynasty of the Achaemenids is thought to have taken over the custom from the kings of Elam. Examples are also found among the succeeding dynasties of the Seleucids and the Arsacids.[17] However, the most famous instance of dynastic incest comes from Egypt. Among the Pharaohs, sibling marriage can be traced back to the eleventh dynasty (*c.*2000 BC).[18] Father–daughter marriages also occurred. Amenhopis IV (Akhenaton), famous for his religious reforms, kept at least two of his daughters as concubines in addition to his chief wife, Nefertiti. After his death, one of these daughters married Tutenkhamen, who was either her brother or her uncle. The Greek dynasty of the Ptolemies also maintained the custom; whether they were following the Ancient Egyptian or the Persian model remains a matter for debate. In 278/277 BC Ptolemy II married his full sister Arsinoe. Of the eleven succeeding Greek rulers of Egypt, eight married their sisters, two a niece, one a cousin who was also his stepmother, and one his real mother. This last was murdered on his wedding-day by an uncle, who then married the widow, his own sister. This ancient Egyptian series of incestuous dynastic marriages ended with queen Cleopatra VII, who married in succession her two young half-brothers Ptolemy XIII (51–47 BC) and Ptolemy XIV (47–42). Her children, however, were born of her relationships with Julius Caesar and Mark Antony.

Dynastic incest can be explained by the notion of 'royal blood'. If the ruler's legitimacy depends on his or her descent from two parents of equally high blood, this limits the choice of suitable spouses, in extreme cases down to his or her siblings. Such a limitation is particularly likely where the royal house is thought to be of divine descent, especially when this notion is coupled with the deification of a recently deceased or living ruler. There is abundant evidence for such an ideology of sacral kingship in Egypt.[19] Ptolemy II had himself and his sister Arsinoe worshipped as *theoi adelphoi*, brother-god and sister-god. Their marriage was paralleled with the mystic wedding of Zeus with his sister Hera. As well as this Greek model, the identification with the divine brother–sister couple of Isis and Osiris was also important for Egyptian notions of kingship. Such myths can decisively influence the marriage customs of ruling families, insofar as the king is thought to have been translated to the divine sphere. They cannot, however, be safely used as evidence for the sexual mores of the societies which hold such beliefs. Just as the *magna mater* cult is an unsure indication of matriarchy, so the widespread incest myths are inconclusive evidence for a widespread practice of incest. People often imagine that their gods enjoy a licence forbidden to dwellers on this earth.

While it remains true that dynastic incest cannot be simply transferred from the ruling houses to the societies under them, it nevertheless seems significant that in two countries whose royal families observed such endogamic practices – Egypt and Iran – the population also tended, over long periods, to marry within the narrowest family circles. This phenomenon is most clearly attested in Egypt,[20] especially from censuses and marriage contracts dating from the first and second centuries AD. The census declarations allow some interesting comparisons. They show that, while sibling marriages were nowhere in the absolute majority, they were frequent enough not to seem exceptional. There is an extreme example in the details given for a weaver's household in AD 189: of twenty-six persons, four were married to siblings. One marriage contract reveals that the bride's parents had practised sibling marriage through three generations.[21] This custom, however, comes to an end in the third century. When Roman citizenship was conferred on the Egyptians by the emperor Caracalla in AD 212, sibling marriage was forbidden.[22]

In Iran, marriage among near kindred is attested over a much longer period.[23] Criticism of the incestuous practices of the Persians begins in Greek sources as early as the fifth century BC, and carries through to the Nestorian authors of the late Sasanian and early Islamic periods, chief among them the aforementioned Mar Aba. However, the reliability of such outside evidence is reduced by the fact that accusations of incest were a favourite way of denigrating another religious or ethnic group. Nevertheless, there is sufficient internal evidence from Iran to put it beyond doubt that such marriages were practised there for centuries. The Persian language has a special term for sibling marriage: *kvaedvadatha* in older documents, giving way to *khvetudas* in more recent texts. The highest form of *kvaedvadatha* was marriage with a sister, mother or daughter. *Kvaedvadatha/khvetudas* occurs frequently in Zoroastrian writings: it figures as the fourth of the seven good works, the ninth of the thirty-three ways to heaven, and the eighth of Zoroaster's ten exhortations to mankind.[24] The high religious value set on sibling marriage by the followers of Zoroaster is culturally unique. Not only was there no taboo on incest, as in Egypt: marriage between close kindred was not merely tolerated, it was socially desirable. It is this emphasis which makes the 'customs of the Magians' so remarkable.

Alongside the normative sources for incestuous marriage as practised in the Persian empire there is a number of individual instances, though they are neither as frequent nor as detailed as the Egyptian censuses. In connection with the theories discussed above it is interesting to note that contemporaries did observe the genetic consequences of Zoroastrian inbreeding. The Nestorian patriarch Jesubocht describes 'the judgement of God, which often manifests itself in the children of such filthy unions, in that there is something abnormal about them: their limbs, eyes, hands and feet and other limbs show some weakness, and their skin is of various colours'.[25] The connection between incestuous marriage and degeneration due to inbreeding is clearly made. Those directly concerned drew no similar consequences, which rather tells against the assumption that incest taboos could arise from such experiences. Another remark by Jesubocht is of interest in relation to the theory of indifference:

> The barrier in human nature shows itself in that these people [the Magians], although they deem their filthy custom to be justified, do not readily engage in such unclean unions unless they have first been inflamed with contemptible lust and have fought stubbornly against their own innate rationality. And once they have taken this step, it often fills them with disgust.[26]

If it is possible to generalize from Jesubocht's observations, they suggest a situation in which the practice of incest appears to be coupled with aversion from it. In that case, the 'customs of the Magians' would tell against the universality of the incest taboo as a social norm, but not against its universality as a sexual attitude towards persons familiar since childhood.

Nobody really knows how marriage customs which would now be reckoned incestuous came to be adopted by a broad cross-section of ancient Egyptian and Iranian society. Some would seek the origin of these customs in dynastic incest.[27] After the collapse of the Ptolemaic dynasty in Egypt, and of the Seleucids in Iran, the marriage customs of the ruling houses ceased to be the prerogative of a high social class, and they were imitated and vulgarized by ordinary people. These hypotheses are unconvincing. Not all the marriage customs of the Egyptian royal house recurred later among the population at large – only sibling marriage. On the other hand, sibling marriage was the only form practised by the Seleucids, whereas the 'customs of the Magians' typically included unions between parents and children. There are also problems with the chronology. The fundamental question, however, is whether dynastic incest based on the principle of 'sacred blood' could really be vulgarized at all. If similar developments can be observed in the ruling families and among the ordinary people of Egypt and Iran, it is worth bearing in mind that both countries belong to a wider area in which strongly endogamic practices are traceable back into the remote past.[28] Perhaps we should see these unions among very close kindred as a special form of an endogamy which had long been prevalent in the Near East.

A comparison of marriage customs in first-century Egypt and Iran reveals a fundamental weakness in the concept of incest taboo: the tendency to lump together sibling marriage with father–daughter and mother–son relationships. Not all cultures subject these relationships to the same kind of taboo, and this applies both to marriage and to sex outside marriage. Gradations appear as far back as the Code of Hammurabi, in which father–daughter incest is punished by exile of the father, mother–son incest by burning both parties alive,[29] but brother–sister incest is not mentioned at all. Any theory of incest has to take account of these differing evaluations of sexual relationships within the nuclear family. The term 'incest taboo', as it has hitherto been used by specialists in the field, tends to level out such distinctions.

The concept of incest taboo also leads to equally unjustified exclusions. Marriages between full siblings or half-siblings are seen as quite separate, as if they were totally different things: if two siblings in a sexual relationship have the same two parents, they are breaking the incest taboo; if they share only one parent, the union is acceptable.[30] Such a distinction might make sense if the function of the incest taboo was to prevent inbreeding. It is less easy to see why supporters of the indifference theory also make such distinctions, and avoid examining the incest taboo in cultures which allow marriage between half-siblings.[31] For half-siblings do, as a rule, grow up together, especially if they are children of successive marriages, so they must be subject to the indifference effect. Half-sibling marriages did occur in several ancient societies over and above those we have already examined.[32] Attic law permitted marriage between half-siblings with the same father, Spartan law between those with the same mother. There are traces of this kind of marriage among the Phoenicians and in pre-Islamic Arabia. According to the Bible, Sarah was Abraham's half-sister, and such marriages must still have been possible in the time of David. Otherwise it is hard to explain why David's beautiful daughter Tamar, when importuned by her half-brother Ammon, tells him to 'speak unto the king; for he will not withhold me from thee'.[33] Evidently the prohibition in Leviticus is of later date.

As well as half-sisters and half-brothers there is a series of other relatives who seem to be heavily taboo as marriage or sexual partners. It surely makes sense to include them in any consideration of the incest taboo, although they are excluded by any definition which confines the taboo to the nuclear family. Among the societies covered by George Murdock's ethnological atlas the ratio of 'forbidden' to 'allowed' is 181 to 5 for father's sister, 170 to 4 for brother's daughter, and 151 to 8 for sister's daughter.[34] The pattern is very clear. It is true that none of these relationships is forbidden in 100 per cent of cases; but, as we have seen, this also applies to parent–child and sibling unions. In historical societies, there is more evidence for marriage with a niece than for that with an aunt. Seeing that most cultures prefer the bridegroom to be older than the bride, the former relationship – if either is permitted at all – is the more likely to occur. An early example of marriage with a niece can be found, once again, in the Bible. Abraham had two brothers, Nahor and Haran; the former was married to the latter's daughter, Milkah.[35] Such marriages are permitted by Mosaic law. The Babylonian Talmud goes so far as to expressly recommend marriage with a sister's daughter.[36] The idea that marriage with a relative is a good work is strikingly similar to the ideas of the Magians, in whose domain the Talmud was composed. The preference for a sister's daughter over a brother's can be plausibly explained. In a patrilinear and patrilocal society the sister's daughter is a more distant relation, who cannot have grown up in the same household; moreover, since women marry at an earlier age, the ages of bride and groom are more likely to be compatible. However, marriage with a niece was not uncontested in Jewish tradition.[37] The Careans, for example, rejected it. European Jews, on the other hand, maintained the custom until the nineteenth century, despite its incompatibility with the mores of society at large. A famous example is the marriage between James Rothschild, head of the Rothschild bank in Paris, and the daughter of his Viennese brother, Salomon – one of the twenty or so endogamous marriages within this banking family.[39] The Habsburg monarchy exempted Jews from its laws against marriage between collaterals.[40]

In the Roman Empire, marriage with a niece was originally forbidden. When in AD 49 the emperor Claudius married Agrippina the younger, daughter of his brother Germanicus, the ban was lifted, though not as regards the sister's daughter – a historical accident which gave rise to a lasting social prohibition on incest. Only under the emperors Constans and Constantius (AD 337–350) was marriage with a niece again generally forbidden, and made punishable by death as a particularly repulsive crime.[41] Such penalties are very interesting because they indicate the degree of the taboo. The abrupt swing from toleration to the death penalty implies that we are dealing not with the 'voice of blood', but with strongly contrasting and competing cultural models. In the Roman Empire this actually meant a conflict between the exogamous traditions of the West and the endogamy of the eastern provinces – a conflict which intensified when citizenship was generalized within the empire.[42] In AD 384/5, the emperor Theodosius I extended the range of forbidden marriages to the children of siblings.[43] Soon afterwards, however, his son Arcadius had to rescind this measure within the eastern empire; he also radically reduced the penalties for marriage with a niece. In Syria and Egypt such marriages remained customary for many more years. Even today, marriage with a cousin, especially a father's brother's daughter, is a preferred form in many eastern countries.[45]

Incest prohibitions in historical societies focused particularly on a cluster of marital and sexual unions which could scarcely have been considered naturally abhorrent: those with female relatives by marriage, such as stepmothers, daughters-in-law and, especially, sisters-in-law. They involve neither a blood relationship nor a common upbringing which might influence subsequent behaviour. The prohibition must therefore have been determined by socio-cultural factors. Proscriptions of this kind are found mainly in societies which have complex family structures, so that a single household may include fathers with married sons, brothers and their wives, and even uncles, nephews and cousins with their wives. The problem of permitted and forbidden unions becomes particularly acute when a woman's husband dies. In some cultures, the widow of a brother, father, son, nephew etc. remains permanently taboo; but in others, one of the dead man's male relations is permitted, or even obliged, to marry the widow. The function of such kindred marriages varies: to provide for the widow and her children within the immediate family; to retain a valuable source of labour; or to produce substitute offspring for a relative who has died childless, the latter function being particularly important in societies which practise ancestor worship. The tension between the two views emerges particularly clearly in Jewish levirate marriages. In the book of Leviticus, the wife of a father, father's brother, son or brother is prohibited, and this prohibition remains if she is widowed.[46] Deuteronomy has a different rule:

> If brethren dwell together, and one of them die, and have no child, the wife of the dead shall not marry without unto a stranger: her husband's brother shall go in unto her, and take her to him to wife, and perform the duty of an husband's brother unto her. And it shall be, that the firstborn which she beareth shall succeed in the name of his brother which is dead, that his name be not put out of Israel.[47]

The same implications emerge from the story of Onan, son of Judah, whose sin – later interpreted in a completely different way – was refusing to engender offspring for his dead brother.[48] These contradictory stipulations made marriage with in-laws controversial in Jewish tradition, but its supporters eventually carried the day.[49] The obligation to marry a childless brother's widow also applied to brothers who were not resident in the same household, as was increasingly the case.

Christendom rejected marriage with in-laws at an early stage, whether or not the brother had died childless.[50] Of the numerous and ever-increasing prohibited degrees imposed by canon law, the ban on unions with brothers and sisters-in-law is the oldest.[51] Even as early as Mar Aba, it is seen as marking a distinction between Christians and Jews. More than a thousand years after the taboo was imposed by Leviticus, the debate over the correct understanding of the Old Testament regulations was revived when Henry VIII strove for the annulment of his marriage to his first wife, Katherine of Aragon. Katherine was the widow of his brother Arthur, who had died young, and he had had a papal dispensation to marry her – which reflects the current attitude towards levirate marriages on the threshold of the events which led to the separation of the Anglican Church.[52] Marriage with a stepmother, which is just as strictly forbidden by Christian tradition, has never had any such world-shaking consequences. There are, however, some notable instances, such as the marriages of the Carolingian princess Judith, daughter of Charles the Bald. In 856 she was married to the English king Aethelwulf; when he died soon after, she was immediately passed on to his son and heir, Aethelbald. Anglo-Saxon custom allowed a stepmother to be 'inherited' in this way, whereas in the Frankish kingdom the practice was regarded as incestuous. In 596, king Childebert II had made it a capital offence – probably under pressure from the church.[53]

Islam permits levirate marriages, and marriage with any other steprelative except a stepmother. The fourth sura of the Quran commands, 'Believers, it is unlawful for you to inherit the women of your deceased kinsmen against their will.' That is to say, widows must consent to their own remarriage within the family, but the principle of remarriage is not in question. The idea that marriage with in-laws is incestuous, taken to excess in the prohibited degrees laid down by various Christian churches, is quite alien to Islamic culture. The Islamic ban on marriage with relations is essentially confined to blood relations, and even here it does not go nearly so far as did the medieval church.

In most historical societies, the range of forbidden partners went far beyond the parent–child unit. Its extent varies widely. Occasionally it includes all the members of a patrilineage, however distantly related they are to one another. In recent European history examples can be found in remote Balkan regions, where remnants of ancient ancestor worship have survived in Christian guise. Here, the fact that two people worship the same household saint is sufficient to prevent them from marrying, because it arouses the suspicion that they may be descended from the same paternal ancestor.[54] This kind of clan exogamy resembles relationships which ethnologists have discovered in many non-European tribal societies. In European Christendom it is more usual for the range of forbidden partners to extend to both paternal and maternal relations. There are especially strong differences amongst cultures in their attitude to step-relatives. However, personal proximity, which excludes from sexual intercourse (and therefore marriage), can go beyond even this kind of kinship. Thus, the fourth sura of the Quran forbids marriage not only with aunts, nieces and step-daughters, but also wet-nurse and sister by milk. The same prohibitions are also found in non-Islamic cultures, for example in Armenia.[55] Applying the theory of indifference, we could see this as a notable corroboration of the innate aversion to sexual intercourse with persons familiar from early childhood. Against this it must be added that many cultures which practise wet-nursing on a large scale have no such prohibitions. This also applies to the incest laws of Western Christendom. It is more probable, therefore, that the ban on marriage between relatives by milk is similar to other incidences arising from artificial kinship. We may think first of the ban on marriage instituted by the spiritual relationship between godparents and godchildren, and their nearest relatives, which began to spread outwards from Byzantium in the sixth century – an obstacle which some authors considered more important than blood relationship.[56] It can be compared with other relationships of godparenthood: for example, in the Balkans there existed also a godparenthood by ritual first haircut.[57] Not dissimilar are the bans on marriage between members of the families of blood brothers.[58] The cultural roots of all marriage prohibitions of this kind are particularly apparent.

Historical sources offer a mixed bag of incest prohibitions applying to blood relations, step-relatives, members of the same household and artificial kindred. They set historians the task of interpreting this whole complex of rules within a set of varying social frameworks. The concept of the so-called 'incest taboo' is not particularly helpful here. It demands a fundamental dichotomy within each set of rules which is not at all justified by the sources. Reading the eighteenth chapter of Leviticus, the fourth sura of the Quran, the marriage laws of Mar Aba and other sources, we have the impression of closed normative systems. Nowhere is there a special taboo on 'nuclear family incest'. In the view of the so-called incest taboo, we shall have to assume a qualitative distinction between nuclear family incest and other forms, even if no such distinction appears in the sources. That is to say, in each set of laws we should have to assume a narrower range of prohibitions which are more deeply rooted than the others – rooted in basic social necessity, perhaps even in human nature. If we distinguish between different rules for the avoidance of incest, we must also find different explanations for them. If the ban on nuclear family incest is 'universal', it must always derive from the same general principle – however diverse the attempts to explain and formulate that principle – whereas no such principle can account for the very variable rules for the avoidance of incest in individual societies.

If we really wish to explain the rules for sexual avoidance in historical societies, we might do better to jettison the concept of incest taboo altogether. It is an academic construct whose implications are often more a hindrance than a help. This applies not only to its prescriptive connection with 'nuclear family incest', ignoring other relationships – with step-sister, stepmother, niece or aunt – which are also heavily tabooed in certain cultures. The concept of incest taboo, as it has previously been used in the literature, also tends to obscure the fundamental difference between the abhorrence of incest as an aspect of behaviour and the prohibition of incest as a social rule. Typically vague are the oft-quoted remarks by Lévi-Strauss, who defines incest as both an instinct and a rule and locates it on the boundary between nature and culture.[59] It is this ambivalent classification which gives the incest taboo its persistent claim to universality. Researchers are therefore obliged to treat all counter-examples as deviations which cannot challenge the viability of the general rule. Dynastic incest can be neglected because it affects only the ruling family, not the whole of society; moreover, since only two important examples have been found, both from the distant past, it is seen as a *quantité négligeable* which casts no doubt on the universality of the incest taboo.[60] Even taking account of the historical fact that there have been societies without any incest taboo at all, there is still one last way to save our academic construct:

> Fox is of the opinion that any attempt to explain the wide dissemination of the incest taboo must distinguish between the beginning of a taboo and its continued existence. Research has justified this assumption. The theory that the incest taboo has arisen in all human societies has been confirmed; in this sense, it is universal. However, the assumption that it has been retained in all societies has been disproved.[61]

It has often been a wearisome task to 'prove' what is in fact assumed by the mere acceptance of the concept of incest taboo. If we do distinguish between avoidance of incest as a more or less important behavioural trait, and bans on incest which turn socially dominant behaviour patterns into coercive constraints, then we can draw some clear conclusions about historical societies: they do not supply evidence for the existence of a universal prohibition on incest. Sexual relationships and marriages between close kindred are usually forbidden, but there is a series of notable exceptions to this rule. Forbidden relationships with close kindred apply not only to parents and full siblings, but also, by degrees, to stepchildren, step-siblings, sons and daughters-in-law, nieces and aunts. There are also gradations within the prohibition on sexual relations between parents and children. Cultures which permit sibling marriages do not necessarily allow relationships with offspring. The strongest taboo must be that on sexual intercourse between mother and son; but even this ban is not universal. At least one past society did not only permit sexual relationships amd marriages between mothers and sons, but actually demanded them. It is the fact of exempting this relationship from any ban on incest which gives the 'customs of the Magians' – the starting point of the present chapter – their peculiar importance in world history. The fact that this is only one culture out of thousands does not quite do justice to its historical significance. The exceptionally endogamic traditions of the Zoroastrians lasted for over a millennium. Zoroastrianism was the state religion of a mighty empire. Its missionary activities and the spread of its marriage customs extended its influence far beyond its own borders. As an example of a radical overturning of incest barriers it surely has more than marginal significance.

The historical fact that no relationship attracts a universally valid incest prohibition does not lead inevitably to the conclusion that abhorrence of incest, as a general trend in human behaviour, has no character of 'universality'. Endogamy among close kindred can be maintained even if it is accompanied by sexual indifference or even rejection. As we have already seen, there is clear evidence that the Persian obligation to marry a close relative met with some resistance.[62] Until very recently, in parts of the Near East where endogamy was strong, it was observed that the maintenance of such customs caused severe emotional problems.[63] Obligatory and forbidden marriages between relatives must surely not be taken to reflect a collective pattern of erotic attraction or repulsion. Thus, abhorring incest is a different thing altogether from placing a ban on it; but the concept of incest taboo runs the two together, making it impossible to investigate their interaction.

Why *are* sexual partnerships with close kindred generally avoided? As the debate stands at present, the theory of the indifference, building on the arguments of Edward Westermarck, seems by far the most plausible explanation. If we accept this theory, we are more or less obliged to abandon the incest taboo with its emphasis on 'nuclear family incest'. According to Westermarck and his followers, the key to explaining the comparative sexual indifference to close kindred is not blood relationship, but close social proximity during childhood. This childhood familiarity, which is decisive for later attitudes of sexual indifference, does not seem to be particularly confined to the 'nuclear family'. Important evidence to back this theory has emerged from observing persons who have not spent their childhood in traditional nuclear families – such as young Jews who have grown up together in kibbutzim. Thus, abhorrence of incest seems to be decided by the pattern of communal living during childhood, not by the blood relationship with natural parents and siblings, as assumed by the concept of 'nuclear family incest'.

If we believe that natural abhorrence of incest depends on proximity to familiar persons during certain phases of childhood development, this gives the problem of incest another interesting historical dimension. The persons included under the taboo would vary according to the current composition of household and family. Considering the great variety of family structures in historical societies, we should *expect a* great variability in the relationships considered incestuous, especially in complex family structures. In laterally extended complex families, cousins soon began to live together; in lineally extended families there would be proximity to nieces and aunts. In complex patrilocal families the intimacy would be with lateral patrilineal kindred. On the other hand, the lack of aversion to incest between close relatives, an aversion to be expected on genealogical grounds, can be explained by particular forms of household. If, in polygamous families, the wives lived comparatively separate lives along with their children, this might eliminate the grounds for avoidance among half-brothers and half-sisters. As for dynastic incest, it is conceivable that royal children, who were reared individually in the unique environment of the court (a kind of extended household), would have failed to develop any aversion to incest even with full siblings. However we are to explain such exceptional cases, the theory of indifference makes it probable that in historical societies the family circle within which children developed barriers against incest was very variously constituted. The concept of incest taboo, with its rigid fixation on the nuclear family, has hitherto directed attention away from this rich array of possibilities.

Not only is it the case that bans on incest within a culture are socially determined; the preconditions for abhorrence of incest also seem to depend on social factors, though these are confined to a smaller number of persons. This leads us to suggest that the two domains may be causally interconnected. We may ask whether very widely differing incest prohibitions were originally connected with the dominance of more or less complex family structures within individual societies. For various reasons, however, this argument must be advanced with caution. Firstly, it is hard to determine which tabooed relationships within households really are to be explained by the phenomenon of indifference. There are other reasons for forbidding sexual relationships with household members, as is shown by bans on 'incest' with in-laws. Such reasons could also have applied to nieces or cousins. Further, it can be shown that there was a series of cultural factors working *against* the construction of incest rules on the basis of natural abhorrence, such as the safeguarding of 'pure blood'; in some cases the overcoming of aversion was even interpreted as a magical or religious act. Finally, we can assume that incest rules, like rules for preferred marriages, can long outlive the social conditions which produced them. We know, for example, that the Jewish levirate arose in a form of household jointly inhabited by married brothers; but it remained a religious duty for thousands of years, independent of that particular family structure. A similar process may affect all incest prohibitions. As a rule, they should not be seen as a direct reflection of contemporary household structures.

Incest prohibitions, as cultural norms, never seem to have a simple explanation. Differing family structures are only one factor among many. Nevertheless, the connection between family structure and incest is not only worth pursuing in order to gain a better understanding of avoidance rules and behaviour among close kindred; it is also important in relation to the family as a historical social form. The classic conception of the incest taboo encourages the idea that the nuclear family is universal and natural. By confronting this view with the variability of incest avoidance and prohibition, we can free the concept of the family from biological determinism.

NOTES

1 This chapter is a revised and extended version of a paper originally published in German as 'Die "Sitten der Magier"'. Zur Relativität der Inzestschranke in historischen Gesellschaften', *Beiträge zur historischen Sozialkunde*, 18/1 (1988), 13–19.
2 Oskar Brown, *Das Buch der Synhados* (Stuttgart, 1900), 130f.
3 Ibid., 133. On the Christian interpretation of the 'burial of an ass', following Jeremiah 22: 19, cf. Martin Illi, *Wohin die Toten gingen. Begräbnis und Kirchhof in der vorindustriellen Stadt* (Zurich, 1992), 112.
4 Edward Sachau, *Syrische Rechtsbücher*, 3 vols. (Berlin, 1907), I, 265.
5 On the religious background to the highly endogamous marriage customs of the Zoroastrians see Nikolaus Sidler, *Zur Universalität der Inzesttabus* (Stuttgart, 1971), 86ff.; Sidler, 'Das Inzest-Tabu', in Gisela Vogler and Karin von Welck (eds.), *Die Braut*, vol. I (Cologne, 1985), 77f.
6 Sachau, *Syrische Rechtsbücher*, II, 74.
7 Deuteronomy 25: 5–6.
8 George P. Murdock, *Social Structure* (New York, 1949), 12.

9 Sidler, *Universalität*, 4f., 152ff.
10 Claude Lévi-Strauss, *The Elementary Structures of Kinship* (Boston, 1969), 8–9, 10.
11 For overviews of incest theories in different disciplines see: Sybil Wolfram, *In-laws and Outlaws: Kinship and Marriage in England* (London and Sydney, 1987), 161ff.; Keith Hopkins, 'Brother–Sister Marriage in Roman Egypt', *Comparative Studies in Society and History*, 22 (1980), 304ff.; Norbert Bischof, *Das Rätsel Ödipus. Die biologischen Wurzeln des Urkonflikts von Intimität und Autonomie* (Munich and Zurich, 1985), 88ff.; Michael Oppitz, *Notwendige Beziehungen – Abriss einer strukturellen Anthropologie* (Frankfurt, 1975), 104ff.; Dieter Claessens, *Das Konkrete und das Abstrakte. Soziologische Skizzen zur Anthropologie* (Frankfurt, 1980), 202.
12 J. Shepher, 'Mate Selections among Second Generation Kibbutz Adolescents and Adults: Incest Avoidance and Negative Imprinting', *Archives of Sexual Behaviour*, 1 (1971), 293ff.
13 A. Wolf, 'Childhood Association, Sexual Attraction and Incest Taboo: A Chinese Case', *American Anthropologist*, 68 (1966), 883f.; Wolf, 'Adopt a Daughter-in-law, Marry a Sister: A Chinese Solution to the Problem of Incest Taboo', *American Anthropologist*, 70 (1968), 864ff.; Wolf, 'Childhood Association and Sexual Attraction: A Further Test of the Westermarck Hypothesis', *American Anthropologist*, 72 (1970), 503ff.
14 Lévi-Strauss, *Elementary Structures*, 24.
15 Sidler, *Universalität*, 8ff.
16 Ibid., 10, 19ff., 128; Bischof, *Rätsel Ödipus*, 28ff.
17 Ernst Kornemann, 'Die Geschwisterehe im Altertum', *Mitteilungen der schlesischen Gesellschaft für Volkskunde*, 24 (1923), 26ff.; Kornemann, 'Mutter-recht', in Pauly-Wissowa (ed.), *Real-Enzyklopädie der klassischen Altertumswissenschaft*, suppl. vol. VI (Stuttgart, 1935), 567.
18 Hopkins, 'Brother–Sister Marriage', 311ff.
19 Sidler, *Universalität*, 81; Jakob Seibert, *Historische Beiträge zu den dynastischen Verbindungen in hellenistischer Zeit* (Wiesbaden, 1967), 81ff.
20 Hopkins, 'Brother–Sister Marriage', 312ff.
21 Ibid., 321.
22 Ibid., 353f. Egon Weiss, 'Endogamie und Exogamie im römischen Kaiserreich', *Zeitschrift der Savigny-Stiftung für Rechtsgeschichte*, 29 (1908), 340ff.
23 Sidler, *Universalität*, 89ff.; Brian Spooner, 'Iranian Kinship and Marriage', *Iran*, 4 (1966), 51ff. Zoroastrianism being a missionary faith, kinship marriage spread far beyond the borders of Iran. A memorial inscription by the high priest Kartir, who lived under five successive Sasanian rulers between AD 242 and 293, mentions missionary expeditions to Antioch, Syria, Tarsus, Cilicia, Caesarea, Cappadocia, Armenia, Georgia, Albania, and the Balkans as far as the 'gates of the Alani'. See Philippe Gignoux, 'L'inscription de Kartir à Sar Mashâd', *Journal Asiatique*, 256 (1968), 396f. Among his religious activities Kartir particularly stresses the promotion of kinship marriage (ibid., 398).
24 Louis J. Luzbetak, *Marriage and Family in Caucasia* (Vienna, 1951), 53.
25 Sachau, *Syrische Rechtsbücher*, III, 35.
26 Ibid.

27 Sidler, *Universalität*, 81ff., 145ff.; Spooner, 'Iranian Kinship', 56.
28 On marriage customs in the east see Jack Goody, *The Development of the Family and Marriage in Europe* (Cambridge, 1983), 10ff.; Emmanuel Todd, *The Explanation of Ideology: Family Structures and Ideological Systems* (Oxford, 1985), 133ff.; A. D. Lee, 'Close Kin Marriage in Late Antique Mesopotamia', *Greek, Roman and Byzantine Studies*, 29 (1988), 403ff.; Michael Mitterauer, 'Christianity and Endogamy', *Continuity and Change*, 6 (1991), 295ff.
29 Sidler, *Universalität*, 27.
30 Ibid., 29, 33, 39.
31 Bischof, following Sidler, also mentions only two critical cases, those of Egypt and Iran.
32 W. K. Lacey, *The Family in Classical Greece* (Mainz, 1968), 109; S. C. Humphreys, *The Family, Women and Death. Comparative Studies* (London, 1983), 25; Raphael Patai, *Sitte und Sippe in Bibel und Orient* (Frankfurt, 1962), 21ff.; Weiss, 'Endogamie', 342.
33 II Samuel 13: 13.
34 Cf. Murdock, *Social Structure*.
35 On endogamy in patriarchal families see Julian Pitt-Rivers, *The Fate of Shechem or the Politics of Sex. Essays in the Anthropology of the Mediterranean* (Cambridge, 1977), esp. table on p. 153.
36 Lazarus Goldschmidt (ed.), *Der Babylonische Talmud*, IV (Berlin, 1966), 531.
37 Shlomo D. Goitein, *A Mediterranean Society*, III (Berkeley, 1978), 26.
38 Ibid., 433.
39 Franz Putz, 'Die österreichische Wirtschaftsaristokratie 1815-1859' (Ph.D. diss., University of Vienna, 1975).
40 Ernst Mayerhofer, *Handbuch für den politischen Verwaltungsdienst in den im Reichsrathe vertretenen Königreichen und Ländern*, V (Vienna, 1901), 13.
41 Goody, *Development of Marriage*, 53-6.
42 Mitterauer, 'Christianity'. The conflict over the marriage of the emperor Heraclius (AD 610-641) with his sister's daughter Martina can also be interpreted as a conflict between Eastern and Western marriage patterns. (Cf. Georg Ostrogorsky, *History of the Byzantine State* (2nd edn, Oxford, 1968), 112-13.) Heraclius was a member of the Armenian family of the Arsacuni, who were descended from the Parthian royal dynasty of the Arsacides. Among other changes, he introduced many Iranian customs into the empire, including emperor worship and insignia. (Cf. Hans Wilhelm Haussig, *Byzantinische Geschichte* (Stuttgart, 1969), 58ff.) His attempt to found a dynasty must also be seen in this context. In marrying his own niece he went further than the fourth-century kindred of Constantine the Great, who confined themselves to marriage between cousins (Goody, *Development of Marriage*, 53-4). The fact that some of his children died young, or were born with deformities, was regarded by some of his Christian contemporaries as God's punishment for his unlawful marriage. The crisis triggered by the marriage, and the ensuing struggle over the inheritance, seem to have helped to reinforce prohibitions on endogamy in the following years.
43 Goody, *Development of Marriage*, 54.
44 Weiss, 'Endogamie', 368; Josef Zhishman, *Das Eherecht der orientalischen Kirche*

(Vienna, 1864), 233f. The conquest of Mesopotamia again raised the problem of close kin marriage in the Byzantine Empire. On the ensuing laws of Constantine (AD 535/6) and his successor Justin II (565–578) see Lee, 'Close Kin Marriage', 403ff.
45 Raphael Patai, 'Cousin-right in Middle Eastern Marriage', *Southwestern Journal of Anthropology*, 11 (1955), 390ff.
46 Leviticus 18: 8–16.
47 Deuteronomy 25: 5–6.
48 Genesis 38: 9.
49 Goitein, *Mediterranean Society*, 210f.; S. Ph. de Vries, *Jüdische Riten und Symbole* (Wiesbaden, 1981), 213ff.
50 Goody, *Development of Marriage*, 63ff.
51 Ibid., 60ff.
52 Ibid., 171ff.
53 Jo Ann McNamara and Suzanne F. Wemple, 'Marriage and Divorce in the Frankish Kingdom', in Susan Mosher Stuart (ed.), *Women in Medieval Society* (Philadelphia: University of Pennsylvania Press, 1976), 99.
54 Edmund Schneeweiss, *Serbokratische Volkskunde*, 1 (Berlin, 1961), 148. More recently, Karl Kaser, 'Ahnenkult und Patriarchalismus auf dem Balkan' *Historische Anthropologie* 1 (1993), 93ff.
55 Luzbetak, *Marriage and Family*, 56.
56 Karl Eduard Zachariae von Lingenthal, *Geschichte des griechisch-römischen Rechts* (Berlin, 1892), 69ff.; Zhishman, *Eherecht*, 264ff.; Evelyne Patlagean, 'Christianisation et parentes spirituelles: la domaine de Byzance', *Annales ESC*, 88 (1978), 628; Joseph H. Lynch, *Godparents and Kinship in Early Medieval Europe* (Princeton, 1986), 223ff.
57 M. E. Durham, *Some Tribal Origins, Laws and Customs of the Balkans* (London, 1928), 303ff.
58 Luzbetak, *Marriage and Family*, 55.
59 See above, n. 10.
60 Bischof, *Rätsel Ödipus*, 32ff.
61 Sidler, *Universalität*, 154.
62 Cf. above, n. 26.
63 Justine MacCabe, 'FBD Marriage: Further Support for the Westermarck Hypothesis of the Incest Taboo?', *American Anthropologist*, 85 (1983), 61ff.

ELEVEN

MASCULINITY AND THE DECADENCE

GEORGE L. MOSSE

> It seems that even vice has now become one of the exact sciences.
> Marcel Proust on reading the sexologists[1]

In all the literature about gender, the concept of masculinity until recently has been taken for granted. It was subsumed under the ideal of an established and settled society. Attention has focused instead upon those whom society excluded or marginalized, for they had been ignored by historians. But the time has come not only to investigate in greater depth the historical image of masculinity as central to modern society, but also the role which those excluded or marginalized by society played in constructing that image. Insider and outsider cannot easily be separated; historically they are linked to one another.

The construction of modern masculinity has known several critical periods: the French Revolution and the subsequent wars, but also the turn of the nineteenth and twentieth centuries, which climaxed and consolidated existing ideas of masculinity. I will focus on this latter, more recent period, because it illustrates best that dialectic between insider and outsider, enemy and comrade, which I have mentioned. The building blocks of the modern ideas of masculinity were already in place by that time. During the French Revolution and the wars which followed, for example, there was an intense preoccupation with manliness.

Indeed, the wars of the age of the French Revolution fought by volunteers and conscripts instead of mercenaries democratized the ideal of manliness. During the German Wars of Liberation a volunteer like Ernst Moritz Arndt seemed to state the obvious when he wrote in 1813, 'I return from a battle fought among men.'[2] But what seems to us self-evident was then fraught with meaning which involved a certain attitude, looks, comportment and behaviour, which stood for an image all of society should take to heart. The accelerated pressures of modernity at the end of the nineteenth century produced a heightened, not a new, concept of masculinity – now there was talk about the 'new man', the 'new German', the 'new Jew' and after the war of the 'new socialist' as well. Such new men at the turn of the century emphasized youth, virility, decisiveness and discipline. But as a rule they put these manly characteristics into the service of a 'higher cause', most frequently that of the nation. All of these manly qualities symbolized that control over the passions demanded by a society in the grip of social and economic change.

Classical models provided the inspiration, often represented in all their nudity. J. J. Winckelmann, at the end of the eighteenth century, had attempted to strip nude Greek statues of male youth of their sensuousness, and now an even greater effort was made to integrate the symbolism of male beauty with middle-class sensibilities. Walter Pater in his *Renaissance* (1873), for example, calls Greek sensuousness childlike: it does not 'fever the conscience' and shame was therefore unknown.[3] Moreover, serenity and restraint are the laws which govern classical Greek sculpture: 'the beauty of Greek statues was a sexless beauty'.[4] Such an ideal of male beauty was projected upon the ideal of masculinity, in order to symbolize its strength.

Whether public symbol or private ideal, the male image was sharpened whenever it faced real or putative enemies and here the *fin de siècle* was a crucial period. Masculinity provided a general bulwark against chaos and the forces of dissolution which seemed so menacing at the time, as the enemies of a settled society became ever more visible and multiplied. Which enemies gave masculinity its particular urgency at the end of the nineteenth century? Economic crisis, labour unrest and the new technology which seemed to speed up time itself provided some of the background. Fears of depopulation, and in France the shock of defeat by Germany, played their role as well. Meanwhile, threats to individual health like syphilis, tuberculosis and hysteria were becoming a general obsession. At the same time, the so-called 'new women', lesbians and homosexuals, were emerging from the shadows and challenging the traditional division between genders, tangible symbols for the times out of joint.

The women's quest for equality and independence, especially strong in England, presented the most effective challenge to the social position of men. This challenge included a critique of male sexuality, centred upon the double standard of moral behaviour expected of men and women. But by and large this was a critique which did not attack the essence of male sexuality: it had no real objection to manly men provided that men and women followed the same moral standard, and women could participate in public life. Indeed, even a radical German feminist could, in the 1890s, credit one of the leaders of the feminist movement with having 'a strong, manly spirit, and an iron will', while her appearance remained 'truly feminine'.[5] Yet the threat to masculinity from the women's liberation movements which were at their height in the 1890s must not be underestimated. However much most of them wanted to preserve the division between the sexes, their demands were alarming enough, and yet it was those who as part of the Decadence sought to reverse normal sexuality who provided the true counter-type against which the ideal of masculinity defined itself, so-called 'abnormal' men and women who challenged the very essence of masculinity. The new mass media gave to the so-called abnormal a greater visibility than it had ever had before. Here the ideal of masculinity was endangered by a general decay, a disorientation, heralded by disease and the diseased.

These enemies were subsumed under the category of vice conceptualized in terms of disease: the corruption of the purity and chastity of manhood stood for the sickness and dissolution of society. Already in 1847 Thomas Couture's painting, *The Romans of the Decadence*, exhibited in Paris, had set the tone. There austere Greek heroes standing tall at the back of the painting provide a startling contrast with the orgy in progress at their feet: men and women in poses of sexual abandon. Moreover, in the foreground two bearded men with prancing feet symbolize homosexuality, while in the background an androgyne-looking boy lying in the arms of a man may be barely discerned. As late as 1917 this painting was praised as a work directed against selfishness and immorality.[6] It foreshadowed the key role which the concept of decadence played in defining the enemies against which manliness measured itself. Jean Baptiste Morel in his famous *Treatise on Decadence* (1857) expressed it well, 'The Incessant progression in Europe, not only of insanity, but of all the abnormal states which have a special relation to the existence of physical and moral evil in society struck my attention.'[7]

The supposed decadence of the age was frequently likened to that of Rome in decline, but just as often it was cast in medical vocabulary. At the same time, descriptions of disease by medical men at the turn of the century were often filled with reference to social conditions as signs or even causes of illness. This was especially true for those physicians concerned with mental health, a term which was said to encompass the whole of the human personality. For example, Oswald Bumke, active from the turn of the century until after the Second World War, an important German alienist, professor at several prestigious German universities, maintained that mental health equalled the movements of the human soul,[8] demonstrating quite clearly how even in their own minds some medical men co-opted what had been a clerical monopoly.

They were seconded by others who were not doctors themselves: thus a woman writer in the *Fortnightly Review* of 1895 held that it was up to the physician, not the moralist, to define the meaning of the *fin de siècle* with its immorality, contempt for tradition and the established order. After all, he was an expert in the two diseases responsible for this condition, degeneration and hysteria.[9] Physicians in turn considered the problems of modernity as facts to be taken into consideration in medical diagnosis, attempting to stop or at least to mitigate the rush of time. For example, Max Nordau, himself a physician, in his famous *Degeneration* (1892) thought that the constant vibrations undergone in railway travel were partly to blame for the shattering of men's nerves, typical of the havoc wrought by the approaching end of the established order.[10]

Nervousness and hysteria lay at the centre of Decadence, whether symbolized by that lack of restraint which, so it was said, had led to the fall of the Roman empire, or to weakness and sterility brought about by 'physical and moral poison' such as alcoholism, the use of opium or debilitating disease. Oswald Bumke was typical of many of his contemporaries when he asserted as part of medical knowledge that the human soul could not function properly without a healthy nervous system, the material foundation for its very existence.[11]

During the last decades of the nineteenth century Jean-Jacques Charcot, chief physician at the Salpêtrière in Paris, had systematized and clearly defined the state of hysteria, while affirming its close relationship to a nervous disposition. But, typically enough, he also extended the scope of hysteria through insisting, contrary to tradition, that it was a male as well as a female disorder. Here he endowed men stricken by that illness with what were usually thought of as female attributes, such as a heightened sensibility.[12] Was the masculine ideal, then, to become a victim of the medical preoccupation with degeneration, hysteria and nervousness, as a formerly solely female disease was linked to the general temper of the times and rapid social change?

The possibility of hysteria among men had been discussed by medical men from the end of the eighteenth century onward, and the male ideal had been preserved through the use of several strategies. Hysteria in men was thought to be transitory, while in women a hysterical condition was always potentially present. Perhaps even more symptomatic of the desire by medical men to safeguard their masculinity was the distancing of the very few pale-faced effeminate and hysterical men from a normal robust manhood.[13] Such men continued to be set apart, and by the end of the century came to exemplify the general preoccupation with nervousness and decadence. French physicians wrote during the 1880s that because of their 'irritable weakness' any sexual act performed by effeminate men would end in profound exhaustion and sterility.[14] Even when they were not characterized as effeminate, the growing awareness of the existence of weak men can be illustrated by German advertisements for cures against nervousness published around 1900: 'Men with weak nerves, here is a guaranteed cure'; 'The sickness of male nerves, its prevention and radical cure' or, simply, 'Weak men! here is a special kind of electricity which has healed thousands'.[15] Such weakness sapped sexual energy, a serious matter at a time when most European societies thought themselves threatened by falling birth-rates.

Effeminate and weak men were often suspected of homosexuality, their love was unproductive, typical of decadents. Sigmund Freud asserted that nervousness was the result of efforts to suppress perverted sexual drives, though for him what was true for sexual deviants in general also held true for normal men who unsuccessfully suppressed or sublimated their libido.[16] Here a stereotype of the outsider was under construction which, through its restlessness, nervous ailments and hysteria, was the very opposite of the image society had of itself. Without the visible presence of such a counter-type society may have found it difficult to project its own image of strength and stability; at the very least, the counter-type gave society's self-representation increased credibility. It should not surprise, given the social function of such outsiders, that effeminate and nervous men, whom Charcot had at least endowed with female sensibility, should, as a rule, be denied the so-called good womanly qualities of steadfastness, sensibility and tenderness.[17]

Nevertheless, during one of Charcot's Tuesday Lessons at the Salpêtrière in 1872/3, while some men subject to hysteria were said to lack all feminine traits, they were to all appearances robust men. And yet Charot too safeguarded the male ideal: for in men all the phenomena associated with hysterical nervousness were never complete. Nevertheless, in the same breath, he went on to describe practically identical cases of male and female hysteria.[18] Male hysteria now became a subject of considerable scientific interest. Books were published about it, and the young Sigmund Freud made his debut at the Vienna Medical Society in 1886 with a paper which included a discussion of male hysteria. The hysterical male, he told a discomfitted audience, is not a rare or peculiar case, but an ordinary case of frequent occurrence.[19]

Social causes were always important to the diagnosis of degeneration as a nervous disease. Richard von Krafft-Ebing, for example, in his much used *Lehrbuch der gerichtlichen Psychopathologie* (Manual of Forensic Psychopathology, 1879) thought that lack of success in social life was a vital cause of mental illness.[20] At the same time older religious ideas continued to make themselves felt, now equated with medical concepts. Thus Benôit-Augustin Morel held that evil and illness coincide as a consequence of original sin, departing from the basic human type created in the image of God.[21] Here too, however, the normal male could be safeguarded from nervousness or hysteria which might place him in dangerous proximity to degeneration, or indeed to the passive attributes women were said to possess. Man was supposed to shape society and to protect women from its dangers, according to Bumke, as both faced social conditions which might lead to degeneration.[22]

Control over the sexual drives was usually considered a sign of mental health, and lack of control indicated mental illness. It is necessary – according to Krafft-Ebing in 1886 – that the civilized human being keep his sexual drives within the limits set by the community. A sense of modesty and shame must prevail. Without such normalcy family and state as the foundations of a legitimate and moral community would cease to exist.[23] Here, for Krafft-Ebing, the man has the advantage: as he wrote in his *Psychopathia sexualis* (1886), for man the love of a woman is just one among many other interests, while a woman's life is dominated by biological concerns, she cannot quench her thirst in merely one embrace.[24] The male ideal once more predominates as exemplary for that normalcy which provides a counter-weight to nervousness and decadence – symbolized in this instance through the control of sexual passion.

The ideal of masculinity and what it represented was challenged as part of the Decadence by the increased visibility and assertiveness of unmanly men and unwomanly women. As I mentioned before, they carried the challenge to the ideal of masculinity to its very doorstep; they provided an image against which masculinity could define itself. From the 1890s onwards such 'degenerates' provided an ever more visible presence and, however small their number, a continuous challenge to normative masculinity. These were not simply normal men with effeminate manners or appearance but so-called abnormal men and women who flaunted their sexual deviance.

The emergence of lesbians and homosexuals into the light of day started slowly in the 1860s and came to a climax in the last decade of the century. To be sure, they had obtained some visibility long before, but as criminals to be condemned rather than in their own right. Friedrich Engels had acted with abhorrence and fear when in 1869 Karl Marx sent him one of the first calls for homosexual rights published that same year and written by Karl Heinrich Ulrichs, onetime German civil servant and journalist: '... The Pederasts are starting to take stock,' Engels wrote, 'and to find that they constitute a power in the state. As yet, an organization is missing,' he continued, 'even though secretly it exists already ... it is lucky that we ourselves are too old to witness the victory of their cause and to pay the price with our own bodies.'[25] The fear of a homosexual conspiracy must have been still greater among those who observed how some of them openly challenged normalcy two decades later. Thus at the opening of Oscar Wilde's play *Lady Windermere's Fan* in 1892 the author and his friends, for the first but not the last time, wore a green carnation in their buttonholes, an emblem which, as Oscar Wilde had it, in individuals was a sign of a subtle artistic temperament, in nations of laxity, if not a decadence of morals.[26] Yet many saw here a symbol not only of decadence but also of homosexuality. Thus Robert Hichens – himself once a member of Wilde's circle of young men – in 1894 associated the green carnation with the gay stereotype: 'all the men who wore them looked the same. They had the same walk, or rather waggle, the same coyly conscious expression, the same wavy motion of the head.'[27] The *Ladies Pictorial* in 1892 denounced the green carnation as unmanly.[28] At the same time *The Artist and Journal of Home Culture* printed Uranian poetry among weighty reviews of the arts.

Men and women living in Paris during the last decade of the century also publicly defended their homosexuality and lesbianism. They did so in books, journals like the very successful *Chat Noir* affiliated to one of Paris's famous cabarets,[29] and, equally important, through their life styles. Some examples must suffice to document a much more extensive and visible 'coming out' than that found in England. Jean Lorrain was a prolific novelist and publicist who wrote openly about pederasty, just as in a decadent mode he glorified prostitutes and androgynes.[30] Here, the linking of such outsiders given to vice led to a specific affirmation of homosexuality. He took his stand without any apology such as the reference to ancient Greece which was supposed to provide homosexuality with a respectable historical tradition. He was called, not without justice, 'the Ambassador from Sodom'.[31]

Robert de Montesquiou is better known, for he was, in all probability, the chief model for Proust's homosexual Baron Charlus, though some of Proust's own self-hate determined this unflattering portrait. He himself congratulated Proust for having in his *Sodom et Gomorrhe* for the first time openly addressed homosexual love.[32] With his companion, Gabriel Yturri, he moved in the homosexual underworld at the turn of the century, but at the same time through his own famous and elaborate festivals, and the salons he visited, frequented the best social circles as well. Both Jean Lorrain and Robert de Montesquiou flaunted their decadence, taking advantage of it in order to construct their own homosexual life style. Both publicly wore rouge, eye-shades and gaudy clothes. They may well have thought their provocative stance their best defence, though Lorrain got into constant brawls because of his looks and behaviour. For all that, their openness about their homosexuality may have been viewed by others as a rather exotic but harmless eccentricity. Nevertheless, these men and others like them, and, as we shall see, lesbians as well, found heterosexual friends and admirers because of a general fascination with the Decadence among a certain upper stratum of society. Such mixing took place here for the first time and, once more, highlighted the danger of the Decadence to the respectable community.

Lesbians occupied a prominent place in the life of Robert de Montesquiou, and certain lesbian groups in Paris at the *fin de siècle* seemed much more vital in their openness than their homosexual counterparts. Here there was a great deal of mixing with heterosexuals but, at the same time, frankness about sexuality. Thus Natalie Barney defended lesbianism in her writings, and took no pains to hide her various lesbian love affairs, while at the same time at the beginning of the new century presiding over one of the most successful salons of Paris frequented by the French literary elite. Looking back in old age over her long life, she proudly quoted Walt Whitman, 'I have never conformed, and nevertheless I exist.'[33] Lilian de Pougy, the most celebrated courtesan of her day, wrote a book, *Idylle-saphique* (1901), which consists of a series of lesbian seduction scenes.[34] Decadent themes weave in and out of the writings and the life style of this circle, best described by Colette in *The Pure and the Impure* (1931).

Such openness and visibility challenged normative society, as did the ever more visible homosexual subculture in the big cities. Magnus Hirschfeld listed over twenty homosexual bars in the Berlin of 1904 (by 1914 there were thirty-eight such places), and the so-called 'Urningsbälle', dances which were held regularly, attracted some 800 people and became one of Berlin's tourist attractions.[35] As a further example, some 320 publications about homosexuality appeared between 1895 and 1905 in Germany alone[36] – not to mention the increasing number of caricatures of homosexuals in journals like the German *Simplicissimus* or the English *Punch*. Such formerly hidden vices became part of the public discourse in France as well, often in books which pointed to Germany, where 'homosexuals find it natural to parade their strange passion in public'.[37] The homosexual scandals of the *fin de siècle* involving the highest levels of society, such as the Eulenburg affair in Germany or the Cleveland Street scandal in England, were taken up greedily by the new mass media. That such scandals involved, above all, members of the aristocracy fuelled the fears of the middle classes that decadence had successfully penetrated the core of government and society.

Homosexuals themselves were aware of the opportunity to redefine masculinity the Decadence provided – not those who attempted to assimilate to or to mimic bourgeois respectability, but men and women like Jean Lorraine or Natalie Barney, proud to take the label 'decadence' as their own and to exploit it as much as possible. Oscar Wilde provides another example, refusing, like Jean Lorraine, to clothe himself in the respectable mantle of the Greek tradition, summoning instead a so-called 'higher philosophy' to his defence. This has been aptly paraphrased as 'dare to live as one wishes to live, not as the middle classes wish one to live; to have the courage of one's desires, instead of only the cowardice of other people.'[38] Such sentiments are repeated among those Parisian homosexuals and lesbians who equated decadence with individual freedom.

The enemy of such freedom was the rigid division between the sexes which true masculinity symbolized, and which was thought essential to the existence of an ordered and settled society. Instead, homosexuals and lesbians met in their admiration of the androgyne who, whether with male or female sexual organs, combined, in Oscar Wilde's words, the grace of Adonis with the beauty of Helen[39] or – more commonly – saw the soul of one gender imprisoned in the body of another. If before 1850 the androgyne had been a symbol of fraternity and solidarity, by the end of the century it had been transformed into a symbol of vice and sexual perversity.[40] Androgyny, however, was a popular literary topic in the milieu in which homosexual and lesbian writers moved; indeed, as Mario Praz has written, the androgyne ideal became an obsession of the Decadent movement.[41] As we have seen, both Lorraine, and even Montesquiou, affected an androgynous appearance, and all her life Natalie Barney longed 'for a past age which made its Apollo effeminate and its Goddesses virile, leading to the triumph of the Androgyne'.[42] Androgyny now served to legitimize so-called sexual deviancy as well as attacks upon normative masculinity and femininity.

The androgyne overcame the division between the sexes through the worship of beauty; this was a theme which would attract many so-called decadents at the *fin de siècle*. Thus Louis Couperus, the foremost Dutch novelist at the turn of the century, in his *De Berg van Licht*, (1905/6) wrote about the young Roman emperor Heliogabal, a man-woman of surpassing grace and beauty. Couperus delights in the description of beautiful objects but also in the details of sensuous and cruel orgies, which in the end lead to the death of the feminized boy-emperor and his beloved male husband. Charles Kains-Jackson's article on the 'new chivalry' (1894) provides an important English example for the significance of beauty as opposed to gender. 'The more spiritual types of English manhood', he wrote, 'already look to beauty first.'[43] Gender does not matter: human beauty must form the basis of all intimate human relationships.

This was a different beauty from that which informed the masculine stereotype, not hard, but soft; it did not project energy but languor instead – that state of near exhaustion which symbolized opposition to true manliness. Moreover, this was no sexless beauty but expressed itself through vivid colours, appealing to the senses. While the androgyne's legendary cruelty and uncontrolled passion was present, for example in Couperus's boy-emperor, the androgyne at the turn of the century fulfilled a liberating function over against gender stereotypes. There was good reason why Oscar Wilde's contemporary and enemy William Ernest Henley around 1890 condemned the '. . . effete and romantic yearning for the hermaphrodite asexuality'.[44] Sexuality here is defined in strictly 'normal', heterosexual terms, while, contrary to Henley, for many so-called decadents the androgyne was strongly sexed. Thus for Colette, the seduction emanating from a person of uncertain or dissimulated sex was a powerful force.[45] But then, the newly found visibility of lesbians and homosexuals, as well as their life style and ideals, must have seemed sterile and destructive to normative sexuality.

The strengthening of masculinity at the *fin de siècle* must be discussed against this background, which, however isolated and literary at first, was seen as confirming the decadence of existing society. Symptoms of decadence did not exist in isolation, but heightened the fear of modernity I have mentioned already. It is no coincidence that from the last decades of the century onwards homosexuality was more actively and publicly persecuted. For example, in England, the Labouchère Amendment to the Criminal Law Bill was passed in 1885 and punished all homosexual acts as 'gross indecencies', while the Netherlands in 1911 put a law directed against all intimate relations among men on the books. Germany had a nation-wide anti-homosexual law (the notorious paragraph 175), and at the beginning of the new century the police opened a 'pink file' containing names of homosexuals.[46] Finally, it seems significant that the new medical science of sexology which emerged in the 1890s was more concerned with the pathological and the deviant rather than the 'normal'.[47]

Christianity took up its traditional role once again. Ever since the end of the eighteenth century, it had played a crucial part in the establishment of respectability. If we take Germany as our example, Christian associations for the protection of morals (*Sittlichkeitsvereine*) multiplied at the turn of the century, another sign of a heightened fear of decadence and social instability. What we want, as one of these associations put it in 1908, is to restore to the nation its moral health with the help of 'true German men'.[48] Protestant clergymen predominated among the members of such associations, together with school-teachers. Not many physicians seemed to have joined such Purity Leagues, though long before the war German Professors of Medicine had issued a proclamation of their own in which they lamented the increase of indecency and called for restraint.[49] Medical expertise was often in demand, especially when it came to the control of prostitution, one of the specific aims of such associations within their general framework of policing all sexuality. The central federation of German moral purity leagues in 1892 attacked Krafft-Ebing's *Psychopathia sexualis* for demanding freedom from criminal prosecution for certain so-called 'abnormal' sexual acts. Homosexuality once again conjured up visions of the fall of the Roman empire. It was a physician, A. Römer, who, also in 1892, in an article written for a journal of the German Purity League entitled 'The Moral Law before the bar of Medical Authority', mounted the attack against Krafft-Ebing, and demanded that in this age of increasing nervousness the state must act in the name of self-preservation.[51]

Medical men possessed perhaps the greatest influence when it came to suggesting cures for so-called degenerate or abnormal behaviour – after all they had medicalized degeneration and thus brought it within their own healing function – always exempting hereditary degeneration which was thought to be beyond anyone's capacity to cure. Apart from the pressures of modernity, so-called bad habits lay at the root of nervous or abnormal sexual behaviour. Krafft-Ebing was in agreement with most physicians in putting masturbation at the top of his list of personal habits which shattered the nerves and perverted the *vita sexualis*. The modern age encouraged masturbation, which led to 'artificially produced pederasts',[52] and stripped men of their manliness.

There is now a vast secondary literature on the history of masturbation and its attempted cures, and nothing more needs to be said here. But beyond the control and punishment of a specific sexual act judged debilitating or abnormal, it was the strength of will power which counted in the end. If the will fails, so a medical dissertation tells us, a human being falls apart and remains incomplete in all that concerns his life. Strength of will was, of course, one of the distinguishing marks of the male ideal as over against so-called 'weak and womanly men'.[53] Damaged will power leads to vice, and in 1908 the journal of one German Moral Purity League called for 'gymnastic of the will', by which it meant strengthening male courage (*Mannesmut*) through sexual and physical education.[54] Here, once more, the ideal of masculinity and sexuality were closely linked.

Will power was usually equated with courage, knowing how to face danger and pain. Steeling the body through sport was universally advocated as one of the best ways to accomplish this end. Angelo Mosso, a renowned Italian physiologist, in addition to praising gymnastics as the best means of perfecting the male body, also admired the way in which English schools encouraged team sports. Sport, he held, develops individual energy, teaches the proper work habits as well as discipline, and in this manner completes the shaping of real men.[55]

Physicians supported and provided the rationale for these means of combating degeneration and the challenges to true manhood. From time to time other methods of control were added: thus marriage was thought a barrier to the practice of vice. A German tract on 'manly honour' of 1889 reminded youths that one day they would be heads of families, and asked how they could rule others if they could not themselves.[56] The autonomy of the ideal male was a constant subtext in such admonitions, as against women's dependency. Personal cleanliness was also put forward as encouraging manliness, and the removal of all temptation – from the exposure of a nude body to the strict supervision of bathing-places advocated almost passionately by Krafft-Ebing.[57]

The masculine ideal was a bulwark erected against decadence; it represented in words, pictures and stone an ideal of chaste manliness which sank deeply into bourgeois consciousness. This ideal provided the standard of judgement, and it is typical that 'outsiders' considered a danger to society, for example homosexuals and lesbians, were always represented for what they were *not* rather than what they were. The counter-type was always negative, the exact opposite in looks, appearance and comportment of the true man.

The indissoluble linkage between insider and outsider, between the true man and the decadent, was to remain in place. The First World War strengthened this connection: on the one side the brave and heroic soldier, calm in the face of death, and on the other, the enemy as nervous shirkers or weaklings, following their illicit passion, lusting, for example, after German women, or – on a French postcard – German soldiers sodomizing each other. The war transmitted a still more trenchant image of masculinity into the post-war world, and so did the stereotype of the unmanly as the mirror-image of manliness.

Masculinity was the rock upon which bourgeois society built much of its own self-image, but the idealized image of masculinity seems equally important for the evolution of so-called abnormal sexuality, largely determined by the counter-image it was made to represent. All those pushed out of society, or existing on its margins, whether, for example, Jews, homosexuals, or Gypsies, shared much the same stereotype and attitudes as far as society itself was concerned. Women shared some of the stereotype of the outsider, for example the lack of robustness, a tendency to sickness and hysteria. However, women were not all *femmes fatales* or the creatures of uncontrolled passion; unlike 'outsiders', in the main they had their solid place in *fin-de-siècle* society as mothers and educators, ruling children and servants, giving tenderness and affection. However, when women left the place assigned to them in the division between the sexes, they became outsiders as well.

Even while the image of manliness was strengthened at the *fin de siècle* at the expense of the unmanly men and unruly women of the Decadence, sexual knowledge and the insights which derived from it had made advances. Thus the notion that masculinity defined itself in large measure against femininity and homosexuality had been modified by most sexologists. Even the sexuality of normal men might contain elements of other so-called 'lesser' sexualities. Nor were manly men chaste and pure because their will power and self-control overcame temptation, but instead they were subject to hidden anxieties about their sex.[58] Though efforts were made to confine any discussion about sexuality to the medical community, this proved impossible; increasingly issues of normal and abnormal, male and female sexuality became part of the public discourse. Men and women were exposed to public discussion of sexual topics which they would not have encountered before the end of the century. Once more, it was sexuality as a topic of public discussion which mattered, not the hidden sexualities which had always existed. Those who opposed this new openness, like the Purity Leagues, greatly furthered that very visibility which they abhorred.

Despite such changes, the ideal of masculinity and its social function remained largely intact. Indeed, it was furthered by the First World War and its aftermath. Eventually, in the Europe of the Dictators, the masculine ideal was refurbished and exalted as the defender of society and the state. Then Josef Weinheber, a leading Nazi poet, summed up once more the ideal of true manhood, brushing aside all the insights gained through the science of sexology in the previous half-century – the myth, not reality, mattered, as it had throughout the construction of masculinity. This extract comes from a poem entitled 'Youth' which was included in the 1940 edition of one of the most popular books of readings for German schools:

> Be hard against yourself,
> Chaste in the glow of your strength and the passion of your sexuality,
> Love and lust must be kept separate from one another
> Just as life and death are opposites
> But life and honour are one.[59]

NOTES

1 George D. Painter, *Marcel Proust. A Biography*, vol. II (New York, 1987), 270.
2 Ernst Moritz Arndt, 'Die Leipziger Schlacht', *Sämmtliche Werke*, 4 (Leipzig, n.d.), 83.
3 Walter Pater, *The Renaissance* (The Modern Library, New York, n.d.), 184.
4 Ibid., 183.
5 Else Lüders, *Minna Cauer, Leben und Werk* (Leipzig, 1925), 55, 59.
6 Albert Boime, *Thomas Couture and the Eclectic Vision* (New Haven and London, 1980), 131.
7 Quoted in Daniel Pick, *Faces of Degeneration* (Cambridge, 1989), 54.
8 Oswald Bumke, *Die Grenzen der geistigen Gesundheit* (Munich, 1929), 5.
9 Janet E. Hogarth, 'Literary Degenerates', *The Fortnightly Review*, NS 57 (April, 1885), 586.
10 Max Nordau, *Degeneration* (New York, 1968), 41.
11 Oswald Bumke, *Gedanken über die Seele*, 4th edn (Berlin and Heidelberg, 1948), 29.
12 J.-M. Charcot, *Leçons sur les maladies du système nerveux faites à la Salpêtrière*, 8th Lesson (Paris, 1872–3), 115.
13 Edward Shorter, *From Paralysis to Fatigue. A History of Psychosomatic Illness in the Modern Era* (New York, 1991), 117, 118; Janet Oppenheimer, *Shattered Nerves* (New York, 1991), 143.
14 Robert A. Nye, 'Sex Difference and Male Homosexuality in French Medical Discourse', *Bulletin of the History of Medicine*, 63 (1989), 40 pp.
15 Advertisements quoted in Ulrich Linse, 'Über den Prozess der Syphilisation, Körper und Sexualität um 1900 in ärztlicher Sicht', in Alexander Schuller and Nikolaus Heim (eds.), *Vermessene Sexualität* (Berlin–Heidelberg, 1987), 167.

16 Sigmund Freud, *Gesammelte Werke*, vol. VII: *Werke aus den Jahren 1906-1909* (London, 1941), 154, 163-4.
17 Nye, 'Sex Difference and Male Homosexuality in French Medical Discourse', 44.
18 Charcot, *Leçons sur les maladies du système nerveux* 8th Lesson, 116.
19 *The Standard Edition of the Complete Psychological Works of Sigmund Freud*, vol. I (1886-95) (London, 1966), 24, 25.
20 Richard von Krafft-Ebing, *Lehrbuch der gerichtlichen Psychopathologie*, vol. III revised edn (Stuttgart, 1892), 72.
21 Günter Mann, 'Dekadenz-Degeneration-Untergangsangst im Licht der Biologie des 19. Jahrhunderts', *Medizinhistorisches Journal*, 20 (1985), 9.
22 Oswald Bumke, *Kultur und Entartung* (Berlin, 1922), 81.
23 Richard von Krafft-Ebing, *Psychopathia sexualis* (Munich, 1984), 60.
24 Ibid., 157.
25 Quoted in Joachim S. Hohmann (ed.), *Der unterdrückte Sexus* (Lollar/Lahn, 1977), 25.
26 Richard Ellmann, *Oscar Wilde* (New York, 1988), 300.
27 Robert Hichens, *The Green Carnation* (London, 1949), 15.
28 Quoted in Neil Bartlett, *Who Was That Man? A Present to Mr Oscar Wilde* (London, 1988), 50.
29 i.e. Jerrold Seigel, *Bohemian Paris* (New York, 1986), 223-4, though nothing is said about the homosexual aspect of the journal.
30 Jean Lorraine, *Modernités* (Paris, 1885), 7, 10, 39.
31 Philippe Jullian, *Jean Lorraine ou le Satyricon 1900* (Paris, 1974), 60.
32 Philippe Jullian, *Robert de Montesquiou* (Paris, 1987), 288.
33 Natalie Barney, *Traits et portraits, suivi de l'amour défendu* (Paris, 1963), 177.
34 George Wickes, *The Amazon of Letters. The Life and Loves of Natalie Barney* (London, 1977), 40.
35 Magnus Hirschfeld, *Berlins drittes Geschlecht* (Berlin and Leipzig, 1904), 37, 55, 43; P. Näcke, 'Ein Besuch bei den Homosexuellen in Berlin. Mit Bemerkungen über die Homosexualität', *Archiv für Kriminalanthropologie und Kriminalistik*, 15 (1904), 246ff.
36 James D. Steakley, *The Homosexual Emancipation Movement in Germany* (New York, 1975), 24.
37 Oscar Meténier, *Les Berlinois chez eux, virtus et vice allemand* (Paris, 1904), 89.
38 Hichens, *The Green Carnation*, 92.
39 Oscar Wilde, 'Portrait of Mr W. H.', in Herbert Read, *Sexual Heretics. Male Homosexuality in English Literature from 1850-1900* (London, 1970), 392.
40 A. J. L. Busst, 'The Image of the Androgyne in the Nineteenth Century', *Romantic Mythologies* (London, 1967), 38, 39.
41 Mario Praz, *The Romantic Agony* (New York, 1956), 332.
42 Natalie Barney, *Nouvelle pensée de l'Amazone* (Paris, 1934), 197.
43 Charles Kains-Jackson, 'The New Chivalry', in Herbert Read, *Sexual Heretics*, 316.
44 William Ernest Henley, 'Rhymes and Rhythms' (1889-93?), in Jerome Hamilton Buckley, *William Ernest Henley* (Princeton, 1945), 148.
45 Colette, *The Pure and the Impure* (New York, 1966), 76.

46 Hans-George Stümke, *Homosexuelle in Deutschland* (Munich, 1989), 144.
47 Lesley Hall, *Hidden Anxieties. Male Sexuality, 1900–1950* (Cambridge, 1991), 21.
48 *Volkswart. Organ der Männervereine zur Bekämpfung der öffentlichen Unsittlichkeit*, November 1915, 145.
49 Ibid., 147.
50 *Streitfragen, Wissenschaftliches Fachorgan der deutschen Sittlichkeits-Vereine*, ed. P. Philips, vol. I (Berlin, 1892), 1.
51 A. Römer, 'Das Sittengesetz vor dem Richerstuhl einer ärtzlichen Autorität', *Streitfragen*, 5ff. A forthcoming work by John F. Fout will analyse these associations in greater detail.
52 Krafft-Ebing, *Psychopathia sexualis*, 228.
53 Erich Grassl, *Die Willensschwäche* (Leipzig, 1937), 216.
54 F. W. Foerster, 'Sexualethik und sexual Pädagogie', *Volkswart*, 1 (1908), 14.
55 Gaetano Bonetta, *Corpo e nazione. L'educazione ginnastica, igienica e sessuale nell'Italia liberale* (Milan, 1990), 130, 131; see also Anso Rabinbach, *The Human Motor, Energy, Fatigue and the Origins of Modernity* (New York, 1990), esp. 133–6.
56 G. Weitbrecht, *Die Sittlichkeit des Mannes Ehre* (Stuttgart, 1889), 7.
57 Krafft-Ebing, *Psychopathia sexualis*, 317.
58 Hall, *Hidden Anxieties*, esp. 114–69.
59 *Hirt's deutsches Lesebuch*, ed. Johannes Eilemann et al. (Breslau, 1940), 243.

TWELVE

'NOT A STRANGER: A DOCTOR': MEDICAL
MEN AND SEXUAL MATTERS IN THE LATE
NINETEENTH CENTURY

ANGUS MCLAREN

At 2.30 in the morning of 12 April 1892 the landlady of a cheap lodging-house on Stamford Street, Lambeth was woken by screams. In the hallway she found 21-year-old Alice Marsh clad in a nightshirt foaming at the mouth and in a bedroom, writhing in pain, 18-year-old Emma Shrivell. In between convulsions the young women said that they had been visited by a man who had given them pills. When the landlady marvelled that they had been so foolish as to take medicine from someone they did not know, Shrivell made the pathetic reply: 'He is not a stranger, he is a doctor.'[1] Three years after the Whitechapel killings of Jack the Ripper, a psychopath was again loose in London. This new serial killer chose as his victims the prostitutes of Lambeth – Shrivell was his fourth and last – and employed strychnine as his weapon.

What drew my attention to this case was that the murderer, Thomas Neill Cream, a doctor trained at McGill College in Montreal, had in North America previously killed three or more women who were seeking abortion. Cream was tried and executed in 1892, the court and press presenting his murders as the incomprehensible acts of a madman. But why was it, I wondered, that serial murders – sex murders – seemed to be a product of the nineteenth century? Were Cream's crimes as inexplicable as they were made out to be? As part of this analysis this chapter is an attempt to put his abortion-related murders in context.

In the late 1890s women dressed as hospital nurses fanned out across the more modest suburbs of London and Manchester distributing advertising postcards puffing the ability of Madame Frain's pills to remove 'obstructions' – a code word for unwanted foetuses. The medicine, which cost 7*d.* a bottle to produce but which sold at prices ranging from 7*s.* 6*d.* to 22*s.*, was completely useless and could not serve, as the advertising implied, as an abortifacient. But the proprietors of 'Madame Frain's Herbal or Medical Institute' of Hackney Road, London, by declaring that they would sell only to customers who swore that they were not pregnant, thought they had struck on a shrewd way of both legally protecting themselves and boosting their product.[2] Indeed, between 1897 and 1899, 1,300 women, who refused to make such a declaration were sent back their money by registered mail.[3] Undeterred, the police raided the Institute and charged its owners with inciting 'women who should read and become cognizant of pamphlets and circulars published in the name of Madame Frain to attempt to administer to themselves noxious things with intent to procure a miscarriage'.[4] Why, asked the crown counsel, would women in needy households pay up to the equivalent of a labourer's weekly salary if not with the serious intent of inducing a miscarriage? Defence counsel responded that although the customers may have thought that the concoction could cause a miscarriage, the defendants knew it could not and therefore there was no case. Dr Luff, Fellow of the Royal College of Physicians, agreed that the medicine was useless. But Mr Justice Darling, the presiding judge, countered that any sort of pill, if taken in sufficient quantities, could be noxious and the case was sent to the jury. The defendants – William Brown, Emmanuel Abrahams and James Fox – were found guilty and sentenced to from nine to twelve months' hard labour in Pentonville Prison.[5]

Most striking about the Madame Frain trial was not so much Mr Justice Darling's creative law-making, as the case's revelation that thousands of women across England in the 1890s were willing to go to enormous lengths to restrict their fertility.[6] Both Europe and North America were going through a demographic transition. In response to the growing expense of maintaining gentility the middle and upper classes had been limiting family size from the mid-century.[7] If middle-class men turned to contraception largely out of a concern at the expenses posed by the large family, middle-class women were drawn to the same tactics out of a desire for some life beyond that of producing and rearing offspring. In the last decades of the century even the fertility of labouring families was restricted. The imposition of compulsory education on the one hand and the restriction of child labour on the other meant that large numbers of children, once a valuable asset in the working-class home, were increasingly viewed as a burden.[8]

The socially conservative Malthusian League began in the 1870s to trumpet the advantages of the small family.[9] Although socialists were generally reluctant to broach the issue, even *The Clarion*, a popular labour paper, was in February 1892 running advertisements for a tract provocatively entitled *Ought Women to be Punished for Having Too Many Children?*[10] But when one moved from theory to practice, problems arose. Although a Dubliner on a visit to London was shocked to see the number of 'antigestatory appliances shown in chemists' windows', condoms, diaphragms and douches were expensive and until well into the twentieth century employed by only a small portion of the population.[11] Withdrawal or *coitus interruptus* would remain the main method of contraception in the working-class household. What if it failed? The most desperate resorted to infanticide and abandonment; in 1895 the bodies of eleven infants were found in Lambeth's streets and gutters.[12] Far more common was the attempt to induce miscarriage.

Women seeking abortion had to face the hostility of clergy, police and doctors. Those few physicians who thought of helping women to control their fertility were warned off by their peers.[13] 'To give directions for the prevention of conception, or instructions in the guilty use of syringes, and other expedients to aid crime or to defeat nature, although not offences within reach of the law, are nevertheless most derogatory and degrading to the assenting practitioner, and a gross abuse of his professional knowledge.'[14] Because the limitation of family size was very much a tabooed subject in both Britain and North America some women were inevitably exploited by quacks like Madame Frain; others were operated on by incompetent abortionists; and the most unfortunate fell into the hands of a man like Thomas Neill Cream. It is quite possible that he killed more women seeking abortion than those known about in London, Ontario, and Chicago, Illinois. While he was awaiting execution the *Toronto Globe* reported that Mr Waters, his solicitor, had a confession in which the murderer admitted that 'he made a practice of poisoning dissolute girls in Canada'.[15]

Crucial to an understanding of Cream's career as an abortionist-murderer is an appreciation of the fact that in the last decades of the nineteenth century women's need for assistance in terminating pregnancies took on a special urgency.[16] Social pressures to restrict family size increased, but adequate contraception was simply not available. Women made unexpectedly pregnant, holding true to a traditional view that they had the right 'to make themselves regular' then turned to attempts to induce miscarriage. Estimates were made that between a sixth and a fifth of all pregnancies were terminated.[17] But in the late 1800s a woman seeking to induce a miscarriage found that because of new laws her options were limited. Although doctors could safely carry out abortions, they claimed to do so only for therapeutic reasons and were vigorously seeking to drive out of business the irregular practitioners, midwives and herbalists associated with the practice.[18]

Doctors deemed abortion 'wrong', but sometimes necessary.[19] A conservative like Dr R. R. Rentoul believed that abortion was only thinkable when a mother's life was in danger. In practice, as an 1896 secret report of the Royal College of Physicians indicated, the policy was to leave to the discretion of the individual practitioner the question of when to act.[20] A therapeutic abortion was considered legitimate if carried out by a regular doctor after consultation with colleagues. And professional etiquette dictated that colleagues not look too closely into each other's affairs. 'Even if a medical practitioner is known to have procured abortion, the presumption is that it was done in the legal exercise of his calling; and the strongest evidence should be forthcoming before he is made answerable for his actions, or, peradventure, the death of his patient.'[21] Any abortion not carried out by a doctor was labelled a 'criminal abortion'. The campaign against such practices in both North America and Britain was part of a process by which the medical profession came to monopolize the delivery of health services.[22] By an 'ideological sleight of hand' doctors declared that abortion was 'murder', but a legitimate operation if physicians decided – in the privacy of their consulting-rooms – that it had to be carried out.[23]

Nineteenth-century doctors in effect succeeded in pushing through a legal revolution. Until the early 1800s abortion before 'quickening' – that is, when the women felt the foetus's movements at about thirteen weeks after conception – was not penalized. Abortion after quickening was punished by a fine or short imprisonment. Even these levies were rarely imposed. In 1803 abortion both before and after quickening was made a crime; only in 1837 was the concept of quickening itself removed.[24] These early statutes were aimed at the abortionist; not until the Offences Against the Person Act of 1861 was the woman herself subject to prosecution. In the United States, where it was estimated that 10 to 30 per cent of pregnancies were terminated, a similar rash of laws criminalizing abortion appeared on the statute books between the 1860s and 1880s.[25] Doctors, lawyers and clergymen, in carrying out their successful campaign of criminalizing abortion, created the conditions in which desperate women were made Cream's potential victims.[26] A woman's worst nightmare – falling into the hands of a killer who posed as an abortionist in order to have his victim become an unwitting accomplice in her own murder – had become reality.

Some middle-class women cajoled their doctors into providing abortions. Only the occasional tragedy brought such transactions before public scrutiny. Ethel Hall, the separated wife of Edward Marshall Hall, who was emerging as one of England's foremost barristers, died in 1890 as a result of being operated on and administered a noxious drug. Her doctor – suspected of forgery and drug trafficking as well – was committed to the Old Bailey to be tried for wilful murder; the charge against her well-connected lover of being an accessory was dropped.[27] Other women, whose demands for medical assistance could not – given the law – be met in an open way, were forced into the back streets. Few working-class women had the temerity to try to convince a regular doctor of their need to terminate a pregnancy; they continued to rely on the services of midwives, the 'Old Queens' of the neighbourhood, and if those were lacking, quack products and commercial abortionists.[28]

A cursory glance at the columns of the popular press and even the religious papers of the 1890s revealed dozens of advertisements for abortifacients – Towles Pennyroyal Pills, Blanchard's Pills, Fenn's Pennyroyal, Steel, Hiera Picra and Bitter Apple Pills, Ottey's Strong Female Pills, Apiol and Steel Pills for Ladies, Tuck's Female Mixture, and Widow Welch's Pills to name only a few.[29] A typical advertisement in the *South London Mail* stated that those who wrote to L. M. Dasmail of Walthamstow would obtain 'Dr Monteith's Electric Female Pills for all Irregularities, Suppressions, and Obstructions of the Female System however Obstinate and Long-Standing'. Some of the medicines contained a few elements of the traditional abortifacients such as aloes, savin, pennyroyal and apiol, but many were no more than candy pills.

If drugs failed, as presumably most would, and self-induction with knitting-needles or douches was unsuccessful, abortionists might be approached. When Cream was charged in Chicago in 1880 for producing abortion the local press commented on the numbers of practitioners offering similar services.

> Some years since a sensational newspaper in this city published an article purporting to expose the professional abortionists. The list included a dozen or twenty quacks, more or less known as such, and we believe no libel suits ever came of the publication . . . It is certain that every large city contains a large number of persons calling themselves doctors or midwives, who undertake the crime of abortion for almost any fee that may be offered them.[30]

In England such practitioners would range from regular doctors such as Charles Whitefoord, convicted in July 1891 of procuring abortion, to irregulars who advertised their ability to treat 'Women's Ailments'.[31] Not surprisingly, midwives such as Elizabeth Berry, Dorothy Davis, Lizzie Ann Mitchell, Annie Stewart and Dinah Clapp were frequently prosecuted for carrying out 'illegal operations'.[32] In 1893 Edith

Bannister, an employee of the London newspaper the *Sun*, died as a result of a bungled abortion; two years later the paper exposed Dr James Ady for using his 'Lambeth Self-Supporting Dispensary' as an abortion clinic.[33] In this twilight world of legal and illegal operations, competent and incompetent practitioners, lurked Cream.[34]

At Blanchard's Hotel in Quebec City in March 1892 Cream struck up a friendship with John Wilson McCulloch. The two travelling agents' talk soon turned to women. Cream led McCulloch to understand that he was an abortionist.

> He next took a bottle out of the cash box and said Do you known what this is? I replied No. He then said It is poison. I said For God's sake what do you do with that? He replied I give it to women to get them out of the family way.

The bottle contained whitish crystals, the size of pinheads, presumably strychnine. When asked how he administered it, Cream showed his friend a box of capsules, saying, 'I give it to them in there.' Cream also produced a pair of false whiskers. 'I said What do you use these for? He replied To disguise my identity so that they would not recognize me again when operating on the women.'[35]

Cream aborted his wife, Flora Brooks; whether he was responsible for her death a year later is impossible to say. He was guilty of the deaths of Kate Hutchinson Gardener in London, Ontario, and Julia Faulkner and Miss Stack in Chicago, Illinois. When awaiting execution it was reported that in Chicago, where 'he owned a house wherein young unmarried women were assisted over their troubles, he took the lives of many'.[36] Killing women who sought abortions was diabolically clever; the victim pathetically made as many efforts as her murderer to hide their relationship.

The subject of abortion held a morbid fascination for Cream. In the letters in which he accused F. W. D. Smith and Walter Harper of giving women poisons under the guise of abortifacients it is difficult not to see a twisted account of his own actions. 'I am writing now', he purportedly warned Donworth, 'to say that if you take any of the medicine he [Smith] gave you for the purposes of bringing on your courses you will die.' He probably accused Lord Russell of Clover's death, not just because his name was in the news due to his messy divorce, but because the Russell family was associated with the defence of birth control. This connection had been made when in 1868 Lord Amberley (Bertrand Russell's father) lost a bitterly contested South Devon election after it was made public that he supported neo-Malthusian doctrines.[37] Amberley was vilified in the press and pulpits for having favoured what the press referred to as 'unnatural crimes'.

Such were Victorian proprieties that at Cream's trial, although the topic of murder was openly discussed, the issue of abortion was carefully skirted. The crown counsel noted that Cream, when in Quebec City, spoke of having drugs 'for the purposes of preventing childbirth' whereas Cream had made it clear they were for provoking miscarriages.[38] Likewise, in referring to the letter sent to F. W. D. Smith that was purportedly written to Donworth the crown counsel avoided any reference to the warning not to take drugs to miscarry.[39] The possible use of strychnine to bring on abortion was also presumably what Geoghegan was discreetly referring to when he put a question in writing to Dr Thomas Stevenson. The court considered the question too indelicate to be aired in public, but one can infer the substance of the query from Stevenson's oral response that 'It is a matter of common medical knowledge in this country. It is supposed to have come from America. It was mentioned in a notorious pamphlet.'[40]

Abortionists sometimes accidentally killed; in 1875 Alfred Thomas Heap was executed in Manchester for having caused the death of a woman he was seeking to abort with a spindle.[41] Some killers involved themselves in abortion. At the 1898 Huntingdon Assizes Justice Hawkins sentenced to death a man who had given strychnine to his pregnant lover, leading her to believe it was an abortifacient.[42] It was popularly believed that Jack the Ripper was an abortionist. In fact one of his victims – Mary Kelly – was three months pregnant.[43] On 10 September 1889 a woman's mutilated, headless body, wrapped in a garment marked with the name 'L. E. Fisher' was found by the police under the arches off Pinchin Street, Whitechapel. Because of the locale her file was included in the Ripper dossier but the *New York Herald* reported in its London edition of 11 September that Dr Thomas Bond, chief surgeon of the Metropolitan Police, concluded that the death resulted from an attempt to procure abortion.[44]

What are we to make of this aspect of the Cream affair? An analysis of Cream's murder of women seeking abortion first directs our attention to the fact that the victims on whom he preyed had already been declared by the state to be outlaws because of their attempts to control their fertility. New abortion laws had created a new class of criminals. A second issue that demands attention is the language in which respectable society described such acts. We know that Cream regarded women who sought abortions as a menace to society who had to be exterminated. What comes as a shock is the discovery of the inflammatory rhetoric in which so many public commentators expressed their feelings of hostility to such women. At best women seeking abortion were typified as 'fallen from virtue'. Lord Brougham in 1858 castigated single women seeking abortion for thus adding 'the deliberate sin of murder to the former one of the passions'.[45] The wife who intended to seek to control her fertility was castigated by Sylvanus Stall as entering 'the marriage relationship for the purpose of practically leading a life of legalized prostitution'.[46] George H. Napheys declared with horror, 'Hundreds of vile men and women in our large cities subsist by this slaughter of the innocents, and flaunt their ill-gotten gains – the price of blood – in our public thoroughfares.' To his disgust he discovered that these clients were married 'virtuous matrons' of the middle classes.[47] Hugh L. Hodge in *Foeticide, or Criminal Abortion* (1869) castigated such women for seeking abortions for the most 'futile and trifling' reasons.[48]

Thomas Radford referred to the 'diabolical arts' used to induce miscarriage.[49] P. H. Chavasse said abortion was simply murder.[50] In 1859 Harvard University professor Walter Channing attacked women for committing 'foeticide, unborn child killing'.[51] H. S. Pomeroy referred to the destruction of unborn life as the 'American sin'.[52] Emma Drake called it 'antenatal infanticide' and in her popular North American tract, *What a Young Wife Ought to Know*, dealt with it in chapter 10, which was entitled, 'The Destruction of Infant Life'.[53] John Cowan similarly spoke, not of abortion, but of 'foeticide'.[54] Augustus K. Gardner warned women, 'You have no right to take precautions or failing in this to resort to murder.'[55] The Canadian Medical Association bemoaned what it called the 'slaughter of the unborn': 'This destruction is equivalent to murder.'[56] In such misogynistic rhetoric the foetus was always presented as male, as a 'potential man'.[57]

Such examples could be multiplied many times over. Of course, it is a large step to move from rhetoric to action. And one could argue that the fact that Cream was ultimately executed proves that the larger society in reality did not desire the deaths of women seeking abortion. But in looking for the sources that might have incited Cream, the public debate over abortion cannot be dismissed. If Cream sought sanctions for his crimes he did not have far to look; the press was full of violent denunciations of women who had recourse to abortion. The respectable referred to abortion as murder and to women who sought abortion as murderers. Was not the appropriate penalty death? Could not Cream, when murdering such women imagine that he was acting in the interests of the greater society? The *Canada Lancet* coolly described the fate of women dying as a consequence of bungled abortions as 'retributive deaths'.[58] Cream, as a 'madman', simply took to its murderously logical conclusion an argument that the rational meant to be no more than a rhetorical exercise.

Turning from the question of the possible source of Cream's motive to the means he adopted leads us to the third issue illuminated by an analysis of his crimes – the fact that being a doctor trained in obstetrics facilitated his homicidal ambitions. The late nineteenth century was the very time when obstetrics and gynaecology were becoming respectable specialities, when the access of the male physician to the female patient finally received full legitimation.[59] James Murphy reminded his colleagues at the first conference of the British Gynaecological Society held in 1891 that a once disdained speciality was now in the forefront of surgery; ovariotomy had 'opened up the whole field of abdominal surgery, so that many men who started as gynaecologists, are now our most brilliant surgeons, successfully attacking the uterus, the spleen, the liver and all the organs contained in the abdomen'.[60] A feminist and doctor like Elizabeth Blackwell believed that women's sexuality was indeed being 'attacked'.[61] The leading gynaecologists accepted with apparent equanimity the fact that the newest and most daring forms of surgery carried the highest risks for their female patients.

A number of gynaecologists were, moreover, only too happy to parade a crude misogyny. At an 1886 meeting of the British Gynaecological Society Charles Routh devoted a paper to the problems posed by 'unfortunate and diseased women' who were under the delusion that they had been molested by their medical attendants or male relatives. As far as Routh was concerned such confidences had to be shown up for the lies that they were; incest was unthinkable.[62]

> Whenever I hear such stories, I suspect the women who tell them, for if, in the history they give of themselves, they can invent such terrible stories about those whom they ought most to love and revere, they seem to me to be very apt to invent and believe other and more terrible stories about their medical attendants, whom they know less of, and which might seriously affect their happiness and future career.[63]

Such perverts posed a danger to every man who came near them. Doctors called to testify in rape cases were accordingly warned by Routh to make every effort to see that no man was ever made a nymphomaniac's victim.

> It is not enough to see if she has been outraged or not; the sign of the rape should be certainly unequivocal. But is she addicted to masturbation? Has her mind been deteriorated by prurient ideas? These

peculiarities are seldom if ever noted. Juries and judges are completely ignorant of the tendencies of such women, and yet these tendencies are the keys to the whole situation.[64]

Routh concluded that great caution was necessary in dealing with any woman who claimed to have been molested. 'Except upon the strongest corroborative evidence, the presumption is they are liars, plausible liars, cunning liars.'[65]

Lawson Tait, the Birmingham surgeon who did more than any other single individual in making gynaecology a speciality, was equally convinced that men were sexually exploited by women.[66] He argued that, though boys were as often raped by women as girls were by men, they were offered no legal protection. During the centuries when rape was a capital crime, Tait speculated, 'thousands of innocent men must have been practically murdered'. Enraged by the passage of the 1885 Criminal Law Amendment Act which appeared to make it even easier for young girls to file rape charges, Tait had the authorities allow him to investigate all such complaints made in the Birmingham area. Out of a hundred cases Tait concluded to his own satisfaction that a mere six prosecutions should be proceeded with. As regards the children and mothers in the other cases, to Tait it was

> an open question as to whether it would not have been far better that many of these children, and the mothers and women concerned with them, aiding, abetting and originating their vile sins, better that one and all of them had been prostitutes openly plying for hire in the market place than have been the vile conspirators and blackmailers that many of them, the great bulk of them, prove to be.[67]

The middle-class 'fussy women' of the Vigilance Committees and the typical 12-year-old girl, a dirty little wretch of a 'bragging, lying disposition, a not unusual disposition of her class', were in concert, according to Tait, making *martyrs* of defenceless men.[68]

One would not have to be psychoanalytically inclined to suspect that men such as Tait and Routh were drawn to the field of gynaecological surgery by some psychological fear of female sexuality. A more mundane explanation would be that since the term 'woman's doctor' could conjure up the image of the abortionist, the gynaecologist sought to prove his loyalty to other males, his respectability to the larger society, by parading an exaggerated anti-feminism.[69]

The breaking of gender boundaries, which interventionist gynaecological surgery represented, created ripples of disquiet in late Victorian society. The antivivisection campaign was in part fuelled by middle-class women's outrage that they, like animals, were being experimented on by male surgeons.⁷⁰ The straps and stirrups of the obstetrical consulting-room conjured up too readily images of pornographic bondage.⁷¹ Feminists referred to the employment of the speculum for the forcible examination of prostitutes under the Contagious Diseases Act as 'instrumental rape'; it continued to be associated with assaults on female dignity long after the Acts were repealed. The antivivisectionists' concerns for the plight of animals and women were entwined in the movement's fiction, which played on the theme of the villainous surgeon who begins by murdering animals and ends up poisoning his wife.⁷²

Such preoccupations help explain why the image of the murdering mad doctor emerged even before Cream appeared on the scene.⁷³ Jack the Ripper was, of course, believed by many to be a doctor. Cream himself believed that murder and medicine were easily linked. In attempting to blame others for his crimes he chose a chemist, an intern and an eminent physician.

A psychopath would no doubt have been drawn to the powerful role played by the physician. Why? Because, as criminologists tell us, murder is the most 'personalized' crime in our society inasmuch as friends and family are the usual victims and perpetrators. In acting as a doctor, the purposes of the potential killer were facilitated because only he could rival friends or relatives in intimacy and contact: 'He wasn't a stranger, he was a doctor.' He could demand from women the sort of trust that would be denied any other man. Women, an obstetrician reminded his colleagues, 'are obliged to believe all that we tell them. They are not in a position to dispute anything we say to them, and, we therefore, may be said to have them at our mercy.'⁷⁴

Cream gave prostitutes hoping to avoid venereal disease and women seeking abortion drugs which killed them. He took advantage of the injunction that doctors were to be trusted. But respectable doctors certainly never lied to their patients regarding the medicines they prescribed. Or did they? Some nineteenth-century physicians, besieged by women seeking to terminate pregnancies, felt that this was one occasion in which honesty was not the best policy. A number flaunted their ability to trick patients who sought abortifacients. The French physician Dr J. P. Munaret, early in the century, boasted that it was his practice to give such women candy pills. '[T]he foetus has the time to grow and strengthen itself while my pills are being used which makes all the more difficult, and dangerous new attempts at abortion. To save a child from death, and a mother from crime, what could be a more wonderful result.'⁷⁵ The English author of *The Young Practitioner* wrote in 1890 that doctors should keep such women 'in ignorance of the innocuousness of the patient assumed abortifacient, lest other means be sought to effect the desired wish and interest'.[76] In short, when it came to abortion the doctor had a right to lie.[77]

Doctors applauded themselves for such trickery and were not bothered by the ethics of their dissimulations. After all, they were administering placebos, not poisons, and were smug in the conviction that they were doing right. But such stratagems were not innocent; as Munaret stated, it made other attempts at abortion 'more difficult and dangerous'. What is really germane was the symbolic importance of the doctor's alone determining what to give his patient while keeping her in ignorance of its effects.[78] Given this professional justification of deceit, Cream's acts – the administering of poisons in the place of abortifacients – appears not a completely isolated incident but the ultimate form of betrayal of the patient.

A review of the violent rhetoric which denounced women who aborted as murderers, the open misogyny of many gynaecologists, and the unapologetic violation of the trust of female patients suggests that the 'voices' that drove Cream on in his killing came as much from the society around him, as from any devil lurking within.[79]

NOTES

1 *Reynolds Newspaper*, 17 April 1892, 5; Charlotte Vogt Deposition, CRIM 1/38/1.
2 *The Lancet* regarded it as a 'grim irony' that Mrs McConville, who also sold abortifacients, thought she could avoid a conflict with the law by keeping accurate accounts of her profits for the benefit of the Income Tax Commissioners. *Lancet*, II (1896), 829.
3 Similar ploys were tried elsewhere. 'Old Dr. Gordon's Pearls of Health, or Female Regulators' came with the warning, 'Not to be taken during first four months of pregnancy'. *Victoria Daily Times*, 24 October 1892, 2.
4 The Medical Defence Union was in February 1892 preparing to press charges against Alfred Harcourt, the purveyor of Widow Winslow's Female Pills, but insisted that it would not lodge a prosecution unless any subsequent fines were paid to it to cover costs. Unqualified Practitioners, MEPO 3 149.
5 *London Times*, 20, 21 November 1899; CRIM 6: Madame Frain Trial; CRIM 9: Calendar of Prisoners; Madame Frain Trial; *British Medical Journal*, II (1899), 1583–4; *Chemist and Druggist*, 23 October 1897, 663–4.
6 Louisa Rebecca Fenn sold an apparently effective abortifacient mixture of aloes and iron on almost as large a scale as 'Madame Frain'. In 1897 the police found at her premises 'hundreds of letters testifying to her [Fenn's] cure, or stating that the medicine had no effect, whilst in other letters people complained that they had had no medicine. Counterfoils of two cheque-books showed that £600. had been paid to newspaper proprietors for advertisements

during six months.' *The Chemist and Druggist*, 26 June 1897, 1004; and see also 24 December 1898, 1011.
7 Joseph A. Banks, *Prosperity and Parenthood: A Study of Family Planning Among the Victorian Middle Classes* (London: Routledge and Kegan Paul, 1954).
8 Curiously enough, the discussion of contraception was considered more shocking than many criminal acts. In France, which had the lowest birth-rate in Europe, the 'ladies covered their faces' when in open court a man denied paternity and stated, 'I had taken precautions.' Joelle Guillais, *Crimes of Passion: Dramas of Private Life in Nineteenth-Century France*, trans. Jane Dunnett (New York: Routledge, 1990), 124.
9 Rosanna Ledbetter, *A History of the Malthusian League, 1877–1927* (Columbus: Ohio State University Press, 1976).
10 *The Clarion*, 13 February 1892.
11 *The Chemist and Druggist*, 10 July 1897, 64; Angus McLaren, *Birth Control in Nineteenth Century England* (London: Croom Helm, 1978), 222–6.
12 MEPO 2 399; Infant Life Protection Act. Report of 27 April 1896 on Dead Bodies (Infants) for Year 1895.
13 The handful of British doctors who supported birth control were listed in Charles R. Drysdale, *The Population Question* (London: Standring, 1892), 74–84.
14 Jukes de Styrap, *The Young Practitioner* (London: H. K. Lewis, 1890), 52; and see also John W. Taylor, *On the Diminishing Birth Rate* (London: British Gynaecological Society, 1904).
15 *Toronto Globe*, 29 October 1892, 1; *Montreal Daily Star*, 28 October 1892, 6.
16 Carl N. Degler, *At Odds: Women and the Family in America from the Revolution to the Present* (New York: Oxford, 1980), 227–48.
17 Norman Barnesby, *Medical Chaos and Crime* (London: Mitchell Kennerley, 1910), 222–3.
18 Angus McLaren, 'Women's Work and the Regulation of Family Size: The Question of Abortion in the Nineteenth Century', *History Workshop*, 4 (1977), 70–81.
19 *Lancet*, 1 January 1881, 15; and see also, Barbara Brookes, *Abortion in England, 1900–1967* (London: Croom Helm, 1988), chapter 3.
20 Sir George Clark, *A History of the Royal College of Phsyicians of London* (Oxford: Clarendon Press, 1964–72), 980–1.
21 *Lancet*, 29 March 1884, 578.
22 James Mohr, *Abortion in America: The Origins and Evolution of National Policy, 1800–1900* (New York: Oxford University Press, 1978); Carroll Smith-Rosenberg, 'The Abortion Movement and the A.M.A., 1850–1880', in Smith-Rosenberg (ed.), *Disorderly Conduct: Visions of Gender in Victorian America* (New York: Knopf, 1985), 217–44; John Keown, *Abortion, Doctors and the Law: Some Aspects of the Legal Regulation of Abortion in England from 1803 to 1982* (Cambridge: Cambridge University Press, 1988).
23 Kristin Luker, *Abortion and the Politics of Motherhood* (Berkeley: University of California Press, 1984), 39.
24 Angus McLaren, *Reproductive Rituals: The Perception of Fertility in England from the Sixteenth to the Nineteenth Century* (London: Methuen, 1984), 113–44.

25 Mohr, *Abortion in America*, 78–82.
26 Gerald Geoghegan, Cream's attorney, in 1891 had unsuccessfully defended a young man for attempting to procure a miscarriage; see *The Times*, 18, 19 December 1891, 12b.
27 Marshall Hall could be seen as indirectly responsible for his wife's death inasmuch as their deed of separation stipulated that she was only to receive maintenance as long as she led a chaste and virtuous life; *The Times*, 12 June 1890, 4e, 11 July 1890, 13c; Edward Marjoribanks, *For the Defence: The Life of Sir Edward Marshall Hall* (New York: Macmillan, 1930), 68–9.
28 Robert Roberts, *The Classic Slum: Salford Life in the First Quarter of the Century* (Manchester: Manchester University Press, 1971), 100.
29 'Quacks and Abortion: A Critical and Analytical Inquiry', *Lancet*, 10 December 1898, 1570–1; and see also 'Report from the Joint Committee on Lotteries and Indecent Advertisements', *Parliamentary Papers*, 9 (1908), 410–15, 457, 475.
30 *Chicago Tribune*, 29 August 1880, 4.
31 *Lancet*, 11 July 1891, 80–1; *East London Advertiser*, 24 September 1898; *The Times*, 10 December 1898, 8d.
32 *Lancet*, 21 February 1891, 463–4; *The Times*, 13 November 1891, 9e; 28 March 1892, 7d; 16 May 1893, 3f; 25 November 1893, 11d.
33 *The Times*, 7 December 1893, 9e; Lionel Rose, *The Massacre of the Innocents: Infanticide in Britain, 1800–1939* (London: Routledge and Kegan Paul, 1986), 87.
34 Gerald Geoghegan, Cream's counsel, defended in December 1892 Dr George Francis, charged with an abortion-related death; *The Times*, 5 December 1892, 14a.
35 W. Teignmouth Shore (ed.), *Trial of Thomas Neill Cream* (London: Hodge, 1923), 93; Fredrick Jarvis Report, 19 July 1892, MEPO 3 144; John Wilson McCulloch deposition: CRIM 1/38/1.
36 *Illustrated Police News*, 26 November 1892, 2.
37 Bertrand and Patricia Russell (eds.), *The Amberley Papers* (New York, 1937), 168–249.
38 Shore, 50.
39 Ibid., 54–5.
40 Ibid., 130; see also the *Pall Mall Gazette*, 20 October 1892.
41 The jury recommended mercy, but the judge insisted on the death penalty; *Lancet*, ii (1893), 153–4.
42 Sir Sydney Smith, *Taylor's Principles and Practices of Medical Jurisprudence*, vol. II (London: Churchill, 1951), 611.
43 There is no proof that, as some twentieth-century authors have speculated, the Ripper was a female abortionist. See Donald Rumbelow, *The Complete Jack the Ripper* (London: W. H. Allen, 1975), 227.
44 MEPO 3 140; and for a coroner's inquest of another woman whose death from an illegal operation was attributed to 'willful murder by some person or persons unknown', see *The Times*, 16 April 1891, 6d.
45 William B. Ryan, *Infanticide: Its Law, Prevalence, Prevention and History* (London: Churchill, 1862), 152.
46 Sylvanus Stall, *What a Young Man Ought to Know* (Toronto: Briggs, 1897), 198.

47 George Napheys, *Physical Life of Women* (London: Homeopathic Publishing Co., 1869), 93; Napheys, *The Transmission of Life: Counsels on the Nature and Hygiene of the Masculine Function* (Philadelphia: Fergus, 1872), 195.
48 Hugh H. Lodge, *Foeticide, or Criminal Abortion* (Philadelphia: Lindsay and Blackiston, 1969), 38.
49 Thomas Radford, *The Value of the Embryonic and Foetal Life, Legally, Socially, and Obstetrically Considered* (London: British Record of Obstetrics, 1848), 10.
50 P. H. Chavasse, *Advice to a Wife*, vol. 1 (Toronto: Musson, 1879), 119.
51 Mohr, *Abortion in America*, 105.
52 H. S. Pomeroy, *The Ethics of Marriage* (New York: Funk and Wagnalls, 1888), 36, 65–9. In 1866 Professor H. R. Storer won an AMA gold medal for an essay opposed to abortion entitled 'Why Not? A Book for Every Woman', which later appeared in an expanded form as *On Criminal Abortion*. John Todd, *Serpent in the Dove's Nest* (Boston, 1867) kept up the attack. See G. J. Barker-Benfield, *The Horrors of the Half-Known Life: Male Attitudes Towards Women and Sexuality in Nineteenth Century America* (New York: Harper, 1976).
53 Emma F. Angell Drake, *What a Young Wife Ought to Know* (Toronto: Vir Publishing, 1908), 123–4.
54 John Cowan, *The Science of the New Life* (New York, 1874), 109.
55 Augustus K. Gardner, *Conjugal Sins Against the Laws of Life and Health* (New York, 1874), 180–1; Mervin N. Olasky, *The Press and Abortion: 1838–1988* (London: Erlbaum, 1988), 24–32.
56 *Canadian Medical Association Journal*, 12 (1922), 166.
57 Radford, *The Value of the Embryonic and Foetal Life*, 11.
58 *Canada Lancet*, December 1871, 185–6; March 1889, 217–18.
59 On earlier suspicions of obstetrics, see Roy Porter, 'A Touch of Danger: The Man Midwife as Sexual Predator', in G. S. Rousseau and Roy Porter (eds.), *Sexual Underworlds of the Enlightenment* (Manchester: Manchester University Press, 1987), 206–32.
60 Ornella Moscucci, *The Science of Woman: Gynaecology and Gender in England, 1800–1929* (Cambridge: Cambridge University Press, 1990), 134.
61 Elizabeth Blackwell, *The Human Element in Sex* (London: Churchill, 1885), 56; and on the linked themes of the secrets of nature being unveiled and the woman dissected, see Ludmilla Jordanova, *Sexual Visions: Images of Gender in Science and Medicine Between the Eighteenth and Twentieth Centuries* (Madison: University of Wisconsin Press, 1989), 99.
62 By the turn of the century the Home Office was aware that incest was common; see Victor Bailey and Sheila Blackburn, 'The Punishment of Incest Act 1908: A Case Study of Law Creation', *Criminal Law Review* (1979), 708–18.
63 C. H. F. Routh, 'On the Etiology and Diagnosis, Considered Specially from a Medico-Legal Point of View, of Those Cases of Nymphomania Which Lead Women to Make False Charges Against Their Medical Attendants', *British Gynaecological Journal*, 2 (1887), 490.
64 Ibid., 501.
65 Ibid., 501. On the fear that 'naturally pure-minded women' when under anaesthesia had 'unfounded dreams' of being molested by their doctors, see Frederick J. Smith, *Lectures on Medical Jurisprudence and Toxicology* (London:

Churchill, 1900), 187–8.
66 Tait's chief work was *Diseases of Women and Abdominal Surgery* (Leicester: Richardson, 1889).
67 Lawson Tait, 'An Analysis of the Evidence in 70 Consecutive Cases of Charges Made Under the New Criminal Law Amendment Act', *Provincial Medical Journal*, 1 May 1894, 236. On Freud and continental discussions of incest and child rape, see Jeffrey Moussaieff Masson, *The Assault on Truth: Freud's Suppression of the Seduction Theory* (New York: Viking, 1985).
68 Was Tait thinking of his own problems when, in the midst of his essay on child rape, he told the story of a nurse who sought to blackmail a doctor? Her threat was to claim that he had seduced and then aborted her with ergot of rye. A nurse's assertion that Tait was the father of her child helped destroy his career. Tait, 'An Analysis', 228; I. Harvey Flack, *Lawson Tait* (London: Heinemann, 1949), 114.
69 On America, see Barker Benfield, *The Horrors of the Half-Known Life*, 83–90.
70 Interestingly enough, the childless Tait, a devotee of blue Persian cats, was a fervent supporter of the antivivisection movement; see Lawson Tait, *The Uselessness of Antivivisection* (London: Victoria Street Society, 1882); Richard D. French, *Antivivisection and Medical Science in Victorian Society* (Princeton: Princeton University Press, 1975); Mary Ann Elston, 'Women and Antivivisection in Victorian England, 1870–1900', in Nicolas Rupke (ed.), *Vivisection in Historical Perspective* (London: Croom Helm, 1987), 259–94.
71 Cora Lansbury, 'Gynaecology, Pornography and Antivivisection', *Victorian Studies*, 28 (1985), 424.
72 H. G. Wells provided the classic depiction of the experimental physiologist as torturer in *The Island of Dr. Moreau* (1986), while George Bernard Shaw likened the vivisectors to contemporary terrorists; both destroyed while claiming to care. George Bernard Shaw, 'The Dynamitards of Science' (1900), cited in Barbara Arnett Melchiori, *Terrorism in the Late Victorian Novel* (London: Croom Helm, 1985), 245; Coral Lansbury, *The Old Brown Dog: Women, Workers and Vivisection in Edwardian England* (Madison: University of Wisconsin Press, 1985), 142.
73 Richard D. Altick, *Victorian Studies in Scarlet* (New York: Norton, 1970), 146–74.
74 Elaine Showalter, *The Female Malady* (New York: Pantheon, 1985), 78.
75 J. M. P. Munaret, *Du médecin des villes et du médecin de campagne* (Paris, 1840), 427.
76 Jukes de Styrap, *The Young Practitioner* (London: H. K. Lewis, 1890), 50.
77 Professional confidentiality provided a warrant for doctors' toleration of lies of omission; for example, not warning a woman that her prospective spouse suffered from a venereal disease; see H. Montgomery Hyde, *A Tangled Web: Sex Scandals in British Politics and Society* (London: Constable, 1986), 101–5; Gail Savage, 'The Wilful Communication of a Loathesome Disease: Marital Conflict and Venereal Disease in Victorian England', *Victorian Studies*, 34 (1990), 35–54; Jill Harsin, 'Syphilis, Wives and Physicians: Medical Ethics and the Family in Late Nineteenth-Century France', *French Historical Studies*, 16 (1989), 72–95.
78 Take the case of the doctor who performed surgery on an unmarried woman,

discovered her to be pregnant and in the 'natural course' of the operation terminated the pregnancy, but never told her. It was not so much what was done as who decided that was significant. Personal communication of Anita Fellman.

79 A number of other nineteenth-century murderers were involved in abortion. When such an operation was forced underground it could obviously be exploited by those who wished to kill. In 1879 the Reverend Anthony Hayden was accused of giving his pregnant servant Mary Stannard arsenic which he claimed was 'quick medicine'. Dr William Palmer, the famous poisoner executed in 1856, recommended abortion to a friend. Dr Edward Pritchard, in 1865 the last man to be executed in public in Scotland, induced a miscarriage in a seduced servant girl. Dr Thomas Smethurst, tried in 1859 for murdering his six- to seven-weeks pregnant mistress, had probably given her an overdose of some poison meant to abort. John Christie, the most infamous of the post-Second World War English serial murderers, ultimately charged with six murders, was known as the 'local abortionist' and used his purported expertise to lure women to his home. Colin Wilson and Patricia Pitman, *Encyclopedia of Murder* (London: Barker 1961), 267–8; George H. Knott (ed.), *Trial of William Palmer* (London: Hodge, 1912), 14; William Roughead (ed.), *Trial of Dr Pritchard* (London: Hodge, 1906), 102; Leonard A. Parry (ed.), *Trial of Dr Smethurst* (Toronto: Canada Law Book Co., 1931), 23–4; F. Tennyson Jesse, *Trials of Timothy John Evans and John Reginald Halliday Christie* (London: Hodge, 1957), 62–6.

THIRTEEN

'MAY THE DOCTOR ADVISE EXTRAMARITAL INTERCOURSE?': MEDICAL DEBATES ON SEXUAL ABSTINENCE IN GERMANY, c. 1900[1]

ANDREAS HILL

IN 1908 Max Marcuse (1877–1963), a dermatologist and venereologist and one of the leading younger 'sexologists', wrote in an article on the sexual life of the German student in *Sexualprobleme*, the most influential sexological periodical in Imperial Germany:[2]

> The increase of venereal diseases, the growing insight into their disastrous effects and the deepened sense of social responsibility on the one hand, and the demand of modern human beings for a harmonious development of all their powers and not least for an activation of their sexual life that meets their needs for happiness on the other hand, have brought about a remarkably lively public discussion about sexual problems – to an extent which would have been thought impossible only a decade ago ... Naturally within this discussion the question about the influence of sexual abstinence on the physical, mental and psychological well-being of human beings plays a prominent part. So does the question about the right and necessity to demand it [i.e. abstinence] – for moral reasons – from the young man until his marriage.[3]

Marcuse had enough insight into the different elements shaping scientific and general knowledge to add: 'The answer [to these questions] reads now this way, now that, according to the *Lebens- und Weltanschauung* of whoever feels competent to respond.'[4]

The question about the beneficial or harmful effects of sexual abstinence involved delicate and highly controversial issues: the right to sexual gratification; the appropriate means and methods to combat venereal diseases and prostitution; birth control and contraception; pre- and extramarital sexual relationships; illegitimate children; celibacy regulations for certain professional groups such as Catholic clerics or female teachers and civil servants; the dangers of masturbation as well as definitions of health and disease. Most of these topics had profound moral and social implications which fuelled the controversies about sexual abstinence. Nevertheless, they were dominated by medical arguments and terminology – not only among doctors but also among other professional groups.

That this issue was widely debated as well as of major importance within the increasing scientific discourse about sexuality was acknowledged at the time by many other prominent figures in the blossoming discipline *Sexualwissenschaft* ('sexual science', i.e. sexology).[5] The impression of contemporaries is confirmed by an extensive bibliometrical analysis of the medical literature on sexual abstinence from 1879 – when the first volume of the *Index medicus* was issued – until 1933, a year that can be taken as an important point also in regard to the development of sexology in Germany. This quantification is mainly based on the relevant German literature – monographs, articles and reviews – listed in the *Index medicus* (from 1879) and the *Index-Catalogue of the Library of the Surgeon-General's Office* (from 1880). Single chapters or paragraphs about the topic in other publications such as the numerous general treatises dealing with normal or pathological sexuality have not been considered for this quantitative analysis since their number does not reflect the chronology of the controversies.

Between 1879 and 1887 no relevant publications have been found; in the following fifteen years between 1888 and 1902 five monographs and two articles were published. After the foundation of the Deutsche Gesellschaft zur Bekämpfung von Geschlechtskrankheiten (German Association for Combating Venereal Diseases) in 1902, a marked increase in the debates can be seen, with nine monographs and sixteen articles for the five-year-period between 1903 and 1907. During the six years from 1908 to 1913 a further expansion occurred with a total of four monographs and sixty-two articles. In the following five years of the First World War the controversies slowed down, with only five papers, and eventually faded away with only two articles on the subject for the entire period of fifteen years between 1919 and 1933, i.e. the era of the Weimar Republic, which otherwise witnessed a sharp increase in scientific publications about sexuality.

A brief look at the *Index-Catalogue of the Library of the Surgeon-General's Office* does also substantiate the thesis of a growing scientific discourse about sexuality in general at the turn of the century. In its first series in 1891 the listed literature runs over about half a page on 'sexual instinct' and two pages on its 'perversions and disorders'. In contrast, the literature in the second series in 1910 amounts to one page of references on 'sexual instinct', one on its 'disorders and abuses', three pages on hygiene, ethics and education related to the 'sexual instinct', three and a half pages on 'inversion', i.e. what elsewhere and later is called homosexuality, seven pages on 'perversions', one and a half pages on the 'psychology of the sexual instinct' and one page on anthropological and folkloric aspects – adding up to nineteen pages headed by the adjective 'sexual'.[6] This expanding medical interest in sexual issues seems to be particularly intensive in the German-speaking countries. No fewer than nine of the eleven periodicals relating to sexual instinct listed in 1910 were published in German; one was in Italian and one in French.[7] M. Wawerzonnek, an author familiar with the bibliometrical extent of the related literature, estimates more than 10,000 monographs and articles related to sexuality during the period between 1886 and 1933.[8]

The medical-intellectual and social-historical background of the debates on sexual abstinence is complex. Medical authorities at the end of the nineteenth century generally agreed that abstinence from sexual intercourse with another person (preferably of the opposite sex) – as it was defined by most of the authors – did not have any harmful effects on body, psyche and intellect, even if maintained over a long period of time. The renowned Berlin specialist for nervous diseases and sexology Albert Eulenburg (1840–1917), editor of the multi-volume standard medical handbook *Real-Encyclopädie der gesamten Heilkunde*[9] and the influential periodical *Deutsche medizinische Wochenschrift*, doubted in his monograph on *Sexuale Neuropathie* (1895) 'that anybody with a decent life-style has ever become diseased, in particular neurasthenic or sexually neurasthenic, only because of sexual abstinence'.[10]

The neurasthenic disorders were to play an important role in the controversies about abstinence. After the term 'neurasthenia' had been coined in 1869 by the American physician George M. Beard (1839–83) the concept of this new disease entity developed quickly; during the late nineteenth century it spread all over Europe and North America and dissolved in the second decade of the twentieth century.[11] 'Neurasthenia' belonged to the 'chronic, general and functional neuroses, i.e. those diseases of the nervous system which – according to our current pathological–anatomical knowledge – are not based upon any macroscopic or microscopic alterations of the tissue, but upon a disorder of its function'.[12] The new concept emerged from and overlapped with those of hypochondria and hysteria. Neurasthenic patients suffered from a broad spectrum of symptoms: irritability, depressive moods, abnormal fatigue, weak memory and concentration, sleep disorders, anxiety, phobias, obsessions, hallucinations, hyperaesthesia and hyperalgesia, allergies, headaches and migraine, spasms and convulsions, loss of appetite, indigestion, palpitations, nervous cardiac weakness, sweatings as well as disorders of the sexual functions. The latter were often subsumed under the term 'sexual neurasthenia' and included such states as sexual hypersensitivity – in its extreme forms, 'satyriasis' and 'nymphomania' – abnormal erections and nocturnal seminal losses (*'Pollutionen'*), 'spermatorrhoea', masturbation, premature ejaculations *(ejaculatio praecox)*, impotency and menstrual disorders. The concept of neurasthenia offered a scientific or pseudoscientific framework – according to one's definition of science – for those doctors who wanted to or had to take seriously the biologically ill-defined diseases and discomforts of their patients.

The author of *Psychopathia sexualis* and the leading figure in the field, Richard von Krafft-Ebing (1840–1902), expressed similar views on sexual abstinence as Eulenburg, but admitted that in individuals with a 'neuropathic' constitution which is often linked with abnormally strong sexual needs abstinence could be 'antihygienic' and lead to nervous disorders.[13] Eulenburg's and Krafft-Ebing's opinions were embedded in widespread theories that saw the underlying, true causes of many diseases as well as social problems – e.g. syphilis, tuberculosis, alcoholism and nervous diseases such as neurasthenia – in a mixture of 'degeneration', 'hereditary strain' and 'neuropathic disposition' on the one hand and 'progressing civilization' on the other.[14] Krafft-Ebing formulated his gloomy analysis of this historical process in an article on 'Nervousness and Neurasthenic States' (1895):

> Countless modern human beings spend their lives not in fresh air, but in gloomy workshops, factories, offices, etc., others in the stressful duties which have been imposed on them by steam and electricity, the means of transport as well as the driving forces of modern times. However, increased work creates the demand for more of the pleasures of life. The progress of civilization has created a life style with greater needs, and the brain has to pay for the gratification of such needs ... One can see them [the human beings in their struggle for existence] in continuous feverish excitement hunting for money, using all their physical and mental powers and all the means which an overhasty cultural development offers in the form of railway, post and telegraph. However, such strained nervous systems develop an increased need for consumption and excitement (coffee, tea, alcohol, tobacco). Hand-in-hand with the improved living-conditions of the modern era it has become increasingly difficult to establish a home of one's own: the man of upper social classes might be able to feed a woman but not to clothe her. The consequences are extramarital sexual intercourse – specially in the big cities – , remaining single and late marriages. When such a modern man of business and work eventually gets married at an advanced age, he is decrepit, debauched and often syphilitic; with the modest remains of his

virility, in the midst of the haste and exhaustion of his professional life, he fathers only sickly, weakly and nervous children.[15]

One phenomenon of this era that was perceived as a particular threat was the increase in prostitution.[16] A joint visit to a brothel was not unusual among (male) students, soldiers and other young men; it was regarded as a suitable initiation rite into the adult world. Within the ruling double moral standard prostitution offered a welcome outlet for the sexual drive of the young, effervescent man, which – according to general medical agreement – was naturally stronger than that of a woman.[17] The prostitute was tolerated as a necessary evil to preserve the chastity of the young middle- or upper-class lady until her marriage, often late in her twenties or thirties.

Nevertheless, with the rise and rapid growth of modern, industrialized cities in the late nineteenth century, prostitution was regarded as a social problem of high priority. Around the turn of the century estimates varied from 100,000 to 200,000 prostitutes in Germany; a contemporary source counted 30,000 in Berlin alone.[18] The 'representatives of purchasable love' seemed to threaten 'public morality', 'public security' and 'public health'[19] since they were seen as the main reservoirs and transmitters of venereal diseases. In many cities in Imperial Germany prostitutes were subjected to surveillance by the police and a regular physical examination by a state-employed doctor. If it was thought necessary, they had to tolerate a sort of imprisonment and in-patient treatment in a hospital. Of course their male clientele was not troubled with similar measures. There was no general obligation to notify venereal diseases and – except for prostitutes – the criminal laws about negligent or wilful physical injury were not applied to the transmission of syphilis or gonorrhoea. However, such measures also became increasingly the object of public discussions.[20]

State control and regulation of 'professional indecency', the so-called *Reglementierung*, was not deemed very efficient and became a highly controversial issue. Critics feared that this system even enhanced the spread of venereal diseases as the male clients were lulled in the false and dangerous conviction of the 'clean', because inspected, prostitute. The call to abolish the regulation system came from different and otherwise opposing directions: conservative leagues fighting for decency and morality, social democrats – under the influence of August Bebel (1840–1913) – as well as various subdivisions of the women's movement, in particular the Deutscher Zweig der Internationalen Abolitionistischen Föderation (German Branch of the International Federation for Abolition).[21] The latter, the so-called abolitionists, demanded equal moral principles for both sexes, i.e. the end of the double standard. Men should be as chaste until marriage and as faithful and monogamous during wedlock as women were supposed to be. For the struggle against prostitution and *Reglementierung* it was of strategic importance to emphasize the harmlessness of sexual abstinence. Both the medical profession – which as a whole, although not unanimously, favoured regulation instead of rigorous prohibition – and the state came under increasing pressure to give up their *laissez-faire* attitudes towards prostitution.

The controversies were intensified by another threat – venereal diseases – which in the eyes of contemporaries grew as fast as prostitution.[22] In Berlin one out of nine or ten inhabitants was thought to have had syphilis during his or her lifetime; syphilis contributed only 20 to 30 per cent, gonorrhoea 60 to 70 per cent of all cases of venereal diseases.[23] The number of patients suffering from venereal diseases in Prussia alone in April 1900 was 41,000. It was calculated that 'among people who get married only in their mid-thirties one out of four or five has been infected with syphilis and that the majority has contracted gonorrhoea at least once, not seldom twice or more often'.[24] Males were infected three times as often as females – figures that substantiate the thesis of the widespread and widely practised double standard.

Not only was the epidemiologic incidence of venereal diseases frightening, but also the growing insight into their effects on the human body and intellect.[25] The prolonged and far-reaching consequences of secondary and tertiary syphilis had been established in the mid-nineteenth century, for example the effects upon various internal organs: *tabes dorsalis* and progressive paralysis were recognized as disastrous effects of this 'scourge of mankind' on the nervous system. The modern theory of hereditary syphilis – developed from the 1860s – hung a sword of Damocles over the descendants of syphilitics as well as over the nation's future. The new knowledge about gonorrhoea was even more revolutionary. Until the 1870s it had been compared with a trivial cold, but during the last three decades of the nineteenth century its serious consequences were discovered: arthritis, meningitis, pericarditis, peritonitis and inflammations of the reproductive organs followed by infertility, especially in women. The Fatherland's military strength seemed to be drowning in the swamps of these illnesses. In contrast to the advancing insight into the etiology, pathogenesis and diagnosis of venereal diseases, the prospects of effective remedies or even a cure remained gloomy. The therapeutic measures were lengthy, unpleasant or painful and had considerable side-effects but little success. Moreover, the health insurance law of 1883 excluded patients from compensation if they had contracted a disease through 'sexual dissipation'.[26] The interest in primary prophylaxis and prevention was comprehensible and controversies about suitable strategies of individual as well as public hygiene were inevitable.

Debates on sexual abstinence developed within this atmosphere of fear and uncertainty that had been brought about with the process of industrialization. In 1899 and 1902 the first international conferences for prophylaxis of venereal diseases were held in Brussels. The Société Internationale de Prophylaxie Sanitaire et Morale de la Syphilis et des Maladies Vénériennes was founded in 1899, with its central office in Brussels and various national branches followed soon. In 1902 the Deutsche Gesellschaft zur Bekämpfung von Geschlechtskrankheiten (German Society for Combating Venereal Diseases, hereafter abbreviated as DGBG)[27] was established by such renowned specialists for dermatology and venereology as Alfred Neisser (1855–1916), discoverer of the pathogen causing gonorrhoea, and Alfred Blaschko (1858–1922), a social democrat and one of the most influential campaigners for *Sozialhygiene* (social hygiene).[28] After one year the DGBG had about 1,600 members. It was not a purely medical organization; at its first conference in 1903 a third of the 180 participants were not doctors, but representatives of various women's associations, headmasters, jurists, clergymen, politicians, public administrators and police officers, as well as representatives of health insurance companies. The official organs were the *Mitteilungen der Deutschen Gesellschaft zur Bekämpfung der Geschlechtskrankheiten* (1903–34) and the more influential periodical *Zeitschrift für Bekämpfung der Geschlechtskrankheiten* (*ZfBdG*, 1903–22). The concept of the DGBG was 'new, since it did not call for further repression by the state, but employed subtly diversified and differentiated components of social control'; its public activities had 'the character of modern propaganda – "from the beginning with the Janus face of enlightenment and guidance, of information and advertising, of education and manipulation"'.[29] The DGBG's broad commitment to such social issues as prostitution, housing shortage, alcoholism, issues of civil and criminal law, as well as sexual education, illustrates that 'the fight against venereal diseases was a fight against the social threats of modern life in a mass-society'.[30]

The DGBG zealously published leaflets and pamphlets and organized lectures to school-leavers, students and other target groups. Their efforts to instruct and to enlighten were aimed chiefly at young men and reflected the shifting focus in the campaigns against venereal diseases: the main person to blame was not any more the prostitute, but the thoughtless, irresponsible, hedonistic man. The first leaflet published by the DGBG in 1903 assured its male readers: 'According to the unanimous judgement of physicians and in contrast to a widespread prejudice, abstinence from sexual intercourse – as a rule – is not unhealthy.'[31] A special, but similar, leaflet was published for women and was mainly directed to female workers, saleswomen and maids whose more independent lifestyle made them another primary target group for the DGBG. The message must not go unheeded: campaigns of unprecedented scale were launched; millions of copies of the leaflet were distributed among young people from all social classes through doctors, health insurance companies, public offices, clubs and the army. Formerly private and intimate issues were dragged into the limelight. Even Marcuse, one of the most vigorous opponents of the DGBG's philosophy, admitted that the campaigns 'had brought about the break with the previous secretiveness *in sexualibus* and had actually made possible the public discussion of all these questions'.[32] Doctors played a prominent role in these efforts towards 'sexual enlightenment'.

Nevertheless, at that very first conference in 1903 critical voices were raised about the DGBG's statement on sexual abstinence. No less a person than Wilhelm Erb (1840–1921), one of the most famous German neurologists, with an international reputation, cautiously pointed out eight male and three female cases in his own practice where he regarded abstinence as the main or joint cause of health disorders.[33] Erb's sceptical views fell on the fertile ground of less moderate doctors who aimed at far-reaching reforms in conventional sexual morality. The debate expanded quickly and various controversial positions were formulated that can be divided roughly into two camps.

The more conservative party – the advocates of abstinence – was supported by the majority of the activists in the DGBG such as Neisser or renowned sexologists as Eulenburg, Albert Moll (1862–1939) and Paul Näcke (1851–1913) as well as the influential psychiatrist and propagandist of degeneration theory August Forel (1848–1931).[34] Their opinions were rooted in the traditional Victorian attitudes towards sexuality.[35] For a normal, healthy person sexual abstinence until marriage was regarded as beneficial and innocuous – or at most causing irrelevant minor discomforts. Only individuals with a 'neuropathic strain' might suffer from its effects. The symptoms – for which abstinence was blamed by the opposing camp – were really caused by an immoral, dissipated life style, particularly by premature and extensively practised masturbation and other 'sexual excesses'. Abstinence was seen as beneficial for the development of physical and mental capacities in adolescents. The possible discomforts were outweighed by the advantages, i.e. the prevention of venereal diseases, illegitimate pregnancies and the social stigmatization that went along with these – especially for women. Nocturnal seminal discharges, for some authors also occasional masturbation in moderation, were seen as sufficient physiological outlets. Of course it was much easier for females than for males to curb their sexual drives – an opinion that was accepted by the liberal opponents of abstinence. To facilitate a chaste life one encouraged a healthy regimen – a balanced diet as well as regular physical and mental exercises – to enhance self-control and will power. Pre- and extramarital sexual intercourse was unacceptable, moreover, as for most of the authors they were synonyms for intercourse with prostitutes. Marriage represented the sole legitimate place for the satisfaction of sexual needs. Protective methods of preventing venereal diseases, as well as contraceptives, were portrayed as unreliable, harmful and immoral since they encouraged illegitimate sexual activities and the separation of sexual pleasures and reproduction. The doctor's personal advice for his patients should follow the generally accepted moral standards and should not be dictated by natural drives. The advocates of abstinence defended their position with medical-scientific arguments and evidence, but their moral considerations and motivations were obvious and often explicit. The prevailing double standard was condemned; lip-service was paid to the public demand that men should live as chastely as was expected of women.

The conservative position found support from the respective sections of the women's movement, from conservative abolitionists, associations fighting for decency and morality, the Catholic and also the Protestant church and such radical moralists as Otto Weininger (1880–1903), author of the bestseller *Geschlecht und Charakter*, who elevated chastity to the highest ideal and rule of life.[36]

The liberal position – campaigning against abstinence – was shaped by such progressive sexual reformers as Marcuse, the Swedish author Anton Nyström (1842–1931) whose works were widely published in German, Magnus Hirschfeld (1868–1935) – a zealous opponent of discrimination against homosexuals – as well as Sigmund Freud (1856–1939), Wilhelm Stekel (1868–1940) and other psychoanalysts.[37] An important institutional platform for the sexual reform movement was established in 1905 with the foundation of the Bund für Mutterschutz (BfM, League for Protection of Mothers) under the leadership of Helene Stöcker (1869–1943), a female doctor of philosophy and one of the central figures in the radical, left-wing bourgeois section of the women's movement.[38] The league soon had between 3,500 and 4,000 members and opened branches in various cities. The official mouthpiece was the periodical *Mutterschutz* (1905–7) which was followed by *Die Neue Generation* (1908–32) and *Sexualprobleme* (1908–14). The BfM advocated cultural, social and legal reforms to support unmarried mothers and their illegitimate children – about 180,000 per year in Germany alone – as well as a fundamental 'reform of sexual ethics'. Celibacy regulations for female teachers and civil servants should be abolished. The league was the most influential organization propagating neo-Malthusianism (i.e. modern) ideas of birth control and contraception in Imperial Germany.[39] Although influenced by psychoanalytical ideas, many of the league's representatives – as well as some who belonged to the conservative position – shared the popular theories of genetics, social Darwinism and eugenics.[40] This might seem surprising at first glance but it has to be seen within the intellectual context: scientific progress – including the 'primary prophylaxis' of the unhealthy, the handicapped, the degenerate – promised to extinguish the evils and sufferings of mankind and to make possible a happy society without disharmonies.

Liberal sexual reformers regarded sexual abstinence over a long period – for example until marriage at the age of 25 or 30 years – as a crucial cause of minor complaints as well as serious diseases not only in the 'neuropathically burdened' but also in the healthy individual with a 'normal' constitution. Listening to, observing and treating their patients, these reforming doctors supposedly established the etiological link between abstinence and such health disorders as neuroses, in particular neurasthenia and sexual neurasthenia, psychoses, 'sexual perversions' such as homosexuality, and even organic diseases, mainly of the reproductive organs. Influenced by the concept of neurasthenia as well as psychoanalysis, the more subjective 'health disorders that lay beyond the stethoscope, the plessimeter and the test-tube' were stressed.[41] Impressive and sometimes dramatic case histories were quoted to support these assumptions. Nocturnal seminal discharges and masturbation did not offer sufficient substitutes for sexual intercourse or were themselves seen as detrimental. The dangers of venereal diseases and illegitimate pregnancy should be prevented by personal hygiene, protective methods and contraceptives such as creams, condoms, sponges, douches and irrigations; the public, unhindered marketing and supply of these goods was called for.

Although the issue of abortion – vigorously debated in the Weimar Republic – did not enter the controversies on abstinence, it was welcomed as a last resort or at least not completely condemned by some of the more radical reformers. Pre- and extramarital sexual intercourse was not regarded as immoral *per se*; in some cases the doctor was even obliged to prescribe it.[42] The desirable alternative beyond abstinence, marriage and prostitution was so-called *freie Liebe* (free love), where emotional and physical attraction were not separated. The final aim was a new ethic in harmony with the natural needs of men and women, a *natürliche Sexualmoral* (natural sexual morality). The sciences that revealed nature's laws, not religion or other traditional institutions, should provide the basis for this new ethic of the *Naturgläubigen* (believers in nature) – as the reformers were called by their adversaries.

A satisfying sexual life was seen as an important condition for health and general well-being. Referring to the sociology of Max Weber (1864–1920), Marcuse also speculated about the interrelations between sexuality and productivity.[43] He attempted to calculate the economic and social profit of a happy, trouble-free sexuality. Acting according to one's physical drives was providing pleasure and gratification and formed happy and therefore 'useful human beings': 'They enjoy working, they live in harmony with their environment, they are friends and willing builders of society.'[44] The reformers conceptualized a liberated yet normative and tamed sexuality that ought to be satisfying as well as pacifying (*befriedigend*). This postulated natural sexuality should dissolve the frictions and contradictions between the individual and society. In this harmony of nature, the individual and society, the dangerous, unpredictable character of the sexual drive should be domesticated. This construction of sexuality installed a subtle, liberal control of its own object, sexual desires and passions. It is not surprising therefore that most sexual reformers stigmatized masturbation, homosexuality and other 'perversions' through the conventional normative terminology of psychopathology; they did so for strategic reasons in their campaigns, i.e. to portray these sexual practices as some of the disastrous effects of abstinence.

The peak of the debates was reached with the eighth annual meeting of the DGBG in 1911 at Dresden. Its central topic was 'Sexual Abstinence and its Effects on Health' and the more pragmatic question: Should the DGBG 'continue its attempts to keep growing adolescents from sexual intercourse or should we abstain from such warnings because of the dangers which could be evoked by sexual abstinence itself'?[45] Most of the speakers repeated their well-known opinions; however, some subtle but meaningful changes loomed on the horizon. One of the earlier campaigners for abstinence, the influential Eulenburg, now blamed continuing abstinence in adults as the 'direct cause of serious physical and mental harms' such as various psychoneurotic states and impotency.[46] He based his views on case histories from his own clinical practice – among others he described a 45-year-old Catholic clergyman with nervous depression and exhaustion – as well as on the relevant literature. Marcuse commented on this shift: 'Eulenburg has completely turned from a Saul into a Paul.'[47] From the more objective standpoint of the historian too the comparison hit the nail on the head; and the connotation of the phrase gives a further example of the almost religious character of these scientific or pseudoscientific debates.

New statistics 'concerning the sexual life of our senior students' contributed to this shift.[48] These enquiries pointed out what pessimistic or realistic contemporaries had already feared or known before: 98.9 per cent of the young men interviewed had sexual intercourse before they reached the safe harbour of marriage, 67.1 per cent as university students and 32.9 per cent as schoolboys. In 40.5 per cent of cases the first sexual intercourse occurred with prostitutes and in 54.5 per cent with so-called 'representatives of the secret prostitution', i.e. maids, saleswomen and waitresses. For contemporaries this was sufficient explanation of the fact that 51.9 per cent had contracted a venereal disease. In the face of these figures mere appeals for abstinence seemed unrealistic and were doomed to failure. The statistics provided good arguments for the liberal forces that propagated and called for protective means such as condoms and creams.

Again for pragmatic reasons the First World War accelerated the decline in the controversies. With hundreds of thousands of men and women separated from their partners, the call for abstinence was more of a lost cause than ever before. Even Karl Touton (born in 1858, he died some time after 1930), a venereologist, one of the DGBG's most vigorous campaigners for abstinence and a personal adversary of Marcuse, was convinced 'that now, during the war, all the educational efforts as far as they point out the advantages of abstinence and the disadvantages of sexual intercourse will be sermons falling on deaf ears'.[49] To prevent a rapid increase of venereal diseases and illegitimate pregnancies, pragmatic solutions were the need of the moment. Instead of slow and unreliable 'ethic and aesthetic' measures, Touton was now favouring the 'hygienic-medical' means, in particular condoms; he was even demanding their obligatory use in the army.[50] Of course such proposals encountered fierce resistance. The associations and clubs for decency and morality were still influential enough to enforce the removal of new vending machines with prophylactic packages in military barracks.[51] But for many contemporaries those protests were deemed increasingly anachronistic, unrealistic and even dangerous. The war might not have made protective methods socially acceptable for everybody, but they became an inevitable measure of personal and public prevention. As a consequence the heated debates about sexual abstinence – as a strategic platform in the controversies about adequate forms of prophylaxis – became redundant or at least less urgent. There was also little prospect of achieving any new methodological breakthroughs. It was difficult to obtain convincing evidence for an etiological link between abstinence and certain diseases; the case histories were often dubious and there was little prospect of performing clinical studies or experiments on the subject.

Beside the general liberalization following the First World War, some further specific factors might have contributed to the decline of the debates. The discovery in 1910 of Salvarsan, the first effective and relatively safe drug against syphilis, had raised (exaggerated) hopes that mankind could be completely released from this scourge and that venereal diseases might lose their terrifying character, hopes that were only fulfilled in the era of penicillin and have been bitterly disappointed with the emergence of AIDS. Hand in hand with the expected medical progress, the moral considerations behind the arguments on hygiene and prophylaxis seemed to become less influential. And the sexual reform movement in the Weimar Republic focused on more concrete issues such as the complete legalization of contraceptives and abortion.[52]

Since the 1980s the HIV-infection and AIDS have created a new awareness of the problematic interactions between sexuality and venereal diseases. The specific combination of a 'real' physical disease and its metaphors confronts us as well as our predecessors with a complicated 'tangle of ideologic, pragmatic and repressive components'.[53] The controversies over sexual abstinence at the beginning of the twentieth century arose within such a tangle. They give yet another example of the medicalization of social and political areas in modern societies, i.e. that such issues were discussed less and less within a theological or explicitly moral discourse, but within a secularized scientific or pseudoscientific one. According to P. Conrad, 'medicalization occurs when traditional or previous forms of social control are no longer efficient or acceptable'.[54] Apparently at the turn of the century new mechanisms of control were needed.

The debates on abstinence were an expression of as well as a stimulus for the expanding publicization of previously private spheres. This modern discourse on sexuality dragged into the public eye what had been hidden behind the closed doors and curtains of Victorianism. The debates illustrate also the shifting focus of the scientific, sexological discourse from *psychopathia sexualis* to so-called normal sexuality and sexual dysfunctions. Sexual reformers encouraged the separation of sex and reproduction, yet not of sex and love. Sexuality was assigned a prominent role in constituting and constructing one's ego. A gratifying, harmonious sexual life was regarded as an important condition for individual and social productivity. This process has been described by such historians as J. D'Emilio, E. B. Freedman, A. Grossmann and L. Birken.[55] The process of liberalization and commercialization of sexuality came along with the development of a modern consumer society whose driving motor was the production and easy, frictionless satisfaction of needs – in contrast to the thrifty economizing and control of physical and intellectual drives and needs of the nineteenth century. The debates on sexual abstinence stand at the beginning – the watershed – of this process of *Modernization of Sex* that came into full flower in the second half of this century.[56]

It might be true that within this process a subtle obligation to sexuality was instituted. Pointing out some of the effects of psychoanalysis, M. Foucault might be right that 'we have been persuaded into feeling guilty of having neglected the sexus for too long'.[57] There can be no doubt that the sexological discourse has contributed to the pathologicalization and discrimination of various sexual desires and behaviour. But to regret the discourses on sexual issues portrayed here would be inappropriate and cynical. The consequences of a tabooed sexuality at that time were disastrous – the lack of free access to protective methods of contraception, abortion, the social stigmatization and discrimination of illegitimate children and pre- and extramarital sexual relationships. Foucault's pronouncement was easy to make from the standpoint of a Western European intellectual living within a relatively liberal society in the 1970s. However, enlightenment and progress are inevitably linked with just those public discourses that Foucault observed with stimulating and necessary scepticism. Of course, there is no conspiracy of oppression by the ruling authorities against the underprivileged majority such as has been constructed by some biased historians;[58] however, it is not enough to cast general suspicion on the discourse as a whole. The empirical historian has to take the trouble to make a detailed analysis of its content, different positions, motivations and intentions as well as of its intellectual and social-historical context; otherwise one is lost in Foucault's diffuse amalgamation of power and knowledge.

NOTES

1 With this question Max Marcuse, one of the protagonists of the debates analysed in this paper, entitled an article which caused considerable sensation: M. Marcuse, 'Darf der Arzt zum außerehelichen Geschlechts-Verkehr raten?', *Monatsschrift für Harnkrankheiten*, vol. 1 (1904), 266–9, 296–322.

 This chapter summarizes some of the results of the author's forthcoming thesis, 'Medizinische Debatten über sexuelle Abstinenz in Deutschland von 1900 bis 1918. Ein Beitrag zur Geschichte der Sexualwissenschaft und der Bekämpfung, von Geschlechtskrankheiten' (Institut für Medizin- und Wissenschaftsgeschichte, Prof. v. Engelhardt, Medizinische Universität Lübeck, Germany). All quotations from German primary and secondary sources have been translated into English by the author.

2 On Marcuse see T. Mayer, 'Der Sexologe Max Marcuse (1877–1963). Seine Beiträge zur Sexualwissenschaft' (Medical dissertation, Freie Universität Berlin, 1986). *Sexualprobleme* – subtitled *Zeitschrift für Sexualwissenschaft und Sexualpolitik* – was edited by Marcuse and appeared monthly from 1908 until 1914.

3 M. Marcuse, 'Das Liebesleben des deutschen Studenten', *Sexualprobleme*, 4 (1908), 667–703, p. 697.

4 Ibid., 697.

5 See, for example, L. Löwenfeld, *Sexualleben und Nervenleiden* (5th edn, Wiesbaden, 1914), vi; P. Fürbringer, 'Samenverluste', in A. Eulenburg (ed.), *Real-Encyclopädie der Gesamten Heilkunde* (4th edn, Berlin and Vienna), vol. XIII (1909), 1–16, p. 6. Fürbringer pointed out the 'unexpected abundance' of publications about sexual abstinence, in contrast to his article in the 3rd edition, vol. XI (1899), 231–46, where there is no hint of such a debate.

6 *Index-Catalogue of the Library of the Surgeon-General's Office*, 1st series, vol. XII (Washington, 1891), 960–3; 2nd series, vol. xv (Washington, 1910), 543–62.

7 Ibid., 552.

8 M. Wawerzonnek, *Implizite Sexualpädagogik in der Sexualwissenschaft 1886 bis 1939* (Cologne, 1984), 20. Apparently he refers to Germany although he does not make this explicit. Wawerzonnek's *Institut für Interdisziplinäre Sexualforschung* (Isestraße 139, D-2000 Hamburg 13, Germany) houses probably one of the world's largest private collections of publications related to sexology.

9 A. Eulenburg, *Real-Encyclopädie der gesamten Heilkunde*, 1st edn (Vienna and Leipzig, 1880–3); 2nd edn (1885–90); 3rd edn (1894–1901); 4th edn (Berlin and Vienna, 1907–27).

10 A. Eulenburg, *Sexuale Neuropathie. Genitale Neurosen und Neuropsychosen der Männer und Frauen* (Leipzig, 1895), 14.

11 G. M. Beard's influential monograph *A Practical Treatise on Nervous Exhaustion* [*Neurasthenia*]; *Its Symptoms, Nature, Sequences, Treatment* (New York, 1880) was immediately translated into German: *Die Nervenschwäche* [*Neurasthenie*]. *Ihre Symptome, Natur, Folgezustände und Behandlung* (Leipzig, 1881). Soon followed G. M.

Beard, *Die sexuelle Neurasthenie. Ihre Hygiene, Ätiologie, Symptome und Behandlung mit einem Capitel über die Diät für Nervenkranke* (Vienna, 1885). For the intellectual and social history of neurasthenia see E. Fischer-Homberger, *Hypochondrie. Melancholie bis Neurose. Krankheiten und Zustandsbilder* (Bern and Stuttgart, 1970); A. Steiner, '*Das nervöse Zeitalter*': *Der Begriff der Nervosität bei Laien und Ärzten in Deutschland und Österreich um 1900* (Zürich, 1964); M. L. Schäfer, 'Zur nosologischen Entwicklung und Wechselbeziehung von Hypochondrie und Neurasthenie', in *Die Psychologie des 20. Jahrhunderts* (Zürich, 1980); F. G. Gosling and J. M. Ray, 'The Right to be Sick. American Physicians and Nervous Patients, 1885–1910', *Journal of Social History*, 20 (1986), 251–67.

12 Ziehen, 'Neurasthenie', in A. Eulenburg (ed.), *Real-Encyclopädie der gesamten Heilkunde*, 3rd edn, vol. XVII (Vienna and Leipzig, 1898), 25–100, p. 25.

13 Richard von Krafft-Ebing, 'Ueber Neurosen und Psychosen durch sexuelle Abstinenz', *Jahrbücher für Psychiatrie*, 7 (1887), 1–6, pp. 2–3. See also R. Hauser's article on 'Krafft-Ebing's Psychological Understanding of Sexual Behaviour' in this volume (chapter 9), as well as her Ph.D. thesis, 'Sexuality, Neurasthenia and the Law: Richard von Krafft-Ebing (1840–1902)' (London University, 1992).

14 For the history of degeneration theory see G. Mann, 'Dekadenz – Degeneration – Untergangsangst im Lichte der Biologie des 19. Jahrhunderts', *Medizinhistorisches Journal*, 20 (1985), 6–35: A. Wettley, 'Zur Problemgeschichte der "dégénérescence"' *Sudhoffs Archiv für Geschichte der Medizin und der Naturwissenschaften*, 43 (1959), 193–212. For the impact of the degeneration theory on a particular disease and social problem, see W. F. Bynum, 'Alcoholism and Degeneration in 19th Century European Medicine and Psychiatry', *British Journal of Addiction*, 79 (1984), 59–70.

15 Richard von Krafft-Ebing, 'Nervosität und neurasthenische Zustände', in *Nothnagels Handbuch der speziellen Pathologie und Therapie* (Vienna, 1895), 9–16, pp. 12–13; here quoted according to Wawerzonnek, *Implizite Sexualpädagogik*, 221. An impressive collection of similar quotations is listed in S. Freud's famous article 'Die kulturelle Sexualmoral und die moderne Nervosität', *Sexualprobleme*, 4 (1908), 107–28.

16 On prostitution in Imperial Germany see for example: R. J. Evans, 'Prostitution, State and Society in Imperial Germany', *Past and Present*, 70 (1976), 106–29; R. Schulte, *Sperrbezirke. Tugendhaftigkeit und Prostitution in der bürgerlichen Welt* (Frankfurt a. M., 1979); V. Konieczka, 'Arten zu sprechen, Arten zu schweigen: Sozialdemokratie und Prostitution im deutschen Kaiserreich', in J. Geyer-Kordesch and A. Kuhn (eds.), *Frauenkörper – Medizin – Sexualität. Auf dem Wege zu einer neuen Sexualmoral* (Düsseldorf, 1986); L. S. Tschirch, 'Die Prostitution aus der Sicht deutschsprachiger medizinischer Autoren der Jahrhundertwende. Ein Beitrag zur medizinischen Vorurteilsforschung' (Medical dissertation, C. A.-Universität Kiel, 1971). See also J. R. Walkowitz, *Prostitution and Victorian Society. Women, Class, and the State* (Cambridge, 1980); A. Corbin, *Les Filles de noce. Misère sexuelle et prostitution aux 19e et 20e siècles* (Paris, 1978).

17 For a classic account of the double standard see K. Thomas, 'The Double Standard', *Journal of the History of Ideas*, 20 (1959), 195–216.

18 R. J. Evans, 'Prostitution, State and Society', 108; G. Behrend, 'Prostitution', in A. Eulenburg (ed.), *Real-Encyclopädie der gesamten Heilkunde*, 3rd edn, vol. XIX (Berlin and Vienna, 1898), 436–50, p. 446.
19 Behrend, 'Prostitution', 442.
20 F. Rühmann, 'Der Einfluß von Konzepten zur Bekämpfung der Geschlechtskrankheiten auf die gesellschaftliche Normierung der Sexualität am Beispiel der Tätigkeit der deutschen Gesellschaft zur Bekämpfung der Geschlechtskrankheiten zwischen 1900 und 1933', *Zeitschrift für Sexualforschung*, 5 (1992), 346–59, pp. 356f.
21 On the women's movement in Germany see R. J. Evans, *The Feminist Movement in Germany 1894–1933* (London, 1976); A. K. Hackett, 'The Politics of Feminism in Wilhelmine Germany, 1890–1918' (Ph. D. dissertation, Columbia University, New York, 1976); B. Greven-Aschoff, *Die bürgerliche Frauenbewegung in Deutschland 1894–1933* (Göttingen, 1981).
22 A detailed history of venereal diseases and their social impact in Germany is still lacking. See F. Rühmann, 1992. For the USA see A. M. Brandt, *No Magic Bullet. A Social History of Venereal Disease in the United States since 1880* (New York, 1985); for Canada see J. Cassel, *The Secret Plague: Venereal Disease in Canada 1838–1939* (Toronto, 1987).
23 M. Joseph, 'Allgemeine Prophylaxe der Geschlechtskrankheiten', in Nobiling-Jankau (ed.), *Handbuch der Prophylaxe* (Munich, 1901), 101.
24 A. Blaschko, 'Geschlechtskrankheiten', in A. Grotjahn and J. Kaup (eds.), *Handwörterbuch der sozialen Hygiene* (Leipzig, 1912), 397–405, pp. 399–400.
25 For an account of the scientific discoveries in this field see W. Schönfeld, *Kurze Geschichte der Dermatologie und Venerologie und ihre kulturgeschichtlichen – Spiegelung* (Hanover, 1954); Brandt, *No Magic Bullet*, 9–12.
26 Rühmann, 'Der Einfluß', 352.
27 See Rühmann, 'Der Einfluß'. The dissertation by M. Kreis, 'Die deutsche Gesellschaft zur Bekämpfung der Geschlechtskrankheiten (DGBG/GBGK) 1902 bis 1987. Ein historischer Abriß' (Universität München, 1988), is a mere compilation of dates, names, figures and lists of contents of congresses and publications – a sort of appendix – without a historical analysis. However, according to personal correspondence there is also a forthcoming thesis on this subject by A. Riesberg, Universität Münster.
28 On the ambivalence of Blaschko's as well as others' 'progressive' position in social hygiene and sexual reform, see U. Linse, 'Alfred Blaschko: Der Menschenfreund als Überwacher – Von der Rationalisierung der Syphilis-Prophylaxe zur sozialen Kontrolle', *Zeitschrift für Sexualforschung*, 2 (1989), 301–16.
29 Rühmann, 'Der Einfluß', 353–4. Rühmann is quoting J. Habermas, *Strukturwandel der Öffentlichkeit* (Berlin, 1974), 241.
30 Rühmann, 'Der Einfluß', 354.
31 Quoted, for example, in W. Waldschmidt, *Die Unterdrückung der Fortpflanzungsfähigkeit und ihre Folgen für den Organismus* (Stuttgart, 1913), 6. This medical dissertation on sexual abstinence compiled all the relevant literature and listed almost 900 titles in its impressive bibliography.
32 M. Marcuse, 'Die sexuelle Aufklärung der Abiturienten', *Sexualprobleme*, 6

(1910), 751–76, p. 773.
33. W. Erb, 'Bemerkungen über die Folgen der sexuellen Abstinenz', *Zeitschrift für Bekämpfung der Geschlechtskrankheiten (ZfBdG)*, 1 (1903), 1–18.
34. On Forel see, for example, A. Wettley, *August Forel. Ein Arztleben im Zwiespalt seiner Zeit* (Salzburg, 1953).
35. For the debates on Victorian sexuality see, for example, C. Z. and P. N. Stearns, 'Victorian Sexuality: Can Historians do it Better?', *Journal for Social History*, 18 (1985), 625–34; P. Gay, *The Bourgeois Experience*, vol. I, *Education of the Senses* (Oxford, 1984), vol. II, *The Tender Passion* (New York, 1986).
36. O. Weininger, *Geschlecht und Charakter* (1st edn, Vienna, 1903; 25th edn, 1923). On Weininger and his ideas about sexuality see C. Sengoopta, 'Science, Sexuality and Gender in the "Fin de Siècle": Otto Weininger as Baedeker', *History of Science*, 30 (1989), 249–79.
37. On M. Hirschfeld see C. Wolff, *Magnus Hirschfeld. A Portrait of a Pioneer in Sexology* (London, 1986); M. Herzer, *Magnus Hirschfeld* (Frankfurt a. M., 1992). For the vast literature on Freud and psychoanalysis see P. Gay, *Freud. A Life For Our Time* (London, 1988). It is worth mentioning that the sexual reform movement influenced Freud and psychoanalysis probably as much as vice versa.
38. On the *BfM* as well as Helene Stöcker see B. Nowacki, *Der Bund für Mutterschutz (1905–1933)* (Husum, 1983); C. Wickert, *Helene Stöcker (1869–1943). Frauenrechtlerin, Sexualreformerin und Pazifistin* (Bonn, 1991).
39. See J. Woycke, *Birth Control in Germany 1871–1933* (London, 1988).
40. For an excellent and exhaustive account, see P. Weindling, *Health, Race and German Politics between National Unification and Nazism 1870–1945* (Cambridge, 1989).
41. Marcuse, 'Darf der Arzt zum außerehelichen Geschlechts-Verkehr raten?', 306.
42. Ibid.
43. M. Marcuse, 'Sexualleben und Arbeitsleistung', *Medizinische Reform*, 19 (1911), 477–82, p. 479; see also his study on the interaction of sexuality and sport: M. Marcuse and M. Kaprolat, 'Sport und sexuelle Abstinenz', *Sexualprobleme*, 7 (1911), 231–48.
44. L. v. Wiese, 'Soziologische Betrachtungen über das Wesen der Askese', in M. Marcuse (ed.), *Archiv für Sexualforschung*, vol. I (1915), 32–42, pp. 39–40.
45. A. Neisser, 'Begrüßungsansprache', *ZfBdG*, 13 (1911), 1–7, p. 4. This volume contains all the contributions delivered at the DGBG conference in 1911.
46. A. Eulenburg, 'Die sexuelle Abstinenz und ihre Einwirkung auf die Gesundheit', *ZfBdG*, 13 (1911), 7–36, p. 36.
47. M. Marcuse, 'Nachwort zu vorstehendem Referat', *Sexualprobleme*, 7 (1911), 577–9, p. 578.
48. E. Meirowsky, 'Über das sexuelle Leben unserer höheren Schüler', *ZfBdG*, 11 (1910/11), 1–27, 41–62; E. Meirowsky and A. Neisser, 'Eine neue sexualpädagogische Statistik', *ZfBdG*, 12 (1912), 341–66, 385–404.
49. K. Touton, 'Krieg und Geschlechtskrankheiten', *Berliner Klinische Wochenschrift*, 52 (1915), 482–4, 523–6, p. 483.
50. Ibid., 524–6.
51. According to K. Touton, 'Geschlechtsleben und Geschlechtskrankheiten in

den Heeren, im Kriege und Frieden', *Berliner Klinische Wochenschrift*, 52 (1915), 56–9, p. 58.

52 See A. Grossmann, 'The New Woman, the New Family and the Rationalization of Sexuality: The Sex Reform Movement in Germany 1928 to 1933' (Doctoral thesis, New Brunswick Rutgers, State University of New Jersey, 1984); Chr. v. Soden, *Die Sexualberatungsstellen der Weimarer Republik 1919–1923* (Berlin, 1988); C. Usborne, *The Politics of the Body in Weimar Germany. Women's Reproductive Rights and Duties* (London, 1992).

53 Rühmann, 'Der Einfluß', 349.

54 P. Conrad, 'On the Medicalization of Deviance and Social Control', in D. Ingleby (ed.), *Critical Psychiatry* (New York, 1980), 112.

55 J. D'Emilio and E. B. Freedman, *Intimate Matters. A History of Sexuality in America* (New York, 1988); A. Grossmann, 'The New Woman'; L. Birken: *Consuming Desire: Sexual Science and the Emergence of a Culture of Abundance, 1871–1914* (Ithaca and London, 1989).

56 P. Robinson, *The Modernization of Sex: Havelock Ellis, Alfred Kinsey, William Masters and Virginia Johnson* (New York, 1976), 1.

57 M. Foucault, *Histoire de la sexualité*, vol. 1: *La Volonté de savoir* (Paris, 1976), translated into English from the German edition: *Sexualität und Wahrheit, I, Der Wille zum Wissen* (Frankfurt a. M., 1977), 190. The secondary literature on Foucault's history of sexuality has become vast; for a critical account see, for example, R. Porter, 'Is Foucault Useful for Understanding Eighteenth and Nineteenth Century Sexuality?', *Contention*, 1 (1991), 61–82.

58 See, for example, J. v. Ussel, *Sexualunterdrückung. Geschichte der Sexualfeindschaft* (Reinbek, 1970).

FOURTEEN

THE DEVELOPMENT OF SEXOLOGY IN THE USA IN THE EARLY TWENTIETH CENTURY

VERN L. BULLOUGH

AMERICAN sex research differed from that in England or on the continent in its concentration on basic heterosexual problems. Richard von Krafft-Ebing, Magnus Hirschfeld and Havelock Ellis all originally had major concerns with variant sexuality.[1] So did Sigmund Freud. Though a few Americans towards the end of the nineteenth century participated in such research, such as Frank Lydston,[2] the main reasons Americans started examining sexuality was because of its association with vice and crime. Even Lydston himself basically used such an approach.[3]

Generally, the American medical establishment itself was reluctant to deal with sexual issues, and when an English version of Havelock Ellis's work on sexual inversion first appeared, an American reviewer stated that Ellis was too inclined to fill his book with the 'pornographic imaginings of perverted minds rather than cold facts, and the data which are collected are seemingly of little value'.[4] John Burnham has argued that American physicians of the time refused to recognize the social aspects of sexual behaviour, and until they did, all they were willing to do was report on individual case studies from their practice.[5]

The official attitudes of American society were characterized by what has been called 'civilized morality', defined by Mark Connelly as the prescriptive system of moral and cultural values, sexual and economic roles, religious sanctions, hygienic rules and idealized behavioural patterns. The viability of such a code depended upon an

> unremitting effort to root out all opportunities for moral lapse. This understanding fueled the purity crusade of the late nineteenth century, particularly the shenanigans of Anthony Comstock and like-minded individuals who were determined to protect American society from salacious books, prostitutes, poker, and other forms of mental or physical

licentiousness. In a sense the purity crusade was an attempt to force the reality of social conditions into line with the dictates of civilized morality.[6]

Two fundamental components of this civilized morality were the conspiracy of silence[7] and the double standard.[8] Institutionalizing the enforcement of this morality was the American Purity Alliance, which had been formed in 1895 through a merger of local and state purity groups.[9] Inevitably such attitudes gave Americans doing sex research a different perspective from that existing on the continent. Few could publicly view sex as dispassionately as Havelock Ellis although they could read Ellis and gradually his ideas were influential in helping to change attitudes, particularly in the period following the First World War.

Key to developments in American sex research was prostitution, since so many 'evils' of the time which concerned the progressive reformers seemed to be related to it: exploitation of children, pornography, disease and crime.[10] Venereal disease was an especial danger since it so damaged the innocent, i.e. wives and children.[11] One of the major figures in emphasizing the dangers was Prince A. Morrow (1836–1913), a New York physician who had translated Alfred Fournier's work on syphilis and marriage into English in 1881 and followed this up with a manual on venereal disease directed towards the medical profession.[12] Prior to Morrow, physicians, when they had been concerned with prostitution and its sequelae, had usually urged that prostitutes be licensed and inspected, something that was anathema to most American reformers, including Morrow himself. It was not clear, however, what the alternatives were. In 1899, Prince attended the first of two international conferences held in Brussels to consider the public health aspects of sexually transmitted diseases. Papers at this conference confirmed Prince's concerns, namely that sexually transmitted diseases were more prevalent than was generally believed and that medical inspection of prostitutes was not effective. At the second international conference, also held in Brussels, in 1902 and which Morrow had helped organize, delegates heard alternatives to reglementation, and Prince was particularly impressed by the success of a French educational campaign to warn youth against the dangers of venereal disease and to urge infected persons to seek treatment.[13]

Convinced that, like many others issues in public health, accurate information and education were the key to dealing with the problems associated with prostitution, he set out to bring this about. In 1904 he published *Social Diseases and Marriage*, the first comprehensive scientific treatise on the subject in English.[14] In it, he wrote at great length about the effects of sexually transmitted diseases on the innocent – sterility among women, congenital blindness in infants, syphilitic insanity, chronic uterine inflammation, and general physical infirmity were all traced back to irregular sexual liaisons by husbands and fathers with prostitutes. Morrow also urged physicians in New York to join together to work to eliminate the social evil in the community. He argued that physicians needed to discuss sexual issues with their patients in order to educate them, since, as long as propriety blocked open discussion of the diseases and their transmission, sexually transmitted diseases would increase.[15]

To emphasize the public health nature of the problems, Morrow launched a social hygiene movement among the medical professionals. In 1905 he formed the Society of Sanitary and Moral Prophylaxis in New York City and within a few years similar groups had taken root across the country.[16] Morrow believed that in an ideal world sex instruction should be given at home at an early age by parents, but he also felt that the majority of parents were not qualified to give it, and that the duty therefore devolved upon teachers. Sex education, he argued, should be an integral part of the course of study in all 'normal' schools (teacher-training schools). This idea appealed not only to the American medical profession but, after some initial resistance, leaders of the American Purity Alliance agreed and in 1908 announced that sex education would be one of their objectives. Sex education, however, was conceived as a way to emphasize sexual purity for both sexes, and to eliminate the false impression instilled in the minds of young men that sexual indulgence was essential to health and that chastity was incompatible with manly vigour. Though Morrow and his followers were willing to admit that sex might well have non-procreative purposes, only husband and wife were to enjoy them and they did not form part of the public discussion.[17]

The movement gained further impetus in 1911 when the two major purity organizations, the American Purity Alliance and the American Vigilance Committee, elected the same officers. This was the first step to their organizational consolidation as the American Vigilance Association, an organization dedicated not only to fighting prostitution but to educating the young about the dangers of immorality. Separately, many of the medically oriented groups which had followed Morrow's ideas met in 1910 and elected him president of a new national organization, the American Federation for Sex Hygiene. In 1913, after Morrow's death, the two surviving organizations, medical and purity, merged formally and symbolically to form the American Social Hygiene Association.[18]

So strong was the campaign for chastity that it even carried over into treatment of soldiers in the First World War. The international moral order visualized by President Woodrow Wilson led to the portrayal of the American soldier as a knight crusading for democracy who kept himself pure for his lady by abstaining from alcohol and sex. Such ascetic dedication not only was supposed to demonstrate the soldier's allegiance to higher ideals but also avoided the taint of venereal disease.[19] President Wilson himself lent his authority to antivenereal fervour: 'The federal government has pledged its word that as far as care and vigilance can accomplish the result, the men committed to its charge will be returned to homes and communities that so generously gave them with no scars except those won in honorable conflict.'[20]

Thus, though military-controlled prostitution had long been part of the American tradition, no such activity could be contemplated or condoned under the new moral regime, and only with reluctance did the War Department establish as the last of its six-point programme for the control of venereal disease the distribution of prophylactic packages. Inevitably, the American policy proved a total failure in Europe, and the major successes against venereal diseases came from those commanders who more or less ignored official policy, which was not finally changed by orders of General Pershing until 1918.[21]

The result of the campaign for education in terms of sex research was the encouragement of what might be called sex research. It was of two types, one given considerable publicity which emphasized morality and the benefits of chastity education, and the other, underground fact-finding research, much less moralistic, which was not published and probably could not be published at that time, although it was some fifteen or twenty years later when sex had become less of a taboo subject. Undoubtedly helping bring about a change in attitudes was the more moralistic research itself. It also made it possible for the medical profession to discuss sex somewhat more openly in professional journals.

A good example of the more moralistic public sex research is a pioneering study of Max J. Exner, a physician associated with the YMCA and the Social Hygiene movement. Exner was a leading sex educator in the second decade of the twentieth century and a strong upholder of the importance of chastity. In his mind sex education was important to curb 'morbid curiosities' and erase sexuality from the consciousness of youth.[22]

Exner, though he later modified some of his moralizing, was one of the leaders in the struggle to keep the American army pure during the

First World War. Even before the United States had entered the war in 1917, he had conducted inspections of American troops involved in the war against 'Pancho' Villa on the Mexican border in 1916. He reported that the character of the military camps was 'sensualizing', with the coarse elements prevailing. In his mind, venereal disease merely represented the physical repercussions of a far more dangerous moral decay. As a result he felt it essential to raise the moral environment of the camps by removing temptations to immortality by cutting down on the sale of liquor and removing the temptations of prostitution.[23]

Exner began his study of 948 college men as an effort to demonstrate that sex education would cut down on what he called 'bad sources' of sexual information, and curtail widespread masturbation which he called 'self-abuse'. Part of his data was gathered from small-group responses to questions, mainly from those active in the YMCA in New York City. This was then supplemented by a mail sample distributed to college students in the Middle West and Pacific Coast. The questionnaire contained thirteen questions, three of which might be said to have dealt specifically with sexual practices while the rest dealt with sex education. The key question was no. 6. It asked whether the individual had ever indulged in any sexual practice at any time. Of the 531 responses to this question, 81 per cent indicated that they had, and those who did were asked in question 7 to indicate what kind of practice. Of the 518 who answered this question, 61.5 per cent 'admit having practiced self-abuse'. Some 36 per cent admitted to having 'indulged in sexual intercourse with women', while an additional 17 per cent said they had practised 'both sexual abuse and intercourse'. Two per cent had indulged 'in various perverted practices' which remained undescribed. The eighth question asked at what ages they had begun their sexual practices, and Exner found that of the 441 who answered this question, 19.7 per cent had begun before the age of 12, and an additional 62.1 per cent had begun before the age of 15, which he called the age of puberty. Between 14 and 17, an additional 32.6 per cent had begun their sexual practices, and only 5.2 per cent after the age of 17. The average age at which some form of sexual practice had first taken place was 13.4 years.

Question 9 asked whether they had received any real sex instruction and, of the 816 who answered it, 94.5 per cent said they had done so. Unfortunately, Exner concluded, the sex information had come too late in their career, with 66.9 per cent receiving it after the age of 14. In fact, the average age was 15.5 years, which he said meant they had to overcome all the misinformation. Instead, he found that most of his sample had received what he called 'bad sources of information' long before they encountered any real sex education. Most of these, 544 of the 676 who answered, had received it from boy associates, while a much smaller number, 33, had received it from girl associates, and an even smaller number, 22, from hired men, farmers or older men. Exner felt that it was very difficult to counter this bad information, which he felt led to 'self-abuse', although he recorded several cases of individuals who had been able to stop masturbating after getting the correct information about its dangers. His conclusion was that sex education emphasizing chastity and the dangers of masturbation should be incorporated very early into the school curriculum. He approved of a biological approach but insisted it emphasize that in humans the sex life had risen to a much higher level than in animals, and this made it essential to relate sex to the highest psychic and spiritual values. Thus it was important 'to create an inspiring atmosphere with reference to sex, through a true and full interpretation of its meaning'.[24] Only then would youthful chastity became a reality.

In spite of Exner's moralizing and his flawed sampling techniques, the study represents the first attempt to use a statistical approach to a study of sex.[25] It is not, however, the first basic study of sexual practices in the United States. Two such studies were initiated in the 1890s, although neither was made public until much later. One of the pioneer researchers was Clelia Mosher (1863–1940), who began her research as a graduate student at the University of Wisconsin in 1892. It grew out of a questionnaire which she had designed for a lecture on 'the marital relation' before the Mothers Club, the members of which were mostly faculty wives. Many of her questions dealt with sex, including their knowledge of sexual physiology before they were married, whether they habitually shared the same bed with their husbands, whether they had a 'venereal' orgasm, and what was considered the true purpose of sexual intercourse. All told, some forty-seven women filled out her questionnaire over the years although, after the first batch of interviews, she gathered data only sporadically from among her patients from about 1900, when she began practising medicine in Palo Alto, to 1920. Her study was not published until 1974 after Carl Degler had discovered it in the Stanford archives.[26]

Mosher found that the majority of women had known little about sex before they were married. One woman said that until she was 18 she did not even know where babies came from. Still, they learned about sex in marriage, and most shared a bed with their husbands. Thirty-five of the forty-four who answered the question said they felt a desire for sexual intercourse, and one wrote that sex was not only agreeable to her but delightful. Thirty-four of the women regularly experienced orgasm during sex and one said that when she did not have an orgasm it was depressing and revolting, while another said the absence of orgasm was 'bad, even disastrous, nervewracking'. The most detailed and personal responses were elicited by a series of questions on 'the true purpose of intercourse', and though nine believed that intercourse was a necessity for men, thirteen claimed it was a necessity for both sexes. While reproduction might be the primary purpose of sex, most (twenty-four women) believed that pleasure exchanged was a worthy purpose in itself. At least thirty of her women used some sort of contraceptive, withdrawal, douching, condoms, cocoa butter, and two used a rubber cap over the cervix. Some felt that intercourse once a month was probably enough, but most felt that it should be more often. Several of her postmenopausal women still enjoyed and desired intercourse. Thirty-three of her women were born before 1870 and of that number thirteen of them before the Civil War. The sample is not really representative of late nineteenth-century America in that 81 per cent of her sample had attended college or normal school and all were economically well-off. Most were married to college graduates. Obviously Americans were much more willing to talk about sex than the official puritanism of the day would indicate.

Another and more significant closeted researcher was the obstetrician-gynaecologist, Robert Latou Dickinson (1861–1950), who might be regarded as the founding father of much of American sex research. Though Dickinson began his research in the 1890s, most of his statistical data was not published until the early 1930s. Some of his physiological findings, however, were published earlier. One of his pioneering studies described an experiment to find out whether reported instances of the vagina gripping the penis during coitus could be confirmed by measurement of pressure exerted by contraction of the *levator ani*. He found that such contraction could be 'readily appreciated' by inserting a finger, something that any gynaecologist could do. To get a more accurate assessment, he greased a wax phallus and inserted it into the relaxed vagina of some female domestic servants who were then asked to contract the muscle firmly. These wax impressions were graphic evidence that the *levator ani* was capable of powerful gripping pressure. He also argued that the rubbing of the semen against the os, rather than sucking action by the uterus, appeared to be the usual means by which sperm reached the mucus of the cervix.[27]

He also did an early study of female masturbation, holding that it often led to the enlargement of the labia minora and hypertrophy about the meatus. Drawing on some 427 cases from his own practice, Dickinson argued that masturbation was common in women and should be recognized and treated, not hysterically denounced. He also noted that the habit by itself produced no serious pathological condition, and reported that self-massage of the pelvic floor on delivery was beneficial for most women.[28] Dickinson later saw masturbation as a normal part of sexual adjustment but in this he was influenced by Havelock Ellis.

Almost anything having to do with female physiology was liable to become the subject for an article by him. For example, some women feared that straddling a bicycle seat might be injurious to them. Dickinson held this was unlikely, although he recognized that under certain condition the bicycle saddle could foster masturbation. He held that this 'danger' could be eliminated if women learned the correct methods for pedalling and kept the bicycle saddle at the correct height and position, all of which he described in some detail.[29] He also demonstrated that the thoracic breathing patterns, so common among women, were pathological conditions caused by excessively tight corsets,[30] although he felt that anti-corset talk was a waste of his breath since women followed the fashion of the time and that the best way to deal with such a problem was to encourage the growth of gymnasiums for women and to encourage them to engage in physical exercise.[31]

Dickinson approached the discussion of sex as a 'Christian' gentleman and an orthodox physician who was rather conservative in his personal life style. He clearly was not a radical social critic, although his ideas on sex were radical. He was very much a part of the American gynaecological establishment, and usually adopted an apologetic tone in bringing up controversial topics with his colleagues. He held that it was the duty of gynaecologists to do sex counselling in order to preserve marriage, since 'no single cause of mental strain in married women is as widespread as sex fears and maladjustments'. Physicians, he believed, as did Morrow before him, were the only people with the knowledge and objectivity to save their patients from their ignorance, and in helping to save marriage, the physicians were only fulfilling their societal duties.[32]

Dickinson's reputation among his colleagues as an outstanding gynaecologist caused them to listen to him, although probably most did not follow his example. Among other things, Dickinson introduced the use of electric cautery in the treatment of cervicitis and he was among the first Americans to use aseptic ligatures for tying the umbilical cord. He also gained widespread prominence for his effectiveness as a medical teacher and was on the faculty of several medical schools and medical centres in New York. He developed a series of rubber models to teach female anatomy, and personally sculpted life-size models to show foetal growth from fertilization to birth.[33] After 1920, as he cut down on his professional practice, he became very active in the campaign for better sex education as well as that for birth control. He was probably the most prominent physician associated with the campaign for birth control and he founded the Committee on Maternal Health in 1923, which began compiling data on contraception.[34]

Probably his most significant contributions were to the study of female sexuality, although little of this was published until 1930. His data grew from his practice. Dickinson believed that the key to effective medical practice was a good patient history, and during the most active years of his gynaecological practice, 1890-1920, he did not accept a patient who had not filled out a four-page questionnaire that not only dealt with the presenting problem but included general and family history. As he examined the patients he also made drawings, at least five, of the uterus, cervix, vulva, and two illustrations of the pelvic difficulty for which they had sought his assistance. The maximum number of drawings for any one patient was sixty-one. He was a master illustrator and could sketch so rapidly that it did not prolong the patient's visit. To speed his sketches, he developed rubber stamps with printed anatomical outlines on them and, after stamping them on the chart, he sketched additional information which he coloured in crayon to add detail. Eventually he turned to photography. A fake flower-pot pedestal, installed at a strategic angle to the examining table, was 'actually a tall hollow box with a camera built in at floor level, and a hinged lid with a mirror on the other side. It stood loaded with a photographic plate, and the shutter-spring set to expose a negative . . . when a switch was pressed.'[35]

As he questioned the patients, he encouraged them to bring up sexual problems which bothered them, and he kept records of their responses. By 1923 he had data on over 5,000 cases, which he turned over to the Committee on Maternal Health. Lura Beam, a writer with a background in education and applied psychology, was called upon to make a preliminary review of the data, and she proposed publication of three books, two of which were actually published. The original 5,200 case histories were divided into two groups, one which included information on 4,000 married women, and the second on 1,200 single women. These served as source material for *A Thousand Marriages* and for *The Single Woman*. This last was based on 350 histories.

One of the advantages of Dickinson's data was that he often saw his patients at different points in their lives and could plot the changes in their attitudes on sexual issues. For example, he illustrated by a sample of thirty cases how 'passion and frigidity' could appear and disappear. At the age of 34 one of his patients became disgusted with coitus but her husband did not. Later the husband also lost interest, but after six years without an orgasm, the woman again became orgasmic and the husband and wife found it difficult to remain apart from one another.[36] The books are a mine of information. For example, he reports that the frequency of intercourse is normally two to three times a week in his married sample, but some 11 per cent had intercourse only once a year or less. He gives information on the length of the period of intromission before ejaculation, the attitudes of brides, sex knowledge of the brides, as well as on more treatment-oriented issues such as frigidity, dyspareunia, minor menstrual disturbances, sexually transmitted diseases, fertility, and such psychological issues as anxiety and fear. One of twelve of his patients in the married sample had some form of venereal disease, usually gonorrhea. It was the Dickinson findings of the changes in sexual response over the life-cycle which makes his studies particularly valuable.

Dickinson reported upon both masturbation and homosexuality in his patients. Interestingly, he found that relatively more married women than single women reported masturbating. He also found that twenty-eight individuals in his sample of single women were involved in some sex relations. When he first saw such women, Dickinson assumed that they might be more masculine than other women, but he soon found this was not the case. Many returned to him over the years and he reported that twenty-seven of those who had lesbian experiences later married and their fertility was normal. Some 12 per cent of his married women had heterosexual intercourse before marriage, and half of those who did so either became pregnant or were infected with a venereal disease.

Dickinson, whose work has often been overlooked by later generations, proved to be innovative in his research in almost every way. He was very much interested in the physiology of intercourse, which had first been studied by Felix Roubaud in the 1870s.[37] Along with W. F. Robie and LeMon Clark, Dickinson was responsible for the introduction of the electrical vibrator or massager, a device producing intense erotic stimulation and even orgasm in some women who previously had been unable to reach climax. It was Dickinson's theory that once a woman had achieved an orgasm, even with a vibrator applied to her genitals, she was more likely to proceed to orgasm during coitus or through digital masturbation. Dickinson also used a glass tube resembling an erect penis in size and shape to observe the behaviour of the vaginal lining and cervix during orgasm. In the process he proved once and for all that female orgasms involved physiological changes in the vagina and cervix.[38]

Though most of the Moser and Dickinson research had been gathered before the First World War, it quite clearly was deemed by both authors to be unpublishable at that time. Proper people did not talk about such things, and the official emphasis was on chastity education. The key to the change in terms of published research was John D. Rockefeller, Jr. Though both he and his father had paid for Christian programmes to help young people maintain high standards of conduct through the YMCA and YWCA, and John D. Jr had been active in the campaign to eliminate prostitution and disease, he gradually came to realize that there was too much that was unknown to deal effectively with such problems. In 1911 he funded the Bureau of Social Hygiene, which grew out of his contact with Katherine Bement Davis (1860–1935). Davis, an adviser to the Bureau, had come to the attention of Rockefeller through her position as warden of the Reformatory for Women at Bedford Hills, a position to which she had been appointed shortly after receiving her Ph.D. from the University of Chicago in 1900. Many of the women in the institution had been prostitutes and, as warden, Davis emphasized education and rehabilitation. Concerned that employment opportunities for poor and working-class women were too often restricted to domestic service, Davis attempted to assist inmates learn a trade, introducing a steam laundry and hat-making shop for this purpose. Since the state budget sometimes proved erratic and insufficient, Davis put her female charges to work renovating the grounds and running the physical plant. Inmates could be found mixing concrete, laying building foundations, grading lawns, cutting ice, and even slaughtering pigs.[39]

Davis believed that with respectable employment and adequate learning, the women could return to society without further danger of law-breaking. She likened her reformatory to an educational institution and often referred to the prison's former inmates as graduates.[40] She also developed a programme to identify different types of offenders and to separate the potentially reformable from the more hardened or irreclaimable. This programme led her to recommend that an offender be studied by experts after being convicted but before being sentenced, a subject on which she wrote a pamphlet.

In 1911, her pamphlet outlining her ideas came to the attention of

John D. Rockefeller, Jr, who, after conferring with Davis, bought land adjacent to the Bedford Hills Reformatory and set up the Laboratory of Social Hygiene under her direction in 1912.[41]

Like his father, John D. Rockefeller, Jr, was convinced that the way to deal with any problem was to gather data and establish a plan of action, after which the solution would appear more or less obvious. What was needed first was the information, and the plan for gathering data was provided by Davis, both with the new laboratory and with the Bureau of Social Hygiene. Through the Bureau, of which Davis was a key member, a number of significant studies of prostitution were carried out over the next half-dozen years. Davis was instrumental in setting these studies in motion and after 1917, as the salaried director of the Bureau of Social Hygiene, in seeing that they were carried through. The Bureau commissioned George J. Kneeland, who had directed the Chicago Vice Commission, to undertake a study of prostitution in New York City.[42] This was followed by studies of prostitution in Europe by Abraham Flexner, a study of European police systems by Raymond B. Fosdick, and a study of prostitution in the United States by Howard Woolston.[43] Davis wrote a chapter in Kneeland's book about the prostitutes committed to her reformatory, and she delayed publication of the Woolston book for several years while she made several revisions. She actively maintained contacts in Europe to assist with the European studies.

Gradually, under her leadership, the Bureau of Social Hygiene became interested in other areas of sexual behaviour, and Rockefeller, Jr, himself became less noticeably involved, perhaps because he had realized that there were no easy solutions to the problems of prostitution. Early in the spring of 1920, Max J. Exner, at the time director of the Department of Educational Activities at the American Social Hygiene Association, tried to persuade Davis to serve as coordinator of a study on the sex life of women which was to be somewhat similar to his own study of men. Davis agreed on the desirability of such a study but believed she needed to consult women physicians about its feasibility. Her correspondents concluded that such a study was needed but opposed the involvement of the YWCA in the project, an involvement proposed by Exner. Exner simply encouraged her to go ahead. Davis then formed a committee to study the sex lives of 5,000 women subject to the approval of John D. Rockefeller, Jr.[44]

Rockefeller not only agreed to her project but made an initial appropriation of $2,000 towards it at a Bureau meeting,[45] and gave financial support in succeeding years until the project was complete.

This marked a departure from the earlier activities of the Bureau of Social Hygiene but one that was a logical extension of its activities. The expansion of interest is clearly indicated when Davis eventually extended her study to include a section on lesbian women,[46] a fact specifically mentioned in the minutes at various times.

The data for the Davis study were drawn from responses to questionnaires – eight pages for married women and twelve pages for the unmarried women, two of which were taken up with definitions. To obtain her subjects, names of women were drawn from alumnae registers of leading women's colleges. A preliminary letter asking for cooperation was originally sent to 20,000 women and the final questionnaire was sent only to those who replied that they were willing to answer the questions. When the answers to the questions from 2,200 respondents were tabulated, it was decided that they needed interpretation, and so Davis went far beyond what had originally been conceived, and did explanatory studies around topics such as the use of contraceptives, frequency of intercourse, the happiness of the married women in terms of general factors of their sex life, in particular autoerotic practices, the periodicity of sex desire, and the prevalence of lesbianism in both samples. About half of the women in the study, both married and unmarried, reported experiencing 'intense emotional relations with women', but the number giving these feelings overt sexual expression was less than 200, a smaller percentage than Kinsey later found.

In spite of her willingness to explore sexual topics, Davis retained some of the reticence about sexuality so common among women of her time. She reported not being surprised to find that a large number of her subjects had 'engaged in various erotic practices', but she did not go on to elaborate what these were.[47] She did, however, discuss masturbation. Some 64.8 per cent of her unmarried college women admitted to masturbating at some time although only 40.1 per cent of her married sample did.[48] Among her married sample, only 71 individuals had sexual intercourse prior to marriage. The vast majority, on the other hand, used some form of contraceptive after marriage (730) and most of those who did not use it themselves approved of the idea in principle. Some 9.3 per cent of the married women had at least one induced abortion, and one had eight such abortions.[49] Of those women she classed as highly erotic, she found that a much higher percentage had received instruction from what she called responsible sources before they were 14. She also found that women who desired intercourse more frequently than they engaged in it with their husband were more likely to be unhappy than where the wives and husbands agreed on the frequency. The mode of greatest frequency was in the once or twice a week category.[50]

Exner, undiscouraged by Davis's decision to do her research on her own, helped push Davis and the Bureau even further into the area of sex research. In 1920 he had hired a young psychology graduate student from Clark University, Earl F. Zinn, as co-ordinator of questionnaires on research projects carried out by the American Social Hygiene Association. Zinn made a series of proposals to Exner about the future of sex research which Exner took to Katharine Bement Davis in 1920, and which, after some modifications suggested by Davis, led to the acceptance of the idea by Rockefeller and the Bureau of Social Hygiene Board. Conscious of the possible consequences to the Bureau of greater involvement in sex research, some of those consulted by Rockefeller and Davis suggested that the research be under the direction of the National Research Council (NRC) even though they would be funded through the Bureau.[51]

Established in 1916 by the National Academy of Sciences to co-ordinate research funding during the First World War, the National Research Council continued to function after the war as a conduit for research funds and projects. Since the Rockefeller Foundation and other Rockefeller groups supported projects of the NRC in other areas, it seemed natural to turn to it to obtain respectability for the new kind of sex research that Zinn and Davis now proposed, namely a systematic and comprehensive research into sex in 'its individual and social manifestations, the prime purpose being to evaluate conclusions now held and to increase our body of scientifically derived data'.[52]

Ultimately, after considerable negotiation, the medical committee of the National Research Council agreed to the project, and a Committee for Research on Sex Problems (CRSP) was set up with an initial budget of $50,000, and this quickly grew much larger.[53] This marked a radical change in the nature of American sex research and led rather quickly to American pre-eminence in the fields it funded. For the most part in its early years, however, the committee refused to fund grants in the kind of social science research which had so far been carried out and instead concentrated much of its early funding on physiology in general and endocrinology in particular.[54] In fact there was a reluctance of the committee in its early years to fund research with the word 'sex' in the title unless it dealt with animals, an indication of the continuation of the American anxieties about sex. The CRSP also refused to carry out any contraceptive research.

The best example of the initial hesitation of the committee to deal with the kind of topics that Davis and Dickinson were already working on is their reaction to the proposed research into sex and marriage by Gilbert V. Hamilton, a New York physician with special training in psychology. Though the five-member committee found it worthy, it refused to support it. Katharine Bement Davis, convinced of its value, managed to have it supported directly by the Bureau of Social Hygiene, of which she was also executive director.

Hamilton studied some 200 married persons, 100 males and 100 females (including 55 married couples), most of them either patients of New York City psychiatrists or friends of such patients. Each subject was examined privately in Hamilton's consulting-rooms and as part of the examination was presented with questions on typed cards, 372 for women who had been pregnant, 357 for those who had not been pregnant, and 334 for all men. Though the questions were presented in typed forms, clients were encouraged to talk out their answers in give-and-take conversations which were taken down word for word without comment. The interviews varied in length from slightly more than two hours to more than thirty. Among other findings Hamilton reported the occurrence of multiple orgasm in some females.[55] Though his findings were an important indicator of what Alfred Kinsey later found, namely a wider range of sexual activity among white, married, college-educated men and women than had been assumed, they were more or less ignored by the scientific community. One reason for this was that an 'undue' number (21 per cent) of the subjects had been upset enough to have needed psychiatric help prior to their participation in the study.[56] Though Hamilton modelled his questionnaire on that used by Davis and had many similar findings, his subjects seem to reflect far more marital unhappiness than those of Davis. His subjects also demonstrated greater sexual variety than hers, but this might be because the interview nature of data-gathering allowed for deeper probing than the use of a mail questionnaire. Interestingly, Hamilton was not allowed to identify the Bureau of Social Hygiene as the source of funding for his project, but could only refer to a 'group of scientific men' which had acted as adviser to his research.[57]

Havelock Ellis, in surveying American sex research in 1931, held that the investigations of Davis, Hamilton and Dickinson (he did not know about Mosher and did not mention Exner) represented a breakthrough in sex research in that they dealt with 'sex relationships among fairly normal people, on a sufficiently large and systematic scale to be treated statistically'.[58] He added that he had long ago realized that there was no rigid rule of normality, and that in reality there was a wide natural range of variations which could be legitimately admitted within the range of normality, and it was the American investigators who had begun to examine this.

With the publication of the studies of Dickinson, Davis and Hamilton, the emphasis on purity and chastity which had been such an important factor in what passed for sex research was being replaced by descriptive studies, increasingly free of the type of moralizing present in the earlier ones. It is worthy of comment that Exner, the exemplar of these traditional ideas, helped usher in the new age, and the Bureau of Social Hygiene, which had started in an effort to deal with the 'social evil', ended up not only establishing American sex research on a much stronger financial basis than it had anywhere else at the time, but also on a more scientific one. Ultimately it was the Committee for Research on Sex Problems which funded Alfred Kinsey, but that came about after Katharine Bement Davis had retired from the committee, and when the committee itself began to feel more comfortable about supporting the kind of studies which previously had been left to the Bureau of Social Hygiene under her leadership. Finally, it deserves mention that the key figure in pushing American sex research in these new directions was a woman, Katharine Bement Davis, and she, in retrospect, was one of those most responsible for helping change opinions about female sexuality since she also helped fund the publication of Dickinson's work. The foundation she had laid rapidly expanded in the 1930s although the money for it came directly from the Rockefeller Foundation itself and not the Bureau of Social Hygiene, which ceased such funding shortly after her retirement. Still the conduit for funding remained the Committee for Research on Sex Problems.

NOTES

1 Richard von Krafft-Ebing, *Psychopathia sexualis* (Stuttgart: Enke, 1886). The first edition of this was only 110 pages and subsequent editions went over 400 pages. The last he personally supervised was the 12th edn, 1903. Magnus Hirschfeld [Theodor Ramien], *Sappho und Sokrates* (Leipzig: Max Spohr, 1896); Havelock Ellis and John Addington Symonds, *Das konträre Geschlechtsgefühl* (Leipzig: Georg Wigand, 1896). For more on this see Vern L. Bullough, *Science in the Bedroom: A History of Modern Sex Research* (New York: Basic Books, 1994).
2 A good example is G. Frank Lydston, 'Lecture on Sexual Perversion, Satyriasis and Nymphomania', a 22-page undated reprint from the *Philadelphia Medical and Surgical Reporter* (reprinted Chicago, 1889?).
3 G. Frank Lydston, *The Diseases of Society: The Vice and Crime Problem* (Philadelphia: J. B. Lippincott, 1905).
4 An anonymous review which appeared in the *American Journal of Insanity*, 59 (1902), 82.
5 John Burnham, 'Early References to Homosexual Communities in American Medical Writings', *Medical Aspects of Human Sexuality*, 7 (1973) 36.

6 Mark Thomas Connelly, *The Response to Prostitution in the Progressive Era* (Chapel Hill; University of North Carolina Press, 1980), 8–9.
7 See John C. Burnham, 'The Progressive Era Revolution in American Attitudes Toward Sex', *Journal of American History*, 59 (1973), 885–908.
8 Keith Thomas, 'The Double Standard', *Journal of the History of Ideas*, 20 (1959), 195–216.
9 See David Pivar, *Purity Crusade, Sexual Morality, and Social Control. 1868–1900* (Westport, Conn.: Greenwood Press, 1973).
10 There is a vast literature on this. See Vern L. Bullough, Barret Elcano, Margaret Deacon and Bonnie Bullough, *Bibliography of Prostitution* (New York: Garland Publishers, 1977), and for the continuing fascination with it see Vern L. Bullough and Lilli Sentz, *Prostitution: A Guide to Sources 1960–1990* (New York: Garland, 1992). See also Vern Bullough and Bonnie Bullough, *Women and Prostitution* (Buffalo: Prometheus Books, 1987), 232–8.
11 See, for example, L. Duncan Bulkley, *Syphilis in the Innocent [Syphilis Insontium], Clinically and Historically Considered with a Plan for the Legal Control of the Disease* (New York: Bailey and Fairchild, 1894). For a detailed overall study see Allan M. Brandt, *No Magic Bullet: A Social History of Venereal Disease in the United States Since 1880* (New York: Oxford University Press, 1985).
12 Alfred Fournier, *Syphilis and Marriage*, trans. Prince Albert Morrow (New York: Appleton, 1881); Prince A. Morrow, *Venereal Memoranda: A Manual for the Student and Practitioners* (New York: W. Wood, 1885).
13 *Conférence internationale pour la prophylaxie de la syphilis et des maladies vénériennes* (Brussels; H. Lansarten, vol. I, 1899; vol.II, 1902). See also Charles Walter Clarke, *Taboo: The Story of the Pioneers of Social Hygiene* (Washington, D.C.: Public Affairs Press, 1961), 49–63.
14 Prince Morrow, *Social Diseases and Marriage: Social Prophylaxis* (New York: Lea Brothers, 1904).
15 Clark, *Taboo*, 57–9; John D'Emilio and Estelle B. Freedman, *Intimate Matters* (New York: Harper and Row, 1988), 204–7.
16 Burnham, 'Progressive Era Revolution', 885–908; see also James F. Gardner, Jr, 'Microbes and Morality: The Social Hygiene Crusade in New York City 1892–1917' (Ph. D. dissertation, Indiana University, 1973), chapter 3.
17 Bryan Strong, 'Ideas of the Early Sex Education Movement in America, 1890–1920', *History of Education Quarterly*, 12 (1972), 129–61.
18 Burnham, 'Progressive Era,' *passim*; Brandt, *No Magic Bullet*, 38; Connelly, *Response to Prostitution*, *passim*; Ruth Rosen, *The Lost Sisterhood: Prostitution in America, 1900–1918* (Baltimore: Johns Hopkins University Press, 1982); Gardner, *Microbes and Morality*, *passim*.
19 Brandt, *No Magic Bullet*, 96.
20 Quoted by Edwin Frank Allen, *Keeping Our Fighters Fit* (New York, 1918), 1.
21 Brandt, *No Magic Bullet*, 96–121.
22 Max J. Exner, 'Sex Education in the Colleges and Universities', *Journal of the Society for Sanitary and Moral Prophylaxis*, 6 (October 1915), 131–3.
23 M. J. Exner, 'Prostitution in its Relation to the Army on the Mexican Border', *Social Hygiene*, 3 (April 1917), 202–11.
24 M. J. Exner, *Problems and Principles of Sex Education: A Study of 948 College Men* (New York: Association Press, 1915). I was unable to consult the original but

did see a reprint of the pamphlet, which said it was unchanged from the original published by the Association Press in 1922.

25 Alfred Kinsey, Wardell B. Pomeroy and Clyde E. Martin, *Sexual Behavior in the Human Male* (Philadelphia: W. B. Saunders Co., 1938), 499, also labelled it as the first statistical study but reported it was badly flawed. Kinsey felt that Exner reported such low figures for masturbation that the study represented a failure to obtain the facts but I am not sure Kinsey saw the original, since the figures as indicated above were very high.

26 Mosher later became a faculty member at Stanford and her findings were found by Carl Degler, a Stanford historian, in vol. 10 of her unpublished works in the Stanford archives; see Carl Degler, 'What Ought to Be and What Was: Women's Sexuality in the Nineteenth Century', *American Historical Review*, 79 (December 1974), 1467–90. The complete survey was published as Clelia Duel Mosher, *The Mosher Survey: Sexual Attitudes of Forty Five Victorian Women*, ed. James Mahood and Kristine Wenburg (New York: Arno Press, 1980). Though most of the women were born in the last half of the nineteenth century, the Degler title was somewhat of a misnomer, and he claimed far more for the findings than he should have done. Two other major surveys reported in this study included women born before 1900 and were much more comprehensive, although none of the others had women born before the Civil War.

27 R. L. Dickinson, 'Studies of the *Levator ani* Muscle', *American Journal of Obstetrics*, 22 (1889), 259–61.

28 Robert Latou Dickinson, 'Hypertrophies of the Labia Minora and their Significance', *American Gynecology*, 1 (1902), 225–54.

29 Robert Latou Dickinson, 'Bicycling for Women from the Standpoint of the Gynecologist', *American Journal of Obstetrics*, 31 (1895), 33.

30 Robert Latou Dickinson, 'The Corset: Questions of Pressure and Displacement', *New York Medical Journal*, 46 (1887), 507–16.

31 This is based upon the statement of his oldest daughter, Dorothy Dickinson Barbour, to Reed, *Private Vice, Public Virtue*, 159. The professional papers of Dickinson are in the Countway Library of Medicine, located in the Harvard Medical School, Boston. Also included there are two documents, 'Incidents in a Happy Life', a 26-page transcript of Dickinson's reminiscences recorded in December 1949 while Dickinson was visiting his daughter and son-in-law, George Barbour, in Cincinnati in December 1949. There is also a manuscript biography of Dickinson by the Barbours covering the period to about 1900. A bibliography of Dickinson's writings can be found in the New York Academy of Medicine Bibliography Department. It was compiled in June 1953.

32 Robert Latou Dickinson, 'Marital Maladjustment: The Business of Preventive Gynecology', *Long Island Medical Journal*, 2 (1908), 1–4.

33 He wrote up his use of models in Robert Latou Dickinson, 'The Application of Sculpture to Practical Teaching in Obstetrics', *American Journal of Obstetrics and Gynecology*, 40 (1940), 662–70.

34 Among his early book-length studies was his co-editorship of the *American Text Book of Obstetrics*, ed. James C. Cameron, Edward P. Davis, Richard C. Norris and Robert L. Dickinson (Philadelphia: W. B. Saunders, 1895; 2nd edn,

1902). Most of his important book-length studies in human sexuality were published after his retirement: R. L. Dickinson and Lura Beam, *A Thousand Marriages* (Baltimore: Williams and Wilkins, 1931); R. L. Dickinson, *Control of Conception* (Baltimore: Williams and Wilkins, 1931); idem, *Human Sex Anatomy* (Baltimore: Williams and Wilkins, 1933; 2nd edn, 1949); R. L. Dickinson and Lura Beam, *The Single Woman* (Baltimore: Williams and Wilkins, 1934); and R. L. Dickinson, *Birth Atlas* (New York: Maternity Center Association, 1940).

35 Quoted from the Barbour papers, by Reed, *Private Vice, Public Virtue*, 156.
36 Dickinson and Beam, *A Thousand Marriages*, 420.
37 Felix Roubaud, *Traité de l'impuissance et de la stérilité chez l'homme et chez la femme*, 2nd edn (Paris: J. B. Baillière and Son, 1876).
38 Dickinson, *Human Sex Anatomy*, 2nd edn, chapter 7, p. 93, fig. 55, 67, 142, 145, 146.
39 For an account of her work at Bedford Hills see Estelle B. Freedman, *Their Sisters' Keepers* (Ann Arbor: University of Michigan Press, 1981), 134, and passim. See also Eugenia C. Lekkerkerker, *Reformatories for Women in the United States* (The Hague: J. B. Wolter, 1931), 105. Davis herself also wrote about this aspect in Katharine Bement Davis, 'The Fresh Air Treatment for Moral Disease', *Proceedings of the Annual Congress of the National Prison Association of the United States*, 1905 and idem, 'Outdoor Work for Women Prisoners', *Proceedings of the National Conference of Charities and Corrections*, 1909.
40 There is a brief biography of her by Ellen Fitzpatrick in *Katharine Bement Davis, Early Twentieth-Century American Women, and the Study of Sex Behavior*, ed. Ellen Fitzpatrick (New York: Garland, 1987). I rely on it for some information.
41 For a first-hand account of the Laboratory, see Davis's introduction to Jean Weidensall, *The Mentality of the Criminal Woman* (Baltimore, Md. Warwick York, 1916), ix–xiv. Weidensall was appointed by Davis to be director of the laboratory and before it closed in 1918, it had undertaken studies of some 761 women at six institutions. One of the purposes had been to find the causes of prostitution but no one or two 'outstanding' causes of prostitution were isolated. Davis herself had left Bedford Hills in 1914 to be Commissioner of Corrections for all of New York City's prisons, a first for a woman.
42 George Kneeland, *Commercialized Prostitution in New York City* (New York: Century, 1913).
43 Abraham Flexner, *Prostitution in Europe* (New York: Century, 1913); Raymond B. Fosdick, *European Police Systems* (New York: Century, 1915), and *American Police Systems* (New York: Century, 1921), and H. B. Woolston, *Prostitution in the United States* (New York: Century, 1921).
44 Katharine Bement Davis to John D. Rockefeller, Jr, 23 April 1920, Rockefeller Family Archives, Rockefeller Boards, Bureau of Social Hygiene, Record Group II (Rockefeller Foundation Archives, Pocantico Hills, North Tarrytown, New York). All future references to manuscripts are from the Rockefeller archives. I have been unable to locate any separate papers of Davis although her period with the Bureau is well covered in the Rockefeller archives.
45 John D. Rockefeller, Jr, to Katharine Bement Davis, 16 October 1920, Rockefeller Family Archives, Rockefeller Boards, Record Group III.
46 The eventual study was Katharine Bement Davis, *Factors in the Sex Life of*

Twenty-two Hundred Women (New York: Harper and Brothers, 1929).
47 Ibid., xvi.
48 Ibid., 152-3.
49 Ibid., 15-21.
50 Ibid., 62-94.
51 See Vern L. Bullough, 'Katharine Bement Davis, Sex Research, and the Rockefeller Foundation', *Bulletin of the History of Medicine*, 61 (1988), 74-89; 'The Rockefellers and Sex Research', *Journal of Sex Research*, 21 (1985), 113-25. See also S. D. Aberle and G. W. Corner, *Twenty-five Years of Sex Research: History of the National Research Council for Research in the Problems of Sex, 1922-47* (Philadelphia: Saunders, 1953).
52 See Earl F. Zinn, 'History, Purpose, and Policy of the National Research Council's Committee for Research on Sex Problems', *Mental Hygiene*, 8 (1924), 94-105.
53 The various stages of the proposal and its progress are in various sections of the Rockefeller archives. See M. J. Exner to John D. Rockefeller, Jr, 7 June 1921 in Rockefeller Family Archives, Rockefeller Boards, Record Group II, and summary note of John D. Rockefeller to Katharine Bement Davis, 23 June 1921, Bureau of Social Hygiene, Minutes, Series 1, Box 3, Rockefeller Archives. 'Request for an Appropriation of $20,000 to the Bureau of Social Hygiene to be Used in Promoting the Working Out of a Plan for Research in the Field of Sex', Rockefeller Family Archives, Rockefeller Boards, Record Group I; Exhibit B, dated 28 October 1921, Conference on Sex Problems, in Rockefeller Family Archives, Rockefeller Boards, Record Group II; Vernon Kellogg, Permanent Secretary, National Research Council, to John D. Rockefeller, 25 March 1922, Rockefeller Family Archives, Rockefeller Boards, Record Group II.
54 For this aspect of American sex research see Aberle and Corner, *Twenty-five Years, passim*, and Vern L. Bullough, *Science in the Bedroom*.
55 Gilbert V. Hamilton, *A Research in Marriage* (New York: A. C. Boni, 1929), 154-5.
56 This is what Kinsey said in Alfred Kinsey, W. Pomeroy and C. Martin, *Sexual Behavior in the Human Male* (Philadelphia: W. B. Saunders, 1948), 25-6.
57 Earl F. Zinn to G. V. Hamilton, 28 May 1928, Bureau of Social Hygiene, Series 3, Box 9.
58 This is in his introduction to Dickinson and Beam, *A Thousand Marriages*, vii.

FIFTEEN

SIGMUND FREUD AND THE SEXOLOGISTS:
A SECOND READING

SANDER L. GILMAN

CERTAINLY one of the most valuable contributions of Frank Sulloway's study of Freud and the biological thought of the nineteenth century was to position Freud within the debates about the meaning and nature of sexuality.[1] Freud was indebted to the sexologists – those professional students of human sexuality, most of them physicians, most of them involved in the definition, identification, treatment of the pathological aspects of human sexuality, as defined by late-nineteenth-century legal codes. Whether it was the radical reinterpreters of sexual pathology, such as Havelock Ellis or Magnus Hirschfeld, or the more conservative commentators on the topic, such as Albert Moll, Freud positioned himself carefully in regard to them. And yet Freud was also careful to position himself in terms of the other great charge, one which Sulloway did not address, of the discussions of the special associations of the racial definition of the Jew and the Jew's (especially the Jewish male's) deviant sexuality.

In the *fin-de-siècle* medical literature there is a clear association of the Jew with sexual crimes, with criminal perversions. This is an ancient topos which harks back to Tacitus's description of the Jews as the 'projectissima ad libidinem gens' – the most sensual of peoples. By the close of the nineteenth century it had become part of the new forensic literature in Germany which described the nature of the Jew; as it was stated in one of the standard forensic studies of the time: 'Further it must be noted that the sexuality of the Semitic race is in general powerful, yes, often greatly exaggerated.'[2] Or, as John S. Billings, the leading American student of Jewish illness and the head of the Surgeon General's Library in Washington, noted, when Jewish males are integrated into Western culture they 'are probably more addicted to ... sexual excesses than their ancestors were'.[3] The physiognomy of the 'sexual' male is 'dark' (Biérent), or has a 'dark complexion' (Bouchereau), or has 'brown skin' and 'long noses'

(Mantegazza).⁴ Jewish physicians of the period understood the implications of this charge. The Viennese Jewish physician Hanns Sachs, who was involved in the earliest development of psychoanalysis, commented in his memoirs on this version of the 'timeworn prejudice that the Jewish . . . mind was abnormally preoccupied with matters of a sexual nature'.⁵ Some Jewish scientists of the *fin de siècle*, such as the Munich neurologist Leopold Löwenfeld, were forced to confront this charge and were unable to dismiss it. He argued, in a study of sexual constitution published in 1911, that the role of racial predisposition in structuring the sexual drives can be confused by the mediating role which climate, nutrition or culture can play.⁶ But he, and his Jewish contemporaries such as Iwan Bloch, have no doubt that racial identity does play some role in structuring sexual constitution. Freud's Jewish lodge brother and one of the original members of the Viennese Psychoanalytic Society, Eduard Hitschmann, believed that 'neuroses, psychoses, suicides, etc. play a more important role among the Jews, . . . they have many more sexual experiences than others and – a fact that must be particularly emphasized – take them much more seriously'.⁷ The Jews' mental states, specifically the psychopathologies associated with the Jews, are closely linked to their intense sexuality.

In terms of the medical world of the *fin de siècle* the criminality of the Jew was also a major factor in understanding the Jew's sexuality. The discussion about the nature of Jew and the Jew's relationship to the world of antisocial activity became a central theme in the medical literature of the late nineteenth century. The statistical evidence of forensic psychiatry argued for a greater rate of criminality, in some specific spheres, among the Jews. Such activity was read as being not only sociopathic but also psychopathic; it was a sign of the degeneracy of the Jews because of their endogamous marriages and the resultant inbreeding.⁸ The etiology for the Jew's hysteria, for example, like the hysteria of the woman, was to be sought in 'sexual excess'.⁹ Specifically in the inbreeding within this endogenous group: 'Being very neurotic, consanguineous marriages among Jews cannot but be detrimental to the progeny.'¹⁰ This view was even advocated by Rudolf Virchow, whose liberal views on Jewish acculturation were paralleled by his sense of the dangers of Jewish consanguinity.¹¹ Virchow pointed out the much greater occurrence of inherited diseases among the Jews. Such dangerous marriages were labelled as a criminal activity, even when such 'inbreeding' was not consanguineous. In historical terms, writers such as Houston Stewart Chamberlain could comment on the origin of the Jews and its 'refreshingly artless expression in the genealogies of the Bible, according to which some of these races owe their origin to incest, while others are descended from harlots'.[12] This was answered, at least in the data gathered by Jewish social scientists and their medical allies, in the claim that either the totality of the image presented was incorrect and correct statistical data could be amassed or that a higher incidence could be found but only for certain crimes (usually economic ones) or among specific subsets (such as Eastern Jews).[13] These were linked in the view that the 'destructive impact of certain professions (such as that of the stock market speculator) on the nerves predisposed individuals to commit sexual crimes'.[14] What is most striking is that the counter-argument, the Jewish 'immunity' from sexual crimes, such as incest, was stressed by other groups.[15] Such immunity was often read as a form of latent criminality, a hidden disposition which was simply not triggered because of the sexual barriers erected by Jewish religious practices. This literature must be set against the ubiquitous charge of Jewish criminal sexuality which haunted European culture of the *fin de siècle*.

The face of the Jew and that of the criminal as sexual criminal had merged in the course of the *fin de siècle* in the portrayal of 'Jack the Ripper' as an Eastern European Jew.[16] The charge was made in 1894 in the anti-Semitic newspapers in Germany, that Jack was an Eastern European Jew functioning as part of the 'International Jewish conspiracy'.[17] This image of the Jewish Jack the Ripper rested on a long association of the image of the Eastern Jew in the West with the image of the mutilated, diseased, different appearance of the genitalia. It is especially in the image of the Eastern Jew as criminal (as described in Western literature) that this view seems to be fixed. The overall medical view is that Jews in the East demonstrate a higher incidence of criminal insanity than do Western Jews. While Eastern Jews argue that they actually evidence a lower rate of criminality,[18] the overall assumption among Western forensic scientists, both Jews and non-Jews, is that the Eastern Jew is dangerous. Rafael Becker reporting from a Jewish mental hospital near Warsaw notes that 13 per cent of the mental patients examined for their legal competency were Jews.[19] In Vienna the legal attempt to identify those who were not German 'by race or language' during the early 1930s led to an on-going representation of the Eastern Jews in Austria as the source of all criminality, including sexual crimes.[20] The theme of the criminality of the Eastern Jew continued into the Nazi period. Joachim Duckart documented the history of a 'criminal community' of Eastern Jews back into the eighteenth century.[21] Though it has been argued that Jews, especially Eastern Jews, presented an overwhelming majority of those individuals involved in sexual commerce in Europe and South

America from the 1880s through the beginning of the 1930s, the image of the Jew as sexual criminal in the medical and forensic debates of the *fin de siècle* rests on the special, sexualized nature of the Jew.[22] It is the debate about race which taints all other views of the social reality of the period.

Within the major psychoanalytic work dealing with criminality, a study written by the Berlin psychoanalyst Franz Alexander and the jurist Hugo Staub in 1929, there is absolutely no mention of the Jewish predisposition for any type of crime.[23] Indeed, race has completely vanished as a category of analysis. Only 'idiots, paretics, schizophrenics, and epileptics' are considered under the label of those criminals showing a 'biological etiology' for crime. All other crimes are committed either by neurotics, whose unresolved Oedipal complex provides the psychological basis for their acts, or by 'normal' criminals, whose acts are examples of the weakness of character deformed by a negative social context. Alexander and Staub actually evoke all of the rhetoric about the Jewish criminal – on all sides of the issue – but in completely removing the category of race from their analysis, they make criminality a universal rather than a racial activity. Sexuality becomes the hallmark of the neurotic criminal with his unresolved Oedipus complex; inheritance, the sign of the 'born criminal' suffering from mental deficiency or impairment, and the social milieu marks the 'normal' criminal. The authors do not create a nosology of crime. They do not place any group in a special relationship to any of these categories. In doing so they avoid all of the debates about the special status of the Jews in relationship to the world of sexuality and crime.

The Jew remains the representation of the male as outsider, the act of circumcision marking the Jewish male as sexually apart, as anatomically different. For *fin-de-siècle* medicine madness was marked not only on the face but also on the genitalia. In the case of the signs of mental degeneration 'precisely the anomalies of the genitalia are of extreme importance and are rarely found alone'.[24] The prostitute was the embodiment of the degenerate and diseased female genitalia in the nineteenth century.[25] From the standpoint of the normative perspective of the European middle class, it is natural that the Jew and the prostitute, Jack and his victims, must be in conflict and that the one 'opens up' the Other, as they are both seen as 'dangers' to the economy, both fiscal and sexual, of the state.[26] This notion of the association of the Jew and the prostitute is also present in the image of 'spending' semen (in an illicit manner) which dominates the literature on masturbation in the eighteenth and early nineteenth centuries. For the Jew and the prostitute are seen as negating factors, outsiders whose sexual images represent all of the dangers felt to be inherent in human sexuality.

The debate about Jewish sexual crimes provides a further reading of the idea of the hidden nature of the Jew. Latent criminality becomes a component of the 'common mental construction' of the Jews. In 1881 there appeared an anonymous, anti-Semitic pamphlet on *The Jews' Role in Crime* which began by asking its audience not to enquire 'Ou est la femme?' in searching for the origin of crime but 'Where is the Jew?'[27] The Jew became the substitute for the woman as the source of criminality in society. The author cited the following statistics from the 1871 Prussian census. In 1871 Jews made up only 1.3 per cent of the population. Thus there were 16,636,990 Protestants; 8,625,840 Catholics; and 339,700 Jews (or '1 Jew for every 74 Germans'). But they were accused of crimes against morality 20 per cent more often than their Catholic or Protestant counterparts (Protestant = 703; Catholic = 372; Jewish = 18). And this argument was made by the author across every arena of criminality. The argument is explicit that Jews are by their very nature criminals and all areas of criminality, including the area of sexual crimes, such as incest, rape, sexual abuse of minors, find them over-represented.

This pamphlet called forth an immediate and intensive rebuttal on the part of Jewish social scientists. S. Löwenfeld attempted to answer it, labelling it a 'statistical cry against the Jew'.[28] Löwenfeld's argument was that while Jews may be accused of certain crimes more frequently than other groups, their conviction rate was actually lower than either the Catholic or the Protestant population; indeed, the number of convictions was less than half that of their representation in the population. He stressed this in specific areas, such as the area of sexual crimes. In 1885 Ludwig Fuld, a lawyer in Mainz, published yet another tabulation of the 'relationship between religion and criminality'. Relying on the 1881 Prussian criminal census, his tabulation of sexual crimes noted that the sexual abuse of minors and statutory rape were the most often punished moral crimes among Jewish men, but also widely spread among non-Jews. Incest, on the other hand, was so rarely to be found that he saw its absence among Jewish men as a relic of the biblical injunction which punishes this crime with death. He saw the lower rate of conviction of Jews for the crime of incest as an atavism which can be traced back to the ethnopsychology of the Jews.[29] At the same time the French Jewish community, in reviewing the crime statistics in France during 1885, argued that these statistics were 'an honor to the Jews' as they revealed a much lower incidence in all areas including incest.[30]

The debate about Jewish criminality, with its subtext about the higher or lower rate of the incidence of sexual crimes among Jews, was serious enough that when the Committee to Defend against Anti-Semitic Attacks began its publication series in 1896, its first statistical study was directed against the literature on Jewish criminality.[31] The statistics on sexual crimes reported in this study are revealing. Covering the period from 1882 to 1892, the statisticians found that, instead of the 44 cases of incest potentially projected for the Jewish population based on its representation in the population, only seven convictions were to be found; in the case of 'unnatural inbreeding' ['Inzucht'], there were 20 cases as against the 50 predicted and 21 cases of 'crimes against morals', which was the number projected.

In 1905 Arthur Ruppin, the founder of Jewish social statistics in Germany, reported similar statistics from the period from 1899 to 1902.[32] Ruppin's rationale for the substantially lower rates of sexual crimes is the 'greater education of the Jews'.[33] Ruppin's work is reflected in his basic study of the sociology of the Jews published in 1904.[34] This view is seconded by Bruno Blau in a pamphlet in 1906 which, however, admits to a higher incidence of certain crimes (such as slander) because of the 'temperament' of the Jews.[35] Here the contrast between evaluations based on nature or nurture can be judged. Ruppin saw the educational level of the Jews as a reflection of the older religious tradition now secularized. This is precisely the aspect of the Jewish mind which is most often evoked when the discussion is of the negative impact of the stresses of civilization on the Jew, given the Jew's predisposition for mental illness. Blau's comment on the temperament of the Jew looked at an argument for criminal activity that was based on character. Character was, however, formed by social stress, by the ghetto experience, according to many commentators. What was clearly an argument based on experience reveals itself to be analogous to one made on inheritance and vice versa. This can be most clearly seen in the comments of one of the leading criminologists of the early twentieth century in his 1910 handbook on sexual crimes: 'The Jew is marked by his intellectual gifts, which in general serve as a preventative against the commission of crime. His ability to think logically and his cleverness provide an antidote to his passion and his sexual excitedness. In other crimes [than sexual ones], especially fraud and perjury these characters are a predisposing criminal factor.'[36]

The view that race was a primary factor in criminality became the flashpoint of debate after the beginning of the twentieth century. In the second volume of the primary German periodical on criminology founded by the most eminent criminologist of his day, Gustav Aschaffenburg, there is a long essay on the topic of race and criminality by the physician Richard Weinberg from Dorpat/Tartu (Estonia).[37] Weinberg argued that criminality is inherently a reflex of race, that it is an inherited proclivity of a group. In looking at the Jews, Weinberg notes the 'general tendency of the Jews for mental illness' and he sees this as a sign of their racial degeneration.[38] This degeneration has a clearly psychological aspect. It is the result of the mixing of races, a sign of the alteration of the character of the second generation of mixed racial types.[39] Madness and criminality result from racial mixing and both are forms of psychological degeneration as represented by physical signs. This is the view of the ideological originator of modern biological anti-Semitism, Count Gobineau, who saw degeneracy of a people as the direct result of the decline of racial homogeneity.[40]

The madness of the Jews, their predisposition to disease, was a result of the inbreeding of the Jews, much as the noble families of Europe had decayed (and lost power) and the population of the Swiss villages had degenerated. This view is stated quite directly in the standard textbook of psychiatry of the *fin de siècle*, that of Emil Kraepelin.[41] Simon Scherbel, a Polish Jew and the son of a rabbi, presented his dissertation to the medical faculty of Berlin University in 1883 on the topic of consanguineous marriages. He was confronted with an absolute contradiction. How can the 'laws of Moses, which are for the most part still valid for Protestants' advocate the marriage of their 'daughters within the tribe'?[42] For it is evident that these laws have 'a negative result'. Jews have higher incidences of deaf-mutism and mental illness.[43] Scherbel responds that the Jew has the necessary disposition for such illnesses, because of his economic or professional status or because of some factor yet unknown, which is triggered more frequently than in his non-Jewish counterpart.[44] The laws which forbid consanguineous marriages are an attempt to avoid 'incest and immorality' in families.[45] The entire debate on consanguineous marriage, from a religious as well as from a medical point of view in the 1920s, was summarized in the *Jewish Lexicon*.[46] The essay by Felix Theilhaber stressed that the result of such marriages is an increased rate of mental illness among the offspring.

In 1909, there are further statistics brought to argue a decrease in the conviction rate for Jews accused of sexually related crimes.[47] In Aschaffenburg's journal, the chief of the Dutch Bureau of Legal Statistics published an essay which asked quite directly: 'Is it racial criminality or is it a criminality which is a product of social circumstances?'[48] He presented the Dutch figures from the period from 1896 to 1906 and argued 'that in spite of the various circumstances in which Jews live, they show the same pattern of criminality'.[49] And this is especially true in the tendency to commit sexually related crimes. They may show fewer cases of incest and sexual criminality, but they are much more involved in the publication of pornography. For de Roos their criminality is the result of the 'combination of the natural disposition and their social and economic circumstances'.[50] Thus in 1911, Rudolf Wassermann was forced to confront the question of the 'racial' cause of Jewish criminality directly. Spurred on by de Roos's essay, Wassermann stated his position most clearly: Jewish criminality mirrors the criminality of the society in which the Jews find themselves and is a purely social reflex rather than the result of inheritance.[51] And indeed this is the general view within the German-speaking Jewish scientific community.[52] Franz von Liszt attempted to further Wassermann's views, stressing that the criminality of any group, including that of the Jews, sprang from the specific social location.[53] What is different in von Liszt's approach is that he assumed that the choice of profession was a reflex of the 'common mental construction' of the Jews.

It is striking that none of the studies suggested the evident control for such assumptions: the rate of criminality and the types of crimes committed by Jewish converts and their offspring. The assumption would be that conversion, given the contemporary discussion of its intent, would at least change the social localization of the convert and would permit the convert to engage in other professions, some of which were *de facto* barred to Jews. The rate of the commission of sexual crimes would also be reflected (positively or negatively) in the change of the structure of the family and of the social context of the Jew. The taboo about seeking to examine the convert can be attributed to the anxiety on all sides of the implications of boundary-crossers.

It is important to clarify what these various 'sexual' crimes were. Incest in the German legal and forensic discourse of the *fin de siècle* is 'Blutschande', the violation of the blood.[54] The origin of this concept is that there is a real 'pollution' of the blood by the sexual contact between relatives.[55] Its origin is the concept of the 'sanguis contumelia' of Roman law.[56] Incest is understood as being 'unnatural' because it comes from an 'unnatural' desire and may lead to 'unnatural', i.e., unhealthy offspring. Incest is a question of law, though there is a substantial debate among forensic scientists about its universal applicability or historical foundation. But it is also seen as a loss of control: 'That the mentally ill tend to commit incest is easily explained, for the mentally ill there is complete loss of control as well as the law of the shortest way'.⁵⁷ Incest is thus an activity which marks the atavistic nature of the mentally ill. In the course of the nineteenth century this concept moves from signifying incestuous behaviour to meaning the violation of the purity of the race.⁵⁸ It is no longer the violation of the taboos created within the narrower definition of the social unity (such as the family); rather it becomes a definition of the boundaries of the wider unity, such as the race. Commit 'Blutschande' and you violate the newly biologically defined taboos inherent in the purity of the racial stock. This act pathologizes the very concept of race by defining what will and does cause racial degeneration, for the very concept of 'Blutschande' implies the degeneration of the race into illness and moral corruption.

It was of little wonder that the very debate about 'incest' was fraught with racialist undertones. For Magnus Hirschfeld, the great German-Jewish sexologist, it was a moral not a legal question. The term which he and other researchers of the period preferred was 'Unzucht' (indecency) rather than 'Blutschande' (incest). 'Inzest' (incest) was forbidden sexual contact between related individuals, but not necessarily related by consanguinity. This view was also stressed by Hermann Rohleder, who distinguished between incestuous relationships, which were forbidden by law, and 'inbreeding' which he interpreted as any sexual contact within the wider blood-relationship.⁵⁹ Thus German and Austrian law at the *fin de siècle* punished sexual contact between in-laws.⁶⁰ The Christian preoccupation with the Jewish custom of the levirate marriage, the obligation of a man to marry the widow of his brother, comes into clear conflict with these European traditions.⁶¹ Within the German understanding of the Jew's sexuality, this aspect of Jewish ritual practice had been a central focus. The 'reader' appended to one of the very first grammars of Yiddish written in German which was to be used to train missionaries to the Jews in the seventeenth century consisted of two texts: one on leprosy and one on the levirate marriage.⁶² The link between the diseased nature of the Jews and the Jews' marital practice was a long-established one. It is unimportant that by Talmudic times such marriages were seen as objectionable; indeed, Abba Saul viewed them as the equivalent to incest.⁶³ This obligation could be avoided through the institution of the ceremony of *chalitsah*.⁶⁴ Even though the levirate marriage was not a common ritual practice in nineteenth-century Europe, it remained a subject of endless fascination. In his history of marriage, one of Freud's major sources, Edvard Westermarck, evoked the practice among the Jews in his discussion of levirate marriage. He cited the obligation 'of a man to marry the widow of his brother if he died childless, and the firstborn should succeed in the brother's name "that his name should be not put out of Israel" '.[65] This type of marriage was one of the keys to the European debate about incest in the nineteenth century.[66] It is the incestuous implications of the levirate marriage which underlie the charge of brother-sister incest often lodged against the Jews, for a sexual relationship between a brother-in-law and his sister-in-law was considered to be the legal equivalent in German and Austrian law to brother-sister incest. C. G. Jung's charge that Freud had sexual relations with his sister-in-law, Minna Bernays, whom he called his 'sister', is an evocation of this calumny.[67]

For German-Jewish scientists such as Hirschfeld 'incest is the most frequent crime of solitary farms and narrow proletarian domiciles',[68] not of the middle-class dwellings of Berlin or Viennese Jewry. It is in these venues, marked by endemic goitre and insanity, that the signs of the degenerate are permitted to be found. Another German-Jewish forensic psychiatrist, Max Marcuse, noted that

> all human beings stem from in-breeding[, f]or the original sexual relationships were incestuous ... In people the marriage of consanguineous parents often evidences severe illnesses and deformities. The dangers of inbreeding can be illustrated by the degeneration and disappearance of many noble families, the racial pathology of the Jews, the endemic constitutional inferiority of people living in mountain villages, in which the inhabitants tend to mix only with themselves.[69]

The acceptance of the view that inbreeding (and certainly incest) results in the decline of the group was a commonplace and was often applied to the Jew as an explanation, as we have seen, for a number of pathological conditions. The 'cure' for the disease of Jewishness would be exogamous rather than endogamous marriages. The cure would be to marry outside the group. In 1904 Heinrich Singer had argued against such positions. For him it is an error to imagine that Jews suffer from the physiological results of inbreeding. 'Mixed marriages', he writes, 'as the sole cure and the preventative of the collapse of the race are not necessary.'[70] Such a cure can be accomplished by Jews moving into professions which are healthier and by the youth undertaking a 'hygienic, body-building education'.

The confusion surrounding the very concept of incest surfaced in the forensic literature of the *fin de siècle*. In 1907 Rudolf Wassermann published his basic introduction to the question of Jewish criminality.[71] Wassermann accepted the question of the criminality of the Jews as one which was appropriate for statistical evaluation, even though there had been a debate in the criminological literature about the effectiveness and appropriateness of using 'religion' as a criterion for the tabulation of such statistics.[72] Wassermann, using the criminal census figures in Germany from 1899 to 1902, tabulated a slightly lower (about 10 per cent) rate of sexual crimes on the part of Jews. But he also noted that during the year of 1895 there had been a 10 per cent higher rate of these crimes among Jews.[73] In general Jews showed a higher rate of crimes against public morality than did Christians, but Christians showed a much high incidence of incest.[74]

For Wassermann, and for many of the other commentators of the period, the Jews' lower rate of sexual crimes was closely tied to their rate of alcohol consumption. This motif, as we have seen in the discussion of the lower incidences of syphilis among Jews, presented a social practice linked to the inheritance of sobriety. Hugo Hoppe, the author of the standard study of Jews and alcohol, sees the Jews as less likely to commit such crimes because of their lower alcohol consumption.[75] Jewish abstinence provided the key to the lower rate of incest. Incest was a crime, as Hirschfeld had noted, committed when one was completely out of rational control. The insane provided him with a perfect model. And alcoholism or at least drunkenness provided precisely the same context. Alcoholism remains the major 'social' context of sexual abuse, although it is seen as an inherited trait which passes other, more devastating inherited traits on to the children of alcoholics. Zola describes his *Nana* as the 'story of a girl descended from four or five generations of drunkards, her blood tainted by an accumulated inheritance of poverty and drink, which in her case had taken the form of a nervous derangement of the sexual instinct'.[76] If alcoholism leads to sexual degeneration and perversity, then the absence of such sociopathic acts on the part of the Jews must be the direct result of their abstinence.

The debates about Jews and alcohol reflect the overall debates about predisposition as opposed to socialization. Wassermann noted that the more visible the Jew is in society the more he is placed in a position where alcohol consumption is needed.[77] Thus the latent criminality of the Jew can be triggered and he can commit sexual crimes. In 1909 Wassermann added to his argument about the social context of the Jew's criminality, seeing the changes of the patterns of Jewish criminality as a reflection of the changes in social status of the Jews.[78] He calculated that 59 per cent of all sexual crimes were committed under the influence of alcohol. Alcohol consumption among Jews remains relatively low into the 1920s.[79] Incest figures for Jews during the period from 1899 to 1916, while higher than in the previous decade, also remain remarkably lower than all other groups.

The association between the illicit sexuality of the Jew and the discourse on criminal sexuality is linked, as has been observed, in the argument that there is a Jewish predisposition for specific forms of mental illness. The 'perverse' sexuality of the Jew lies at the heart of this charge, for it is the inbreeding of the Jew which predisposes him to specific psychopathologies, precisely those such as 'homosexuality, from which the Jew is understood to suffer'. The 'degenerate' Jew becomes closely associated with models of 'degenerate' sexuality. Ludwig Woltmann, the noted eugenist and anthropologist, sees in the 'physical collapse of the Jews the degeneration of their nervous systems'.[80] The 'degenerate', the greater category into which the nosologies of the nineteenth century placed the 'pervert', was – according to Max Nordau, one of the very first supporters of Theodor Herzl's Zionism, quoting B. A. Morel – the 'morbid deviation from an original type'.[81] The difference between the original type, the middle-class, heterosexual, Protestant, white male, and the outsider was a morbid one – the outsider was diseased. Thus there is a general parallel drawn between the feminization of the Jew and the homosexual in the writings of assimilated Jews, Jews who did not seek to validate their difference from the majority during the late nineteenth century but did see themselves as potentially at risk by being perceived as such morbid deviations from the norm. Nowhere is this illustrated with greater force than in an essay written in 1897 by the future foreign minister of the Weimar Republic, Walter Rathenau. Rathenau, who begins his essay by 'confessing' to his identity as a Jew, condemns the Jews as a foreign body in the cultural as well as the political world of Germany: 'Whoever wishes to hear its language can go any Sunday through the Thiergartenstrasse midday at twelve or evenings glance into the foyer of a Berlin theater. Unique Vision! In the midst of a German life, a separate, strange race ... On the sands of the Mark Brandenburg, an Asiatic horde.' As part of this category of difference, Rathenau sees the physical deformities of the Jewish male – his 'soft weakness of form', his femininity (associated with his 'orientalism') – as the biological result of his oppression. This was a restructuring of the charge that Jews were inherently feminine, rather than a social reaction to their stigmatization.[82] Theologians such as David Friedrich Strauss, the great critic of Christianity, were quite able to speak of the 'especially female' nature of the Jews.[83] (Freud read this text as a young man and it made a considerable impression on him.)[84] The evils of Christianity lie in the mentality of their Jewish origin – a view to which Nietzsche, and many of the 'Christian' critics of Christianity during the late nineteenth century ascribed. And physicians such as

Moses Julius Gutmann could translate this discussion of the 'common mental construction' of the Jews into a reading of the anthropometric statistics of the woman as parallel to those of the male Jew. Thus the Jew has an arm span less than equivalent to his height, as does the woman.[85] It is of little surprise therefore that the Jew is seen as overwhelmingly at risk of being (or becoming) a homosexual. Moses Julius Gutmann observes that 'all of the comments about the supposed stronger sexual drive among Jews have no basis in fact; most frequently they are sexual neurasthenics. Above all the number of Jewish Homosexuals is extraordinarily high.'[86] This view is echoed by Alexander Pilcz, Freud's colleague in the Department of Psychiatry at the University of Vienna, who noted that 'there is a relatively high incidence of homosexuality among the Jews'.[87] It is the very biological (or 'ontological') difference of the Jew which is the source of his feminized nature. Among Jews, according to a lecture in 1920 by the Professor of Anthropology at the University of Vienna, Robert Stigler,

> the physical signs of the sexual characteristics are noticeably vague. Among them, the women are often found to have relatively narrow pelvis and relatively broad shoulders and the men to have broad hips and narrow shoulders. . . . It is important to note the attempt on the part of the Jews to eliminate the role which secondary sexual characteristics instinctively play among normal people through their advocacy of the social and professional equality of man and woman.[88]

Only Havelock Ellis denied this association, noting that among his homosexual patients only 'two are more or less Jewish'. His (British) surprise is that 'frequent presence of the German element' among his patients.[89] This charge of the general tendency of all Jews (male and female) towards homosexuality, as represented by their social and political acts as well as their biological reality, had to be modified by Jews such as Rathenau to provide a space where they were able to escape the stigma of feminization.

'Feminization' is here to be understood both in its general, cultural sense and in its very specifically medical sense. 'Feminization' or the existence of the 'feminized man' is a form of 'external pseudo-hermaphrodism'.[90] It is not true hermaphrodism, but rather the sharing of external, secondary sexual characteristics, such as the shape of the body or the tone of the voice. The concept begins in the middle of the nineteenth century with the introduction of the term 'infeminisce', to feminize, to describe the supposed results of the castration of the male.[91] By the 1870s, the term is used to describe the 'feminisme' of the male through the effects of other diseases, such as tuberculosis.[92] And

Henry Meige, at the Salpêtrière, saw this feminization as a form of atavism, in which the male returns to the level of the 'sexless' child.[93] 'Feminization' was the direct result of actual castration or the physiological equivalent, such as intensely debilitating illness. And it reshaped the body. Freud, citing Taruffi, rejected any simple association of the form of the body of the hermaphrodite with the sexual preference of the homosexual.[94] He separated out the 'common mental construction' of the homosexual from his/her physical form.

Freud's response to his own potential 'deviancy' was complicated. In the 1890s he confronted the question of the relationship between inheritance and trauma as the two major sources for all mental illness. His struggle with the idea of predisposition and inheritance can be seen in his reading of Leopold Löwenfeld's work. Löwenfeld, one of Freud's most assiduous supporters, confronted the question of the racial predisposition of the Jews in his textbook of 1894. In his discussion of the etiology of neurasthenia and hysteria he examined the role which 'race and climate' might play in the origin of these diseases:

> Concerning the claimed predisposition of the Semitic race, one can only state the fact that among the Israelites today there is an unusually large number of neurasthenics and hysterics. Whether this is the result of a specific predisposition of the race seems very questionable. Historically, there is no trace of such a predisposition to be shown. The epidemics of mass hysteria observed in earlier centuries never affected members of the Semitic race. I believe it more likely that the great predisposition of the Israelites does not rest in racial qualities, but in their present quality of life. Among these would come into consideration – in East Europe, the physical poverty as well as the extraordinary moral pressure, the practice of early marriage, and the great number of children – in the West, the great number of Israelites who undertake intellectual activities.[95]

Freud read Löwenfeld's textbook very carefully. The opening pages are full of debates about the inheritability of hysteria and its relationship to trauma. Thus Löwenfeld claims that 'inheritance plays a major role in the origins of neurasthenia and hysteria through the existence of an abnormal constitution of the nervous system'. Freud retorts: 'From where?' in the margin. Tucked away in a footnote, Löwenfeld quotes a source which claimed to have seen a large number of cases of hysteria 'without a trace of hereditary neurosis'.[96] Freud chuckles: 'Bravo! Certainly acquired.' These comments reflected Freud's preoccupation with the universal question of whether all human beings could be divided into the healthy and the degenerate, the mentally sound and the hysteric. Löwenfeld's rejection of the predisposition for hysteria for *all* Jews meant it was possible to focus on the universal rather than the racialist question. And yet Löwenfeld's distinction between Eastern Jews with their mix of social and sexual causes for their mental states and Western Jews with their (highly sought) intellectual status shows that even there a dichotomy between the religious and the secular Jew is sought. Freud seems never to have reached this section of the book; his eye remains fixed on the universal question and does not seem to enter into the debate about the Jews and madness. But in fact, he enters this debate in a complicated manner.

Freud's essay on '"Civilized" Sexual Morality and Modern Nervous Illness' (1908) is in many ways an unspoken dialogue on the association of race and insanity in contemporary science. In that paper Freud links the repressive nature of modern society with the deformation of human sexuality. He begins with a paraphrase of the work of the contemporary Prague philosopher and co-founder of *Gestalt* psychology Christian von Ehrenfels, who held an essentially ethnopsychological position (for many of the same reasons as did Freud). Ehrenfels had solicited Freud's contribution to a new periodical, *Sexual Problems*, which first appeared in 1908.[97] The magazine was one of the successors of the older journal, *Mother Protection*, the official publication of a eugenics group to which Freud and Ehrenfels belonged. Upon founding the journal, Ehrenfels immediately wrote to Freud for a contribution and received the essay from him.

Ehrenfels stated, in the extract cited by Freud, that 'the innate character of a people' could be compared with their 'cultural attainments' in order to differentiate between 'civilized' and 'natural' sexual morality.[98] 'Civilized' morality produces 'intense and productive cultural activities', while 'natural sexual morality maintains "health and efficiency"'. The disease of the cities, of urban life, is thus a product of the civilizing process. It is a necessary, though unfortunate, result of the suppression of human sexuality in culture. It is a problem of modern life, not of Jews in modern society.

Christian von Ehrenfels's monograph is a most interesting point of departure for Freud.[99] Published in a series of short monographs on 'marginal questions' in neurology and psychology edited by Freud's friend Leopold Löwenfeld in Munich, Ehrenfels's text is explicitly indebted to Freud for much of its psychological framework. Highly influenced (like Freud) by a Darwinian model of sexual selection, Ehrenfels could not only contrast 'natural' and 'civilized' morality, but just as easily write of the competition between the 'higher' and the 'lower' races and about the 'great problem of our time': resolving the demand of race in the light of the 'liberal-humanistic fiction of the equality of all people'.[100] For Ehrenfels, the purpose of 'natural sexual morals' (which is for him a natural law) 'is to conserve or improve the constitution of the tribe or people'.[101] He saw the need for the 'white, yellow, and black' races to remain 'pure' and to avoid any sexual interbreeding. As with most of the racial scientists of his time, he justified colonial expansion with the rationale that the 'sexual mission' of some races was best accomplished 'if they place their generative powers in the service of others'.[102] As the rhetoric of this statement seems to indicate throughout Ehrenfels's discussion of race, his prime example is the 'Oriental'. Indeed, Freud underlines the passage in his text where Ehrenfels warns of the risk of the 'Yellow Peril' overwhelming Europe. Freud's own writing reflects this image in his formulation of 1915, in which he stated that the war which had been expected before 1914 was assumed to be between the 'civilized' ('white') and 'primitive' ('darker') races.[103] It is clear in this formulation that the Jews, seen as a people of culture, were to be considered to be 'white' and, therefore, civilized.

The monograph, however, concludes with an index, prepared by the author and intended by him to enable his monograph to be used as a handbook for those seeking direct advice on topics of sexual morality. The final entry makes reference to the discussion on racial sexuality and concludes the volume with the following observation: 'These same directives are applicable to the Jewish problem, in as much as these are the result of differences in their constitution and not − as is actually generally the case − the result of resolvable differences in their social milieu.'[104] All of the discussions about race are, in fact, encoded references to the Jewish question. It is the claim for an innate, biologically rooted difference of the Jews which is the subtext of Ehrenfels's study of sexual ethics, for the Jews are understood as biologically different. Their strengths, like the strengths of each of the races, are preserved only when they remain within their own group. Intermixing leads to the corruption and the weakening of the race. Rather than intermixing with the Aryan the Jews, Ehrenfels implies, through their activity in Western culture, can place 'their generative powers in the service of others'.

Ehrenfels's demands for the purity of the race were not merely theoretical. Ehrenfels himself was an active spokesperson for eugenics and spoke on 'breeding reform' in December 1908 before the Vienna Psychoanalytic Society. There again he warned about the dangers of monogamy as well as the threat of the 'annihilation of the white race by the yellow race'.[105] And yet the racial theorist who advocated the purity of the race and the distinction between 'healthy' and 'civilized morality' in the 'higher' and 'lower' races was himself Jewish by descent even though raised as a Christian. Ehrenfels publicly acknowledged his own personal Jewish background and saw the rise of political anti-Semitism as a social anathema.[106] The real danger, Ehrenfels again stated in a talk given in 1911, is the 'Yellow Peril', the 'hordes of Mongols' poised to confront the 'Caucasian' race: 'Among 100 whites there stand two Jews. The German peasant has been awakened and armed with the holy weapons of his ancestors – not to struggle against 80 million Mongols but to confront two Jews! Is this not the height of folly!'[107]

Ehrenfels's response to the nature of the Jew can be best read in his review of Otto Weininger's *Sex and Character*, published in one of the most widely read eugenics journals of his day.[108] Weininger had published his revised dissertation, *Sex and Character*, in 1903, and killed himself shortly thereafter in the house in Vienna in which Beethoven had died.[109] Weininger's book both became an immediate best-seller and established him as a serious contributor to the discourse about the relationship between race and gender at the beginning of the century.[110] This is a work of intensive, undisguised self-hatred which had an unprecedented influence on the scientific discourse about Jews and women at the turn of the century. Thus the lesbian feminist Charlotte Perkins Gilman saw Weininger's work as a major contribution to the science of gender.[111] And Ludwig Wittgenstein, the homosexual, partly 'Jewish' Catholic philosopher, accepted and incorporated aspects of Weininger's 'philosophy' into his worldview.[112] Christian von Ehrenfels immediately identified the central problem in Weininger's work as the author's rejection of heterosexuality. But Ehrenfels is careful to separate Weininger's rejection of heterosexuality (and the parallel sexual ambiguity) from any discussion of Jewish identity. In regard to Weininger's overt anti-Semitism, Ehrenfels sees all of his traits as falling within Weininger's representation of the Jew. He is 'superficial, impious, frivolous, impertinent, and publicity seeking'. In other words, he sees Weininger as living out his own internalized negative self-image of the Jew in his own writing. For Ehrenfels, the central link to this classic of early twentieth-century sexology is Weininger's own reflection of the ambiguities of all identity formation – either as a male or as a Jew, but not as a gay Jew.

By 1911 Ehrenfels comes to deny any substantial physiological difference between Aryans and Jews. Indeed, he comes to see the Jews as suffering from all the diseases and dangers of modern society: 'They suffer more than we do from the present sexual and economic order.'[113] Primary among these are mental diseases. Jews are, therefore, simply exaggerated Aryans. Indeed, this seems a response to Oskar Rie's comment following his paper in Vienna – 'would the Mongols, in taking over our culture, not take over our potential for degeneration as well'[114] – for a number of thinkers of the period assumed that the Jews were the example of the worst cast of the impact of civilization because of their weak nervous system. Franz Kafka mentions a response which Ehrenfels made to a presentation by Felix Theilhaber on the 'decline of German Jewry' to a public audience in Prague during January of 1912.[115] Theilhaber had recapitulated the thesis of his controversial book, that urbanization, the struggle for profit, as well as mixed marriages and baptism were causing German Jewry to vanish. (The latter argument was a social variant on the older biological argument that 'mixed marriages between Jews and Aryans had a noticeably lower fecundity'.)[116] Ehrenfels's response, as Kafka noted, was a 'comic scene' in which the philosopher (whose Jewish antecedents were well known) 'smiling spoke in favor of mixed races'. Freud and Ehrenfels both found themselves in an unresolvable tension between accepting the discourse of science about race and the need to position themselves in regard to this discourse. Freud represses this discourse; Ehrenfels eventually valorizes it.

Freud's model for the image of the healthy family in '"Civilized" Sexual Morality and Modern Nervous Illness' is clearly not a Jewish one as represented in nineteenth-century images of Jewish sexuality. It is of a family, 'living in simple, healthy, country conditions', which became ill when the members 'had successfully established themselves in the metropolis, and in a short space of time had brought their children to a high level of culture'.[117] It is, however, the Jews who are the prime examples for such social deformation in Freud's own primary sources. Freud argued that these authorities were essentially correct but that they

> leave out of account precisely the most important of the etiological factors involved. If we disregard the vaguer ways of being 'nervous' and consider the specific forms of nervous illness, we shall find that the injurious influence of civilization reduces itself in the main to the harmful suppression of the sexual life of civilized peoples (or classes) (*Kulturvölker* [oder Schichten]) through the 'civilized' sexual morality prevalent in them.[118]

Not race (Ehrenfels's point of departure) – but civilization or class determines pathology. But what do Freud's sources say? Otto

Binswanger stated that 'among the European races the Jews present the greatest number of cases of neurasthenia'.[119] Wilhelm Erb, at a birthday celebration for the King of Baden, commented on the increased nervousness among the 'Semites, who already are a neurotically predisposed race. Their untamed desire for profit and their nervousness, caused by centuries of imposed life style (*auferlegte Lebensweise*) as well as their inbreeding (*Inzucht*) and marriage within families (*Familienheiraten*) predisposes them to nervousness.'[120] Richard von Krafft-Ebing, in one of the standard medical handbooks of the day, simply quoted Erb, that 'Jews are especially prone to nervousness'.[121] None of this Freud commented upon. His desire was to move the argument about the madness of the Jews away from the question of race and to universalize it.

Human sexuality becomes the universal wellspring of psychoanalytic theory. There are many potential threads to Freud's discovery/construction of this fact. One of them which was quite evident is Freud's careful repression of the discourse on Jewish psychopathology and its relationship to sexual deviancy in the medical literature of his time. Freud 'reads around' this problem, confronts all of its presuppositions – predisposition, inheritance, trauma – and concludes that what was present was the ubiquitous presence of human sexuality – in all of its manifestations – within the course of human development. Here too Freud masks the discussion of the meaning of the sexuality of the Jew. In 1926 Freud (in his essay on lay analysis) referred (in English) to female sexuality as the 'dark continent' of the human psyche:

> But we need not feel ashamed of this distinction; after all, the sexual life of adult women is a 'dark continent' for psychology. But we have learnt that girls feel deeply their lack of a sexual organ that is equal in value to the male one; they regard themselves on that account as inferior, and this 'envy for the penis' is the origin of a whole number of characteristic feminine reactions.[122]

Elsewhere I have sketched the implications of this phrase in terms of the medicalization of the black female body during the nineteenth century.[123] But note Freud's vocabulary concerning the sense of inferiority attributed to the woman because of her '"envy for the penis"'. The question of the woman's attribution of meaning to the female genitalia, specifically the clitoris, is raised by Freud in this context: 'women possess as part of their genitals a small organ similar to the male one; and this small organ, the clitoris, actually plays the same part in childhood and during the years before sexual intercourse as the large organ in men'.[124] The view that the clitoris is a 'truncated penis' is generally rejected in contemporary psychoanalytic theory. To date the only explanation for this view has been found in the arguments about homologous structures of the genitalia.[125] But little attention has been given to what Freud could have understood within this generally accepted model.

The image of the clitoris as a 'truncated penis', as a less than intact penis, reflects the popular *fin-de-siècle* Viennese view of the relationship between the body of the male Jew and the body of the woman. The clitoris was known in Viennese slang of the *fin de siècle* simply as the 'Jew' (*Jud*).[126] The phrase 'for a woman to masturbate' is to 'play with the Jew'. The 'small organ' of the woman becomes the *pars par toto* for the Jew with his circumcised, shortened organ. This pejorative synthesis of both bodies because of their 'defective' sexual organs reflects the *fin-de-siècle* Viennese definition of the essential male as the antithesis of the female and the Jewish male.

But the clitoris, the 'Jew', becomes a sign of masculinity for Freud. In his *Three Essays on the Theory of Sexuality* Freud stresses the fact that the 'assumption that all human beings have the same (male) form of the genital' is the primary fantasy of all children (male and female) about the structure of the body.[127] According to this view, all children believe that they have a penis and may lose it (male) or had a penis and lost it (female). The clitoris, the 'truncated penis', becomes the sign of the missing (castrated) penis. In Freud's own theory the unitary fantasy of a 'male' penis is transmuted into the image of the clitoris as a parallel to the penis (at least in terms of masturbatory activity). In the genital stage the little boy and the little girl masturbate using their 'penis/clitoris'. It is a unitary 'male' penis which unites all the fantasies of the genitalia.

Everyone, male and female, seems to relate to this male organ. The woman must transcend her own fantasy of castration and her penis envy. She must not remain fixated at the level of masculine sexuality but must move to the higher level of vaginal (i.e., reproductive) sexuality. As late as his essay on female sexuality (1931), Freud stressed the need for female sexuality to develop from the early masturbatory emphasis on the masculine genital zone, the clitoris, to the adult sexuality of vaginal intercourse. The clitoris, the 'Jew', is the sign of the masculine which must be abandoned if and when the female is to mature into an adult woman.[128] The 'Jew' is the male hidden within the body of the female for Freud. The 'Jewish' nature of 'castrated' female sexuality is replaced by the universal 'male' nature of the child's fantasy of the human body. It is this masculine aspect of the woman which must be transcended if she is to define herself antithetically to the male. But with which male is she to identify herself? For the body of the Jewish male is not identical with that of the Aryan. The Jew's penis is different and visibly so. It is the Aryan which is the 'healthy', 'normal' baseline which determines the pathological difference of the male Jew. In Freud's discussion of the nature of the female body the distinction between male Aryan and male Jew is repressed, to be inscribed on the body of the woman. All of this displacement is coloured by the discourse on the Jewish male body (and mind) present within the medical (and sexological literature) of the time. Here is the second reading of Frank Sulloway's history of Freud and sexology – a subliminal one, but one which helped shape the rhetoric of Freud's own argument.

NOTES

1 Frank Sulloway, *Freud, Biologist of the Mind: Beyond the Psychoanalytic Legend* (New York: Basic Books, 1979), 277–319.
2 Erich Wulffen, *Der Sexualverbrecher* (Berlin: P. Langenscheidt, 1910), 302. This was considered to be one of the major innovative contributions to criminology of the day. See the review in the *Jahrbuch für sexuelle Zwischenstufen*, NS 3 (1911), 376–8.
3 John S. Billings, 'Vital Statistics of the Jews', *North American Review*, 153 (1891), 70–84, p. 84.
4 All of these *fin-de-siècle* sources are cited by Havelock Ellis, *Studies in the Psychology of Sex*, vol. v (7 vols., Philadelphia: F.A. Davis, 1900–28), 185–6. (In the Freud Library, London.)
5 Hanns Sachs, *Freud: Master and Friend* (Cambridge, Mass.: Harvard University Press, 1946), 19.
6 Leopold Löwenfeld, *Über die sexuelle Konstitution und andere Sexualprobleme* (Wiesbaden: J.F. Bergmann, 1911), 75–6. (In the Freud Library, London.)
7 *Protokolle der Wiener Psychoanalytischen Vereinigung*, vol. II, ed. Herman Nunberg and Ernst Federn (4 vols., Frankfurt a. M.: Fischer, 1976–81), 41; translation from *Minutes of the Vienna Psychoanalytic Society*, vol. II, trans. M. Nunberg (4 vols., New York: International Universities Press, 1962–75), 45.
8 The overall literature on this topic is available in M.L. Rodriques de Areia and A.M. Elias Abade (eds.), *Consanguinidade: Bibliografia* (Coimbra: Instituto de Antropologia, Universidade de Coimbra, 1983).
9 Cecil F. Beadles, 'The Insane Jew', *Journal of Mental Science*, 46 (1900), 732.
10 Maurice Fishberg, *The Jews: A Study of Race and Environment* (New York: Walter Scott, 1911), 349.
11 Rudolph Virchow, 'Über Erblichkeit I. Die Theorie Darwins', *Deutsche Jahrbücher für Politik und Literatur*, 6 (1863), 339–58, p. 354.
12 Houston Stewart Chamberlain, *Foundations of the Nineteenth Century*, trans. John Lees, vol. I (2 vols., London: John Lane Bodley Head, 1913), 366. On Freud's reading of Chamberlain see Sigmund Freud, *Gesammelte Werke:*

Chronologisch Geordnet (19 vols., Frankfurt a. M.: S. Fischer, 1952–87). (Referred to in the notes as *GW*.) Here supplementary volume, 787.

13 On the question of Jews and crime, and the anxiety about violence, in the nineteenth century see Paul Briones, *Tough Jews: Political Fantasies and the Moral Dilemma of American Jewry* (New York; Basic Books, 1990), 106–112.

14 Wulffen, *Der Sexualverbrecher*, 302.

15 D. Ackner, 'The Crime of Incest', *Medical and Legal Journal*, 48 (1980), 79–91.

16 See the discussion in 'The Jewish Murderer: Jack the Ripper, Race, and Gender', in Sander L. Gilman, *The Jew's Body* (New York: Routledge, 1991), 104–27.

17 Peter Pulzer, *The Rise of Political Anti-Semitism in Germany and Austria* (London: Peter Halban, 1988), 6.

18 B. Goldberg, 'Zur Kriminalität der Juden in Russland', *Zeitschrift für Demographie und Statistik der Juden*, 8 (1912), 127–30.

19 Rafael Becker, 'Die Häufigkeit jüdischer Krimineller unter den geisteskranken Verbrecher in Poler', *Psychiatrische-Neurologische Wochenschrift*, 33 (1931), 362–4.

20 Walter Pötsch, *Die jüdische Rasse im Lichte der Straffälligkeit: Zuchtstätten der Minderrassigkeit* (Ratibor: Hans W. Pötsch, 1933).

21 Joachim Duckar, *Die Juden von Betsche: Ein Beitrag zum 'Wirken' der Juden im deutschen Osten*, vol. 1, *Veröffentlichungen des Rassenpolitischen Amtes der NSDAP* (Meseritz: P. Matthias, 1939).

22 See Edward Bristow, *Prostitution and Prejudice: The Jewish Fight Against White Slavery, 1870–1939* (New York: Schocken, 1983) and his essay 'History versus Memory: Jews and White Slavery', *Moment*, 9 (1984), 44–9, which has an overview of the critical literature on this topic.

23 Franz Alexander and Hugo Staub, *Der Verbrecher und seine Richter: eine psychoanalytischer Einblick in die Welt der Paragraphen* (Vienna: Internationaler Psychoanalytischer Verlag, 1929); trans. Gregory Zilborg as *The Criminal. The Judge. and the Public: A Psychological Analysis* (New York: Macmillan, 1931). (Both in the Freud Library, London.)

24 Paul Näcke, 'Über den Wert der sog. Degenerationszeichem', *Monatsschrift für Kriminalpsychologie und Strafrechtsreform*, 1 (1904), 99–111, pp. 110–11.

25 See Sander L. Gilman, *Sexuality: An Illustrated History* (New York: Wiley, 1989), 231–62.

26 See the discussion by Alain Corbin, 'Commercial Sexuality in Nineteenth-Century France: A System of Images and Regulations', *Representations*, 14 (1986), 209–19.

27 *Der Juden Antheil am Verbrechen: auf Grund der amtlichen Statistik über die Thätigkeit der Schwurgerichte, in vergleichender Darstellung mit den christlichen Confessionen* (Berlin: Otto Hentze, 1881).

28 S. Löwenfeld, *Die Wahrheit über der Juden Antheil am Verbrechen* (Berlin: Stuhr, 1881).

29 Ludwig Fuld, *Das jüdische Verbrecherthum: eine Studie über den Zusammenhang zwischen Religion und Kriminalität* (Leipzig: Theodor Huth, 1885), 24–5. He also notes that the rates of convictions for incest in the census are for Protestants = 31 convictions; Catholics = 25 convictions; and Jews = 1 conviction.

30 *Archives Israélites: recueil politique et religieux hebdomadaire*, 46 (13 August 1885), 260–1.
31 *Die Kriminalität der Juden in Deutschland* (Berlin: Siegfried Cronbach, 1896). This is followed up by *Die wirtschaftliche Lage, soziale Gliederung und die Kriminalstatistik der Juden* (Berlin: Verlag des Vereins zur Abwehr des Antisemitismus, 1912).
32 Arthur Ruppin, 'Die Kriminalität der Christen und Juden in Deutschland 1899–1902', *Zeitschrift für Demographie und Statistik der Juden*, 1 (1905), 6–9.
33 Ibid., 9.
34 Arthur Ruppin, *Die Juden der Gegenwart* (Berlin: S. Calvary, 1904), chapter 15.
35 Bruno Blau, *Die Kriminalität der deutschen Juden* (Berlin: Louis Lamm, 1906).
36 Wulffen, *Der Sexualverbrecher*, 303.
37 Richard Weinberg, 'Psychische Degeneration, Kriminalität und Rasse', *Monatsschrift für Kriminalpsychologie und Strafrechtsreform*, 2 (1906), 720–30.
38 Ibid., 727.
39 Ibid., 729.
40 Arthur de Gobineau, *The Inequality of Human Races*, trans. Adrian Collins (New York: Howard Fertig, 1967), 168–80.
41 Emil Kraepelin, *Psychiatrie: ein Lehrbuch für Studierende und Ärzte*, vol. 1 (4 vols., Leipzig: Johann Ambrosius Barth, 1909), 189. (In the Freud Library, London.) See Kurt Kolle, *Kraepelin und Freud: Beitrag zur neueren Geschichte der Psychiatrie* (Stuttgart: Georg Thieme, 1957).
42 Simon Scherbel, *Über Ehen zwischen Blutsverwandten* (Berlin: Gustav Schade, 1883), 8.
43 Ibid.: deaf-mutism, 12, 27; mental illness, 40–2.
44 Ibid., 43–4.
45 Ibid., 9.
46 Felix A. Theilhaber, 'Blutverwandte, Ehen unter', *Jüdisches Lexikon*, vol. 1, ed. Georg Herlitz and Bruno Kirschner (4 vols. in 5, Berlin: Jüdischer Verlag, 1927–30), 1088–92. (In the Freud Library, London.)
47 Bruno Blau, 'Die Kriminalität der Juden in Deutschland während der Jahre 1903–1906', *Zeitschrift für Demographie und Statistik der Juden*, 5 (1909), 49–53.
48 J. R. B. de Roos, 'Über die Kriminalität der Juden', *Monatsschrift für Kriminalpsychologie und Rechtsreform*, 6 (1909–10), 193–205.
49 Ibid., 197.
50 Ibid., 205.
51 Rudolf Wassermann, 'Ist die Kriminalität der Juden Rassenkriminalität?' *Zeitschrift für Demographie und Statistik der Juden*, 7 (1911), 36–9.
52 Anonymous, 'Die Kriminalität der deutschen Juden', *Ost und West*, 12 (1912), 713–16.
53 Franz von Liszt, *Das Problem der Kriminalität der Juden* (Giessen: Alfred Töpelmann, 1907).
54 Magnus Hirschfeld, *Geschlecht und Verbrechen* (Leipzig: Verlag für Sexualwissenschaft, 1930).
55 Ibid., 325.
56 Herbert Maisch, *Incest*, trans. Colin Bearne (London: Andre Deutsch, 1973),

11–64. Compare Jack Goody, 'A Comparative Approach to Incest and Adultery', *British Journal of Sociology*, 7 (1956), 286–305.
57 Hirschfeld, *Geschlecht und Verbrechen*, 326.
58 Christina von Braun, 'Die "Blutschande" – Wandlung eines Begriffs: Vom Inzesttabu zu den Rassengesetzen', *Die schamlose Schönheit des Vergangenen: Zum Verhältnis von Geschlecht und Geschichte* (Frankfurt a. M.: Verlag Neue Kritik, 1989), 81–112.
59 Hermann Rohleder, *Monographien über die Zeugung beim Menschen*, vol. II: *Die Zeugung unter Blutsverwandten* (7 vols., Leipzig: Thieme, 1911–12), 3–8.
60 Hirschfeld, *Geschlechte und Verbrechen*, 329.
61 Isser Yehuda Unterman, *Shevet mi-Yehudah: Berure Sugyot, Hidushe Torah ve-Hikre Halakhah be-a Rba ah Helka Shulhan Arukh* (Jerusalem: Mosad ha-Rab Kook, 1983).
62 Johann Christoph Wagenseil, *Belehrung der Jüdisch-Teutschen Red- und Schreibart* (Königsberg: Paul Friedrich Rhode, 1699). See my *Jewish Self-Hatred: Anti-Semitism and the Secret Language of the Jews* (Baltimore: Johns Hopkins University Press, 1986), 74.
63 *Yebamot*, 39b.
64 *Yebamot*, 109a.
65 Edvard Westermarck, *The History of Marriage*, vol. III (3 vols., London: Macmillan, 1921), 216. (In the Freud Library, London, in the translation by L. Katscher and R. Grazer (Berlin: H. Barsdorf, 1902).) Of interest in this context is Westermarck's response to Freud, *Freuds Teori um Oedipuskomplexen* (Stockholm: Albert Bonnier, 1934). On the function of this tradition within the anthropological literature see Howard Eilberg-Schwartz, *The Savage in Judaism: An Anthropology of Israelite Religion and Ancient Judaism* (Bloomington: Indiana University Press, 1990), 36. On Westermarck see Timothy Stroup ed.), *Edward Westermarck: Essays on His Life and Works* (Helsinki: Societas Philosophica Fennica, 1982).
66 See the discussion of this theme in Hjalmar J. Nordin, 'Die eheliche Ethik der Juden zur Zeit Jesu', trans. W. A. Kastner and Gustave Lewié, *Beiwerke zum Studium der Anthropophyteia*, 4 (1911), 99–104, a periodical which Freud both contributed to and used extensively (see the *Standard Edition* (n. 98 below): *SE*, vol. X, 215, n. 1; vol. XI, 233–5; vol. XII, 177–203; vol. XXI, 106–7). On the political implications of this theme see N. F. Anderson, 'The "Marriage with a Deceased Wife's Sister Bill" Controversy: Incest Anxiety and the Defense of Family Purity in Victorian England', *The Journal of British Studies*, 21 (1982), 67–86.
67 See the discussion in William J. McGrath, *Freud's Discovery of Psychoanalysis*, 280.
68 Hirschfeld, *Geschlechte und Verbrechen*, 326.
69 Max Marcuse (ed.), *Handwörterbuch der Sexualwissenschaft* (Bonn: A. Marcus and E. Webers, 1926), 311. (In the Freud Library, London.)
70 Heinrich Singer, *Allgemeine und spezielle Krankheitslehre der Juden* (Leipzig: Benno Konegen, 1904), 22–3.
71 Rudolf Wassermann, *Beruf, Konfession und Verbrechen: eine Studie über die Kriminalität der Juden in Vergangenheit und Gegenwart* (Munich: Ernst Reinhardt, 1907).

72 Ibid., 4–5.
73 Ibid., 39–41.
74 Ibid., 46–7.
75 Hugo Hoppe, *Alkohol und Kriminalität in allen ihren Beziehungen* (Wiesbaden: J. F. Bergmann, 1906); 'Die Kriminalität der Juden und der Alkohol', *Zeitschrift für Demographie und Statistik der Juden*, 2 (1907), 38–41.
76 Emile Zola, *Nana*, trans. George Holden (Harmondsworth: Penguin, 1972), 221.
77 Wassermann, *Berufe*, 55.
78 Rudolf Wassermann, 'Die Kriminalität der Juden in Deutschland in den letzten 25 Jahren (1882–1906)', *Monatsschrift für Kriminalpsychologie und Rechtsreform*, 6 (1909), 609–19.
79 Felix A. Theilhaber, 'Alkoholgenuss der jüdischen Jugend', *Zeitschrift für Demographie und Statistik der Juden*, NS 3 (1926), 128–34.
80 Ludwig Woltmann, 'Rassenpsychologie und Kulturgeschichte', *Politisch-anthropologische Revue*, 3 (1905), 350–7, p. 355.
81 Cited from the English translation, Max Nordau, *Degeneration* (New York: Appelton, 1895), 16.
82 See his essay 'Höre, Israel!' *Die Zukunft* (6 March 1897), 454–62.
83 David Friedrich Strauss, *Der alte und der neue Glaube: ein Bekenntnis* (Leipzig: G. Hirzel, 1872), 71.
84 H. Knöpfmacher, 'Sigmund Freud in High School', *American Imago*, 36 (1979), 287–300; Robert R. Holt, 'Freud's Adolescent Reading: Some Possible Effects on his Work', in Paul Stepansky (ed.), *Freud: Appraisals and Reappraisals*, vol. III (3 vols., Hillsdale, N. J.: Analytic Press, 1988), 167–92, pp. 185–8.
85 M. J. Gutmann, *Über den Lentingen Stand der Rasse- und Krankheitsfrage der Juden* (Berlin: Rudolph Müller and Steinecke, 1920), 18.
86 Ibid., 25–6.
87 Cited by Hans F. K. Günther, *Rassenkunde des jüdischen Volkes* (Munich: J. F. Lehmann, 1931), 273. (First published in 1922.)
88 Robert Stigler, 'Die rassenphysiologische Bedeutung der sekundären Geschlechtscharaktere', *Sitzungsberichte der anthropologischen Gesellschaft in Wien* (1919/20), 6–9, p. 7. Published as a special number of the *Mitteilungen der anthropologischen Gesellschaft in Wien*, 50 (1920).
89 Havelock Ellis, *Studies in the Psychology of Sex*, vol. II: *Sexual Inversion* (Philadelphia: F. A. Davis, 1920), 264. (In the Freud Library, London.)
90 Freud's primary source on this topic was Cesare Taruffi, *Hermaphrodismus und Zeugungsunfähigkeit: eine systematische Darstellung des Missbildungen der menschlichen Geschlechtsorgane*, trans. R. Teuscher (Berlin: H. Barsdorf, 1903), 96–103.
91 Ibid., 97.
92 Ferdinand-Valère Faneau de la Cour, *Du féminisme et de l'infantilisme chez les tuberculeux* (Paris: A. Parent, 1871).
93 Henri Meige, 'L'infantilisme, féminisme et les hermaphrodites antiques', *L'Anthropologie*, 15 (1895), 257–64.
94 *SE*, vol. VII, 141–2.
95 Leopold Löwenfeld, *Pathologie und Therapie der Neurasthenie und Hysterie* (Wiesbaden: J. F. Bergmann, 1894), 44–5. (In the Freud Library, London.)

96 Ibid., 19 (inheritance); 20, note (on hysteria).

97 On the background to the essay see Wilhelm Hemcker, '"Ihr Brief war mir so wertvoll . . ." Christian von Ehrenfels und Sigmund Freud – eine verschollene Korrespondenz', in Jean Clair, Cathrin Pichler and Wolfgang Pircher (eds.), *Wunderblock – eine Geschichte der modernen Seele* (Vienna: Löcker, 1989), 561–70. See also Peter Brückner, *Sigmund Freuds Privatlektüre* (Cologne: Verlag Rolf Horst, 1975), 62.

98 Sigmund Freud, *Standard Edition of the Complete Psychological Works of Sigmund Freud*, vol. IV, and trans J. Strachey, A. Freud, A. Strachey and A. Tyson (24 vols., London: Hogarth, 1955–74, referred to in the notes as *SE*), 181.

99 Christian von Ehrenfels, *Sexualethik* (Wiesbaden: J. F. Bergmann, 1907). (In the Freud Library, London with extensive marginalia.) This is reprinted in Christian von Ehrenfels, *Philosophische Schriften*, vol. III, ed. Reinhard Fabian (4 vols., Munich: Philosophia Verlag, 1982–90), 265–356. All references are to this edition.

100 On his debt to Freud, *Sexualethik*, 296, n. 1; on the problem of our time, 362; on the question of the 'higher' and 'lower' races see his essay 'Über den Einfluss des Darwinismus auf die moderne Soziologie', *Volkswirtschaftliche Wochenschrift* (Vienna), 42 (1904), 256–9 and *Die Wage* (Vienna), 7 (1904), 363–4, 382–5; *Philosophische Schriften*, vol. III, 251–64.

101 *Sexualethik*, 275.

102 Ibid., 276.

103 *SE*, vol. XIV, 274.

104 *Sexualethik*, 356.

105 *Protokolle der Wiener Psychoanalytischen Vereinigung*, vol. II, ed. Herman Nunberg and Ernst Federn (4 vols., Frankfurt a. M.: Fischer, 1976–81), 84–91; translation from *Minutes of the Vienna Psychoanalytic Society*, vol. II, trans. M. Nunberg (4 vols., New York: International Universities Press, 1962–75), 93–100, p. 93. He also discussed Fritz Wittels's monograph on sexuality, vol. I, 74–83; vol. II, 82–92.

106 On Ehrenfels's sense of his own Jewish ancestry see Max Brod, *Streitbares Leben* (Munich: Herbig, 1969), 211.

107 Christian von Ehrenfels, 'Rassenproblem und Judenfrage', *Prager Tageblatt*, 36 (1 December, 1911), 1–2. Reprinted in *Philosophische Schriften*, vol. IV, 334–42, p. 337.

108 Christian von Ehrenfels, 'Geschlecht und Charakter', *Politisch-anthropologische Revue*, 3 (1905); 481–4, p. 483.

109 On Weininger see my *Jewish Self-Hatred*, 244–51; Jacques Le Rider and Norbert Leser (eds.), *Otto Weininger: Werk und Wirkung* (Vienna: Osterreichischer Bundesverlag, 1984); Peter Heller, 'A Quarrel over Bisexuality', in Gerald Chapple and Hans H. Schulte (eds.) *The Turn of the Century: German Literature and Art, 1890–1915* (Bonn: Bouvier, 1978), 87–116; Peter Gay, *Freud. A Life for Our Time* (New York: W. W. Norton, 1988), 154–5; Katherine Arens, 'Characterology: Hapsburg Empire to Third Reich', *Literature and Medicine*, 9 (1989), 128–55, and her *Structures of Knowing: German Psychologies of the Nineteenth Century* (Dordrecht and Boston: Kluwer Academic Publishers, 1989); H. Rodlauer, *Von 'Eros und Psyche' zu 'Geschlecht und Charakter'*:

Unbekannte Weininger-Manuskripte im Archiv der Osterreichischen Akademie der Wissenschaften (Vienna: Verlag der Osterreichischen Akademie der Wissenschaften, 1987), 110–39; Franco Nicolino, *Indagini su Freud e sulla psicoanalisi* (Naples: Liguori editore, n.d.), 103–10.

110 See, for example, the discussion in Carl Dallago, *Otto Weininger und sein Werk* (Innsbruck: Brenner-Verlag, 1912) and Emil Lucka, *Otto Weininger: Sein Werk und seine Persönlichkeit* (Berlin: Schuster and Loeffler, 1921), esp. 37–80.

111 Charlotte Perkins Gilman, 'Review of Dr Weininger's *Sex and Character*', *The Critic*, 12(1906), 414.

112 Jacques Le Rider, 'Wittgenstein et Weininger', *Wittgenstein et la Critique du Monde Moderne* (Brussels: La Lettre Volée, 1990), 43–65.

113 Ehrenfels, *Philosophische Schriften*, vol. IV, 341.

114 Nunberg and Federn, *Protokolle der Wiener Psychoanalytischen Vereinigung*, vol. II, 84–91; translation from *Minutes of the Vienna Psychoanalytic Society*, vol. II, 93–100, p. 99.

115 Franz Kafka, *Tagebücher*, ed. Hans-Gerd Koch, Michael Müller and Malcolm Pasley (Frankfurt: S. Fischer, 1990), 370–1.

116 Heinrich Singer, *Allgemeine und spezielle Krankheitslehre der Juden* (Leipzig: Benno Konegen, 1904), 25.

117 *SE*, vol. IV, 182.

118 Ibid., 185; *GW*, vol. VIII, 148.

119 Otto Binswanger, *Die Pathologie und Therapie der Neurasthenie* (Jena: Gustav Fischer, 1896), 46. *SE*, vol. IX, 184–5.

120 Wilhelm Erb, *Über die wachsende Nervosität unserer Zeit. Akademische Rede zum Geburtsfeste . . . Karl Friedrich am 22. November 1893* (Heidelberg: Universitäts-Buchdruckerei J. Horing, 1893), 22.

121 Richard von Krafft-Ebing, *Nervosität und Neurasthenische Zustände* (Vienna: Alfred Holder, 1895), 57. (This was also published as part of vol. XII of Hermann Nothnagel (ed.), *Specielle Pathologie und Therapie* (24 vols., Vienna: Alfred Hölder, 1894–1908), 54.

122 *SE*, vol. XX, 212.

123 Sander L. Gilman, *Difference and Pathology: Stereotypes of Sexuality, Race, and Madness* (Ithaca, N.Y.: Cornell University Press, 1985), 76–108.

124 *SE*, vol. XV, 155.

125 See, for example, F. D. F. Souchay, *De l'homologie sexuelle chez l'homme* (Paris: Rignoux, 1855). This topic is central to the argument in Thomas Laqueur, *Making Sex: Body and Gender from the Greeks to Freud* (Cambridge, Mass: Harvard University Press, 1990).

126 Karl Reiskel, 'Idioticon viennense eroticum', *Anthropophyteia*, 2 (1905), 1–13, p. 9. Freud makes reference to this volume in *SE*, vol. X, 215, n. 1. On Freud's relation to the editor of the journal see Johannes Reichmeyr, 'Friedrich Salomon Krauss und Sigmund Freud – Begegnung unorthodoxer Gelehrte', *Luzifer Amor*, 1 (1988), 133–55, and Mirjam Morad, 'Friedrich Salomon Krauss. Vom Blick in die Seele zum Seelenzergliederer', in Clair et al. (eds.), *Wunderblock*, 501–6.

127 *SE*, vol. VII, 195.

128 *SE*, vol. XXI, 232–3.

SIXTEEN

'THE ENGLISH HAVE HOT-WATER BOTTLES':
THE MORGANATIC MARRIAGE BETWEEN
SEXOLOGY AND MEDICINE IN BRITAIN
SINCE WILLIAM ACTON

LESLEY A. HALL

'CONTINENTAL people have sex life; the English have hot-water bottles':[1] British traditions of discretion in matters of sexual conduct are expressed in the comment 'it doesn't matter what people do as long as they don't do it in the street and frighten the horses'. In such circumstances, could a 'British school' of sexology ever emerge?

Medical men, licensed to investigate other taboo facets of human existence, permitted, even compelled, to take some notice of sexual phenomena, consulted not merely about genital infections but also the functional disorders, have unrivalled opportunities to delve into others' sexual life. The newly respectable British medical profession of the mid-nineteenth century experienced some ambivalence in this matter. Interest in sexual phenomena veered perilously close to stigmatized quackery. Practitioners like Messrs Sloan and Co. (boasting membership of the Royal College of Surgeons), and Dr De Roos (with his famous Waxwork Museum) vaunting himself the 'only Legally-Qualified Practitioner in Berners Street', who blatantly advertised treatment for venereal diseases and 'Generative Disability and Seminal Weakness' in 'The Victims of Their Own Follies', were not models most mid-Victorian medical men aspired to emulate.[2] The ambiguous relationship between the British medical profession and the development of a science of sexology was at best a 'morganatic marriage': a union not establishing equality of rank between the partners, or conferring parental high status upon the offspring. Most doctors, while they wanted to get the study of sex off the streets and out of the hands of quacks, went no further towards granting it respectability than, as it were, setting it up in a discreet villa in St John's Wood.

Foucault has described sexuality as 'an especially dense transfer point for relations of power',[3] and he pointed out that sexual discourses proliferated during the nineteenth and twentieth centuries. Significant questions can asked about who might participate in particular debates,

350

and who was excluded and ought not listen. The 1860s in Britain were a crucial period in defining these questions of authority and exclusion for the medical profession.

The serious and scholarly study of sexual phenomena, though distasteful, was agreed to be needful, even praiseworthy. 'Secret diseases' should be wrested from the hands of quacks through their discussion 'by men of honour, probity, and intelligence', for example, William Acton, whose *The Functions and Disorders of the Reproductive Organs in Youth, Adult Age and Advanced Life, considered in their Physiological, Social and Psychological Aspects* was first published in 1857. The *Lancet* reviewer of the third edition, 1862, praised Acton's undertaking of identifying himself 'with all the aspects of the sexual question' and the 'honesty, boldness, and manifest good intent' with which he had done so.[4]

Acton, often dismissed as merely a propagandist for 'Victorian' ideas of female sexlessness, is more properly regarded as a revolutionary innovator initiating serious medical debate on sex, by no means antithetical to a figure such as Havelock Ellis. Acton's project was certainly seen by contemporaries as somewhat daring. The *Lancet* reviewer claimed that 'Mr Acton has never feared to touch pitch', while Sir James Paget, sometimes seen as Acton's antithesis,[5] paid obituary tribute that 'he practised honourably in the most dangerous of specialities ... wrote decently on subjects not usually decent ... never used the opportunities which his practice offered for quackery or extortion'.[6] Havelock Ellis confirmed Acton's importance by describing him in 1918 as 'the chief English authority on sexual matters', though deprecating his actual teachings.[7] As late as 1930, a *Lancet* reviewer alluded to 'Acton, the British pioneer in this subject'.[8]

Acton's respectability was more or less assured by the fact that he was writing for medical colleagues, in a serious and scholarly work by no means cheap, displaying classical learning and including lengthy quotes in foreign tongues, not intended to be popularly accessible, though it had some circulation among the lay public. Its message that sex was dangerous, primarily important from the reproductive aspect, contributed to his favourable reception.

Acton's acceptance contrasts with the fate of a couple of other contemporary practitioners operating in the field of sexual disorders. One of the first tests of the powers of the British General Medical Council concerned Samuel La'mert, a Licentiate of the Society of Apothecaries, and Bavarian MD. He was struck off the recently established Medical Register in 1863 for publishing 'an indecent and unprofessional treatise': *Self-Preservation: A Medical Treatise on Nervous and Physical Debility, Spermatorrhoea, Impotence and Sterility, with Practical*

Observations on the Use of the Microscope in the Treatment of Diseases of the Generative System. The Court of Queen's Bench upheld the ruling on appeal, without examining the work.[9]

It was not the matter of La'mert's work that caused scandal – his arguments about the dangerous neglect of this delicate subject by the profession parallel those in the pages of *The Lancet*,[10] and like Acton he warned of the dangers of over-indulgence in sexual pleasures[11] – it was its manner. *Self-Preservation* was a cheap volume aimed at the general public, incorporating advertisements for La'mert's Bedford Square practice, and testimonials from grateful patients. La'mert's son, Lima Abraham, a Licentiate of the Royal College of Physicians of Edinburgh, manifested eagerness to dissociate himself from his father's dubious practice, alleging false inclusion as joint author of *Self-Preservation*.[12]

The fascinating *cause célèbre* which erupted in 1866 and 1867 around Isaac Baker Brown and his clitoridectomies performed at the London Surgical Home involved complex factors, one being the question of who might be privy to medical discussions on sexual matters. The reviewer of Baker Brown's book *On the Curability of Certain Forms of Insanity, Epilepsy, and Hysteria in Females* in the *British Medical Journal* observed that a serious medical work on the subject of female masturbation should not 'bear . . . those outward *facies* which belong to the class of works which lie upon drawing-room tables', or have the author's name prominently externally displayed in gilt letters.[13] 'A Provincial FRCP' wrote to the *British Medical Journal* deploring Baker Brown's distribution of the *Report* of his London Surgical Home, with its lists of 'female diseases enough to make the blood of any layman curdle', to 'half the nobility in the Kingdom'.[14] The *British Medical Journal* editorialized on 'the disgust which reasonable and thinking men must feel at the public discussion, before mixed audiences, of sexual abuses'. Such 'a dirty subject' was 'one with which only a strong sense of duty can induce professional men to meddle . . . as far as possible in strictly technical language'.[15]

Baker Brown was perceived, by some at least of his colleagues, as improperly exciting 'the attention of non-medical persons, and especially of women, to the subject of Self-Abuse in the Female Sex'. Addressing audiences of clergymen was one of the practices for which he was condemned during the meeting of the Obstetrical Society considering his expulsion, as was his wide dissemination of circulars about the London Surgical Home.[16] Clergymen, it would appear, were among those to be excluded from medical debates on these touchy subjects. Some years later *The Lancet* was to compare doctors to 'the old type of priests who combined moral and medical functions', suggesting a quite remarkable degree of professional rivalry.[17]

This issue of audience and accessibility dogged the production of works on sexology well into the mid-twentieth century, with questions of who might be permitted to produce and who peruse these works and for what purpose. Acton's fearless tackling of the subject was commended, given that 'many men in the profession ... would fear associating their name and reputation with discussions of this kind',[18] but many doctors shrank even from discreet and professional association with sexual matters: after the examples of La'mert and Baker Brown the line may have seemed too fine a one to tread. While doctors might with propriety counsel and warn of the lurking dangers of sex, it was a duty they took up with great reluctance, if repeated exhortations by the leading medical journals may be believed.[19] Sexual matters might be a fit field for medical intervention, but the idea of their utter disgustingness persisted. Doctors prefaced discussions on sex with elaborate disclaimers about the unfortunate necessity of mentioning the subject at all.

In 1878 C. H. F. Routh claimed that he had been induced to discuss the evils of contraception only at the desire of 'distinguished members of the profession'. Aware of 'the responsibility of having one's notions misconstrued', nevertheless he was 'ready to fulfil a manly and generous part'. It was 'almost defilement even thus cursorily to allude to these vile practices' of 'sexual fraudulency, conjugal onanism', but the medical man's duty, unpleasant though it might be, to do so in order to point out the dangers.[20]

H. A. Allbutt, unfortunately for him, neglected Routh's precautions. *The Wife's Handbook* (1886), addressed to the lay public, at a price placing it within the reach of all but the poorest classes, did not condemn, but rather recommended, the use of contraception in certain circumstances. According to the *British Medical Journal* in 1889, Allbutt 'might have ventilated his views without let or hindrance from professional authority had he been contented to address them to medical men instead of to the public'.[21] It seems improbable that he would have met a favourable reception had he done so; however, he might have avoided deletion from the Medical Register.

As late as 1923 *The Practitioner*, a journal for the medical profession, in an issue devoted to birth control, found eminent medical persons of both sexes ready to deny the slightest hint of legitimacy to such a disgusting and physically deleterious practice. Just possibly contraception might be meted out in certain ultra-deserving cases on medical grounds: but some contributors assumed contra-indication of further pregnancies implied cessation of conjugal relations.[22]

By the end of the nineteenth century sex was gradually becoming more widely recognized as a legitimate subject for scientific investigation. Darwin's *Origin of Species* had opened up new approaches to the problem as a phenomenon bearing intimately upon the processes of evolution from the angle of biology. In 1889 a small volume entitled *The Evolution of Sex* was published in the Contemporary Science Series under the editorship of Havelock Ellis. The authors were Patrick Geddes, biologist, sociologist, educationist and town-planner, and J. Arthur Thomson, a zoologist (neither of them medical men). This work, a cheap and deliberately accessible volume, doubtless had a far wider circulation than Ellis's own multi-volume *Studies in the Psychology of Sex*, and moreover, probably accorded far more closely with prevalent ideas.

Geddes and Thomson's biological approach derived lessons for human behaviour from the description of the far less charged reproductive activities of much lower life-forms. Underlying all their arguments was the belief in 'the divergent evolution of the sexes', which they expressed in terms of 'anabolic' or constructive and conservative energies, assigned by them to the female, and 'katabolic' or disruptive and destructive energies, assigned by them to the male. The 'average truth throughout the world of animals' appeared to be 'the preponderating passivity of the females, the predominant activity of the males': at least, in the cochineal insect and the threadworm.[23] The study of insects and arachnids demonstrated that males 'are especially liable to exhaustion', but not – since it went unmentioned – also especially liable to be eaten by the female after mating.[24] Although the authors declared that it was 'full time to re-emphasise, this time of course with all scientific relativity instead of a dogmatic authority, the biological factors of the case',[25] their appeal to science did not seem to take them very far from the teachings of 'dogmatic authority'.

It is not clear what impact, if any, this work and its general approach had on the medical profession. It does not seem to have been reviewed by the major medical journals, and Geddes claimed it was 'boycotted by the physiologists, zoologists and botanists' because of his estrangement from the leading physiological school of the time, associated with Burdon-Sanderson and Schäfer.[26] Contemporary British physiologists were squeamish about sexual phenomena. The French scientist Brown-Séquard's use of testicular extracts for rejuvenation was greeted with scepticism by the British profession. The impetus which this 'organotherapy' gave to investigation into the gonadal secretions was ignored for some time by British endocrinologists, in spite of the important work on other glandular secretions being done by E. A. Schäfer and his school.²⁷ Although the physiology of other major organ systems had been explored long before, it was not until 1910 that F. H. A. Marshall's *The Physiology of Reproduction* .collated studies from a wide variety of uncoordinated fields to reveal how very little was known on the subject. Both Marshall, and the gynaecologist Blair Bell in *The Sex Complex* (1916), cited Geddes and Thomson's work – by then over twenty years old – as a significant contribution.²⁸

The new sexology of the turn of the century, however, is usually far more often associated, particularly in its medicalizing aspect, with the pathological and the deviant than with investigations into 'normal' functioning. Opinions on this development differed, and its influence upon the British medical profession is open to question. Because works on sex bore warnings (up to the mid-twentieth century at least) that their sale was restricted to members of the medical profession (and sometimes also to 'serious students of sexual problems') this is no guarantee that they were either purchased or read by doctors. (There is some evidence, though, that booksellers would not sell such works to members of the public without medical authorization.)²⁹

Writers in the medical press might concede that 'many morally disgusting subjects ... have to be studied by the doctor and by the jurist': but though perhaps 'valuable as a book of reference', Krafft-Ebing's *Psychopathia sexualis* was 'not to be left about for general reading'.³⁰ Nationalistic prejudice was also involved. Arthur Cooper's *The Sexual Disabilities of Man and their treatment* (1908) was favourably contrasted by *The Lancet* with 'turbid continental outpourings',³¹ which may have alluded to the works of Sigmund Freud as well as those of Krafft-Ebing. W. H. R. Rivers, while promulgating the value of Freud's theories in the abreactive treatment for shellshock in 1917, deplored the Freudians' over-emphasis on sex.³² As late as 1920 Sir Robert Armstrong-Jones could declare to the Medico-Psychological Society that Freud's system was 'probably applicable to life on the Austrian and German frontiers, but not to virile, sport-loving open-air people like the British'.³³ Early psychoanalytic writings gained more sympathetic attention in Britain among the educated and enquiring lay public than the medical profession: even then Jung was preferred to Freud.³⁴

The towering native figure of British sexology was Henry Havelock Ellis (1859–1939), a man of considerable eccentricity and polymathic learning, who received a revelation of his life's work, to elucidate the mysteries of sex, while employed as a school-teacher in a remote area of Australia. Gaining a medical qualification as a necessary first step was a wise tactical move. Returning to England to study medicine, after much trial he obtained in 1889 the Licentiate of the Society of Apothecaries, the minimum necessary diploma, and soon abandoned practice to devote himself to his life's work. He must be one of the few Licentiates of the Society of Apothecaries ever to have become a Fellow of the Royal College of Physicians, an honour bestowed in 1938 shortly before his death. His own sex-life seems to have been unorthodox: a urolagnist, he had numerous amorous friendships with women, besides being married twice (the first time to the predominantly lesbian Edith Lees), but it seems questionable whether any of these were fully consummated. Ellis, although praised by the profession for having qualified in medicine as an essential preliminary to his great work, unlike, for example, Acton, did not derive the data incorporated into his studies from clinical practice. His work was based on the study of an enormous variety of sources: medical writings, anthropological research, the work of biologists, literature from many countries, and, as Ellis and his works became more widely known, personal or epistolary confidences. Ellis's approach was synthetic rather than analytical, covering vast aeons of history and the entire world, with a lack of dogmatism extremely refreshing in such a field, although he did not wholly avoid contemporary assumptions.[35]

The initial volume of the *Studies*, *Sexual Inversion*, was confiscated in 1897 during the seizure from the publisher of material suspected to be politically subversive. However, the subject of the book was particularly sensitive so soon after the imprisonment of Oscar Wilde. *The Lancet* admitted that a work of 'scientific enquiry into a subject which, though odious in itself, has yet to be faced, cannot possibly be included under the head of indecent literature'. The *British Medical Journal* likewise conceded that 'nothing about the book itself ... pander[s] to the prurient mind'. 'Such a book', however, might 'become indecent if offered to the general public with a wrong motive'. The medical press was agreed that the subject, though 'extremely disagreeable', was undoubtedly 'one of those unpleasant matters with which members of the medical profession should have some acquaintance'. There were 'proper claims for discussion' of the 'subject of sexual inversion', though this should be limited 'to persons of particular attainments', implicitly supposed to be medical men, and possibly jurists. It was 'especially important that such matters should not be discussed by the man in the street, not to mention the boy and girl in the street'.[36] Doctors should not 'object to dealing with filth for the purpose of elucidating a scientific principle or obtaining a valuable datum'.[37] Nevertheless, it was inappropriate to extend the debate to the lay public or disseminate this dangerous knowledge among them.

The consequences of so doing were never explicitly stated. (Frightened horses perhaps?)

Ellis qualified (just) to investigate, and even speak on, matters of sexuality. But to whom could he unfold his investigations? Once the *Sexual Inversion* furore had died down Ellis apparently enjoyed the esteem of fellow members of his profession. As early as 1902 a reviewer in the *British Medical Journal* commended Ellis's 'serious and honest attempts to deal with his subject', though regretting such 'honesty of purpose' was not 'turned to better account'.[38] By 1910, the *Lancet's* reviewer was recommending *Sex in Relation to Society* 'to the medical world and to serious students of social problems'.[39] Ellis, like Acton before him, had become the acceptable medical man who had taken on the unlovely task of dealing with sexual matters, to be held up against quacks, or foreigners like Krafft-Ebing. It must have helped that he wrote in 'delicate, grave, rectory English', sustaining 'in the most difficult circumstances' the 'inveterate appearance ... of being a character out of *Cranford*'.[40] As well as displaying this chastity of style, *Studies in the Psychology of Sex* were clearly the result of serious scholarly labours, published in limited, exsspensive editions that were hard to obtain, and never in their entirety in the UK, although Ellis did also produce more popular works. Well before his death he had become the Grand Old Man of British sexology. By the early 1930s the medical press was recommending Ellis's short compendium *Psychology of Sex* as a textbook in medical schools (if not for a wider audience), paying tribute to his illumination of this murky subject for the benefit of other practitioners.[41]

By the time of Ellis's death in 1939 the climate of sexual discussion had allegedly changed radically, due in part to his efforts. To J. A. Ryle, founder of the discipline of social medicine, the contrast between the reception of *Sexual Inversion* and 'the respect now shown [1943] to the memory of Havelock Ellis' was 'a measure of our change in outlook'. But Ryle pertinently asked: 'How many practitioners, how many teachers of medical students, I wonder, have read his *Psychology of Sex* or *Sex in Relation to Society*, or given serious thought to the teaching which in turn they might have given to others?'[42] It could even possibly be argued that Ellis, by his very stature in the field, his almost single-handed efforts to elevate sexology to the dignity of a science in its own right, valued by the medical profession but not merely, as it had been with Acton, an aspect of clinical practice, had in fact effected a closure of the entire field in Britain.

Yet he was not alone. Among the others in the field must be included Edward Carpenter (1844–1929), a passionate advocate of the rights of homosexuals in an era when it could be remarked at the very highest levels of society, 'I thought fellas like that shot themselves'.[43] Carpenter's *Love's Coming of Age* (1896) was exceedingly influential and much reprinted.[44] The treatment of his *The Intermediate Sex* by the *British Medical Journal* in 1909 contrasts sharply with the praise received by Ellis and the approval accorded Arthur Cooper, contemporary medical men writing on allied subjects. The reviewer began his four-column attack by complaining of having 'been subjected to so many publications of this character since *Psychopathia Sexualis* and *Sexual Inversion*'. He concluded with the suggestion that 'Urnings' ought to emigrate to 'some land where their presence might be welcome, and thus serious people in England might be spared the waste of time reading a low-priced book of no scientific or literary merit, advocating the culture of unnatural and criminal practices'. Since the reviewer mentioned the book's low price once, and its cost (3s. 6d) twice, perhaps this pricing (and indeed general orientation) for a popular audience was even more of an offence than the subject matter to which he took overt exception.[45] Carpenter was dismissively referred to as late as 1939 as what Ellis might have been lacking the benefits of medical training.[46]

Marie Stopes (1880–1958), the sexologist as agony aunt, wrote and published *Married Love: A New Contribution to the Solution of Sex Difficulties* (1918) while still certifiably a virgin, according to the court which had granted the annulment of her first marriage. Stopes was not a medical doctor but a palaeobotanist, with degrees from London and Munich. Finding her marriage inexplicably unsatisfactory, she undertook a course of study among the books in the British Museum Reading Room still shelved under the rubric of 'Cupboard', and reached the conclusion (or so she subsequently claimed) that her marriage had never been consummated. She felt that 'knowledge gained at such a cost' ought to be deployed for the wider good.[47] She therefore wrote *Married Love*, a runaway bestseller from its first appearance early in 1918.[48] Stopes is usually remembered as a propagandist for birth control but contraception was only one aspect of her ideals of marital sex: Ellis himself paid tribute to her idea of a cycle of recurrent sexual desire in women.[49]

Contributions to sexology did not emerge solely outside the medical profession. Kenneth Walker, FRCS (1882–1966), produced a plethora of works for the profession and the general public, based on his clinical experience. He had the advantage of being one of the finest genito-urinary surgeons of the age, allegedly attending on royalty and certainly attending Sir Henry Wellcome.[50] Walker was also, however, a student of Gurdjieff and Ouspensky, amongst other interests not usually associated with the practice of surgery, and was considered 'more of a philosopher than most surgeons are'.[51]

There was 'a select and courageous group of women doctors ... pioneers in sexual reform', considered 'heretical and shocking' for their contributions to the advancement of sexual knowledge, the dissemination of sex education, and the improvement of control over fertility. Numbered among them were Joan Malleson (1900–56), and Helena Wright (1887–1982), former medical missionary in China, both influential figures in the body eventually entitled the Family Planning Association. Work in birth-control clinics revealed to both of them the frequency of common sexual problems (especially those of women) and gave them insights into them which were embodied in their practice and in their writings. Wright, in *The Sex Factor in Marriage* and elsewhere, defended the significance of the clitoris in female sexual arousal and satisfaction throughout a period when clitoral orgasm was being condemned as inferior to the vaginal variety.[52]

Norman Haire (1892–1952), who practised in Harley Street, wrote on sexual matters himself and sponsored translations of, and edited, continental works on the subject.[53] He was in touch with developments worldwide, visiting and studying at Magnus Hirschfeld's Institute for Sexual Science in Berlin and active in the World League for Sexual Reform, as well as the British Society for the Study of Sex Psychology. Haire wrote to Havelock Ellis of this body that 'to be of any service in England it must work largely through the medical profession'. Himself of Australian origin, he commented that 'the English medical profession is a powerful priesthood'.[54]

All these writers had a propagandist aim as well as the intention to push back the frontiers of sexual knowledge. They produced accessible writings directed at a lay audience to lift the dark clouds of sexual ignorance which troubled so many. While assuming the medical profession's particular claims to knowledge in this field, they believed this knowledge ought to be more widely disseminated. Acute recognition of the ignorance of many doctors and their reluctance to have anything to do with sexual problems encountered almost unconscious belief in the authority of medical science. Lay authors often appealed to or recommended medical authorities. Writers such as A. Herbert Gray or Leslie Weatherhead in religiously orientated works on sexual conduct were prone, in long-standing social purity tradition,[55] to appeal to the medical benefits as well as moral value of their advice, and to incorporate chapters specially written by medics on 'The Physical Facts'.[56] The relationship between the actual medical profession and this rise of a medicalized discursive system for speaking about sex is extremely problematic. Doctors themselves implicitly differentiated between what could be admitted within the profession and what could be said to the public. Kenneth Walker was scathing about other doctors in works intended for colleagues,[57] but writing for the public, advised the family physician as a first resort in cases of marital difficulty.[58]

Doctors who broke the barriers as to whom they might communicate with, and in what terms, ran risks, as Norman Haire found when the publisher of his edited translation of the *Encyclopaedia of Sexual Knowledge* was prosecuted in 1934. It was not so much the book itself – 'a bulky volume of fairly high price' – that was the problem but the advertising pamphlet issued by the publisher, considered inappropriate for a serious scientific work. Haire hastily disclaimed having had any control over the content and dissemination of this pamphlet.[59] Another Harley Street doctor, Eustace Chesser, specialist in gynaecology and psychology, had his marriage manual *Love without Fear* prosecuted for obscenity in 1942. The usual procedure in such cases was for the defendant to plead guilty and pay a small fine. Chesser took the calculated risk of trial by jury, appealing to the common sense of the 'man in the street', and was vindicated (what the repercussions of conviction on his career and status would have been are not clear, but it would hardly have done him good). The defence contended that 'in the year 1942' it was 'ridiculous and absurd to suggest that the discussion of sex and sex relationship in a book is obscene'. Nevertheless, it was emphasized that the book was for sale to the married and those about to be married only, in reputable bookshops such as Harrods and W. H. Smith, at a price calculated to keep it out of the hands of the merely pruriently curious (who beset all debates about the wider dissemination of sexual information).[60]

It would appear that Chesser had hit on an interesting, but not unique, point in appealing to lay common sense. The Mass Observation organization was set up in the 1930s to produce 'an anthropology of ourselves'. Among its wide-ranging investigations, it endeavoured to scrutinize al fresco courtship behaviour among holidaymakers at Blackpool,[61] and during the war conducted Government-sponsored research into public opinion (and knowledge) about venereal diseases.[62] In 1947 it undertook a 'Sex Survey' on 'what people's attitudes really are to sex morality in this country'. One of its outstanding discoveries was 'the contrast between our own initial expectation of inhibition, embarrassment and rebuff – and the friendly and cooperative manner with which our questions were answered'. Only 1 per cent of the random street sample refused to continue responding once they had learnt of the survey's emphasis. The 'street sample' as well as the probably rather untypical liberal middle-class members of the Mass Observation Panel of observers, took a view on issues such as the desirability of sex education that tended to differ from the rigidly restrictive views expressed by 'Leaders of Opinion', such as the medical profession, the clergy and teachers.[63]

Mass Observation's approach, using lay observers approaching interviewees in the street, contrasts vividly with the agonizings as to the proper way of acquiring both sample and interviewers of the Royal College of Obstetricians and Gynaecologists in 1944 when they undertook an 'Enquiry into Family Limitation and its Influence on Human Fertility during the Past Fifty Years' for the Royal Commission on Population. They anticipated difficulties in 'questioning a representative sample of the normal married female population'. Because of the 'very tactful approach' needed, 'the Committee were convinced that only qualified members of the medical profession who stood to the women in the relation of doctor to patient were suitable persons to act as interviewers'. Thus doctors specially hired to conduct the interviews approached married women in general hospital wards.[64] While the Royal College's survey accumulated considerable amounts of statistical data, Mass Observation's less rigid approach provided much richer qualitative material. The embarrassment or rudeness or otherwise of 'the street sample' in the 1942-3 venereal disease survey formed a pertinent element of the information gleaned.[65]

Prejudice against investigations into sexual behaviour continued. Eustace Chesser, already mentioned, undertook a survey of the *Sexual, Marital, and Family Relationships of the Englishwoman* in the early 1950s, a large detailed survey considering many variables. He collaborated with a number of other people: his 'Advisory Committee' included Kenneth Walker, and nearly 1,500 doctors assisted in gathering data.[66] However, in spite of Chesser's medical status and the co-operation of fellow members of the profession, the production of this work apparently caused scandal among his colleagues.[67] No reviews of the volume appeared in either the *British Medical Journal* or *The Lancet*. The refusal within the last few years of government funding to the survey of sexual behaviour in Britain subsequently funded by the Wellcome Trust indicates that similar prejudices are far from extinct.

While doctors continued to take a somewhat custodial attitude towards sexual information, and were regarded in and out of the profession as repositories of sexual knowledge, it is very arguable whether they knew more about the matter than the average person.

Sex was dealt with fleetingly and peripherally, if at all, in medical school curricula. A 1949 commentator (almost certainly Alex Comfort, then a young doctor) on the Goodenough report on medical schools remarked in *The Lancet* that though the doctor was 'the one person who might be expected to provide informed advice', patients often complained that 'problems ... arising out of sexual abnormality or sexual ignorance find the least satisfactory reception'. He was forced to admit that 'the newly qualified doctor today is no better off, so far as the teaching given him is concerned, than his counterpart of 1914. Indeed, he often shares all the prejudices of his time.'[68] Elsewhere Comfort claimed that 'sex education of the public in England has almost certainly outstripped sex education of doctors', and that 'the patient with a specifically sexual problem' was 'very often willing to discuss it with anyone except his own medical adviser'.[69]

In 1962 Clifford Allen asserted that 'psychosexual diseases' had become 'an acceptable part of the corpus of respectable medicine'[70] but in 1979 psychosexual medicine could still be described as 'this new branch of the profession', over eighty years after the publication of the first volume of *Studies in the Psychology of Sex*.[71] Writers of recent textbooks for the general practitioner faced with sexual problems in the surgery have pointed out that most doctors prefer 'to avoid the subject rather than reveal their embarrassment, ignorance and therapeutic impotence'.[72] Patients found that 'the doctor either didn't know how to help them, or just didn't want to know about their problems'.[73] A leader in *The Lancet* in 1988 remarked that more was known about the Human Immunodeficiency Virus than about people's actual sexual practices in the privacy of their bedrooms.[74]

It may be argued that we have now gone far beyond the simplistic appeal to 'science' and aggregation of statistics on sexual behaviour, that the whole debate is far more sophisticated, to do with the complex structuring and manifestation of sexual roles within society. Doctors' 'false traditions and antiquated prejudices'[75] on problems of sexuality are, however, by no means outmoded. During the 1980s the *British Medical Journal* printed a discreet small advertisement for the Gay Medical Association, causing furore which led to a leader entitled 'Intolerance 1980s Style', in turn generating further heated correspondence.[76] Far from being aware of recent debates on questions of sexual identity, doctors agitated by the issue did not seem to have got as far as 1897 in their thinking and their comments would not have seemed out of place at the trial of Oscar Wilde.

Nevertheless, a British school of sexology, with both lay and medical representatives, can be traced. On the whole its character has been pragmatic and empirical, lacking the theoretical constructs emanating from the continent, as one might expect, given the British empirical intellectual tradition. Those who took an interest in the science of sex – very few – did so on a more or less amateur basis. It was no route to professional posts or the acclaim of colleagues, although considerable financial rewards could accrue (Norman Haire's Harley Street practice was extremely profitable). It was a subject pursued on the whole by individuals in some way 'outsiders', by reason of their gender, sexual orientation, ethnicity or national origin, or interests placing them outside the mainstream.

The contribution of the medical profession to both the creation of the field and the dissemination of its findings was deeply ambiguous. Terms of debate on sex were ever-increasingly medicalized, yet the actual profession manifested recurrent anxiety about the spread of serious, non-didactic discussion of sexual phenomena beyond those who had an allegedly legitimate claim to pursue this study (whether they actually pursued it or not). The fear persisted that without precautions, in some way the entire subject would get loose, run into the streets, and frighten the horses.

NOTES

1 Entire chapter on 'Sex', G. Mikes, *How to be an Alien* (London, 1946), quoted in *The Best of Mikes* (London, 1962), 22.
2 Advertisements and handbills, c.1857–8, in William Acton's 'Social Evil Abstracts' scrapbook, part I, Fawcett Library, London Guildhall University.
3 M. Foucault, *The History of Sexuality*, vol. 1: *An Introduction* (Harmondsworth, 1979), 103.
4 *Lancet*, I (1862), 518–19. *The Lancet* took spermatorrhoea seriously: articles by J. L. Milton appeared in 1854, and a further series by M. Wilson during 1856–7.
5 M. J. Peterson, 'Dr Acton's Enemy: Medicine, Sex, and Society in Victorian England', *Victorian Studies*, 29 (1986), 569–90.
6 *Proceedings of the Royal Medical and Chirurgical Society of London*, 7 (1876), 74–6.
7 H. Ellis, *The Erotic Rights of Women and the Objects of Marriage* (London, 1918), 9.
8 *Lancet*, I (1930), 1187.
9 S. La'mert, *Self-Preservation: A Medical Treatise on Nervous and Physical Debility, Spermatorrhoea, Impotence and Sterility, with Practical Observations on the Use of the Microscope in the Treatment of Diseases of the Generative System* (London, c.1850s–1860s); *British Medical Journal*, I (1863), 567; II (1863), 586–7; *Lancet*, II (1863), 634–35.
10 Ibid., 'Introduction', ix.
11 Ibid., 23.
12 *BMJ*, II (1863), 586–7; *Lancet*, II (1863), 634–5.

13 *BMJ*, I (1866), 440.
14 Ibid., 478.
15 *BMJ*, II (1866), 665.
16 *Lancet*, II (1866), 566; *BMJ*, I (1867), 395–410.
17 *Lancet*, II (1889), 1042.
18 *Lancet*, I (1862), 518.
19 e.g., *Lancet*, II (1870), 89–90, 124–6, 159–60, 224–5.
20 C. H. F. Routh, *On the Moral and Physical Evils Likely to Follow if Practices Intended to Act as Checks to Population be not Strongly Discouraged and Condemned* (London, 1879).
21 *BMJ*, II (1889), 88.
22 *The Practitioner*, July 1923: A. L. McIlroy, 'The Harmful Effects of Artificial Contraceptive Methods', 25–35.
23 P. Geddes and J. A. Thomson, *The Evolution of Sex* (London, 1889), 17.
24 Ibid., 257.
25 Ibid., 269.
26 P. Boardman, *The Worlds of Patrick Geddes, Biologist, Town Planner, Re-educator, Peace-warrior* (London and Boston, 1978), 299.
27 M. Borell, 'Organotherapy, British Physiology, and Discovery of the Internal Secretions', *Journal of the History of Biology*, 9 (1976), 235–68; 'Setting the Standards for a New Science: Edward Schäfer and Endocrinology', *Medical History*, 22 (1978), 282–90; 'Organotherapy and the Emergence of Reproductive Technology', *Journal of the History of Biology*, 18 (1985), 1–30.
28 F. H. A. Marshall, *The Physiology of Reproduction* (London, New York, Bombay and Calcutta, 1910), 'Introduction', 1; W. Blair Bell, *The Sex Complex: A Study of the Relationships of the Internal Secretions to the Female Characteristics and Functions in Health and Disease* (London, 1916), 'Introduction', 3; 'Sex Characteristics', 13.
29 W. Gallichan, *The Poison of Prudery: An Historical Survey* (London, 1929), 147; Marie Stopes's papers in the Contemporary Medical Archives Centre at the Wellcome Institute for the History of Medicine, CMAC PP/MCS/A.158, correspondent re attempt to purchase *Contraception*, 1923.
30 *BMJ*, I (1893), 1325–6; R. von Krafft-Ebing, *Psychopathia sexualis: With Especial Reference to the Antipathetic Sexual Instinct. A Medico-forensic Study*, first published in German, 1886 (London, 1893).
31 *Lancet*, II (1908), 1373.
32 *Lancet*, I (1917), 912–14.
33 *Lancet*, II (1920), 404.
34 D. Rapp, 'The Early Discovery of Freud by the British General Public', *Social History of Medicine*, 3 (1990), 217–43.
35 P. Grosskurth, *Havelock Ellis: A Biography* (London, 1980) is the most recent biography; see also chapter on Ellis in P. Robinson, *The Modernization of Sex* (New York, 1976), 1–41: still a good study of Ellis's thought, though Robinson points out in a recent reprint that the book is very much of its time.
36 *Lancet*, II (1898), 1344–5; *BMJ*, II (1898), 1466.
37 *BMJ*, I (1902), 339–40.
38 Ibid.

39 *Lancet*, I (1910), 1207.
40 Review of Ellis's *Essays in Wartime*, in J. Marcus (ed.), *The Young Rebecca: Writings of Rebecca West 1911–1917* (London, 1982), 332–5.
41 *Lancet*, I (1933), 1348; *BMJ*, I (1933), 1057.
42 *Lancet*, I (1943), 415.
43 Allegedly by King George V.
44 E. Carpenter, *Love's Coming of Age: A Series of Papers on the Relation of the Sexes* (London, 1896): thirteen editions by 1930.
45 *BMJ*, I (1909), 1547.
46 *Lancet*, II (1939), 164.
47 M. Stopes, *Married Love. A New Contribution to the Solution of Sex Difficulties* (London, 1918), Author's Preface, xiii.
48 P. Eaton and M. Warnick, *Marie Stopes: A Checklist of Her Writings* (London 1977); R. Hall, *Marie Stopes: A Biography* (London, 1977).
49 H. Ellis, *Eonism and Other Supplementary Studies, Studies in the Psychology of Sex*, vol. VII, (Philadelphia, 1928), section IV, 'The Menstrual Curve of Sexual Impulse', 213–36.
50 *BMJ*, II (1936), 318.
51 *Lancet*, I (1966), 300; Sir J. P. Ross and W. R. Lefanu, *Lives of the Fellows of the Royal College of Surgeons, 1965–1973* (London, 1981), 377–8.
52 Transcript of broadcast obituary of Dr Joan Malleson, *Woman's Hour*, December 1956, in Family Planning Association archives in the Contemporary Medical Archives Centre at the Wellcome Institute for the History of Medicine, CMAC: SA/FPA/A.14/58.2; B. Evans, *Freedom to Choose: The Life and Work of Dr Helena Wright, Pioneer of Contraception* (London, 1984); H. Wright, *The Sex Factor in Marriage: A Book for those who are or are about to be Married* (London, 1930); *More About the Sex Factor in Marriage: A Sequel to The Sex Factor in Marriage* (London, 1947).
53 N. Haire, *Hymen, or the Future of Marriage* (New York, 1928); (ed.), *Some More Medical Views on Birth Control* (London, 1928); (ed.), English translation of A. Costler and A. Willy, *Encyclopaedia of Sexual Knowledge* (London, 1934).
54 Havelock Ellis papers, British Library Additional Manuscripts 70540, Haire to Ellis, 20.8.1923.
55 e.g., 'JEH' (J. E. Hopkins), 'True Manliness', A. T. Barnett, 'The Testimony of Medical Men', White Cross League tracts published during the 1880s, reprinted in *The Blanco Book* (London, 1913), 115–43, 217–48.
56 Rev. A. H. Gray, *Men, Women, and God: A Discussion of Sex Questions from the Christian Point of View* (London, 1923), Appendix 'Some of the Physical Facts' by Dr Charles Gray (Revd Gray's brother); L. Weatherhead, *The Mastery of Sex through Psychology and Religion* (London, 1931), Appendix 'The Physical Facts' – 'based on notes specially written for this book by Dr Greaves'.
57 K. M. Walker, *Male Disorders of Sex* (London, 1930), 65.
58 K. M. Walker, *Marriage: A Book for the Married and about to be Married* (London, 1951), 33–7; *Love, Marriage and the Family* (London, 1957), 75–6.
59 *BMJ*, II (1934), 95, 152.
60 E. Chesser, *Love without Fear: A Plain Guide to Sex Technique for Every Married Adult* (London, 1941); A. Craig, 'Recent Developments in the Law of Obscene

Libel', in Dr A. Pillay and A. Ellis (eds.), *Sex, Society and the Individual: Selected Papers, Revised and Brought up to Date, from Marriage Hygiene [1934–1937] and the International Journal of Sexology [1947–1952]* (Bombay, 1953), 302–27.

61 A. Calder and D. Sheridan (eds.), *Speak for Yourself: A Mass Observation Anthology 1937–1949* (Oxford, 1985), 48–62.

62 Tom Harrisson-Mass Observation Archive at the University of Sussex: A9, 'Sexual Behaviour 1929–1950', includes this material.

63 Mass Observation File Report no. 3010A: findings were never published in full.

64 'Report on an Enquiry into Family Limitation and its Influence on Human Fertility during the Past Fifty Years' by E. Lewis-Faning, B.Sc., Ph.D., Conducted at the Request of the Royal Commission on Population'; held in the Royal College of Obstetricians and Gynaecologists. Published by HMSO in 1949 as *Papers from the Royal Commission on Population*, vol. I.

65 Mass Observation, A9 'Sexual Behaviour 1929–1950', Box 1/A Venereal Disease Survey, December 1942 (London).

66 E. Chesser, J. Maizels, L. Jones and B. Emmett, *The Sexual, Marital and Family Relationships of the English Woman* (London, 1956), 'Introduction'.

67 Dr Eric Trimmer (former editor, *Journal of Sexual Medicine*) indicates that the British Medical Association was somewhat perturbed: letter to *The Times*, 15.9.89; also verbal communication.

68 *Lancet*, I (1949), 744.

69 A. Comfort, 'Sex Education in the Medical Curriculum', *International Journal of Sexology*, 3 (1950), 175–7. Supporting evidence may be found in L. A. Hall, *Hidden Anxieties: Male Sexuality 1900–1950* (Oxford and Cambridge, Mass., 1991), chapter 6, 139–69.

70 C. Allen, *Textbook of Psychosexual Disorders* (London, 1962), ix.

71 M. Aylett, review of Eric Trimmer's *Basic Sexual Medicine*, *Journal of the Royal College of General Practitioners*, 29 (1979), 440.

72 C. Fairburn, M. G. Dickson and J. Greenwood, *Sexual Problems and Their Management* (Edinburgh, 1983), 'Introduction' by J. Bancroft, i.

73 G. R. Freedman, *Sexual Medicine* (Edinburgh, 1983), 107.

74 *Lancet*, I (1988), 31.

75 H. Ellis, *Psychology of Sex: The Biology of Sex – The Sexual Impulse in Youth – Sexual Deviation – The Erotic Symbolism – Homosexuality – Marriage – The Art of Love* (London, 1933), 2.

76 *BMJ*, II (1985), 1747.

SEVENTEEN

TAINTED LOVE

RICHARD DAVENPORT-HINES AND CHRISTOPHER PHIPPS

The first and only principle of sexual ethics: the accuser is always in the wrong.

Theodor Adorno

If I partake of my pleasure prudently and gingerly it will no longer be pleasure for me.

Lope de Vega

Men are rewarded or punished not for what they do, but rather for how their acts are defined. This is why men are more interested in better justifying themselves than in better behaving themselves.

Thomas Szasz

A LATE TWENTIETH-CENTURY PANDEMIC

The most recently emergent fatal human epidemic has two names and two acronyms. The Human Immunodeficiency Virus (HIV) and Acquired Immunodeficiency Syndrome (AIDS) are related medical phenomena with far-reaching social, economic, political and demographic implications, arguably far-reaching sexual implications and some minor artistic meanings. It is impossible in this brief essay to do more than sketch the subject.[1] We have chosen to focus on some of the medical and social paradoxes raised by HIV and AIDS. The duality of the pandemic has a resonance beyond its nomenclature.

HIV is a virus transmissible in body fluids such as semen and blood (but not sweat or saliva) which results in the breakdown of the human immunity system and facilitates the outbreak of a variety of opportunistic and ultimately fatal infections. Among the most common illnesses for people with AIDS (PWA) are a skin cancer called Kaposi's sarcoma, pneumocystis carinii pneumonia (PCP) and cryptococcal meningitis, but the list of AIDS-associated clinical conditions grows steadily longer. The interval between infection with HIV and the (attributed) onset of AIDS varies considerably between patients; so too do patients' responses to treatment.[2] The two most common routes of infection have been sexual intercourse and the shared use of needles by intravenous (IV) drug-users; in the 1980s haemophiliacs and other hospital patients requiring blood transfusions were also infected with HIV by contaminated blood products.

Since the early 1980s HIV has caused heartbreak, waste and loss on an enormous scale. By mid-1992 a cumulative total of 501,272 cases of AIDS had been reported to the World Health Organisation (WHO) from 191 countries. This is a certain and acknowledged understatement: more realistic estimates suggest a toll of between 2 million and 2.6 million cases globally. In any event, the delay between initial infection and the onset of AIDS means that these figures are like a frozen frame from a film of the epidemic taken a decade ago. WHO predicts that 50 per cent of people with HIV will develop AIDS within ten years of infection, 90 per cent within twenty years. To run the film forward we must look at the numbers of people diagnosed as seropositive with HIV (HIV+). By July 1992 WHO estimated that between 10 and 12 million adults and children worldwide were HIV+; in the same month the International AIDS Center at Harvard (IACH) projected that these figures would have risen to nearly 20 million by 1995. It is clear that the death toll has not yet peaked on any continent: in Africa one adult in 40 may be HIV+; in the USA the ratios are one man in 75 and one woman in 700; and in Europe one man in 200 and one woman in 1,400. In south-east Asia HIV has arrived later but with explosive results, so that over one million people have been infected since the late 1980s. IACH now estimates that across the world up to 24 million adults will have AIDS by 2000 and between 38 million and 110 million will be HIV+.

Though the lives of people with AIDS can be prolonged, and techniques of treatment are steadily improving in the industrialized world, there is no cure.

FIRST WORLD, OR THIRD?

AIDS is a global catastrophe but not a monolithic one. The experiences of people living in, say, the Caribbean, sub-Saharan Africa, south-east Asia or the developed world vary. Social and medical responses must struggle to accommodate this pluralism: 'AIDS cannot be stopped in any country unless it is stopped in all countries', as an official of the WHO declared in 1988.³ If any categorization is helpful in the face of this complexity, it is between rich AIDS and poor AIDS. In any epidemic there are differences of perception and experience between rich and poor communities. Inadequate housing and diet, or poor working conditions, often increase vulnerability to infection. Poor education, exhaustion and despair can make people less receptive to ideas of preventive medicine. The poor are likely to have meagre access to medical care and medicines. They are less likely to be able to organize their communities to deal with health issues. All along the line they are likely to be told what to do by people of alien traditions and sympathies. In these respects the HIV epidemic has resembled earlier epidemics, but more than most it has compounded the traditional social dichotomy between the sick and the well with a schism between the rich sick and the poor sick.

In rich AIDS most of the activism, including publicity about safer sex, has originated from within those communities most heavily stricken with the virus: so we have the vital, campaigning work of the Gay Men's Health Crisis in New York, for example. But in poor AIDS 'solutions', or codes of behaviour, are imposed on those perceived by others to be at risk: such is the experience of First World health agencies working with sub-Saharan black Africans, for example. Everywhere AIDS is supremely a personal disaster, but in prosperous parts of the world it has secondary associations with notions of individual self-expression and liberation. Elsewhere it is linked more fundamentally to questions of familial and national survival.

In the USA and Europe ACT UP (AIDS Coalition to Unleash Power) has organized demonstrations and confrontations as well as directly participating in policy-making and cultivating news media.⁴ In Britain the previously staid Haemophilia Society has been forced into a role of AIDS activism.⁵ Along with issues of medical treatment, vaccine trials and access to new therapies, activists from the rich world have laudably lobbied on such questions as the privacy of people with HIV, contact-tracing, the ethics of antibody testing, and discrimination against PWA and those who have tested positive.⁶ These concerted intra-community efforts of the First World have endured many hardships; hopes for success from the fragmented work of aid agencies in the Third World look even bleaker.

The neglect of PWA outside the developed world can be shown in innumerable ways. Since the identification of AIDS in 1981, 97 per cent of the money spent on its research has been spent in the industrialized world. Some 30,000 research papers on HIV and AIDS were published in 1981–91, of which only 3 per cent concerned African populations, although 25 per cent of AIDS patients lived in Africa. Only 11 per cent of the world budget on AIDS care goes to the 70 per cent of PWA who live outside North America or Western Europe. In the developed world one PWA may have $100,000 spent on treatment, but the annual health budgets of many Third World countries amount to less than $1 per head of population. 'A few AIDS cases would bankrupt us, just in terms of taking care of them', a politician from the (Pacific) Marshall Islands declared in 1991.[7]

Once the existence of HIV was recognized in the 1980s, differences in its African epidemiology were spotted. The ratio of male to female cases was approximately 1:1 in sub-Saharan Africa, compared to 13:1 in the developed world. One set of hypotheses to explain this posited that HIV had originated in Africa, and had reached a more advanced stage in its epidemiological history, a view that was fiercely resented by African leaders, and jeopardized African governmental co-operation with AIDS workers. Other theories focused on sexual behaviour: it was hypothesized, for example, that heterosexual anal intercourse was more common among Africans, and various oppressive stereotypes of African sexual 'promiscuity' were constructed. Such theories were influenced by cultural bias about Africans, and had the effect of privileging certain lines of research while marginalizing other possibilities. The susceptibility of Africans to HIV, and the level of its heterosexual transmission, may be related to the high levels of background infection, malnutrition, and other immunosuppressant conditions that exist in Africa. Unsterilized needle use in African clinics may be another significant means of HIV transmission. Little is known, except that methodologically questionable data or prurient comment on African sexual habits have seldom helped either scientific understanding of the virus or the prevention of its transmission.[8]

Stigmatizing people from Uganda, the Bahamas or Pacific islands as 'promiscuous' because their sexual culture does not conform to the idealization of British suburban domesticity is unconstructive. Heated imaginations have also been at work in some accounts of Western capitalists visiting underdeveloped countries like Haiti and spreading HIV. These denunciations are easier, but less helpful, than addressing the hopeless degradation of PWA in places such as Haiti.[9]

WHO estimates that in 1992 there were about 6.5 million cases of HIV infection in sub-Saharan Africa, with seroprevalence in some of the worst affected countries (Burundi, Malawi, Mozambique, Rwanda, Tanzania, Uganda, Zambia and Zimbabwe) doubling every one or two years. In Uganda, with a current population of 16 million, it is estimated that about 180,000 people will be dying of AIDS-related diseases by 2000. Currently in some areas of sub-Saharan Africa (as in a few US cities) about 25 per cent of women of childbearing age are HIV+. On present predictions, there will be 10 million infants born by 2000 who are HIV+, and a further 10 million uninfected children will be AIDS orphans – 'the grandparents' burden', as they are called in Africa. These bare figures cannot convey the personal misery; they can, however, point to some of the national and international repercussions of such a disaster. The destruction of families and communities has far-reaching demographic implications and is already disrupting food production. The fact that 68 per cent of those tested HIV+ in Zambia's copperbelt are skilled technicians is not only an unimaginable personal tragedy, but calamitous for Zambian mining and foreign exchange earnings. The high levels of seroprevalence attributed to the personnel in some African armies, or at some sub-Saharan universities, are other indicators of potential economic disruption and political instability. The World Bank in 1992 predicted that by 2015 AIDS would have reduced the gross domestic product of typical sub-Saharan countries by about 22 per cent.[10]

It is not simply a question, though, of rich world and poor world, but of rich PWA and poor PWA. By the early 1990s health policy experts in the USA saw AIDS as 'a chronic disease that was spreading most rapidly among the disadvantaged, especially among blacks and Hispanics'. In 1991 it became the fifth most prevalent cause of death among US women of childbearing age; but as 72 per cent of these cases were black or Hispanic women, this fact was somehow erased from most people's experience and 'Middle America' could still consign PWA to a 'moral ghetto'.[11] Such distortions of experience are central to the phenomenon of AIDS and have deplorable consequences for the limitation of its spread.

TARGETING

Prevention of HIV infections is in everyone's interest. The best chances of prevention involve public health education: either propaganda in favour of continence, or education in techniques of 'safer sex'. The former option failed throughout the centuries when syphilis was a potentially fatal sexually transmitted infection.[12] It has nevertheless kept some appeal – most sinisterly for right-wing moralists and religious fundamentalists.[13] The range of policies which offer most hope are all based on promoting 'safer' sexual practices. Targeting is basic to all such publicity.

Paradoxically, with few exceptions, propaganda has tended to be targeted at *groups* perceived to be 'at risk' of infection rather than being targeted at risky activities. In developed countries the targets have been gay men, IV drug-users, sex workers, non-monogamous heterosexuals and, because of their potential sexual contacts with foreigners, tourists and business travellers. Targeting types of individual rather than activities, while convenient, is probably less effective: it is certainly more inaccurate in establishing who is at greater risk of exposure to the virus. Socially it has perpetuated a culture of ignorance, blame and complacency that facilitates the spread of infection. In Britain, the 'gay plague' of popular mediaspeak in the mid-1980s has mutated into 'the myth of heteroscxual AIDS' in the early 1990s. In the USA the increasing association of HIV with the underclass continues to undermine the effectiveness of responses to the pandemic. The pre-articulate belief still seems to be that only other people get AIDS.

The origins of mis-targeting are easy to find. The social construction of AIDS, and reactions to it (including those of physicians and policy-makers), have been shaped by publicity. This pandemic has been media-mediated.[14] The first medical descriptions of AIDS were published in the USA in 1981 and noted that 'these patients were all homosexuals'. In advanced literate countries the association with male homosexuality has persisted. This process of media synthesis has been complex and contradictory. Thus in Japan, where the death in 1987 of a Kobe prostitute (the eighteenth AIDS-related death in Japan, and the first woman) was a key media event comparable to Rock Hudson's death in California in 1985, it has not stopped 'the generalized perception ... that anyone other than "normal" Japanese ... is likely to have AIDS and should be avoided'.[15]

In the industrialized world most governments responded tardily to AIDS. People like gay men, IV drug-users and sex workers identified as at risk from HIV infection were often already marginalized or devalued; once they were identified as at high risk from HIV infection, they were ostracized still further. The treatment in prison of people with HIV has been disgraceful: the fact that the manual at Stafford prison stipulates that prisoners with AIDS should be led on chains during hospital visits was part of the attitude which in 1991 led Lord Justice Woolf to describe the segregation and humiliation of British HIV+ prisoners as a 'travesty of justice'.[16] This devaluation of people with AIDS has harmed members of supposedly high-risk groups and continues to be an obstacle to the global prevention of AIDS. In France it has been heinous. Whereas the British and Dutch governments recognized gay men as a social constituency and co-operated with them in health education, the French government would not. An extensive system of needle exchanges was introduced in Britain in 1986, but in 1992 there were still no state-funded legal needle exchanges in France. The infection by HIV of half the country's 3,000 haemophiliacs as the result of reckless mismanagement by the government agency in charge of blood products was an integral part of this official culture of contempt for PWA. As a result France in 1992 had 500 per cent more cases of AIDS than Britain, with an estimated 250,000 cases of HIV. Overall the French experience amounts to what Hannah Arendt called 'administrative massacre'.[17]

In countries other than France IV drug-users have been seen as human flotsam worth little effort to save. As a senior health official of a Third World country said privately at an AIDS forum in the early 1990s, 'there is no point in our having needle exchange clinics because we hang all our drug users'.[18] HIV has spread rapidly among drug injectors in Bangkok, New York, and various cities in Scotland, Switzerland and Italy.[19] In the Bahamas the HIV epidemic is also drug-related. On these Atlantic islands, where one in eighty people tested is HIV+, the health crisis began with an upsurge in crack-cocaine addiction (stimulated by criminals in the USA), followed by the sale of sex to buy drugs, which led to a 2,000 per cent increase in genital ulcer disease. In these conditions HIV flourished – not merely among drug-users so despised by the authorities. Elsewhere hostility or contempt has often been manifest: Scottish police, for example, created many obstacles to the provision of clean syringes at a critical period in the 1980s; IV drug-users have been marginalized in important HIV voluntary organizations; and their perspective on the pandemic has been largely erased from the historical record by gay memoirs or media shots of sick children.[20]

The system of sexual categorization that has dominated discourse on AIDS is flawed. It is trapped in the peculiarly Teutonic imperatives of classification associated with Richard von Krafft-Ebing's *Psychopathia sexualis* (1886), or the equally rigid needs of nineteenth-century French medico-jurisprudence. In matters of sexual desire the difference within a person can be as important as the differences between people; yet the *Sunday Times* reported that several British air stewardesses have contracted HIV 'after having affairs with homosexual colleagues' without noticing any anomaly in their use of the word 'homosexual' about men who have been enjoying intercourse with women.[21] Individual sexuality is complicated, with no fixed correspondence among the components of sexual desire, practice, self-perceived identity, official definition or cultural construction. A French survey of

1989–92 showed that of people who had had homosexual intercourse at least once, 82 per cent of men and 78 per cent of women had had intercourse with people of both sexes. In Brazil there is a long tradition of same-sex behaviour without the labelling of 'homosexuality' or 'bisexuality'. Two Brazilian males engaged in anal intercourse would be distinguished as the active masculine penetrator and the passive feminine penetrated. They would not necessarily perceive their behaviour as 'homosexual', a label which would seem meaningless to most Brazilians.[22] This mentality makes nonsense of safer sex propaganda or sexual education which is based on the identification of risk groups rather than targeted at risky behaviour, such as unprotected anal sex.

In Britain in the 1980s targeting presented other AIDS-related paradoxes. Most of the early AIDS activists were gay men: they wanted to prevent the victimization of both gay men and PWA, they resented depictions of either group as victims, and yet the responses of some of them were conditioned by their victimized outlook. In the early years of activism organizations like the Gay and Lesbian Switchboard, the Terrence Higgins Trust and Body Positive, all of which wanted to avert a homophobic backlash, pressed for public-health campaigns directed at the whole population rather than at gay men solely. Paradoxically, this also suited right-wing moralists who wanted (to use one of their clichés) to turn back the rising tide of 1960s permissiveness. One result of the temporary combination of these wishes was the government's public health campaign of 1986–7 directed at the entire nation. There has since been criticism of this campaign: that its technically accurate assertion 'We are all at risk' gave the inaccurate impression that everyone was at equal short-term risk, that this led to cynicism and complacency, and created resistance to the safer sex message. Some of its harshest critics have had hidden agendas about the enforcement of suburban values or the humiliation of minorities. Given the state of knowledge in the mid-1980s, it would have been hard for the government to take any other course of action. The truth is that the campaigns of 1986–7 succeeded in raising national awareness of AIDS: the level of knowledge within the general population is now high, with 90 per cent of people knowing by 1988 how HIV is transmitted. Its slogan 'Don't die of ignorance' became a catchphrase. These levels of knowledge about HIV are preferable to the 'abysmal ignorance' about other sexually transmitted diseases (STD), such as genital herpes, especially among the sexually active young. Since 1988 some efforts at prevention have attempted to target smaller, more vulnerable groups (ethnic and otherwise) or high-risk activities (while also trying to maintain a high level of public awareness), but with only moderate success. A 1989 survey of public health advertising concluded:

> heterosexual and homosexual subjects agree about the groups that are more at risk than others. Equally, it is clear that homosexuals, including those in stable relationships, recognise their potential susceptibility but feel that they have 'got the message'. However, heterosexuals still do not see themselves at risk. It is still someone else's problem: others are likely to contract HIV, not them; others have only themselves to blame if they do contract HIV, it is not their fault; and those people who are at risk, are NOT LIKE ME.[23]

The prerequisite of HIV prevention campaigns is that members of target populations see the relevance to themselves, accept the messages and are motivated to change their behaviour. Public health campaigns work best when integrated with more effective sex education. In the Netherlands, where sex education in schools begins at the age of 8, 95 per cent use contraceptives when they first have intercourse; in the USA, where traditionally there has been almost no formal sex education, 95 per cent do not. In Britain the follow-through from the AIDS campaigns to sex education is feeble. A survey of *The Sexual Health of Young Adults in England* (1991) found that 62 per cent of respondents wanted protection against pregnancy and only 19 per cent against the risk of HIV infection. They therefore abandoned condoms in favour of contraceptive pills. While 56 per cent of sexually active 16-year-old women used condoms with their partners, the proportion fell to 38 per cent among 19-year-olds; male usage fell from 77 per cent at 16 to 47 per cent by 19. The positive side of condoms needs to be sold in sex education classes: the caption (*c.*1988) for advertisements for Mates condoms – 'They're awfully fiddly to put on. Isn't that half the fun?' – is the sort of message pupils should be receiving. They should be taught too that though some men find that condoms reduce sensitivity, this may have the bonus of helping them to last longer before coming; though some women may dislike the friction of condoms inside them, this can be eroticized by the use of lubricating gels.[24]

PROFESSIONAL MEDICAL ATTITUDES

AIDS presents many paradoxes, not least in the vexed issue of its medical treatment. Despite increasingly effective clinical response, men, women and children continue to die in large numbers. Another paradox — in the developed world, at least — is that despite a huge financial, intellectual and emotional commitment by physicians and nurses engaged in either research or patient care, the AIDS community is in some respects isolated, and sympathy and commitment to PWA are not universal in the medical community. Historically STD, and 'pox-doctors' who treat them, have suffered from low status, poor resources and public near-invisibility. Some of this has been changed by HIV. In Britain, for example, Michael Adler of Middlesex Hospital, Charles Farthing of St Stephen's Hospital and Anthony Pinching, of St Mary's, Paddington, adopted a high campaigning profile in the mid-1980s, and met some resentment from the medical hierarchy for doing so. They also worked closely with gay activists and HIV charities such as the Terrence Higgins Trust, as did the government's chief medical officer, Sir Donald Acheson, whose receptivity was outstanding and earned the plaudits of many lobbyists. Yet the energy and open-mindedness of physicians and nurses confronted with the immediate reality of PWA cannot be assumed in the general medical community. A survey of US doctors in 1991 found that half would not treat people with HIV if they had the choice, and nearly one-third saw nothing wrong in withholding such treatment. In the same year a medical survey of over 500 British doctors training to become general practitioners found that half would not accept an IV drug-user on their list, only 12 per cent found it easy to discuss sex with homosexual patients and only 37 per cent felt able to offer counselling on HIV or AIDS.[25]

In the early days of HIV policy-making in the USA epidemiology was the most influential medical specialism; scientific discoveries about the virus, and the development of a test for it, moved the balance of power towards virologists. Many AIDS physicians and activists continue to argue that insufficient funds have been allotted to research to improve the health of infected and at-risk people. In Britain, from the early recognition of the AIDS crisis until 1988, the medical input to policy-making came from a heterogeneous group of venereologists, virologists, immunologists, haematologists and psychologists. Since then both the media and Whitehall officialdom have re-presented the ideas and images of AIDS, turning it from 'plague' to 'chronic disease'. AIDS funding has been decentralized to health and local authorities (who sometimes divert the money to non-AIDS-related services), and a professional network of AIDS co-ordinators, counsellors and health education experts has emerged. This increasingly institutionalized response has in turn provoked a backlash against the AIDS community as expensive, over-professionalized and surplus to requirements.[26]

In many countries there have been over-zealous media intrusions into the lives of medical practitioners with HIV or AIDS, wrong-headed contamination fears and ugly threats of sanctions. The infection with HIV by David Acer, a bisexual Florida dentist, of several of his patients, and the television appearances of one of them, Kimberly Bergalis (1968–91), aroused ferocious fears in the United States. The possibility of accidental transmission seems remote. The likeliest explanation is that, suffering dementia, Acer deliberately infected patients. Nevertheless, there are strong practical and ethical reasons for arguing that health-care professionals infected with HIV should be permitted to continue their work for as long as they are capable.[27]

It must be acknowledged that AIDS still excites frantic fears of contagion in some people. Even in 1991 a man with HIV could be charged with assault after spitting at Devon police, and, just as significantly, this complete non-story could still make the national newspapers, complete with irrelevant reference to the man's antibody status. Though the paranoia which surrounded the epidemic until the mid-1980s has somewhat abated, in 1989 Curtis Weeks was sentenced in Texas to life imprisonment for attempted murder after spitting at a prison guard, who 'panicked, removed his clothes, then rinsed himself with Clorox', and has since had himself tested for HIV on ten occasions.[28]

COPERNICAN OR REACTIONARY?

The AIDS regime raises yet another set of paradoxes. Public attitudes towards sexual minorities and those with STD; notions of prevention and cure in modern medicine; and the possibilities of changing sexual habits on either a personal or community basis: tracing the continuities and discontinuities in these three themes is basic to understanding the contemporary phenomenon of AIDS.

In the industrialized world AIDS has simultaneously transformed notions of sexuality associated with the liberation of the 1960s and 1970s, brought discourse on sexuality to a new and energetic phase and yet has also caused a recrudescence of sexual anxieties, notably homophobia, and a revival of sanctimony. Responses to AIDS have been reactionary and regressive but also Copernican: reactionary because some of the opprobrium, scapegoating and viciousness attached to earlier STD has been fastened to AIDS; Copernican because it is hard to imagine any previous epoch that would have held World Syphilis Day, as World AIDS Day is now marked globally each December (or Britain's National Condom Week every August).

In the brief epoch between the discovery of antibiotics and the identification of AIDS there was in the developed world a tendency among patients presenting at STD clinics to regard venereal infections as inconvenient but not life-threatening. This reflected their faith in the power of medical technology, and the hegemony of the medical profession in some cultures like the USA. For this generation the belief that cure is better than prevention has proved chimerical.

As with other aspects of AIDS, the evidence about changes in sexual behaviour suggests that much has changed and much has stayed the same.[29] We can touch on only two aspects of behaviour: condom usage and numbers of sexual partners. Some pointers are given by surveys of sexual behaviour undertaken in France in 1989–92 and in Britain in 1990–1 (the results of which of which have just become available at time of writing). The French reported a 'relatively high level of condom use in young people and in those most exposed to the risk of contamination by STDs or by AIDS, although a considerable proportion of these people still do not use condoms, especially with new partners'. In France 'young people change partners more frequently than older people', which seems neither new nor surprising, but also 'are less likely to have more than one sexual partner at any one time', which may reflect some AIDS-mediated change of behaviour.[30]

PROSTITUTION

'Prostitutes and opera singers survive revolutions', W. H. Auden noted,[31] but in the world of contemporary prostitution, only sex-workers in developed countries have much chance of surviving lethal epidemics of STD. Research into prostitution and the transmission of HIV reveals some encouraging indicators, and much that is dreadful.

The association of HIV with IV drug-use and the tradition of people entering prostitution in order to pay for their hard drug habits are at first sight ominous. Research in Birmingham, Edinburgh, London and Sheffield suggests that 14–20 per cent of female prostitutes may be injecting drugs, though the figure may be higher in Glasgow. Most HIV-testing studies on European women prostitutes indicate a rate of HIV infection under 5 per cent; although Spanish research found that over 50 per cent of drug-injecting prostitutes were HIV+, only 3.5 per cent of a sample of Glaswegian drug-injecting women prostitutes were seropositive. As to the users of such sex-workers, a survey of 1991 by Birmingham's AIDS project co-ordinator found that of about 1,200 women prostitutes in the city each see on average

22 clients weekly. Between 1 in 5 and 1 in 12 adult Birmingham men use a prostitute annually: few clients are under 20, the greatest number being between 20 and 40, with 18 per cent in their fifties, 7.2 per cent in their sixties, 1.6 per cent in their seventies and 1 per cent in their eighties. About 43 per cent are married.[32]

Yet the level of knowledge about HIV is high among British women prostitutes. Owing to condom use, or non-penetrative sex, there are signs that heterosexual prostitution is not crucial to the spread of HIV infection in Britain. In some other countries, though, the position is disastrous. Two instances from Asia present the worst scenarios. In India HIV infections are spreading at great speed through needle abuse, unhygienic bloodbanks, government apathy, but above all, the ignorance of the poor and the crushing poverty that drives people into prostitution in the stews of districts like Kamatipura in Bombay. Thailand is also badly affected. HIV infection among tested army recruits has risen from 0.5 per cent in 1989 to 3.2 per cent in 1992, but with strong regional fluctuations: 20 per cent of recruits in the northern province of Prayou test HIV+. In the country's second city, Chiang Mai, no AIDS cases had been recorded in 1987. By the end of 1991 reported cases had reached nearly 150, and in the first quarter of 1992 this figure doubled. African A-type HIV, a strain common among Thai prostitutes, is spreading in Japan. The Japanese health ministry reported in December 1992 that 60 per cent of Japanese men with HIV had been infected through heterosexual acts abroad. Before 1989 there were only two reports to Britain's Communicable Disease Surveillance Centre of HIV infection attributable to heterosexual exposure in Thailand. In 1989–90 five more reports were received, and another seventeen in 1991–2. The overall British tally is twenty-one men and three women, aged 24 to 50, of whom by December 1992 nine were asymptomatic, five were symptomatic but without an AIDS indicator disease, and four had AIDS. This crisis in Thailand's tourist sex business has created a demand for 'uncontaminated' women, especially Burmese; as a result, AIDS is becoming endemic in the Burmese–Thai border region, where one hill-tribe, the Akah, is threatened with extinction by AIDS. There are persistent rumours that the Burmese government is killing by lethal injections sex-workers who return from Thailand with AIDS.[33]

CONCLUSION

Historians and policy-makers from the medical community have much debated the continuities and discontinuities of AIDS. It is a new kind of epidemic, fashioned by the rhetoric, the economic and social divisions, the mass tourism and the scientific advances of the late twentieth century; yet in other respects its circumstances resemble long-established chronic diseases. The fact that this is the first epidemic of the information age – entailing the mediation of the media in defining images of AIDS and the potential sophistication of techniques in targeting people who need preventive advice – distinguishes it from its predecessors. Yet at the same time it has drawn anachronistic responses as 'the wrath of God', and reactionary punitive attitudes towards the ill as transgressors. Most of all it is a reminder of the millennial truism that the poor are always with us.

NOTES

1 There has been a deluge of publications about the pandemic. Its course in the period to 1985 has been described in Randy Shilts, *And the Band Played On* (New York, 1987). Perhaps a better guide is Mirko D. Grmek, *History of AIDS* (Princeton, 1990). See also Douglas Crimp (ed.), *AIDS, Cultural Analysis/Cultural Activism* (Cambridge, Mass., and London, 1988); Erica Carter and Simon Watney (eds.), *Taking Liberties: AIDS and Cultural Politics* (London, 1989).
2 The connection between HIV and AIDS has been famously contested: see, for example, Jad Adams, *AIDS: The HIV Myth* (London, 1989).
3 Quoted by Susan Sontag, *Illness as Metaphor – AIDS and its Metaphors* (London, 1991), 177.
4 For a virulent view of AIDS activism, see Larry Kramer, *Reports from the Holocaust* (New York, 1989).
5 Paul Wilkinson, 'HIV Adverts Censured', *The Times*, 15 May 1991.
6 Thomson Prentice, 'Unconscious Patients Might be Tested for HIV Infection', *The Times*, 11 January 1991.
7 James Pringle, 'Growing Shadow of AIDS Darkens Pacific Paradise', *The Times*, 4 September 1991; T. Prentice, 'AIDS in Africa Ignored', *The Times*, 23 December 1991.
8 Randall Packard and Paul Epstein, 'Medical Research on AIDS in Africa', in Elizabeth Fee and Daniel Fox (eds.), *AIDS: The Making of a Chronic Disease* (Berkeley and Oxford, 1992), 346–73. See generally Ed Hooper, *Slim: A Reporter's Own Story of AIDS in East Africa* (London, 1990).
9 Philip Wearne, 'Sisters Offer a Mercy Lifeline to Haiti's Poor', *The Times*, 6 January 1991.
10 Tony Barnett and Piers Blaikie, *AIDS in Africa: Its Present and Future Impact* (London, 1992).
11 Daniel Fox, 'The Politics of HIV Infection: 1989–1990 as Years of Change', in Fee and Fox (eds.), *AIDS Chronic Disease*, 125; Charles Bremner, 'Middle America Consigns Aids Patients to Moral Ghetto', *The Times*, 3 June 1991.
12 Historical perspectives are given by Theodor Rosebury, *Microbes and Morals* (New York, 1971); Allan Brandt, *No Magic Bullet* (New York and Oxford,

1985); Elizabeth Fee and Daniel Fox (eds.), *AIDS, the Burdens of History* (Los Angeles and London, 1988); Richard Davenport-Hines, *Sex, Death and Punishment* (London, 1990); Claude Quétel, *History of Syphilis* (Oxford and Baltimore, 1990). A contemporary perspective is in Dennis Altman, *AIDS and the New Puritanism* (London, 1986; published New York 1986 as *AIDS in the Mind of America*).

13 Barbara Amiel, 'Aids Flourishes in a Culture of Soft Soap', *The Times*, 9 June 1991; Louise Hidalgo, 'Carey Casts Doubt on Condom Approach', *The Times*, 23 September 1991; B. Amiel, 'And Still We Try to Wish away our Plague', *The Times*, 17 November 1991; Brian Appleyard, 'The Face of AIDS', *Sunday Times*, 1 December 1991. For the Conservative Family Campaign's so-called Charter, see Bill Frost, 'Aids Charter Launched', *The Times*, 28 August 1991.

14 See Anthony Vass, *AIDS, A Plague in Us* (St Ives, 1986); Simon Watney, *Policing Desire: Pornography, AIDS and the Media* (London, 1987).

15 James Dearing, 'Foreign Blood and Domestic Politics: The Issue of AIDS in Japan', in Fee and Fox, *AIDS Chronic Disease*, 329–30, 340.

16 Quentin Cowdry, 'Woolf Sets off Urgent Review of AIDS Policy', *The Times*, 4 April 1991; 'Prisoners with Aids Led on Chains', *The Times*, 27 September 1991.

17 Simon Watney, 'How France Created an AIDS Epidemic', *The Independent*, 20 November 1992. For the case of US blood, see Harvey Sapolsky and Stephen Boswell, 'The History of Transfusion AIDS: Practice and Policy Alternatives', in Fee and Fox, *AIDS Chronic Disease*, 170–90.

18 Private information. For the social construction of the British fascination with drug use as a symptom of national crisis, see Marek Kohn, *Dope Girls: The Birth of the British Drug Underground* (London, 1992).

19 Philip Jacobsen, 'Damned to Life in a Zurich Park', *The Times*, 15 June 1991.

20 Don Des Jarlais et al. 'The First City: HIV among Intravenous Drug Users in New York City', Fee and Fox, *AIDS Chronic Disease*, 279–93. AIDS-related memoirs include Paul Monette, *Borrowed Time* (London, 1988); Emmanuel Dreuilhe, *Mortal Embrace* (New York, 1988; London, 1989); Jack Pollock, *Dear M* (London, 1991); Derek Jarman, *Modern Nature* (London, 1991) and *At Your Own Risk* (London, 1992). One memoir of a family with HIV is Elizabeth Glaser with Laura Palmer, *In the Absence of Angels* (New York, 1991). There is a host of lightly fictionalized memoirs of AIDS including Peter McGehee, *Boys Like Us* (New York, 1991); Denis Belloc, *Slow Death in Paris* (London, 1992); Hervé Guibert, *To the Friend Who Did Not Save My Life* (London, 1992).

21 'Aids Danger for Air Crews', *Sunday Times*, 10 March 1991.

22 Analyse des Comportements Sexuels en France, 'AIDS and Sexual Behaviour in France', *Nature*, 360 (3 December 1992), 408; Paula Treichler, 'AIDS and HIV Infection in the Third World', in Fee and Fox, *AIDS Chronic Disease*, 394; on Brazil generally, see João Trevisan, *Perverts in Paradise* (London, 1986).

23 Janet Stockdale et al., 'The Self in Relation to Mass Media Representations of HIV and AIDS – Match or Mismatch?', *Health Education Journal*, 48 (1989), 129. See also K. Wellings, 'Tracking Public Views of AIDS', *Health Education Journal*, 47 (1988), 34–6; T. Prentice, 'AIDS Campaign has Failed to Make Impact', *The Times*, 7 August 1991; Janet Stockdale, 'Charity Poster Advertis-

ing – An Effective Medium?' paper at ICFM National Fundraising Convention, Birmingham, 2 July 1992. The AIDS Media Research Project at Glasgow University has extensively researched this subject: some of their findings are summarized in David Miller et al., 'Message Misunderstood', *Times Higher Education Supplement*, 3 July 1992.

24 T. Prentice, 'Teenagers are more Worried about Pregnancy than AIDS', *The Times*, 14 August 1991. On British sex education, see Barnados, *HIV/AIDS: Who's Telling the Children?* (London, 1992); Ian Nash, 'Facts that Breed Fictions' and Clare Jenkin, 'Telling It Like It Really Is', both in *Times Education Supplement*, 10 July 1992. On condoms, see Jane Austin, 'A Pack of Three without the Shame', *Independent*, 3 August 1992.

25 Nick Nuttall and Alan McGregor, 'Kissing Gets a Health Warning', *The Times*, 28 November 1991; T. Prentice, 'Trainee GPs Ill Informed about Aids', *The Times*, 7 October 1991.

26 Sheila Gunn, 'AIDS Funding is Siphoned off for Building Work', *The Times*, 23 October 1991; John Furbisher and Grace Bradberry, 'More Staff than Patients in Booming AIDS Industry', *Sunday Times*, 19 July 1992.

27 Martin Fletcher, 'Fear Prompts Hardline Aids Vote', *The Times*, 20 July 1991; Liz Gill, 'Ring of No Confidence', *The Times*, 25 July 1991. For the case of a HIV+ British ophthalmologist mendaciously denounced by the *News of the World* as 'desperately ill' with 'the killer disease', see David Utting, 'Trial by Tabloid', *Independent on Sunday*, 12 July 1992. General comment includes T. Prentice, 'Cutting down the Risk', *The Times*, 11 March 1991; Prentice, 'Patients of Aids Virus Surgeon Told Remote Risk', ibid., 9 April 1991; Prentice, 'Specialists Underline HIV Risk to Patients', ibid., 9 August 1991.

28 'Spitting Charge', *The Times*, 18 July 1991; 'Tide of Lawsuits Portrays Society Ravaged by AIDS', *New York Times*, 23 August 1992.

29 Caroline Lees, 'Aids Puts a Brake on Teen Romance', *Sunday Times*, 6 January 1991; T. Prentice, 'Unsafe Sex Risks Being Ignored', *The Times*, 19 June 1991; Tim Rayment, 'Joy of Sex Revised for AIDS Era', *Sunday Times*, 7 July 1991. These and most other sources on the subject are impressionistic but not empirical.

30 ACSF, 'AIDS and Sexual Behaviour', 408–9; Anne Johnson et al., 'Sexual Lifestyles and HIV Risk', *Nature*, 360 (3 December 1992), 410–12.

31 Edward Mendelson (ed.), *The English Auden* (London, 1977), 401.

32 Neil McKeganey and Marina Barnard, *AIDS, Drugs and Sexual Risk: Lives in the Balance* (Milton Keynes, 1992); Thomas Stuttaford, 'HIV off the Kerb', *The Times*, 10 October 1991.

33 Christopher Gunness, 'Deadly Trail of AIDS in Sex Slaves' Wake', *Independent on Sunday*, 29 November 1992; Fred Lenihan, 'Thailand tries again to Tackle AIDS', *British Medical Journal*, 305 (5 December 1992), 1385; Ahilya Noone et al., 'HIV Transmission, Travel and Thailand', ibid., 1431; on HIV in Thailand and the Philippines, see Jon Swain, 'Asia Threatened by an Aids Timebomb', *Sunday Times*, 29 December 1991. On France, see Philip Jacobson, 'Aids Team Closes Door on Bordellos', *The Times*, 23 March 1991. On India, see Derek Brown, 'Dark Tide of AIDS in a Sea of Suffering', *Guardian*, 8 August 1992; cf. Andrea Dabrowski, 'Mexican Prostitutes Join Condom Campaign', *The Times*,

3 June 1991. For longer-term scholarly perspectives, see Luise While, *The Comforts of Home: Prostitution in Colonial Nairobi* (Chicago, 1991) and more generally Ronald Hyam, *Empire and Sexuality* (Manchester, 1990). For a fictional treatment of AIDS and the colonial legacy, see Nigel Krauth, *JF Was Here* (London, 1992).

INDEX

Aba, Mar *see* Mar Aba
abortifacients 99
   maternal milk 195
   patent nostrums 267–8, 271, 278 n6
   placebos 277–8
   poisons 267, 272, 273, 277, 278
abortion 86, 99, 148, 267–83, 294, 296, 297, 315
   in ancient Greece 34
   criminal 13, 270–4
   laws 273
   by midwives 269
   by quacks 267–8, 269
   self-induction 271
   serial murders (Cream case) 267, 269–75, 277–8
   therapeutic 270
Abraham 239
Abrahams, Emmanuel, defendant in 'Madame Frain' trial 268
abstinence *see* sexual abstinence
Acer, David, HIV+ dentist 377
Achaemenids, Persian dynasty 235
Acheson, Sir Donald 376
acquired immune deficiency syndrome *see* AIDS
ACT UP (AIDS Coalition to Unleash Power) 369
Acton, William 12, 350, 352, 353, 356, 357
   Functions and Disorders of the the Reproductive Organs 351
Acts of Parliament (Great Britain)
   Contagious Diseases Acts (1864, 1866, 1869) 277
   Criminal Law Amendment Act (1885) 276; Labouchère amendment 260
   Offences Against the Person Act (1861) 270
Adam and Eve *see* Bible
addiction *see* alcoholism; drug-addiction
Addison, Joseph 11
Addy, J. 83

Adler, Michael 376
adolescence
   and masturbation 141
   and sexual abstinence 292, 294–5
   see also puberty; sex education
Adorno, Theodor 367
adultery 84
   excessive marital sex as 89
   in Indian tradition 76
   punishment of married women 90
advice literature 11–12, 351–4, 356, 358–62
   and corruption of innocence 139–40;
      authors' apologia 141–5
   in early modern England 83–91
   in eighteenth-century England 134–57
   on marriage 31, 134–57
   for mothers 199, 200
   sex manuals: ancient Indian/Chinese 51;
      Graeco-Roman 36, 39; midwives' 34, 93, 94, 95, 113
   women's health guides 113
Ady, James 272
Aethelbald, king of the West Saxons 242
Aethelwulf, king of the West Saxons 242
Africa
   dynastic incest in Hima kingdoms 235
   erotic practices 136
   female breast shapes 197
   HIV/AIDS epidemic 368, 369–71
Agrippina the younger, daughter of Germanicus Casear 240
AIDS 6, 7, 296, 367–83
   activism 369, 374, 376
   at-risk groups 371–5
   economic factors 369–70, 371, 376
   low status of patients 372, 376, 377
   treatment 368, 369, 375
alchemy 126
alcoholism 254, 287, 290, 306
   among Jews 333
Alexander, Franz 326
Alexandria (third century BC) 36

INDEX

'algolagnia' (Schrenk-Notzing) 48, 214
alienists *see* psychiatry
Allbutt, H. A., *Wife's Handbook* 353
Allen, Clifford 362
Allestree, James 120
Allestree, Richard, *The Ladies Calling* 120–1
allometry (Huxley) 169–71, 172
Amazons (myth) 195
Amenhotep IV (Akhenaton), Egyptian pharaoh 235
amenorrhoea 109
American Federation for Sex Hygiene 305
American Psychiatric Association, *Diagnostic and Statistical Manual of Mental Disorders* 48
American Purity Alliance 304, 305
American Social Hygiene Association 305, 314, 316
American Vigilance Association 305
Ames, Nicholas, defendant in sexual assault case 96
Ammonius (Christian ascetic) 55
anaesthesia, sexual (Krafft-Ebing) 215
anal intercourse 15, 90, 98, 99, 147
  and spread of HIV 370, 374
  see also pederasty
anatomy 215
  ancient Greek 10
  female 86: early modern theories 107–33
  gender comparisons 10, 91, 110–13
  male 85, 107
  midwives' knowledge of 86
  Vesalian 116
  see also genitalia; neuroanatomy; pathological anatomy
ancestor worship 241
androgynes 68, 145, 335–6
  during Decadence 255, 256, 257–60
  homosexuals' admiration for 259–60
  ideal of beauty 260
Anglican church 118, 120, 122, 127, 128, 242
  view of marriage 83–4
Anglo-Saxons, marriage with stepmother 242
animals
  coital behaviour: human comparisons 231, 232, 354; as source of sexual knowledge 98
  courtship behaviour 51, 95, 139, 160–6: colour/beauty 159, 160, 161, 162; combat 160, 169, 170, 171, 173; display 160, 163, 164–5, 172; and female physiology 165–7, 172, 173, 174
  experimentation *see* vivisection
  mammals 184–209
  monogamous 159, 167–8, 169
  in mythology 191–2

polygamous 159, 167, 169, 173
secondary sex characteristics 163–4, 171, 172
sex with *see* bestiality
sexual selection theory 158–83
  theory of indifference 233–4
Annalistes 83
anthropology 15, 286, 334
  see also Magi
antibiotics 296, 377
antiquity 8–9, 15, 135, 212, 219
  Greek and Roman sexology 29–46
  incest in Magian society 231–50
anti-Semitism 325, 327, 328, 329, 339
antivivisection movement 276–7
Antonius, Marcus, Roman triumvir 236
anxiety, and sexual information 12
Aphrodite (myth) 190
Arabia, pre-Islamic, incest laws 239
Arcadius, Eastern Roman emperor 240
Archilochus, on fellatio 35
Arendt, Hannah 373
Aristotle 2, 110, 149, 184
  on generation 85
  lactation theory 191
  physiological theory 113–14
  on role of passive partner 30
  taxonomy 186–7, 204
  Historia animalium 186, 191
  Politics 34
Aristotle's Book of Problems 136
Aristotle's Complete Midwife 136
Aristotle's Master-Piece 2, 94, 136, 137, 145, 146, 148, 149
Armenia, incest taboo 243
Armstrong, John, *Oeconomy of Love* 147
Armstrong-Jones, Sir Robert 355
Arndt, Ernst Moritz 251
Arnulf of Villers, St 56
Arsacids, Persian dynasty 235
Arsinoe, sister of Ptolemy II 236
art
  anatomical 110
  Graeco-Roman erotic 30, 32, 36–8
  male beauty in 252
Artemidoros, *Dream Book* 30, 32, 38, 39
Arthur, prince 242
Artist and Journal of Home Culture 257
asceticism
  Christian 9, 52–8
  Indian tradition 64, 65, 69–72, 75, 77
Aschaffenburg, Gustav, on race and criminality 329
Asia, south-east, HIV/AIDS epidemic 368
assault, sexual 14, 96–7
associationism 222, 223
Astell, Mary, 'Essay in Defence of the Female Sex' 116

astrology 113, 136, 138
Astyanassa, sex manual 31
Atalanta (myth) 37–8
Athens (fifth century BC) 29, 30
 erotic vase-paintings 30, 36
 pederasty 30
Attic law, and marriage of half-siblings 239
Augustine of Hippo, St 135, 195
Augustus, Roman emperor 36, 37
Austria 210, 211
 incest laws 331, 332
 see also Vienna
autopsies *see* dissections
Avicenna 90
Āyurveda, on menstruation 63, 67, 69, 71, 73, 75, 77

Bacon, Francis, first baron Verulam 5, 121, 127–8
 on bodily fluids 116
 on gender relations 126
 Masculine Birth of Time 118
Bahamas, HIV/AIDS epidemic 373
Bannister, Edith, death during abortion 271–2
Barnes, Ann, complainant in sexual assault case 96
Barney, Natalie, decadent lesbian 258, 259
Baxter, Ethelreda, complainant in sexual assault case 97
Beam, Lura 311
Beard, George, on neurasthenia 286
beauty
 androgynes' ideal 260
 female: of breast 195, 197, 198; and male pleasure 33
 male: and animal courtship 159, 160, 161, 162; in Greek sculpture 252; stereotype 260
Beauvais Cathedral 58
Bebel, August 288
Becker, Rafael 325
Beethoven, Ludwig van 339
Bell, Rudolph M. 56
Bell, W. Blair, *The Sex Complex* 355
Belot, *Les Baigneuses de Trouville* 222
Benedict, St 57
Bergalis, Kimberly, death from AIDS 377
Berlin 286
 Institute for Sexual Science 359
 prostitution 288
 'Ürningsballe' 212, 258
 venereal diseases 289
Bernays, Minna 332
Bernheim, Hippolyte Marie 223
Berry, Elizabeth, midwife 271
bestiality 30, 90

Bible 3, 142, 187
 Adam and Eve 3, 84, 217
 on incest 327
 on intermarriage 239–40
 on origin of Jews 324–5
 prohibition of sex during menstruation 89
 see also Deuteronomy; Leviticus
Billings, John Shaw 323
Binet, Alfred, association theory 221, 222, 223
Binswanger, Otto, on Jews' predisposition for neurasthenia 340–1
biology 247
 and female nature 256
 and Freud's theories 323
 inbreeding avoidance theory 233
 and Jews 334, 335, 338
biology, evolutionary 8, 10
 mutation theory 162, 164
 mutual selection theory 166
 natural selection theory 158–83 *passim*
 sexual selection theory 158–83
birds
 in Aristotle's taxonomy 186
 courtship behaviour 162–3, 164–9, 171, 172
 in Linnaeus's taxonomy 185, 186
Birken, L. 297
Birmingham, prostitution survey (1991) 378
birth control *see* contraception
birth-rate, decline 252, 255
Black Death (1347–51) 57
Blackwell, Elizabeth, physician 275
Blainville, Henri de, taxonomy 188
Blaschko, Alfred 290
Blau, Bruno, on Jewish temperament 328
blindness, congenital (venereal) 305
Bloch, Iwan 14
 on race and sexual constitution 324
blood 107
 in Aristotle's taxonomy 186–7
 as body essence 127
 chemical composition 117
 circulation 117
 in seventeenth-century physiology 116
 transfusion, and spread of HIV 367, 368, 379
 in Willis's physiology 115
 see also menstrual blood
body *see* anatomy; female body; mind/body relationships; physiology
Body Positive 374
body-snatchers 118
Bond, Thomas, Metropolitan Police surgeon 273
bondage 51
Bose, D. M. 68
Boyle, Robert 125

Brackley, Deborah 100
brain 222
 and gender theory 11, 113–16, 123, 124, 125, 215
 role in pain inhibition 50
 as seat of hysteria 107
 tumour 126
 Willis's doctrine 113–16
Brazil, HIV/AIDS epidemic 374
breast-feeding *see* lactation
breasts, female
 beauty of 195, 197, 198, 201–2
 in cultural history 185, 190–7, 198, 202
 in Jainist texts 71
Bridewell Prison, London 90
Britain *see* Great Britain
British Gynaecological Society 275
British Medical Journal 352, 353, 356, 357, 358, 361, 362
British Society for Sex Psychology 158, 173
British Society for the Study of Sex Psychology 359
Brooke, H., on sexual excess 88
Brooks, Flora 272
brothels *see* prostitution
Brougham, Henry Peter, baron Brougham and Vaugh 274
Brown, Isaac Baker 352–3
 Curability of . . . Insanity, Epilepsy, and Hysteria in Females 352
Brown, William, defendant in 'Madame Frain' trial 268
Brown-Séquard, Charles Edouard, 'organotherapy' (rejuvenation) 354
Buchan, William, *Observations on the Prevention and Cure of the Venereal Disease* 138–9
Buddha (Prince Siddhārtha), on nature of woman 69
Buddhism, Indian 69, 219
Buffon, comte de *see* Leclerc, G.-L.
Bullough, Vern L. ix, 9, 16, 47–62, 303–22
Bumke, Oswald, German alienist 253–4, 256
Bund für Mutterschutz 292–3
Burdon-Sanderson, Sir John Scott 354
Bureau of Social Hygiene (USA) 313–17, 318
Burma, HIV/AIDS epidemic 379
Burnham, John 303
Burton, Robert, *Anatomy of Melancholy* 135
Butler, A., *Butler's Lives of the Saints* 56
Byzantium, incest laws 243

Cadogan, William, attack on wet-nursing 200, 201
Caesar, Gaius Julius 37, 236
Caligula, Roman emperor 200
Canada Lancet 274

Canadian Medical Association 274
cancer, skin 367
Canterbury Cathedral 58
Caracalla, Roman emperor 237
Carakasaṃhitā 67–8
carnal knowledge
 Christian attitudes 3, 4, 5, 137
 see also advice literature; sex education
Carpenter, Edward 357–8
 The Intermediate Sex 358
 Love's Coming of Age 358
Carson, A. 39
Cartwright, Thomas, Puritan theologian 88
Casanova de Seingalt, Giacomo Girolamo 4
case histories
 Anne Conway 125–8
 Dickinson's patients 311
Castlehaven, second earl of 90
castration 335, 336, 342
Catholic church 327
 celibacy of clerics 88, 284, 295
 and morality 292
Cato 38
Catullus 38
 on impotence 35
Cavendish, Margaret, duchess of Newcastle 122–3
 approval of pathological anatomy 119
 natural philosophy 123
Cecil, William, baron Burghley 87
celibacy *see* sexual abstinence
Cellier, Elizabeth, midwife 86, 124–5
censorship, of advice literature 137, 138, 149
cerebral localization (Willis) 115
cervix 309, 311, 313
 cervicitis 310
Chamberlain, Houston Stewart 324–5
Chamberlen family, use of obstetrical forceps 124
Chamberlen, Peter (1572–1626), surgeon/accoucheur 124
Chamberlen, Peter (1601–83), physician/accoucheur 86
Channing, Walter 274
Charcot, Jean Martin, on hysteria 254, 255
Charles II, king of Great Britain 123
Charles the Bald, king of France 242
Chartier, Roger 149
chastity *see* sexual abstinence
chastity symbols 192, 193
Chat Noir 257
Chaumette, Pierre-Gaspard, on woman's domestic role 202
Chavasse, P. H. 274
chemistry
 of blood 117
 medical 108

Chesser, Eustace
　Love without Fear 360
　Sexual, Marital and Family Relationships of the Englishwoman 361
Cheyne, George, on hysteria 116
childbirth 82, 91, 195
　fear of 87, 99
　and female oral culture 96
　in Jewish tradition 191
　male control of 124, 199, 200–1, 275, 277
　pain in 84
　see also midwives
Childebert II, king of the Franks 242
children
　abuse of 47, 49, 59, 327
　communal upbringing and 'indifference' 234, 246
　compulsory education 268
　feral 192
　illegitimate 284, 293, 297
　labouring 268
　prostitution 13
　sexual behaviour 135
　sexual fantasies 342
　see also family; infants
chlorosis *see* greensickness
Christian of Aquila, St 55
Christianity 331, 334, 339
　asceticism 9, 52–8
　and carnal knowledge 3, 4, 5, 137
　condemnation of sex manuals 31, 32
　cult of relics 221
　and incest 241, 242, 243, 333
　maternal imagery 192, 195
　and misogyny 10, 219
　and morality 83–4, 261
　suffering and salvation 9, 52–8, 126
　see also Nestorian Christians
Christie, John, murderer 283 n79
Chrysostom, St John 136
circumcision 326, 342, 343
Civil War
　American (1861–65) 309
　English (1642–46) 5, 86, 119
civilization/industrialization
　and disease 287–8, 290
　effect on Jews 328, 337–41
Clapp, Dinah, midwife 271
Clarion 268–9
Clark, LeMon 312
classical antiquity *see* antiquity
classification
　of sado-masochism (Krafft-Ebing) 47–8, 58
　see also taxonomy
Claudius, Roman emperor 240
Clement of Alexandria, St 31
Cleopatra, queen of Egypt 236

Cleveland Street scandal (1899–90) 259
clitoris
　clitoridectomy 352
　and orgasm 359
　as 'truncated penis' 341–3
Cochin, Charles and Gravelot, Hubert François, portrayal of Nature as virgin 192, 193
coitus *see* animals, coital behaviour; heterosexual intercourse; homosexuality, male
coitus interruptus 99, 148, 269, 309
Colette, Sidonie Gabrielle 260
　The Pure and the Impure 258
colostrum 199, 200
Comber, Thomas, dean of Carlisle 86
Comfort, Alex 51, 362
Committee to Defend against Anti-Semitic Attacks (Germany) 328
Committee on Maternal Health (USA) 311
Commune of Paris (1793) 202
Communicable Disease Surveillance Centre (UK) 379
Compleat Doctoress 109
Comstock, Anthony 303
conception 34, 39, 89, 93, 94, 96, 139, 144
　ancient theories 85–6
　early modern theories 86–9
　heat theory 108
　in Indian texts 67–8, 69, 75–6
　sexual pleasure and 87, 100
condoms *see* contraception
Connelly, Mark 303
Constans I, Roman emperor 240
Constantius, Eastern Roman emperor 240
consumerism 297
consumption, maternal milk as therapy 195
Contagious Diseases Acts (1864, 1866, 1869) 277
contraception 5, 92–3, 98–9, 148, 150, 268–9, 272, 273, 284, 292, 293, 296, 297, 309, 315, 316, 353, 358, 359, 361, 375
　coitus interruptus 99, 148, 269, 309
　condoms 269, 293, 295–6, 309, 375, 377, 378, 379
　creams 293, 295, 309
　and depopulation 148–9
　diaphragms 269, 309
　douches 269, 293, 309
　oral 6, 375
　rhythm method 87
　sexual abstinence 99
　withdrawal method *see* coitus interruptus
Conway, Anne, viscountess Conway, case history 125–8
Conway, Edward, third viscount Conway 128
Cooper, Arthur 358

INDEX 389

Sexual Disabilities of Man and their Treatment 355
copulation *see* heterosexual intercourse
Cotta, J. 100
Couperus, Louis, *De Berg van Licht* 260
courtship 212
 behaviour: of animals 160–6, 169–74: of birds 162–9, 171, 172
 etiquette (classical Athens) 30
Couture, Thomas, *Romans of the Decadence* 253
Cowan, John 274
Cowley, Abraham 122
Cowper, Sarah, diarist 97
Crawford, Patricia ix, 10, 11, 82–106, 135
Cream, Thomas Neill, abortionist/serial murderer 267, 269–75, 277–8
criminal abortion *see* abortion
Criminal Law Amendment Act (1885) 260, 276
criminality
 and madness 329
 and mental deficiency 326
 and race 328–9
 and spread of HIV 373
 see also Jews/Judaism
Crooke, Helkiah, on conception 86, 87
Crosby, David, Baptist minister 97
Culpeper, Nicholas 96
 on conception 87
 on sexual excess 88
 Practice of Physick 109
culture *see* society
Cunningham, Joseph T. 162
'curse' *see* menstruation
Cuvier, G.L.C.F.D., baron *see* Geoffroy Saint-Hilaire, E. and Cuvier, Georges
Cyrene (ancient Greek prostitute) 31

Daphnis and Chloe see Longus
Darling, Charles John, judge in 'Madame Frain' trial 268
Darnton, Robert 149
Darwin, Charles Robert
 natural selection theory 158–83 *passim*
 sexual selection theory 8, 158–83, 337
 Descent of Man, and Selection in Relation to Sex 158, 160
 Origin of Species 149, 354
Darwin, Erasmus 145
Dasmail, L. M., patent-medicine vendor 271
Daubenton, Louis, critique of Linnaeus 187
Davenport-Hines, Richard ix, 6, 367–83
David, Jacques-Louis, 'Fountain of Regeneration' 202, 203
David, king of Israel 239
Davis, Dorothy, midwife 271

Davis, Katherine Bement 313, 317, 318
 sexual behaviour study 314–17
De Roos, 'Dr', unorthodox venereal disease treatment 350
deaf-mutism 329
Deak, E. 219
death penalty
 for adultery 90
 for bestiality 90
 for criminal abortion 273
 for incest 327
 for infanticide 99
 for marriage with niece 240
 for marriage with stepmother 242
 pregnancy plea 92
 for rape 276
 for sex during menstruation 89
 for sodomy 90
Decadence 13
 masculinity and 251–66
Defoe, Daniel, on sexual excess 89
degeneration 13–14, 254, 262, 287, 291, 332
 hereditary 261
 and inbreeding 233, 237–8
 among Jews 324, 334
 mental 256, 326, 329
 racial 331, 340
 sexual 333
Degler, Carl 308
Dekker, R. and Van de Pol, L., *Female Transvestism in Early Modern Europe* 146
D'Emilio, J. 297
demography 268
 depopulation 148–9, 198–9, 252, 255
 implications of AIDS pandemic 371
Denmark, reversal of population decline 199
Denton, William, physician 95
dependence, sexual (Krafft-Ebing) 214, 216–17
Desert Fathers (ascetic sect, c. fourth century AD) 53, 56–7
Dessoir, Max 222
Deuteronomy, on levirate marriage 241
Deutsche Gesellschaft zur Bekämpfung von Geschlechtskrankheiten 285, 290–1, 294–5
Deutsche medizinische Wochenschrift 286
Deutscher Zweig der Internationalen Abolitionistischen Föderation 288–9
deviancy, sexual 6, 15, 355
 classification 13–14
 of Jews 14, 15, 323–49
 see also androgynes; homosexuality
Dewar, Douglas 162
d'Hancarville, Pierre F. Hugues, baron, *Monumens de la vie privée des douze Césars* 37

diagnosis
  of deviants 14
  of nervous disorders 254, 256
  of sado-masochism (Krafft-Ebing) 47–8, 211
Diana of Ephesus, fertility symbol 190, 192, 193, 194, 201
diaries, women's 97
Dickinson, Robert Latou 2
  sexual behaviour study 309–13, 316, 317, 318
  The Single Woman 311
  A Thousand Marriages 311
diet *see* regimen
Diez, *Suicide* 221
Digambaras (Jainist sect) 70–2
dildos 36, 142, 312–13
dissections 136
  patients' permission for 118–19
  Vesalius's 117–18
  Willis's 116–17, 126
divorce 145
Dixon, Dwight 47–62
Dixon, Joan 47–62
Dostoevsky, Fyodor Mikhailovich, *The Gambler* 216
Drake, Emma, *What a Young Wife Ought to Know* 274
dreams, interpretation of, in Artemidoros 30, 32, 38
Drosophila, sexual selection in 163, 164
drug therapies, for venereal diseases 296
drug-addiction
  crack-cocaine 373
  opium 254
  and spread of HIV 368, 370, 372, 373, 376, 378
Duckart, Joachim 325
Durant, John 162, 166, 172
dyspareunia 146, 312

early modern period
  female anatomy and English medicine 107–33
  sexual knowledge in England 82–106
earth, metaphor for female 38–9, 67, 86, 127–8
ecstasy, through pain 51, 53–4, 55–6, 58
education
  female 123, 124
  Jewish superiority 328
  male 120
  midwives' 124–5
  see also sex education
effeminacy 14
  see also androgynes
Egypt, ancient, dynastic incest 235–7, 238, 240

Ehrenfels, Christian von
  on modern society and sexuality 337–40
  on nature of Jews 339
  on race 338–40
eighteenth century
  English sexual advice literature 134–57
  zoological taxonomy 184–209
Eisenstein, Elizabeth 11
ejaculation 5, 71, 108, 312
  female 109–10
  male 110, 215, 216
  see also semen
Elephantis (midwife), sex manual 34, 36
Elias, Norbert, on knightly male character 122
Elizabeth I, queen of England 87
Ellis, Henry Havelock 8, 174, 304, 310, 317, 323, 335, 351, 354, 355–7, 358, 359
  on sado-masochism 48
  on sexual inversion 303, 356–7
  Man and Woman 14, 158
  Psychology of Sex 357
  Sex in Relation to Society 357
  Sexual Inversion 356–7
  Studies in the Psychology of Sex 14, 158, 362
embryology 145, 191
emotions
  hormonal influence 165
  in humoral theory 115
endocrinology
  animal studies 174
  'rejuvenation' therapy 354–5
  see also hormones
endorphins 50, 53
Engels, Friedrich 257
England *see* Great Britain
Enlightenment *see* eighteenth century
epidemiology *see* AIDS
epilepsy 114, 352
epistemology, medical, and gender 116–18
Erasmus, Desiderius, attack on wet-nursing 200
Erb, Wilhelm
  on Jews' nervous disposition 341
  on sexual abstinence 291
erection 5, 30, 220
erotic disposition 14
erotica 3, 12, 83, 137–8, 150
eroticism 8
  African 136
  in antiquity 135
Escholle des filles 137, 150
ethnography 13
etiology, of hysteria 109, 324
eugenics 293, 334, 337, 338–9
  sexual restraint and 88
Eulenburg, Albert 214
  on sexual abstinence 287, 291, 295

INDEX 391

Sexuale Neuropathie 286
evolution *see* biology, evolutionary
exercise, physical, for women 310
exhibitionists 15
Exner, Max J. 314, 316, 317, 318
   sexual behaviour study 306-8
experimentation, human/animal 117

family 16, 151
   Christian concept 3
   domestic violence 13
   Freud's model 340
   history 134
   social context 83, 145
   see also children; incest; marriage; mothers
Family Planning Association 359
fantasies, sexual 213-14, 215, 220, 342
Farthing, Charles 376
Faulkner, Julia, murder victim 272
fear
   of AIDS 377
   of childbirth 87, 99
   in Dickinson's survey 312
   in imagery of female 29-30, 71
   male fears of women's desires 97-8
Felix of Cantalice, St 55
fellatio 99, 147
   in Graeco-Roman literature 35, 37, 38
felony, sexual offences as 90
female
   deceitfulness 32-3
   diseases *see* gynaecology
   domestic role 109, 185, 197, 201-2
   see also mothers
   earth metaphor 38-9, 67, 86, 127-8
   education 123, 124
   healers 82, 96
   see also midwives
   innate impurity 63, 66-7, 191
   intellect 121, 128
   modesty 87, 93, 95, 96, 97, 98
   moisture theories 108-13
   objectification of, in Graeco-Roman mythology 29, 31, 38
   patients 107, 118-19, 124, 125
   sexuality 6, 215-16, 341, 358: menstruation and 63-81; statistical studies: Chesser's 361; Davis's 314-17 Dickinson's 309-13; Mosher's 308-9; voracity 30, 63, 64-5, 67, 69, 71
   subordination 9, 10, 48, 91, 115, 118, 127-8, 212, 354
   traditional knowledge 82-3, 108, 128
   as victims (fear/force) 29-30, 71
   virtues 121
   see also anatomy; gender; menstruation; physiology
female body 72, 135

   in early modern English medicine 107-33
   Indian ascetics' aversion to 69-71
   see also anatomy; genitalia
feminists 4, 5, 6, 134, 292, 293
   objections to interventionist gynaecology 276-7
   rights movement (1890s) 252
feminization, of Jews 335-6
Fenn, Louisa Rebecca, patent-medicine vendor 278 n6
Ferrand, Jacques, *De la maladie d'amour* 135
fertility 268, 273, 312, 359
   in ancient Greece 34
   in Indian tradition 75-6, 77
   symbols: Diana of Ephesus 190, 192, 193, 194, 201; female breasts 190-9; Isis 202
fetishism 47, 211, 213, 221-3
fevers
   meningeal 125-6
   theories of 117
fin de siècle 323-49
   abortion debates 267-83
   Jews and sexuality 323-49
   masculinity and the Decadence 251-66
   sexual abstinence debates 284-302
Finn, Frank 162
First World War (1914-18) 264, 285, 304, 313, 316
   chastity campaigns 295-6, 306-7
   and masculine ideal 263
fish, in Aristotle's taxonomy 186
Fisher, L. E. 273
'fits of the mother' 85, 91
   marriage as therapy 109
flagellation 47, 48, 213-14, 220
   mass 57-8
   self- 56-8
flattery, in Graeco-Roman sex manuals 32
Flaubert, Gustave 136
Flexner, Abraham, study of prostitution in Europe 314
fluids/solids, physiological theories 107-8, 109, 113, 115, 116, 128
foetus
   deformed 90-1, 145, 147; as punishment 90
   gender of 34, 68, 74
   growth of 311
   health of 87
   influence of sexual excess 88, 89
   nourishment of 69
   quickening of 99
   superiority of male 91
   see also abortion
folklore, sexual 136
Fontanus, Nicholas, *Woman's Doctour* 109
food, women portrayed as 31

Forberg, Karl Friedrich, *Apophoreta or Manual of Classical Erotology* 37
Forel, Auguste Henri 223
  on sexual abstinence 291
forensic science, incest debate 330–1
foreplay *see* heterosexual intercourse
fornication 85
  by married men 90
Fortnightly Review 254
Fosdick, Raymond B. 314
Foucault, Michel 9, 12, 83, 145, 297–8, 350
  on repression myth 7, 137, 150
  History of Sexuality 29, 135
Foucaultians 4
Fournier, Alfred, on syphilis and marriage 304
Fox, George, *Journal* 126–7
Fox, James, defendant in 'Madame Frain' trial 268
Frain, Madame
  Herbal or Medical Institute, London 268
  Pills to Remove Obstructions 267–8, 269
France
  crime statistics 327
  Festival of the Supreme Being (1794) 202
  maternal lactation 201
  responses to HIV/AIDS 372–3: AIDS survey (1989–92) 373–4, 378
  sex education campaign 304
  wet-nursing 198, 200
Frances of Rome, St 55
Franco-Prussian War (1870–71) 252
Frankel, Simon J. ix, 8, 158–83
Frederick II, 'the Great', king of Prussia 201
free love 4, 294
Freedman, E. B. 297
French Revolution (1789–99)
  ideal of masculinity 251
  and repression of women 202
  women as symbols (Marianne) 190, 202
Freud, Sigmund 5, 8, 9, 13, 174, 210, 292, 303, 323, 324, 332, 334, 335, 337, 355
  on incest taboo 15
  on inheritance and trauma 336–7
  on male hysteria 255–6
  on Oedipus complex 15
  penis envy theory 6, 7, 341–3
  on sado-masochism 48
  on sexuality of Jews 341–3
  '"Civilized" Sexual Morality and Modern Nervous Illness' 337, 340–1
  Three Essays on the Theory of Sexuality 14, 342
Freudians 6
Freudo-Marxists 4, 5
frigidity 312
Fromm, Eric, on sado-masochism 51

fruit flies *see* Drosophila
Fuld, Ludwig, on religion and criminality 327
fur fetish 47, 213

Galen 90
  on generation 85
  physiological theory 113–14, 115
  uterine theory 191
Gardener, Kate Hutchinson, murder victim 272
Gardner, Augustus K. 274
Gay and Lesbian Switchboard 374
Gay Medical Association 362
Gay Men's Health Crisis, New York 369
Gay, Peter 134
Gebhard, Paul, on sado-masochism 51
Geddes, Patrick and Thomson, J. Arthur, *Evolution of Sex* 354, 355
gender 8, 10, 151
  conceptualization of 10–11, 14, 16, 82, 110, 146, 204; masculinity 251–66 *passim*
  decadents' view of 260
  of foetus 34, 68, 74
  medical epistemology and 116–18
  'neurocentric' theory 107–8, 113–16, 120, 123, 127, 128
  politics of 184; in taxonomy 197–204
  and race 339
  see also female; male
General Medical Council 351
general practitioners 362, 376
generation *see* conception
genetics 293
  Drosophila experiments 163, 164
  Huxley's work 170
  see also heredity; incest, inbreeding avoidance theory
genital herpes 374
genitalia 144, 145
  anatomy 10–11, 145
  female 91, 140, 341–3: in Jainist texts 71; in Vesalius 111, 113, 117–18
  gender comparisons 110–13
  of Jews 325, 326
  male 9, 91, 140, 341–3
  of prostitutes 326
Geoffroy Saint-Hilaire, Etienne, and Cuvier, Georges, 'Mammalogie' 189
Germanicus Caesar 240
Germany 251, 252, 323
  abortion 294
  anti-Semitism 325, 327–8, 340
  chastity debates 12, 284–302
  criminal censuses (1899–1902) 333
  feminist movement (1890s) 253
  health insurance law (1883) 289–90

homosexuality 258-9, 261
incest laws 331, 332
Moral Purity Leagues 261, 262, 263
psychiatry 210, 253-4, 255
Gesner, Conrad 184
Gestalt psychology 337
Giddens, Anthony 8
Gilman, Charlotte Perkins, lesbian feminist 339
Gilman, Sander L. ix-x, 13, 14, 15, 323-49
Giuliani, Veronica, St 192
Gobineau, Arthur de, on racial degeneration 329
Goethe, Johann Wolfgang von 195
Elective Affinities 8
goitre, endemic 332
Goldman, R. P. 72
gonorrhoea 289, 290, 312
Goodenough, Sir William Macnamara, Committee on Medical Education (1942-44) 362
Gouge, William, on sin/sexuality 84, 89
gout, and sexual excess 89
Graham, James 149
Gravelot, Hubert François *see* Cochin, C. and Gravelot, H. F.
Gray, A. Herbert 359
Great Britain 350
  fin de siècle homosexuality 259, 260-1
  medicine and female physiology 107-33
  responses to HIV/AIDS 372-3, 374-5, 376, 378-9
  sex surveys: Chesser's (1950s) 361; Mass Observation Organization (1947) 360-1; sexual behaviour (1990-1) 378
  sexual advice literature (before 1800) 134-57
  sexual knowledge (1500-1750) 10, 82-106
  women's rights movement (1890s) 252, 253
  see also medical profession, British
Greatrakes, Valentine 'the stroker' 125
Greece, ancient 237
  anatomy 10
  dynastic incest 235-6
  homosexuality 257, 259
  ideal of female beauty 195
  ideal of male beauty 252
  sexology 8-9, 29-46
  see also myths
Greek language 35
  sexual vocabularies 31
greensickness 85, 91, 95
  copulation as cure 145
Gregory of Nice, St 143
Groller, Balduin, *Gräfin Aranka* 219
Grossmann, A. 297

Guillemeau, Jacques 96
Gurdjieff, George Ivanovich 359
Gutenberg, Johannes Gensfleisch 11, 135, 137
Gutmann, Moses Juius 335
gynaecology
  in advice literature 136
  in antiquity 34-5
  Dickinson's work 309-13
  intercourse as therapy 34-5, 85, 109, 145
  interventionist 276-7
  as medical speciality 275, 278
  popular knowledge 113
  seventeenth-century nosology 109

Habsburg dynasty 240
Haemophilia Society (UK) 369
haemophiliacs, and HIV 368, 373
Haire, Norman 359, 363
  (ed. and trans.) *Encyclopaedia of Sexual Knowledge* 360
Haiti, HIV/AIDS epidemic 370
Hall, Ethel, murder victim 270-1
Hall, Lesley A. x, 12, 350-66
Hall, Sir Edward Marshall 270
Hallett, J. P. 37
Hamilton, Gilbert V., sexual behaviour study 316-17, 318
Hammurabi, Babylonian king, legal code 238
Haran, brother of Abraham 239
Harper, Walter 272
Harris, W., on sex during pregnancy 89
Hart, J., on sexual excess 88
Harvard University *see* International AIDS Center
Harvey, William 113, 125
  cardiovascular theory 114, 117
Hauser, Renate x, 9, 13, 210-27
Hawaii, dynastic incest in 235
Hayden, Revd Anthony, murderer 283 n79
headaches, Anne Conway's 125-8
health
  of foetus 87
  of infants 198-9, 200
  of married women 91
  and sexual activity 85, 88, 145, 294
  of virgins/widows 91
health insurance, German system (1883) 289-90
health-care professionals, and spread of HIV 377
Heap, Alfred Thomas, criminal abortionist 273
heart
  Harvey's work 114
  in Willis's theory 114-15
heat, in reproduction theory 108-9, 110

Hector and Andromache (myth) 38
Helen of Troy 31, 259
Heliogabalus, Roman emperor 260
Helmont, F. M. Van 125
Helmont, Jean Baptiste van
  chemical theory 127
  pathological theory 117
Henley, William Ernest, condemnation of
  androgynes 260
Henry II, king of England 58
Henry VIII, king of England 241–2
herbalists, and abortion 269
heredity 145, 341
  diseases 287, 289
  HIV 371
  Jewish 324, 328
  and mental deficiency 326
  and psychopathology 332, 336
hermaphrodites *see* androgynes
Herodas, on female sexuality 36
herpes *see* genital herpes
Herrup, Cynthia 90
Herzl, Theodor 334
heterosexual intercourse 140, 307
  and conception 68, 146–7
  female dissatisfaction 215–16
  foreplay 51, 140
  frequency 89, 145, 309, 312, 315
  in Graeco-Roman art 36–7
  as gynaecological therapy 34–5, 85, 109, 145
  in Indian texts 64, 71, 74
  marital *see* marriage
  physiology 309–13
  pleasure in 34, 145, 146, 148, 309
  positions 31–2, 33, 34, 36, 37, 38, 39, 140, 144, 147, 150
  problems 303
  and spread of HIV 370, 372, 375, 378–9
  see also incest; marriage
heterosexuality 339
  as 'normality' 6, 7, 16, 83
Hichens, Robert 257
Higgins, Terence *see* Terence Higgins Trust
Highmore, Nathaniel, physician 85, 120
Hilder, Thomas, condemns contraception 99
Hill, Andreas x, 12, 284–302
Hinduism 63
  and carnal knowledge 4
  and female sexuality 10
Hippocrates 2, 110
  on generation 85–6, 93
Hippocratic corpus 38
  Diseases of Women 34–5
  Sacred Disease 114
Hirschfeld, Magnus 14, 258, 292, 303, 323, 331, 333
  on incest 332
  Institute for Sexual Science (Berlin) 359
historiography, sexual 4, 6, 16
  Graeco-Roman 8–9
Hitschmann, Eduard, on Jews' sexuality 324
HIV 296, 362, 367–83
  see also AIDS
Hodge, Hugh L., *Foeticide, or Criminal Abortion* 274
Holden, Mary, almanack writer 94
Homo sapiens 8, 191
homosexuality, female *see* lesbianism
homosexuality, male 6, 13, 14, 15, 16, 47, 98, 134, 147, 212, 252, 255, 262, 263, 285, 293, 294, 339
  in ancient Greece/Rome 29, 30, 36, 253, 257, 259; role of passive partner 30, 34
  and fetishism 222
  hypnotic therapy 211, 219–21
  among Jews 334, 335, 336
  masochistic 219–21
  persecution of gays 260–1, 292
  rights movement 257, 358, 369, 374, 376
  sadistic 221
  and spread of HIV 368, 372–6
  visibility during Decadence 256–60
Hoppe, Hugo, on Jews and alcohol 333
Horace 29, 219
hormones 173, 174
  female (animals) 165
hospitals, lying-in 125
Houlbrooke, R. 83
Hudson, Rock 372
human experimentation 117
human immunodeficiency virus *see* HIV
humiliation/torture 51, 213
humoral theory 119
  in Galenic physiology 115
  of menstruation 75
  of pregnancy and lactation 199
  in seventeenth-century physiology 116
Hunt, Lynn 202
Hunter, John, taxonomy 188
Huxley, Sir Julian Sorell 8
  on avian courtship 164–9, 171, 172
  critique of sexual selection theory 158–83
  on mutual selection 166–7
  on relative growth (allometry) 169–71, 172
  'Courtship Activities in the Red-throated Diver' 168, 169
  'Courtship Habits of the Great Crested Grebe' 165–6
  Evolution, the Modern Synthesis 173
  Problems of Relative Growth 171
  'Sex Biology and Sex Psychology' 158
Huxley, Thomas Henry 158

hybridization 163
hydrotherapy, as infertility therapy 87
hygiene, personal 262, 293, 296
hypnosis, Krafft-Ebing's use of 210, 211, 219–21, 223
hypochondria 286
hysteria 252, 254, 286
  Charcot's work 254–5
  copulation as cure 145
  etiology theories: heredity 336; uterine 109; Willis's 113–16
  female 254, 255, 263, 324, 352
  among Jews 324, 336, 337
  male 254–6
  mass 336
  psychological factors 215
  seventeenth-century debates 107–9

illegitimacy 93
  prosecution of mothers 90
Ilma (Krafft-Ebing's patient) 211
imagery
  maternal 190–7, 199
  of Nature as female 190–9, 202
  woman as earth 38–9, 67, 86, 127–8
  see also dreams
imagination, in Krafft-Ebing's psychopathology 214
impotence 37, 68, 138, 145, 220, 287, 295
  in Graeco-Roman literature 34–6
Incas, dynastic incest among 235
incest 13, 15, 275, 329, 332
  and alcoholism 333
  definition 330–1
  dynastic 235–9, 238, 244, 246
  health of offspring 329, 330, 332
  inbreeding avoidance theory 233, 237
  indifference theory 233–4, 237–8, 239, 243, 245, 246–7
  in Magian society 231–50
  in nuclear family 235, 239, 243, 244, 245–6, 247
  taboo 232–5, 239, 240–1
  see also Jews/Judaism, levirate marriage
Index medicus 285
Index-Catalogue of the Library of the Surgeon-General's Office 285
India 10
  HIV/AIDS epidemic 379
  masochism in literature 219
  menstruation and female sexuality 63–81
Indiana University 2
Indra (Indian god) 65, 66–7, 73, 75
industrialization *see* civilization
inequity 30, 38
  between heterosexual partners 29
  between homosexual partners 29
infanticide 99, 269

infants
  abandonment of 269
  and HIV 371
  mortality 200; relation to wet-nursing 198–9
  and venereal diseases 305
  see also lactation
infertility 68, 84, 88, 289, 305
  advice literature 87, 138
  in ancient Greece 34
  and degeneration 254, 255
  in Indian tradition 76
Ingram, M. 83
inheritance, legal aspects 92
  see also heredity
initiation rites, in classical Athens 30
innocence, corruption of, by advice literature 139–40
  authors' apologia 141–5
insanity 352
  and criminality 325, 329
  erotic 135
  and incest 330–1, 333
  among Jews 328, 340
  and menstruation 218
  social causes 256
  syphilitic 305
intellect, female 128
  inferiority of 121
International AIDS Center, Harvard University 368
International Code of Zoological Nomenclature 189
inversion, sexual 13, 15, 285, 303, 356–7
Isis and Osiris (myth) 236
Islam
  and carnal knowledge 4
  incest laws 242, 243
  status of women 218
Italy
  homosexuality in 220–1
  Renaissance *see* Vesalius

Jack the Ripper 13, 273, 277
  portrayal as Jew 325, 326
Jacobsen, J. P., *Niels Lyhne* 219
Jäger, *Discovery of the Soul* 222
Jainism 63
  view of women 70–2, 75
James II, king of Great Britain 98
James della Marcca, St 56
Japan, responses to HIV/AIDS 372, 379
Jardin des Plantes, Paris 187
Jeake, Samuel, diarist 98
Jerome, St 54
Jesubocht, Nestorian patriarch, condemnation of incest 237–8
Jesus Christ 127

birth of 195
on marital love 84
sufferings of 52, 56, 57
see also Christianity
Jewish Lexicon 329
Jews/Judaism 52, 263
  and alcoholism 333
  circumcision 326, 342, 343
  and civilization 339–41
  criminality 324, 325, 328, 329–30, 332–3; of Eastern Jews 325–6, 337; latent 327, 333–4
  deviant sexuality 14, 15, 323–49
  feminization 334–5
  and hysteria 336, 337
  impurity of women 191
  inbreeding 324, 325, 328, 329, 332, 341
  incest 333
  levirate marriage 231, 232, 239–40, 241, 246, 247, 331–2
  and mental illness 328, 329, 334, 340
  nature 323, 326, 327, 328, 330, 338, 339
  nervous disposition of 324, 340, 340–1
  physiognomy (male) 323–4, 325
  and prostitution 326–7
  and sexual deviation 14, 15
  Jews' Role in Crime 327
Jinner, Sarah, almanack writer 94, 98
Job 52
John Paul II, pope 52
Johnson, Virginia E. 49
Jones, Rice 127
Jordanova, Ludmilla 143
Judaeo-Christian tradition 52
Judah 241
Judith, daughter of Charles the Bald 242
Jung, Carl Gustav 174, 332, 355
jury of matrons 92
Justin the Martyr, St 31

Kafka, Franz 340
Kains-Jackson, Charles 260
Kakar, Sudhir 63, 76
Kaposi's sarcoma 367
Katherine of Aragon, first queen of Henry VIII 242
Keller, Evelyn Fox 108, 125
Kelly, Mary, murder victim 273
King, Helen x, 8–9, 10, 29–46
Kinsey, Alfred Charles 2, 8, 51, 315, 317, 318
  Kinsey Reports 2
  Sexual Behavior in the Human Male 2
Kinsey Institute, Indiana 1
Kleist, Heinrich von, 'Kätchen von Heilbronn' 216, 217
Kneeland, George J., study of prostitution in New York City 314

knowledge, sexual *see* advice literature; sex education
Kolodny, Robert C. 49
Kraepelin, Emil 329
Krafft-Ebing, Richard von 13, 262, 303, 357
  on fetishism 221–3
  on Jews' nervous disposition 341
  on masochism 212–21
  psychological theories 210–27
  on sado-masochism 9, 47–8, 58, 59
  on sexual abstinence 287
  on sexual dependence 214, 216–17
  use of hypnosis 210, 219–21, 223
  'Comments on "Sexual Dependence" and Masochism' 216
  Lehrbuch der Gerichtlichen Psychopathologie 256
  'Nervousness and Neurasthenic States' 287–8
  'On Inborn Sexual Anaesthesia' 215
  Psychopathia sexualis 14, 47–8, 210, 211, 218, 221, 223, 256, 261, 287, 355, 373
  Psychosis menstrualis 218

Laboratory of Social Hygiene (Bedford Hills, USA) 314
Labouchère, Henry Du Pré, amendment to Criminal Law Bill (1885) 260
lactation 69, 91, 184–209
  advantages of 197–202
  medicinal uses of milk 195
  in mythology 191–2
  sexual activity during 89
  see also wet-nursing
Ladies Dispensatory 200
Ladies' Pictorial 257
Lais (midwife), sex manual 34
Lambeth Self-Supporting Dispensary 272
La'mert, Lima Abraham 352
La'mert, Samuel 353
  Self-Preservation 351–2
Lancet 351, 352–3, 355, 357, 361, 382
language *see* semantics
Laqueur, Thomas 10, 11, 108, 110, 140
  Making Sex 146
Latin language 35, 94
  early modern medical literature 84–5, 120
  sexual discourse 86–7, 136
  sexual vocabularies 31
  use for explicit details 212
law
  and adultery 90
  annulment of marriage 92, 241–2, 358
  biological aspects of women's crimes 218
  church courts 83, 90

and illegitimacy 90
obscenity cases 3, 360
paternity/inheritance suits 92, 93
on rape 87–8
sexual assault cases 14; women's evidence 96–7
sexual dependence and criminality 217
see also psychiatry, forensic
lay healers 123–4
  female 124, 129
lay medical knowledge 86–7
lay sexual knowledge 91–100
  female 92, 113; oral tradition 94–7
  male 91, 94, 96
  see also advice literature; sex education
Leake, John, medical advice for women 93
Leclerc, Georges-Louis, comte de Buffon, critique of Linnaeus 187, 188, 190
Lees, Edith 356
Lemnius, L., on marital sex 84
leprosy 331
lesbianism 13, 30–1, 90, 211, 252, 262, 312, 315, 339, 356
  visibility during Decadence 256–7, 258, 259, 260
Leslie, Julia xi, 10, 63–81
Lévi-Strauss, Claude 15
  on incest taboo 233, 234, 244
levirate marriage *see* Jews/Judaism
Leviticus
  prohibition of levirate marriage 239, 241, 243
  prohibition of sex during menstruation 89
liberation movements, sexual 3–5, 6–7, 134
libido
  female *see* female, sexuality
  male 6–7, 220, 255
  nature of 145
lifespan, and sexual excess 88
Linnaeus, Carolus 8, 195
  attack on wet-nursing 199, 200, 201
  'mammalia' in taxonomy 184, 185–91, 197, 202, 204
  Fauna Suecica 192, 194
  'Step Nurse' 199
  Systema naturae 184, 185, 187, 188
  Tour of Lapland 187–8
Liszt, Franz von 330
literacy
  female 92, 93
  male 92, 93, 120
literature
  forensic 323, 332–3
  homosexuality in 257–60
  masochism in 219
  sexual dependence in 216
  traditional Indian 64–76
  see also advice literature

Lobel, E. 32
Lombroso, Cesare 221
London Surgical Home 352
longevity, of country folk 119
Longus, *Daphnis and Chloe* 35, 38, 39
Lorrain, Jean, decadent homosexual 257, 259
Louis IX, king of France 58
Louis XV, king of France 199
love
  of boys 33–4
  and fetishism 222
  homosexual 258
  lesbian 258
  male/female responses 217
  marital 33–4, 84, 121, 148–9
  in medieval tradition 219
  as motive for sado-masochism 48
  nature of 145
  philtres 98
  Polycrates's treatise 33
  and sexual dependence 216
  and sexuality 297
'lovesickness' 135
Löwenfeld, Leopold 324
  on race and psychopathologic etiology 336–7
Löwenfeld, S., Jewish sociologist 327
Lucretius, on conception 39
lust 145–6
  marriage as cure for 85, 109
  and masturbation 141–2
  in monastic communities 88
Lydston, Frank 303
Lydwina of Schiedam, St 55–6

Macarius the Younger (Christian ascetic) 53–4
  Spiritual Homilies 54
MacBride, E. W. 171
McCulloch, John Wilson 272
Macfarlane, A. 83
McLaren, Angus xi, 12–13, 99, 148, 150, 267–83
McMath, J. 93
  conception theory 86
  on hydatidiform moles 90–1
Madame Frain *see* Frain
madness *see* insanity
Magi/Magians (Zoroastrian tribe in Sasanian Empire), incest customs 13, 15, 231–50
Mahābhārata 64–5
male
  anatomy 85, 107
  character 122–3, 354
  libido 6–7, 220, 252, 255
  as 'outsider' 326

role in heterosexual intercourse 215–16
sexuality *see* sex research
superiority 83–5, 91, 100, 115, 118, 127–8
see also gender; genitalia; homosexuality, male; masculinity
Malleson, Joan, family planning pioneer 359
Malthus, Thomas 149
see also neo-Malthusians
Malthusian League 268
mammae *see* breasts, female
'mammalia' (Linnaeus's taxonomy) 184, 185–91, 197, 202, 204
mammals 184–209
manual sex 99
Manusmṛti 65
Mar Aba, Nestorian patriarch, condemnation of incest 231–2, 237, 241, 243
Mar Timotheos, Nestorian patriarch 232
Marcuse, Max, on sexual abstinence 284, 291, 292, 294, 295
Marianne, French symbol of freedom 190, 202
Mārkaṇḍeyapurāṇa 65
marriage 134, 222, 284, 293, 294, 295
  ancient customs 15
  annulment of 92, 241–2, 358
  as cure for lust 85, 262
  duties of spouses 121–2
  as gynaecological therapy 109
  and health 85, 110
  as ideal for females 91
  in Indian texts 64–76
  love 33–4, 84, 121, 148–9
  in medical texts 82
  and procreation 86, 146–7, 148–9
  sexual relations 83–4, 91, 145–7, 201, 292, 305, 308–9, 315–17, 353, 358; advice on 31, 134–57, 360
  sexuality (excess) 89
  spouse abuse 49, 59
  and venereal diseases 304
  see also incest; sex research
Marriage Promoted 148
Marsh, Alice, Lambeth prostitute 267
Marshall, F. H. A., *Physiology of Reproduction* 355
Marten, John 143
  Gonosologium novum 138, 145–6
  Treatise of all the Symptoms of the Venereal Disease 138, 147
Martensen, Robert L. xi, 10–11, 107–33
Martial 38
Marx, Karl 257
Mary I, queen of England 87
Mary of Modena, queen of James II 87
Mary, Virgin 192, 195

masculinity
  classical model 252
  and Decadence 251–66
  ideal of 251–2, 254–5, 260–1, 262–4
  sadism and 48
masochism 9, 15, 47–62, 211
  and Christian asceticism 52–8
  as cultural phenomenon 218
  definition 47
  hypnotic therapy 219–20
  Krafft-Ebing's work 212–21
mass media
  abortifacient advertising 271
  and AIDS crisis 369, 372, 373, 377, 380
  and Decadence 253; homosexual scandals 259
Mass Observation Organization (UK) 360–1
Masters, William H. 49
masturbation 8, 15, 38, 90, 215, 220, 294
  dangers of 261–2, 284, 287
  eighteenth-century controversy 11, 140–4, 147, 149
  female 275, 309–10, 312–13, 315, 342, 352
  and fetishism 221–3
  male 261–2, 292, 293, 307, 308, 326
  as medical therapy 90, 109
materialism 126
Mayr, Ernest 173
mechanism, seventeenth-century theories 114, 115
media *see* mass media
medical profession
  American 303, 304, 305, 306, 310; responses to HIV/AIDS epidemic 376–7
  British: early modern period 118–19; and HIV/AIDS epidemic 375–6; and sex education 12–13; and sexology (nineteenth–twentieth centuries) 267–83, 350–66; treatment of women 124; *see also* physicians
  German 261; chastity debates 12, 284–302
Medical Register (British) 351, 353
medical texts
  English (1500–1750) 82, 84–91
  Indian 67–9
medicine
  early modern, female anatomy/physiology 107–33
  role of pathological anatomy 117–19
Medico-Psychological Society 355
Meghavijaya, *Yuktipradodh* 70–1
Meige, Henry 336
melancholy, copulation as cure 145
meningitis, cryptococcal 367

menopause 84, 309
menstrual blood 108, 109–10, 113, 191
  role in conception 67–9, 71, 85–6
menstruation 38, 91, 95, 109
  as 'curse' 10, 191
  disorders of 287, 312
  and female inferiority 10
  and female sexuality 10, 63–81
  in Hippocratic corpus 34
  in Indian tradition 63–81; ascetic texts 69–72; medical texts 67–9; normative discourse 72–6
  in Jewish tradition 191
  precipitation of 86
  and psychosis 218
  sexual abstinence during 68, 73–6, 89, 98
mental deficiency, and crime 326
mental illness *see* insanity
Merchant, Carolyn 108, 128, 192
Mesopotamia *see* Magi/Magians
microscope 119
Middle Ages 9, 10, 192
  Christian asceticism 55–8
  concept of uniqueness of man 187, 191
  cult of Virgin Mary 192, 195
  female fluids theories 109
  'lovesickness' 135
  neo-Aristotelian gender theory 110
  tradition of courtly love 219
Middlesex Hospital 376
midwives 93, 94, 100, 124
  and abortion 269, 271
  in antiquity 34
  encouragement of lactation 200
  masturbation of patients 90, 109
  professionalization of 124–5
  rivalry with male physicians 200–1
  role in sex education 34, 82, 93, 94, 95, 96, 113, 129
  training of 199
milk, maternal *see* lactation
Milkah, niece of Abraham 239
mind/body relationships 108, 115, 116, 126
Minerva (myth) 117, 122
miscarriage, procuration of *see* abortion
misogyny 10, 109
  among gynaecologists 275, 278
Mitchell, Lizzie Ann, midwife 271
Mitteilungen der Deutschen Gesellschaft zur Bekämpfung der Geschlechts-krankheiten 290
Mitterauer, Michael xi, 13, 15, 231–50
Möbius, Paul Julius 14
  psychological analysis of Rousseau 213
moisture, female, traditional theories 108–13
mole, hydatidiform *see* foetus, deformed
Molière [Jean Baptiste Poquelin] 222

Moll, Albert 14, 223, 323
  on sexual abstinence 291
monasteries
  illicit sexuality in 88
  see also asceticism
Mongols 339, 340
monogamy 338
  animal 159, 167–8, 169
  human 218, 222
monsters *see* foetus, deformed
Monteith's Electric Female Pills 271
Montesquiou, Robert de, decadent homosexual 257–8, 259
moon, and menstrual cycle 91
morality 82, 296, 338
  British attitudes 147, 360
  Christian churches' view 83–4, 261
  condemnation of abortion 273–4
  male/female double-standard 252, 288, 289, 304
  purity movements: in Germany 261, 262, 263; in USA 303–7, 318
More, Henry 126, 128
Morel, Benedict-Augustin 334
  on original sin 256
Morel, Jean Baptiste, *Treatise on Decadence* 253
Morgan, Lloyd 165
Morgan, Thomas Hunt 165, 171
  on *Drosophila* 168
  mutation theory 162, 164
  Evolution and Adaptation 162
  Genetic . . . Evidence Relating to Secondary Sexual Characters 164
Morrow, Prince Albert 310
  social hygiene movement 305
  Social Diseases and Marriage 304–5
Moser, Charles *see* Weinberg, M. S., Williams, C. J. and Moser, C.
Moses 329
Mosher, Clelia, sexual behaviour study 308–9, 313, 317
Mosse, George L. xi, 13, 14, 251–66
Mosse, Rudolf 218
Mosso, Angelo 262
mothers 86
  advice literature 199, 200
  in dreams 38
  and sexual excess 88–9
  unmarried 90; support of 293
  see also childbirth; 'fits of the mother'; lactation
Munaret, J. P., French physician 277–8
murder 283 n79
  Cream case 269–75, 277–8
  see also infanticide
Murdock, George P. 232, 239
Murphy, James 275

Mutterschutz 293, 337
Myerowitz, M. 33, 36
myths 29
   Egyptian, Isis and Osiris 236
   Graeco-Roman: Aphrodite 190; Atalanta 37–8; Diana of Ephesus 190, 192–4, 201; Hector and Andromache 38; Minerva 117, 122; Pandora 31, 32; Philosophia-Sapienta 195, 196; Romulus and Remus 192; Zeus 117, 122, 192, 236
   Indian tradition 63, 65–7, 73, 75
   lactation in 191–2
   virgins in 195

Nacke, Paul, on sexual abstinence 291
Nahor, brother of Abraham 239
Napheys, George H. 274
narcissism 8, 15
National Condom Week (UK) 377
National Research Council (USA), Committee for Research on Sex Problems 316, 318
natural philosophy 116, 119, 122, 123
   Anne Conway writings 125–7
natural selection theory *see* biology, evolutionary
Nature
   female breast as symbol 190–9
   female personification 192–5, 199, 202
   Rousseau's concept 201–2
Nature 168, 170
Nazis, anti-Semitism 325
Nefertiti, queen of Akhenaton 235
Neisser, Alfred, on sexual abstinence 290, 291
neo-Lamarckians 162, 171
neo-Malthusians 272, 293
Nero, Roman emperor 47, 200
nervous disorders 261
   and Decadence 254–5
   Jews' predisposition for 334, 340–1
   see also hysteria; neurasthenia
Nestorian Christians 231–2, 237–8
Netherlands
   Bureau of Legal Statistics 329–30
   persecution of homosexuals 260–1
   responses to HIV/AIDS 372–3
   sex education 375
Neue Generation 293
neurasthenia 215, 220, 286–7, 293
   etiology of 336
   among Jews 335, 341
   sexual 287, 293
neuroanatomy
   'neurocentric' gender theory (Willis) 11, 107–8, 113–16, 120, 123, 127, 128
neurology 337

Krafft-Ebing's study 210
   and syphilis 289
neuroses 293
   and crime 326
   functional 286
   hereditary 336
New York City
   AIDS 373
   Gay Men's Health Crisis 369
   prostitution study 314
   sex research study (Exner) 307
   Society of Sanitary and Moral Prophylaxis 305
New York Herald 273
Newcastle, duchess of *see* Cavendish, Margaret
Newtonians 116
Nietzsche, Friedrich Wilhelm 334
nineteenth century 12–13, 14
   British medical profession and sexology 267–83, 350–4
   see also fin de siècle
Noble, William, defendant in sexual assault case 97
nocturnal seminal emissions *see* semen
Nollius, H., on sexual frequency 89
Nordau, Max 334
   Degeneration 254
Norwich Consistory Court 97
nosology, gynaecological 116
Nystrom, Anton 292

objectification of women 29, 31, 38
obscenity
   advice literature as 139–45
   erotica as 3, 360
obstetrical forceps 124
Obstetrical Society 352
obstetrics
   male take-over of 199, 200–1
   as medical speciality 275, 277
Oedipus complex 15, 326
Offences Against the Person Act (1861) 270
Oldenburg, Henry 121
Oliver, John, condemns contraception 99
Onan, son of Judah 241
Onania 139, 140–4, 147, 148, 150
onanism *see* coitus interruptus; masturbation
opium addiction 254
oral intercourse *see* fellatio
oral tradition, female sexual knowledge 82–3
'organotherapy' (Brown-Séquard) 354
orgasm 5, 51
   female 7, 108, 109, 308, 309, 312–13, 317, 359
   simultaneous, and conception 86, 87
original sin (Morel) 256

orthogenesis theory 170-1
Osborn, Henry Fairfield, *Origin and Evolution of Life* 170
Osiris *see* Isis and Osiris
Ostervald, Jean Frédéric, *Traité contre l'impureté* 144
Ouspensky, Peter Demianovich 359
ovaries 91
ovariotomy 275
Ovid 29-30, 36, 38
  on flattery 32, 33
  on impotence 35-6
  Art of Love 33, 37
  Cures for Love 33
ovulation 95
  courtship behaviour and 172
Oxford University 107, 114, 120, 127
  Sheldonian Theatre 120, 122

Pachon (Christian ascetic) 55
Paget, Sir James 351
pain
  in childbirth 84
  and Christian asceticism 52-8
  and ecstasy 51, 53-6, 58
  historical concepts 52-9
  in intercourse *see* dyspareunia
  physiology of 50-1
  see also masochism
Palladius 53-4, 55
Palmer, William, Rugeley poisoner 283 n79
palmistry 136
Pandora (myth) 31, 32
Paracelsus
  chemical theory 127
  pathological theory 117
paralysis
  of the insane 210
  peripheral 210
  venereal 289
Paré, Ambroise
  advice on conception 86
  on hydatidiform moles 90
Paris
  Commune (1793) 202
  visibility of homosexuals (1890s) 257-8, 259
Parker, Holt 31, 32, 33
Parrhasius of Ephesus, painter of erotic *tabellae* 37
passions, nervous fluid and 115
passivism *see* sexual dependence
patent medicines, abortifacients 267-8, 278 n6
Pater, Walter, *Renaissance* 252
paternity 92, 93
pathological anatomy 116-19

patients, female 107, 124, 125
  Anne Conway 125-8
  elite 118-19
pederasty 257, 261
  in ancient Greece/Rome 29, 30
penetration 30, 36, 38, 90
penicillin 296
penis 309
  in Vesalius's anatomy 113
penis envy 6, 7, 341-3
Pennant, Thomas, taxonomy 188
Pepys, Samuel 96, 98
  purchase of *L'eschollle des filles* 137, 150
Pericles 29
Perkins, William, marriage advice 84, 89
permissiveness (1960s) 6, 374, 377
Pershing, John Joseph 306
Persia *see* Magi/Magians
personality
  defects 48
  and mental health 253
perversions 13, 14-15, 16, 285, 293, 294, 334
  criminal, of Jews 323
Peter, German wild boy 192
Petronius 136
phallus, fetish 7
Philaenis, sex manual (fourth century BC) 32, 33, 34, 36, 39
Philosophia-Sapienta (myth) 195, 196
Philosophical Transactions 121
philosophy
  as male pursuit 122
  see also natural philosophy
Phipps, Christopher xi, 6, 367-83
Phoenicians, incestuous marriages 239
photography 311
physicians 119, 120, 277
  advice for mothers 199
  and contraception 269
  and degeneration 254
  female, and sexual reform 359
  laymen's distrust of 100
  and male hysteria 253-5
  sexual knowledge 83, 84-9, 113
  take-over of midwifery 199, 200-1
  and therapeutic abortion 270
  see also medical profession
physiognomy 136
  of male Jews 323-4, 325, 326
physiology 216
  of coitus 309-13
  female 91, 212, 215, 309-13; early modern theories 107-33
  gender comparisons 10, 110
  male 262
  of pain 50-1
  of reproduction 145

see also anatomy; animals, courtship behaviour
Pilcz, Alexander 335
Pill, The *see* contraception, oral
Pinching, Anthony 376
plants, Linnaeus's taxonomy 185
Plato 2, 110
  location of reason 115
  on primacy of brain 114
  uterine theory 191
Pliny the Elder 34
pneumonia (*Pneumocystis carinii*) 367
Poeton, Edward, *The Midwiues Deputy* 96
poetry, Graeco-Roman 35–6
poisons
  abortifacients 272, 273, 277, 278
  arsenic 283 n79
  strychnine 267, 272, 273
politics, gender, and taxonomy 197–204
Polycrates, treatise on love 33
polygamy
  animal 159, 167, 169, 173
  human inclination (male) 218
Pomeroy, H. S. 274
popular knowledge *see* advice literature; lay sexual knowledge
population *see* demography
pornography 138, 150, 330
Porter, Roy xii, 11–12, 134–57
positions *see* heterosexual intercourse
Pougy, Lilian de, *Idylle-saphique* 258
Poulton, Edward, rejection of sexual selection theory 162, 165
Practitioner 353
Praz, Mario 259
pregnancy 199
  diseases of 109
  illegitimate 292, 293, 295, 312
  Indian tradition 74–5
  and mitigation of death penalty 92
  promotion of 147, 150
  and rape 88
  regimen during 68–9
  sex during 88–9
  social context 83, 92
  see also abortion
Prévost, Abbé Antoine François, *Manon Lescaut* 216
primates
  man's place among 187, 191
  see also mammals
printing
  and culture 149, 150
  role in dissemination of knowledge 11–12, 85, 94
Pritchard, Edward, murderer 283 n79
prostitution 2, 88, 217, 220, 257, 261, 295
  and abortion 267

  in ancient Greece/Rome 31, 32, 38
  child 13
  in Europe (Flexner's study) 314
  and fetishism 222
  in Germany 284, 288, 290, 291, 294; regulation 288–9
  Jews and 326–7
  masochistic techniques 214, 218
  and murder 269–75, 277–8
  punishment for 90
  and spread of HIV 372, 378–9
  and spread of venereal diseases 288
  in USA 303, 305, 306, 307; regulation 304; rehabilitation 313, 314
Protestant church 327, 329
  and morality 292
  opposition to celibacy 88
  view of sexuality 84
Proust, Marcel 251, 257–8
  Sodom et Gomorrhe 258
Prussia
  censuses (1871, 1881) 327
  law on maternal lactation (1794) 185, 201
  venereal diseases 289
Ps-Lucien, *Affairs of the Heart* 33–4
psychiatry 253–4, 329
  forensic 13, 14, 210–11, 256, 324, 332
  and sexual deviancy 135
  view of sado-masochism 48–9
psychoanalysis 5, 48, 174, 276, 292, 293, 297, 324, 341, 342, 355
  and criminality 326
psychology 286
  Gestalt 337
  Krafft-Ebing's theories 13, 47–8, 58, 59, 210–27
psychopathies, sexual 5, 14–15, 16, 47–62
  classifications 14, 210, 211, 214
  of Jews 324, 334, 341
  see also masochism; sadism
psychopaths 277
  serial murderers 267
psychoses 293
  mass 219
Ptolemy II, Egyptian pharaoh 236
Ptolemy XIII, Egyptian pharaoh 236
Ptolemy XIV, Egyptian pharaoh 236
puberty 85, 307
  in Indian tradition 76
  see also adolescence
public health 304
  in Germany 284–302 *passim*
  responses to AIDS pandemic 371–5, 379–80
  'safer sex' campaigns 369, 371–2, 374, 375
Punch 259

purity movements *see* morality
Pycraft, W. P., *Courtship of Animals* 165

quacks 138, 350, 351, 357
  and abortion 267–8, 269, 271
Quaife, G. R. 83
Quakers 125–8
questionnaires *see* sex research
Quran, marriage prohibitions 242, 243

Rabelais, François 4
race 15
  and civilization 337–41
  and criminality 326, 328–9
  and degeneration 329
  and gender 339
  and incest 330–1
  and insanity 337
  purity of 331, 338–9
Radford, Thomas 274
Ranters (Antinomian sect, *c.*1645) 5, 88–9
rape 48–9, 59, 275–6, 327
  legal attitudes to 87–8
Rare Verities. The Cabinet of Venus Unlocked 94
Rathenau, Walter 334
Raulin, Joseph 199
Ray, John 184
  taxonomy 186–7
Rayes, Gilles de, child abuser 47
Reagan, Ronald Wilson 7
reason
  as male attribute 191
  women's capacity for 117, 120–1, 122
Reformation 83
Reformatory for Women (Bedford Hills, USA) 313, 314
regimen
  to avoid fornication 85
  for chastity 292
  for men 34–5
  during menstruation 68
  during pregnancy 68–9
  for women 34–5
Reich, Wilhelm 5
'rejuvenation' therapy (Brown-Séquard) 354
Renaissance, anatomical texts 110–13
Rentoul, R. R., physician 270
repression 4, 6
  myth of (Foucault) 7, 137, 150
Restoration, English (1660) 84, 120, 124–5
Richards, O. W., 'Sexual Selection and Allied Problems in Insects' 171–2
Richepin, Jean, *La Glu* 219
Richlin, Amy 29, 37
Rie, Oskar 340
Rita of Cascia, St 56
Rivers, W. H. R. 355

Robie, W. F. 312
Robinson, Nicholas, 'nerve doctor' 116
Robours, Marie Anel le, French midwife 200, 201
Rockefeller, John Davison Jr 313, 314, 316
Rockefeller Foundation 316, 318
Rogers, Daniel, on sexual frequency 89
Rohleder, Hermann 331
Roman Empire
  decline of 253, 254, 261
  incestuous marriages 240
Rome, ancient, sexology 8–9, 29–46
Römer, A., 'Moral Law before the Bar of Medical Authority' 261
Romulus and Remus (myth) 192
Roos, J. R. B. de 330
Roper, Lyndal 90
Rothschild, James 240
Rothschild, Simon 240
Roubaud, Felix 312
Rousseau, Jean Jacques
  attack on wet-nursing 201–2
  masochistic tendency 47–8, 58, 213
  Confessions 47–8, 58
  Emile 201
Routh, Charles H. F., gynaecologist 275–6
  on evils of contraception 353
Royal College of Obstetricians and Gynaecologists, Enquiry into Family Limitation (1944) 361
Royal College of Physicians of Edinburgh 352
Royal College of Physicians of London 86, 120, 124, 125, 268, 356
Royal College of Surgeons of England 350
Royal Commission on Population (UK, 1944) 361
Royal Society of London 121, 122, 124
Rueff, Jacob 96
  The Expert Midwife 93
Ruppin, Arthur, on sociology of Jews 328
Rusbridger, Alan, *Concise History of the Sex Manual* 137
Russell, Bertrand Arthur William, third earl Russell 272
Russell, John, first earl Russell 272
Russell, John, viscount Amberley 272
Russett, Cynthia Eagle 12
Ryle, John Alfred 357

Sachau, Edward 15
Sacher-Masoch, Leopold von 53, 212, 218, 219
  Venus in Pelz 47, 213
Sachs, Hanns, Jewish physician 324
Sade, Louis-Donatien-François-Alphonse de, marquis 47, 53
  Juliette 47

Justine 47
sadism 9, 211
  definition 47
sado-masochism 47–62
  cultural dimensions 51–2
  historical concepts 52–9
  social definition 49–51
  see also masochism
St Mary's Hospital, London 376
St Stephen's Hospital, London 376
Salpêtrière, Paris 254, 255, 336
Salvarsan 296
salvation
  Christian view 9, 52–8
  of women (Jainism) 70–1
Sand, Georges, *Leone Leoni* 216
Sanskrit language 64
Sarah, wife of Abraham 239
Sasanians, Persian dynasty (AD 226–637) *see* Magi/Magians
Schäfer, Sir Edward Albert Sharpey- 354, 355
Scherbel, Simon, on consanguineous marriages 329
Schiebinger, Londa xii, 8, 108, 110, 184–209
Schrenck-Notzing, Albert von 221
  on 'algolagnia' 48, 214
Schull, A. F. 171
Scotland, HIV/AIDS epidemic 373, 378
Secrets des dames 109
seed, male/female 110
'seeds', female 127
Seleucids, Persian dynasty 235, 238
self, concepts of, in antiquity 135
self-abuse *see* masturbation
self-definition, sexuality and 8
self-punishment 55–8
Selous, Edmund, on avian courtship 162–3, 164
semantics
  Greek/Latin sexual vocabularies 31
  sex as semantic construct 7
semen 68, 71, 309
  Aristotle's theory 191
  ejaculatio praecox 287
  nocturnal emissions 287, 292, 293
  secretion of 88
  and transmission of HIV 367
  waste of 88, 326
sex education 12–13
  and AIDS epidemic 371–2, 374–5
  in England (1500–1750) 82–106
  Graeco-Roman 35–6
  in Great Britain 359, 361
  midwives' role 34, 82, 94, 95, 96, 113, 129
  in USA 305, 306–8, 311
  see also advice literature

sex manuals *see* advice literature
sex offenders *see* deviancy; psychopathies
sex research
  French AIDS survey 373–4, 378
  in Great Britain: Chesser's survey 361; Mass Observation Organization 360–1; *Sexual Health of Young Adults in England* 375, 378
  in USA 303–22: Davis's study 314–17; Dickinson's study 309–13; Exner's study 306–8; Gilbert's study 316–17; Mosher's study 308–9
sexual abstinence 88, 307, 313
  benefits of 284, 291–2, 296
  and control of HIV 371
  German debates 12, 284–302
  harmful effects 284, 287, 291–2, 293, 294, 295
  US campaigns 305–6, 318
sexual behaviour, Krafft-Ebing's psychology of 210–27
sexual disorders 323
  British medical profession and 350–66
  see also psychopathies
Sexual Health of Young Adults in England (1991) 375
sexual knowledge *see also* advice literature; sex education; sex research
sexual selection theory 158–83, 337
sexuality
  of Jews 14, 15, 323–49
  see also female; male
sexually transmitted diseases *see* AIDS; genital herpes; venereal diseases
Sexualprobleme 284, 293, 337
Shakespeare, William 88
Shapiro, H. A. 36
Sharp, Jane, midwife 82, 93, 94, 96
  Midwives Book 124
Sharpey-Schäfer, Sir Edward Albert *see* Schäfer, Sir Edward Albert Sharpey-
Sheldon, Gilbert, archbishop of Canterbury 120
shellshock 355
Shenute (Christian ascetic) 56–7
Shrivell, Emma, Lambeth prostitute 267
Siegesbeck, Johann 189
Simplicissimus 259
sin, Christian view of 84
Singer, Heinrich 332
Sinibaldus, Joannes, *Geneanthropeiae, sive de Hominis Generatione Decateuchon* 136
Slack, Paul 93
slander 328
Slaughter, Alice 98
Sloan, quack 350
Smethurst, Thomas, murderer 283 n79
Smith, F. W. D. 272, 273

Smṛticandrikā 74
social conditions
  and criminality 329–30
  and disease 253
  and spread of HIV 369
social Darwinism 293
social hygiene movement
  Germany 290
  USA 305, 306
socialism 268
Société Internationale de Prophylaxie . . .
  de la Syphilis et des Maladies
  Vénériennes 290
society
  English, class and medical information 94,
    95, 118–19, 124
  incest and 231–50 *passim*
  male/female relations 120, 121–2
  and sexuality 49–51, 83, 303, 337, 357
  status of women 218
Society of Apothecaries of London 351, 356
Society of Friends *see* Quakers
Society of Sanitary and Moral Prophylaxis
  (New York) 305
sodomy *see* anal intercourse; pederasty
solids *see* fluids/solids
Solon, on sexual frequency 89
Soranus of Ephesus, *Gynaecology* 34
soul
  in Aristotle 186
  Anne Conway's view 127
  of foetus 91
  and mental health (Bumke) 254
  Willis's view 127
  see also salvation
Sourvinou-Inwood, C. 37
South America 325–6
South London Mail 271
Spartan law, and marriage of half-siblings
  239
speculum, gynaecological 277
sport, and masculinity 262
Sprat, Thomas, *History of the Royal Society*
  121, 122
Stack, Miss, murder victim 272
Stall, Sylvanus 274
Starling, Ernest H., research on hormones
  165
statistics *see* sex research
Staub, Hugo 326
Stedman, Joanna 197
Stedman, John 197
Stekel, Wilhelm 292
Stengers, J. and Van Neck, A., *Histoire d'une
  grande peur: la masturbation* 140
sterility *see* infertility
Stevenson, Thomas, medical witness in
  Cream trial 273

Stewart, Annie, midwife 271
Stigler, Robert, on feminization of Jews 335
stillbirth, proof of 99
Stöcker, Helene, leader of Bund für
  Mutterschutz 293
Stone, Lawrence 83, 84, 99
  Uncertain Unions 134
Stone, Sarah 95
Stopes, Marie, *Married Love* 358
Stout, William, on illicit sexuality 85
Strauss, David Friedrich 334
strychnine (Cream murders) 267, 272, 273
Sturtevant, A. H. 164, 165, 171
  on secondary sexual characteristics 163–4,
    168
  'Experiments on . . . the Problem of
    Sexual Selection in *Drosophila*' 163
Suetonius, *Life of Tiberius* 36, 37
Sulloway, Frank 323, 343
Sun 272
Sunday Times 373
superstition 88
  on wet-nursing 200
Sutton, R. F. 36
Śvetāmbaras (Jainist sect) 70, 72
symbols 7, 56
  chastity 192, 193
  female breast 190–9, 202
  fertility: Diana of Ephesus 190, 192, 193,
    194, 201; Isis 202
symposia, Graeco-Roman 36
syphilis 252, 287, 289, 304, 305, 333, 371
  drug therapies 296
  hereditary 289
Syria, incest laws 240
Szasz, Thomas 367

tabes dorsalis 289
Tacitus 323
Tait, Robert Lawson, study of rape trials
  276
Taittirīyasaṃhitā 66
Taiwan, Sim-pua marriages 234
Talmud 240, 331
Tamar, daughter of David 239
Tannahill, Reay, *Sex in History* 6
Tantschatantra 219
taxonomy
  Aristotle's 186
  botanical 185
  and gender politics 197–204
  zoological, 'mammalia' (Linnaeus) 184–
    209
Taylor, Gordon Rattray, *Sex in History* 6
Taylor, Jeremy
  on male domination 121
  rules for widows 91
technique, sexual 139

in Graeco-Roman myths 37
see also heterosexual intercourse
Terence Higgins Trust 374, 376
Tertullian 143
testes 113
testicular extracts, and 'rejuvenation' 354
Thailand, HIV/AIDS epidemic 379
Thatcher, Margaret Hilda, baroness 7
Theilhaber, Felix
  on decline of German Jewry 340
  on inbreeding 329
Theodorus Pricianus, on impotence 35
Theodosius I, Roman emperor 240
theological discourse, sexuality in 82, 83–5
therapy
  for AIDS 368, 369, 375
  heterosexual intercourse as 34–5, 85, 109, 145
  for infertility 87
  medico-psychological 14
  'rejuvenation' 354–5
  uses of maternal milk 195
  for venereal diseases 289, 295, 296
  see also hypnosis
Third World, and spread of HIV/AIDS 373
Thomas à Becket, St 58
Thomson, J. Arthur see Geddes, P. and Thomson J. A.
Tiberius, Roman emperor 36, 37, 47
Timotheos, Mar see Mar Timotheos
Tissot, S.-A.-A.D., Onanism 140, 143
Tonga, dynastic incest in 235
Toronto Globe 269
tourism, and spread of HIV 372, 379
Touton, Karl, on sexual abstinence 295
transvestism
  female 146
  see also androgynes
trauma 341
  and mental illness 336
Tryambaka, Strīdharmapaddhati 64
  on menstruation 72–6
Tsantsanoglou, K. 33
tuberculosis 252, 287, 335
Tutenkhamen, Egyptian pharaoh 235
twentieth century 2, 16
  1960s permissiveness 6, 374, 377
  AIDS pandemic 367–83
  British medical profession and sexology 354–60
  sex research in USA 303–22
  sexual abstinence debates 12, 284–302
  sexual campaigns 5, 134
  sexual selection theory 158–83
  see also fin de siècle

Uganda, HIV/AIDS epidemic 370–1

Ulrich, Karl Heinrich, on homosexuals' rights 257
umbilical cord 310
urbanization see civilization
urolagny 356
USA 16
  criminalization of abortion 270
  HIV/AIDS epidemic 368, 369, 371, 372, 376
  prostitution 303, 304, 305, 306
  purity movement 303–4
  sex education 375
  sex research 2, 303–22
  venereal diseases 304, 306
uterus 309, 311
  body domination theory 123, 124, 128, 135
  in childbirth 199
  diseases of 34–5
  early theories 115–16, 191
  inflammation of 305
  role in conception 86, 108
  as seat of hysteria 107, 109
  suffocation of 85, 91
  in Vesalius's anatomy 113, 117

vagina 309, 313, 342
  and orgasm 359
Van Neck, A. see Stengers, J. and Van Neck, A.
Van de Pol, Lotte see Dekker, R. and Van de Pol, L.
Vega, Lope de 367
venereal diseases 5, 199, 277, 284, 289, 293, 295
  in advice literature 136, 138–9
  British survey 360, 361
  fear of 93, 99
  prophylaxis 290, 292, 295, 296, 306
  and sexual excess 89
  therapies 289, 295, 296; unorthodox 350
  in USA 304, 306, 307, 312, 313
Venette, Nicolas, Tableau de l'amour conjugal 136, 137, 139, 140, 142–3, 144–9
Verney, Sir Ralph 95
Vesalius, Andreas 116
  dissections 117–18
  imagery of uterus 113, 117, 191
  De humani corporis fabrica 110–13, 118
Vicinus, Martha 85
Vicq d'Azyr, Félix, taxonomy 188
victims
  of child abuse 49, 59
  of rape 48, 59
  in sado-masochistic relationships 51
  of spouse abuse 49, 59
  women as 29–30, 71
Vienna

anti-Semitism 325, 342
Krafft-Ebing's work 210
Medical Society 255
Psychoanalytic Society 324, 338, 340
University 335
Vigilance Committees (1890s) 276
Virchow, Rudolf Ludwig Karl 324
virginity, and marriage annulment 92
virgins
  beauty of breasts 195
  diseases of 109
  health of 91, 110
  image of Nature as 192–5
viruses *see* HIV
vitalism 125, 126, 127, 188
vivisection 117

Wack, Mary, *The 'Viaticum' and its Commentaries* 135
Waddell, Helen 53
Wagner, Peter, 'Some Pornographic Aspects of the *Onania*' 150
Walker, Kenneth, genito-urinary surgeon 358, 360, 361
Wallace, Alfred Russel, rejection of sexual selection theory 159–62, 167, 169, 173
Wallace, Robert 145
Walpole, Horace, fourth earl of Orford 123
Warner, Marina 195
Wassermann, Rudolf, on Jewish criminality 330, 332–4
Waters, Toronto solicitor for T. N. Cream 269
Wawerzonnek, M. 286
Weatherhead, Leslie 359
Weber, Max 294
Wedde, Johannes 219
Weeks, Curtis 377
Weeks, Jeffrey 32
Weimar Republic 285, 294, 296, 334
Weinberg, Martin S., Williams, C. J. and Moser, C., model of sado-masochism 49–51, 59
Weinberg, Richard, on Jews and mental degeneration 329
Weinheber, Josef, Nazi poet 264
Weininger, Otto, *Geschlecht und Charakter* 292, 339
Wellcome, Sir Henry Solomon 358
Wellcome Trust 361
Westermarck, Edvard Alexander 15, 245
  on levirate marriage 331–2
Westfall, Richard 120
wet-nursing 89, 197
  eighteenth-century attacks on 185, 197–202
  and infant mortality 198–9, 200

Whatley, William, on sex during menstruation 98
White, Charles 197
Whitefoord, Charles, conviction for abortion 271
Whitman, Walt 258
widows
  diseases of 109
  health of 91, 110
Wilde, Oscar 259, 260, 356, 362
  Lady Windermere's Fan 257
Williams, Colin J. *see* Weinberg, M. S., Williams, C. J. and Moser, C.
Willis, Thomas 119, 121, 124
  concept of hysteria 107–8, 113
  dissections 116–19, 126
  'neurocentric' gender theory 107–8, 113–16, 120, 123, 127, 128
  treatment of Anne Conway 125–6
  Cerebri anatome 113–16, 122
  Pathology of the Brain and Nervous Stock 118
Wilson, Thomas Woodrow 306
Winckelmann, J. J. 252
Winkler, Jack 30
Winstanley, Gerard, on sexual excess 88
Wisconsin University, Mothers' Club 308–9
wisdom, female personification of 195, 196
witchcraft 145
Wittgenstein, Ludwig 339
Woltmann, Ludwig 334
womb *see* uterus
women *see* female
Woolf, Sir Harry (Kenneth), Lord Justice 372
Woolston, Howard, study of prostitution in USA 314
World AIDS Day 377
World Bank 371
World Health Organisation 368, 369
World League for Sexual Reform 359
Wren, Sir Christopher 113, 122
Wright, Helena, family planning pioneer 359
  Sex Factor in Marriage 359

'Yellow Peril' (Ehrenfels) 338, 339
Young Men's Christian Association (YMCA) 306, 307, 313
Young Practitioner 277–8
Young, Wayland, *Eros Denied* 6
Young Women's Christian Association (YWCA) 313, 314

Zambia, HIV/AIDS epidemic 371
Zeitlin, F. I. 35, 39
Zeitschrift für Bekämpfung der Geschlechtskrankheiten 290
Zeus (myths) 117, 122, 192, 236

Ziegler, Philip 57–8
Zinn, Earl F. 316
Zionism 334
Zola, Emile 212
   Um eine Liebesnacht 219
   Nana 333

zoology
   mammals and sexology 184–209
   sexual selection theory 158–83
   see also animals
Zoroaster (Zarathustra) 232, 237
Zoroastrianism *see* Magi